THE **GOVT** SOLUTION

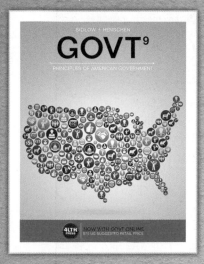

SIDLOW • HENSCHEN

GOVT⁹

PRINCIPLES OF AMERICAN GOVERNMENT

4LTR PRESS NOW WITH GOVT ONLINE
$75 US SUGGESTED RETAIL PRICE

Print
+
Online

MANAGE MY COURSE ▾   STUDENT

GOVT9

CHAPTER **1**

America in the 21st Century

CHAPTER **2**

The Constitution

GOVT⁹ delivers all the key terms and core concepts for the **Principles of American Government** course.

GOVT Online provides the complete narrative from the printed text with additional interactive media and the unique functionality of **StudyBits**—all available on nearly any device!

What is a StudyBit™? Created through a deep investigation of students' challenges and workflows, the StudyBit™ functionality of **GOVT Online** enables students of different generations and learning styles to study more effectively by allowing them to learn their way. Here's how they work:

COLLECT WHAT'S IMPORTANT
Create StudyBits as you highlight text, images or take notes!

WEAK
FAIR
STRONG
UNASSIGNED

RATE AND ORGANIZE STUDYBITS
Rate your understanding and use the color-coding to quickly organize your study time and personalize your flashcards and quizzes.

StudyBit™

TRACK/MONITOR PROGRESS
Use Concept Tracker to decide how you'll spend study time and study YOUR way!

 85%

PERSONALIZE QUIZZES
Filter by your StudyBits to personalize quizzes or just take chapter quizzes off-the-shelf.

CORRECT
INCORRECT
INCORRECT
INCORRECT

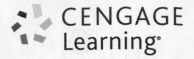

GOVT9

Edward Sidlow • Beth Henschen

Product Manager: Clinton Kernen

Content Developers: Victoria Castrucci, Colin Grover

Product Assistant: Lauren Dame

Marketing Manager: Valerie Hartman

Sr. Content Project Manager: Ann Borman

Manufacturing Planner: Ron Montgomery

Art Director: Bethany Casey

Intellectual Property Analyst: Alexandra Ricciardi

Intellectual Property Project Manager: Erika Mugavin

Internal Designer: Chris Miller/CMiller Design

Cover Designer: Lisa Kuhn/Curio Press, LLC

Cover Image: Alex Belomlinsky/DigitalVision Vectors/ Getty Images

Indexer: Terry Casey

Production Service: Lachina

Design elements: 2016 elections: iStockphoto.com/Getty Images; America at odds: ©Stillfx/Shutterstock.com; Perception v Reality: E+/Getty Images; The Rest of the World: iStockphoto.com/Getty Images; Join the Debate: iStockphoto.com/Getty Images

For product information and technology assistance, contact us at **Cengage Learning Customer & Sales Support, 1-888-915-3276**

For permission to use material from this text or product, submit all requests online at www.cengage.com/permissions.

Further permissions questions can be emailed to **permissionrequest@cengage.com**.

Library of Congress Control Number: 2016957446

ISBN-13: 978-1-337-09978-3

Cengage Learning
20 Channel Center Street
Boston, MA 02210
USA

Cengage Learning is a leading provider of customized learning solutions with employees residing in nearly 40 different countries and sales in more than 125 countries around the world. Find your local representative at **www.cengage.com/global**.

Cengage Learning products are represented in Canada by Nelson Education, Ltd.

To learn more about Cengage Learning Solutions, visit **www.cengage.com**.

Purchase any of our products at your local college store or at our preferred online store **www.cengagebrain.com**.

Printed in the United States of America

Print Number: 02   Print Year: 2017

SIDLOW / HENSCHEN

GOVT⁹

BRIEF CONTENTS

Alex Belomlinsky/DigitalVision Vectors/Getty Images

CONTENTS

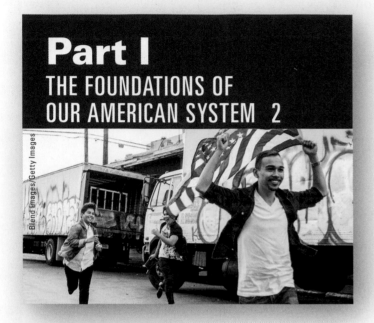

Part I
THE FOUNDATIONS OF OUR AMERICAN SYSTEM 2

Part II OUR LIBERTIES AND RIGHTS 72

AFP/Getty Images

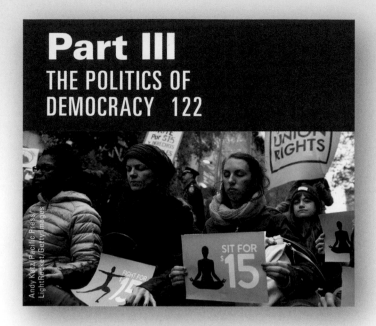

Part III
THE POLITICS OF DEMOCRACY 122

Andy Katz / Pacific Press / LightRocket / Getty Images

10 POLITICS AND THE MEDIA 216

Part IV
INSTITUTIONS 236

Orhan Cam/Shutterstock.com

11 THE CONGRESS 236

Part V
PUBLIC POLICY 334

SKILL PREP

A Study Skills Module

Welcome!

With this course and this textbook, you've begun what we hope will be a fun, stimulating, and thought-provoking journey into the world of American government and politics.

In this course, you will learn about the foundation of the American system, culture and diversity, interest groups, political parties, campaigns, elections, the media, our governing institutions, public policy, and foreign policy. Knowledge of these basics will help you think critically about political issues and become an active citizen.

We have developed this study skills module to help you gain the most from this course and this textbook. Whether you are a recent high school graduate or an adult returning to the classroom after a few years, you want

results when you study. You want to be able to understand the issues and ideas presented in the textbook, talk about them intelligently during class discussions, and remember them as you prepare for exams and papers.

This module is designed to help you develop the skills and habits you'll need to succeed in this course. With tips on how to be more engaged when you study, how to get the most out of your textbook, how to prepare for exams, and how to write papers, this guide will help you become the best learner you can be!

STUDY PREP

What does it take to be a successful student? You may think success depends on how naturally smart you are. However, the truth is that successful students aren't born, they're made. Even if you don't consider yourself "book smart," you can do well in this course by developing study skills that will help you understand, remember, and apply key concepts.

Reading for Learning

Your textbook is the foundation for information in a course. It contains key concepts and terms that are important to your understanding of the subject. For this reason, it is essential that you develop good reading skills. As you read your textbook with the goal of learning as much of the information as possible, work on establishing the following habits:

FOCUS

Make an effort to focus on the book and tune out other distractions so that you can understand and remember the information it presents.

TAKE TIME

To learn the key concepts presented in each chapter, you need to read slowly, carefully, and with great attention.

REPEAT

To read for learning, you have to read your textbook a number of times. Follow a preview-read-review process:

1. **PREVIEW: Look over the chapter title, section headings, and highlighted or bold words. This will give you a good preview of important ideas in the chapter.** Notice that each major section heading in this textbook has one or more corresponding **Learning Objectives.** You can increase your understanding of the material by rephrasing the headings and subheadings in your textbook into questions, and then try to answer them. Note graphs, pictures, and other visual illustrations of important concepts.

   QUICK TIP! Log in to GOVT9 Online with the access code in the front of your textbook to find interactive figures and tables from the chapters, to quiz yourself on the important material in the book.

2. **READ: It is important to read with a few questions in mind:** What is the main point of this paragraph or section? What does the author want me to learn from this? How does this relate to what I read before? Keeping these questions in mind will help you be an attentive reader who is actively focusing on the main ideas of the passage.

   QUICK TIP! In GOVT9 Online, create StudyBits from Key Terms and definitions, photos, figures, and your text highlights. You can include notes in your StudyBits, and add your own tags—such as "Midterm Exam"—so you can collect them all later.

Also during this phase, it is helpful to take notes while reading in detail. You can mark your text or write an outline, as explained later in this module. Taking notes will help you read actively, identify important concepts, and remember them. When it comes time to review for the exam, the notes you've made should make your studying more efficient.

QUICK TIP! In GOVT9 Online, create practice quizzes from filtered StudyBits or use all quiz questions from the chapter to test yourself before exams.

3. **REVIEW: When reviewing each section of the text and the notes you've made, ask yourself this question: What was this section about?** You'll want to answer the question in some detail, readily identifying the important points. Use the Learning Objectives in the text to help focus your review.

QUICK TIP! Tear out the Chapter Review cards in the back of the textbook for on-the-go review!

A reading group is a great way to review the chapter. After completing the reading individually, group members should meet and take turns sharing what they learned. Explaining the material to others will reinforce and clarify what you already know. Getting a different perspective on a passage will increase your knowledge, because different people will find different things important during a reading.

Take Notes

Being *engaged* means listening to discover (and remember) something. One way to make sure that you are listening attentively is to take notes. Doing so will help you focus on the professor's words and will help you identify the most important parts of the lecture.

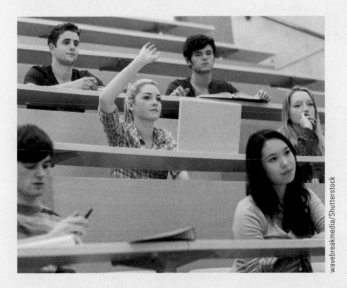

wavebreakmedia/Shutterstock

The physical act of writing makes you a more efficient learner. In addition, your notes provide a guide to what your instructor thinks is important. That means you will have a better idea of what to study before the next exam if you have a set of notes that you took during class.

Make an Outline

As you read through each chapter of your textbook, you might want to make an outline—a simple method for organizing information. You can create an outline as part of your reading or at the end of your reading. Or you can make an outline when you reread a section before moving on to the next one. The act of physically writing an outline for a chapter will help you retain the material in this text and master it.

To make an effective outline, you have to be selective. Your objectives in outlining are, first, to identify the main concepts and, second, to add the details that support those main concepts.

Your outline should consist of several levels written in a standard format. The most important concepts are assigned Roman numerals; the second-most important, capital letters; and the third-most important, numbers. Here is a quick example.

I. What Are Politics and Government?
  A. Defining Politics and Government
    1. Politics and Conflict
    2. Government and Authority
  B. Resolving Conflicts
  C. Providing Public Services
    1. Services for All and Services for Some
    2. Managing the Economy
  D. Defending the Nation and Its Culture
II. Different Systems of Government
  A. Undemocratic Systems
    1. Monarchy
    2. Dictatorship
  B. Democratic Systems
    1. The Athenian Model of Direct Democracy
    2. Direct Democracy Today
    3. Representative Democracy
    4. Types of Representative Democracy
  C. Other Forms of Government

Mark Your Text

If you own your own textbook for this course and plan to keep it, you can (improve) your learning by marking your text. By doing so, you will identify the most important concepts of each chapter, and at the same time, you'll be making a handy study guide for reviewing material at a later time. Marking allows you to become an active participant in the mastery of the material. Researchers have shown that the physical act of marking, just like the physical acts of note-taking during class and outlining, increases concentration and helps you better retain the material.

WAYS OF MARKING

The most common form of marking is to underline important points. The second-most commonly used method is to use a felt-tipped highlighter or marker, in yellow or some other transparent color. You can put a check mark next to material that you do not understand. Work on better comprehension of the checkmarked material after you've finished the chapter. Marking also includes circling, numbering, using arrows, jotting brief notes, or any other method that allows you to remember things when you go back to skim the pages in your textbook prior to an exam.

QUICK TIP! Don't forget about the StudyBit functionality when highlighting in GOVT9 Online! Change colors of your highlights to rate your understanding of each StudyBit, and use them in your review in the Studyboard.

TWO POINTS TO REMEMBER WHEN MARKING

▶ **Read one section at a time before you do any extensive marking.** You can't mark a section until you know what is important, and you can't know what is important until you read the whole section.

▶ **Don't overmark.** Don't fool yourself into thinking that you have done a good job just because each page is filled with arrows, circles, and underlines. Be selective in your marking, so that each page allows you to see the most important points at a glance. You can follow up your marking by writing out more in your subject outline.

> Researchers have shown that the physical act of marking, just like the physical acts of note-taking during class increases concentration and helps you better retain the material.

Try These Tips

Here are a few more hints that will help you develop effective study skills.

▶ **Do schoolwork as soon as possible after class.** The longer you wait, the more likely you will be distracted by television, the Internet, video games, or friends.

▶ **Set aside time and a quiet, comfortable space where you can focus on reading.** Your school library is often the best place to work. Set aside several hours a week of "library time" to study in peace and quiet. A neat, organized study space is also important. The only work items that should be on your desk are those that you are working on that day.

▶ **Reward yourself for studying!** Rest your eyes and your mind by taking a short break every twenty to thirty minutes. From time to time, allow yourself a break to do something else that you enjoy. These interludes will refresh your mind, give you more energy required for concentration, and enable you to study longer and more efficiently.

▶ **To memorize terms or facts, create flash (or note) cards.** On one side of the card, write the question or term. On the other side, write the answer or definition. Then use the cards to test yourself or have a friend quiz you on the material.

QUICK TIP! In GOVT9 Online, flash cards are available for all key terms (with definitions). Create more flash cards from your StudyBits or anything in the online narrative, and rate your understanding on each while you study!

▶ **Mnemonic (pronounced ne-mon-ik) devices are tricks that increase our ability to memorize.** A well-known mnemonic device is the phrase ROY G BIV, which helps people remember the colors of the rainbow—red, orange, yellow, green, blue, indigo, violet. You can create your own mnemonic devices for whatever you need to memorize. The more fun you have coming up with them, the more useful they will be.

▶ **Take notes twice.** First, take notes in class. Writing down your instructor's key points will help you be a more active, engaged listener. Taking notes will also give you a record of what your instructor thinks is important. Later, when you have a chance, rewrite your notes. The rewrite will act as a study session for you to think about the material again.

TEST PREP

You have worked hard throughout the term, reading the book, paying close attention in class, and taking good notes. Now it's test time, and you want to show mastery of the material you have studied. To be well prepared, you should know which reading materials and lectures will be covered. You should also know whether the exam will contain essays, objective questions, or both. Finally, you should know how much time you will have to take the exam. The following steps can help to reduce any anxiety you may feel, allowing you to approach the test with confidence.

Follow Directions

Students are often in a hurry to start an exam, so they take little time to read the instructions. The instructions can be critical, however. In a multiple-choice exam, for example, if there is no indication that there is a penalty for guessing, then you should never leave a question unanswered. Even if only a few minutes are left at the end of an exam, you should guess on the questions that you remain uncertain about.

Additionally, you need to know the weight given to each section of an exam. In a typical multiple-choice exam, all questions have equal weight. In other types of exams, particularly those with essay questions, different parts of the exam carry different weights. You should use these weights to apportion your time. If the essay portion of an exam accounts for 20 percent of the total points on the exam, you should not spend 60 percent of your time on the essays.

Finally, you need to make sure you are marking the answers correctly. Some exams require a No. 2 pencil to fill in the dots on a machine-graded answer sheet. Other exams require underlining or circling. In short, you have to read and follow the instructions carefully.

Objective Exams

An objective exam consists of multiple-choice, true/false, fill-in-the-blank, or matching questions that have only one correct answer. Students usually commit one of two errors when they read objective exam questions: (1) they read things into the questions that do not exist, or (2) they skip over words or phrases. Most test questions include key words such as:

> ALL   > NEVER
>   > ALWAYS   > ONLY

If you miss any of these key words, you may answer the question incorrectly even if you know the information being tested.

Whenever the answer to an objective question is not obvious, start with the process of elimination. Throw out the answers that are clearly incorrect. Typically, the easiest way to eliminate incorrect answers is to look for those that are meaningless, illogical, or inconsistent. Often, test authors put in some answers that make perfect sense and are indeed true, but do not answer the question under study. Here are a few more tips that will help you become an efficient, results-oriented student.

▶ **Review your notes thoroughly** as part of your exam preparation. Instructors usually lecture on subjects they think are important, so those same subjects are also likely to be on the exam.

- **Create a study schedule** to reduce stress and give yourself the best chance for success. At times, you will find yourself studying for several exams at once. When this happens, make a list of each study topic and the amount of time needed to review that topic.

- **Form a small group for a study session.** Discussing a topic out loud can improve your understanding of that topic and will help you remember the key points that often come up on exams.

- **Study from old exams.** Some professors make old exams available, either by posting them online or by putting them on file in the library. Old tests can give you an idea of the kinds of questions the professor likes to ask.

- **Avoid cramming just before an exam.** Cramming tires the brain unnecessarily and adds to stress, which can severely hamper your testing performance. If you've studied wisely, have confidence that you will be able to recall the information when you need it.

- **Be sure to eat** before taking a test so you will have the energy you need to concentrate.

- **Be prepared.** Make sure you have everything you will need for the exam, such as a pen or pencil. Arrive at the exam early to avoid having to rush, which will only add to your stress. Good preparation helps you focus on the task at hand.

- **When you first receive your exam, make sure that you have all the pages.** If you are uncertain, ask your professor or exam proctor. This initial scan may uncover other problems as well, such as illegible print or unclear instructions.

- **With essay questions, look for key words** such as "compare," "contrast," and "explain." These will guide your answer. Most important, get to the point without wasting your time (or your professor's) with statements such as "There are many possible reasons for . . . ."

- **Review your answers** when you finish a test early. You may find a mistake or an area where some extra writing will improve your grade.

- **Keep exams in perspective.** Worrying too much about a single exam can have a negative effect on your performance. If you do poorly on one test, it's not the end of the world. Rather, it should motivate you to do better on the next one.

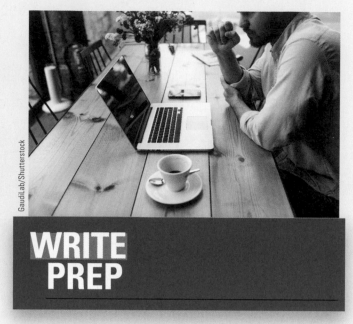

WRITE PREP

A key part of succeeding as a student is learning how to write well. Whether writing papers, presentations, essays, or even e-mails to your instructor, you have to be able to put your thoughts into words and do so with force, clarity, and precision. In this section, we outline a three-phase process that you can use to write almost anything.

Phase 1: Getting Ready to Write

First, make a list. Divide the ultimate goal—a finished paper—into smaller steps that you can tackle right away. Estimate how long it will take to complete each step. Start with the date your paper is due and work backward to the present: For example, if the due date is December 1, and you have about three months to write the paper, give yourself a cushion and schedule November 20 as your targeted completion date. Then list what you need to get done by October 1 and November 1.

PICK A TOPIC

To generate ideas for a topic, any of the following approaches work well:

- **Brainstorm with a group.** There is no need to create in isolation. You can harness the energy and the natural creative power of a group to assist you.

- **Speak it.** To get ideas flowing, start talking. Admit your confusion or lack of clear ideas. Then just speak. By putting your thoughts into words, you'll start thinking more clearly.

- **Use free writing.** Free writing, a technique championed by writing teacher Peter Elbow, is also very effective when trying to come up with a topic. There's only one rule in free writing: Write without stopping. Set a time limit— say, ten minutes—and keep your fingers dancing across the keyboard the whole time. Ignore the urge to stop and rewrite. There is no need to worry about spelling, punctuation, or grammar during this process.

REFINE YOUR IDEA

After you've come up with some initial ideas, it's time to refine them:

- **Select a topic and working title.** Using your instructor's guidelines for the paper, write down a list of topics that interest you. Write down all of the ideas you think of in two minutes. Then choose one topic. The most common pitfall is selecting a topic that is too broad. "Political Campaigns" is probably not a useful topic for your paper. Instead, consider "The Financing of Modern Political Campaigns."

- **Write a thesis statement.** Clarify what you want to say by summarizing it in one concise sentence. This sentence, called a *thesis statement*, refines your working title. A thesis is the main point of the paper—it is a declaration of some sort. You might write a thesis statement such as "Recent decisions by the Supreme Court have dramatically changed the way that political campaigns are funded."

SET GOALS

Effective writing flows from a purpose. Think about how you'd like your reader or listener to respond after considering your ideas.

- If you want to persuade someone, make your writing clear and logical. Support your assertions with evidence.

> There is no need to create in isolation. Brainstorm ideas for a topic with a group. Ask for feedback from your instructor or a friend as you prepare an outline and revise your first draft.

- If your purpose is to move the reader into action, explain exactly what steps to take, and offer solid benefits for doing so.

To clarify your purpose, state it in one sentence—for example, "The purpose of this paper is to discuss and analyze the role of women and minorities in law enforcement."

BEGIN RESEARCH

At the initial stage, the objective of your research is not to uncover specific facts about your topic. That comes later. First, you want to gain an overview of the subject. Say you want to advocate for indeterminate sentencing. You must first learn enough about determinate and indeterminate sentencing to describe the pros and cons of each one.

MAKE AN OUTLINE

An outline is a kind of map. When you follow a map, you avoid getting lost. Likewise, an outline keeps you from wandering off topic. To create your outline, follow these steps:

1. **Review your thesis statement** and identify the three to five main points you need to address in your paper to support or prove your thesis.

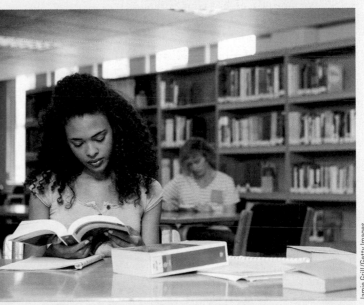

2. **Next, focus on the three to five major points** that support your argument and think about what minor points or subtopics you want to cover in your paper. Your major points are your big ideas. Your minor points are the details you need to fill in under each of those ideas.

3. **Ask for feedback.** Have your instructor or a classmate review your outline and offer suggestions for improvement. Did you choose the right points to support your thesis? Do you need more detail anywhere? Does the flow from idea to idea make sense?

DO IN-DEPTH RESEARCH

Dig in and start reading. Keep a notebook, tablet, or laptop handy and make notes as you read. It can help to organize your research into three main categories:

1. **Sources** (bibliographical information for a source),

2. **Information** (nuggets of information from a correctly quoted source)

3. **Ideas** (thoughts and observations that occur to you as you research, written in your own words)

You might want to use these categories to create three separate documents as you work. This will make it easy to find what you need when you write your first draft.

When taking research notes, be sure to:

▸ Copy all of the information correctly.

▸ Include the source and page number while gathering information. With Internet searches, you must also record the date a site was accessed.

▸ Stay organized; refer to your outline as you work.

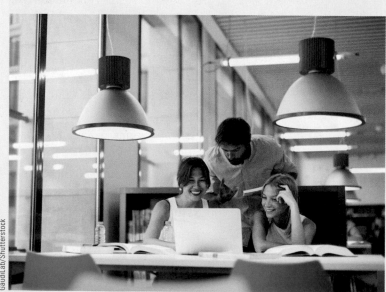

Gaudilab/Shutterstock

Phase 2: Writing a First Draft

To create your draft, gather your notes and your outline (which often undergoes revision during the research process). Then write about the ideas in your notes. It's that simple. Just start writing. Write in paragraphs, with one idea per paragraph. As you complete this task, keep the following suggestions in mind:

▸ **Remember that the first draft is not for keeps.** You can worry about quality later. Your goal at this point is simply to generate words and ideas.

▸ **Write freely.** Many writers prefer to get their first draft down quickly and would advise you to keep writing, much as in free writing. You may pause to glance at your notes and outline, but avoid stopping to edit your work.

▸ **Be yourself.** Let go of the urge to sound "scholarly" and avoid using unnecessary big words or phrases. Instead, write in a natural voice.

▸ **Avoid procrastination.** If you are having trouble getting started, skip over your introduction and just begin writing about some of your findings. You can go back later and organize your paragraphs.

▸ **Get physical.** While working on the first draft, take breaks. Go for a walk. From time to time, practice relaxation techniques and breathe deeply.

▸ **Put the draft away for a day.** Schedule time for rewrites, and schedule at least one day between revisions so that you can let the material sit. After a break, problems with the paper or ideas for improvement will become more evident.

Phase 3: Revising Your Draft

During this phase, keep in mind the saying, "Write in haste; revise at leisure." When you are working on your first draft, the goal is to produce ideas and write them down. During the revision phase, however, you need to slow down and take a close look at your work. One guideline is to allow 50 percent of writing time for planning, researching, and writing the first draft. Then use the remaining 50 percent for revising.

Here are some good ways to revise your paper:

1. **READ IT OUT LOUD.** The combination of speaking and hearing forces us to pay attention to the details. Is the thesis statement clear and supported by enough evidence? Does the introduction tell your reader what's coming? Do you end with a strong conclusion that expands on your introduction rather than just restating it?

2. **HAVE A FRIEND LOOK OVER YOUR PAPER.** This is never a substitute for your own review, but a friend can often see mistakes you miss. With a little practice, you will learn to welcome feedback, because it provides one of the fastest ways to approach the revision process.

3. **CUT.** Look for excess baggage. Also, look for places where two (or more) sentences could be rewritten as one. By cutting text you are actually gaining a clearer, more polished product. For efficiency, make the larger cuts first—sections, chapters, pages. Then go for the smaller cuts—paragraphs, sentences, phrases, words.

4. **PASTE.** The next task is to rearrange what's left of your paper so that it flows logically. Look for consistency within paragraphs and for transitions from paragraph to paragraph and section to section.

5. **FIX.** Now it's time to look at individual words and phrases. Define any terms that the reader might not know. In general, focus on nouns and verbs. Too many words add unnecessary bulk to your writing. Write about the details, and be specific. Also, check your writing to ensure that you:

   ▶ **Prefer the active voice.** Write *"The research team began the project"* rather than *"A project was initiated,"* which is a passive statement.

   ▶ **Write concisely.** Instead of *"After making a timely arrival and observing the unfolding events, I emerged totally and gloriously victorious,"* be concise with *"I came, I saw, I conquered."*

   ▶ **Communicate clearly.** Instead of *"The speaker made effective use of the television medium, asking in no uncertain terms that we change our belief systems,"* you can write specifically, *"The senatorial candidate stared straight into the television camera and said, 'Take a good look at what my opponent is doing! Do you really want six more years of this?'"*

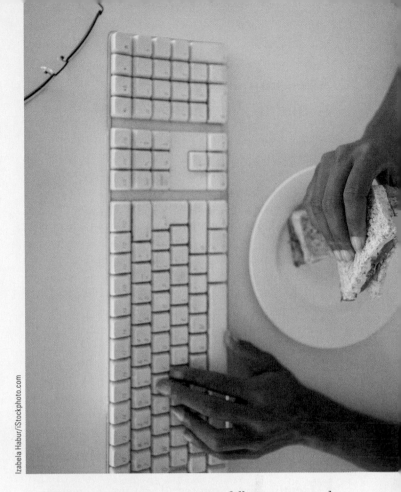

Izabela Habur/iStockphoto.com

6. **PREPARE.** Format your paper following accepted standards for margin widths, endnotes, title pages, and other details. Ask your instructor for specific instructions on how to cite the sources used in writing your paper. You can find useful guidelines in the *MLA Handbook for Writers of Research Papers.* If you are submitting a hard copy (rather than turning it in online), use quality paper for the final version. For an even more professional appearance, bind your paper with a plastic or paper cover.

7. **PROOFREAD.** As you ease down the home stretch, read your revised paper one more time, and look for the following:

   ▶ A clear thesis statement.

   ▶ Sentences that introduce your topic, guide the reader through the major sections of your paper, and summarize your conclusions.

   ▶ Details—such as quotations, examples, and statistics—that support your conclusions.

   ▶ Lean sentences that have been purged of needless words.

   ▶ Plenty of action verbs and concrete, specific nouns.

   ▶ Spelling and grammar mistakes. Use contractions sparingly, if at all. Use spell-check by all means, but do not rely on it completely, as it will not catch everything.

Academic Integrity: Avoiding Plagiarism

Using another person's words, images, or other original creations without giving proper credit is called *plagiarism*. Plagiarism amounts to taking someone else's work and presenting it as your own—the equivalent of cheating on a test. The consequences of plagiarism can range from a failing grade to expulsion from school.

To avoid plagiarism, ask an instructor where you can find your school's written policy on this issue. Don't assume that you can resubmit a paper you wrote for another class for a current class. Almost all schools will regard this as plagiarism even though you wrote the paper. The basic guidelines for preventing plagiarism are to cite a source for each phrase, sequence of ideas, or visual image created by another person. While ideas cannot be copyrighted, the specific way that an idea is *expressed* can be. You also need to list a source for any idea that is closely identified with a particular person. The goal is to clearly distinguish your own work from the work of others. There are several ways to ensure that you do this consistently:

▸ **Identify direct quotes.** If you use a direct quote from another source, put those words in quotation marks. If you do research online, you might copy text from a website and paste it directly into your notes. This is a direct quote. You must use quotation marks or if the quote is long, an indented paragraph.

▸ **Paraphrase carefully.** Paraphrasing means restating the original passage in your own words, usually making it shorter and simpler. Students who copy a passage word for word and then just rearrange or delete a few phrases are running a serious risk of plagiarism. Remember to cite a source for paraphrases, just as you do for direct quotes. When you use the same sequence of ideas as one of your sources—even if you have not paraphrased or directly quoted—cite that source.

▸ **Note details about each source.** For books, include the author, title, publisher, publication date, location of publisher, and page number. For articles from print sources, record the author, date, article title, and the name of the magazine or journal as well. If you found the article in an academic or technical journal, also include the volume and number of the publication. A librarian can help identify these details.

▸ **Cite online sources correctly.** If your source is a website, record as many identifying details as you can find—author, title, sponsoring organization, URL, publication date, and revision date. In addition, list the date that you accessed the page. Be careful when using Internet resources, as not all sites are considered legitimate sources. For example, many professors don't regard Wikipedia as an acceptable source.

▸ **Include your sources as endnotes or footnotes to your paper.** Ask your instructor for examples of the format to use. You do not need to credit wording that is wholly your own. Nor do you need to credit general ideas, such as the suggestion that people use a to-do list to plan their time. But if you borrow someone else's words or images to explain the idea, do give credit.

▸ **When in doubt, don't.** Sometimes you will find yourself working against a deadline for a paper, and in a panic, you might be tempted to take "shortcuts." You'll find a source that expressed your idea perfectly, but you must cite it or completely rephrase the idea in your own words. Professors are experts at noticing a change in tone or vocabulary that signals plagiarism. Often, they can simply Google a phrase to find its source online. Do not let a moment's temptation cause you to fail the course or face an academic integrity hearing.

LOFFLOW/Shutterstock

TAKE ACTION

A Guide to Political Participation

It's easy to think of politics as a spectator sport—something that politicians do, pundits analyze, and citizens watch. But there are many ways to get engaged with politics, to interact with the political world and participate in it, and even to effect change.

GET INFORMED

Find Out Where You Fit and What You Know

- You already have some opinions about a variety of political issues. Do you have a sense of where your views place you on the political map? Get a feel for your ideological leanings by taking *The World's Smallest Political Quiz:* **theadvocates.org/quiz**.

- Which Founder Are You? The National Constitutional Center can help you with that. Go to **constitutioncenter.org/foundersquiz** to discover which Founding Father's personality most resembles your own.

- The U.S. Constitution is an important part of the context in which American politics takes place. Do you know what the Constitution says? *Take the Constitution I.Q. Quiz:* **constitutionfacts.com**. Was your score higher than the national average?

- At the National Constitution Center, you can explore the interactive Constitution and learn more about the provisions in that document: **constitutioncenter.org/interactive-constitution**.

- Find out what those who want to become U.S. citizens have to do—and what they have to know. Go to the U.S. Citizenship and Immigration Services Web site at **uscis. gov/**. What is involved in applying for citizenship? Take the *Naturalization Self-Test* at **https://my.uscis. gov/prep/test/civics**. How did you do?

Think about How Your Political Views Have Been Shaped

- Consider how agents of political socialization—your family, your schools, and your peers, for example—have contributed to your political beliefs and attitudes. Then have conversations with people in your classes or where you live about the people, institutions, and experiences that influenced the way they view the political world. Try to understand how and why your views might differ.

- Explore how your views on political issues compare with those of a majority of Americans. There are a number of good polling sites that report public opinion on a range of topics.

  o The Pew Research Center for the People & the Press conducts monthly polls on politics and policy issues: **people-press.org**.

  o Public Agenda reports poll data and material on major issues: **publicagenda.org**.

  o The results of recent polls and an archive of past polls can be found at Gallup: **gallup.com**.

  o The Roper Center for Public Opinion Research is a leading archive of data from surveys of public opinion: **ropercenter.cornell.edu**.

GET CONNECTED

News

Keep up with news—print, broadcast, and online. Don't avoid certain news sources because you think you might not agree with the way they report the news. It's just as important to know how people are talking about issues as it is to know about the issues themselves.

- One way to follow the news is to get your information from the same place that journalists do. Often they take their cues or are alerted to news events by news agencies such as the nonprofit cooperative Associated Press: **ap.org**.

- Installing a few key apps on your phone or tablet can help you stay informed. Try downloading the Associated Press (AP) app for timely updates about news around the world. There are tons of other great political apps—some are fairly polarizing, some are neutral, and still others are just plain silly.

Blogs

The blogosphere affords views of politics that tend to be slanted according to the political orientation of the blog sponsor. In the last several decades, blogs have surged in popularity as a source for political news and opinion.

Social Media

Staying connected can be as simple as following local, national, or international politics on social media. President Barack Obama, Senator Elizabeth Warren, House Speaker Paul Ryan, and even the White House have Instagram accounts worth following. Most politicians and political outlets are also on Twitter and Facebook.

Check the Data

- It's not always easy to figure out whether a news report or public statement is accurate. PolitiFact, a project of the *Tampa Bay Times*, is a good place to go to get the facts: **politifact.com**. Check out the Truth-O-Meter, and get it on your smartphone or tablet.

- A project of the Annenberg Public Policy Center, **factcheck.org** is a nonpartisan, nonprofit "consumer advocate" for voters that monitors the factual accuracy of what political players are saying in TV ads, speeches, and interviews.

Keep Up during Election Season

- Project Vote Smart offers information on elections and candidates: **votesmart.org**.
- Nate Silver's FiveThirtyEight features election analysis, in addition to covering sports and economics: **fivethirtyeight.com**.
- Stay connected to the horse-race aspect of electoral politics by tracking election polls. There are many good sources:
  - For a comprehensive collection of election polls, go to the RealClearPolitics website: **realclearpolitics.com/polls**. RealClearPolitics is a good source for other political news and opinions as well.
  - Polls for U.S. federal elections, including state-by-state polls, can be found at **electoral-vote.com**.
  - HuffPost Pollster publishes pre-election poll results combined into interactive charts: **elections.huffingtonpost.com/pollster**. During presidential elections, additional maps and electoral vote counts can be found at HuffPost Politics Election Dashboard.
- If you have the opportunity, attend a speech by a candidate you're interested in.

Rawpixel.com/Shutterstock

Monitor Money and Influence in Politics

The Center for Responsive Politics Web site is an excellent source for information about who's contributing what amounts to which candidates: **opensecrets.org**. You can also use the lobbying database to identify the top lobbying firms, the agencies most frequently lobbied, and the industries that spend the most on lobbying activities.

Connect with Congress

You can, of course, learn a lot about what's going on in Congress from the Web sites of the House of Representatives and the Senate: **house.gov** and **senate.gov**. Look up the names and contact information for the senators and the representative from your area. If you want your voice to be heard, simply phone or e-mail your senators or your representative. Members of Congress listen to their constituents and often act in response to their constituents' wishes. Indeed, next to voting, contacting those who represent you in Congress is probably the most effective way to influence government decision making.

Check GovTrack to find out where your representative and senators fall on the leadership and ideology charts, and learn about their most recently sponsored bills and votes on legislation: **govtrack.us**.

Dragon Images/Shutterstock

financial health, accountability and transparency,
and reporting of results.

Design Your Own Ways to Take Action

- Start a network to match those who need assistance and those who want to help. For example, there may be people on your campus who, because of a disability or recent injury, need someone to help carry belongings, open doors, or push wheelchairs.

- Do you want to raise awareness about an issue? Is there a cause that you think needs attention? Talk with friends. Find out if they share your concerns. Turn your discussions into a blog. Create videos of events you think are newsworthy and share them online. Sign or start a petition.

Join a Group on Campus

You probably see flyers promoting groups and recruiting members posted all over campus. Chances are, there's a group organized around something you're interested in or care about.

Maybe it's an organization that works to bring clean water to remote parts of the world. The American Red Cross may be looking for help with campus blood drives. You'll find groups organized around race, culture, or political parties; groups that go on spring break trips to serve communities in need; service organizations of all kinds; and groups that focus on the environment. The list goes on and on.

If you have an interest that isn't represented by the groups on your campus, start your own. Your college or university should have an office of campus life (or something similar) that can help you establish a student organization.

Vote (but Don't Forget to Register First)

- You can learn about the laws governing voting in your state by going to the Web site of the National Confer-

GET INVOLVED

Take an Interest in Your Community—Offer to Help

Every community—large and small—can use energetic people willing to help where there is a need. Local non-profit agencies serving the homeless, battered women, or troubled teens often welcome volunteers who are willing to pitch in.

The Internet also has abundant resources about nonprofits and charities and how you can get involved:

- **Idealist.org** is a great place to find organizations and events that are looking for employees, interns, and volunteers. Filter by type and area of focus (women, disaster relief, animals, etc.) to find a cause that fits you.

- **Tinyspark.org** is a watchdog for nonprofits and charity organizations. It highlights individuals and groups that are doing good things around the globe and investigates those who may not be doing as much good as you'd think. Tinyspark also has a podcast.

- **Charitynavigator.org** is another tool for checking on charities. It evaluates and rates charities on ence of State Legislatures and its link to Voter Identification Requirements: **ncsl.org/research/ elections-and-campaigns/voter-id.**

- **Register: Enter "register to vote in [your state]" in a search engine.** The office in your state that administers voting and elections will have a Web site that outlines the steps you will need to follow. You can also find out how to obtain an absentee ballot.

- **If you want to view a sample ballot to familiarize yourself with what you'll see at the polls, you will probably be able to view one online.** Just enter "sample ballot" in a search engine. Your local election board, the League of Women Voters, or your district library often post a sample ballot online.

- **Vote: Familiarize yourself with the candidates and issues before you go to the polls.** If you'd like to influence the way things are done in your community, state, or Washington, D.C., you can do so by helping to elect local, state, and federal officials whose views you endorse and who you think would do a good job of running the government. Make sure you know the location and hours for your polling place.

Support a Political Party

Getting involved in political parties is as simple as going to the polls and casting your vote for the candidate of one of the major parties—or of a third party. You can also consider becoming a delegate to a party convention. Depending on the state, parties may hold conventions by U.S. House district, by county, or by state legislative district. In many states, the

lowest-level conventions (or, in some states, caucuses) are open to anyone who shows up. Voting rights at a convention, however, may be restricted to those who are elected as precinct delegates in a party primary.

In much of the country, precinct delegate slots go unfilled. If this is true in your area, you can become a precinct delegate with a simple write-in campaign, writing in your own name and persuading a handful of friends or neighbors to write you in as well. Whether you attend a convention as a voting delegate or as a guest, you'll have a firsthand look at how politics operates. You'll hear debates on resolutions. You might participate in electing delegates to higher-level conventions—perhaps even the national convention if it is a presidential election year.

© LHF Graphics/Shutterstock

Work for a Campaign

Candidates welcome energetic volunteers. So do groups that are supporting (or opposing) ballot measures. While sometimes tiring and frustrating, working in campaign politics can also be exhilarating and very rewarding.

Find the contact information for a campaign you're interested in on its website, and inquire about volunteer opportunities. Volunteers assemble mailings, answer the telephone, and make calls to encourage voters to support their candidate or cause. Even if you have little free time or are not comfortable talking to strangers, most campaigns can find a way for you to participate.

Joseph Sohm/Shutterstock

Be Part of Campus Media

Do you have a nose for news and do you write well? Try reporting for the university newspaper. Work your way up to an editor's position. If broadcast media are your thing, get involved with your college radio station or go on air on campus TV.

Engage with Political Institutions, Government Agencies, and Public Policymakers— at Home and Abroad

- **Visit the government websites for your state and community and learn about your representatives.** Contact them with your thoughts on matters that are important to you. Attend a city council meeting. You can find the date, location, and agenda on your city's website. And if you're passionate about a local issue, you can even sign up to speak.

- **Check to see if internships or volunteer opportunities are available close to home.** Your U.S. representative has a district office, and your U.S. senators also have offices in various locations around the state. If you plan to be in Washington, D.C., and want to visit Capitol Hill, book a tour in advance through your senators' or representative's offices. That's also where you can obtain gallery passes to the House and Senate chambers.

- **Spend some time in Washington, D.C.** Many colleges and universities have internship programs with government agencies and institutions. Some have semester-long programs that will bring you into contact with policymakers, journalists, and a variety of other prominent newsmakers. Politics and government will come alive, and the contacts you make while participating in such programs can often lead to jobs after graduation.

- **If you're interested in the Supreme Court** and you're planning a trip to Washington D.C., try to watch oral arguments. Go to the Court's website to access the link for oral arguments: **supreme court.gov**. You'll find the argument calendar and a visitor's guide. (The secret is to get in line early.)

- **Become a virtual tourist.** If you can't make it to Washington, D.C., for a semester-long program or even a few days, take the U.S. Capitol Virtual Tour: **www.aoc.gov/virtual-tours/capitolbldg/ tourfiles**.

- **You can take a virtual tour of the Supreme Court** at the Web site of the Oyez Project at IIT Chicago-Kent College of Law: **www.oyez.org/tour**. You can also listen to Supreme Court oral arguments wherever you are. Go to the Oyez site and check out ISCOTUSnow (blogs.kentlaw.iit.edu/iscotus/).

- **Check with the study-abroad office** at your college or university. Studying abroad is a great way to expand your horizons and get a feel for different cultures and the global nature of politics and the economy. There are programs that will take you almost anywhere in the world.

- **Participate in the Model UN Club** on your campus (or start a Model UN Club if there isn't one). By participating in Model UN, you will become aware of international issues and conflicts and gain hands-on experience in diplomacy.

GET INFORMED.
GET CONNECTED.
GET INVOLVED.

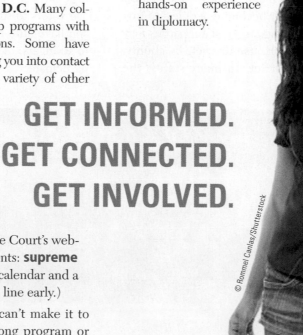

Every day in America, almost 12,000 people turn age 18 and become eligible to vote. Each vote makes a difference!

Rock the Vote! is the largest nonprofit and nonpartisan organization providing the tools college students need to get registered to vote. It also provides resources around becoming a more active citizen.

Go to the website below and get involved. Let your voice be heard!

Go to the Rock the Vote website below and ...

Blend Images/Getty Images

1

AMERICA IN THE TWENTY-FIRST CENTURY

LEARNING OUTCOMES *After reading this chapter, you should be able to:*

1-1 Explain what is meant by the terms *politics* and *government*.

1-2 Identify the various types of government systems.

1-3 Summarize some of the basic principles of American democracy and basic American political values.

1-4 Define common American ideological positions, such as "conservatism" and "liberalism."

After finishing this chapter, go to **PAGE 21** for **STUDY TOOLS**

AMERICA AT ODDS | Must We Give Up Some of Our Freedoms to Destroy ISIS?

oneinchpunch/Shutterstock.com

The threat of terrorism in the homeland is here to stay. As of 2016, for the first time in years, terrorism became the American public's number-one concern. This development followed the massacres in Paris in November 2015 (more than 130 dead) and shootings in San Bernardino, California, in December (14 dead). In Paris, the terrorists were part of a group called ISIS, and the killers in San Bernardino were inspired by ISIS as well. What, then, is ISIS?

The term *ISIS* represents the English initials of the group's former name, the Islamic State in Iraq and Syria. (An alternative is the Islamic State in Iraq and the Levant—ISIL.)[1] ISIS later shortened its name to the *Islamic State*. Uniquely among terrorist groups, it has established a government in territory seized from Iraq and Syria. In addition to fighting in these countries, ISIS has told its followers worldwide through Twitter and other social media to kill residents of Western nations.

How much of our freedom and our privacy, if any, should we sacrifice in our attempts to defeat ISIS and other terrorist groups?

Security First

Some point out that the oldest purpose of government is to protect its citizens from foreign and domestic violence. It follows that destroying ISIS is "job one." We should be willing to make sacrifices to defeat it. We will have to accept additional "snooping" by espionage and law enforcement agencies such as the National Security Agency (NSA). The government must use all possible means to analyze phone, e-mail, and social media data to identify terrorists. This will cost us some of our privacy. Remember, though: the NSA is not interested in 99.9 percent of what Americans are doing, saying, or thinking.

No one thinks twice today about security measures when we fly. We accept that it is better to stop terrorists from blowing up planes than to enjoy the freedom to board a flight without a security check. Polls show that a majority of Americans worry that the United States won't go far enough in monitoring potential terrorists. These citizens have got it right.

Freedom Is Fragile—Don't Crush It

Others say that America has spent two centuries developing and protecting our freedoms, the most important of which are found in the Bill of Rights. Now is not the time to start revoking these freedoms. The Bill of Rights requires the government to obtain a warrant from a court before conducting searches. That warrant must "particularly describe the place to be searched, and the persons or things to be seized." Given such language, how can the government indiscriminately collect information on every phone call, e-mail, and social media post?

True, our freedoms can exist only when they are protected by the government. But history shows that governments can also abuse their power and commit terrible crimes. We can recover from any particular terrorist incident, but we might not be able to recover from losses of our liberty.

Defeating ISIS is a laudable goal, but we must not stifle our vibrant free society. Security at any cost is, to say the least, a bad policy choice.

Where do you stand?

1. Most Muslims loathe and reject the term *Islamic State* because it presents the group as the legitimate leaders of Islam. Many call it *Daesh*, which is the equivalent of *ISIL* in Arabic. *Daesh* resembles a number of Arab insults. Should Americans adopt this term?

2. Many Americans are more afraid of a terrorist attack than a heart attack. Yet death from terrorism is very rare, while heart disease kills more of us than anything else. Why might relatively rare events often be so frightening?

Explore this issue online

- You can find more detailed arguments for and against NSA surveillance online. Look up "nsa pro outline" using a search engine such as Google. You'll find both pro and con arguments from Debate Central, a project of the National Center for Policy Analysis.

INTRODUCTION

Regardless of how Americans feel about government, one thing is certain: they can't live without it. James Madison (1751–1836) once said, "If men were angels, no government would be necessary." Today, his statement still holds true. People are not perfect. People need an organized form of government and a set of rules by which to live.

Government performs a wide range of extremely important functions. From the time we are born until the day we die, we constantly interact with various levels of government. Most (although not all) students attend government-run schools. All of us travel on government-owned streets and highways. Many of us serve in the military—a completely government-controlled environment. A few of us get into trouble and meet up with the government's law enforcement system. Every citizen after reaching the age of sixty-five can expect the government to help with medical and living expenses. To fund all these functions, the government collects taxes.

In a representative democracy such as ours, it is politics that controls what the government decides to do. What combination of taxes and government services is best? When should our leaders use military force against foreign nations or rebellions in foreign countries? As discussed in this chapter's opening *America at Odds* feature, how do we balance national security and civil liberties? How the nation answers these and many other questions will have a major impact on your life—and participation in politics is the only way you can influence what happens.

1–1 WHAT ARE POLITICS AND GOVERNMENT?

> **LO** Explain what is meant by the terms *politics* and *government*.

institution An ongoing organization that performs certain functions for society.

social conflict Disagreements among people in a society over what the society's priorities should be.

Even if—contrary to Madison's observation—people were perfect, they would still need to establish rules to guide their behavior. They would somehow have to agree on how to divide up a society's resources, such as its land, among themselves and how to balance individual needs and wants against those of society generally.

These perfect people would also have to decide *how* to make these decisions. They would need to create a process for making rules and a form of government to enforce those rules. It is thus not difficult to understand why government is one of humanity's oldest and most universal **institutions**.

As you will read in this chapter, a number of different systems of government exist in the world today. In the United States, we have a democracy in which decisions about pressing issues ultimately are made politically by the people's representatives in government.

Because people rarely have identical thoughts and feelings about issues, it is not surprising that in any democracy citizens are often at odds over many political and social problems. Throughout this book, you will read about contemporary controversies that have brought various groups of Americans into conflict with one another.

Differences in political opinion are part and parcel of a democratic government. Ultimately, these differences are resolved, one way or another, through the American political process and our government institutions.

1–1a Defining Politics and Government

Politics means many things to many people. There are also many different notions about the meaning of government. How should we define these two central concepts?

Politics and Conflict To some, politics is an expensive and extravagant game played in Washington, D.C., in state capitols, and in city halls, particularly during election time. To others, politics involves all of the tactics and maneuvers carried out by the president and Congress. Most formal definitions of politics, however, begin with the assumption that **social conflict**— disagreements among people in a society over what the society's priorities should be—is inevitable. Conflicts will naturally arise over how the society should use its scarce resources and who should receive various benefits, such as status, health care, and higher education. Resolving

> "THE ULTIMATE RULERS OF OUR DEMOCRACY ARE . . . THE VOTERS OF THIS COUNTRY."
>
> FRANKLIN D. ROOSEVELT
> THIRTY-SECOND PRESIDENT
> OF THE UNITED STATES
> 1933–1945

such conflicts is the essence of **politics**. Political scientist Harold Lasswell perhaps said it best in his classic definition of politics as the process of determining "who gets what, when, and how" in a society.[2]

Government and Authority

Disputes over how to distribute a society's resources inevitably arise because valued resources, such as property, are limited, while people's wants are unlimited. To resolve such disputes, people need ways to determine who wins and who loses, and how to get the losers to accept those decisions. Who has the legitimate power—the *authority*—to make such decisions? This is where governments step in.

Faculty member (center) with students. *In what ways are teachers at state colleges and universities different from other government employees?*

From the perspective of political science, **government** can best be defined as the individuals and institutions that make society's rules and also possess the power and authority to enforce those rules. Generally, in any country, government uses its authority to serve at least three essential purposes:

▶ It resolves conflicts,

▶ it provides public services, and

▶ it defends the nation and its culture against attacks by other nations.

1–1b Resolving Conflicts

Governments decide how conflicts will be resolved so that public order can be maintained. Governments have **power**—the ability to influence the behavior of others. Power is getting someone to do something that he or she would not otherwise do. Power may involve the use of force (often called coercion), persuasion, or rewards. Governments typically also have **authority**, which they can exercise only if their power is legitimate. As used here, the term *authority* means the ability to use power that is collectively recognized and accepted by society as legally and morally correct. Power and authority are central to a government's ability to resolve conflicts by making and enforcing laws, placing limits on what people can do, and developing court systems to make final decisions.

For example, the judicial branch of government—specifically, the United States Supreme Court—resolved the highly controversial question of whether the Second Amendment to the Constitution grants individuals the right to bear arms. In 2008 and 2010, the Court affirmed that such a right does exist. Because of the Court's stature and authority as a government body, there was little resistance to its decision, even from gun control advocates.

1–1c Providing Public Services

Another important purpose of government is to provide **public services**—essential services that many individuals cannot provide for themselves. Governments undertake projects that individuals usually would not or could not carry out on their own. These projects include building and maintaining roads, establishing welfare programs, operating public schools, and preserving national parks. Governments also

politics The process of resolving conflicts over how society should use its scarce resources and who should receive various benefits, such as public health care and public higher education.

government The individuals and institutions that make society's rules and possess the power and authority to enforce those rules.

power The ability to influence the behavior of others, usually through the use of force, persuasion, or rewards.

authority The ability to legitimately exercise power, such as the power to make and enforce laws.

public services Essential services that individuals cannot provide for themselves, such as building and maintaining roads, establishing welfare programs, operating public schools, and preserving national parks.

provide such services as law enforcement, fire protection, and public health and safety programs. As Abraham Lincoln once stated:

> The legitimate object of government is to do for a community of people, whatever they need to have done, but cannot do, *at all,* or cannot, *so well* do, for themselves—in their separate, individual capacities. In all that the people can individually do as well for themselves, government ought not to interfere.[3]

Services for All and Services for Some   Some public services are provided equally to all citizens of the United States. For example, government services such as national defense and domestic law enforcement allow all citizens, at least in theory, to feel that their lives and property are safe. Laws governing clean air and safe drinking water benefit all Americans.

Other services are provided only to citizens who are in need at a particular time, even though they are paid for by all citizens through taxes. Such services include health and welfare benefits. For example, a program such as Social Security Disability Insurance provides a source of income to people whose ability to work is limited by a notable disability. Americans contribute to the program through the Social Security payroll tax regardless of whether they ever become disabled.

Managing the Economy   One of the most crucial public services that the government is expected to provide is protection from hardship caused by economic recessions or depressions. From 2008 on, this governmental objective became more important than almost any other, due to the severity of the recession that began in December 2007.

One of the most damaging consequences of the recession has been high rates of unemployment, which have continued into the present, even though the recession officially ended in June 2009 when economic growth resumed. True, the official unemployment rate was 5.0 percent in early 2016, down from a high of 10 percent. Yet large numbers of discouraged workers remained out of the workforce and were not counted in the unemployment figures. When many Americans continue to face economic hardships, they often have negative views about how well our government is "running the ship."

1–1d Defending the Nation and Its Culture

Historically, matters of national security and defense have been given high priority by governments and have demanded considerable time, effort, and expense. The U.S. government provides for the common defense and national security with its Army, Navy, Marines, Air Force, and Coast Guard. The departments of State, Defense, and Homeland Security, plus the Central Intelligence Agency, National Security Agency, and other agencies, also contribute to this defense network.

As part of an ongoing policy of national security, many departments and agencies in the federal government are constantly dealing with other nations. The Constitution gives our national government exclusive power over relations with foreign nations. No individual state can negotiate a treaty with a foreign nation.

Of course, in defending the nation against attacks by other nations, a government helps to preserve the nation's culture, as well as its integrity as an independent unit. Failure to defend successfully against foreign attacks may have significant consequences for a nation's culture. For example, consider what happened in Tibet in the 1950s. When that country was taken over by the

Photo by Petty Officer 1st Class Rob Simpson.S/ Department of Defense

An MH-60 Jayhawk helicopter hoists a Coast Guard officer from the water near San Diego. The U.S. Navy is vastly superior to any other naval force. *What benefits do we gain by our control of the high seas?*

People's Republic of China, the conquering Chinese set out on a systematic program, the effective result of which was large-scale cultural destruction.

Attacks by foreign governments are not the only threat that nations must address. Since the terrorist attacks on the World Trade Center and the Pentagon in 2001, defending the homeland against future terrorist attacks has become a priority of our government. Terrorists often operate independently of any foreign authority, even if they are inspired from abroad. Examples include the Boston Marathon bombing in April 2013 and the massacre in San Bernardino, California, in December 2015.

CRITICAL THINKING

▶ *Would it be a good idea to send U.S. ground forces to attack ISIS in Iraq or Syria, or would doing so lead to even greater problems than we already face? Explain your answer.*

1–2 DIFFERENT SYSTEMS OF GOVERNMENT

LO Identify the various types of government systems.

Through the centuries, the functions of government just discussed have been performed by many different types of structures. A government's structure is influenced by a number of factors, such as a country's history, customs, values, geography, resources, and human experiences and needs. No two nations have exactly the same form of government. Over time, however, political analysts have developed ways to classify different systems of government. One of the most meaningful ways is according to *who* governs. Who has the power to make the rules and laws that all must obey?

1–2a Undemocratic Systems

Before the development of modern democratic systems, the power of the government was typically in the hands of an authoritarian individual or group. When such power is exercised by an individual, the system is called **autocracy**. Autocrats can gain power by traditional or nontraditional means.

Monarchy One form of autocracy, known as a **monarchy**, is government by a king or queen, an emperor or empress—or a person with some other aristocratic title, such as emir, grand duke, or prince. In a monarchy, the monarch, who usually acquires power through inheritance, is the highest authority in the government.

Historically, many monarchies were *absolute monarchies,* in which the ruler held complete and unlimited power. Until the eighteenth century, the theory of "divine right" was widely accepted in Europe. This **divine right theory**, variations of which had existed since ancient times, held that God gave those of royal birth the unlimited right to govern other men and women. In other words, those of royal birth had a "divine right" to rule, and only God could judge them. Thus, all citizens were bound to obey their monarchs, no matter how unfair or unjust they seemed to be. Challenging this power was regarded not only as treason against the government but also as a sin against God.

Most modern monarchies, however, are *constitutional monarchies,* in which the monarch shares governmental power with elected lawmakers. Over time, the monarch's power has come to be limited, or checked, by other government leaders and perhaps by a constitution or a bill of rights. Most constitutional monarchs today serve merely as ceremonial leaders of their nations, as in Spain, Sweden, and the United Kingdom (Britain).

Dictatorship Undemocratic systems that are not supported by tradition are called **dictatorships**. Often, a dictator is a single individual, although dictatorial power can be exercised by a group, such as the Communist Party of China. Dictators are not accountable to anyone else.

A dictatorship can be *totalitarian*, which means that a leader or group of leaders seeks to control almost all aspects of social and economic life. The leadership establishes the goals of society. Citizens must conform to the government's dictates in all fields of endeavor—in the economy, in literature and entertainment, and even in private conversation. Typically, these collective goals benefit only the leaders, and are damaging to the nation as a whole.

Examples of the totalitarian form of government

autocracy A form of government in which the power and authority of the government are in the hands of a single person.

monarchy A form of autocracy in which a king, queen, or other aristocrat is the highest authority in the government. Monarchs usually obtain their power through inheritance.

divine right theory The theory that a monarch's right to rule was derived directly from God rather than from the consent of the people.

dictatorship A form of government in which absolute power is exercised by an individual or group whose power is not supported by tradition.

> "People often say that, in a democracy, decisions are made by a majority of the people. Of course, that is not true. Decisions are made by a majority of . . . the people who vote—a very different thing."
>
> ~ WALTER H. JUDD,
> U.S. REPRESENTATIVE FROM MINNESOTA, 1943–1963

1–2b Democratic Systems

The most familiar form of government to Americans is **democracy**, in which the supreme political authority rests with the people. The word *democracy* comes from the Greek *demos,* meaning "the people," and *kratia,* meaning "rule." The main idea of democracy is that government exists only by the consent of the people and reflects the will of the majority. Figure 1–1 shows the extent of democracy in the world today—with "democratic" defined as "free."

The Athenian Model of Direct Democracy

Democracy as a form of government began long ago. In its earliest form, democracy was simpler than the system we know today. What we now call **direct democracy** exists when the people participate directly in government decision making. In its purest form, direct democracy was practiced in Athens and several other ancient Greek city-states about 2,500 years ago. Every Athenian citizen participated in the governing assembly and voted on all major issues. Some consider the Athenian form of direct democracy ideal because it demanded a high degree of citizen participation. Others point out that most residents in the Athenian city-state (women, foreigners, and slaves) were not considered citizens. Thus, they were not allowed to participate in government.

democracy A system of government in which the people have ultimate political authority. The word is derived from the Greek *demos* ("the people") and *kratia* ("rule").

direct democracy A system of government in which political decisions are made by the people themselves rather than by elected representatives. This form of government was practiced in some parts of ancient Greece.

include Adolf Hitler's Nazi regime in Germany from 1933 to 1945 and Joseph Stalin's dictatorship in the Soviet Union (Russia) from 1929 to 1953. A more contemporary example of a totalitarian dictator is the latest leader of North Korea, Kim Jong-un.

FIGURE 1–1   FREE AND UNFREE NATIONS OF THE WORLD, JANUARY 2016

In this classification of nations by Freedom House, green means free, yellow means partly free, and blue means unfree. Bear in mind that these are the assessments of a single organization. *Why might another organization come up with a different system of classification?*

Sources: Arch Puddington and Tyler Roylance, *Freedom in the World 2016—Anxious Dictators, Wavering Democracies: Global Freedom under Pressure* (Washington, D.C.: Freedom House, 2016). Outline map adapted from Wikimedia.

Citizens of Calais, Vermont, raise yellow cards to register their vote on Town Meeting Day. Some New England towns use town meetings to engage in a form of direct democracy. *Why doesn't the United States as a nation have direct democracy?*

Direct Democracy Today Clearly, direct democracy is possible only in small communities in which citizens can meet in a chosen place and decide key issues and policies. Nowhere in the world does pure direct democracy exist today. Some New England towns, though, and a few of the smaller political subunits, or cantons, of Switzerland still use a modified form of direct democracy.

Another modern institution with some of the characteristics of direct democracy is the ballot proposal, in which the voters themselves decide a specific question rather than letting their elected officials resolve the issue. Ballot proposals are used in many American states. In one type, the *referendum*, the legislature sends a ballot proposal to the voters. The *initiative* differs in that a question is placed on the ballot by gathering signatures, not by action of the legislature. A related process is *recall*, an initiative to remove an elected official immediately, before his or her term of office comes to an end.

Representative Democracy Although the founders of the United States were aware of the Athenian model and agreed that government should be based on the consent of the governed, they believed that direct democracy would deteriorate into mob rule. They thought that large groups of people meeting together would ignore the rights and opinions of people in the minority and would make decisions without careful thought. They believed that representative assemblies were superior because they would enable public decisions to be made in a calmer and more deliberate manner.

In a **representative democracy**, the will of the majority is expressed through smaller groups of individuals elected by the people to act as their representatives. These representatives are responsible to the people for their conduct and can be voted out of office. Our founders preferred to use the term **republic**, which means essentially a representative system with one qualification.

A democratic republic, by definition, has no king or queen. Rather, the people are sovereign. In contrast, a representative democracy may be headed by a monarch. For example, as Britain evolved into a representative democracy, it retained its monarch as the head of state (but with no real power).

Types of Representative Democracy In the modern world, there are basically two forms of representative democracy: presidential and parliamentary. In a *presidential democracy*, the lawmaking and law-enforcing branches of government are separate but equal. For example, in the United States, Congress is charged with the power to make laws, and the president is charged with the power to carry them out.

In a *parliamentary democracy*, the lawmaking and law-enforcing branches of government are united. In Britain, for example, the prime minister and the cabinet are members of the legislature, called Parliament, and are responsible to that body. A **parliament** thus both enacts the laws and carries them out.

representative democracy A form of democracy in which the will of the majority is expressed through groups of individuals elected by the people to act as their representatives.

republic Essentially, a representative system in which there is no king or queen and the people are sovereign.

parliament The national legislative body in countries governed by a parliamentary system, such as Britain and Canada.

1-2c Other Forms of Government

Monarchy, dictatorship, and *democracy* are three of the most common terms for describing systems of government, but there are others. For example, the term *aristocracy,* which in Greek means "rule by the best," describes a government run by members of old, noble families. Aristocracies have rarely had complete power, but have usually shared power with other forces, such as a monarch. *Plutocracy,* a somewhat similar form, means "government by the wealthy." The term typically refers to systems in which the rich have a disproportionate influence.

A difficult form of government for Americans to understand is *theocracy*—a term derived from the Greek words meaning "rule by the deity" or "rule by God." In a theocracy, there is no separation of church and state. Rather, the government rules according to religious precepts. In Iran, the Council of Guardians, an elected group of religious leaders, ensures that laws and lawmakers conform to their interpretation of the teachings of Islam.

CRITICAL THINKING

▶ *Chinese Communist leader Mao Zedong (1893–1976) once said, "Political power grows out of the barrel of a gun." Was Mao right? Why or why not?*

 1-3 AMERICAN DEMOCRACY

LO Summarize some of the basic principles of American democracy and basic American political values.

limited government
A form of government based on the principle that the powers of government should be clearly limited either through a written document or through wide public understanding.

"This country, with all its institutions, belongs to the people who inhabit it. Whenever they shall grow weary of the existing government, they can exercise their constitutional right to amend it, or their revolutionary right to dismember or overthrow it."[4]

With these words, Abraham Lincoln underscored the most fundamental concept of American government: the people, not the government, are ultimately in control.

1-3a The British Legacy

In writing the U.S. Constitution, the framers incorporated two basic principles of government that had evolved in England: *limited government* and *representative government*. In a sense, then, the beginnings of our form of government are linked to events that occurred centuries earlier in England. They are also linked to the writings of European philosophers, particularly the English political philosopher John Locke (1632–1704). From these writings, the founders of our nation derived ideas to justify their rebellion against Britain and their establishment of a "government by the people."

Limited Government At one time, the English monarch claimed to have almost unrestricted powers. This changed in 1215, when King John was forced by his nobles to accept the Magna Carta, or the Great Charter. This monumental document provided for a trial by a jury of one's peers (equals). It prohibited the taking of a free man's life, liberty, or property except through due process of law. The Magna Carta also forced the king to obtain the nobles' approval of any taxes he imposed on them. Government thus became a contract between the king and his subjects.

The importance of the Magna Carta to England cannot be overemphasized, because it clearly established the principle of **limited government**—a government on which strict limits are placed, usually by a constitution. This form of government is characterized by institutional checks to ensure that it serves public rather than private interests. Hence, the Magna Carta signaled the end of the monarch's absolute power. Although many of the rights provided under the original Magna Carta applied only to the nobility, the document formed the basis of the future constitutional government for England and eventually the United States.

Representative Government In a representative government, the people, by whatever means, elect individuals to make governmental decisions for all of the citizens. Usually, these representatives of the people are elected to their offices for specific periods of time. In England, as mentioned earlier, this group of representatives is called a *parliament*. The English form of government provided a model for Americans to follow. Each of the American colonies established its own legislature.

In 1689, the English Parliament passed the English Bill of Rights, which further extended the concepts of limited and representative government. This document included several important ideas:

▶ **The king or queen could not interfere with parliamentary elections.**

▶ **The king or queen had to have Parliament's approval to levy (collect) taxes or to maintain an army.**

▶ **The king or queen had to rule with the consent of the people's representatives in Parliament.**

The English colonists in North America were also English citizens, and nearly all of the major concepts in the English Bill of Rights became part of the American system of government.

Political Philosophy: Social Contracts and Natural Rights Our democracy resulted from what can be viewed as a type of **social contract** among early Americans to create and abide by a set of governing rules. Social-contract theory was developed in the seventeenth and eighteenth centuries by philosophers such as John Locke. According to this theory, individuals voluntarily agree with one another, in a "social contract," to give up some of their freedoms to obtain the benefits of orderly government. The government is given adequate power to secure the mutual protection and welfare of all individuals.

Locke also argued that people are born with **natural rights** to life, liberty, and property. He theorized that the purpose of government was to protect those rights. If it did not, it would lose its legitimacy and need not be obeyed. As you will read in Chapter 2, when the American colonists rebelled against British rule, such concepts as natural rights and a government based on a social contract became important theoretical tools in justifying the rebellion.

1-3b Principles of American Democracy

We can say that American democracy is based on at least five fundamental principles:

▶ **Equality in voting.** Citizens must have equal opportunities to express their preferences about policies and leaders.

▶ **Individual freedom.** All individuals must have the greatest amount of freedom possible without interfering with the rights of others.

▶ **Equal protection of the law.** The law must entitle all persons to equal protection.

▶ **Majority rule and minority rights.** The majority should rule, while guaranteeing the rights of minorities.

▶ **Voluntary consent to be governed.** The people who make up a democracy must collectively (not individually) agree to be governed by the rules laid down by their representatives.

These principles frame many of the political issues that you will read about in this book. They also frequently lie at the heart of America's political conflicts. Does the principle of minority rights mean that minorities should receive preferential treatment in hiring and firing decisions to make up for past mistreatment? Does the principle of individual freedom mean that individuals can express whatever they want on the Internet, including hateful, racist comments? Above all, how much should the government *do*? We address that last question in this chapter's *Join the Debate* feature.

Such conflicts over individual rights and freedoms and over society's priorities are natural and inevitable. Resolving these conflicts is what politics is all about. The key point is that Americans are frequently able to reach acceptable compromises because of their common political heritage.

1-3c American Political Values

Historically, as the nations of the world emerged, the boundaries of each nation normally coincided with the boundaries of a population that shared a common ethnic heritage, language, and culture. From its beginnings as a nation, however, America has been defined less by the culture shared by its diverse population than by the ideas that make up its political culture.

A **political culture** can be defined as a patterned set of ideas, values,

social contract
A voluntary agreement among individuals to create a government and to give that government adequate power to secure the mutual protection and welfare of all individuals.

natural rights
Rights that are not bestowed by governments but are inherent within every man, woman, and child by virtue of the fact that he or she is a human being.

political culture
The set of ideas, values, and attitudes about government and the political process held by a community or a nation.

For much of America's history, there was little discussion about whether our government had grown too large. The government, after all, wasn't that big. Since the Great Depression of the 1930s, however, the government has grown by leaps and bounds.

Americans are at odds over the proper size of government. Indeed, the size of government lies at the very heart of the differences between Republicans and Democrats. Republicans have called for trillions of dollars in federal budget cuts over the next decade. Democrats, however, believe that cuts of this size may endanger important programs such as Medicare and Medicaid. (Medicare provides health-care funding to the elderly, and Medicaid provides it to low-income persons.)

Big Government Must Shrink

Many of those who believe that big government must shrink admit that government programs can help many people who need, for example, medical care or education. The problem is that once government programs are in place, they expand. The result is an "assisted society." Opponents of big government believe that too many people spend too much time seeking government assistance rather than taking care of their problems by themselves or with the help of family and friends.

Conservatives argue that government spending must be held back to avoid higher taxes. Even if the government supports its spending by borrowing, it will have to make up the difference by imposing new taxes at some time in the future. The federal budget deficit cannot rise forever, and most of us know that. Further, the government is inefficient. Private citizens can almost always make better use of funds than the government can, so taxing the people to allow government spending wastes resources. Finally, taxing some people to support other people is fundamentally unfair.

We Need What the Government Does

Liberals reject the argument that taxation must injure the economy. In the 1990s, Democrats under President Bill Clinton raised taxes to reduce the federal budget deficit. Conservatives predicted disaster. In fact, America then experienced some of the strongest economic growth in its history.

More generally, liberals argue that we need the programs that a big government can provide. Medicare, Medicaid, Social Security, and national defense together make up well over half of all federal spending. The first three programs assist people who cannot get by with just the help of family or friends. Most of the smaller programs, such as education and veterans' benefits, serve equally important purposes.

Liberals agree that government should do whatever it can to limit wasteful spending. But when we must choose between higher taxes and eliminating crucial services, we will simply have to pay for the benefits we need. America can do this. Until December 2012, when taxes on the wealthiest increased, taxes were lower as a share of the economy than in any year since the 1950s.

Critical Analysis

Are tax increases a legitimate policy option—or should they be out of the question?

and ways of thinking about government and politics. Our political culture is passed from one generation to another through families, schools, and the media. This culture is powerful enough to win over most new immigrants. Indeed, some immigrants come to America precisely because they are attracted by American values.

The ideals and standards that constitute American political culture are embodied in the Declaration of Independence, one of the founding documents of this nation, which will be discussed further in Chapter 2 and presented in its entirety in Appendix A. The political values outlined in the Declaration of Independence include natural rights (to life, liberty, and the pursuit of happiness), equality under the law, government by the consent of the governed, and limited government powers. In some ways, the Declaration of Independence defines Americans' sense of right and wrong. It presents a challenge to anyone who might wish to

A young girl celebrates the Fourth of July. *What function does "flag waving" have?*

overthrow our democratic processes or deny our citizens their natural rights.

The rights to liberty, equality, and property are fundamental political values shared by most Americans. These values provide a basic framework for American political discourse and debate because they are shared, yet Americans often interpret their meanings quite differently. The result of these differences can be sharp conflict in the political arena.

Liberty The term *liberty* can be defined as a state of being free from external controls or restrictions. In the United States, the Constitution sets forth our *civil liberties* (see Chapter 4), including the freedom to practice whatever religion we choose and to be free from any state-imposed religion. Our liberties also include the freedom to speak freely on any topic and issue. Because people cannot govern themselves unless they are free to voice their opinions, freedom of speech is a basic requirement in a true democracy.

Clearly, though, if we are to live together with others, there have to be some restrictions on individual liberties. If people were allowed to do whatever they wished, without regard for the rights or liberties of others, chaos would result. Hence, a more accurate definition of **liberty** would be: *the freedom of individuals to believe, act, and express themselves as they choose so long as doing so does not infringe on the rights of other individuals in the society.*

While almost all Americans believe strongly in liberty, differing ideas of what liberty should mean have led to some of our most heated political disputes. Should women be free to obtain abortions? Should employers be free to set the wages and working conditions of their employees? Should individuals be free to smoke marijuana? Over the years, Americans have been at odds over these and many other issues that concern liberty.

Equality The goal of **equality** has always been a central part of American political culture. The Declaration of Independence confirmed the importance of equality to early Americans by stating, "We hold these Truths to be self-evident, that all Men are created equal." Because of the goal of equality, the Constitution prohibited the government from granting titles of nobility. (The Constitution did not prohibit slavery, however—see Chapter 2.)

But what, exactly, does *equality* mean? Does it mean simply political equality—the right to vote and run for political office? Does it mean that individuals should have equal opportunities to develop their talents and skills? What about those who are poor, suffer from disabilities, or are otherwise at a competitive disadvantage? Should it be the government's responsibility to ensure that such individuals also have equal opportunities?

Although most Americans believe that all persons should have the opportunity to fulfill their potential, few contend that it is the government's responsibility to totally eliminate the economic and social differences that lead to unequal opportunities. Indeed, some contend that efforts to achieve equality, in the sense of equal treatment for all, are fundamentally incompatible with the value of liberty.

Property As noted earlier, the English philosopher John Locke asserted that people are born with natural rights and that among these rights are life, liberty, and *property*. The Declaration of Independence makes a similar assertion: people are born with certain "unalienable" rights, including the right to life, liberty, and the *pursuit of happiness*. For Americans, property and the pursuit of happiness are closely related. Americans place a great value on home ownership, on material possessions, and on their businesses. Property gives its owners political power and the liberty to do what they want—within limits.

> **liberty** The freedom of individuals to believe, act, and express themselves as they choose so long as doing so does not infringe on the rights of other individuals in the society.
>
> **equality** A concept that holds, at a minimum, that all people are entitled to equal protection under the law.

Property and Capitalism. Private property in America is not limited to personal possessions such as automobiles and houses. Property also consists of assets that can be used to create and sell goods and services, such as factories, farms, and shops. Private ownership of wealth-producing property is at the heart of our capitalist economic system. **Capitalism** enjoys such widespread support in the United States that we can reasonably call it one of the nation's fundamental political values. In addition to the private ownership of productive property, capitalism is based on *free markets*—markets in which people can freely buy and sell goods, services, and financial investments without undue constraint by the government. Freedom to make binding contracts is another element of the capitalist system. The preeminent capitalist institution is the privately owned corporation.

Capitalism and Government. Although capitalism is supported by almost all Americans, there is no equivalent agreement on the relationship between capitalism and the government. Is it best for the government to leave businesses alone in almost all circumstances—or would this lead to excessive inequality and unethical business practices that injure consumers? As with the values of liberty and equality, Americans are divided over what the right to property should mean.

1–3d Political Values and a Divided Electorate

Differences among Americans in interpreting our collectively held values underlie the division between the Republican and Democratic parties. Election results in the twenty-first century suggest that the voters are split right down the middle. Elections have often been close. In 2000, for example, Republican George W. Bush won the presidency in one of the closest presidential elections in U.S. history. In election years since 2000, support for the two major parties has swung back and forth, sometimes dramatically. The years 2006 and 2008 were very good for the Democrats, at first because of public dissatisfaction with the war in Iraq and later because of the economic crisis that struck while Bush was still president. The Republicans, in turn, enjoyed banner years in 2010 and 2014, based in part on the widespread belief that President Barack Obama and the Democrats were going too far in an attempt to carry out their liberal party platform. Despite the earlier swing to the Democrats and the later Republican victories, the underlying reality remained—the nation was closely divided in its political preferences.

The 2012 Elections Republican successes in 2010 were backed up by the growth in new conservative movements such as the Tea Party. Founded after Barack Obama became president, the grassroots **Tea Party movement** opposed current levels of government and taxation, and also resisted political compromise. Tea Party activism had its limits, however. By 2012, many moderate voters were apparently concerned that Republican threats to popular social programs outweighed Democratic fondness for "big government."

Also, in a presidential election year such as 2012, more Democratic-leaning young people and minority group members could be expected to vote. (Often, such voters stay home in *midterm election years* such as 2010 and 2014, when presidential candidates are not on the ballot.) In the end, President Obama won reelection by a comfortable margin.

The Current Environment The political battles of the twenty-first century have been intense. Public opinion polls report that increasing numbers of Republicans and Democrats consider the other party to be not merely misguided, but a danger to the country. The 2016 elections, therefore, were certain to be consequential, whether or not they were close.

For the Democrats, a key question was whether they could preserve social programs such as the Affordable Care Act, better known as "Obamacare." (This program was designed to substantially increase the number of citizens with health-care insurance.) Republicans sought to obtain sufficient control of the government to lock in conservative policies for years to come. We describe the election results in this chapter's *Elections 2016* feature.

Republican prospects were clouded by a division in their ranks. For years, a core Republican objective had been cuts in tax rates, especially for upper-income Americans. Republican leaders were willing to fund such reductions by cutting programs such as Social Security and Medicare. Many ordinary Republicans, however, saw these programs as a right earned by years of paying taxes. For many of these people, opposition to immigration was the number one issue. In contrast,

---

capitalism An economic system based on the private ownership of wealth-producing property, free markets, and freedom of contract. The privately owned corporation is the preeminent capitalist institution.

Tea Party movement A grassroots conservative movement that arose in 2009 after Barack Obama became president. The movement opposes big government and current levels of taxation, and also rejects political compromise.

In the 2016 elections, Republican Donald J. Trump was elected the forty-fifth president of the United States. The Republicans retained control of the U.S. Senate and House of Representatives. For the first time since December 2010, one party was in full control of the national government. Trump was expected to fill a vacancy in the United States Supreme Court, guaranteeing that the Republicans would enjoy a sympathetic hearing from the judiciary. If Democrat Hillary Clinton had won the presidency, the nation might have continued on a course broadly similar to that of the last six years, with a Democratic president constrained by at least a Republican House of Representatives. Clinton did, in fact, win the popular vote. American presidential elections are decided in the electoral college, however, and there Trump's victory margin was decisive. Still, Democrats enjoyed a net gain of two senators and eight members of the House, but this was far from enough to threaten Republican control of either chamber. The practical consequences of the Republican sweep were not immediately clear. That party was expected to pass much conservative legislation, but any new laws would need Trump's approval. On many points, Trump's nationalist politics differed from traditional Republican small-government conservatism. Negotiations between Trump and the Republicans in Congress were inevitable, but most observers expected them to succeed.

business-oriented establishment Republicans often supported immigration and steps to improve the status of illegal immigrants.

1-3e Political Values in a Changing Society

From the earliest English and European settlers to the many cultural groups that today call America their home, American society has always been multicultural. Until recently, most Americans accepted that American society included numerous ethnic and cultural groups, but they expected that the members of these groups would abandon their cultural distinctions and assimilate the language and customs of earlier Americans. One of the outgrowths of the civil rights movement of the 1960s, however, was an emphasis on *multiculturalism*, the belief that the many cultures that make up American society should remain distinct and be protected—and even encouraged—by our laws.

Despite the growth in multiculturalism, Americans of all backgrounds remain committed to the values described in the last few sections of this text. Inevitably, however, different groups interpret these values in varying ways, thus adding to our political divisions. African Americans, for example, given their collective history, often have a different sense of what equality should mean than do Americans whose ancestors came from Europe.

Race and Ethnicity The racial and ethnic makeup of the United States has changed dramatically in the last two decades and will continue to change, as shown in Figure 1–2. Already, non-Hispanic whites are a minority in California. For the nation as a whole, non-Hispanic whites will be in the minority before 2050. Some Americans fear that rising numbers of immigrants will threaten traditional American political values and culture. Others are confident that newcomers will adopt American values. Even as new Hispanic and Asian citizens assimilate into American culture, they remain more likely to vote for Democrats than Republicans. In other words, demographic change may provide a substantial future benefit to the Democratic Party. In recent elections, however, this benefit has been counteracted by another effect. A growing number of non-Hispanic whites—especially older ones—have been drawn to conservatism by their concern over the changing nature of American society. We take a closer look at the immigration issue in this chapter's *Perception vs. Reality* feature.

An Older Society In 2010, Americans aged 65 or above made up 13 percent of the total population. By 2040, however, that figure is expected to exceed 21

FIGURE 1–2   DISTRIBUTION OF THE U.S. POPULATION BY RACE AND HISPANIC ORIGIN, 2010 TO 2050

By 2050, minorities will constitute a majority of the U.S. population.

Year	White	Hispanic	Asian	Black	Other
2050	47.3	26.5	8.4	12.8	5.0
2040	51.3	24.1	7.6	12.7	4.3
2030	55.5	21.6	6.7	12.6	3.7
2020	59.6	19.0	5.8	12.4	3.2
2010	63.7	16.3	4.7	12.2	3.0

Percent (0–100)

■ White ■ Hispanic ■ Asian ■ Black ■ Other

Data for 2010 are from the 2010 census. Data for 2020 through 2050 are Census Bureau projections.

Figures do not necessarily sum to 100%, because of rounding. Hispanics may be of any race. The chart categories "White," "Black," "Asian," and "Other" are limited to non-Hispanics.

"Other" consists of the following non-Hispanic groups: "American Indian," "Alaska Native," "Native Hawaiian," "Other Pacific Islander," and "Two or More Races."

Sources: U.S. Bureau of the Census and authors' calculations.

ideology Generally, a system of political ideas that are rooted in religious or philosophical beliefs concerning human nature, society, and government.

conservatism A set of political beliefs that include a limited role for the national government in helping individuals and in the economic affairs of the nation, as well as support for traditional values and lifestyles.

percent. The aging of America means that in future years there will be more retired people collecting Social Security, Medicare, and private pensions, compared with the number of working adults. Inevitably, the question of how to share the national income among the generations will become an ever-greater problem. In many foreign countries, however, the aging population poses a much greater threat than in the United States. Our population is expected to grow throughout the coming century. Nations such as Germany, Japan, Russia, and even China can expect to see their populations shrink, which will make it much harder for them to support their older citizens.

CRITICAL THINKING

▶ *It's an old saying: "Your freedom to swing your arm ends where my nose begins." Can you think of other examples where one person's liberty interests conflict with those of another person?*

1–4 AMERICAN POLITICAL IDEOLOGY

LO Define common American ideological positions, such as "conservatism" and "liberalism."

In a general sense, **ideology** refers to a system of political ideas. These ideas typically are rooted in religious or philosophical beliefs about human nature, society, and government.

When it comes to ideology, Americans are often placed in two broad political camps: conservatives and liberals. The term *conservative* originally referred to persons who wished to conserve—keep—traditional social and political habits and institutions. The term *liberal* referred to those who wanted to be free from tradition and to establish new policies and practices. In today's American political arena, however, these simple definitions of *liberalism* and *conservatism* are incomplete. Both terms mean much more.

1–4a Conservatism

Modern American **conservatism** does indeed value traditions—specifically, American ones. For much of U.S. history, business enterprise was largely free from government control or regulation. That freedom began to break down during the administration of Franklin D. Roosevelt (1933–1945). Roosevelt's New Deal programs, launched in an attempt to counter the effects of

Do Immigrants Take American Jobs?

America was founded by immigrants, and few restrictions on immigration existed until the twentieth century. Today, however, immigration is a major issue. A special concern is the large number of unauthorized immigrants, also called illegal immigrants. There are probably about 11.3 million of these people currently in the country. The number of unauthorized immigrants has been stable since 2008 due to a collapse in rates of immigration from Mexico. (In fact, the annual number of Mexican immigrants—legal and illegal—returning home now exceeds the number of new arrivals.) Still, many people fear that immigrants, whether legal or illegal, take jobs away from American citizens.

The Perception

Many believe that increased immigration leads to more competition for jobs. Low-skilled immigrants drive down the wages of low-skilled citizens. Even highly skilled immigrants can take jobs away from engineers and other educated individuals born in the United States.

The Reality

Immigrants fill jobs, but they also create them. Economic growth can increase the amount of employment that is available. And economic studies show that highly skilled immigrants promote economic growth, increasing employment even among high-tech workers.

The number of well-educated immigrants from China, India, and other Asian countries is growing rapidly. The annual number of immigrants from Asia now exceeds the number from Latin America. A quarter of the engineering and technology companies started in the United States from 1995 to 2005 had at least one founder who was foreign-born. Some of the world's brightest brains and most cutting-edge innovators come to the United States to study—and often to stay. Foreign students earn 44 percent of U.S. science and engineering doctorates. Yet many of these students are forced to leave the country after graduation because there are not enough visas available for professionals.

Even low-skilled immigrants benefit the overall economy. The United States has jobs available at the bottom as well as the top. With unemployment at 10 percent in 2009 and 2010, farmers on the West Coast still could not find U.S. citizens willing to pick fruits and vegetables.

Studies suggest that while low-skilled—and especially illegal—immigrants may have an impact on low-end wages, those most likely to not be hired are *other low-skilled immigrants*. These immigrants often speak English poorly, if at all. That gives native-born citizens an employment advantage in most parts of the country. They can compete successfully for jobs that require English competency, such as store-clerk positions. More immigration means more economic growth, and more of all kinds of jobs, including jobs that require English-speaking applicants.

Blog On

Enter "immigration and american jobs" into an Internet search engine such as Google. One result of the search will be an informative New York Times *article with that exact title.*

the Great Depression, involved the government in the American economy to an extent previously unknown. Roosevelt gave conservatives a common cause: opposition to the New Deal and to big government. One tradition that conservatives sought to maintain, therefore, was a version of capitalism that was free of government regulation or control. Another is that groups that held a preeminent position in American society in the past—such as business and religious leaders—should continue to receive respect.

The Conservative Movement The emergence of the conservative movement in the 1950s and 1960s was essential to the development of modern conservatism. Previously, economic conservatives were often seen as individuals who feared that government activity might personally cost them wealth or power. The conservative movement, in contrast, was

> **conservative movement**
> An ideological movement that arose in the 1950s and 1960s and continues to shape conservative beliefs.

Donald Trump introduces Indiana governor Mike Pence as his vice-presidential running mate. *How is Trump different from past Republican candidates?*

1-4b Liberalism

While modern American **liberalism** can trace its roots to the New Deal programs of Franklin D. Roosevelt, the ideology did not take its fully modern form until the 1960s, during the Johnson administration. Johnson went well beyond the programs of Roosevelt with new economic initiatives, such as Medicare and Medicaid. These programs—and more recent health-care reforms—reflect the strong liberal belief that the social and economic outcomes that exist in the absence of government action are frequently unfair. Conservatives commonly accuse liberals of valuing "big government" for its own sake. Liberals reject that characterization and argue that big government is simply a necessary tool for promoting the common welfare.

clearly ideological. It provided a complete way of viewing the world, and it attracted millions of followers who were not necessarily motivated by narrow economic self-interest. The conservative movement emerged as a major force in 1964, when Arizona senator Barry Goldwater won the Republican presidential nomination on a relatively radical platform. Goldwater was soundly defeated by Democrat Lyndon B. Johnson (1963–1969). In 1980, however, Republican Ronald Reagan became the first "movement conservative" to win the White House.

Conservatism Today A key element in conservative thinking is the belief that the distribution of social and economic benefits that would exist if the government took little or no action is usually optimum. Conservatives believe that individuals and families should take responsibility for their own economic circumstances, and if that means that some people have less, so be it. Conservatives also place a high value on the principle of order, on family values, and on patriotism. Conservatism has always included those who want society and the government to reflect traditional religious values, and Christian conservatives remain an important part of the conservative coalition today. As one result, many conservatives continue to oppose same-sex marriages, even though the United States Supreme Court legalized such unions nationwide in June 2015.[5]

liberalism A set of political beliefs that include the advocacy of active government, including government intervention to improve the welfare of individuals and to protect civil rights.

The Civil Rights Revolution In the 1960s, liberals in the Democratic Party were able to commit their party firmly to the cause of African American equality, permanently overriding those Democratic conservatives who still supported legal segregation of the races. In a matching development, conservatives in the Republican Party began to appeal to traditionalist whites who were upset by the African American civil rights movement. As the party of Lincoln, the Republicans had once been the natural political home of African Americans. This was no longer true. Support for minority rights of all kinds became an integral part of liberal ideology, while conservatism came to include skepticism toward minority claims. As one example, consider the Black Lives Matter movement that arose in 2015 following claims that many police officers were too willing to use deadly force against African Americans. Democratic presidential candidates expressed sympathy for the movement, but most Republican candidates accused it of being antipolice.

Other Liberal Values The Vietnam War (1965–1975) also influenced liberal thinking. Although American participation in the conflict was initiated by President Johnson, liberals swung against the war more strongly than other Americans. Liberalism therefore came to include a relatively negative view of American military initiatives abroad. (That distrust has declined in recent years, however.)

Liberals strongly favor the separation of church and state. They generally think that the government should avoid laws that endorse or impose traditional religious values. Examples include laws that limit the rights of gays and lesbians. These beliefs sharply contrast with those of

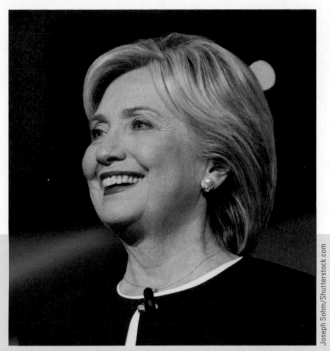

Democratic presidential candidate Hillary Clinton speaks to the International Union of Painters and Allied Trades, a labor union, just before the Nevada presidential caucuses. *What is her ideology?*

1-4c The Traditional Political Spectrum

Traditionally, liberalism and conservatism have been regarded as falling within a political spectrum that ranges from the left to the right. As illustrated in Figure 1–3, modern conservatives typically identify themselves politically as Republicans. Similarly, liberals—or progressives—identify with the Democratic Party. The identification of the parties with specific ideologies is clear today but was not always so noticeable in the past. Conservative Democrats and liberal Republicans were once common, but they are now rare.

People whose views fall in the middle of the traditional political spectrum are generally called **moderates**. By definition, moderates do not classify themselves as either liberal or conservative. Moderates may vote for either Republicans or Democrats, although in public opinion polls Democrats are about twice as likely as Republicans to identify themselves as moderates. Still, a large number of moderates do not support either major political party and often describe themselves as *independent* (see Chapter 7).

1-4d Beyond Conservatism and Liberalism

religious conservatives. In this area, at least, liberals do not stand for big government, but rather the reverse.

Liberals and Progressives Not all political labels are equally popular, and the term *liberal* has taken a particular beating in the political wars of the last several decades. One result is that most politicians who might have called themselves liberals in the past have labeled their philosophy **progressivism** instead. The term *progressive* dates back to the first years of the twentieth century, when it referred to a reform movement that was active in both major political parties. Later, the progressive label fell into disuse, until it was resurrected in recent years.

Many Americans do not adhere firmly to a particular political ideology. Some are not interested in political issues. Others may have opinions that do not neatly fit under the liberal or conservative label. For example, conservatives typically support restrictions on the availability of abortion. They also may favor banning the procedure altogether.

progressivism
Today, an alternative, more popular term for the set of political beliefs also known as liberalism.

moderates Persons whose views fall in the middle of the political spectrum.

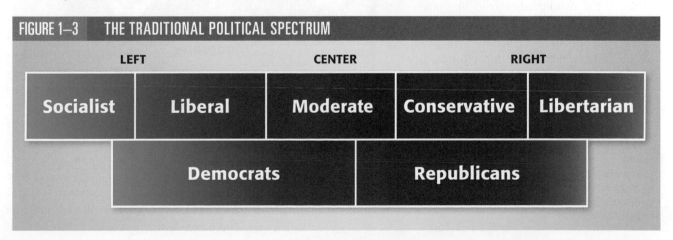

FIGURE 1–3   THE TRADITIONAL POLITICAL SPECTRUM

LEFT		CENTER		RIGHT
Socialist	Liberal	Moderate	Conservative	Libertarian
	Democrats		Republicans	

Liberals usually favor the right to have an abortion. Many liberals believe that the government ought to guarantee that everyone can find a job. Conservatives generally reject this idea. Millions of Americans, however, support restrictions on abortion while supporting government jobs programs. Many other citizens would oppose both of these positions. Conservatism and liberalism, in other words, are not the only ideological possibilities.

Socialism   To the left of liberalism on the traditional ideological spectrum lies **socialism**. This ideology has relatively few adherents in the United States, although a handful of Democrats and independents accept the label, including senator and 2016 presidential candidate Bernie Sanders (D., Vt.). In much of the world, however, the main left-of-center party descends from the socialist tradition. These *social democrats* have a stronger commitment to egalitarianism than do U.S. liberals and a greater tolerance for strong government. Indeed, in the first half of the twentieth century, most socialists advocated government ownership of major businesses. Few social democrats endorse such proposals today, however.

Social democrats strongly support democracy, but early in the twentieth century an ultra-left breakaway from the socialist movement—the Communists—established a series of brutal dictatorships, initially in Russia (the Soviet Union). Communists remain in power in China and a few other nations. Despite Communist rule, in recent years capitalist businesses have thrived in China.

Libertarianism   Even as socialism is weak in America compared with the rest of the world, the right-of-center ideology of **libertarianism** is unusually strong. Libertarians oppose almost all government regulation of the economy and government redistribution of income.

Many ardent conservatives share these beliefs. What distinguishes true libertarians, however, is that libertarians also oppose government involvement in issues of private morality. In this belief, they often have more in common with liberals than they do with conservatives. For most people, however, economic issues remain the more important ones, and a majority of libertarians ally with conservatives politically and support the Republicans.

Economic Progressives, Social Conservatives   Many other voters are liberal on economic issues even as they favor conservative positions on social matters. These people support government intervention to promote both economic "fairness" *and* moral values. Low-income people frequently are economic progressives and social conservatives. A large number of African Americans and Hispanics fall into this camp. While it is widespread within the electorate, this "anti-libertarian" point of view has no agreed-upon name.

In sum, millions of Americans do not fit neatly into the traditional liberal–conservative spectrum. We illustrate an alternative, two-dimensional political classification in Figure 1–4.

CRITICAL THINKING

▶ *Suppose you are a representative in Congress who ran for office on a platform that clearly articulated your strong beliefs. Should you be willing to compromise with others in the hopes of obtaining at least some of what you favor—or is it better to stand on principle, even if you lose?*

socialism   A political ideology, often critical of capitalism, that lies to the left of liberalism on the traditional political spectrum. Socialists are scarce in the United States but common in many other countries.

libertarianism   The belief that government should do as little as possible, not only in the economic sphere, but also in regulating morality and personal behavior.

FIGURE 1–4   A TWO-DIMENSIONAL POLITICAL CLASSIFICATION

Social Liberty ⬌ Social Order

Economic Liberty

Libertarian: Robert Heinlein, science fiction writer

Conservative: Justice Clarence Thomas

Moderates

Economic Equality

Liberal/Progressive: Maya Angelou, author

Social Conservative/ Economic Progressive: His Holiness Pope Francis

Olga Popova/Shutterstock.com; Steven Petteway, Collection of the Supreme Court of the United States. Chris Felver/Getty Images. giulio napolitano/Shutterstock.com.

AMERICA AT ODDS | America in the Twenty-First Century

As you learned in this chapter, Americans are united by a common political culture. At the same time, however, Americans are at odds over how much weight should be given to various fundamental principles. We can summarize these most basic disputes as follows:

- *How much of a problem does terrorism pose for the United States? Is it severe enough that we should strengthen domestic intelligence gathering? Send U.S. troops into combat abroad? Restrict immigration from targeted countries? Or are concerns about terrorism often overblown and likely to lead to responses that are more troublesome than terrorism itself?*

- *How large should our government be? Should it offer a wide range of services, along with the resulting taxes—or should it provide relatively few services and collect less in taxes?*

- *Should businesses be strictly regulated to ensure the common good—or should regulation be minimized to promote economic freedom and growth?*

- *More generally, should we place a greater value on economic liberty and property rights—or on economic egalitarianism and improving the condition of those who are less well off?*

- *How active should the government be in promoting moral behavior? Should the government support traditional values—or place a high value on social liberty?*

STUDY TOOLS 1

READY TO STUDY? IN THE BOOK, YOU CAN:

- ☐ Review what you've read with the following chapter quiz.
- ☐ Check your answers in Appendix D at the back of the book.
- ☐ Rip out the Chapter Review Card, which includes key terms and chapter summaries.

ONLINE AT WWW.CENGAGEBRAIN.COM, YOU CAN:

- ☐ Learn more about U.S. ambassador to the United Nations Samantha Power in Major Players in American Government.
- ☐ Explore various online resources in the VOX and Pew Research websites in the Internet Resources tool.
- ☐ Interact with figures from the text, and watch quick animation clips.
- ☐ Prepare for tests with quizzes.
- ☐ Review the key terms with Flash Cards.

FILL-IN

Learning Outcome 1–1

1. _____ can best be defined as the individuals and institutions that make society's rules and also possess the power and authority to enforce those rules.

2. In any country, government generally serves at least three essential purposes: _____, _____, _____.

Learning Outcome 1–2

3. In a/an _____, the power and authority of the government are in the hands of a single person.

4. In a/an _____, the will of the majority is expressed through groups of individuals elected by the people to act as their representatives.

Learning Outcome 1–3

5. The philosopher John Locke argued that people are born with natural rights to _____, _____, _____.

6. American democracy is based on five fundamental principles: _____, _____, _____, _____, _____.

Learning Outcome 1–4

7. When it comes to ideology, Americans are often placed in two broad political camps: _____, _____.

8. Arizona senator Barry Goldwater and President Ronald Reagan were well-known political _____.

9. People whose views fall in the middle of the traditional political spectrum are generally called

_____.

10. _____ oppose almost all government regulation of the economy and government redistribution of income, while also opposing government involvement in issues of private morality.

MULTIPLE CHOICE

Learning Outcome 1–1

11. Political scientist Harold Lasswell defined _____ as the process of determining "who gets what, when, and how" in a society.
    a. government **b.** power **c.** politics

12. When the government's ability to exercise power is widely viewed as legitimate, we say that the government
    a. has authority. **b.** is representative. **c.** is limited.

Learning Outcome 1–2

13. The system of government in the United States is best described as a _____ democracy.
    a. parliamentary **b.** presidential **c.** direct

14. In _____, there is no separation of church and state, and the government rules through religious precepts.
    a. a plutocracy **b.** an aristocracy **c.** a theocracy

Learning Outcome 1–3

15. Which of the following best describes a social contract?
    a. The set of ideas, values, and attitudes about government and politics held by a community or a nation.
    b. A voluntary agreement among individuals to create a government and to give that government adequate power to secure the mutual protection and welfare of all individuals.
    c. An economic system based on the private ownership of wealth-producing property, free markets, and freedom of contract.

16. Because of the political value of _____, Article I, Section 9, of the U.S. Constitution prohibits the government from granting titles of nobility.
    a. equality **b.** liberty **c.** multiculturalism

Learning Outcome 1–4

17. Today's Republican Party differs from the party that existed a century ago in that it
    a. no longer has strong support from business interests.
    b. is less reliant on the support of religious conservatives.
    c. no longer enjoys the support of most African Americans.

18. American liberalism took its fully modern form in the _____.
    a. 1960s, during the administration of Lyndon Johnson.
    b. 1990s, during the administration of Bill Clinton.
    c. 2000s, during the administration of Barack Obama.

GOVT ONLINE

ACCESS TEXTBOOK CONTENT ONLINE— INCLUDING ON SMARTPHONES!

Includes Videos & Other Interactive Resources!

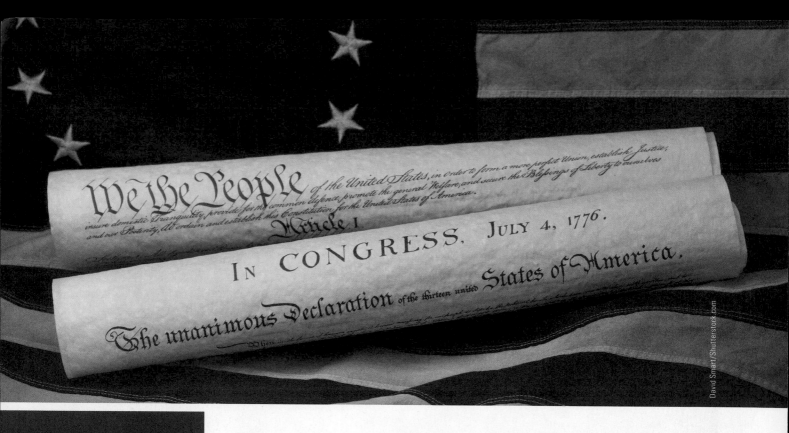

2

THE CONSTITUTION

LEARNING OUTCOMES *After reading this chapter, you should be able to:*

2-1 Point out some of the influences on the American political tradition in the colonial years.

2-2 Explain why the American colonies rebelled against Britain.

2-3 Describe the structure of government established by the Articles of Confederation and some of the strengths and weaknesses of the Articles.

2-4 List the major compromises made by the delegates at the Constitutional Convention, and discuss the Federalist and Anti-Federalist positions on ratifying the Constitution.

2-5 Summarize the Constitution's major principles of government, and describe how the Constitution can be amended.

After finishing this chapter, go to **PAGE 47** for **STUDY TOOLS.**

Library of Congress

AMERICA AT ODDS | Should We Call a New Constitutional Convention?

The convention at which our Constitution was written was held more than 225 years ago. That Constitution is now the oldest one on the planet. It has been amended twenty-seven times, always through proposals initiated by Congress. Another mechanism is possible, however. Article V of the Constitution allows amendments to be proposed by a new constitutional convention. Two-thirds of the states (currently thirty-four states) would have to petition for such a convention. Three-quarters of the states would have to ratify any amendment for it to go into effect. The Constitution provides no details about how such a convention would be run, however. How many delegates would each state send? Would proposed amendments require a two-thirds vote by the delegates—or a simple majority? From 1973 to 1992, Congress tried more than twenty times to approve rules for such a convention, if one should be called. All attempts failed.

A Convention Will Allow the States to Regain Their Lost Power

Those in favor of a new convention argue that it is the only way to reduce the size and scope of the federal government and bring back power to the states. Supporters of such a convention include Texas governor Greg Abbott and Senator Marco Rubio (R., Fla.), a 2016 presidential candidate. Most of Abbott's nine proposed constitutional amendments strengthen the power of the states at the expense of the federal government. For example, one would allow two-thirds of the states to overturn any ruling by the United States Supreme Court.

One amendment proposed by Abbott and Rubio—to force Congress to balance the federal budget—already has twenty-seven active petitions filed with Congress. The Balanced Budget Amendment Task Force is targeting thirteen additional states. Once thirty-four states have filed their petitions, Congress would have to act. Supporters say that the time is right for a convention. Such a possibility was included in the Constitution for a reason—to allow the states to take back control from an overmighty national government.

The Folly of a Constitutional Convention

Opponents argue that a new constitutional convention would be pure folly. Let's assume, though, that such a convention has been called and its rules of procedure sorted out. Is it possible to limit the topics discussed at such a gathering? Many experts believe that the answer is "no." A convention could issue an entirely new constitution, just as the first one did. Such a document might include anything. It could repeal some of our basic rights or discriminate against unpopular groups. Also, while it is conservatives who dream of such a convention today, they have no guarantee that they would have a majority when it met. Many states would surely send liberal delegations.

We are not even sure that once thirty-four states demand a convention, Congress would call one. Congress could require that all state petitions have the same wording and thus make advocates start over. Indeed, no legal mechanism exists to force Congress to call a convention, no matter how many states request one. Only the voters can make members of Congress act—by threatening their reelection. As of today however, voters couldn't care less about this issue.

Where Do You Stand?

1. Would you be in favor of your state petitioning Congress for a new constitutional convention? Why or why not?

2. Other than the ones mentioned here, can you think of important constitutional amendments that might be proposed at a new convention?

Explore this Issue Online

- The National Constitutional Center in Philadelphia has additional details on what a new constitutional convention would involve. Find these by searching online for "constitutional convention doing the math."

- Noah Rothman, himself a conservative, asks how conservatives can simultaneously claim to revere the existing Constitution and ask for a rewrite. Find his article by searching for "constitutional convention noah rothman."

INTRODUCTION

The Constitution, which was written more than two hundred years ago, continues to be the supreme law of the land. Time and again, its provisions have been adapted to the changing needs and conditions of society. The challenge before today's citizens and political leaders is to find a way to apply those provisions to a society and an economy that could not possibly have been anticipated by the founders. Will the Constitution survive this challenge? Most Americans assume that it will—and with good reason: no other written constitution in the world today is as old as the U.S. Constitution. Americans tend to revere their Constitution—which is why a new constitutional convention, as discussed in the chapter-opening *America at Odds* feature, is unlikely.

To understand the principles of government set forth in the Constitution, you have to go back to the beginnings of our nation's history.

2-1 THE BEGINNINGS OF AMERICAN GOVERNMENT

> **LO** Point out some of the influences on the American political tradition in the colonial years.

When the framers of the Constitution met in Philadelphia in 1787, they brought with them some valuable political assets. One asset was their English political heritage (see "American Democracy" in Chapter 1). Another was the hands-on political experience they had acquired during the colonial era. Their political knowledge and experience enabled them to establish a constitution that could meet not only the needs of their own time but also the needs of generations to come.

The American colonies had been settled by individuals from many nations, including France, Germany, Ireland, the Netherlands, Spain, and Sweden. The majority of the colonists, though, came from England and Scotland. The British colonies in North America were established by private individuals and private trading companies, and were under the rule of the British

Mayflower Compact
A document drawn up by Pilgrim leaders in 1620 on the ship *Mayflower*. The document stated that laws were to be made for the general good of the people.

Crown. The colonies, which were located along the Atlantic seaboard of today's United States, eventually numbered thirteen.

Although American politics owes much to the English political tradition, the colonists derived most of their understanding of social compacts, the rights of the people, limited government, and representative government from their own experiences. Years before Parliament adopted the English Bill of Rights or John Locke wrote his *Two Treatises on Government* (described in Chapter 1), the American colonists were already putting the ideas expressed in those documents into practice.

2-1a The First English Settlements

The first permanent English settlement in North America was Jamestown, in what is now Virginia.[1] Jamestown was established in 1607 as a trading post of the Virginia Company of London.[2]

Plymouth Colony The first New England colony was founded by the Plymouth Company in 1620 at Plymouth in what is today Massachusetts. Most of the settlers at Plymouth were Pilgrims, a group of English Protestants who came to the New World on the ship *Mayflower*. Even before the Pilgrims went ashore, they drew up the **Mayflower Compact**, in which they set up a government and promised to obey its laws.

The reason for the compact was that the group was outside the territory assigned to the Virginia Company, which had arranged for them to settle in what is now New York, not Massachusetts. Fearing that some of the passengers might decide that they were no longer subject to any rules of civil order, the leaders on board the *Mayflower* agreed that some form of governmental authority was necessary.

The Mayflower Compact was essentially a social contract. It has historical significance because it was the first of a series of similar contracts among the colonists to establish fundamental rules of government.[3] The Compact reflected the fact that Plymouth was essentially a religious colony, and early colonial attitudes toward religion were different from those of the revolutionary era. We address that point in this chapter's *Join the Debate* feature.

More Colonies, More Constitutions The Massachusetts Bay Colony was established as another trading outpost in New England in 1628. In 1636, following disputes in the Massachusetts Bay Colony, settlers from Massachusetts organized the Connecticut Colony at Hartford. In 1639, they adopted America's

JOIN THE DEBATE

Was the United States Meant to Be a Christian Nation?

The Pilgrims established a religious colony when they landed in New England. In early Virginia, failure to attend Church of England services was a serious crime. By the time the Constitution was written, several states still had established (state-supported) churches. Christian beliefs were strong among the population in that era. Most Americans considered themselves to be part of a Christian—indeed, a Protestant—people. (Anti-Catholicism was widespread.)

Yet the Declaration of Independence never refers to Christ. The Constitution does not contain the word *God*. It refers to religion twice. Article VI states: "no religious Test shall ever be required as a Qualification to any Office or public Trust under the United States." The world-famous First Amendment begins: "Congress shall make no law respecting an establishment of religion, or prohibiting the free exercise thereof."

Considering these facts, was the United States meant to be a Christian nation—or not? The answer to that question depends in part on what we mean by "Christian nation."

Yes, America Is a Christian Nation

By *nation*, do we mean a country's government or its people? If we say "people," it is hard to deny that the United States has been a Christian nation. According to the Pew Research Center, 70.6 percent of Americans today consider themselves to be Christian. Some conservatives, however, have argued that "Christian nation" should mean more than that. Most of the founders, even those whose private commitment to Christianity was questionable, agreed that religion was essential to a just and harmonious society. The founders would have been astonished to learn that public school teachers today may not lead their students in prayer. According to Christian conservatives, constitutional principles are inseparable from Christianity, and the First Amendment means only that the government must not pick and choose among Christian churches. Limits on "anti-Western" religions, such as bans on Islamic mosques, are appropriate.

The "Christian Nation" Idea Would Violate Our Rights

It is hard to imagine how the founders could have sought to establish a Christian nation when many of them were not Christians at all, in the modern sense. George Washington never took communion or referred to Christ. John Adams was a Unitarian—that is, he did not believe that Jesus was divine. Thomas Jefferson thought likewise. It is impossible to say what James Madison and James Monroe believed, because they avoided issues of doctrine even in their private correspondence. Not until Andrew Jackson (1829–1837) did we have a president who openly endorsed Christianity in the way we now expect of political candidates.

Opponents of the "Christian nation" concept argue that the First Amendment should be interpreted strictly. It is essential to tolerate the adherents of all religions—including Muslims and, for that matter, atheists. This is an issue about which the founders were quite explicit.

Critical Analysis

Christian conservatives argue that discrimination against Christians is widespread in modern America. Is anti-Christian discrimination a problem? Why or why not?

first written constitution, which was called the Fundamental Orders of Connecticut. This document called for the laws to be made by an assembly of elected representatives from each town. The document also provided for the popular election of a governor and judges.

Other colonies, in turn, established fundamental governing rules. The Massachusetts Body of Liberties protected individual rights. The Pennsylvania Frame of Government, passed in 1682, and the Pennsylvania Charter of Privileges of 1701 established principles that were later expressed in the U.S. Constitution and the **Bill of Rights** (the first ten amendments to the Constitution). By 1732, all thirteen colonies had been established, each with its own political documents and constitution (see Figure 2–1).

2–1b Colonial Legislatures

As mentioned, the British colonies in America were under the rule of the British monarchy. Britain, however, was thousands of miles away—it took two months to sail across the Atlantic. Thus, to a significant extent, colonial legislatures carried on the "nuts and bolts" of colonial government. These legislatures, or *representative*

Bill of Rights The first ten amendments to the U.S. Constitution. They list the freedoms—such as the freedoms of speech, press, and religion—that a citizen enjoys and that cannot be infringed on by the government.

assemblies, consisted of representatives elected by the colonists. The earliest colonial legislature was the Virginia House of Burgesses, established in 1619. By the time of the American Revolution, all of the colonies had representative assemblies. Many had been in existence for more than a hundred years.

Through their participation in colonial governments, the colonists gained crucial political experience. Colonial leaders became familiar with the practical problems of governing. They learned how to build coalitions among groups with diverse interests and how to make compromises. Indeed, by the time of the American Revolution in 1776, Americans had formed a complex, sophisticated political system.

The colonists benefited from their political experiences. They were quickly able to establish their own constitutions and state governments after they declared their independence from Britain in 1776. Eventually, they were able to set up a national government as well.

2–2 THE REBELLION OF THE COLONISTS

LO Explain why the American colonies rebelled against Britain.

Scholars of the American Revolution point out that by and large, the American colonists did not want to become independent of Britain. For the majority of the colonists, Britain was the homeland, and ties of loyalty were strong. Why, then, did the colonists revolt against Britain and declare their independence? What happened to sever the political, economic, and emotional bonds that tied the colonists to Britain? The answers to these questions lie in a series of events in the mid-1700s that culminated in a change in British policy toward the colonies. Table 2–1 shows some major political events in early U.S. history.

One of these events was the Seven Years' War (1756–1763) between Britain and France. (In North America, the fighting began in 1754, and Americans call that conflict the *French and Indian War.*) The British victory in the Seven Years' War permanently altered the relationship between Britain and its American colonies. After successfully ousting the French from North America, the British expanded their authority over the

FIGURE 2–1 THE THIRTEEN COLONIES BEFORE THE AMERICAN REVOLUTION

The western boundary of the colonies was set by the Proclamation Line of 1763, which banned European settlement in western territories that were reserved for Native Americans. Note that Vermont, which is striped, was claimed by both New York and New Hampshire. *What would have happened if the founders had tried to limit the number or powers of new states?*

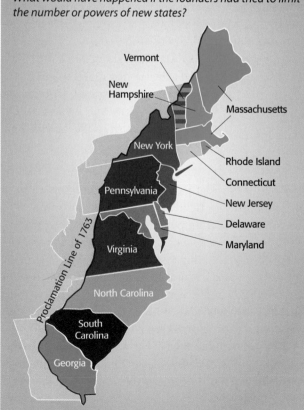

TABLE 2–1	SIGNIFICANT EVENTS IN EARLY U.S. POLITICAL HISTORY
1607	Jamestown established; Virginia Company lands settlers.
1620	Mayflower Compact signed.
1628	Massachusetts Bay Colony set up.
1639	Fundamental Orders of Connecticut adopted.
1641	Massachusetts Body of Liberties adopted.
1682	Pennsylvania Frame of Government passed.
1701	Pennsylvania Charter of Privileges adopted.
1732	Last of thirteen colonies established (Georgia).
1754	French and Indian War breaks out.
1765	Stamp Act; Stamp Act Congress meets.
1773	Boston Tea Party.
1774	First Continental Congress meets.
1775	Second Continental Congress; Revolutionary War begins.
1776	Declaration of Independence signed.
1777	Articles of Confederation drafted.
1781	Last state signs Articles of Confederation.
1783	"Critical period" in U.S. history begins; weak national government until 1789.
1786	Shays' Rebellion.
1787	Constitutional Convention held.
1788	Constitution ratified.
1791	Bill of Rights ratified.

colonies. To pay its war debts and to finance the defense of its expanded North American empire, Britain needed revenues. The British government decided to obtain some of these revenues by imposing taxes on the American colonists and exercising more direct control over colonial trade.

At the same time, Americans were beginning to distrust the expanding British presence in the colonies. Having fought alongside British forces, Americans thought that they deserved more credit for the victory. The British, however, attributed the victory solely to their own efforts.

Furthermore, the colonists began to develop a sense of identity separate from the British. Americans were shocked at the behavior of some of the British soldiers and the cruel punishments meted out to enforce discipline among the British troops. The British, in turn, had little good to say about the colonists alongside whom they had fought. They considered them brutish, uncivilized, and undisciplined. It was during this time that the colonists began to use the word *American* to describe themselves.

2–2a "Taxation without Representation"

In 1764, the British Parliament passed the Sugar Act, which imposed a tax on all sugar imported into the American colonies. Some colonists, particularly in Massachusetts, vigorously opposed this tax and proposed a boycott of certain British imports. This boycott developed into a "nonimportation" movement that soon spread to other colonies.

The Stamp Act of 1765 The following year, in 1765, Parliament passed the Stamp Act, which imposed the first direct tax on the colonists. Under the act, all legal documents and newspapers had to use specially embossed (stamped) paper that was purchased from the government. Items such as playing cards and dice were also subject to this requirement.

The Stamp Act generated even stronger resentment among the colonists than the Sugar Act. James Otis, Jr., a Massachusetts attorney, declared that there could be "no taxation without representation." The American colonists were not represented in the British Parliament. They viewed Parliament's attempts to tax them as contrary to the principle of representative government. The British saw the matter differently. From the British perspective, it was only fair that the colonists pay taxes to help support the costs incurred by the British government in defending its American territories. Troops were permanently stationed in the colonies following the Seven Years' War.

In October 1765, nine of the thirteen colonies sent delegates to the Stamp Act Congress in New York City. The delegates prepared a declaration of rights and grievances, which they sent to King George III. This action marked the first time that a majority of the colonies had joined together to oppose British rule. The British Parliament repealed the Stamp Act.

Further Taxes and the Coercive Acts Soon, however, Parliament passed new laws designed to bind the colonies more tightly to the central government in London. Laws that imposed taxes on glass, paint, lead, and many other items were passed in 1767. The colonists protested by boycotting all British goods. In 1773, anger over taxation reached a powerful climax at the Boston Tea Party, in which colonists dressed as Mohawk Indians dumped almost 350 chests of British tea into Boston Harbor as a gesture of tax protest.[4]

The British Parliament was quick to respond to the Tea Party. In 1774, Parliament passed the Coercive Acts (sometimes called the "Intolerable Acts"), which closed Boston Harbor and placed the government of Massachusetts under direct British control.

2–2b The Continental Congresses

In response to the "Intolerable Acts," New York, Pennsylvania, and Rhode Island proposed a colonial congress. The Massachusetts House of Representatives requested that all colonies select delegates to send to Philadelphia for the congress.

The First Continental Congress The First Continental Congress met on September 5, 1774, at Carpenter's Hall in Philadelphia. Of the thirteen colonies, only Georgia did not participate. The congress decided that the colonies should send a petition to King George III to explain their grievances, which they did. The congress also called for a continued boycott of British goods and required each colony to establish an army.

To enforce the boycott and other acts of resistance against Britain, the delegates to the First Continental Congress urged that "a committee be chosen in every county, city and town . . . whose business it shall be attentively to observe the conduct of all persons." The committees of "safety" or "observation," as they were called, organized militias, held special courts, and suppressed the opinions of those who remained loyal to the British Crown. Committee members spied on neighbors' activities and reported to the press the names of those who violated the boycott against Britain. The names were then printed in the local papers, and the transgressors were harassed and ridiculed in their communities.

The Second Continental Congress Almost immediately after receiving the petition from the First Continental Congress, the British government condemned the actions of the congress as open acts of rebellion. Britain responded with even stricter and more repressive measures. On April 19, 1775, British soldiers (Redcoats) fought against colonial citizen soldiers (Minutemen) in the towns of Lexington and Concord in Massachusetts—the first battles of the American Revolution.

First Continental Congress A gathering of delegates from twelve of the thirteen colonies, held in 1774 to protest the Coercive Acts.

Second Continental Congress The congress of the colonies that met in 1775 to assume the powers of a central government and to establish an army.

Less than a month later, delegates from all thirteen colonies gathered in Pennsylvania for the Second Continental Congress, which immediately assumed the powers of a central government. The Second Continental Congress declared that the militiamen who had gathered around Boston were now a full army. It also named George Washington, a delegate to the congress who had some military experience, as its commander in chief.

The delegates to the Second Continental Congress still intended to reach a peaceful settlement with the British Parliament. One declaration stated specifically that "we [the congress] have not raised Armies with ambitious Designs of separating from Great Britain, and establishing independent States." The continued attempts to effect a reconciliation with Britain, even after the outbreak of fighting, underscore the colonists' reluctance to sever their relationship with the home country.

> ## "WE HAVE IT IN OUR POWER
> ### TO BEGIN
> ### THE WORLD OVER AGAIN."
>
> PATRICK HENRY
> AMERICAN PLANTER AND POLITICIAN
> 1736–1799

2–2c Breaking the Ties: Independence

Public debate about the problems with Britain continued to rage, but the stage had been set for declaring independence. One of the most rousing arguments in favor of independence was presented by Thomas Paine, a former English schoolmaster and corset maker, who wrote a pamphlet called *Common Sense.*

Paine's *Common Sense* Paine's pamphlet was published in Philadelphia in January 1776. In it, Paine addressed the crisis using "simple fact, plain argument, and common sense." He mocked King George III and attacked every argument that favored loyalty to the king. He called the king a "royal brute" and a "hardened, sullen-tempered Pharaoh [Egyptian king in ancient times]."[5]

Paine's writing went beyond a personal attack on the king. He contended that America could survive economically on its own and no longer needed its British connection. He wanted the developing colonies to become a model republic in a world in which other nations were oppressed by strong central governments.

None of Paine's arguments was new. In fact, most of them were commonly heard in tavern debates throughout the land. Instead, it was the wit and eloquence of Paine's words that made *Common Sense* so effective:

A government of our own is our natural right: and when a man seriously reflects on the precariousness of human affairs, he will become convinced, that it is infinitely wiser and safer, to form a constitution of our own in a cool and deliberate manner, while we have it in our power, than to trust such an interesting event to time and chance.[6]

Revolution and the Popular Mind Many historians regard Paine's *Common Sense* as the single most important publication of the American Revolution. The pamphlet became a best seller. More than one hundred thousand copies were sold within a few months after its publication. (The equivalent in today's publishing world would be a book that sells between 9 million and 11 million copies in its first year of publication.) It put independence squarely on the agenda. Above all, *Common Sense* helped sever the remaining ties of loyalty to the British monarch, thus removing the final psychological barrier to independence. Indeed, later John Adams would ask,

What do we mean by the Revolution? The War? That was no part of the Revolution. It was only an effect and consequence of it. The Revolution was in the minds of the people, and this was effected, from 1760 to 1775, in the course of fifteen years before a drop of blood was drawn at Lexington.[7]

Independence from Britain—The First Step
By June 1776, the Second Continental Congress had voted for free trade at all American ports with all countries except Britain. The congress had also suggested that all colonies establish state governments separate from Britain. The colonists realized that a formal separation from Britain was necessary if the new nation was to obtain supplies for its armies and commitments of military aid from foreign governments. On June 7, 1776, the first formal step toward independence was taken when Richard Henry Lee of Virginia placed the following resolution before the congress:

RESOLVED, That these United Colonies are, and of right ought to be, free and independent States, that they are absolved from allegiance to the British Crown, and that all political connection between them and the state of Great Britain is, and ought to be, totally dissolved.

The congress postponed consideration of Lee's resolution until a formal statement of independence could be drafted. On June 11, a "Committee of Five" was appointed to draft a declaration that would present to the world the colonies' case for independence.

Library of Congress Prints and Photograph Division

Thomas Paine, the author of *Common Sense*. Paine argued that the United States could stand on its own economically. *How important do you think that argument was?*

The Significance of the Declaration of Independence Adopted on July 4, 1776, the Declaration of Independence is one of the world's most famous documents. Like Paine, Thomas Jefferson, who wrote most of the document, elevated the dispute between Britain and the American colonies to a universal level. Jefferson opened the second paragraph of the declaration with the following words, which have since been memorized by countless American schoolchildren and admired the world over:

We hold these Truths to be self-evident, that all Men are created equal, that they are endowed by their Creator with certain unalienable Rights, that among these are Life, Liberty, and the Pursuit of Happiness—That to secure these Rights, Governments are instituted among Men, deriving their just Powers from the Consent of the Governed, that whenever any Form of Government becomes destructive of these Ends, it is the Right of the People to alter or to abolish it, and to institute new Government.

Three members of the committee chosen to draft a declaration of independence are shown here: Benjamin Franklin, John Adams, and Thomas Jefferson. *What would the British have done if they had managed to arrest these people?*

Library of Congress Prints and Photographs Division [LC-USZ62-96219]

The concepts expressed in the Declaration of Independence clearly reflect Jefferson's familiarity with European political philosophy, particularly the works of John Locke.[8] Jefferson's "life, liberty, and the pursuit of happiness" is clearly modeled on Locke's "life, liberty, and property."

From Colonies to States Even before the Declaration of Independence, some of the colonies had transformed themselves into sovereign states with their own permanent governments. In May 1776, the Second Continental Congress had directed each of the colonies to form "such government as shall . . . best be conducive to the happiness and safety of their constituents [those represented by the government]."

Before long, all thirteen colonies had created constitutions. Eleven of the colonies had completely new constitutions. The other two,

unicameral legislature
A legislature with only one chamber.

Rhode Island and Connecticut, made minor modifications to old royal charters. Seven of the new constitutions contained bills of rights that defined the personal liberties of all state citizens. All constitutions called for limited governments.

Republicanism Many citizens were fearful of a strong central government because of their recent experiences under the British Crown. They opposed any form of government that resembled monarchy in any way. This antiroyalist—or *republican*—sentiment pervaded the colonies.

The Impact of Republicanism. Wherever antiroyalist sentiment was strong, the legislature—composed of elected representatives—became all-powerful. In Pennsylvania and Georgia, for example, **unicameral** (one-chamber) **legislatures** were unchecked by any executive authority. Indeed, the executive branch was extremely weak in all thirteen states.

The republican spirit was strong enough to seriously interfere with the ability of the new nation to win the Revolutionary War. (For example, republican sentiments made it difficult for the national government to raise the funds needed to adequately supply General Washington's army.) Republicans of the Revolutionary Era (not to be confused with supporters of the later Republican Party) were suspicious not only of executive authority in their own states but also of national authority as represented by the Continental Congress.

This antiauthoritarian, localist impulse contrasted with the *nationalist* sentiments of many of the nation's founders, especially such leaders as George Washington and Alexander Hamilton. Nationalists favored an effective central authority. Of course, many founders, such as Thomas Jefferson, harbored both republican and nationalist impulses.

Who Were the Republicans? Like all political movements of the time, the republicans were led by men of "property and standing." Leaders who were strongly republican, however, tended to be less prominent than their nationalist or moderate counterparts. Small farmers may have been the one group that was disproportionately republican. Significantly, small farmers made up a majority of the voters in every state.

CRITICAL THINKING

▶ *The American colonists did not have the right to elect members of the British Parliament. How might American history have been different if the British had permitted such representation?*

2–3 THE CONFEDERATION OF STATES

LO Describe the structure of government established by the Articles of Confederation and some of the strengths and weaknesses of the Articles.

Republican sentiments influenced the thinking of the delegates to the Second Continental Congress, who formed a committee to draft a plan of confederation. A **confederation** is a voluntary association of *independent* states (see Chapter 3). The member states agree to let the central government undertake a limited number of activities, such as forming an army, but do not allow the central government to place many restrictions on the states' own actions. The member states typically can still govern most state affairs as they see fit.

On November 15, 1777, the Second Continental Congress agreed on a draft of the plan, which was finally signed by all thirteen colonies on March 1, 1781. The **Articles of Confederation**, the result of this plan, served as this nation's first national constitution and represented an important step in the creation of our system of government.[9]

2–3a The Articles of Confederation

The Articles of Confederation established the Congress of the Confederation as the central governing body. This congress was a unicameral (one-chamber) assembly of representatives—or ambassadors, as they were called—from the various states. Although each state could send from two to seven representatives to the congress, each state, no matter what its size, had only one vote. The issue of sovereignty was an important part of the Articles of Confederation:

> Each State retains its sovereignty, freedom, and independence, and every power, jurisdiction, and right, which is not by this Confederation expressly delegated to the United States in Congress assembled.

The structure of government under the Articles of Confederation is shown in Figure 2–2.

confederation A league of independent states that are united only for the purpose of achieving common goals.

Articles of Confederation The nation's first constitution, which established a national form of government following the American Revolution. The Articles provided for a confederal form of government in which the central government had few powers.

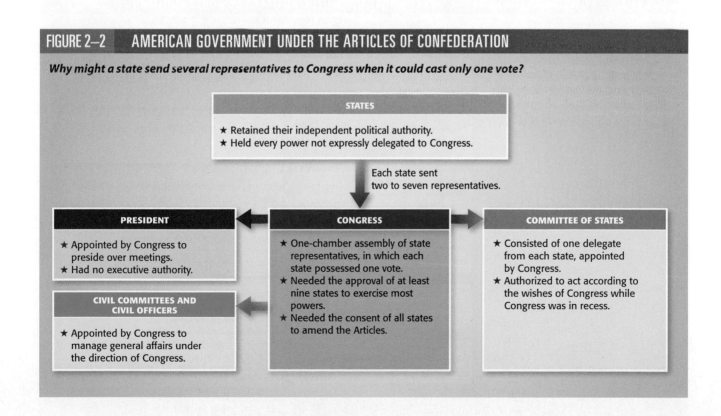

FIGURE 2–2 AMERICAN GOVERNMENT UNDER THE ARTICLES OF CONFEDERATION

Why might a state send several representatives to Congress when it could cast only one vote?

STATES
- ★ Retained their independent political authority.
- ★ Held every power not expressly delegated to Congress.

Each state sent two to seven representatives.

PRESIDENT
- ★ Appointed by Congress to preside over meetings.
- ★ Had no executive authority.

CIVIL COMMITTEES AND CIVIL OFFICERS
- ★ Appointed by Congress to manage general affairs under the direction of Congress.

CONGRESS
- ★ One-chamber assembly of state representatives, in which each state possessed one vote.
- ★ Needed the approval of at least nine states to exercise most powers.
- ★ Needed the consent of all states to amend the Articles.

COMMITTEE OF STATES
- ★ Consisted of one delegate from each state, appointed by Congress.
- ★ Authorized to act according to the wishes of Congress while Congress was in recess.

Powers under the Articles Congress had several powers under the Articles of Confederation, and these enabled the new nation to achieve a number of objectives (see Figure 2–3). The Northwest Ordinance settled states' claims to many of the western lands and established a basic pattern for the government of new territories. Also, the 1783 peace treaty negotiated with Britain granted to the United States all of the territory from the Atlantic Ocean to the Mississippi River and from the Great Lakes and Canada to what is now northern Florida.

Weaknesses under the Articles In spite of these accomplishments, the central government created by the Articles of Confederation was quite weak. The Congress of the Confederation had no power to raise revenues for the militia or to force the states to meet military quotas. Essentially, this meant that the new government did not have the power to enforce its laws. Even passing laws was difficult because the Articles of Confederation provided that nine states had to approve any law before it was enacted. Figure 2–4 lists powers that the central government lacked under the Articles of Confederation.

The Articles and the Constitution Nonetheless, the Articles of Confederation proved to be a good "first draft" for the Constitution, and at least half of the text of the Articles would later appear in the Constitution. The Articles were an unplanned experiment that tested some of the principles of government that had been set forth earlier in the Declaration of Independence. Some argue that without the experience of government under the Articles of Confederation, it would have been difficult, if not impossible, to arrive at the compromises that were necessary to create the Constitution several years later.

2–3b A Time of Crisis—The 1780s

The Revolutionary War ended on October 18, 1781. The Treaty of Paris, which confirmed the colonies' independence from Britain, was signed in 1783. Peace with the British may have been won, but peace within the new nation was hard to find. The states bickered among themselves and refused to support the new central government in almost any way. As George Washington stated, "We are one nation today and thirteen tomorrow. Who will treat [with] us on such terms?"

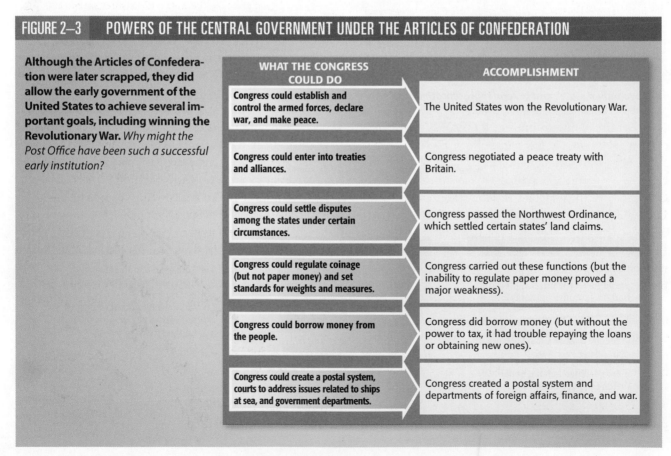

FIGURE 2–3   POWERS OF THE CENTRAL GOVERNMENT UNDER THE ARTICLES OF CONFEDERATION

Although the Articles of Confederation were later scrapped, they did allow the early government of the United States to achieve several important goals, including winning the Revolutionary War. *Why might the Post Office have been such a successful early institution?*

WHAT THE CONGRESS COULD DO	ACCOMPLISHMENT
Congress could establish and control the armed forces, declare war, and make peace.	The United States won the Revolutionary War.
Congress could enter into treaties and alliances.	Congress negotiated a peace treaty with Britain.
Congress could settle disputes among the states under certain circumstances.	Congress passed the Northwest Ordinance, which settled certain states' land claims.
Congress could regulate coinage (but not paper money) and set standards for weights and measures.	Congress carried out these functions (but the inability to regulate paper money proved a major weakness).
Congress could borrow money from the people.	Congress did borrow money (but without the power to tax, it had trouble repaying the loans or obtaining new ones).
Congress could create a postal system, courts to address issues related to ships at sea, and government departments.	Congress created a postal system and departments of foreign affairs, finance, and war.

The government's lack of certain powers under the Articles of Confederation taught the framers of the Constitution several important lessons, which helped them create a more effective government under that new document. *Why would the inability of the national government to regulate interstate commerce have been so important?*

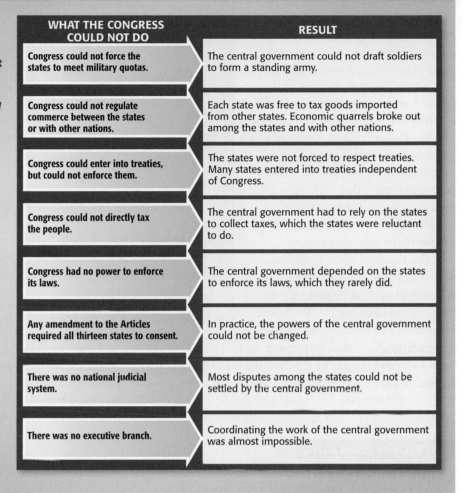

WHAT THE CONGRESS COULD NOT DO	RESULT
Congress could not force the states to meet military quotas.	The central government could not draft soldiers to form a standing army.
Congress could not regulate commerce between the states or with other nations.	Each state was free to tax goods imported from other states. Economic quarrels broke out among the states and with other nations.
Congress could enter into treaties, but could not enforce them.	The states were not forced to respect treaties. Many states entered into treaties independent of Congress.
Congress could not directly tax the people.	The central government had to rely on the states to collect taxes, which the states were reluctant to do.
Congress had no power to enforce its laws.	The central government depended on the states to enforce its laws, which they rarely did.
Any amendment to the Articles required all thirteen states to consent.	In practice, the powers of the central government could not be changed.
There was no national judicial system.	Most disputes among the states could not be settled by the central government.
There was no executive branch.	Coordinating the work of the central government was almost impossible.

Indeed, the national government, such as it was, did not have the ability to prevent the various states from entering into agreements with foreign powers, despite the danger that such agreements could completely disrupt the confederation, pitting state against state. When Congress proved reluctant to admit Vermont into the Union, Britain began negotiations with influential Vermonters with the aim of annexing the district to Canada. Britain also held a variety of forts on territory that was undeniably American by treaty. Likewise, Spain occupied forts as far north as Memphis.

The states increasingly taxed each other's imports and at times even prevented trade altogether. By 1784, the new nation was suffering from a serious economic depression. States started printing their own money at dizzying rates, which led to inflation. Banks were calling in old loans and refusing to issue new ones. Individuals who could not pay their debts were often thrown into prison.

Shays' Rebellion The tempers of indebted farmers in western Massachusetts reached the boiling point in August 1786. Former Revolutionary War captain Daniel Shays, along with approximately two thousand armed farmers, seized county courthouses and disrupted the debtors' trials. Shays and his men then launched an attack on the national government's arsenal in Springfield. **Shays' Rebellion** continued to grow in intensity and lasted into the winter, when it was finally stopped by the Massachusetts volunteer army, which was paid by Boston merchants.[10]

Similar disruptions occurred throughout most of the New England states and in some other areas as well. The upheavals were an important catalyst for change. The revolts frightened American political and business leaders and caused more and more Americans to realize that a *true* national government had to be created.

Shays' Rebellion A rebellion of angry farmers in western Massachusetts in 1786, led by former Revolutionary War captain Daniel Shays.

The Annapolis Meeting The Virginia legislature called for a meeting of representatives from all of the states in Annapolis, Maryland, on September 11, 1786, to consider extending national authority to issues of commerce. Five of the thirteen states sent delegates, two of whom were Alexander Hamilton of New York and James Madison of Virginia. Both of these men favored a strong central government.[11] They persuaded the other delegates to issue a report calling on the states to hold a convention in Philadelphia in May of the following year.

The Congress of the Confederation at first was reluctant to give its approval to the Philadelphia convention. By mid-February 1787, however, seven of the states had named delegates to the Philadelphia meeting. Finally, on February 21, the Congress called on the states to send delegates to Philadelphia "for the sole and express purpose of revising the Articles of Confederation." That Philadelphia meeting became the **Constitutional Convention**.

Alexander Hamilton was among the key delegates to the Constitutional Convention that convened on May 25, 1787. *What kind of government did he want America to have?*

fifty-five of the seventy-four delegates had arrived.[12] Only Rhode Island, where feelings were strong against creating a more powerful central government, did not send any delegates.

CRITICAL THINKING

▶ *Given that all Americans would have benefited from an army capable of keeping the peace and defending the country, why would the states have been so reluctant to fund the national government?*

2–4 DRAFTING AND RATIFYING THE CONSTITUTION

LO List the major compromises made by the delegates at the Constitutional Convention, and discuss the Federalist and Anti-Federalist positions on ratifying the Constitution.

Constitutional Convention The convention of delegates from the states that was held in Philadelphia in 1787 for the purpose of amending the Articles of Confederation. In fact, the delegates wrote a new constitution (the U.S. Constitution) that established a federal form of government.

Although the convention was supposed to start on May 14, 1787, few of the delegates had actually arrived in Philadelphia on that date. The convention formally opened in the East Room of the Pennsylvania State House on May 25, after

2–4a Who Were the Delegates?

Among the delegates to the Constitutional Convention were some of the nation's best-known leaders. George Washington was present, as were Alexander Hamilton, James Madison, George Mason, Robert Morris, and Benjamin Franklin (who, at eighty-one years old, had to be carried to the convention on a portable chair).

Some notable leaders were absent, including Thomas Jefferson and John Adams, who were serving as ambassadors in Europe, and Patrick Henry, who did not attend because he "smelt a rat." (Henry was one of Virginia's most strongly republican leaders.)

For the most part, the delegates were from the best-educated and wealthiest classes. Thirty-three delegates were lawyers, nearly half of the delegates were college graduates, three were physicians, and seven were former chief executives of their respective states. Six owned large plantations, at least nineteen owned slaves, eight were important business owners, and twenty-one had fought in the Revolutionary War.

In other words, the delegates to the convention constituted an elite assembly. No ordinary farmers or merchants were present. Indeed, in his classic work on the Constitution, Charles Beard maintained that the Constitution was produced primarily by wealthy bondholders who had made loans to the government under the Articles and wanted a strong central government that could prevent state governments from repudiating debts.[13] Later historians, however, rejected Beard's thesis, concluding that bondholders played no special role in writing the Constitution.

2-4b The Virginia Plan

James Madison had spent months reviewing European political theory before he went to the Philadelphia convention. His Virginia delegation arrived before anybody else, and he immediately put its members to work. On the first day of the convention, Governor Edmund Randolph of Virginia was able to present fifteen resolutions outlining what was to become known as the *Virginia Plan*. This was a masterful political stroke on the part of the Virginia delegation. Its proposals immediately set the agenda for the remainder of the convention.

The fifteen resolutions contained in the Virginia Plan proposed an entirely new national government under a constitution. The plan, which favored large states such as Virginia, called for the following:

- A **bicameral** (two-chamber) **legislature**. The lower chamber was to be chosen by the people. The smaller, upper chamber was to be chosen by the elected members of the lower chamber. The number of representatives would be in proportion to each state's population (the larger states would have more representatives). The legislature could void any state laws.
- A national executive branch, elected by the legislature.
- A national court system, created by the legislature.

The smaller states immediately complained because they would have fewer representatives in the legislature. After two weeks of debate, they offered their own plan—the *New Jersey Plan*.

2-4c The New Jersey Plan

William Paterson of New Jersey presented an alternative plan favorable to the smaller states. He argued that because each state had an equal vote under the Articles of Confederation, the convention had no power to change this arrangement. The New Jersey Plan proposed the following:

- Congress would be able to regulate trade and impose taxes.
- Each state would have only one vote.

- Acts of Congress would be the supreme law of the land.
- An executive office of more than one person would be elected by Congress.
- The executive office would appoint a national supreme court.

2-4d The Compromises

Most delegates were unwilling to consider the New Jersey Plan. When the Virginia Plan was brought up again, however, delegates from the smaller states threatened to leave, and the convention was in danger of dissolving. On July 16, Roger Sherman of Connecticut broke the deadlock by proposing a compromise plan. Compromises on other disputed issues followed.

The Great Compromise Roger Sherman's plan, which has become known as the **Great Compromise** (or the Connecticut Compromise), called for a legislature with two chambers:

- A lower chamber (the House of Representatives), in which the number of representatives from each state would be determined by the number of people in that state.
- An upper chamber (the Senate), which would have two members from each state. The members would be elected by the state legislatures.

The Great Compromise gave something to both sides: the large states would have more representatives in the House of Representatives than the small states, yet each state would be granted equality in the Senate—because each state, regardless of size,

bicameral legislature
A legislature made up of two chambers, or parts.

Great Compromise A plan for a bicameral legislature in which one chamber would be based on population and the other chamber would represent each state equally. Also known as the Connecticut Compromise.

Delegates to the Constitutional Convention sign the final document under the view of George Washington, the convention chair. *What advantages may have followed from naming Washington to preside over the convention?*

would have two senators. The Great Compromise thus resolved the small-state/large-state controversy.

The Three-Fifths Compromise A second compromise had to do with how many representatives each state would have in the House of Representatives. Although slavery was legal in parts of the North, most slaves and slave owners lived in the South. Indeed, in the southern states, slaves constituted about 40 percent of the population. Counting the slaves as part of the population would thus greatly increase the number of southern representatives in the House. The delegates from the southern states wanted the slaves to be counted as persons, but the delegates from the northern states disagreed.

Eventually, the **three-fifths compromise** settled this deadlock: each slave would count as three-fifths of a person in determining representation in Congress.

three-fifths compromise A compromise reached during the Constitutional Convention by which three-fifths of all slaves were to be counted for purposes of representation in the House of Representatives.

interstate commerce Trade that involves more than one state.

(The three-fifths compromise was eventually overturned in 1868 by the Fourteenth Amendment.)

Slave Importation The three-fifths compromise did not satisfy everyone at the Constitutional Convention. Many delegates wanted slavery to be banned completely in the United States. The delegates compromised on this question by agreeing that Congress could prohibit the importation of slaves into the country beginning in 1808. The issue of slavery itself, however, was never really addressed by the delegates to the Constitutional Convention. As a result, the South won twenty years of unrestricted slave trade and a requirement that escaped slaves who had fled to the northern states be returned to their owners. Domestic slave trading was untouched.

Banning Export Taxes The South's economic health depended in large part on its exports of agricultural products. The South feared that the northern majority in Congress might pass taxes on these exports. This fear led to yet another compromise: the South agreed to let Congress have the power to regulate **interstate commerce** as well as commerce with other nations. In exchange, the Constitution guaranteed that no export taxes would be imposed on products exported by the states. Today, the United States is one of the few countries that does not tax its exports.

2–4e Defining the Executive and the Judiciary

The Great Compromise was reached by mid-July. Still to be determined was the makeup of the executive branch and the judiciary.

The Executive   One of the weaknesses of the Confederation had been the lack of an independent executive authority. The Constitution remedied this problem by creating an independent executive—the president— and by making the president the commander in chief of the army and navy and of the state militias when called into national service. The president was also given extensive appointment powers, although Senate approval was required for major appointments.

To insulate the presidency from the masses, the position was to be filled by members of an *electoral college,* not directly by the people. Each state was to have a number of *electors* (members of the electoral college) equal in number to the total number of senators and representatives from that state.[14] In the long run, the electoral college failed to prevent ordinary voters from choosing the president. As of 1796, electors were typically pledged to specific presidential candidates. Voting for an elector was therefore equivalent to voting for a presidential candidate. For a number of decades, electors in several states were selected by the state legislature, not the people. By 1796, however, the creation of political parties meant that voters could effectively choose the presidential candidate of a particular party by voting for that party's state legislative candidates. The creation of the electoral college did accomplish one goal—it kept the national Congress from choosing the president.

The Judiciary and the Impeachment Process
Another problem under the Confederation was the lack of a judiciary that was independent of the state courts. The Constitution established the United States Supreme Court and authorized Congress to establish other "inferior" federal courts.

To protect against possible wrongdoing, the Constitution also provided a way to remove federal officials from office—through the impeachment process. The Constitution provides that a federal official who commits "Treason, Bribery, or other high Crimes and Misdemeanors" may be *impeached* (accused of, or charged with, wrongdoing) by the House of Representatives and tried by the Senate. If found guilty of the charges by a two-thirds vote in the Senate, the official can be removed from office and prevented from ever assuming another federal government post.

2–4f The Final Draft Is Approved

A five-man Committee of Detail handled the executive and judicial issues, plus other remaining work. In August, it presented a rough draft to the convention. In September, a committee was named to "revise the stile [style] of, and arrange the Articles which had been agreed to" by the convention. The Committee of Style was headed by Gouverneur Morris of Pennsylvania.[15] On September 17, 1787, the final draft of the Constitution was approved by thirty-nine of the remaining forty-two delegates (some delegates had left early).

As we look back on the drafting of the Constitution, an obvious question emerges: Why didn't the founders ban slavery outright? Certainly, many of the delegates thought that slavery was morally wrong and that the Constitution should ban it entirely. Many Americans have since regarded the framers' failure to deal with the slavery issue as a betrayal of the Declaration of Independence, which proclaimed that "all Men are created equal."

A common argument supporting the framers' action (or lack of it) with respect to slavery is that they had no alternative but to ignore the issue. If they had taken a stand on slavery, the Constitution certainly would not have been ratified. Indeed, if the antislavery delegates had insisted on banning slavery, the delegates from the southern states might have walked out of the convention—and there would have been no Constitution to ratify. For another look at this issue, however, see this chapter's *Perception vs. Reality* feature.

2–4g The Debate over Ratification

The ratification of the Constitution set off a national debate of unprecedented proportions. The battle was fought chiefly by two opposing groups—the **Federalists** (those who favored a strong central government and the new Constitution) and the **Anti-Federalists** (those who opposed a strong central government and the new Constitution).

In the debate over ratification, the Federalists had several advantages. They assumed a positive name, leaving their opposition with a negative label.

Federalists A political group, led by Alexander Hamilton and John Adams, that supported the adoption of the Constitution and the creation of a federal form of government.

Anti-Federalists A political group that opposed the adoption of the Constitution.

PERCEPTION VS. REALITY

The Slavery Issue

In the Declaration of Independence, Thomas Jefferson, a Virginia slave owner, pronounced that "all Men are created equal." Jefferson considered slavery a "hideous blot" on America. George Washington, also a slave owner, regarded the institution of slavery as "repugnant." Patrick Henry, another southerner, also publicly deplored slavery. Given such views among the leading figures of the era, why didn't the founders stay true to the Declaration of Independence and free the slaves?

The Perception

Most Americans assume that southern economic interests and racism alone led the founders to abandon the principles of equality expressed in the Declaration of Independence. African slaves were the backbone of American agriculture, particularly for tobacco, the most profitable export. Without their slaves, southern plantation owners would not have been able to earn such high profits. Presumably, southerners would not

have ratified the Constitution unless it protected the institution of slavery.

The Reality

The third chief justice of the United States Supreme Court, Oliver Ellsworth, declared that "as population increases, poor laborers will be so plenty as to render slaves useless. Slavery in time will not be a speck in our country."[16] He was wrong, of course. But according to historian Gordon S. Wood, Ellsworth's sentiments mirrored those of most prominent leaders in the United States in the years leading up to the creation of our Constitution. Indeed, great thinkers of the time firmly believed that the liberal principles of the Revolution would destroy the institution of slavery.

At the time of the Constitutional Convention, slavery was disappearing in the northern states (it would be eliminated there by 1804). Many founders thought the same thing would happen in the southern states. After all, there were more antislavery societies in the

South than in the North. The founders also thought that the ending of the international slave trade in 1808 would eventually end slavery in the United States. Consequently, the issue of slavery was taken off the table when the Constitution was created simply because the founders had a mistaken belief about the longevity of the institution. They could not have predicted that, within a relatively short time, rapid growth of cotton production in the southern states would give slavery a new lease on life.[17]

Blog On

"Slavery and the Constitution" is just one of many subjects that you can read about in the Legal History Blog, which you can find at legalhistoryblog.blogspot .com. If you enter "slavery" into the box at the top left of the screen, you will see the postings on this topic.

(Instead, the Anti-Federalists could well have called themselves republicans and their opponents nationalists.) The Federalists also had attended the Constitutional Convention and thus were familiar with the arguments both in favor of and against various constitutional provisions. The Anti-Federalists, in contrast, had no actual knowledge of those discussions because almost none of them had attended the convention.

The Federalists also had time, funding, and prestige on their side. Their impressive list of political thinkers and writers included Alexander Hamilton, John Jay, and James Madison. The Federalists could communicate with one another more readily because many of them were bankers, lawyers, and merchants who lived in urban areas, where communication was easier. Accordingly, the Federalists organized a quick and effective ratification

campaign to elect themselves as delegates to each state's ratifying convention.

The Federalists Argue for Ratification Alexander Hamilton, a leading Federalist, enlisted John Jay and James Madison to help him write newspaper columns in support of the new Constitution. In a period of less than a year, these three men wrote a series of eighty-five essays in defense of the Constitution. These essays, which were printed in newspapers throughout the states, are known collectively as the *Federalist Papers*.

Generally, the papers attempted to allay the fears expressed by the Constitution's critics. One fear was that the rights of those in the minority would not be protected. Many critics also feared that a republican form of government would not work in a nation the size of the United States. Various groups, or **factions**, would struggle for power, and chaos would result.

Madison responded to the latter argument in *Federalist Paper* No. 10 (see Appendix C), which is considered a classic in political theory. Among other things, Madison argued that the nation's size was actually an advantage in controlling factions: in a large nation, there would be so many diverse interests and factions that no one faction would be able to gain control of the government.[18]

The Anti-Federalists' Response Perhaps the greatest advantage of the Anti-Federalists was that they stood for the status quo. Usually, it is more difficult to institute changes than it is to keep what is already known and understood. Among the Anti-Federalists were such patriots as Patrick Henry and Samuel Adams. Patrick Henry said of the proposed Constitution, "I look upon that paper as the most fatal plan that could possibly be conceived to enslave a free people."

In response to the *Federalist Papers*, the Anti-Federalists published their own essays. They also wrote brilliantly, attacking nearly every clause of the new document. Many Anti-Federalists contended that the Constitution had been written by aristocrats and would lead the nation to aristocratic **tyranny** (the exercise of absolute, unlimited power). Other Anti-Federalists feared that the Constitution would lead to an overly powerful central government that would limit personal freedom.[19]

The Anti-Federalists argued vigorously that the Constitution needed a bill of rights. They warned that without a bill of rights, a strong national government might take away the political rights won during the American Revolution. They demanded that the new Constitution clearly guarantee personal freedoms.

The Federalists generally did not think that a bill of rights was necessary. Some worried that listing specific rights might imply that other rights could be denied. (The Ninth Amendment addressed that issue.) Nevertheless, to gain the necessary political support, the Federalists finally promised to add a bill of rights to the Constitution as the first order of business under the new government. This promise turned the tide in favor of the Constitution.

2-4h Ratification

The contest for ratification was close in several states, but the Federalists finally won in all of the state conventions. In 1787, Delaware, Pennsylvania, and New Jersey voted to ratify the Constitution, followed by Georgia and Connecticut early in the following year. Even though the Anti-Federalists were perhaps the majority in Massachusetts,

a successful political campaign by the Federalists led to ratification by that state on February 6, 1788.

Following Maryland and South Carolina, New Hampshire became the ninth state to ratify the Constitution on June 21, 1788, thus formally putting the Constitution into effect. New York and Virginia had not yet ratified, however, and without them the Constitution would have no true power. That worry was dispelled in the summer of 1788, when both Virginia and New York ratified the new Constitution. North Carolina waited until November 21 of the following year to ratify the Constitution, and Rhode Island did not ratify until May 29, 1790.

2-4i Did a Majority of Americans Support the Constitution?

Some historians have called the Constitution an aristocratic document that lacked majority support. We cannot conclusively say what most Americans thought of the Constitution, however, because the great majority of adults did not have the right to vote.

Slaves, women, and Indians, of course, could not vote. Furthermore, free men could not vote unless they held sufficient property. A typical voting requirement, used by several states, was possession of land or other property worth forty British pounds. At the time, this sum would buy about a hundred acres of average U.S. farmland. Many of the men who could not vote, it has been argued, were strong republicans.

Still, support for the Constitution seems to have been widespread in all social classes. Both rich and poor Americans were troubled by the weakness of the national government under the Articles of Confederation.

CRITICAL THINKING

▶ *Suppose that Rhode Island had refused to ratify the Constitution and join the Union. Would American history have been seriously altered by such an event?*

 2-5 **THE CONSTITUTION'S MAJOR PRINCIPLES OF GOVERNMENT**

LO Summarize the Constitution's major principles of government, and describe how the Constitution can be amended.

The framers of the Constitution were fearful of the powerful British monarchy,

faction A group of individuals forming a cohesive minority.

tyranny The arbitrary or unrestrained exercise of power by an oppressive individual or government.

against which they had so recently rebelled. At the same time, they wanted a central government strong enough to prevent the kinds of crises that had occurred under the weak central authority of the Articles of Confederation. The principles of government expressed in the Constitution reflect both of these concerns.

2–5a Limited Government, Popular Sovereignty, and the Rule of Law

The Constitution incorporated the principle of limited government, which means that government can do only what the people allow it to do through the exercise of a duly developed system of laws. This principle can be found in many parts of the Constitution. For example, while Articles I, II, and III indicate exactly what the national government *can* do, the first nine amendments to the Constitution list the ways in which the government *cannot* limit certain individual freedoms.

Popular Sovereignty Implicitly, the principle of limited government rests on the concept of popular sovereignty. Remember the phrases that frame the Preamble to the Constitution: "We the People of the United States . . . do ordain and establish this Constitution for the United States of America." In other words, it is the people who form the government and decide on the powers that the government can exercise. If the government exercises powers beyond those granted to it by the Constitution, it is acting illegally.

The Rule of Law The idea that no one, including government officers, is above the law is often called the **rule of law**. Ultimately, the viability of a democracy rests on the willingness of the people and their leaders to adhere to the rule of law. A nation's written constitution may guarantee numerous rights and liberties for its citizens. Yet, unless the government of that nation enforces those rights and liberties, the law does not rule the nation. Rather, government leaders decide what the rules will be.

rule of law A basic principle of government that requires those who govern to act in accordance with established law.

federal system A form of government that provides for a division of powers between a central government and several regional governments.

commerce clause The clause in Article I, Section 8, of the Constitution that gives Congress the power to regulate interstate commerce (commerce involving more than one state).

2–5b The Principle of Federalism

The Constitution also incorporated the principle of *federalism,* or a **federal system** of government, in which the central (national) government shares sovereign powers with the various state governments. Federalism was the solution to the debate over whether the national government or the states should have ultimate sovereignty.

National Powers The Constitution gave the national government significant powers—powers that it had not had under the Articles of Confederation. For example, the Constitution expressly states that the president is the nation's chief executive as well as the commander in chief of the armed forces. The Constitution also declares that the Constitution and the laws created by the national government are supreme—that is, they take precedence over conflicting state laws. Other powers given to the national government included the power to coin money, to levy and collect taxes, and to regulate interstate commerce, a power granted by the **commerce clause**. Finally, the

Neftali/Shutterstock.com

James Madison (1751–1836). Madison's contributions at the Constitutional Convention in 1787 earned him the title "Master Builder of the Constitution." *Why might he have been the one chosen to draft the Bill of Rights?*

national government was authorized to undertake all laws that are "necessary and proper" for carrying out its expressly delegated powers.

State Powers Because the states feared too much centralized control, the Constitution also allowed for many states' rights. These rights include the power to regulate commerce within state borders and generally the authority to exercise any powers that are not delegated by the Constitution to the central government.

2–5c Separation of Powers

As James Madison once said, after you have given the government the ability to control its citizens, you have to "oblige it to control itself." To force the government to "control itself" and to prevent the rise of tyranny, Madison devised a scheme, the **Madisonian Model**, in which the powers of the national government were separated into different branches: legislative, executive, and judicial.[20] The legislative branch (Congress) passes laws, the executive branch (the president) administers and enforces the laws, and the judicial branch (the courts) interprets the laws. By separating the powers of government, the framers ensured that no one branch would have enough power to dominate the others. This principle of **separation of powers** is laid out in Articles I, II, and III of the Constitution.

2–5d Checks and Balances

A system of **checks and balances** was also devised to ensure that no one group or branch of government can exercise exclusive control. Even though each branch of government is independent of the others, it can also check the actions of the others.

Look at Figure 2–5 and you can see how this is done. As the figure shows, the president checks Congress by

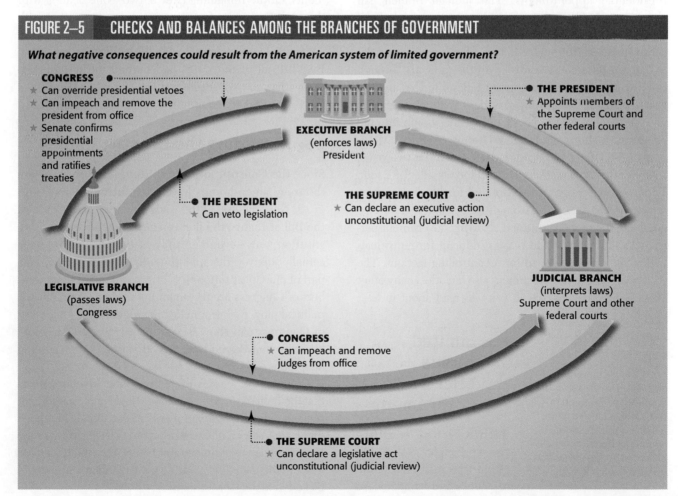

FIGURE 2–5   CHECKS AND BALANCES AMONG THE BRANCHES OF GOVERNMENT

What negative consequences could result from the American system of limited government?

CONGRESS
★ Can override presidential vetoes
★ Can impeach and remove the president from office
★ Senate confirms presidential appointments and ratifies treaties

THE PRESIDENT
★ Appoints members of the Supreme Court and other federal courts

EXECUTIVE BRANCH
(enforces laws)
President

THE PRESIDENT
★ Can veto legislation

THE SUPREME COURT
★ Can declare an executive action unconstitutional (judicial review)

LEGISLATIVE BRANCH
(passes laws)
Congress

JUDICIAL BRANCH
(interprets laws)
Supreme Court and other federal courts

CONGRESS
★ Can impeach and remove judges from office

THE SUPREME COURT
★ Can declare a legislative act unconstitutional (judicial review)

Nicola Sturgeon is the first (prime) minister of Scotland. Here, she responds during question time at the Scottish Parliament in Edinburgh. *Should members of the U.S. Congress have an opportunity to directly question the president? Why or why not?*

holding a **veto power**, which is the ability to return bills to Congress for reconsideration. Congress, in turn, controls taxes and spending, and the Senate must approve presidential appointments. The judicial branch can check the other branches of government through *judicial review*—the power to rule congressional or presidential actions unconstitutional.[21] In turn, the president and the Senate exercise some control over the judiciary through the president's power to appoint federal judges and the Senate's role in confirming presidential appointments.

Among the other checks and balances built into the American system are staggered terms of office. Members of the House of Representatives serve for two years, members of the Senate for six, and the president for four. Federal court judges are appointed for life but may be impeached and removed from office by Congress for misconduct. Staggered terms and changing government personnel were supposed to make it difficult for individuals within the government to form controlling factions. The American system of government also includes many other checks and balances, which you will read about in later chapters of this book.

veto power A constitutional power that enables the chief executive (president or governor) to reject legislation and return it to the legislature with reasons for the rejection. This either prevents or delays the bill from becoming law.

2–5e Limited versus Effective Government

Such American constitutional principles as the separation of powers and a system of checks and balances are not universal among representative democracies. Compared with the United States, many countries place less emphasis on limited government and a higher value on "effective government." (The alternative term "efficient government" is also used.) The *parliamentary system* is a constitutional form that reflects such values. We describe it in this chapter's *The Rest of the World* feature.

2–5f The Bill of Rights

To secure the ratification of the Constitution in several important states, the Federalists had to promise a Bill of Rights. At the state ratifying conventions, delegates set forth specific rights that should be protected. James Madison considered these recommendations as he labored to draft the Bill of Rights.

After sorting through more than two hundred state recommendations, Madison came up with sixteen amendments. Congress tightened the language somewhat and eliminated four of the amendments. Of the remaining twelve, two—one dealing with the apportionment of representatives and the other with the compensation of the members of Congress—were not ratified by the states during the ratification process.[22] By 1791, all of the states had ratified the ten amendments that now constitute our Bill of Rights. We discuss the Bill of Rights in depth in Chapter 4.

2–5g Amending the Constitution

Since the Constitution was written, more than eleven thousand amendments have been introduced in Congress. Nonetheless, in the years since the ratification of the Bill of Rights, the first ten amendments to the Constitution, only seventeen proposed amendments have actually survived the amendment process and become a part of our Constitution. It is often contended that members of Congress use the amendment process simply as a political ploy. By introducing an amendment, a member of Congress can show her or his position on an issue, knowing that the odds against the amendment's being adopted are high.

One of the reasons there are so few amendments is that the framers, in Article V, made the formal amendment process difficult (although it was easier than it had been under the Articles of Confederation). There are two ways to propose an amendment and two ways to ratify one. As a result, there are four possible ways for an amendment to be added to the Constitution.

The Parliamentary Alternative

An alternative to our form of government is the *parliamentary system*. Britain—the United Kingdom—has a typical parliamentary system. In contrast to the American system, the British one is based on the *fusion* of powers rather than the *separation* of powers.

First, a Few Basics

Members of Parliament (MPs) are elected just as we elect members of Congress. Here the similarity ends. British voters do not directly choose a chief executive, as we do when we vote for president. Rather, the chief executive is chosen by the lower house of Parliament—the House of Commons, analogous to our House of Representatives. (There is an upper house, the House of Lords, but it has little power.)

Each political party selects a leader well before the general elections. If one party wins a majority of the seats in the House of Commons, it can name its leader as the prime minister—the chief executive of the nation.

The Fusion of Powers

MPs who join the *government* (what we would call the administration) keep their seats in Parliament. The prime minister is both the chief executive of the nation and the leader of his or her party in the legislature. The legislature and the executive are fused, not separated. In contrast, the U.S. Constitution explicitly requires members of Congress who join the president's administration to resign from Congress.

Americans often view the parliamentary system as undemocratic because voters cannot choose the chief executive. Citizens of parliamentary countries do not see the system in quite that way, however. Voters know who the party leaders are in advance of the elections. When they vote, they are choosing a party and its leader. The identity of their own local MP usually has little impact on how they cast their ballots.

What the parliamentary system really does is prevent voters from choosing a chief executive from one party and a legislative representative from another. In America after the

2010 and 2012 elections, for example, Democratic president Barack Obama faced a House of Representatives controlled by the Republicans. That kind of divided government is impossible under the parliamentary system.

Coalition Governments

The parliamentary system does encourage the formation of multiple major parties, thus providing voters with more options than is common in America. But what if no party wins a majority in the lower house of Parliament? Two options are possible. The largest party can form a *minority government* with the acquiescence of other parties. Alternatively, two, three, or more parties can agree to form a *coalition government*. Many countries that use the parliamentary system are normally governed by coalitions.

Critical Analysis
Why is it so hard to form effective third parties in the United States?

Methods of Proposing an Amendment The two methods of proposing an amendment are as follows:

1. Following presentation of a proposed amendment, a two-thirds vote in the Senate and in the House of Representatives is required. All of the twenty-seven existing amendments have been proposed in this way.

2. If two-thirds of the state legislatures request that Congress call a national amendment convention, then Congress must call one. The convention may propose amendments to the states for ratification. No such convention has ever been convened.

The notion of a national amendment convention is exciting to many people. Many leaders, however, are uneasy about the prospect of convening a body that conceivably could do what the Constitutional Convention did—create a new form of government. We discussed this issue in the chapter-opening *America at Odds* feature.

Methods of Ratifying an Amendment There are two methods of ratifying a proposed amendment:

1. Three-fourths of the state legislatures can vote in favor of the proposed amendment. This method is considered the "traditional" ratification method and has been used twenty-six times.

2. The states can call special conventions to ratify the proposed amendment. If three-fourths of the states approve, the amendment is ratified. This

method has been used only once—to ratify the Twenty-first Amendment.[23]

You can see the four methods for proposing and ratifying amendments in Figure 2–6. As you can imagine, to meet the requirements for proposal and ratification, any amendment must have wide popular support throughout the country.

CRITICAL THINKING

▶ *Is amending the Constitution too difficult? Why or why not?*

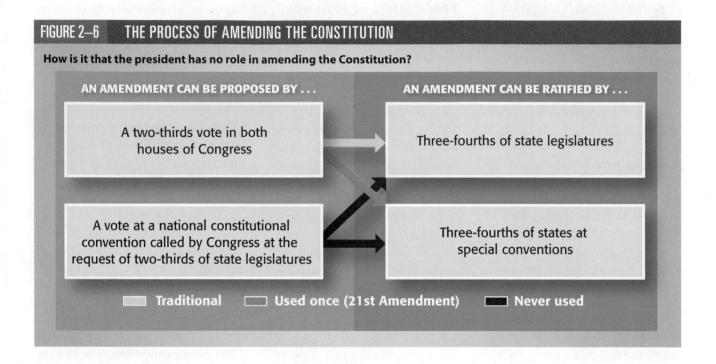

FIGURE 2–6   THE PROCESS OF AMENDING THE CONSTITUTION

How is it that the president has no role in amending the Constitution?

AN AMENDMENT CAN BE PROPOSED BY ...

A two-thirds vote in both houses of Congress

A vote at a national constitutional convention called by Congress at the request of two-thirds of state legislatures

AN AMENDMENT CAN BE RATIFIED BY ...

Three-fourths of state legislatures

Three-fourths of states at special conventions

☐ Traditional   ☐ Used once (21st Amendment)   ■ Never used

AMERICA AT ODDS   The Constitution

Americans engaged in intense disputes about the ratification of the Constitution, as you have learned in this chapter. The most important of these disputes was over the relative power of the states and the national government. This dispute is central to the topic of federalism, which we will take up in Chapter 3. Proposed constitutional amendments have also been the source of many controversies throughout U.S. history. These controversies include the following:

- *The Equal Rights Amendment of 1972 stated, "Equality of rights under the law shall not be denied or abridged by the United States or by any state on account of sex." The amendment failed to win approval from enough states. Should it be revived—or are equal rights for women unacceptable because women could not then be exempted from a military draft?*

- *Progressive groups have called for a constitutional amendment to overturn the Supreme Court's decision in* Citizens United v. Federal Election Commission. *In that case, the Court removed many existing limits on contributions to*

political campaigns. Should we reimpose such limits to curb corruption—or would that violate freedom of speech?

- *Conservatives have campaigned for a constitutional amendment to require the federal government to balance its budget. Would such a measure be desirable—or would it introduce a disastrous lack of flexibility into national finances?*

- *What about an amendment to ban the destruction of the American flag as an act of protest? Is such a ban important to the dignity of our fallen soldiers—or would it be an unacceptable limit on free speech?*

STUDY TOOLS 2

READY TO STUDY? IN THE BOOK, YOU CAN:

☐ Review what you've read with the following chapter quiz.

☐ Check your answers in Appendix D at the back of the book.

☐ Rip out the Chapter Review Card, which includes key terms and chapter summaries.

ONLINE AT WWW.CENGAGEBRAIN.COM, YOU CAN:

☐ Explore various online resources in the National Constitution Center and U.S. Constitution websites with the Internet Resources tool.

☐ Interact with figures from the text, and watch quick animation clips.

FILL-IN

Learning Outcome 2–1

1. Even before the Pilgrims went ashore, they drew up the _____, in which they set up a government and promised to obey its laws.

Learning Outcome 2–2

2. After the Seven Years' War, the British government decided to obtain revenues to pay its war debts and to finance the defense of its North American empire by _____.

3. The British Parliament imposed several taxes on the colonists, including the _____.

Learning Outcome 2–3

4. The Articles of Confederation established the _____ as the central governing body.

5. _____, a rebellion of angry farmers in western Massachusetts in 1786, along with similar uprisings throughout most of the New England states, emphasized the need for a true national government.

Learning Outcome 2–4

6. At the Constitutional Convention in 1787, the delegates forged the Great Compromise, which established a bicameral legislature composed of the _____.

7. The Constitution provides that a federal official who commits "_____" may be impeached by the House of Representatives and tried by the Senate.

8. During the debate over ratification, the Anti-Federalists argued that the Constitution needed a _____ because a strong national government might take away the political rights won during the American Revolution.

Learning Outcome 2–5

9. The principle of dividing governmental powers among the legislative, the executive, and the judicial branches of government is known as the _____.

10. Among the checks and balances built into the American system of government is the court's power of _____.

MULTIPLE CHOICE

Learning Outcome 2–1

11. The majority of American colonists came from
   a. Germany and Spain.
   b. France and Ireland.
   c. England and Scotland.

Learning Outcome 2–2

12. Before the mid-1700s, the majority of American colonists were
   a. secretly planning to declare their independence from Britain.
   b. loyal to the British monarch and viewed Britain as their homeland.
   c. politically indifferent.

Learning Outcome 2–3

13. Under the Articles of Confederation, the new nation
   a. could not declare war.
   b. could enter into treaties and alliances.
   c. could regulate interstate commerce.

Learning Outcome 2–4

14. The three-fifths compromise reached at the Constitutional Convention had to do with
   a. how slaves would be counted in determining representation in Congress.
   b. the imposition of export taxes.
   c. the regulation of commerce.

Learning Outcome 2–5

15. All of the existing amendments to the Constitution have been proposed
   a. by a two-thirds vote in the Senate and in the House of Representatives.
   b. by a vote in three-fourths of the state legislatures.
   c. at national constitutional conventions.

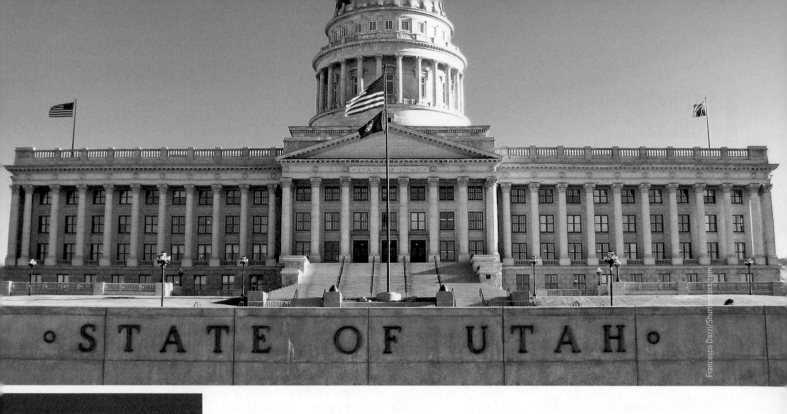

Francesco Dazzi/Shutterstock.com

°STATE OF UTAH°

3 FEDERALISM

LEARNING OUTCOMES *After reading this chapter, you should be able to:*

3-1 Explain what federalism means, how federalism differs from other systems of government, and why it exists in the United States.

3-2 Indicate how the Constitution divides governing powers in our federal system.

3-3 Summarize the evolution of federal-state relationships in the United States over time.

3-4 Describe developments in federalism in recent years.

3-5 Explain what is meant by the term fiscal federalism.

After finishing this chapter, go to **PAGE 70** for **STUDY TOOLS**.

Peter Kim/Shutterstock.com

AMERICA AT ODDS | Should Recreational Marijuana Be Legal?

The history of marijuana in America is long and varied. Before the 1920s, marijuana was either not regulated or lightly regulated throughout the United States. By the mid-1930s, however, pot was illegal almost everywhere. Current national law is based on the Controlled Substances Act of 1970, which lists marijuana as a "Schedule I" substance with no medical use and a high potential for abuse.

Times have changed, and so have state laws. According to a Gallup poll, a majority of Americans now favor legalizing marijuana. As of early 2016, marijuana remains fully illegal in twenty-one states. Twenty have legalized it for medical purposes, however, and fifteen have decriminalized it—that is, no longer treat its use as a criminal offense. (These two categories overlap.) Alaska, Colorado, Oregon, and Washington have legalized marijuana for both recreational and medical purposes. The same is true for the cities of Portland and South Portland in Maine and the District of Columbia. As of 2016, at least a dozen states were contemplating looser marijuana laws, either through a vote of the people or through state legislative action. With our federal system, though, the national government can still arrest individuals for possession and use of marijuana everywhere.

Legalize Marijuana at Our Peril

Opponents of marijuana legalization say that if you like the huge expense of alcohol and tobacco abuse, then you will love the costs of legal marijuana. Use of alcohol and tobacco is common—65 percent of Americans use alcohol, and 30 percent use tobacco. If we were to add legalized marijuana to that list, how many people would abuse the drug? More than do so now, surely.

Just as long-term use of alcohol and tobacco affects the body and the brain, so, too, does long-term marijuana use. The results are memory loss, reduced ability to concentrate, and poor coordination. Long-term abuse from an early age yields diminished attention spans and reduced ability for abstract reasoning. Adolescents face the greatest risk if we legalize marijuana.

A final point: Legalization advocates claim that legal pot will cut crime rates. Yet most drug-related violence and gang activity is not due to marijuana. Most violence follows from the production and sale of cocaine, heroin, and methamphetamines. Do we want to legalize these?

The Benefits Outweigh the Costs

Those in favor of marijuana legalization point out the obvious: In a typical year, forty to fifty million Americans use marijuana recreationally at least once. If we were to repeal current federal legislation and let the states do as they wish, we would relieve our overworked police, courts, and prisons. Arresting hundreds of thousands of people each year for marijuana use is simply a waste of resources. Those who are arrested, even if they do not serve time in prison, will have a police record for life, reducing their chances for employment.

Tobacco smokers die an average of seven years before nonsmokers. Thousands of people die from alcohol poisoning each year, but it is essentially impossible to die of a pot overdose. Marijuana users are not as aggressive as those who are intoxicated with alcohol—a third of those arrested for crimes were drunk when they broke the law. What sense does it make to ban marijuana when these legal drugs are so much more dangerous?

Where do you stand?

1. Instead of legalizing marijuana, would it make sense to ban alcoholic beverages? Why or why not?
2. What benefits might states gain if they legalize the recreational use of marijuana?

Explore this issue online:

- John Hawkins argues against marijuana legalization on the conservative Townhall blog. Find the article by searching for "hawkins marijuana."
- Renee Jacques and Todd Van Luling make the case for legalization on the Huffington Post site. Search for "marijuana should be legal everywhere."

INTRODUCTION

Clearly, those who work for the national government would like the states to cooperate fully in the implementation of national policies. At the same time, those who work in state government don't like to be told what to do by the national government, especially when the implementation of a national policy is costly for the states. (Sometimes, this attitude can lead to conflicts, such as the one described in the chapter-opening *America at Odds* feature.) Finally, those who work in local governments would like to run their affairs with the least amount of interference from both their state governments and the national government.

Such conflicts arise because our government is based on the principle of **federalism**, which means that government powers are shared by the national government and the states. When the founders of this nation opted for federalism, they created a practical and flexible form of government capable of enduring for centuries. At the same time, however, they planted the seeds for future conflict between the states and the national government over how government powers should be shared. As you will read in this chapter—and throughout this book—many of today's most pressing issues have to do with which level of government should exercise certain powers.

3-1 FEDERALISM AND ITS ALTERNATIVES

LO Explain what federalism means, how federalism differs from other systems of government, and why it exists in the United States.

There are various ways of ordering relations between central governments and local units. Federalism is one of these ways. Learning about federalism and how it differs from other forms of government is important to understanding the American political system.

3-1a What Is Federalism?

federalism A system of shared sovereignty between two levels of government— one national and one subnational—occupying the same geographic region.

Nowhere in the Constitution does the word *federalism* appear. This is understandable, given that the modern concept of federalism was an invention of the founders.

Since the Federalists and the Anti-Federalists argued more than two hundred years ago about what form of government we should have, hundreds of definitions of federalism have been offered. Basically, as mentioned in Chapter 2, government powers in a *federal system* are divided between a central government and regional, or subdivisional, governments.

Defining Federalism Although the definition given here seems straightforward, its application certainly is not. After all, almost all nations—even the most repressive totalitarian regimes—have some kind of subnational governmental units. Thus, the existence of national and subnational governmental units by itself does not make a system federal. *For a system to be truly federal, the powers of both the national units and the subnational units must be specified and limited.*

Under true federalism, individuals are governed by two separate governmental authorities (national and state authorities) whose expressly designated powers cannot be altered without changing the fundamental nature of the system—for example, by amending a written constitution. Table 3–1 lists some of the countries that have a federal system of government.[1]

TABLE 3-1 COUNTRIES THAT HAVE A FEDERAL SYSTEM TODAY

What influence might the example of the United States have had on the adoption of federal systems in other countries?

Country	Population (in Millions)
Argentina	43.6
Australia	24.0
Austria	8.7
Brazil	205.5
Canada	36.0
Ethiopia	92.2
Germany	81.3
India	1,282.9
Malaysia	30.8
Mexico	122.3
Nigeria	187.0
Pakistan	192.5
Switzerland	8.3
United States	323.6

Source: Official estimates by governments of the listed nations or by the United Nations.

U.S. Federalism in Practice Federalism in theory is one thing—federalism in practice is another. As you will read shortly, the Constitution sets forth specific powers that can be exercised by the national government and provides that the national government has the implied power to undertake actions necessary to carry out its expressly designated powers. All other powers are "reserved" to the states. The broad language of the Constitution, though, has left much room for debate over the specific nature and scope of certain powers, such as the national government's implied powers and the powers reserved to the states. Thus, the actual workings of our federal form of government have depended, to a great extent, on the historical application of the broad principles outlined in the Constitution.

To further complicate matters, the term *federal government*, as it is used today, refers to the national, or central, government. When individuals talk of the federal government, they mean the national government based in Washington, D.C. They are not referring to the federal *system* of government, which is made up of both the national government and the state governments.

3-1b Alternatives to Federalism

Perhaps an easier way to define federalism is to discuss what it is *not*. A majority of the nations in the world today have a **unitary system** of government. In such a system, the constitution vests all powers in the national government. If the national government so chooses, it can delegate some activities to subnational units. In a unitary system, any subnational government is a "creature of the national government." The governments of Britain, France, Israel, Japan, and the Philippines are examples of unitary systems.

In the United States, because the Constitution does not mention local governments (cities and counties), we say that city and county governmental units are "creatures of state government." That means that state governments can—and do—both give powers to and take powers from local governments. The individual American states, in other words, are also unitary systems.

The Articles of Confederation, discussed in Chapter 2, created a confederal system, a second alternative to federalism. In a **confederal system**, the national government exists and operates only at the direction of the subnational governments. Few true confederal systems are in existence today, although some people contend that the European Union—a group of twenty-eight European nations that has established many common institutions—qualifies as such a system.

3-1c Federalism—An Optimal Choice for the United States?

The Articles of Confederation failed because they did not allow for a sufficiently strong central government. The framers of the Constitution, however, were also fearful of tyranny and a too-powerful central government. The outcome had to be a compromise—a federal system.

Advantages of Federalism The appeal of federalism was that it retained state powers and local traditions while establishing a strong national government capable of handling common problems, such as national defense. A federal form of government also furthered the goal of creating a division of powers (to be discussed shortly). There are other reasons why the founders opted for a federal system, and a federal structure of government continues to offer many advantages for U.S. citizens.

Advantage: Size. One of the reasons a federal form of government is well suited to the United States is our country's large size. Even when the United States consisted of only thirteen states, its geographic area was larger than that of England or France. In those days, travel was slow and communication was difficult, so people in outlying areas were isolated. The news of any particular political decision could take several weeks to reach everyone. Therefore, even if the framers of the Constitution had wanted a more centralized system (which most of them did not), such a system would have been unworkable.

Look at Figure 3–1. As you can see, to a great extent the practical business of governing this country takes place in state and local governmental units. Indeed, the most common type of governmental unit in the United States is the *special district*—an independent unit of government that is separate from general-purpose local governments such as counties, cities, and townships. Special districts enjoy substantial administrative and financial independence.

A special district is generally concerned with a specific issue such as solid waste disposal, mass transportation, or fire protection. Often, the jurisdiction of special districts crosses the boundaries of other governmental units, such as cities or counties. Special districts also tend to have fewer restrictions than other local governments as

unitary system
A centralized governmental system in which local or subdivisional governments exercise only those powers given to them by the central government.

confederal system
A league of independent sovereign states, joined together by a central government that has only limited powers over them.

FIGURE 3–1 GOVERNMENTAL UNITS IN THE UNITED STATES TODAY

How could the number of governments in the United States create problems for voters?

THE NUMBER OF GOVERNMENTS IN THE UNITED STATES TODAY

Government	Number
Federal government	1
State governments and District of Columbia	51
Local governments	
Counties	3,031
Municipalities (mainly cities or towns)	19,522
Townships (less extensive powers)	16,364
Special districts (water, sewer, and so on)	37,203
School districts	12,884
Subtotal local governments	89,004
Total	**89,056**

PERCENTAGE OF ALL GOVERNMENTS IN THE UNITED STATES TODAY

Townships 18.4%
School districts 14.5%
Counties 3.4%
States (& D.C.) 0.06%
Federal 0.001%

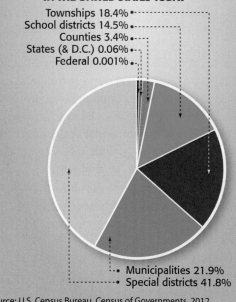

Municipalities 21.9%
Special districts 41.8%

Source: U.S. Census Bureau, Census of Governments, 2012

to how much debt they can incur and so are created to finance large building projects.

Advantage: Experimentation. The existence of numerous government subunits in the United States also makes it possible to experiment with innovative policies and programs at the state or local level. Many observers, including Supreme Court justice Louis Brandeis (1856–1941), have emphasized that in a federal system, state governments can act as "laboratories" for public-policy experimentation. For example, many states have adopted minimum-wage laws that establish a higher minimum wage than the one set by national legislation. State governments also have a wide variety of policies on how or whether state employees can form labor unions.

Depending on the outcome of a specific experiment, other states may (or may not) implement similar programs. State innovations can also serve as models for federal programs. For instance, California was a pioneer in air-pollution control. Many of that state's regulations were later adapted by other states and eventually by the federal government.

Advantage: Subcultures. We have always been a nation of different political subcultures. The Pilgrims who founded New England were different from the settlers who established the agricultural society of the South. Both of these groups were different from those who populated the Middle Atlantic states. The groups that founded New England had a religious focus, while those who populated the Middle Atlantic states were more business oriented. Those who settled in the South were more individualistic than the other groups. That is, they were less inclined to act as a collective and more inclined to act independently of each other. A federal system of government allows the political and cultural interests of regional groups to be reflected in the laws governing those groups.

As we noted earlier, nations other than the United States have benefited from the principle of federalism. One of them is Canada. Because federalism permits the expression of varying regional cultures, Canadian federalism naturally differs from the American version, as you will discover in this chapter's *The Rest of the World* feature.

Some Drawbacks to Federalism Federalism offers many advantages, but it also has some drawbacks. Consider that although federalism in many ways promotes greater self-rule, or democracy, some scholars point out that local self-rule may not always be in society's best interests. These observers argue that the smaller the political unit, the higher the probability that it will be dominated by a single political group, which may or may not be concerned with the welfare of many of the local unit's citizens. For example, entrenched segregationist politicians in southern states denied African Americans their civil rights and voting rights for decades, as we discuss further in Chapter 5.

Canadian versus American Federalism

By land area, Canada is the second-largest country in the world. Physically, the country seems designed for a federal system of government. And indeed, Canada has a federal system similar in some ways to that of the United States—but it also has some big differences. When the 1867 Constitution Act created modern Canada, the United States had just concluded the Civil War. Canada's founders blamed that war on the weakness of the U.S. central government. Therefore, the Canadian Constitution gave far more power to the central government than did the U.S. Constitution.

The Powers of Lower-Level Governments

Our lower levels of government are called states, whereas in Canada they are called provinces. Right there, the powers of the central government are emphasized. The word *state* implies sovereignty. A *province*, however, is never sovereign and is typically set up for the convenience of the central government.

In the United States, the powers of the national government are limited to those listed in the Constitution. In the Canadian Constitution, it is the powers of the provinces that are limited by a list. The Tenth Amendment to the U.S. Constitution reserves residual powers to the states or to the people. In Canada, residual powers rest with the national government. Under the 1867 Canadian Constitution, the central government could veto any provincial legislation. No such clause appears in the U.S. Constitution.

The Provinces Gain Strength

Over time, the powers of the U.S. federal government grew at the expense of the states. The opposite happened in Canada. By the end of the nineteenth century, the Canadian government in practice had abandoned the power to veto provincial legislation. The Great Depression of the 1930s strengthened the national government in the United States. In Canada, it strengthened the provinces.

Two Languages

Another striking difference between Canada and the United States is that Canada has two national languages. A majority of Canadians speak English, but most of the population of Québec speak French. The Parti Québécois (PQ), which wants Québec to be a separate country, gained power in that province in 1976 and 1994. Both times, it held referendums on whether Québec should demand "sovereignty-association," a euphemism for independence. In 1995, the PQ almost obtained a majority vote for its position. The PQ returned to power in 2012 but without enough votes to hold another referendum. In 2014, it was defeated by the Liberal Party. Nevertheless, the possibility exists that Canada could actually break apart someday.

Critical Analysis

The Canadian Constitution is based on the principles of "peace, order, and good government." Contrast that phrase with the words in the Declaration of Independence—"life, liberty, and the pursuit of happiness." How do the statements differ?

Powerful state and local interests can impede national plans. State and local interests often diverge from those of the national government. For example, the health-care reforms adopted by the national government in 2010 sought to expand the number of poor persons eligible for Medicaid. As of 2016, however, nineteen states have refused to participate in the expansion program, even though the national government picks up the entire cost until 2020. Finding acceptable solutions to such conflicts has not always been easy. Indeed, as will be discussed shortly, in the 1860s, war—not politics—decided the outcome of a struggle over states' rights.

Federalism has other drawbacks as well. One of them is the lack of uniformity of state laws, which can complicate business transactions that cross state borders. Another problem is the difficulty of coordinating government policies at the national, state, and local levels. Additionally, the simultaneous regulation of business by all levels of government creates red tape that imposes substantial costs on the business community.

In a federal system, there is always the danger that national power will be expanded at the expense of the states. President Ronald Reagan (1981–1989) once said, "The Founding Fathers saw the federalist system as constructed something like a masonry wall. The States are the bricks, the national government is the mortar. . . . Unfortunately, over the years, many people have increasingly come to believe that Washington is the whole wall."[2]

CRITICAL THINKING

▶ *The national government imposed a uniform highway speed limit on the entire country from 1974 until its repeal in 1995. Why should we leave speed limits to the states—or why should they be a federal responsibility?*

3–2 THE CONSTITUTIONAL DIVISION OF POWERS

LO Indicate how the Constitution divides governing powers in our federal system.

The founders created a federal form of government by dividing sovereign powers into powers that could be exercised by the national government and powers that were reserved to the states. Although there is no systematic explanation of this **division of powers**, the original Constitution, along with its amendments, provides statements on what the national and state governments can (and cannot) do.

3–2a The Powers of the National Government

The Constitution delegates certain powers to the national government. It also prohibits the national government from exercising certain powers.

division of powers
A basic principle of federalism established by the U.S. Constitution, by which powers are divided between the national and state governments.

expressed powers
Constitutional or statutory powers that are expressly provided for by the U.S. Constitution; also called *enumerated powers.*

implied powers
The powers of the federal government that are implied by the expressed powers in the Constitution, particularly in Article I, Section 8.

necessary and proper clause Article I, Section 8, Clause 18, of the Constitution, which gives Congress the power to make all laws "necessary and proper" for the federal government to carry out its responsibilities; also called the *elastic clause.*

Powers Delegated to the National Government The national government possesses three types of powers: expressed powers, implied powers, and inherent powers.

Expressed Powers. Article I, Section 8, of the Constitution expressly enumerates twenty-seven powers that Congress may exercise. Two of these **expressed powers**, or *enumerated powers,* are the power to coin money and the power to regulate interstate commerce. Constitutional amendments have provided for other expressed powers. For example, the Sixteenth Amendment, added in 1913, gives Congress the power to impose a federal income tax.

One power expressly granted to the national government is the right to regulate commerce not only among the states, but also "with the Indian Tribes." As a result, relations between Native American tribal governments and the rest of the country have always been a national responsibility. A further consequence is that state governments face significant limits on their authority over Indian reservations within their borders.

Implied Powers. The constitutional basis for the **implied powers** of the national government is found in Article I, Section 8, Clause 18, often called the **necessary and proper clause**. This clause states that Congress has the power to make "all Laws which shall be necessary and proper for carrying into Execution the foregoing [expressed] Powers, and all other Powers vested by this Constitution in the Government of the United States, or in any Department or Officer thereof." The necessary and proper clause is often referred to as the *elastic clause,* because it gives elasticity to our constitutional system.

The U.S. Flag flies above the Texas state flag in Austin, Texas. *What type of power did the national government use when it annexed California?*

An example of an implied power is the power to print paper currency such as dollar bills. The Constitution says only that Congress has the power to "coin money," presumably in the form of gold or silver coins. Congress also has the expressed power to borrow, however, and on that basis it eventually issued paper currency that represented sums owed by the government.[3]

Inherent Powers. The national government also enjoys certain inherent powers—powers that governments must have simply to ensure the nation's integrity and survival as a political unit. For example, any national government must have the inherent ability to make treaties, regulate immigration, acquire territory, wage war, and make peace. While some inherent powers are also enumerated in the Constitution, such as the powers to wage war and make treaties, others are not. For example, the Constitution does not speak of regulating immigration or acquiring new territory. Although the national government's inherent powers are few, they are important.

Federal Lands. One inherent power is older than the Constitution itself—the power to own land. The United States collectively owned various western lands under the Articles of Confederation. The Northwest Territory, which included the modern states of Illinois, Indiana, Michigan, Ohio, Wisconsin, and part of Minnesota, joined United States' lands together with lands given up by New York and Virginia. The Northwest Territory was organized during the ratification of the Constitution. Indeed, establishing the territory as the collective property of the entire Union was necessary to secure support for ratification in several states, including Maryland.

The United States then sold land to new settlers—land sales were a major source of national government income throughout much of the 1800s. To this day, the national government owns most of the acres in many far western states, a fact that annoys many Westerners. We discuss that issue in this chapter's *Join the Debate* feature.

Powers Prohibited to the National Government The Constitution expressly prohibits the national government from undertaking certain actions, such as imposing taxes on exports, and from passing laws restraining certain liberties, such as the freedom of speech or religion. Most of these prohibited powers are listed in Article I, Section 9, and in the first eight amendments to the Constitution. Additionally, the national government is implicitly prohibited from exercising certain powers. For example, most authorities believe that the federal government does not have the power to create a national public school system, because such power is not included among those that are expressed and implied.

3–2b The Powers of the States

The Tenth Amendment to the Constitution states that powers that are not delegated to the national government by the Constitution nor prohibited to the states "are reserved to the States respectively, or to the people." The Tenth Amendment thus gives numerous powers to the states, including the power to regulate commerce within their borders and the power to maintain a state militia.

Police Powers In principle, each state has the ability to regulate its internal affairs and to enact whatever laws are necessary to protect the health, safety, welfare, and morals of its people. These powers of the states are called police powers. The establishment of public schools and the regulation of marriage and divorce have traditionally been considered to be entirely within the purview of state and local governments.

Because the Tenth Amendment does not specify what powers are reserved to the states, these powers have been defined differently at different times in our history. In periods of widespread support for increased regulation by the national government, the Tenth Amendment tends to recede into the background. When the tide of support turns, the Tenth Amendment is resurrected to justify arguments supporting increased states' rights (see, for example,

> "THE GREAT DIFFICULTY LIES IN THIS:
> *YOU MUST FIRST ENABLE THE GOVERNMENT TO CONTROL THE GOVERNED; AND IN THE NEXT PLACE, OBLIGE IT TO CONTROL ITSELF.*"
> ~ JAMES MADISON, FOURTH PRESIDENT OF THE UNITED STATES, 1809–1817

inherent powers
The powers of the national government that, although not always expressly granted by the Constitution, are necessary to ensure the nation's integrity and survival as a political unit.

police powers The powers of a government body that enable it to create laws for the protection of the health, safety, welfare, and morals of the people. In the United States, most police powers are reserved to the states.

JOIN THE DEBATE

Should Most Federal Lands Be Transferred to the States?

Extensive federal land ownership was in the news in 2016 when about twenty armed "insurgents" seized a building at the Malheur National Wildlife Refuge near Burns, Oregon. These people were protesting the national government's continued ownership and administration of public lands in western states. Initially, the authorities took a "wait and see" attitude toward the demonstration. After more than three weeks, however, state police and the FBI arrested eight protesters while they were away from the refuge. One of the protestors was killed during the arrest.

Currently, the federal government owns at least half of the land in Alaska, Arizona, California, Colorado, Idaho, Nevada, New Mexico, Oregon, Utah, and Wyoming. Should these federal lands be turned over to state or local authorities? Or even sold to private parties?

The Federal Government Should Not Manage So Much Land

Some Westerners argue that there is no good reason to keep so much land in federal hands. These people contend that federal land management is inefficient. They think it would be better if management were undertaken by governments closer to the people—state or local governments.

A group of U.S. senators and representatives has sponsored legislation called the Federal Lands Freedom Act that, among other things, would give states unlimited power to regulate the development of energy resources on federal lands.

When the government owns land, the use of that land is determined by politics, not markets. Groups that can lobby the government most effectively come out on top. For many years, cattle ranchers had the most influence in determining land use. More recently, environmentalists have gained substantial influence over land use. At a minimum, politicking over the use of federal lands should take place at the state or local level rather than in Washington, D.C. Some libertarians argue that the lands should be sold off altogether. Private owners would put land to its most profitable use—which would also be the most socially beneficial use.

If You Give the Land to the States, They Won't Use It Wisely

True, the national government sometimes has difficulty managing its vast acreage. Yet opponents of any transfer contend that the states are even less able to manage land effectively. Where would states find the sums needed to fight forest or range fires? The obvious

answer is that states would have to sell off some of their land.

Federal lands are currently managed under a "multiple-use" principle. Some lands are leased for grazing, logging, mining, or oil and natural gas production. Most lands are also open to hikers and hunters. Some are even open to snowmobiles and off-road vehicles. Do people seriously believe that private owners would allow the public to use their lands for recreational purposes?

Land could even be bought by foreign interests. The Chinese have invested heavily in farmland in the Canadian provinces of Alberta and Saskatchewan. Do the people who graze cattle think they can get a better deal from the Chinese? Federal grazing fees are about a tenth of what a private owner would charge.

We are *all* owners of the federal lands. Why should western states obtain large amounts of our property without paying for it?

Critical Analysis

Given that a majority of Oregonians live in metro Portland or Eugene, do you think Oregon voters would endorse different public land policies than U.S. voters would? Why or why not?

the discussion of the new federalism later in this chapter). Because the United States Supreme Court is the ultimate arbiter of the Constitution, the outcome of disputes over the extent of state powers often rests with the Court.

Powers Prohibited to the States   Article I, Section 10, denies certain powers to state governments,

such as the power to tax goods that are transported across state lines. States are also prohibited from entering into treaties with other countries. In addition, the Thirteenth, Fourteenth, Fifteenth, Nineteenth, Twenty-fourth, and Twenty-sixth Amendments prohibit certain state actions. (The complete text of these amendments is included in Appendix B.)

The fact remains that, under the Constitution, the states have considerable scope for action under their police powers. Some have even argued that state-level laws and regulations can be more burdensome than national legislation. This chapter's *Perception vs. Reality* feature reports on that concern.

3–2c Interstate Relations

The Constitution also contains provisions relating to interstate relations. The states have constant commercial and social interactions among themselves, and these interactions often do not directly involve the national government. The relationships among the states in our federal system of government are sometimes referred to as *horizontal federalism*.

The Full Faith and Credit Clause   The Constitution's full faith and credit clause requires each state to honor every other state's public acts, records, and judicial proceedings. This constitutional mandate posed a problem in the years from 2004 to 2015, when same-sex marriage was legal in some—but not all—of the states. Already in 1996, members of Congress feared that one

PERCEPTION VS. REALITY
The Best Government Is Local Government

Our government has certainly grown in size since World War II. Many Americans complain about "big government." These people contend that government does too much. Taxes are too high. Regulations take away our freedom. The "government" in question is the one in Washington, D.C.

The Perception

Big government is the problem, and big government means the federal government. Government closest to the people governs best. Therefore, state and local governments should have more power, and the federal government should have less.

The Reality

In recent years, more and more commentators have begun arguing that regulations imposed by state and local governments are even more costly than the ones imposed by the feds. Consider housing policies. The zoning regulations that control housing construction are almost entirely local. Typically, zoning restricts development to ensure low population densities in our major urban areas. City dwellers want to keep out new high-rises. Suburbanites want to stop the construction of town houses and apartment buildings. As a result, cities with highly productive industries, such as Boston, New York, Los Angeles, San Francisco, and Seattle, don't have enough housing for all the people who would like to live there.

The law of supply and demand takes its course: the cost of the housing that does exist rises astronomically. Americans willing to move in search of economic opportunity are priced out. Instead, they go to places where the cost of housing is tolerable—places such as Houston, which has no zoning code. *But jobs don't pay as well in Houston as they do in San Francisco.* The national cost of excessive residential zoning, therefore, may run into hundreds of billions of dollars.

As another example, look at state (and sometimes local) occupational licensing requirements. Of course, it's generally agreed that not everyone who wants to should be a surgeon or a lawyer. We need to be sure that people who handle matters of life and death know what they are doing. But do we really need to license interior designers, as is done in Florida? Do barbers really have to be licensed? Should dental hygienists be required to work for dentists, who then get a cut of their income? Some 29 percent of American workers need a state-issued license to do their jobs legally.

Excessive licensing not only makes the services we buy more expensive, but also restricts job opportunities. These restrictions simply serve the interests of those already in particular trades by reducing the number of competitors.

Blog On

New York Magazine *columnist Jonathan Chait is best known for his aggressive criticism of conservatives. In "The Worst Governments in America Are Local," however, he takes on both political parties. Find this article by searching on "chait worst governments."*

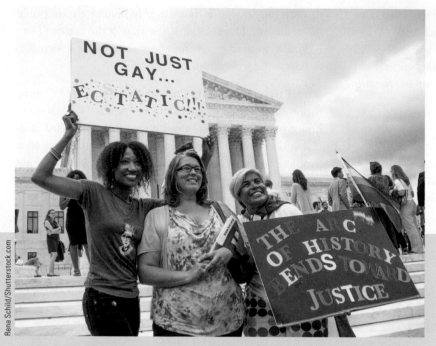

Supporters of same-sex marriage celebrate at the United States Supreme Court after it legalized same-sex marriage in all fifty states in June 2015. *Why has same-sex marriage been an issue for our federal system?*

find that the second part of the law, which banned national recognition of such marriages, was unconstitutional.[4] As a result, same-sex couples were now eligible for hundreds of national benefits available to married partners. *Windsor* was, in a way, a vindication of states' rights— the national government could not interfere with state decisions on whether to recognize same-sex marriage.

Obergefell v. Hodges By 2015, thirty-seven states and the District of Columbia permitted same-sex marriage. In June of that year, in *Obergefell v. Hodges,* the Supreme Court found laws against same-sex marriage to be unconstitutional throughout the entire United States.[5] With that ruling, the question of whether DOMA violated the full faith and credit clause became irrelevant.

or more states might recognize such marriages. If a gay couple was legally married in one state, would all the others be forced to recognize the marriage? To prevent this result, Congress passed the Defense of Marriage Act (DOMA), which provided that no state was required to treat a relationship between persons of the same sex as a marriage, even if the relationship was considered a marriage in another state. A second part of the law barred the national government from recognizing same-sex marriages in states that legalized them. The constitutionality of both parts of the law was subject to debate.

In November 2003, the Massachusetts Supreme Judicial Court found that same-sex couples had the right to marry in that state. The following year, Massachusetts became the first state in the nation to authorize gay marriages. The question of whether DOMA violated the full faith and credit clause was no longer hypothetical. From 2008 on, an ever-larger number of states joined Massachusetts, and the question of DOMA's constitutionality became increasingly important.

United States v. Windsor The United States Supreme Court never took up the question of whether DOMA violated the full faith and credit clause. In 2013, however, in *United States v. Windsor,* the Court did

concurrent powers Powers held by both the federal and the state governments in a federal system.

Interstate Compacts Horizontal federalism also includes agreements, known as *interstate compacts,* among two or more states to regulate the use or protection of certain resources, such as water or oil and gas. California and Nevada, for example, have formed an interstate compact to regulate the use and protection of Lake Tahoe, which lies on the border between those states.

3–2d Concurrent Powers

Concurrent powers can be exercised by both the state governments and the federal government. Generally, a state's concurrent powers apply only within the geographic area of the state and do not include functions that the Constitution delegates exclusively to the national government, such as the coinage of money and the negotiation of treaties.

An example of a concurrent power is the power to tax. Both the states and the national government have the power to impose income taxes—and a variety of other taxes. States, however, are prohibited from imposing tariffs (taxes on imported goods), and, as noted, the federal government may not tax articles exported by any state.

Figures 3–2 and 3–3 summarize the powers granted and denied by the Constitution and lists other concurrent powers.

FIGURE 3—2   POWERS GRANTED BY THE CONSTITUTION

The Constitution grants certain powers to the national government and certain powers to the state governments, while denying them other powers. Some powers, called *concurrent powers,* can be exercised at either the national or the state level, but generally the states can exercise these powers only within their own borders. *There are limits on what states can do using their police powers. Give some examples of actions that would not be allowed.*

NATIONAL
- To coin money
- To conduct foreign relations
- To regulate interstate commerce
- To declare war
- To raise and support the military
- To establish post offices
- To admit new states
- To exercise powers implied by the necessary and proper clause

CONCURRENT
- To levy and collect taxes
- To borrow money
- To make and enforce laws
- To establish courts
- To provide for the general welfare
- To charter banks and corporations

STATE
- To regulate intrastate commerce
- To conduct elections
- To provide for public health, safety, welfare, and morals
- To establish local governments
- To ratify amendments to the federal Constitution
- To establish a state militia

3–2e The Supremacy Clause

The Constitution makes it clear that the federal government holds ultimate power. Article VI, Clause 2, known as the **supremacy clause**, states that the U.S. Constitution and the laws of the federal government "shall be the supreme Law of the Land." In other words, states cannot use their reserved or concurrent powers to counter national policies. Whenever state or local officers, such as judges or sheriffs, take office, they become bound by an oath to support the U.S. Constitution. National government power always takes precedence over any conflicting state action.[6]

CRITICAL THINKING

▶ *Under current court rulings, it is very difficult for states to collect taxes on goods that their citizens buy through the Internet. National legislation, however, could make such tax collection more feasible. Should Congress pass such legislation? Why or why not?*

3–3 THE STRUGGLE FOR SUPREMACY

LO Summarize the evolution of federal-state relationships in the United States over time.

Much of the political and legal history of the United States has involved conflicts between the supremacy of the national government and the desire of the states to preserve their sovereignty. The most extreme example of this conflict was the Civil War in the 1860s. Through the years, because of the Civil War and several important Supreme Court decisions, the national government has increased its power.

3–3a Early United States Supreme Court Decisions

Two Supreme Court cases, both of which were decided in the early 1800s, played a key role in establishing the constitutional foundations for the supremacy of the national government. Both decisions were issued while John Marshall was chief justice of the Supreme Court. In his thirty-four years as chief justice (1801–1835), Marshall did much to establish the prestige and the independence of the Court.

In *Marbury v. Madison,*[7] Marshall clearly enunciated the principle of *judicial review,* under which the courts can determine that laws or executive actions are unconstitutional. Judicial review has since become an important part of the checks and balances in the American system of government. William Marbury was appointed a judge by president John Adams, a member of the Federalist Party, when Adams was about to leave office. The incoming president, Thomas Jefferson, was leader of the rival Republican Party. Adams sought to pack the judiciary, thus preventing Jefferson from filling judicial posts. James Madison, now secretary of state under Jefferson, refused to issue Marbury's appointment. Marshall's court found Marbury's suit to be unconstitutional on a technicality, thus resolving

supremacy clause
Article VI, Clause 2, of the Constitution, which makes the Constitution and federal laws superior to all conflicting state and local laws.

FIGURE 3–3   POWERS DENIED BY THE CONSTITUTION

The Constitution grants certain powers to the national government and certain powers to the state governments, while denying them other powers. *What would happen if the states had the right to coin their own money?*

NATIONAL
- To tax articles exported from any state
- To violate the Bill of Rights
- To change state boundaries without consent of the states in question

CONCURRENT
- To grant titles of nobility
- To permit slavery
- To deny citizens the right to vote

STATE
- To tax imports or exports
- To coin money
- To enter into treaties
- To impair obligations of contracts
- To abridge the privileges or immunities of citizens or deny due process and equal protection of the laws

a troublesome issue. Under Marshall's leadership, the Supreme Court also established, through the following cases, the superiority of federal authority under the Constitution.

McCulloch v. Maryland (1819)

The issue in *McCulloch v. Maryland,*[8] a case decided in 1819, involved both the necessary and proper clause and the supremacy clause. When the state of Maryland imposed a tax on the Baltimore branch of the Second Bank of the United States, the branch's chief cashier, James McCulloch, declined to pay the tax. The state court ruled that McCulloch had to pay it, and the national government appealed to the United States Supreme Court.

The Necessary and Proper Clause. The case involved much more than a question of taxes. At issue was whether Congress had the authority under the Constitution's necessary and proper clause to charter and contribute capital to the Second Bank of the United States. A second constitutional issue was also involved: If the bank was constitutional, could a state tax it? In other words, was a state action that conflicted with a national government action invalid under the supremacy clause?

Chief Justice Marshall pointed out that no provision in the Constitution grants the national government the *expressed* power to form a national bank. Nevertheless, if establishing such a bank helps the national government exercise its expressed powers, then the authority to do so could be implied. Marshall also said that the necessary and proper clause included "all means that are appropriate" to carry out "the legitimate ends" of the Constitution.

The Doctrine of National Supremacy. Having established this doctrine of implied powers, Marshall then answered the other important constitutional question

before the Court and established the doctrine of *national supremacy.* Marshall declared that no state could use its taxing power to tax an arm of the national government. If it could, the Constitution's declaration that the Constitution "shall be the supreme Law of the Land" would be empty rhetoric without meaning. From that day on, Marshall's decision became the basis for strengthening the national government's power.

Gibbons v. Ogden (1824)

As Chapter 2 explained, Article I, Section 8, gives Congress the power to regulate commerce "among the several States." But the framers of the Constitution did not define the word *commerce.* At issue in *Gibbons v. Ogden*[9] was how the *commerce clause* should be defined and whether the national government had the exclusive power to regulate commerce involving more than one state.

The New York legislature had given Robert Livingston and Robert Fulton the exclusive right to operate steamboats in New York waters, and Livingston and Fulton licensed Aaron Ogden to operate a ferry between New York and New Jersey. Thomas Gibbons, who had a license from the U.S. government to operate boats in interstate waters, decided to compete with Ogden, but he did so without New York's permission. Ogden sued Gibbons in the New York state courts and won. Gibbons appealed.

In ruling on the case, Chief Justice Marshall defined *commerce* as including all business dealings, including steamboat travel. Marshall also stated that the power to regulate interstate commerce was an *exclusive* national power and had no limitations other than those specifically found in the Constitution. Since this 1824 decision, the national government has used the commerce clause repeatedly to justify its regulation of almost all areas of economic activity.

3-3b The Civil War—The Ultimate Supremacy Battle

The great issue that provoked the Civil War (1861–1865) was the future of slavery. Because people in different sections of the country had radically different beliefs about slavery, the slavery issue took the form of a dispute over states' rights versus national supremacy. The war brought to a bloody climax the ideological debate that had been outlined by the Federalist and Anti-Federalist factions even before the Constitution was ratified.

A Shift to States' Rights As just discussed, the Supreme Court headed by John Marshall interpreted the commerce clause in such a way as to increase the power of the national government at the expense of state powers. By the late 1820s, however, a shift back to states' rights had begun, and the question of the regulation of commerce became one of the major issues in federal-state relations. When the national government, in 1828 and 1832, passed laws imposing tariffs (taxes) on goods imported into the United States, southern states objected, believing that such taxes were against their interests.

One southern state, South Carolina, attempted to *nullify* the tariffs, or to make them void. South Carolina claimed that in conflicts between state governments and the national government, the states should have the ultimate authority to determine the welfare of their citizens. President Andrew Jackson was prepared to use force to uphold national law, but Congress reduced the tariffs. The crisis passed temporarily.

Courtesy of the Supreme Court of the United States Washington, DC

John Marshall, chief justice of the United States Supreme Court (1801–1835). *How did Marshall strengthen the national government?*

> "We here highly resolve that … This Nation … shall have a new birth of freedom; and that government of the people, by the people, for the people, shall not perish from the earth."
>
> ~ ABRAHAM LINCOLN,
> GETTYSBURG ADDRESS, 1863

States' Rights, Slavery, and Secession The defense of slavery and the promotion of states' rights were both important elements in the South's decision in favor of **secession**—withdrawal from the Union—in 1860 and 1861. Indeed, the two concepts were commingled in the minds of Southerners of that era. Which of these two was the more important remains a matter of controversy even today. Modern defenders of states' rights and those who distrust governmental authority often present southern secession as entirely a matter of states' rights. Liberals and those who champion the rights of African Americans see slavery as the sole cause of the crisis. The declarations of secession issued by the southern states left little doubt as to the importance of slavery.

When the South was defeated in the war, the idea that a state has a right to secede from the Union was defeated also. Although the Civil War occurred because of the South's desire for increased states' rights, the result was just the opposite—an increase in the political power of the national government.

3-3c Dual Federalism—From the Civil War to the 1930s

Scholars have devised various models to describe the relationship between the states and the national government at different times in our history. These models are useful in describing the evolution of federalism after the Civil War.

The model of **dual federalism** assumes that the states and the national government are more or

secession The act of formally withdrawing from membership in an alliance; the withdrawal of a state from the federal Union.

dual federalism A system of government in which the federal and the state governments maintain diverse but sovereign powers.

less equals, with each level of government having separate and distinct functions and responsibilities. The states exercise sovereign powers over certain matters, and the national government exercises sovereign powers over others.

For much of our nation's history, this model of federalism prevailed. After the expansion of national authority during the Civil War, the courts again tended to support the states' rights to exercise police powers and tended to strictly limit the powers of the federal government under the commerce clause. In 1918, for example, the Supreme Court ruled unconstitutional a 1916 federal law excluding from interstate commerce the products created through the use of child labor. The law was held unconstitutional because it attempted to regulate a local problem.[10] The era of dual federalism came to an end in the 1930s, when the United States was in the depths of the greatest economic depression it had ever experienced.

3–3d Cooperative Federalism and the Growth of the National Government

The model of **cooperative federalism**, as the term implies, involves cooperation by all branches of government. This model views the national and state governments as complementary parts of a single governmental mechanism, the purpose of which is to solve the problems facing the entire United States. For example, federal law enforcement agencies, such as the Federal Bureau of Investigation, lend technical expertise to solve local crimes, and local officials cooperate with federal agencies.

Roosevelt's New Deal Cooperative federalism grew out of the desire to solve the pressing national problems caused by the Great Depression, which began in 1929. In an attempt to bring the United States out of the Depression, President Franklin D. Roosevelt (1933–1945) launched his **New Deal**, which involved many government spending and public-assistance programs. Roosevelt's New Deal legislation not only ushered in an era of cooperative federalism, which has more or less continued until the present day, but also marked the real beginning of an era of national supremacy.

Before the period of cooperative federalism could be truly established,

President Franklin D. Roosevelt proposed many new federal programs during the Great Depression. *How did our conception of federalism change during his presidency?*

it was necessary to obtain the concurrence of the United States Supreme Court. As mentioned, in the early part of the twentieth century, the Court held a very restrictive view of what the federal government could do under the commerce clause. In the 1930s, the Court ruled again and again that various economic measures were unconstitutional.

In 1937, Roosevelt threatened to "pack" the Court with up to six new members who presumably would be more favorable to federal action. This move was widely considered to be an assault on the Constitution, and Congress refused to support it. Later that year, however, Roosevelt had the opportunity—for the first time since taking office—to appoint a new member of the Supreme Court. Hugo Black, the new justice, tipped the balance on the Court. After 1937, the Court ceased its attempts to limit the scope of the commerce clause.

Cooperative Federalism and the "Great Society" The 1960s and 1970s saw an even greater expansion of the national government's role in domestic policy. The Great Society legislation of President Lyndon B. Johnson (1963–1969) created Medicaid, Medicare, the Job Corps, Operation Head Start, and other programs. The Civil Rights Act of 1964 prohibited discrimination in public accommodations, employment, and other areas on the basis of race, color, national origin, religion, or gender. In the 1970s, national laws protecting consumers, employees, and the environment imposed further regulations on

cooperative federalism A model of federalism in which the states and the federal government cooperate in solving problems.

New Deal The policies ushered in by the Roosevelt administration in 1933 in an attempt to bring the United States out of the Great Depression.

the economy. Today, few activities are beyond the reach of the regulatory arm of the national government.

Nonetheless, the massive social programs undertaken in the 1960s and 1970s also resulted in greater involvement by state and local governments. The national government simply could not implement those programs alone. For example, Head Start, a program that provides preschool services to children of low-income families, is administered by local nonprofit organizations and school systems, although it is funded by federal grants.

The model in which every level of government is involved in implementing a policy is sometimes referred to as **picket-fence federalism**. In this model, the policy area is the vertical picket on the fence, while the levels of government are the horizontal support boards.

Cornerstones of Cooperative Federalism

The regulatory powers that the national government enjoys today rest on constitutional cornerstones laid by the Supreme Court decisions discussed at the beginning of this section. The commerce clause and the doctrine of federal preemption have been crucial.

The Commerce Clause. From 1937 on, the Supreme Court consistently upheld Congress's power to regulate domestic policy under the commerce clause. Even activities that occur entirely within a state were rarely considered to be outside the regulatory power of the national government. For example, in 1942 the Supreme Court held that wheat production by an individual farmer intended wholly for consumption on his own farm was subject to federal regulation. The Court reasoned that the home consumption of wheat reduced the demand for wheat and thus could have an effect on interstate commerce.[11]

In 1980, the Supreme Court acknowledged that the commerce clause had "long been interpreted to extend beyond activities actually in interstate commerce to reach other activities that, while wholly local in nature, nevertheless substantially affect interstate commerce."[12] Today, Congress can regulate almost any kind of economic activity, no matter where it occurs. In recent years, though, the Supreme Court has, for the first time since the 1930s, occasionally curbed Congress's regulatory powers under the commerce clause. You will read more about this development shortly.

Federal Preemption. John Marshall's validation of the supremacy clause of the Constitution has also had significant consequences for federalism. One important effect of the supremacy clause today is that the clause allows for federal **preemption** of certain areas in which the national government and the states have concurrent powers. When Congress chooses to act exclusively in an area in which the states and the national government have concurrent powers, Congress is said to have *preempted* the area. In such cases, the courts have held that a valid federal law or regulation takes precedence over a conflicting state or local law or regulation covering the same general activity.

CRITICAL THINKING

▶ *Although marijuana is illegal under national law, Alaska, Colorado, Oregon, and Washington have moved to legalize and tax it. Should the federal government take a hands-off approach or crack down on these states? In either case, why?*

 3–4 FEDERALISM TODAY

LO Describe developments in federalism in recent years.

By the 1970s, some Americans had begun to question whether the national government had acquired too many powers. Had the national government gotten too big? Had it become, in fact, a threat to the power of the states and the liberties of the people? Should steps be taken to reduce the regulatory power and scope of the national government? Since that time, the model of federalism has evolved in ways that reflect these and other concerns.

3–4a The New Federalism— More Power to the States

Starting in the 1970s, several administrations attempted to revitalize the doctrine of dual federalism, which they renamed the "new federalism." The **new federalism** involved a shift from *nation-centered* federalism to *state-centered* federalism. One of the major goals of the new federalism was to return to the states certain powers that had been exercised by the national government since the 1930s. The term

picket-fence federalism A model of federalism in which specific policies and programs are administered by all levels of government—national, state, and local.

preemption A doctrine rooted in the supremacy clause of the Constitution that provides that national laws or regulations governing a certain area take precedence over conflicting state laws or regulations governing that same area.

new federalism A plan to limit the federal government's role in regulating state governments and to give the states increased power in deciding how they should spend government revenues.

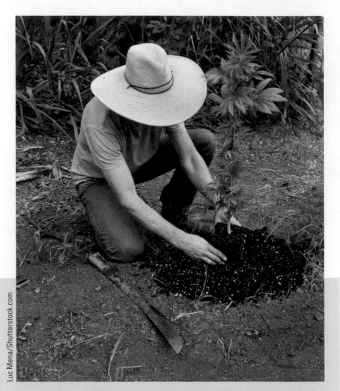

A marijuana grower tends a new plant on an outdoor farm. Alaska, Colorado, the District of Columbia, Oregon, and Washington have legalized recreational marijuana. *Should other states follow? Why or why not?*

Limiting the Power of the National Government

In a landmark 1995 decision, *United States v. Lopez*,[13] the Supreme Court held, for the first time in sixty years, that Congress had exceeded its constitutional authority under the commerce clause. The Court concluded that the Gun-Free School Zones Act of 1990, which banned the possession of guns within one thousand feet of any school, was unconstitutional because it attempted to regulate an area that had "nothing to do with commerce."

In a 1997 decision, the Court struck down portions of the Brady Handgun Violence Prevention Act of 1993, which obligated state and local law enforcement officers to do background checks on prospective handgun buyers until a national instant-check system could be implemented. The Court stated that Congress lacked the power to "dragoon" state employees into federal service through an unfunded **federal mandate** of this kind.[14]

In 2000, the Court invalidated a key provision of the federal Violence Against Women Act of 1994, which allowed women to sue in federal court when they were victims of gender-motivated violence, such as rape. The Court upheld a federal appellate court's ruling that the commerce clause did not justify national regulation of noneconomic, criminal conduct.[15]

Forcing the National Government to Act

In *Massachusetts v. Environmental Protection Agency*,[16] Massachusetts and several other states sued the Environmental Protection Agency (EPA) for failing to regulate greenhouse-gas emissions. The states asserted that the agency was required to do so by the Clean Air Act of 1990. The EPA argued that it lacked the authority under the Clean Air Act to regulate greenhouse-gas emissions alleged to promote climate change. In a 2007 decision, the Court ruled for the states, holding that the EPA did have the authority to regulate such emissions and should take steps to do so.

3-4c The Shifting Boundary between Federal and State Authority

Clearly, the boundary between federal and state authority has been shifting. Notably, issues relating to the federal structure of our government, which at one time were not at the forefront of the political arena, have in recent years been the subject of heated debate among Americans and their leaders. The federal government and the states seem to be in a constant tug-of-war over federal regulations, federal programs, and federal demands on the states.

The Politics of Federalism The Republican Party is often viewed as the champion of states' rights. Certainly,

devolution—the transfer of powers to political subunits—is often used to describe this process.

Although a product of conservative thought and initiated by Republicans, the devolutionary goals of the new federalism were also espoused by Democrats during the Clinton administration (1993–2001). An example of the new federalism is the welfare reform legislation passed by Congress in 1996, which gave the states more authority over welfare programs.

3-4b The Supreme Court and the New Federalism

devolution The surrender or transfer of powers to local authorities by a central government.

federal mandate A requirement in federal legislation that forces states and municipalities to comply with certain rules.

During the late 1900s and the early 2000s, the Supreme Court played a significant role in furthering the cause of states' rights. A variety of decisions either limited the power of the federal government or enhanced the power of the states.

the party has claimed such a role. For example, when the Republicans took control of both chambers of Congress in 1995, they promised devolution—which, as already noted, refers to a shifting of power from the national level to the individual states. Smaller central government and a state-centered federalism have long been regarded as the twin pillars of Republican ideology. In contrast, Democrats usually have sought greater centralization of power in Washington, D.C.

Since the Clinton administration, however, there have been times when the party tables seem to have turned. As mentioned earlier, it was under Clinton that welfare reform legislation giving more responsibility to the states—a goal that had been endorsed by the Republicans for some time—became a reality. Conversely, the No Child Left Behind Act of 2001, passed at the request of Republican president George W. Bush, gave the federal government a much greater role in education and educational funding than ever before. Finally, the Bush administration made repeated attempts to block California's medical-marijuana initiative and Oregon's physician-assisted suicide law.

The Supreme Court Weighs In Again

In the last several years, the Supreme Court has again issued rulings that have affected the shape of our federal system. Sometimes, that has meant upholding the authority of the national government, as in an immigration case involving Arizona. More often, the Court has extended the rights of the states, as it did in opinions on health-care reform and voting rights.

Immigration. In 2012, in *Arizona v. United States*, the Supreme Court confirmed national authority over immigration by striking down three provisions of a tough Arizona immigration law.

The rejected provisions would have (1) subjected illegal immigrants to criminal penalties for activities such as seeking work, (2) made it a state crime for immigrants to fail to register with the federal government, and (3) allowed police to arrest people without warrants if they had reason to believe that the individuals were deportable.

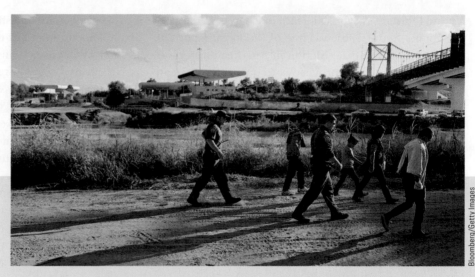

U.S. Border Patrol agents escort a family of migrants that turned themselves in along the Rio Grande River. Migrants may choose to turn themselves in if there is a chance they can win asylum status in the United States. *Do we have an obligation to take in migrants whose lives are threatened in their home countries?*

The Court did allow Arizona to check the immigration status of individuals arrested for reasons other than immigration status. But it reserved the right to rule against Arizona on that issue, too, if the state was shown to practice racial discrimination in its arrests.[17]

Health-Care Reform. Another 2012 ruling concerned the constitutionality of the Affordable Care Act, popularly known as Obamacare. In this case, *National Federation of Independent Business v. Sebelius*, the Court upheld most of the law. Two of Chief Justice John Roberts's arguments, however, seemed to set new limits on the powers of the national government.

Writing the majority opinion, Roberts contended that the federal government cannot, under the commerce clause of the Constitution, *require* individuals to purchase something—in this case, health-care insurance. The government can encourage such behavior through the tax code, however. Roberts also stated that the national government cannot force the states to expand Medicaid by threatening to take away all of their Medicaid funds if they do not. Roberts argued that cutting the states off completely would do too much damage to their budgets.[18]

Although Obamacare survived the decision, the case did appear to demonstrate that the Court was more willing to challenge the national government on its use of the commerce clause than at any time since 1937. Indeed, four of the nine justices advocated positions on the commerce clause that, in terms of recent legal understanding, were almost revolutionary.

Voting Rights. As you will learn in Chapter 5, the Voting Rights Act of 1965 was one of the most important pieces of civil rights legislation in American history. It included a variety of provisions to guarantee African Americans and others the right to vote. (This right was widely violated in many Southern states at the time.) One provision was known as *preclearance*. State or local governments with a history of voting rights violations could not change voting procedures or district boundaries without approval by either the U.S. Attorney General or the U.S. District Court for the District of Columbia.

In June 2013, in *Shelby County v. Holder*, the Court held that the methods used to determine whether a state or local government should be subject to preclearance were obsolete.[19] The preclearance system was therefore unconstitutional until Congress could agree on new methods for determining eligibility. The chances that a divided Congress would be able to pass such legislation anytime soon were negligible.

The ruling was seen as a great victory for the rights of the affected states. The ruling does not prevent the national government from suing state and local governments *after* new procedures or district boundaries are put in place. Such lawsuits, however, are less effective than the preclearance system.

CRITICAL THINKING

▶ *Some states authorize and regulate medical marijuana. In a 2015 law, Congress sought to keep the Justice Department from cracking down on these states. Was this a wise step? Why or why not?*

3–5 THE FISCAL SIDE OF FEDERALISM

LO Explain what is meant by the term fiscal federalism.

fiscal federalism The allocation of taxes collected by one level of government (typically the national government) to another level (typically state or local governments).

categorical grant A federal grant targeted for a specific purpose as defined by federal law.

Since the advent of cooperative federalism in the 1930s, the national

> "TAXES, *AFTER ALL, ARE THE DUES THAT WE PAY FOR THE PRIVILEGE OF MEMBERSHIP IN AN* ORGANIZED SOCIETY."
>
> ~ FRANKLIN D. ROOSEVELT, THIRTY-SECOND PRESIDENT OF THE UNITED STATES, 1933–1945

government and the states have worked hand in hand to implement programs mandated by the national government. Whenever Congress passes a law that preempts a certain area, the states are, of course, obligated to comply with the requirements of that law.

As already noted, a requirement that a state provide a service or undertake some activity to meet standards specified by a federal law is called a *federal mandate*. Many federal mandates concern civil rights or environmental protection. Recent federal mandates require the states to provide persons with disabilities with access to public buildings, sidewalks, and other areas; to establish minimum water-purity and air-purity standards; and to extend Medicaid coverage to all poor children.

To help the states pay for some of the costs associated with implementing national policies, the national government gives back some of the tax dollars it collects to the states in the form of grants. As you will see, the states have come to depend on grants as an important source of revenue. When taxes are collected by one level of government (typically the national government) and spent by another level (typically state or local governments), we call the process **fiscal federalism**.

3–5a Federal Grants

Even before the Constitution was adopted, the national government granted lands to the states to finance education. Using the proceeds from the sale of these lands, the states were able to establish elementary schools and, later, *land-grant colleges*. Cash grants started in 1808, when Congress gave funds to the states to pay for the state militias. Federal grants were also made available for other purposes, such as building roads and railroads.

Only in the twentieth century, though, did federal grants become an important source of funds to the states. The major growth began in the 1960s, when the dollar amount of grants quadrupled to help pay for the Great Society programs of the Johnson administration. Grants became available for education, pollution control, conservation, recreation, highway construction and maintenance, and other purposes. There are two basic types of federal grants: categorical grants and block grants.

Categorical Grants A **categorical grant** is targeted for a specific purpose as defined by federal law. The federal government defines hundreds of categories of state and local spending. Categorical grants give the national government control over how states use the funds by imposing certain conditions. For example, a categorical grant may require that the funds be used for the purpose of repairing interstate highways and that the projects cannot pay below the local prevailing wage. Depending on the project, the government might require that an environmental impact statement be prepared.

Block Grants A **block grant** is given for a broad area, such as criminal justice or mental-health programs. The term *block grant* was coined in 1966 to describe a series of programs initiated by President Johnson, although a number of federal grants issued earlier in our history shared some of the characteristics of modern block grants. Block grants now constitute a growing percentage of all federal aid programs.

A block grant gives the states more discretion over how the funds will be spent. Nonetheless, the federal government can exercise control over state decision-making through these grants by using **cross-cutting requirements**, or requirements that apply to all federal grants. Title VI of the 1964 Civil Rights Act, for example, bars racial discrimination in the use of all federal funds, regardless of their source.

3–5b Federal Grants and State Budgets

Currently, about one-fifth of state and local revenue comes from the national government. In fiscal year 2016, the federal government transferred about $665 billion to state and local governments— more than half a trillion dollars. By far, the largest transfer was for Medicaid, the health-care program for the poor. It totaled $351 billion. The federal government provided the states with about $57 billion for education. Highway grants ran about $46 billion.

When the media discuss state and local budgets, they typically refer just to the general fund budgets, which are largely supported by state and local taxes. But, in fact, state and local taxes support slightly more than half of state and local spending. Federal funds aren't listed in general fund budgets. Further, about one-quarter of state and local spending goes to fee-for-service operations, in which governments charge for the services they provide. This spending applies to:

▸ functions such as water supplies, sewers, and other public utilities;

▸ fees charged by government-owned hospitals;

▸ airport fees; and

▸ college tuition.

Typically, these operations are also excluded from general fund budgets. Figure 3–4 summarizes state and local revenue sources.

> **block grant** A federal grant given to a state for a broad area, such as criminal justice or mental-health programs.
>
> **cross-cutting requirements** Requirements that apply to all federal grants.

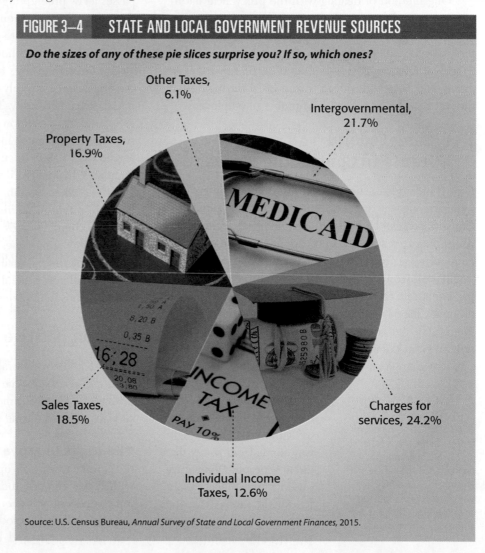

FIGURE 3–4   STATE AND LOCAL GOVERNMENT REVENUE SOURCES

Do the sizes of any of these pie slices surprise you? If so, which ones?

- Other Taxes, 6.1%
- Intergovernmental, 21.7%
- Property Taxes, 16.9%
- Charges for services, 24.2%
- Sales Taxes, 18.5%
- Individual Income Taxes, 12.6%

Source: U.S. Census Bureau, *Annual Survey of State and Local Government Finances*, 2015.

3-5c Federalism and Economic Cycles

Unlike the federal government, state governments are supposed to balance their budgets. A practical result is that when a major recession occurs, the states are faced with severe budget problems. Because state citizens are earning and spending less, state income and sales taxes fall. During a recession, state governments may be forced either to reduce spending and lay off staff—or to raise taxes. Either choice helps make the recession worse. State spending patterns tend to make economic booms more energetic and busts more painful—in a word, they are *procyclical*.

The federal government has no difficulty in spending more on welfare, unemployment compensation, and Medicaid during a recession. Also, the federal government often cuts tax rates in a recession to spur the economy. It makes up the difference by going further into debt. In a recession, the actions of the federal government are normally *anticyclical*.

One method of dealing with the procyclical nature of state spending is to increase federal grants to the states during a recession. Such grants were included in the February 2009 stimulus legislation championed by President Obama. By the middle of 2010, however, the grants had largely dried up. From 2010 through 2012, the states laid off a substantial number of employees.

3-5d Using Federal Grants to Control the States

Grants of funds to the states from the national government are one way that the Tenth Amendment to the U.S. Constitution can be bridged. Remember that the Tenth Amendment reserves all powers not delegated to the national government to the states and to the people. You might well wonder, then, how the federal government has been able to exercise control over matters that traditionally have been under the authority of state governments. The answer involves the giving or withholding of federal grant dollars.

For example, in 1984 the national government forced the states to raise the minimum drinking age to twenty-one by threatening to withhold federal highway funds from states that did not comply. Obamacare raised questions about forcing the states to expand Medicaid, as mentioned earlier in this chapter.

competitive federalism A model of federalism in which state and local governments compete for businesses and citizens, who in effect "vote with their feet" by moving to jurisdictions that offer a competitive advantage.

The education reforms embodied in the No Child Left Behind Act relied on federal funding for their implementation as well. The states received block grants for educational purposes and, in return, had to meet federally imposed standards for testing and accountability. In time, No Child Left Behind proved to be unpopular. Conservatives disliked the degree of national control imposed by the act. Teachers complained that too much class time was devoted to "teaching to the test." Also, some of the national standards were impossibly strict. As a result, the Obama administration was able to gain substantial leverage over the states by waiving the harshest requirements in exchange for state concessions. In December 2015, No Child Left Behind was replaced by the Every Student Succeeds Act. The new legislation lets states create their own evaluation systems and standards.

3-5e The Cost of Federal Mandates

As mentioned earlier, when the national government passes a law preempting an area in which the states and the national government have concurrent powers, the states must comply with that law in accordance with the supremacy clause of the Constitution. Thus, when such laws require the states to implement certain programs, the states must comply—but compliance with federal mandates can be costly. The cost of compliance has been estimated at $29 billion annually, but some believe the true figure to be much higher. Although Congress passed legislation in 1995 to curb the use of unfunded federal mandates, that legislation was more rhetoric than reality.

Even when funding is provided, it may be insufficient, resulting in an *underfunded* federal mandate. As mentioned earlier, for example, states receive block grants for educational purposes in return for meeting standards imposed by the national government. Critics argue that the national government does not supply the states with enough funds to implement these programs properly.

3-5f Competitive Federalism

The debate over federalism is sometimes reduced to a debate over taxes. Which level of government will raise taxes to pay for government programs, and which will cut services to avoid raising taxes?

The Right to Move How states answer that question gives citizens an option: they can move to a state with fewer services and lower taxes, or to a state with more services but higher taxes. Political scientist Thomas R. Dye calls this model of federalism **competitive federalism**. State and local governments compete for

If Ohio has very strict environmental regulations, however, that same business may choose not to build there, no matter how beneficial the tax advantages, because complying with the regulations would be costly. Although Ohio citizens lose the opportunity for more jobs, they may enjoy better air and water quality than citizens of the state where the new factory is ultimately built.

Advantages and Disadvantages of Competition Some observers consider such competition an advantage: Americans have several variables to consider when they choose a state in which to live. Others consider it a disadvantage: a state that offers more social services or lower taxes may experience an increase in population as people "vote with their feet" to take advantage of that state's laws. The resulting population increases can overwhelm the state's resources and force it to cut social services or raise taxes. Regulations that make it easier to build new housing may also draw in new residents. Recent studies suggest that much of the difference in population growth rates among states in recent decades may be due to differences in the cost of housing (see this chapter's *Perception vs. Reality* feature.)

It appears likely, then, that the debate over how our federal system functions, as well as the battle for control between the states and the federal government, will continue. The Supreme Court, which has played umpire in this battle, is also likely to continue issuing rulings that influence the balance of power.

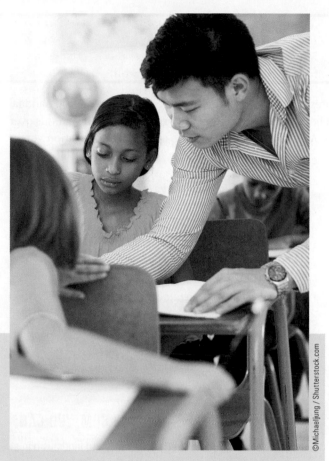

An elementary school teacher helps his students. Under the 2015 Every Student Succeeds Act, states will design tests to determine whether schools are doing an adequate job of teaching their students. *Are such tests desirable? Why or why not?*

©Michaeljung / Shutterstock.com

businesses and citizens. If the state of Ohio offers tax advantages for locating a factory there, for example, a business may be more likely to build its factory in Ohio, thereby providing more jobs for Ohio residents.

CRITICAL THINKING

▶ *What kinds of factors might cause you to consider moving to a different state? Are any of these factors under the control of state governments? Local governments?*

AMERICA AT ODDS | Federalism

The topic of federalism raises one of the most enduring disputes in American history—the relative power of the national government versus that of the state governments. As you read in the last two chapters, Americans have been at odds over the strength of the central government since well before the American Revolution. The issue of centralization versus decentralization has taken a number of specific forms:

- *Is it right for the national government to use its financial strength to pressure states into taking actions such as raising the drinking age by threatening to withhold subsidies—or are such pressures an abuse of the federal system?*

- *Should the national government let some states get away with legalizing recreational marijuana—or should it crack down on these states?*

- *Should the commerce clause be interpreted broadly, granting the federal government much power to regulate* the economy—or should it be interpreted as narrowly as possible to keep the government from interfering with the rights of business owners?

- *Should the federal government have a role in setting national policies for public education—or should that be left entirely to the states?*

- *Should the federal government establish a national system for funding health care—or should that, too, be left to the states or to the private sector?*

STUDY TOOLS 3

READY TO STUDY? IN THE BOOK, YOU CAN:

- ☐ Review what you've read with the following chapter quiz.
- ☐ Check your answers in Appendix D at the back of the book.
- ☐ Rip out the Chapter Review Card, which includes key terms and chapter summaries.

ONLINE AT WWW.CENGAGEBRAIN.COM, YOU CAN:

- ☐ Learn about undocumented immigrants and federalism in a short video.
- ☐ Explore various online resources in the *New York Times* Civil War website.
- ☐ Interact with figures from the text, and watch quick animation clips.
- ☐ Prepare for tests with quizzes.
- ☐ Review the key terms with Flash Cards.

FILL-IN

Learning Outcome 3–1

1. The advantages of a federal system of government in the United States include _____.

Learning Outcome 3–2

2. The constitutional basis for the implied powers of the national government is the _____ clause.

3. The Constitution's _____ clause requires each state to honor every other state's public acts, records, and judicial proceedings.

Learning Outcome 3–3

4. In *McCulloch v. Maryland,* a case decided in 1819, the United States Supreme Court established the doctrines of _____.

5. Cooperative federalism grew out of the need to solve the pressing problems caused by _____.

Learning Outcome 3–4

6. The relationship of national, state, and local levels of government in implementing massive social programs in the 1960s and 1970s is often referred to as _____ federalism.

7. A _____ is a requirement in federal legislation that forces states and municipalities to comply with certain rules.

8. When tax revenue collected by one level of government is passed on to another level, we call this _____.

Learning Outcome 3–5

9. The national government forced the states to raise the minimum drinking age to twenty-one by _____.

10. In 2015, the Every Student Succeeds Act replaced the earlier _____ Act, which according to many people had given the national government too much control over education.

MULTIPLE CHOICE

Learning Outcome 3–1

11. In a unitary system,
    a. subdivisional governments exercise only those powers given to them by the central government.
    b. sovereign states are joined together by a central government that has only limited powers over them.
    c. there are no local or subdivisional governments.

12. There are ____ governmental units in the United States today.
    a. 51   b. nearly 3,000   c. almost 90,000

Learning Outcome 3–2

13. Article I, Section 8, of the U.S. Constitution enumerates twenty-seven powers that Congress may exercise. Two of these _____ powers are the power to coin money and the power to regulate interstate commerce.
    a. concurrent   b. expressed   c. inherent

14. The relationships among the states in our federal system of government are sometimes referred to as _____ federalism.
    a. picket-fence   b. cooperative   c. horizontal

Learning Outcome 3–3

15. The era of _____ federalism came to an end in the 1930s.
    a. dual   b. new   c. competitive

Learning Outcome 3–4

16. The welfare reform legislation passed by Congress in 1996 is an example of _____ federalism.
    a. dual   b. cooperative   c. new

Learning Outcome 3–5

17. Block grants
    a. are targeted for specific purposes by law.
    b. are federal grants given to a state for broad areas, such as criminal justice or mental-health programs.
    c. give the states less discretion than categorical grants over how funds will be spent.

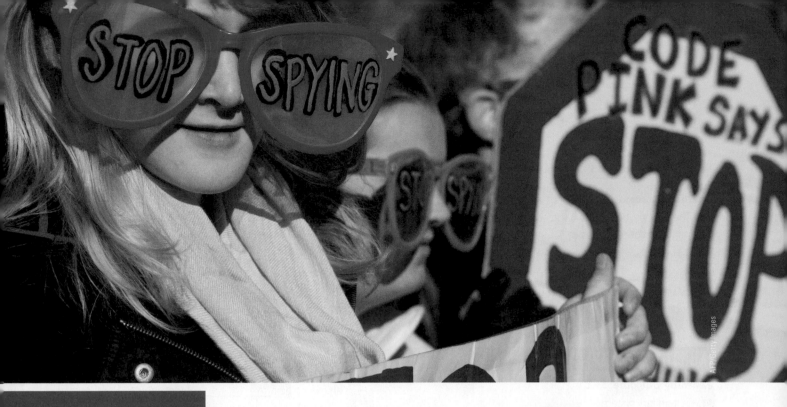

4

CIVIL LIBERTIES

LEARNING OUTCOMES *After reading this chapter, you should be able to:*

4-1 Define the term *civil liberties*, explain how civil liberties differ from civil rights, and state the constitutional basis for our civil liberties.

4-2 List the religious freedoms guaranteed by the First Amendment, and explain how the courts have interpreted and applied these freedoms.

4-3 Describe how freedom of speech is protected by the First Amendment, and show how the courts have implemented this freedom.

4-4 Discuss why Americans are increasingly concerned about privacy rights.

4-5 Summarize how the Constitution and the Bill of Rights protect the rights of accused persons.

After finishing this chapter, go to **PAGE 95** for **STUDY TOOLS**.

AMERICA AT ODDS

Do U.S. Citizens Really Need Military-Style Rifles?

Anatoly Vartanov/Shutterstock.com

The Second Amendment to the U.S. Constitution states that the people have the right "to keep and bear arms." The Supreme Court has ruled that this right is enjoyed by individuals, not just state militias. In these rulings, however, the Court has also said that the national and state governments may limit the types of weapons that individuals may hold. Should ordinary citizens have a right to own rifles based on military weapons?

This issue came to the fore after a shooter killed twenty-six children and teachers in December 2012 at the Sandy Hook Elementary School in Connecticut. The shooter used a semiautomatic rifle based on the military's M4 carbine. In December 2015, Islamist terrorists—a married couple—killed fourteen people and seriously injured twenty-two more at a holiday party for employees of the Public Health Department in San Bernardino, California. The weapons included two military-style rifles. Still, Americans remain at odds about whether military-style rifles and high-round magazines should be legal.

The Second Amendment Means What It Says

Those who do not believe that Congress should ban military-style rifles maintain that such weapons are fully covered by the constitutional right to bear arms. The most popular military-style rifle is the AR-15, based on the military's M16. Other rifles are based on the similar but lighter M4. These civilian rifles are semiautomatic, which means that the trigger must be pulled once for each shot. That makes these weapons different from fully automatic military weapons that can spray bullets like water from a hose. Plenty of civilian weapons other than the AR-15 are semiautomatic, including many handguns and deer rifles. Yet they were exempt from the recent proposed legislation to limit military-style arms.

From 1994 to 2004, the Federal Assault Weapons Ban outlawed such weapons. This law did not reduce the national murder rate. Although the murder rate fell throughout this period, the decline would have occurred even if these weapons had not been banned. After all, only 2.6 percent of all murders are committed using any type of rifle.

Citizens Don't Need Military-Style Rifles

Although the National Rifle Association claims that semiautomatic military-style rifles are useful for hunting, target practice, and home defense, they are not. The AR-15's .223 caliber ammunition is too light for deer hunting and useless for waterfowl. The low-power .22 rimfire cartridge—not the high-power .223—is the international standard for target competition. An ordinary 12-gauge shotgun is vastly superior for home protection, and a handgun is best for self-defense in other circumstances.

The AR-15/M16 was designed in 1957 for the U.S. Army. This rifle, and its more recent M4 version, is optimized for one purpose only—killing the largest number of enemy possible on the battlefield. How can such a weapon be legitimate in a civilian context? Let's face it: military-style rifles are popular because they appeal to owners' dangerous fantasies of domestic chaos or insurrection. *World War Z* is not an acceptable basis for national policy.

Where do you stand?

1. Under the Second Amendment, what limits, if any, should be placed on the kinds of weapons that ordinary civilians can own?
2. Could a citizens' militia possibly be effective against an attempt to install a dictator?

Explore this issue online:

- For a defense of the right to bear the AR-15, search on "lott wsj assault weapons" for an article by John Lott.
- Justin Peters criticizes the usefulness of the AR-15— enter "slate peters AR-15."
- Finally, Matt Steinglass attacks the fantasies of AR-15 owners at "economist gun treason Steinglass."

INTRODUCTION

The debate over military-style rifles, discussed in the chapter-opening *America at Odds* feature, is but one of many controversies concerning our civil liberties. **Civil liberties** are legal and constitutional rights that protect citizens from government actions.

Perhaps the best way to understand what civil liberties are and why they are important to Americans is to look at what might happen if we did not have them. If you were a student in China, for example, you would have to exercise some care in what you said and did. That country prohibits various kinds of speech, notably any criticism of the leading role of the Communist Party. If you criticized the government in e-mail messages to your friends or on your website, you could end up in court on charges that you had violated the law—and perhaps even go to prison.

Note that some Americans confuse *civil liberties* (discussed in this chapter) with *civil rights* (discussed in the next chapter) and use the terms interchangeably. Scholars, however, make a distinction between the two. They point out that civil liberties are limitations on government action, setting forth what the government *cannot* do. Civil rights, in contrast, specify what the government *must* do—for example, ensure equal protection under the law for all Americans.

 4-1

THE CONSTITUTIONAL BASIS FOR OUR CIVIL LIBERTIES

LO Define the term *civil liberties,* explain how civil liberties differ from civil rights, and state the constitutional basis for our civil liberties.

civil liberties Individual rights protected by the Constitution against the powers of the government.

writ of *habeas corpus* An order that requires an official to bring a specified prisoner into court and explain to the judge why the person is being held in jail.

bill of attainder A legislative act that inflicts punishment on particular persons or groups without granting them the right to a trial.

***ex post facto* law** A criminal law that punishes individuals for committing an act that was legal when the act was committed.

The founders believed that the constitutions of the individual states contained ample provisions to protect citizens from government actions. Therefore, the founders did not include many references to individual civil liberties in the original version of the Constitution. Many of our liberties were added by the Bill of Rights, ratified in 1791. Nonetheless, the original Constitution did include some safeguards to protect citizens against an overly powerful government.

4–1a Safeguards in the Original Constitution

Article I, Section 9, of the Constitution provides that the writ of *habeas corpus* (a Latin phrase that roughly means "produce the body") will be available to all citizens except in times of rebellion or national invasion. A **writ of *habeas corpus*** is an order requiring that an official bring a specified prisoner into court and explain to the judge why the prisoner is being held in jail. If the court finds that the imprisonment is unlawful, it orders the prisoner to be released. If our country did not have such a constitutional provision, political leaders could jail their opponents without giving them the opportunity to plead their cases before a judge. Without this opportunity, many opponents might conveniently be left to rot away in prison.

The Constitution also prohibits Congress and the state legislatures from passing bills of attainder. A **bill of attainder** is a legislative act that directly punishes a specifically named individual (or a group or class of individuals) without a trial. For example, no legislature can pass a law that punishes a named Hollywood celebrity for unpatriotic statements.

Finally, the Constitution prohibits Congress from passing *ex post facto* laws. The Latin term *ex post facto* roughly means "after the fact." An ***ex post facto* law** punishes individuals for committing an act that was legal when it was committed.

4–1b The Bill of Rights

As you read in Chapter 2, one of the contentious issues in the debate over ratification of the Constitution was the lack of protections for citizens from government actions. Although many state constitutions provided such protections, the Anti-Federalists wanted more. The promise of the addition of a bill of rights to the Constitution ensured its ratification.

The Bill of Rights was ratified by the states and became part of the Constitution on December 15, 1791. Look at the text of the Bill of Rights in Table 4–1. As you can see, the first eight amendments grant the people specific rights and liberties. The remaining two amendments reserve certain rights and powers to the people and to the states.

Basically, in a democracy, government policy tends to reflect the view of the majority. A key function of the Bill of Rights, therefore, is to protect the rights of those in the minority against the will of the majority. When there is disagreement over how to interpret the Bill of Rights, the courts step in.

TABLE 4–1 THE BILL OF RIGHTS AND WHAT IT MEANS

Amendment I.
Religion, Speech, Press, Assembly, and Petition

Congress shall make no law respecting an establishment of religion, or prohibiting the free exercise thereof; or abridging the freedom of speech, or of the press; or the right of the people peaceably to assemble, and to petition the Government for a redress of grievances.

Congress may not create an official church or enact laws limiting the freedom of religion, speech, the press, assembly, and petition. These guarantees, like the others in the Bill of Rights (the first ten amendments), are not absolute—each right may be exercised only with regard to the rights of other persons.

Amendment II.
Militia and the Right to Bear Arms

A well regulated Militia, being necessary to the security of a free State, the right of the people to keep and bear Arms, shall not be infringed.

Each state has the right to maintain a volunteer armed force. Although individuals have the right to bear arms, states and the federal government may regulate the possession and use of firearms by individuals.

Amendment III.
The Quartering of Soldiers

No Soldier shall, in time of peace be quartered in any house, without the consent of the Owner, nor in time of war, but in a manner to be prescribed by law.

Before the Revolutionary War, it had been common British practice to quarter soldiers in colonists' homes. Military troops do not have the power to take over private houses during peacetime.

Amendment IV.
Searches and Seizures

The right of the people to be secure in their persons, houses, papers, and effects, against unreasonable searches and seizures, shall not be violated, and no Warrants shall issue, but upon probable cause, supported by Oath or affirmation, and particularly describing the place to be searched, and the persons or things to be seized.

Here, the word warrant *refers to a document issued by a magistrate or judge indicating the name, address, and possible offense committed. Anyone asking for a warrant, such as a police officer, must be able to convince the magistrate or judge that an offense probably has been committed.*

Amendment V.
Grand Juries, Self-Incrimination, Double Jeopardy, Due Process, and Eminent Domain

No person shall be held to answer for a capital, or otherwise infamous crime, unless on a presentment or indictment of a Grand Jury, except in cases arising in the land or naval forces, or in the Militia, when in actual service in time of War or public danger; nor shall any person be subject for the same offense to be twice put in jeopardy of life or limb; nor shall be compelled in any criminal case to be a witness against himself, nor be deprived of life, liberty, or property, without due process of law; nor shall private property be taken for public use, without just compensation.

There are two types of juries. A grand jury considers physical evidence and the testimony of witnesses and decides whether there is sufficient reason to bring a case to trial. A petit jury hears the case at trial and decides it. "For the same offense to be twice put in jeopardy of life or limb" means to be

tried twice for the same crime. A person may not be tried for the same crime twice or forced to give evidence against herself or himself. No person's right to life, liberty, or property may be taken away except by lawful means, called the due process of law. Private property taken for public purposes must be paid for by the government.

Amendment VI.
Criminal Court Procedures

In all criminal prosecutions, the accused shall enjoy the right to a speedy and public trial, by an impartial jury of the State and district wherein the crime shall have been committed, which district shall have been previously ascertained by law, and to be informed of the nature and cause of the accusation; to be confronted with the witnesses against him; to have compulsory process for obtaining witnesses in his favor, and to have the Assistance of Counsel for his defence.

Any person accused of a crime has the right to a fair and public trial by a jury in the state in which the crime took place. The charges against that person must be made clear. Any accused person has the right to a lawyer to defend him or her and to question those who testify against him or her, as well as the right to call people to speak in his or her favor at trial.

Amendment VII.
Trial by Jury in Civil Cases

In Suits at common law, where the value in controversy shall exceed twenty dollars, the right of trial by jury shall be preserved, and no fact tried by a jury, shall be otherwise re-examined in any Court of the United States, than according to the rules of the common law.

A jury trial may be requested by either party in a dispute in any case involving more than $20. If both parties agree to a trial by a judge without a jury, the right to a jury trial may be put aside.

Amendment VIII.
Bail, Cruel and Unusual Punishment

Excessive bail shall not be required, nor excessive fines imposed, nor cruel and unusual punishments inflicted.

Bail is that amount of money that a person accused of a crime may be required to deposit with the court as a guarantee that she or he will appear in court when requested. The amount of bail required or the fine imposed as punishment for a crime must be reasonable compared with the seriousness of the crime involved. Any punishment judged to be too harsh or too severe for a crime shall be prohibited.

Amendment IX.
The Rights Retained by the People

The enumeration in the Constitution, of certain rights, shall not be construed to deny or disparage others retained by the people.

Many civil rights that are not explicitly enumerated in the Constitution are still held by the people.

Amendment X.
Reserved Powers of the States

The powers not delegated to the United States by the Constitution, nor prohibited by it to the States, are reserved to the States respectively, or to the people.

Those powers not delegated by the Constitution to the federal government or expressly denied to the states belong to the states and to the people. This clause in essence allows the states to pass laws under their "police powers."

The United States Supreme Court, as our nation's highest court, has the final say as to how the Constitution, including the Bill of Rights, should be interpreted. The civil liberties that you will read about in this chapter have all been shaped over time by Supreme Court decisions. For example, it is the Supreme Court that determines where freedom of speech ends and the right of society to be protected from certain forms of speech begins.

4-1c The Incorporation Principle

For many years, the courts assumed that the Bill of Rights limited only the actions of the national government, not the actions of state or local governments. In other words, if a state or local law was contrary to a basic freedom, such as the freedom of speech or the right to due process of law, the federal Bill of Rights did not come into play. The founders believed that the states, being closer to the people, would be less likely to violate their own citizens' liberties. Moreover, state constitutions, most of which contain bills of rights, protect citizens against state government actions. The United States Supreme Court upheld this view when it decided, in *Barron v. Baltimore* (1833), that the Bill of Rights did not apply to state laws.[1]

Eventually, however, the Supreme Court began to take a different view. Because the Fourteenth Amendment played a key role in this development, we look next at the provisions of that amendment.

The Right to Due Process   In 1868, three years after the end of the Civil War, the Fourteenth Amendment was added to the Constitution. The **due process clause** of this amendment requires that state governments protect their citizens' rights. (A similar requirement, binding on the federal government, was provided by the Fifth Amendment.) The due process clause reads, in part, as follows:

> No State shall . . . deprive any person of life, liberty, or property, without due process of law.

The right to **due process of law** is simply the right to be treated fairly under the legal system. That system and its officers must follow "rules of fair play" in making decisions, in determining guilt or innocence, and in punishing those who have been found guilty. Due process has two aspects—procedural and substantive.

Procedural Due Process. *Procedural* due process requires that any governmental decision to take life, liberty, or property be made equitably. For example, the government must use "fair procedures" in determining whether a person will be subjected to punishment or have some burden imposed on him or her. Fair procedure has been interpreted as requiring that the person have at least an opportunity to object to a proposed action

due process clause
The constitutional guarantee, set out in the Fifth and Fourteenth Amendments, that the government will not illegally or arbitrarily deprive a person of life, liberty, or property.

due process of law
The requirement that the government use fair, reasonable, and standard procedures whenever it takes any legal action against an individual; required by the Fifth and Fourteenth Amendments.

before an impartial, neutral decision maker (who need not be a judge).

Substantive Due Process.   *Substantive* due process focuses on the content, or substance, of legislation. If a law or other governmental action limits a *fundamental right*, it will be held to violate substantive due process, unless it promotes a *compelling* or *overriding state interest*. All First Amendment rights plus the rights to interstate travel, privacy, and voting are considered fundamental. Compelling state interests could include, for example, the public's safety.

Other Liberties Incorporated   The Fourteenth Amendment also states that no state "shall make or enforce any law which shall abridge the privileges or immunities of citizens of the United States." For some time, the Supreme Court considered the "privileges and immunities" referred to in the amendment to be those conferred by state laws or constitutions, not the federal Bill of Rights.

Starting in 1925, however, the Supreme Court gradually began using the due process clause to say that states could not abridge a civil liberty that the national government could not abridge. In other words, the Court *incorporated* the protections guaranteed by the national Bill of Rights into the liberties protected under the Fourteenth Amendment. As you can see in Table 4–2, the Supreme Court was particularly active during the 1960s in broadening its interpretation of the due process clause to ensure that states and localities could not infringe on civil liberties protected by the Bill of Rights.

Today, the liberties still not incorporated include the right to a grand jury hearing. The right to refuse to quarter soldiers has been affirmed by a U.S. appeals court, but not by the Supreme Court, and so that liberty is fully guaranteed in only a few states. The right to bear arms described in the Second Amendment was incorporated only in 2010.

Who is Covered Under the Fourteenth Amendment?   The language of the due process clause refers to "persons," not citizens. The choice of words was deliberate. The authors of the amendment sought in this way to avoid questions about who was covered by the guarantee. One group of persons has only limited protection, however—noncitizens seeking to enter or remain in the United States. The government can bar noncitizens from entry into the country without raising any constitutional questions. We discuss some consequences of this fact in this chapter's *The Rest of the World* feature.

Noncitizens living in the United States can be deported even if their presence here is lawful. In 1903,

TABLE 4–2 INCORPORATING THE BILL OF RIGHTS INTO THE FOURTEENTH AMENDMENT

Year	Issue	Amendment Involved	Court Case
1925	Freedom of speech	I	*Gitlow v. New York*, 268 U.S. 652.
1931	Freedom of the press	I	*Near v. Minnesota*, 283 U.S. 697.
1932	Right to a lawyer in capital punishment cases	VI	*Powell v. Alabama*, 287 U.S. 45.
1937	Freedom of assembly and right to petition	I	*De Jonge v. Oregon*, 299 U.S. 353.
1940	Freedom of religion	I	*Cantwell v. Connecticut*, 310 U.S. 296.
1947	Separation of church and state	I	*Everson v. Board of Education*, 330 U.S. 1.
1948	Right to a public trial	VI	*In re Oliver*, 333 U.S. 257.
1949	No unreasonable searches and seizures	IV	*Wolf v. Colorado*, 338 U.S. 25.
1961	Exclusionary rule (See "The Rights of the Accused" section later in this chapter.)	IV	*Mapp v. Ohio*, 367 U.S. 643.
1962	No cruel and unusual punishments	VIII	*Robinson v. California*, 370 U.S. 660.
1963	Right to a lawyer in all criminal felony cases	VI	*Gideon v. Wainwright*, 372 U.S. 335.
1964	No compulsory self-incrimination	V	*Malloy v. Hogan*, 378 U.S. 1.
1965	Right to privacy	Various	*Griswold v. Connecticut*, 381 U.S. 479.
1966	Right to an impartial jury	VI	*Parker v. Gladden*, 385 U.S. 363.
1967	Right to a speedy trial	VI	*Klopfer v. North Carolina*, 386 U.S. 213.
1969	No double jeopardy	V	*Benton v. Maryland*, 395 U.S. 784.
1982	Right to refuse to quarter soldiers	III	*Engblom v. Carey*, 677 F.2d 957 (2d Cir.)
2010	Right to bear arms	II	*McDonald v. Chicago*, 561 U.S. 3025.

however, the Supreme Court ruled that the government could not deport someone without a hearing that meets constitutional due process standards.[2] Still, the courts have often accepted government arguments that non-citizens cannot make constitutional claims. Under the Antiterrorism and Effective Death Penalty Act of 1996, the government has the power to deport noncitizens for alleged terrorism without any court review of the deportation order, based on secret evidence that the deportee is not allowed to see. Under this law, residents can also be deported for actions that would otherwise be protected by the First Amendment.[3]

CRITICAL THINKING

▶ Congress often passes laws that are so narrowly defined that only one individual or corporation is covered by the legislation. Should such laws be considered bills of attainder and thus unconstitutional? Why or why not?

4–2 FREEDOM OF RELIGION

LO List the religious freedoms guaranteed by the First Amendment, and explain how the courts have interpreted and applied these freedoms.

The First Amendment sets forth some of our most important civil liberties. Specifically, the First Amendment guarantees the freedoms of religion, speech, the press, and assembly, as well as the right to petition the government. In the pages that follow, we look closely at the first three of these freedoms and discuss how, over time, Supreme Court decisions have defined their meaning and determined their limits.

The First Amendment prohibits Congress from passing laws "respecting an establishment of religion, or prohibiting the free exercise thereof." The first part of this amendment is known as the **establishment clause**. The second part is called the **free exercise clause**.

4–2a Laws on Religion in the Colonies

That freedom of religion was the first freedom mentioned in the Bill of Rights is not surprising. After all, many colonists came to America to escape religious persecution. Nonetheless, these same colonists showed

establishment clause The section of the First Amendment that prohibits Congress from passing laws "respecting an establishment of religion."

free exercise clause The provision of the First Amendment stating that the government cannot pass laws "prohibiting the free exercise" of religion.

As we have explained, the United States government has almost complete freedom to ban foreign citizens from entering this country. Such persons have no constitutional protections until they actually enter, and their protections are limited while they are here. The United States is hardly the only country to ban entry by foreigners, however. Britain exercises similar powers.

Britain Takes Offense at Donald Trump

As noted in the chapter-opening *America at Odds* feature, in December 2015, terrorist attacks in California by a Muslim couple killed fourteen and injured many more. The husband was a native-born citizen, but the wife was an immigrant. Donald Trump, a leading Republican presidential candidate, then called for a ban on all Muslims entering the country until we can "figure out what is going on." His Republican and Democratic rivals chastised him for lumping all Muslims together as potential terrorists.

Within weeks of Trump's remarks, a woman in Aberdeen, Scotland, where Trump owns a golf course, started a petition to ban Trump from entering Britain. (The theory seemed to be that turnabout is fair play.) The petition amassed almost six hundred thousand signatures. Britain has adopted a law that whenever parliament receives a petition with at least one hundred thousand signatures on it, a committee of the House of Commons must hold a debate on the question.

The debate was duly held—and the committee voted to ban Trump. In reality, however, a mere parliamentary committee has no power to do much of anything in Britain. Only the executive branch can take action. The notion of banning Trump was opposed by David Cameron, the conservative prime minister, and also by the leader of Her Majesty's loyal opposition.

American Analogues

The United States has a program similar to the British petition plan. If the White House website receives a petition with one hundred thousand signatures, the administration promises to make a written response. The White House has received hundreds of such petitions. Among the most famous was a demand that the federal government build a Star Wars–style Death Star. The White House response was entitled "This Isn't the Petition Response You're Looking For."

Also, the federal government has banned many politicians, authors, musicians, and artists from entry. The government only needs to decide that these people are politically unacceptable. For example, the British singer Yusuf Islam (formerly known as Cat Stevens) was banned a decade ago for obscure reasons. At about the same time, the government banned the entry of Narendra Modi, currently the prime minister of India. At the time he was banned, Modi was the chief minister (governor) of the Indian state of Gujarat. The state had experienced anti-Muslim riots that led to thousands of deaths, and the American government blamed Modi for not taking adequate steps to halt the killings.

Critical Analysis

Should the U.S. House of Representatives hold debates in response to citizen petitions? Why or why not?

little tolerance for religious freedom within the communities they established. For example, in 1610 the Jamestown colony enacted a law requiring attendance at religious services on Sunday "both in the morning and the afternoon." Repeat offenders were subjected to particularly harsh punishments. For those who twice violated the law, for example, the punishment was a public whipping. For third-time offenders, the punishment was death.

These examples of religious laws provide a context that is helpful in understanding why, in 1802, President Thomas Jefferson—a great proponent of religious freedom and tolerance—wanted the establishment clause to be "a wall of separation between church and state." The context also helps to explain why even state leaders who supported state religions might have favored the establishment clause—to keep the national government from interfering in such state matters. After all, the First Amendment says only that *Congress* can make no law respecting an establishment of religion. It says nothing about whether the *states* can make such laws.

4–2b The Establishment Clause

The establishment clause forbids the government from establishing an official religion or church. This makes the United States different from countries that are ruled by religious governments, such as the Islamic government of Iran. It also makes us different from nations that have in the past strongly discouraged the practice of any religion at all, such as the People's Republic of China.

The Establishment Clause in Practice What does this separation of church and state mean in practice? For one thing, religion and government, though constitutionally separated in the United States, have never been enemies or strangers. The establishment clause does not prohibit government from supporting religion in *general*. Religion remains a part of public life.

Most government officials take an oath of office in the name of God, and our coins and paper currency carry the motto "In God We Trust." Clergy of different religions serve in each branch of the armed forces. Public meetings and even sessions of Congress open with prayers. (The Supreme Court endorsed such practices as recently as 2014 in *Town of Greece v. Galloway*.)[4] Indeed, the establishment clause often masks the fact that Americans are, by and large, religious and prefer that their political leaders be people of faith.

The Wall of Separation The "wall of separation" that Thomas Jefferson referred to, however, does exist and has been upheld by the Supreme Court on many occasions. An important ruling by the Supreme Court on the establishment clause came in 1947. The case involved a New Jersey law that allowed the state to pay for bus transportation of students who attended parochial schools (schools run by churches or other religious groups).

The Court stated: "No tax in any amount, large or small, can be levied to support any religious activities or institutions." Nevertheless, the Court upheld the New Jersey law because it did not aid the church *directly* but provided for the safety and benefit of the students.[5] The ruling both affirmed the importance of separating church and state and set the precedent that not *all* forms of state and federal aid to church-related schools are forbidden under the Constitution.

A full discussion of the various church-state issues that have arisen in American politics would fill volumes. Here, we examine three of these issues: prayer in the schools, the teaching of evolution versus creationism or intelligent design, and government aid to parochial schools.

THE FIRST AMENDMENT TO THE CONSTITUTION MANDATES SEPARATION OF CHURCH AND STATE. *NONETHELESS, REFERENCES TO GOD ARE COMMON IN PUBLIC LIFE, AS THE PHRASE "IN GOD WE TRUST" ON THIS COIN DEMONSTRATES.*

magicoven/Shutterstock.com

4–2c Prayer in the Schools

Public opinion polls reveal that a substantial majority of Americans believe that public school teachers ought to be able to lead students in prayer. The Supreme Court disagrees, however.

The Regents' Prayer Case On occasion, some public schools have promoted a general sense of religion without proclaiming allegiance to any particular church or sect. Whether the states have a right to allow this was the main question presented in 1962 in *Engel v. Vitale*,[6] also known as the "Regents' Prayer case." The State Board of Regents in New York had composed a nondenominational prayer (a prayer not associated with any particular church) and urged school districts to use it in classrooms at the start of each day. The prayer read as follows:

> Almighty God, we acknowledge our dependence upon Thee, and we beg Thy blessings upon us, our parents, our teachers, and our Country.

Some parents objected to the prayer, contending that it violated the establishment clause. The Supreme Court agreed and ruled that the Regents' Prayer was unconstitutional. Speaking for the majority, Justice Hugo Black wrote that the First Amendment must at least mean "that in this country it is no part of the business of government to compose official prayers for any group of the American people to recite as a part of a religious program carried on by government."

Since the *Engel v. Vitale* ruling, the Supreme Court has continued to shore up the wall of separation between church and state in a number of decisions. For example, in a 1980 case, the Supreme Court ruled that a Kentucky law requiring that the Ten Commandments be posted in all public schools violated the establishment clause.[7] Many groups around the country opposed this ruling.

Moments of Silence and Other Issues

Another controversial issue is whether "moments of silence" in the schools are constitutional. In 1985, the Supreme Court ruled that an Alabama law authorizing a daily one-minute period of silence for meditation and voluntary prayer was unconstitutional. Because the law specifically endorsed prayer, it appeared to support religion.[8] Since then, the lower courts have generally held that a school may require a moment of silence, but only if it serves a clearly secular purpose (such as to meditate on the day's activities).[9]

Yet another issue concerns prayers said before public school sporting events, such as football games. In 2000, the Supreme Court held that student-led pre-game prayer using the school's public-address system was unconstitutional.[10]

In sum, the Supreme Court has ruled that public schools, which are agencies of government, cannot sponsor religious activities. It has *not*, however, held that individuals cannot pray, when and as they choose, in schools or in any other place. Nor has it held that the schools are barred from teaching *about* religion, as opposed to engaging in religious practices.

4–2d Evolution Versus Creationism

Certain religious groups have long opposed the teaching of evolution in public schools. These groups contend that evolutionary theory, a theory with overwhelming scientific support, directly counters their religious belief that human beings did not evolve but were created fully formed, as described in the biblical story of the creation. In fact, surveys have shown that up to one-third of Americans believe that humans were directly created by God rather than having evolved from other species. The Supreme Court, however, has held that state laws forbidding the teaching of evolution in the schools are unconstitutional.

For example, in a case decided in 1968, the Supreme Court held that an Arkansas law prohibiting the teaching of evolution violated the establishment clause because it imposed religious beliefs on students.[11] In 1987, the Supreme Court also held unconstitutional a Louisiana law requiring that the biblical story of the creation be taught along with evolution. The Court deemed the law unconstitutional in part because it had as its primary purpose the promotion of a particular religious belief.[12]

Evolution Versus Intelligent Design. Some activists have advocated the concept of "intelligent design" as an alternative to the teaching of evolution. This concept posits that an intelligent cause, rather than an undirected process such as natural selection, lies behind the creation and development of the universe and living things. Proponents of intelligent design claim that it is a scientific theory and thus that its teaching does not violate the establishment clause in any way. Opponents contend that the "intelligent cause" is simply another term for God.

These arguments were tested in 2004 in Dover, Pennsylvania, when the local school board required ninth-grade

iStockPhoto.com/Digitalskillet

A student Bible study group. If public high schools allow student clubs to use school facilities after hours, they must allow religious groups the same rights as any other organizations. *Why would that be so?*

biology classes to use a textbook that endorsed intelligent design. In November 2005, the board members who supported the requirement were voted out of office. In December, a federal district court judge ruled that intelligent design was not science, that it was inherently religious, and that the school board's actions were unconstitutional.[13]

"Teach the Controversy" Various groups continue their efforts to restrict the teaching of evolution. One strategy is a campaign known as "Teach the Controversy," promoted by the Discovery Institute, an anti-evolution group. Proponents of this campaign argue that it is only fair to present both sides of the question—that is, both evolution and other views, such as intelligent design. Biologists, however, point out that there is no controversy within the scientific community. Evolution is a "theory" only in the sense that scientists speak of a "theory of gravity." Debate over evolution exists solely in the domains of religion and politics. If the controversy is taught at all, it should be taught in classes that deal with those topics. Indeed, the Dover ruling just mentioned dismissed the "teaching the controversy" tactic as insincere at best.

4-2e Aid to Parochial Schools

Americans have long been at odds over whether public tax dollars should be used to fund activities in parochial schools. Over the years, the courts have often had to decide whether specific types of aid do or do not violate the establishment clause. Aid to church-related schools in the form of transportation, equipment, or special educational services for disadvantaged students has been held permissible. Other forms of aid, such as funding teachers' salaries and paying for field trips, have been held unconstitutional.

The *Lemon* Test Since 1971, the Supreme Court has held that, to be constitutional, a state's school aid must meet three requirements: (1) the purpose of the financial aid must be clearly secular (not religious), (2) its primary effect must neither advance nor inhibit religion, and (3) it must avoid an "excessive government entanglement with religion." The Court first used this three-part test in *Lemon v. Kurtzman*,[14] and hence it is often referred to as the *Lemon* test.

In the 1971 *Lemon* case, the Court denied public aid to private and parochial schools even for the salaries of teachers of secular courses and for textbooks and instructional materials in certain secular subjects. The Court held that the establishment clause is designed to

> "The purpose of separation of church and state is to keep forever from these shores the ceaseless strife that has soaked the soil of Europe in blood for centuries."
>
> ~ JAMES MADISON, DRAFTER OF THE BILL OF RIGHTS AND U.S. PRESIDENT, 1809–1817

prevent three main evils: "sponsorship, financial support, and active involvement of the sovereign [the government] in religious activity."

School Voucher Programs Another contentious issue has to do with the use of **school vouchers**—educational certificates, provided by state governments, that students can use at any school, public or private. In an effort to improve their educational systems, a number of school districts have been experimenting with voucher systems. Thirteen states and the District of Columbia now have limited voucher programs, under which some schoolchildren may attend private elementary or high schools using vouchers paid for by taxpayers' dollars. In six of these states, vouchers are limited to children with special needs.[15]

In 2002, the United States Supreme Court ruled that a voucher program in Cleveland, Ohio, was constitutional. Under the program, the state provided up to $2,250 to low-income families, who could use the funds to send their children to either public or private schools. The Court concluded that the taxpayer-paid voucher program did not unconstitutionally entangle church and state because the funds went to parents, not to schools. The parents theoretically could use the vouchers to send their children to nonreligious private academies or charter schools, even though 95 percent used the vouchers at religious schools.[16]

Despite the 2002 Supreme Court ruling,

Lemon **test** A three-part test enunciated by the Supreme Court in the 1971 case of *Lemon v. Kurtzman* to determine whether government aid to parochial schools is constitutional.

school voucher An educational certificate, provided by a government, that allows a student to use public funds to pay for a private or a public school chosen by the student or his or her parents.

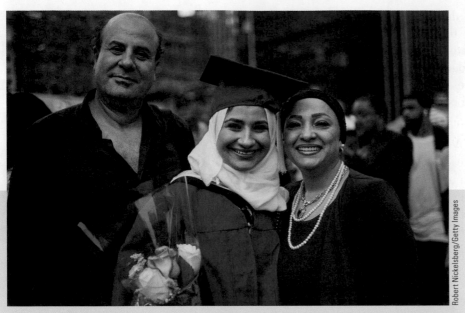

In New York City, a Hunter College graduate stands with her parents following graduation ceremonies. She is a first-generation Syrian American. *What civil liberties protect her right to wear a head scarf at a public college?*

States.[18] Reynolds was a member of the Latter-Day Saints (Mormons) who had two wives. Polygamy, or the practice of having more than one spouse simultaneously, was encouraged by the customs and teachings of his church at that time. Polygamy was prohibited by federal law, however. Reynolds was convicted and appealed the case, arguing that the law violated his constitutional right to freely exercise his religious beliefs. The Court did not agree. It said that to allow Reynolds to practice polygamy would make religious doctrines superior to the law. In 1890, the Latter-Day Saints issued a manifesto prohibiting new polygamist marriages.

several constitutional questions surrounding school vouchers remain unresolved. For example, some state constitutions are more explicit than the federal Constitution in denying the use of public funds for religious education. Even after the Supreme Court ruling in the Ohio case, a Florida court ruled in 2002 that a voucher program in that state violated Florida's constitution.[17]

4-2f The Free Exercise Clause

As mentioned, the second part of the First Amendment's statement on religion consists of the free exercise clause, which forbids the passage of laws "prohibiting the free exercise of religion." This clause protects a person's right to worship or to believe as he or she wishes without government interference. No law or act of government may violate this constitutional right.

Belief and Practice Are Distinct The free exercise clause does not necessarily mean that individuals can act in any way they want on the basis of their religious beliefs. There is an important distinction between belief and practice. The Supreme Court has ruled consistently that the right to hold any *belief* is absolute. The right to *practice* one's beliefs, however, may have some limits. As the Court itself once asked, "Suppose one believed that human sacrifice were a necessary part of religious worship?"

The Supreme Court first dealt with the issue of belief versus practice in 1878 in *Reynolds v. United*

Medical Treatment for Children Another issue under the free exercise clause is the right to refuse medical treatment. In most cases, adults have such a right. The right of parents to refuse treatment for their children, however, is much more limited. The courts have long held that a refusal by a parent to allow lifesaving treatments for a child can be considered a serious crime.

This principle also extends to vaccination. As a public health measure, states may require all children attending public schools to be vaccinated against common diseases. Typically, state law allows parents to opt out for religious reasons. Some states allow opt-outs based on philosophical beliefs as well. Such opt-outs are not required by the Constitution, however. Mississippi, West Virginia, and as of 2015 California, allow no opt-outs except when a physician advises that a vaccination might endanger a child's health.

Vaccination has been in the news lately because of a movement against vaccination among some Americans. Although medical science is united in its support for vaccination, some parents have chosen not to have their children vaccinated. In turn, the increase in the number of unvaccinated children has left some communities open to outbreaks of diseases such as measles. As a result, several states have sought to toughen their vaccination laws.

Religious Practices and the Workplace The free exercise of religion in the workplace was bolstered by Title VII of the Civil Rights Act of 1964, which requires employers to accommodate their employees' religious practices unless such accommodation causes an employer to suffer an "undue hardship." Thus, if an employee claims that religious beliefs prevent him or her from working on a particular day of the week, such as Saturday or Sunday, the employer must try to accommodate the employee's needs if possible.

Several cases have come before lower federal courts concerning employer dress codes that contradict the religious customs of employees. In 1999, the Third Circuit Court of Appeals ruled in favor of two Muslim police officers in Newark, New Jersey, who claimed that they were required by their faith to wear beards and would not shave them to comply with the police department's grooming policy.[19] Since then, Muslims, Rastafarians, and others have refused to change their dress or grooming habits and have been successful in court. For example, in 2015, the Supreme Court ruled against Abercrombie & Fitch, a chain of clothing stores. The company had refused to hire a young Muslim woman who wore a headscarf for religious reasons.[20] "This is really easy," Justice Antonin Scalia said in announcing the decision.

Insurance for Birth Control A recent free exercise controversy involved the question of whether businesses could be required to supply health-insurance coverage for birth control measures. Such coverage was required in health-insurance plans that met the standards of the 2010 Affordable Care Act. Churches and other religious organizations that objected to contraception on principle were exempt from the requirement. In 2012, however, the government ruled that universities, hospitals, and similar organizations had to provide coverage for contraception even if they were affiliated with churches that opposed birth control.

The result was a storm of opposition from organizations such as the Roman Catholic Church, which rejects contraception. These groups argued that they were being forced to support activities to which they were morally opposed. Such a requirement was, in their opinion, a violation of their free exercise rights. An alternative view was that the churches were attempting to impose their religious values on employees not directly involved in religious activities.

President Barack Obama proposed a compromise under which church-affiliated hospitals and schools would not have to pay for the insurance coverage, but employees would still receive the benefit. This plan satisfied many schools and hospitals. It was not acceptable to the Catholic bishops, however, who filed a lawsuit aimed at overturning the requirement.

In 2014, in *Burwell v. Hobby Lobby*, the Supreme Court held that a closely held for-profit corporation could be exempted from the requirement to provide certain forms of birth control coverage if its owners objected on religious grounds.[21] The ruling was based on congressional legislation rather than the free exercise clause. It therefore left many questions unanswered.

CRITICAL THINKING

▶ *The establishment of religious chaplains in the armed forces has been justified on the basis that, without them, service members on active duty would have no access to religious services and counseling. Do you agree with this argument? Why or why not?*

4-3 FREEDOM OF EXPRESSION

LO Describe how freedom of speech is protected by the First Amendment, and show how the courts have implemented this freedom.

No one in this country seems to have a problem protecting the free speech of those with whom they agree. The real challenge is protecting unpopular ideas. The protection needed is, in Justice Oliver Wendell Holmes's words, "not free thought for those who agree with us but freedom for the thought that we hate." The First Amendment is designed to protect the freedom to express *all* ideas, including those that may be unpopular. Many foreign nations do not protect unpopular ideas in the way that the United States does. Also, in the United States, private organizations—such as Facebook—are not bound by the First Amendment.

> "Free speech is the whole thing, the whole ball game. Free speech is life itself."
>
> ~ SALMAN RUSHDIE,
> INDIAN-BORN BRITISH WRITER, BORN 1947

The First Amendment has been interpreted to protect more than merely spoken words. It also protects **symbolic speech**—speech involving actions and other nonverbal expressions. Some common examples include

symbolic speech
The expression of beliefs, opinions, or ideas through forms other than verbal speech or print; speech involving actions and other nonverbal expressions.

picketing in a labor dispute or wearing a black armband in protest of a government policy. Even burning the American flag as a gesture of protest has been held to be protected by the First Amendment.

4–3a The Right to Free Speech Is Not Absolute

Although Americans have the right to free speech, not *all* speech is protected under the First Amendment. Our constitutional rights and liberties are not absolute. Rather, they are what the Supreme Court—the ultimate interpreter of the Constitution—says they are.

Although the Court has zealously safeguarded the right to free speech, at times it has imposed limits on speech in the interests of protecting other rights of Americans. These rights include security against harm to one's person or reputation, the need for public order, and the need to preserve the government. As Justice Holmes once said, even "the most stringent protection of free speech would not protect a man in falsely shouting fire in a theatre and causing a panic."[22] We look next at some of the ways that the Court has limited the right to free speech.

4–3b Subversive Speech

At times in our nation's history, various individuals have opposed our form of government. The government, in responding to these individuals, has drawn a line between legitimate criticism and the expression of ideas that may seriously harm society. Clearly, the government may pass laws against violent acts. But what about subversive or **seditious speech**, which urges resistance to lawful authority or advocates overthrowing the government?

As early as 1798, Congress took steps to curb seditious speech when it passed the Alien and Sedition Acts. The Sedition Act made it a crime to utter "any false, scandalous, and malicious" criticism of the government. The acts were considered unconstitutional by many but were never tested in the courts. Several dozen individuals were prosecuted under the Sedition Act, and some were actually convicted. In 1801, President Thomas Jefferson pardoned those sentenced under the act, and it was not renewed after it expired in 1801.

The Bad Tendency and Clear and Present Danger Tests During World War 1, Congress passed the Espionage Act of 1917, which prohibited attempts to interfere with operations of the military forces, the war effort, or the process of recruitment. A 1918 amendment to the act, the Sedition Act, made it a crime to "willfully utter, print, write, or publish any disloyal . . . or abusive language about the government."

In judging whether this restriction on free speech was constitutional, the Supreme Court used several tests. The predominant test at the time was the *bad tendency test,* which held that speech could be restricted if it was likely to have harmful consequences. Using this broad test, the Court upheld the Espionage Act's restrictions on speech in several cases.[23]

The Court used a somewhat different rule in the 1919 case of *Schenck v. United States,* although the outcome was still to uphold the Espionage Act. Under the *clear and present danger test,* expression could be restricted if it would cause a dangerous condition, actual or imminent, that Congress had the power to prevent.[24]

The Imminent Lawless Action Test The current standard for evaluating the legality of speech opposing the government was established by the Supreme Court in 1969. Under the **imminent lawless action test**, speech can be forbidden only when it is "directed to inciting . . . imminent [immediate] lawless action."[25] This is a hard standard for prosecutors to meet. As a result, subversive speech receives far more protection today than it did in the past.

4–3c Limited Protection for Commercial Speech

Advertising, or **commercial speech**, is also protected by the First Amendment, but not as fully as regular speech. Generally, the Supreme Court has considered a restriction on commercial speech to be valid as long as the restriction

1. Seeks to implement a substantial government interest.

2. Directly advances that interest.

3. Goes no further than necessary to accomplish its objective." Problems arise, though, when restrictions on commercial advertising achieve one substantial government interest yet are contrary to the interest in protecting free speech and the right of consumers to be informed. In such cases, the courts have to decide which interest takes priority.

seditious speech
Speech that urges resistance to lawful authority or that advocates the overthrow of a government.

imminent lawless action test The current Supreme Court doctrine for assessing the constitutionality of subversive speech. To be illegal, speech must be "directed to inciting . . . imminent lawless action."

commercial speech Advertising statements that describe products. Commercial speech receives less protection under the First Amendment than ordinary speech.

Liquor advertising is a good illustration of this kind of conflict. In one case, Rhode Island argued that its law banning the advertising of liquor prices served the state's goal of discouraging liquor consumption (because the ban discouraged bargain hunting and thus kept liquor prices high). The Supreme Court, however, held that the ban was an unconstitutional restraint on commercial speech. The Court stated that the First Amendment "directs us to be especially skeptical of regulations that seek to keep people in the dark for what the government perceives to be their own good."[26]

4–3d Unprotected Speech

Certain types of speech receive no protection under the First Amendment. Speech has never been protected when the speech itself is part of a crime. An act of fraud, for example, often may be carried out entirely through spoken words. Accused fraudsters who attempted to defend their actions by standing on their First Amendment rights would get nowhere. Other types of unprotected speech include defamation (libel and slander) and obscenity.

Libel and Slander   No person has the right to libel or slander another. **Libel** is a published report of a falsehood that tends to injure a person's reputation or character. **Slander** is the public utterance (speaking) of a statement that holds a person up for contempt, ridicule, or hatred. To prove libel or slander, certain criteria must be met. The statements made must be untrue, must stem from an intent to do harm, and must result in actual harm.

The Supreme Court has ruled that public figures (public officials and others in the public limelight) cannot collect damages for remarks made against them unless they can prove the remarks were made with "reckless" disregard for accuracy. Generally, it is believed that because public figures have greater access to the media than ordinary persons do, they are in a better position to defend themselves against libelous or slanderous statements.

The End of Obscenity   Traditionally, obscenity was a form of expression not protected under the First Amendment. The courts, however, have found the term **obscenity** hard to define. In 1973, the Supreme Court finally came up with a three-part test in *California v. Miller*.[27] To be ruled obscene, a work must

1. excite unwholesome sexual desire under present-day community standards,
2. offensively depict prohibited sexual conduct, and
3. lack serious literary, artistic, political, or scientific value. Under "community standards," the definition of obscenity could vary from one part of the country to another.

Comedian and actor Russell Brand won a substantial libel settlement from the *Sun on Sunday*, a London newspaper. The *Sun* falsely accused Brand of cheating on his girlfriend. *Why would a celebrity such as Brand have a harder time winning such a case in the United States?*

The *Miller* test was handed down at a time when American attitudes toward sexual expression were undergoing a revolution. A few years earlier, major literary works such as *Ulysses* by James Joyce and *Lady Chatterley's Lover* by D. H. Lawrence were illegal. By the early 1980s, however, it was possible in almost all parts of the country to rent pornographic videotapes that left nothing to the imagination.

The Internet was the final blow to the concept of obscenity. By the end of the twentieth century, U.S. officials no longer tried to impose obscenity restrictions on printed or visual material. Attempts by Congress in 1996 and 1998 to ban Internet obscenity that might be seen by minors were ruled unconstitutional by the Supreme Court.[28]

libel A published report of a falsehood that tends to injure a person's reputation or character.

slander The public utterance (speaking) of a statement that holds a person up for contempt, ridicule, or hatred.

obscenity Indecency or offensiveness in speech, expression, behavior, or appearance.

Remaining Restrictions on Pornography
Several types of restrictions survive. The First Amendment applies only to governments, so private, voluntary restrictions are possible. Most mainstream movie theaters, for example, will not show a film that has received a "no [child] 17 or under admitted" (NC-17) rating from the Motion Picture Association of America. In addition, the government retains the right to impose restrictions on activities that it subsidizes or media that it controls, such as the broadcast spectrum. Thus, restrictions on radio and broadcast television remain in effect.

Finally, the courts have upheld laws aimed at protecting children. Making or possessing pornographic videos or photographs of underage persons remains a serious crime, based on the argument that such depictions are acts of child abuse. Ironically, this argument demonstrates the collapse of obscenity as a legal concept—child pornography is *not* banned because it is obscene. Writings or drawings, including animation, that depict underage sexuality are tolerated because no actual children are involved.

4-3e Free Speech for Students?

America's schools and college campuses experience an ongoing tension between the guarantee of free speech and the desire to restrain speech that is offensive to others. Typically, cases involving free speech in the schools raise the following question: Where should the line between unacceptable speech and merely offensive speech be drawn? Schools at all levels—elementary schools, high schools, and colleges and universities—have grappled with this issue.

Elementary and High Schools Generally, the courts allow elementary schools wide latitude to define what students may and may not say to other students. At the high school level, the Supreme Court has allowed some restraints to be placed on the freedom of expression. For example, as you will read shortly in the discussion of freedom of the press, the Court allows school officials to exercise some censorship over high school publications. And, in a controversial 2007 case, the Court upheld a school principal's decision to suspend a high school student who unfurled a banner reading "Bong Hits 4 Jesus" at an event off the school premises. School officials maintained that the banner appeared to advocate illegal drug use in violation of school policy. Many legal commentators and scholars strongly criticized this decision.[29]

> "THE ONLY SECURITY OF ALL IS IN A *FREE PRESS*. . . . IT IS NECESSARY, TO KEEP THE WATERS PURE."
>
> ~ THOMAS JEFFERSON, THIRD PRESIDENT OF THE UNITED STATES 1801–1809

Colleges and Universities A difficult question that many colleges and universities face today is whether the right to free speech includes the right to make hateful remarks about others based on their race, gender, or sexual orientation. Some claim that allowing people with extremist views to voice their opinions can lead to violence. In response to this question, several universities have gone so far as to institute speech codes to minimize the disturbances that hate speech might cause. Speech codes at public colleges have been ruled unconstitutional on the ground that they restrict freedom of speech.[30] Such codes continue to exist on many college campuses, however.

Race-based incidents on university campuses gave rise to free speech questions in 2015. At the University of Oklahoma (UO), a YouTube video showed fraternity brothers chanting a racist song. The lyrics, which proclaimed that blacks would never join the fraternity, were highly insulting to African Americans and possibly threatening as well. UO promptly closed the fraternity and expelled two students. Some observers thought that this reaction violated the students' First Amendment rights. The students in question did not contest their punishment, however—perhaps because doing so might have exposed them to further public humiliation.

At the University of Missouri, a series of racial insults and threats—plus questionable responses by the administration—led to a strike by the football team. The school's chancellor and the president of the state university system then resigned. The issue of free speech arose when protesting students tried to prevent campus reporters from covering their activities. At Yale, a school statement cautioned against insensitive Halloween costumes. The statement was criticized by a lecturer who later resigned. In response to such incidents, conservatives claimed that free speech on college campuses was threatened by "political correctness."

4-3f Freedom of the Press

The framers of the Constitution believed that the press should be free to publish a wide range of opinions and information, and generally the free speech rights just discussed also apply to the press. The courts have placed certain restrictions on freedom of the press, however. Over the years, the Supreme Court has developed various guidelines and doctrines to use in deciding whether freedom of speech and the press can be restrained.

The Preferred-Position Doctrine One major guideline, called the *preferred-position doctrine,* states that certain freedoms—including freedom of speech and of the press—are so essential to a democracy that they hold a preferred position. According to this doctrine, any law that limits these freedoms should be presumed unconstitutional unless the government can show that the law is absolutely necessary. The idea behind this doctrine is that freedom of speech and the press should rarely, if ever, be diminished, because spoken and printed words are the prime tools of the democratic process.

Prior Restraint Stopping an activity before it actually happens is known as *prior restraint.* With respect to freedom of the press, prior restraint means *censorship,* which occurs when an official removes objectionable materials from an item before it is published or broadcast. An example of censorship and prior restraint would be a court's ruling that two paragraphs in an upcoming article in the local newspaper had to be removed before the article could be published. The Supreme Court has generally ruled against prior restraint, arguing that the government cannot curb ideas before they are expressed.

In certain circumstances, however, the Court has allowed prior restraint. For example, in a 1988 case, a high school principal deleted two pages from the school newspaper just before it was printed. The pages contained stories on students' experiences with pregnancy and discussed the impact of divorce on students at the school. The Supreme Court, noting that students in school do not have exactly the same rights as adults in other settings, ruled that high school administrators can censor school publications. The Court said that school newspapers are part of the school curriculum, not a public forum. Therefore, administrators have the right to censor speech that promotes conduct inconsistent with the "shared values of a civilized social order."[31]

CRITICAL THINKING

▶ *Libel and slander are hard to prove in the United States. Should it be easier to win libel and slander suits than it is now? Why or why not?*

4-4 THE RIGHT TO PRIVACY

LO Discuss why Americans are increasingly concerned about privacy rights.

In a dissenting opinion written in 1928, Supreme Court justice Louis Brandeis stated that the right to privacy is "the most comprehensive of rights and the right most valued by civilized men."[32] The majority of the justices on the Supreme Court at that time did not agree. In the 1960s, however, Court opinion began to change.

In 1965, in the landmark case of *Griswold v. Connecticut,*[33] the Supreme Court held that a right to privacy is implied by other constitutional rights guaranteed in the First, Third, Fourth, Fifth, and Ninth Amendments. For example, consider the words of the Ninth Amendment: "The enumeration in the Constitution, of certain rights, shall not be construed to deny or disparage others retained by the people." In other words, just because the Constitution, including its amendments, does not specifically mention the right to privacy does not mean that this right is denied to the people.

Although Congress and the courts have acknowledged a constitutional right to privacy, the nature and scope of this right are not always clear. For example, Americans continue to debate whether the right to privacy includes the right to have an abortion or the right of terminally ill persons to commit physician-assisted suicide. Since the terrorist attacks of September 11, 2001, another pressing privacy issue has been how to monitor potential terrorists to prevent another attack without violating the privacy rights of all Americans.

4-4a The Abortion Controversy

One of the most divisive and emotionally charged issues debated today is whether the right to privacy means that women can choose to have abortions.

Abortion and Privacy In 1973, in the landmark case of *Roe v. Wade,*[34] the Supreme Court, using the *Griswold* case as a precedent, held that the "right of privacy . . . is broad enough to encompass a woman's decision whether or not to terminate her pregnancy." The right is not absolute throughout pregnancy, however. The Court also said that any state could impose certain regulations to safeguard the health of the mother after the first three months of pregnancy and, in the final stages of pregnancy, could act to protect potential life.

Since the *Roe v. Wade* decision, the Supreme Court has adopted a more conservative approach and has upheld restrictive state laws requiring counseling, waiting periods, notification of parents, and other actions prior to abortions.[35] Yet the Court has never overturned the *Roe* decision. In fact, in 1997 and again in 2000, the Supreme Court upheld laws requiring "buffer zones" around abortion clinics to protect those entering the clinics from unwanted counseling or harassment by anti-abortion groups.[36] In 2014, however, the Court ruled that

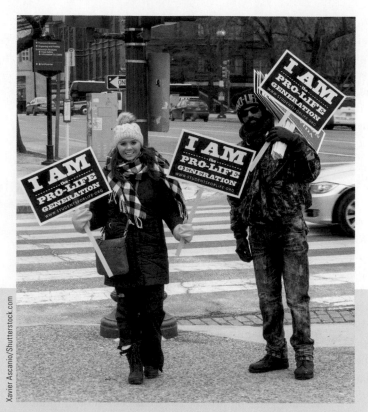

Pro-life activists at the annual March for Life in Washington, D.C. The activists gather every year to mark the anniversary of *Roe v. Wade,* the Supreme Court decision that legalized abortion. *Why does abortion continue to be an explosive topic?*

a thirty-five-foot buffer zone established by Massachusetts was excessive.[37]

Partial-Birth Abortions In 2000, the Supreme Court invalidated a Nebraska statute banning "partial-birth" abortions, a procedure used during the second trimester of pregnancy.[38] Abortion rights groups contend that the procedure, known to physicians as "intact dilation and extraction," is sometimes the best way to protect the health of the mother. In any event, the government should not outlaw particular medical procedures. Anti-abortion activists disagree, and claim that the procedure destroys the life of a fetus that might be able to live outside the womb.

Undeterred by the fate of the Nebraska law, President George W. Bush signed the Partial Birth Abortion Ban Act in 2003. In a close (five-to-four) and controversial 2007 decision, the Supreme Court upheld the constitutionality of the 2003 act.[39]

Many were surprised at the Court's decision on partial-birth abortion, given that the federal act banning this practice was quite similar to the Nebraska law that had been struck down by the Court in 2000, just seven years

earlier. The Court became more conservative in 2006, however, when President George W. Bush appointed Justice Samuel Alito to replace Justice Sandra Day O'Connor. Dissenting from the majority opinion in the case, Justice Ruth Bader Ginsburg said that the ruling was an "alarming" departure from three decades of Supreme Court decisions on abortion.

In reality, how easy is it for women to access abortion services today? We examine that question in this chapter's *Perception versus Reality* feature.

4–4b Do We Have the "Right to Die"?

Whether it is called euthanasia (mercy killing) or assisted suicide, it all comes down to one basic question: Do terminally ill persons have, as part of their civil liberties, a right to die and to be assisted in the process by physicians or others? Phrased another way, are state laws banning physician-assisted suicide in such circumstances unconstitutional?

In 1997, the issue came before the Supreme Court, which characterized the question as follows: Does the liberty protected by the Constitution include a right to commit suicide, which itself includes a right to assistance in doing so? The Court's clear and categorical answer to this question was no. To hold otherwise, said the Court, would be "to reverse centuries of legal doctrine and practice, and strike down the considered policy choice of almost every state."[40]

Although the Court upheld the states' rights to ban such a practice, the Court did not hold that state laws *permitting* assisted suicide were unconstitutional. In 1997, Oregon became the first state to implement such a law. Four additional states now allow the practice—Montana, New Mexico, Vermont, and Washington. Oregon's law was upheld by the Supreme Court in 2006.[41]

4–4c Privacy and Personal Information

A major concern among Americans in recent years is that their personal information could be collected by individuals or organizations that use the data improperly. Some kinds of data have been collected and disseminated for many years. Any economically active person has a credit rating, and a poor credit rating can make it impossible to borrow money for a car or house. Recently, information

PERCEPTION VS. REALITY

The Availability of Abortion

Before 1973, abortion was illegal in much of the United States. In that year, the United States Supreme Court issued its decision in *Roe v. Wade*. The outcome of this landmark case seemed to settle the abortion issue once and for all. Women had the right to terminate their pregnancies.

The Perception

The highest court in the land made it clear—women can have an abortion if they so decide, and no state laws may prevent this, at least during the first trimester of pregnancy. During the second trimester, only state laws that limit the procedure to protect the health of pregnant women are constitutional. It follows that abortion should be freely available throughout the land.

The Reality

The pro-life and pro-choice sides of the abortion debate seem to agree on one thing. In practice, *Roe v. Wade* is no longer the law of the land. Since 2010, state legislatures have adopted a total of 288 new laws aimed at limiting access to abortion, according to the Guttmacher Institute.

Twenty-eight states have imposed a waiting period between required counseling and the time an abortion can be performed. Seventeen states require that counseling include statements that the medical profession considers false or unproven. Twenty place limits on how late in the pregnancy an abortion can be performed that are stricter than specified in *Roe v. Wade*. Nine require an ultrasound before an abortion can be performed.

Other legislation is aimed at closing down abortion clinics. Twenty-four states require that abortion facilities must meet structural standards equivalent to those for surgical facilities. In some states, this requirement is easy to meet. In Texas, however, many clinics would have to move into new and expensive custom-built facilities. Five states require that clinic physicians have admitting privileges at a local hospital. The states can then rely on hospitals to refuse such privileges.

Most of these new laws violate *Roe v. Wade* and subsequent Supreme Court rulings. Supporters of abortion rights, however, have been reluctant to challenge the laws because they are afraid that the Supreme Court might narrow abortion rights further. Still, recent laws have forced abortion clinics to defend themselves in court. As a result, dozens of state laws have been overturned by the federal courts. In June 2016, the Supreme Court struck down the Texas law that set clinic structural standards and required hospital admitting privileges. Still, for all practical purposes, women today cannot get an abortion in several small-population Great Plains and Rocky Mountain states.

Blog On

For up-to-date information on state laws concerning abortion, visit the Guttmacher Institute website at www.guttmacher.org/statecenter.

---

technology has made it easier for businesses and other institutions to collect vast quantities of personal data. Grocery stores, for example, may collect data on every purchase you make in an effort to sell you more goods. Another looming privacy issue is the use of drones to collect information. Both governments and private parties may be tempted to use such devices as they become more widespread.

Privacy Legislation The 1960s marked the beginning of Congress's attempts to pass laws protecting the privacy rights of individuals. The 1966 Freedom of Information Act allows any person to request copies of information about her or him contained in government files. In 1974, Congress passed the Privacy Act, which restricts government disclosure of data to third parties.

The Driver's Privacy Protection Act, passed in 1994, prevents states from disclosing or selling a driver's personal information without the driver's consent.[42] In late 2000, the federal Department of Health and Human Services issued a regulation protecting the privacy of medical information. Health-care providers and insurance companies are restricted from sharing confidential information about their patients. In 2011, however, the Supreme Court struck down a Vermont law that prevented pharmacies from selling the prescription records of physicians to drug companies. The Court concluded that such limits violated free speech rights.[43]

The vast amount of information available about individuals on the Internet has led to additional attempts to safeguard privacy. In Europe, for example, courts have come up with a new doctrine aimed at protecting privacy—the "right to be forgotten." In some cases, individuals can obtain a court order requiring Google and other search engines to remove personal information from their search results. (The information is not deleted, but it becomes difficult to locate.) Most experts doubt that such a right could be extended to the United States because of our First Amendment guarantees of free speech. California, however, has adopted a new law that requires websites to let persons under the age of eighteen erase material that they have posted on the sites.

Online Harassment

The Internet gives individuals a potent platform for communicating information about each other, including highly damaging information and even outright lies. The resulting online harassment has been called *cyberbullying*. Recently, several cyberbullies have been charged with crimes.

Cases of Cyberbullying. One example is the case of a Rutgers student who committed suicide after his roommate secretly taped a sexual encounter he had with another man and then posted it online. The roommate was convicted of multiple computer-related crimes but is appealing his convictions. Another example is a woman who pretended online to be a boy so as to harass one of her daughter's classmates. The young victim committed suicide. The woman's conviction was overturned on appeal, because the statute under which she was charged was inapplicable. Both of these cases raise troubling questions about whether verbal harassment may be protected by the First Amendment. Forty-one states now have laws against online harassment, however.

Revenge Porn. Another form of harassment is the practice of posting online sexually explicit photographs or videos of a former partner. Such postings may even include the name, address, or employer of the victim. This practice, aptly dubbed *revenge porn*, can have devastating effects on the targeted person. If the photos go into wide circulation, it may be impossible to track them down and delete them.

Still, a revenge porn victim may have more legal options than a victim of cyberbullying. Twenty-six states and the District of Columbia now outlaw the act explicitly, and legislation is pending in an additional eleven. Victims can also pursue civil lawsuits on a variety of grounds. If, as is often the case, a posted photo was taken by the victim—if it was a "selfie"—the victim may even be able to allege copyright violation. Perpetrators who took the photos themselves, however, have claimed First Amendment rights to do what they wish with the images.

Cyberbullying is a major problem, especially among younger people. *Why is it so hard for the law to address this issue?*

SpeedKingz/Shutterstock.com

4–4d Personal Privacy and National Security

Since the terrorist attacks of September 11, 2001, the news media and Congress have debated how the United States can strengthen national security while still protecting civil liberties, particularly the right to privacy.

The USA Patriot Act Several laws and programs that infringe on Americans' privacy rights were created in the wake of 9/11 in an attempt to protect the nation's security. For example, the USA Patriot Act of 2001 gave the government broad latitude to investigate people who are only vaguely associated with terrorists. Under this law, the government can access personal information on American citizens to an extent never before allowed.

The Federal Bureau of Investigation was also authorized to use "National Security Letters" to demand personal information about individuals from private companies (such as banks and phone companies). The companies supplying the information are not allowed to inform their customers about the requests. In one of the most controversial programs, the National Security Agency (NSA) was authorized to monitor certain domestic phone calls without first obtaining a warrant. When Americans learned of the NSA's actions in 2005, the ensuing public furor forced the Bush administration to obtain warrants for such activities.

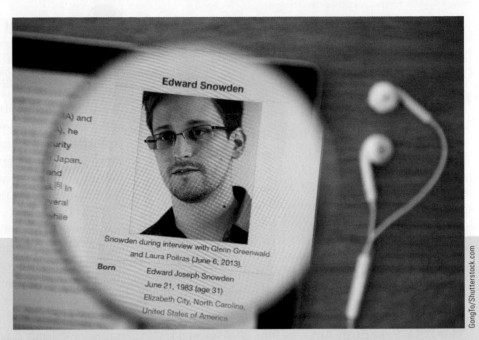

Edward Snowden, who leaked secret materials from the National Security Agency. *Should Snowden be pardoned or prosecuted to the full extent of the law?*

National Security Under President Obama

During his 2008 campaign, Obama promised to make a clean break with the policies of the Bush administration on national security. It did not take long, however, for observers to realize that the differences between the Obama and Bush administrations were more a matter of presentation than of substance. For example, Obama restated the Bush policy that suspected terrorists could be held indefinitely without trial.

Another issue was the treatment of individuals who passed national security information to the press. By 2013, the administration had brought felony charges against seven such persons under the Espionage Act of 1917. It had been almost thirty years since the government last charged anyone under the act based on leaks to the press. One of the most serious cases involved Private First Class Bradley Manning, who was convicted in 2013 of giving huge amounts of classified material to WikiLeaks, a website. Before conviction, Manning was held in solitary confinement under conditions some considered abusive. (Manning has since chosen to become a woman and has adopted the first name of Chelsea.)

The NSA Revelations

In June 2013, materials released to the press by Edward Snowden, a national security contractor, revealed that surveillance by the NSA has been more universal than most people had previously assumed. Snowden, aware of the treatment of leakers such as Manning, was in Hong Kong by the time his identity was released. Learning that the Chinese government might turn him over to the United States, he fled to Russia, where he was granted asylum.

Collecting Metadata. Under one NSA program publicized by Snowden's revelations, the agency had been collecting information about every land-line phone call made in the entire United States—not the content of the call, but the time, number called, and number calling. (Such information *about* phone calls—as opposed to actual contents of communications—has been called *metadata*.) Although this program was undertaken pursuant to a secret court-ordered search warrant, its scope seems hard to square with the text of the Fourth Amendment, which states that "no Warrants shall issue, but upon probable cause . . . and particularly describing the place to be searched, and the persons or things to be seized."

Cloud Computing. Another program, known as PRISM, was designed to accumulate vast quantities of data from the servers of corporations such as AOL, Apple, Facebook, Google, Skype, and others. The information included e-mails, chats, photos, and more, and was collected worldwide. In particular, the NSA considered itself free to access any data stored on a U.S. server by a foreign citizen. As a former NSA chief put it, "The

Fourth Amendment is not an international treaty." This policy threatened to create major problems for American companies that offer "cloud computing" services worldwide. (In *cloud computing*, users store their information on a remote server so that they can access it from any system, anywhere.)

Bugging Foreign Leaders. It was also revealed that the NSA had collected massive quantities of data on foreign phone calls. The agency tapped the telephones of dozens of foreign leaders, including German chancellor Angela Merkel, Brazil's president Dilma Rousseff, and dozens of others. It bugged the offices of European Union negotiators in advance of trade talks with the United States. Other surveillance also seemed to be aimed more at gaining U.S. economic advantage than at combating terrorism. These revelations created serious diplomatic problems for the U.S. government.

The USA Freedom Act In June 2015, several key provisions of the USA Patriot Act expired. Debate in Congress on whether to renew the provisions was fierce. Supporters of civil liberties squared off against defenders of the intelligence community. In an unusual coalition, Republican libertarians united with left-leaning Democrats in an attempt to place limits on the NSA's activities. The result was the USA Freedom Act.

The new act reauthorized most of the provisions of the USA Patriot Act. Still, it also sought to control the NSA's collection of metadata on domestic phone calls. Further it attempted to shine some light on the Foreign Intelligence Surveillance Court (FISC). This secret court is responsible for authorizing searches by the NSA and other intelligence agencies. The FISC must now release justifications for key rulings. A new panel is to review search requests and challenge them if necessary.

Civil liberties advocates argued that the new legislation would have little practical effect—massive data sweeps would continue under the authority of other laws.

probable cause Cause for believing that there is a substantial likelihood that a person has committed or is about to commit a crime.

double jeopardy The prosecution of a person twice for the same criminal offense; prohibited by the Fifth Amendment in all but a few circumstances.

self-incrimination Providing damaging information or testimony against oneself in court.

CRITICAL THINKING

▸ *Could the government's current policies on screening airline passengers be considered a violation of privacy rights? Why or why not?*

4–5 THE RIGHTS OF THE ACCUSED

LO Summarize how the Constitution and the Bill of Rights protect the rights of accused persons.

The United States has one of the highest murder rates in the industrialized world. It is therefore not surprising that many Americans have extremely strong opinions about the rights of persons accused of criminal offenses. Indeed, some Americans complain that criminal defendants have too many rights.

Why do criminal suspects have rights? The answer is that all persons are entitled to the protections afforded by the Bill of Rights. If criminal suspects were deprived of their basic constitutional liberties, all people would suffer the consequences, because there is nothing to stop the government from accusing anyone of being a criminal. In a criminal case, a state official (such as the district attorney, or D.A.) prosecutes the defendant, and the state has immense resources that it can bring to bear against the accused person. By protecting the rights of accused persons, the Constitution helps to prevent the arbitrary use of power by the government.

4–5a The Rights of Criminal Defendants

The basic rights, or constitutional safeguards, provided for criminal defendants are set forth in the Bill of Rights. These safeguards include the following:

▸ The Fourth Amendment protection from unreasonable searches and seizures.

▸ The Fourth Amendment requirement that no warrant for a search or an arrest be issued without **probable cause**—cause for believing that there is a substantial likelihood that a person has committed or is about to commit a crime.

▸ The Fifth Amendment requirement that no one be deprived of "life, liberty, or property, without due process of law." As discussed earlier in this chapter, this requirement is also included in the Fourteenth Amendment, which protects persons against actions by state governments.

▸ The Fifth Amendment prohibition against **double jeopardy**—being tried twice for the same criminal offense.

▸ The Fifth Amendment provision that no person can be required to be a witness against (incriminate) himself or herself. This is often referred to as the constitutional protection against **self-incrimination**. It is the basis for a criminal suspect's "right to remain silent" in criminal proceedings.

JOIN THE DEBATE

Is the Death Penalty a Cruel and Unusual Punishment?

The Eighth Amendment to the U.S. Constitution explicitly states that the government cannot inflict "cruel and unusual punishments." But what exactly is considered "cruel and unusual"? What about the death penalty, also called capital punishment?

Criminals have been executed in America since the earliest days of the republic. In addition to murder, a variety of crimes have been punished by death. In the 1700s, for example, citizens were executed for robbery, forgery, and illegally cutting down trees.

No state executes people for such crimes today. Furthermore, although a majority of Americans continue to support the death penalty for crimes such as murder, fewer states are executing people at all. Nineteen states—most recently, Nebraska—and the District of Columbia have abolished the death penalty. Several governors have announced that they will not authorize executions even though their states permit them. Pharmaceutical companies have refused to sell to the states the drugs that are necessary for executions by lethal injection. Only twenty-eight persons were executed in the United States in 2015, the lowest number in twenty-four years. Do these developments suggest that in our modern world the death penalty itself is seen as cruel and unusual, and therefore a violation of the Eighth Amendment?

An Eye for an Eye Makes the Whole World Blind

Some argue that the death penalty is inappropriate even for someone who has committed murder. Violence and death may always be with us, but the law should not encourage violent sentiments. Already in 1764, the Italian jurist Cesare Beccaria asserted that "the death penalty cannot be useful, because of the example of barbarity it gives men."

Face it—capital punishment is barbaric whether it is carried out by a firing squad, an electric chair, a gas chamber, lethal injection, or hanging. Nations other than the United States that frequently employ capital punishment are not ones that we would seek to emulate: they include China, Iran, North Korea, and Saudi Arabia. Almost all of our allies have abolished the practice.

There Is Nothing Cruel and Unusual about Executing a Murderer

Strangely enough, some who are against capital punishment have argued that life in prison without parole is crueler than death. Prisoners are confined in an environment of violence where they are treated like animals, and the suffering goes on for decades. If you think about it, this is an argument that the death sentence can be merciful.

In any event, capital punishment is not cruel and unusual as meant by the Eighth Amendment. Indeed, the current method of execution used in most states—lethal injection— appears quite civilized compared with methods of execution used in England back in the 1700s, which included drawing and quartering and burning at the stake. Practices such as these are what the founders sought to ban.

Critical Analysis

Can there be a humane method of extinguishing someone's life? Why or why not?

▶ The Sixth Amendment guarantees of a speedy trial, a trial by jury, a public trial, and the right to confront witnesses.

▶ The Sixth Amendment guarantee of the right to counsel at various stages in some criminal proceedings. The right to counsel was strengthened in 1963 in *Gideon v. Wainwright*.[44] The Supreme Court held that if a person is accused of a felony and cannot afford an attorney, an attorney must be made available to the accused person at the government's expense.

▶ The Eighth Amendment prohibitions against excessive bail and fines and against cruel and unusual punishments. Should the death penalty be considered a cruel and unusual punishment? We discuss that question in this chapter's *Join the Debate* feature.

4–5b The Exclusionary Rule

Any evidence obtained in violation of the constitutional rights spelled out in the Fourth Amendment normally is not admissible at trial. This rule, which has been applied in the federal courts since at least 1914, is known as the **exclusionary rule**. The rule was extended to state court proceedings in 1961.[45]

The reasoning behind the exclusionary rule is that it forces law enforcement personnel to gather evidence properly. If they do not, they will be unable to introduce the evidence at trial to convince the jury that the defendant is guilty.

In a 2014 landmark case, the Supreme Court brought the exclusionary rule into the modern age. The Court held unanimously that searching the digital contents of a cell phone during an arrest is unconstitutional unless law enforcement personnel have a search warrant. Chief Justice John Roberts wrote: "Modern cell phones are not just another technological convenience. With all they contain and all they may reveal, they hold for many Americans 'the privacies of life.' The fact that technology now allows an individual to carry such information in his hand does not make the information any less worthy of the protection for which the Founders fought."[46]

a katz/Shutterstock

Following the death of Freddie Gray while in police custody in Baltimore, protests took place around the country. Attempts to march resulted in more than one hundred arrests in New York City. *Is it appropriate for cities to ban protesters from marching in the streets without a parade permit?*

4–5c The *Miranda* Warnings

In the 1950s and 1960s, one of the questions facing the courts was not whether suspects had constitutional rights—that was not in doubt—but how and when those rights could be exercised. For example, could the right to remain silent (under the Fifth Amendment's prohibition against self-incrimination) be exercised during pretrial interrogation proceedings or only during the trial? Were confessions obtained from suspects admissible in court if the suspects had not been advised of their right to remain silent and other constitutional rights?

To clarify these issues, in 1966 the Supreme Court issued a landmark decision in *Miranda v. Arizona.*[47] In

exclusionary rule A criminal procedural rule stating that illegally obtained evidence is not admissible in court.

***Miranda* warnings** A series of statements informing criminal suspects, on their arrest, of their constitutional rights, such as the right to remain silent and the right to counsel; required by the Supreme Court's 1966 decision in *Miranda v. Arizona.*

that case, the Court enunciated the *Miranda* **warnings** that are now familiar to almost all Americans:

> Prior to any questioning, the person must be warned that he has a right to remain silent, that any statement he does make may be used against him, and that he has a right to the presence of an attorney, either retained or appointed.

The Erosion of *Miranda* As part of a continuing attempt to balance the rights of accused persons against the rights of society, the Supreme Court has made a number of exceptions to the *Miranda* ruling. In an important 1991 decision, the Court stated that a suspect's conviction will not be automatically overturned if the suspect was coerced into making a confession. If the other evidence admitted at trial was strong enough to justify the conviction without the confession, then the fact that the confession was obtained illegally can be, in effect, ignored.[48]

In another case related to *Miranda,* in 1994 the Supreme Court ruled that a suspect must unequivocally and assertively state his right to counsel in order to stop police questioning. Saying "Maybe I should talk to a lawyer" during an interrogation after being taken into custody is not enough. The Court held that police officers are not required to decipher the suspect's intentions in such situations.[49] In 2011, however, the Court ruled that because children are more susceptible to pressure than adults, police officers must take extra care in ensuring the *Miranda* rights of child suspects.[50]

Recording Confessions *Miranda* may eventually become obsolete regardless of any decisions made in the courts. A relatively new trend in law enforcement has been for agencies to digitally record interrogations and confessions. Thomas P. Sullivan, a former U.S. attorney in Chicago, and his staff interviewed personnel in more than 230 law enforcement agencies in thirty-eight states that record interviews of suspects who are in custody. Sullivan found that nearly all police officers said the procedure saved time and money, created valuable evidence to use in court, and made it more difficult for defense attorneys to claim that their clients had been illegally coerced.[51] Some scholars have suggested that recording all custodial interrogations would satisfy the Fifth Amendment's prohibition against coercion and in the process render the *Miranda* warnings unnecessary.

CRITICAL THINKING

▶ *In many states, public defenders—court-appointed attorneys—suffer from low pay and excessive workloads. Why might this be so?*

AMERICA AT ODDS | Civil Liberties

Civil liberties represent a contentious topic, and Americans are at odds over many civil liberties issues. Almost all Americans claim to believe in individual rights, but how should this freedom be defined? Often, one right appears to interfere with another. Some of the resulting disputes include the following:

- *Should the First Amendment's establishment clause be interpreted strictly, so that no one's rights are infringed on by government sponsorship of religion—or should it be interpreted loosely, to recognize that the United States is a very religious country?*

- *What kinds of religious practices should be allowed under the free exercise clause? For example, should religious groups that limit or ban participation by gay men and lesbians receive the same government benefits as any other group—or should they be penalized for discrimination?*

- *Should advertising receive the same free speech rights as any other kind of speech—or should advertisers be held accountable for making false claims?*

- *Has the government gone too far in restricting liberties in an attempt to combat terrorism—or are the restrictions trivial compared with the benefits?*

- *Consider the most intense controversy of all: Should women have a privacy right to terminate a pregnancy for any reason—or should abortion be a crime?*

STUDY TOOLS 4

READY TO STUDY? IN THE BOOK, YOU CAN:

☐ Review what you've read with the following chapter quiz.

☐ Check your answers in Appendix D at the back of the book.

☐ Rip out the Chapter Review Card, which includes key terms and chapter summaries.

ONLINE AT WWW.CENGAGEBRAIN.COM, YOU CAN:

☐ Learn about the right to keep and bear arms in a short video.

☐ Explore various online resources in the National Coalition Against Censorship webpage Internet Resources tool.

☐ Interact with figures from the text, and watch quick animation clips.

☐ Prepare for tests with quizzes.

☐ Review the key terms with Flash Cards.

FILL-IN

Learning Outcome 4–1

1. The _____ clause of the Fourteenth Amendment to the U.S. Constitution guarantees that state governments will not arbitrarily deprive any person of life, liberty, or property.

Learning Outcome 4–2

2. The *Lemon* test, enunciated by the Supreme Court in 1971 to determine whether government aid to parochial schools is constitutional, states that the aid must _____.

Learning Outcome 4–3

3. The current Supreme Court standard for assessing the constitutionality of _____ is the imminent lawless action test.

4. _____ is a published report of a falsehood that tends to injure a person's reputation or character.

Learning Outcome 4–4

5. Under the USA Patriot Act of 2001, the FBI is authorized to use _____ to demand personal information about individuals from private companies, such as banks and phone companies.

6. In _____, the Supreme Court held that the "right of privacy . . . is broad enough to encompass a woman's decision whether or not to terminate her pregnancy."

Learning Outcome 4–5

7. The _____ Amendment includes protection from unreasonable searches and seizures.

8. Upon arrest, suspects must be advised of their constitutional rights through _____.

MULTIPLE CHOICE

Learning Outcome 4–1

9. A/An _____ is an order requiring that an official bring a specified prisoner into court and explain to the judge why the prisoner is being held.
   a. *ex post facto* law
   b. writ of *habeas corpus*
   c. bill of attainder

10. The Supreme Court has used the incorporation principle to
    a. extend First Amendment protections to corporations.
    b. require state governments to observe protections listed in the national Bill of Rights.
    c. guarantee all citizens the right to vote.

Learning Outcome 4–2

11. The Supreme Court has ruled that public schools
    a. cannot sponsor religious activities.
    b. are allowed to determine for themselves the number of religious exercises they will sponsor.
    c. are barred from teaching about religion.

Learning Outcome 4–3

12. The Supreme Court's _____ doctrine states that certain freedoms are so essential that any law limiting these freedoms should be presumed to be unconstitutional unless the government can show that it is absolutely necessary.
    a. prior-restraint
    b. due-process
    c. preferred position

Learning Outcome 4–4

13. The Supreme Court, in *Griswold v. Connecticut* (1965), held that a right to privacy is implied by other constitutional rights guaranteed in the
    a. Magna Carta.
    b. First, Third, Fourth, Fifth, and Ninth Amendments.
    c. Declaration of Independence.

Learning Outcome 4–5

14. The Fifth Amendment
    a. includes a protection against self-incrimination.
    b. guarantees a speedy trial and a trial by jury.
    c. guarantees the right to counsel at various stages in some criminal proceedings.

GOVT
ONLINE
STUDY YOUR WAY
WITH STUDYBITS!

WEAK

FAIR

STRONG

UNASSIGNED

Rate and Organize StudyBits

Collect What's Important

Create Flashcards From Your StudyBits

Track/Monitor Your Progress

85%

CORRECT

INCORRECT

INCORRECT

INCORRECT

Personalize Your Quizzes

4LTR
PRESS

Access GOVT ONLINE at www.cengagebrain.com

5 CIVIL RIGHTS

Michael B. Thomas/Getty Images News/Getty Images

LEARNING OUTCOMES *After reading this chapter, you should be able to:*

5-1 Explain the constitutional basis for our civil rights and for laws prohibiting discrimination.

5-2 Discuss the reasons for the civil rights movement and the changes it caused in American politics and government.

5-3 Describe the political and economic achievements of women in this country over time, and identify some obstacles to equality that women continue to face.

5-4 Summarize the struggles for equality that other groups in America have experienced.

5-5 Explain what affirmative action is and why it has been so controversial.

After finishing this chapter, go to **PAGE 120** for **STUDY TOOLS**.

AMERICA AT ODDS

Do the Police Use Excessive Force against African Americans?

A katz//Shutterstock.com

In 2015 and 2016, Americans were confronted with a major issue—police relations with minority communities. Above all, the question has been whether law enforcement officers have employed excessive force against African Americans—especially young men. Incidents in which unarmed black men were killed during interactions with police have led to riots in cities as varied as Ferguson, Missouri, and Baltimore, Maryland. Protests and expressions of concern have taken place across the nation.

Another issue: police regularly subject black drivers and pedestrians, especially young men, to investigatory stops—stops made without evidence of a crime. African Americans refer to these stops as the "crime of driving while black." Whites, including white males, almost never experience investigatory stops. Of course, the more often African Americans are stopped, the more likely it is that an incident will turn out badly. Is police racism, then, a serious problem in this country?

The Police Are Just Trying to Do Their Job

Those who defend the police say racism, while it may exist in some forces, is not the whole story. After all, many of the officers involved in recent incidents—such as the death of Freddie Gray while in custody in Baltimore—are themselves African American.

There are other reasons why men of color—black and Latino—are arrested more frequently than whites. Through no fault of their own, many young men in black and Latino neighborhoods grow up in an environment that seems designed to push them toward a life of crime. Finding a job seems impossible. Criminals, in contrast, receive respect and money. And it is a fact that African Americans are far more likely to commit many kinds of crime than white Americans.

Furthermore, police advocates contend that demonstrations and activism make it harder for police officers to do their jobs. Police may pull back and make fewer arrests if they fear that the community will resist rather than support them. In Baltimore, murder rates are 150 percent of what they were before the Freddie Gray incident.

The Police Have Created the Problem, Not the Protestors

African Americans say they have good reasons to be afraid of the police. Consider the statistics. The Propublica website calculates that black teens are twenty-one times more likely than white teens to be shot and killed by police. Consider, too, that most complaints about police brutality are never investigated. Even when a complaint is investigated, only rarely is the officer convicted, particularly when a minority male is the alleged victim. And when there is a conviction, the disciplinary action is often trivial.

It is a long-standing truism that the police cannot combat crime all by themselves. They need the cooperation of the local community if they are to be effective. Victims must be prepared to report crimes to the authorities. Witnesses must be willing to come forward and talk. If members of an impoverished African American or Latino community are afraid that any interaction with the police can have disastrous consequences, they will avoid the police at all costs. And in fact, the police are seen as an army of occupation in many neighborhoods. Such a force can only breed resentment, not solve crimes.

Where do you stand?

1. Do you think having officers wear cameras to record interactions with the public would be a good solution? Why or why not?

2. There is a disparity in drug arrests among racial groups. Will that gap be reduced in states that have legalized recreational marijuana? Why or why not?

Explore this issue online:

- FBI director James Comey discusses police-community relations at "comey georgetown university."

- For a description of investigatory stops, see an article by Charles Epp and Steven Maynard-Moody at "how to rebuild trust epp moody."

INTRODUCTION

As noted in Chapter 4, people sometimes confuse civil rights with civil liberties. Generally, though, the term **civil rights** refers to the rights of all Americans to equal treatment under the law, as provided by the Fourteenth Amendment.

As you will read in this chapter, the struggle of various groups in American society to obtain equal treatment has been a long one, and it continues. African Americans make up one such group, and we discussed an issue that concerns them in this chapter's opening *America at Odds* feature.

In a sense, the history of civil rights in the United States is a history of discrimination against various groups. Discrimination against women,

> **ALL AMERICANS ARE ENTITLED TO *EQUAL TREATMENT UNDER THE LAW,* AS PROVIDED BY THE FOURTEENTH AMENDMENT.**

African Americans, and Native Americans dates back to the early years of this nation. More recently, other groups, including persons with disabilities and gay men and lesbians, have struggled for equal treatment under the law. This chapter discusses each of these groups. Inevitably, though, a single short chapter must omit discussion of some groups that have experienced discrimination. Two such groups are American Muslims and older Americans.

Central to any discussion of civil rights is the interpretation of the equal protection clause of the Fourteenth Amendment to the Constitution. For that reason, we look first at that clause.

civil rights The rights of all Americans to equal treatment under the law, as provided by the Fourteenth Amendment to the Constitution.

equal protection clause Section 1 of the Fourteenth Amendment, which says that no state shall "deny to any person within its jurisdiction the equal protection of the laws."

fundamental right A basic right of all Americans, such as First Amendment rights. Any law or action that prevents some group of persons from exercising a fundamental right is subject to the *strict scrutiny standard.*

strict scrutiny standard A standard under which a law or action must be necessary to promote a compelling state interest and must be narrowly tailored to meet that interest.

suspect classification A classification, such as race, that provides the basis for a discriminatory law. Any law based on a suspect classification is subject to strict scrutiny by the courts, meaning that the law must be justified by a compelling state interest.

5–1 THE EQUAL PROTECTION CLAUSE

LO Explain the constitutional basis for our civil rights and for laws prohibiting discrimination.

You read about the due process clause of the Fourteenth Amendment in Chapter 4. Equal in importance to the due process clause is the **equal protection clause** in Section 1 of that amendment, which reads as follows: "No State shall . . . deny to any person within its jurisdiction the equal protection of the laws." Section 5 of the amendment provides a legal basis for federal civil rights legislation: "The Congress shall have power to enforce, by appropriate legislation, the provisions of this article."

The equal protection clause has been interpreted by the courts, and especially the United States Supreme Court, to mean that states must treat all persons equally and may not discriminate *unreasonably* against a particular group or class of individuals. The task of distinguishing between reasonable and unreasonable discrimination is difficult. Generally, in deciding this question, the Supreme Court balances the constitutional rights of individuals to equal protection against government interests in protecting the safety and welfare of citizens.

Over time, the Court has developed various tests, or standards, for determining whether the equal protection clause has been violated. These standards are strict scrutiny, intermediate scrutiny, and ordinary scrutiny (the rational basis test).

5–1a Strict Scrutiny

If a law or action prevents some group of persons from exercising a **fundamental right** (such as one of our First Amendment rights), the law or action will be subject to the **strict scrutiny standard**. Under this standard, the law or action must be necessary to promote a *compelling state interest* and must be narrowly tailored to meet that interest. A law based on a **suspect classification**, such as race, is also subject to strict scrutiny by the courts, meaning that the law must be justified by a compelling state interest.

5-1b Intermediate Scrutiny

Because the Supreme Court had difficulty deciding how to judge cases in which men and women were treated differently, another test was developed—the *intermediate scrutiny standard*. Under this standard, also known as *exacting scrutiny*, laws based on gender classifications are permissible if they are "substantially related to the achievement of an important governmental objective."

For example, a law punishing males but not females for statutory rape (sex with an underage person) has been ruled valid by the courts. The reasoning is that there is an important governmental interest in preventing teenage pregnancy in those circumstances, and almost all of the harmful consequences of teenage pregnancies fall on young females.[1] A law prohibiting the sale of beer to males under twenty-one years of age and to females under eighteen years would not be valid, however.[2]

Generally, since the 1970s, the Supreme Court has scrutinized gender classifications closely and has declared many gender-based laws unconstitutional. In 1979, the Court held that a state law allowing wives to obtain alimony judgments against husbands but preventing husbands from receiving alimony from wives violated the equal protection clause.[3] In 1982, the Court declared that Mississippi's policy of excluding males from the School of Nursing at Mississippi University for Women was unconstitutional.[4]

5-1c The Rational Basis Test (Ordinary Scrutiny)

A third test used to decide whether a discriminatory law violates the equal protection clause is the **rational basis test**. This test is employed only when there is no classification—such as race or gender—that would require a higher level of scrutiny. When applying this test to a law that classifies or treats people or groups differently, the courts ask whether the discrimination is rational. In other words, is it a reasonable way to achieve a legitimate government objective? Few laws tested under the rational basis test—or the *ordinary scrutiny standard,* as it is also called—are found invalid, because few laws are truly unreasonable.

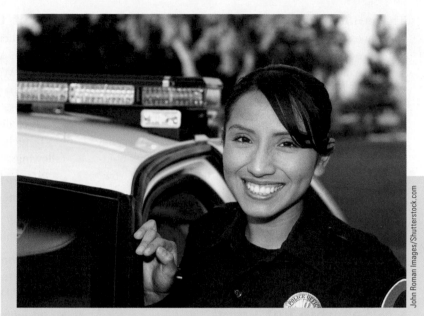

Increasingly, women are filling traditionally male jobs, such as police officer. *What benefits can a police force obtain by hiring more women officers?*

John Roman Images/Shutterstock.com

A municipal ordinance that prohibits certain vendors from selling their wares in a particular area of the city, for example, will be upheld if the city can meet this rational basis test. The rational basis for the ordinance might be the city's legitimate interest in reducing traffic congestion in that particular area.

CRITICAL THINKING

▶ *When evaluating cases of discrimination against gay men or lesbians, some judges have employed the rational basis test, while others have applied intermediate scrutiny. Which standard do you consider appropriate, and why?*

5-2 AFRICAN AMERICANS

LO Discuss the reasons for the civil rights movement and the changes it caused in American politics and government.

The equal protection clause was originally intended to protect the newly freed slaves after the Civil War (1861–1865). In the early years after the war, the U.S. government made an effort to protect the rights of African Americans living in the states of the former Confederacy. The

rational basis test
A test (also known as the *ordinary scrutiny standard*) used by the Supreme Court to decide whether a discriminatory law violates the equal protection clause of the Constitution. It is used only when there is no classification—such as race or gender—that would require a higher level of scrutiny.

Thirteenth Amendment (which granted freedom to the slaves), the Fourteenth Amendment (which guaranteed equal protection under the law), and the Fifteenth Amendment (which stated that voting rights could not be abridged on account of race) were part of that effort.

By the late 1880s, however, southern legislatures had begun to pass a series of *segregation* laws—laws that separated the white community from the black community. Such laws were commonly called "Jim Crow" laws (from a song that was popular in minstrel shows that caricatured African Americans). Some of the most common Jim Crow laws called for racial segregation in the use of public facilities, such as schools, railroads, and, later, buses. These laws were also applied to housing, restaurants, hotels, and many other facilities.

5-2a Separate But Equal

In 1892, a group of Louisiana citizens decided to challenge a state law that required railroads to provide separate railway cars for African Americans. A man named Homer Plessy, who was seven-eighths European and one-eighth African, boarded a train in New Orleans and sat in the railway car reserved for whites. When Plessy refused to move at the request of the conductor, he was arrested for breaking the law.

Four years later, in 1896, the Supreme Court provided a constitutional basis for segregation laws. In *Plessy v. Ferguson,*[5] the Court held that the law did not violate the equal protection clause if *separate* facilities for blacks were *equal* to those for whites.

The lone dissenter, Justice John Marshall Harlan, disagreed: "Our Constitution is colorblind, and neither knows nor tolerates classes among citizens." The majority opinion, however, established the **separate-but-equal doctrine**, which was used to justify segregation in many areas of American life for nearly sixty years. Separate facilities for African Americans, when they were provided at all, were in practice almost never truly equal.

5-2b Violence and Vote Suppression

Segregation was far from the only problem faced by African Americans in the years following the abolition of slavery. Perhaps the most important was denial of the right to vote.

separate-but-equal doctrine A Supreme Court doctrine holding that the equal protection clause of the Fourteenth Amendment did not forbid racial segregation as long as the facilities for blacks were equal to those for whites.

Loss of the Franchise The Fifteenth Amendment explicitly extended the *franchise* (the right to vote) to African Americans, and for several decades following the Civil War, blacks were in fact able to vote throughout much of the former Confederacy. In the 1880s and 1890s, however, Southern leaders launched major efforts to disenfranchise black voters. They used a number of techniques to accomplish this goal, including the following:

▸ *Literacy tests,* which African Americans were guaranteed to fail.

▸ The *poll tax,* a tax on voting, which disenfranchised poor whites as well as blacks.

▸ The *grandfather clause,* which effectively limited voting to those whose ancestors could vote before the Civil War.

▸ The *white primary,* which prevented African Americans from voting in Democratic primary elections.

Social Control through Violence These restrictive laws were backed up by the threat of violence directed at African Americans who were brave enough to try to vote. The *Ku Klux Klan* was famous for its use of force to keep black citizens "in their place," but white violence was not limited to Klan members. The threat of *lynching*—execution and even torture at the hands of a mob—was employed to keep African Americans from voting. Violence and economic coercion were also used to impose an elaborate code of conduct on African Americans. They were expected to behave humbly toward whites.

5-2c The *Brown* Decisions and School Integration

In the late 1930s and the 1940s, the Supreme Court gradually moved away from the separate-but-equal doctrine discussed earlier. The major breakthrough, however, did not come until 1954, in a case involving an African American girl who lived in Topeka, Kansas.

In the 1950s, Topeka's schools, like those in many cities, were segregated. Mr. and Mrs. Oliver Brown wanted their daughter, Linda Carol Brown, to attend a white school a few blocks from their home instead of an all-black school that was twenty-one blocks away. With the help of lawyers from the National Association for the Advancement of Colored People (NAACP), Linda's parents sued the board of education to allow their daughter to attend the nearby school. (NAACP is always pronounced as "N-double-A-C-P.")

In 1954, in *Brown v. Board of Education of Topeka,*[6] the Supreme Court reversed *Plessy v. Ferguson.* The

Court unanimously held that segregation by race in public education is unconstitutional. Chief Justice Earl Warren wrote as follows:

> Does segregation of children in public schools solely on the basis of race, even though the physical facilities and other "tangible" factors may be equal, deprive the children of the minority group of equal educational opportunities? We believe that it does. . . . [Segregation generates in children] a feeling of inferiority as to their status in the community that may affect their hearts and minds in a way unlikely ever to be undone. . . . We conclude that in the field of public education the doctrine of "separate but equal" has no place. Separate educational facilities are inherently unequal.

In 1955, in *Brown v. Board of Education*[7] (sometimes called *Brown II*), the Supreme Court ordered desegregation to begin "with all deliberate speed," an ambiguous phrase that could be (and was) interpreted in a variety of ways.

Reactions to School Integration The Supreme Court ruling did not go unchallenged. Bureaucratic loopholes were used to delay desegregation. Another reaction was "white flight." As white parents sent their children to newly established private schools, some formerly white-only public schools became 100 percent black. In Arkansas, Governor Orval Faubus used the state's National Guard to block the integration of Central High School in Little Rock in 1957. A federal court demanded that the troops be withdrawn. Only after President Dwight D. Eisenhower federalized the Arkansas National Guard and sent in additional troops did Central High finally become integrated.

By 1970, *de jure* **segregation**—segregation that is established by law—had been abolished by school systems. But that meant only that no public school could legally identify itself as being reserved for all whites or all blacks. It did not mean the end of *de facto* **segregation**—segregation that is not imposed by law but is produced by circumstances, such as neighborhoods populated mostly by African Americans. Attempts to overcome *de facto* segregation have included redrawing school district lines, reassigning pupils, and busing.

Busing As it applies to civil rights, **busing** is the transporting of students by bus to schools physically outside their neighborhoods in an effort to achieve racially desegregated schools. The Supreme Court first endorsed busing in 1971 in a case involving the school system in Charlotte, North Carolina.[8] Following this decision, the Court upheld busing in several northern cities.[9]

Nevertheless, busing was unpopular with many groups from its inception. By the mid-1970s, the courts

A member of the Ku Klux Klan in Miami, Florida, in 1939. He was part of a campaign to intimidate potential black voters. *How successful were campaigns such as this in the South?*

had begun to retreat from their former support for busing. In 1974, the Supreme Court rejected the idea of busing children across school district lines.[10] In 1986, the Court refused to review a lower court decision that ended a desegregation plan in Norfolk, Virginia.[11] Today, courts no longer issue busing orders to end *de facto* segregation. Indeed, *de facto* segregation in America's schools is still widespread.

5-2d The Civil Rights Movement

In 1955, one year after the first *Brown* decision, an African American woman named Rosa Parks, a long-time activist in the NAACP, boarded a public bus in Montgomery, Alabama. When it became crowded, she refused to move to the "colored section" at the

de jure segregation Racial segregation that occurs because of laws or decisions by government agencies.

de facto segregation Racial segregation that occurs not as a result of government actions but because of social and economic conditions and residential patterns.

busing The transportation of public school students by bus to schools physically outside their neighborhoods to eliminate school segregation based on residential patterns.

rear of the bus. She was arrested and fined for violating local segregation laws. Her arrest spurred the local African American community to organize a year-long boycott of the entire Montgomery bus system.

The protest was led by a twenty-seven-year-old Baptist minister, the Reverend Dr. Martin Luther King, Jr. During the protest period, he was jailed and his house was bombed. Yet, despite white hostility and what appeared to be overwhelming odds against them, the protesters were triumphant in the end.

In 1956, a federal court prohibited the segregation of buses in Montgomery, and the era of the **civil rights movement**—the movement by minorities and concerned whites to end racial discrimination—had begun. The movement was led by a number of groups and individuals, including Martin Luther King, Jr., and his Southern Christian Leadership Conference (SCLC). Other groups, such as the Congress of Racial Equality (CORE), the NAACP, the Student Nonviolent Coordinating Committee (SNCC), and the Urban League, also sought to secure equal rights for African Americans.

> ## "INJUSTICE ANYWHERE IS A THREAT TO JUSTICE EVERYWHERE."
> ~ MARTIN LUTHER KING, JR.
> U.S. CIVIL RIGHTS LEADER,
> 1929–1968

Nonviolence as a Tactic   Civil rights protesters in the 1960s began to apply the tactic of nonviolent **civil disobedience**—the deliberate and public refusal to obey laws considered unjust—in civil rights actions throughout the South. Activists were trained in the tools of nonviolence—how to use nonthreatening body language, how to go limp when dragged or assaulted, and how to protect themselves from clubs and police dogs.

civil rights movement
The movement in the 1950s and 1960s, by minorities and concerned whites, to end racial discrimination.

civil disobedience
The deliberate and public act of refusing to obey laws thought to be unjust.

sit-in A tactic of nonviolent civil disobedience. Demonstrators enter a business, college building, or other public place and remain seated until they are forcibly removed or until their demands are met.

Greensboro: An Example. In 1960, for example, four African American students in Greensboro, North Carolina, sat at the "whites only" lunch counter at Woolworth's and ordered food. The waitress refused to serve them, and the store closed early, but more students returned the next day to sit at the counter, with supporters picketing outside. **Sit-ins** spread to other lunch counters across the South.

In some instances, students participating in sit-ins were heckled or even dragged from Woolworth's by angry whites. But the protesters never reacted with violence. They simply returned to their seats at the counter, day after day. Within months of the first sit-in, lunch counter managers began to reverse their policies of segregation.

The National Reaction.   As the civil rights movement gained momentum, media images increasingly showed nonviolent protesters being assaulted by police, sprayed with fire hoses, and attacked by dogs. These pictures shocked and angered Americans across the country. The resulting public backlash led to nationwide demands for reform. The March on Washington for Jobs and Freedom, led by Martin Luther King, Jr., in 1963, aimed in part to demonstrate widespread public support for legislation to ban discrimination in all aspects of public life.

Civil Rights Legislation   As the civil rights movement demonstrated its strength, Congress began to pass civil rights laws. While the Fourteenth Amendment prevented the *government* from discriminating against individuals or groups, the private sector—businesses, restaurants, and the like—could still freely refuse to employ and serve nonwhites. Therefore, Congress sought to address this issue.

The Civil Rights Act of 1964.   The Civil Rights Act of 1964 was the first and most comprehensive civil rights law. It forbade discrimination on the basis of race, color, religion, gender, and national origin. The major provisions of the act were as follows:

▶ It outlawed discrimination in public places of accommodation, such as hotels, restaurants, movie theaters, and public transportation.

▶ It provided that federal funds could be withheld from any federal or state government project or facility that practiced any form of discrimination.

▶ It banned discrimination in employment.

▶ It outlawed arbitrary discrimination in voter registration.

▶ It authorized the federal government to sue to desegregate public schools and facilities.

Voting and Housing Rights.   Other significant laws were passed by Congress during the 1960s as well. The Voting Rights Act of 1965 made it illegal to interfere with anyone's right to vote in any election held in this

Civil rights leader the Reverend Dr. Martin Luther King, Jr. (1929–1968), at the March on Washington in 1963. King gave his most celebrated speech ("I have a dream") at this event. *What were the goals of the demonstration?*

5–2e African Americans in Politics Today

As mentioned earlier, in many jurisdictions African Americans were prevented from voting for years after the Civil War, despite the Fifteenth Amendment (1870). These discriminatory practices persisted in the twentieth century. In the early 1960s, only 22 percent of African Americans of voting age in the South were registered to vote, compared with 63 percent of voting-age whites. In Mississippi, the most extreme example, only 6 percent of voting-age African Americans were registered to vote. Such disparities led to the enactment of the Voting Rights Act of 1965, which ended discriminatory voter-registration tests and gave federal voter registrars the power to prevent racial discrimination in voting.

Today, the percentages of eligible blacks and whites registered to vote are nearly equal. As a result of this dramatic change, political participation by African Americans has increased, as has the number of African American elected officials.

Representation in Office   More than nine thousand African Americans now serve in elective office in the United States. Following the 2016 elections, forty-seven African Americans were members of Congress.

A number of African Americans have achieved high office in the executive branch, including Colin Powell, who served as President George W. Bush's first secretary of state, and Condoleezza Rice, his second secretary of state. Of course, in 2008 Barack Obama, a U.S. senator from Illinois, became the first African American president of the United States. Obama's election reflects a significant change in public opinion. Fifty years ago, only 38 percent of Americans said that they would be willing to vote for an African American as president. Today, this number has risen to more than 90 percent. Nonetheless, only two African Americans have been elected to a state

country. (We discuss restrictions on voting rights further in Chapter 8.) The Civil Rights Act of 1968 prohibited discrimination in housing.

The Black Power Movement   Not all African Americans embraced nonviolence. Several outspoken leaders in the mid-1960s were outraged at the slow pace of change in the social and economic status of blacks.

Malcolm X, a speaker and organizer for the Nation of Islam (also called the Black Muslims), rejected the goals of integration and racial equality espoused by the civil rights movement. He called instead for black separatism and "black pride." Although he later moderated some of his views when he converted to a more orthodox version of Islam, his rhetorical style and powerful message influenced many African American young people.

Both Malcolm X and Martin Luther King, Jr., were assassinated—Malcolm X in 1965 and King in 1968. In the late 1960s, a series of "race riots" (actually, insurrections against perceived police abuses) shook African American neighborhoods across the nation. The riots helped destroy much of the goodwill generated by nonviolent civil disobedience. By the end of the decade, the high tide of the civil rights movement was clearly over.

governorship since the Reconstruction period that followed the Civil War.

The Supreme Court Weakens the Voting Rights Act

In June 2013, the Voting Rights Act received a significant setback at the hands of the Supreme Court. In *Shelby County v. Holder*, the Court ruled that Section 4 of the Voting Rights Act was unconstitutional.[12] This section defined which state and local governments were subject to special federal oversight.

These governments could not change voting procedures or district boundaries without *preclearance*, or approval, from the federal government. The governments identified by Section 4 had a history of voting rights violations in the 1960s, but the Court argued that basing current law on events that far in the past was unacceptable. In principle, Congress could adopt a new Section 4. The chances of such a measure passing a highly polarized Congress any time soon are remote, however. Meanwhile, the Department of Justice can still challenge election procedures after they have been implemented, but such lawsuits are less effective than the preclearance system.

The Impact of Voting Restrictions

Progressives feared that the Court's decision would result in new state laws that would make it difficult for many low-income persons to vote. Indeed, in recent years, a substantial number of new laws have threatened to reduce turnout among poor—and minority—voters. These laws have included limits on early voting and requirements that voters produce photographic IDs. In several states, federal judges blocked the new laws in time for the 2016 elections. In North Carolina, a judge stated that the legislature had targeted black voters with "surgical precision." Failure to open enough voting sites in black areas was also a major problem.

5–2f Continuing Challenges

Although African Americans no longer face *de jure* segregation, they continue to struggle for income and educational parity with whites. Recent census data show that average incomes in black households are only 59 percent of those in non-Hispanic white households. The poverty rate for blacks is roughly three times that for whites. The loss of jobs caused by the recent Great Recession tended to make matters worse for African Americans and other minority group members.

Problems with Law Enforcement

Criminal activity is commonplace in the impoverished neighborhoods where many African Americans live. As a result, African Americans are disproportionately victimized by crime. They are also arrested for crimes in numbers that substantially exceed their share of the population.

Some statistics suggest that African Americans probably do commit a disproportionate share of violent crime. Other statistics paint an alternative picture, however. Blacks

2016 ELECTION

The United States failed to reach one milestone in 2016—it did not elect the nation's first woman president. Still, more minority group members were elected. The Latino and Asian American presence in Congress reached new heights. The number of African Americans elected to the House was the same as in 2014, however. The Senate gained one additional black member, Kamala Harris (D., Calif.).

Harris had ancestors from India, and she therefore also qualified as an Asian American. Another notable addition to the Senate was Tammy Duckworth (D., Ill.). Of Thai origin on her mother's side, Duckworth lost both legs in Iraq when her helicopter was shot down. Still, the total number of women in Congress was down by one.

In other respects, the 2016 elections were not encouraging to women and minority group interests. Donald Trump's crude speech and behavior toward women set a poor example. Trump gained initial attention by questioning the citizenship of the first African American president, Barack Obama. He began his presidential campaign by calling Mexican immigrants "rapists."

are nearly four times as likely to be arrested for possession of marijuana as are whites, even though studies show that the two groups use "weed" at similar rates. African Americans make up 12 percent of the total population of drug users, but almost 40 percent of those arrested for drug offenses and 60 percent of those in state prisons for drug offenses.

Indeed, African Americans constitute nearly 1 million of the 2.3 million persons in prison. Add Hispanics, and these two groups make up 60 percent of all prisoners, even though they represent about 30 percent of the U.S. population. Such data raise the suspicion that U.S. law enforcement is biased against minority group members. We examined that question in further detail in the chapter-opening *America at Odds* feature.

Problems with Education The education gap between blacks and whites also persists despite continuing efforts by educators and by government to reduce it. Federal legislation aimed at this goal has included the No Child Left Behind Act, now replaced by the Every Student Succeeds Act. Recent studies show that, on average, African American students in high school read and do math at the level of whites in junior high school. Also, while black students have narrowed the gap with whites in earning high school diplomas, the disparity has widened for college degrees.

These problems tend to feed on one another. Schools in poorer neighborhoods generally have fewer educational resources available, resulting in lower achievement levels for their students. A persistent problem is that as talented teachers gain experience, they often transfer from struggling schools to schools in prosperous neighborhoods where students are better prepared. Thus, some educational experts suggest that it all comes down to money. In fact, many parents of minority students in struggling school districts are less concerned about integration than they are about funds for their children's schools.

Class versus Race in Educational Outcomes
Researchers have known for decades that when students enrolled at a particular school come almost entirely from impoverished families, regardless of race, the performance of the students at that school is seriously depressed. When low-income students attend schools where the majority of the students are middle class, again regardless of race, their performance improves dramatically—without dragging down the performance of the middle-class students. These studies appear to provide evidence for the Supreme Court's earlier ruling in *Brown v. Board of Education*. Because of this research and recent Supreme Court rulings that have struck down some racial integration plans, several school

systems have adopted policies that integrate students on the basis of socioeconomic class, not race.

CRITICAL THINKING

▶ *Why might low-income students do better in their studies, on average, when most of their classmates are middle class instead of poor?*

5–3 WOMEN

LO Describe the political and economic achievements of women in this country over time, and identify some obstacles to equality that women continue to face.

In 1848, Lucretia Mott and Elizabeth Cady Stanton organized the first "woman's rights" convention in Seneca Falls, New York. The three hundred people who attended approved a Declaration of Sentiments: "We hold these truths to be self-evident: that all men *and women* are created equal." In the following years, other women's groups held conventions in various cities in the Midwest and the East. With the outbreak of the Civil War, though, women's rights advocates devoted their energies to the war effort.

5–3a The Struggle for Voting Rights

The movement for political rights gained momentum again in 1869, with the founding of two organizations devoted to gaining **suffrage**—the right to vote—for women. The National Woman Suffrage Association, formed by Susan B. Anthony and Elizabeth Cady Stanton, saw suffrage as only one step on the road toward greater social and political rights for women. In contrast, the American Woman Suffrage Association, founded by Lucy Stone and others, believed that the right to vote should be the only goal.

The Suffrage Campaign By 1890, the two organizations had joined forces, and the resulting National American Woman Suffrage Association had indeed only one goal—enfranchisement (being given the right to vote). When little progress was made, small, radical splinter groups took to the streets. Parades, hunger strikes, arrests, and jailings soon followed.

World War I (1914–1918) marked a turning point in the battle for women's rights. The war offered many opportunities for women. Several thousand women served in the U.S. Navy, and about a million women

suffrage The right to vote; the franchise.

joined the workforce, holding jobs vacated by men who had entered military service.

The Nineteenth Amendment After the war, President Woodrow Wilson wrote to Carrie Chapman Catt, one of the leaders of the women's movement: "It is high time that [that] part of our debt should be acknowledged." Two years later, in 1920, seventy-two years after the Seneca Falls convention, the Nineteenth Amendment to the Constitution was ratified: "The right of citizens of the United States to vote shall not be denied or abridged by the United States or by any State on account of sex."

5–3b The Feminist Movement

For many years after winning the right to vote, women engaged in little independent political activity. In the 1960s, however, a new women's movement arose—the feminist movement. Women who faced discrimination in employment and other circumstances were inspired in part by the civil rights movement and the campaign against the war in Vietnam.

The National Organization for Women (NOW), founded in 1966, was the most important new women's organization. But the feminist movement also consisted of thousands of small, independent "women's liberation" and "consciousness-raising" groups established on campuses and in neighborhoods throughout the nation. Feminism, the goal of the movement, meant full political, economic, and social equality for women.

Combating Gender Discrimination During the 1970s, NOW and other organizations sought to win passage of the Equal Rights Amendment (ERA) to the Constitution, which would have written equality into the heart of the nation's laws. The amendment did not win support from enough state legislatures, however, and it failed. Campaigns to change state and national laws affecting women were much more successful. Congress and the various state legislatures enacted a range of measures to provide equal rights for women. The women's movement also enjoyed considerable success in legal action. Courts at all levels accepted the argument that *gender discrimination* violated the Fourteenth Amendment's equal protection clause.

Abortion and Other Issues In addition to fighting against gender discrimination, the feminist movement took up a number of other issues important to women. Some campaigns, such as the one to curb domestic violence, have been widely supported. Others have resulted in heated debate. Perhaps the most controversial issue of all has been the right to have an abortion, which we discussed in Chapter 4.

feminism A doctrine advocating full political, economic, and social equality for women.

U.S. Department of the Army

A woman soldier presents flag patches to members of the Women's Olympic Basketball Team. In 2013, the Department of Defense ruled that women could apply for front-line combat positions. *Why would some women want to serve in combat units?*

5-3c Women in American Politics Today

More than ten thousand members have served in the U.S. House of Representatives. Only 1 percent of them have been women, and women continue to face a "men's club" atmosphere in Congress. In 2002, however, a woman, Nancy Pelosi (D., Calif.), was elected minority leader of the House of Representatives. She was the first woman to hold this post. Pelosi again made history when, after the Democratic victories in the 2006 elections, she was elected Speaker of the House of Representatives, the first woman ever to lead the House. After the Republicans took control of the House in 2011, Pelosi again became minority leader.

In the 2016 elections, women continued to win a substantial number of seats in Congress. Twenty-one women were elected to the Senate, and eighty-three were elected to the House.

Women have also been underrepresented in the executive branch. Franklin D. Roosevelt (1933–1945) appointed the first woman to a cabinet post—Frances Perkins, who was secretary of labor from 1933 to 1945. A variety of women have held cabinet posts in more recent administrations. All of the last three presidents have appointed women to the most senior cabinet post—secretary of state. Bill Clinton (1993–2001) appointed Madeleine Albright to this position, George W. Bush (2001–2009) picked Condoleezza Rice for the post in his second term, and most recently, Barack Obama chose New York senator Hillary Clinton to be secretary of state during his first term.

In addition, Ronald Reagan (1981–1989) appointed the first woman to sit on the Supreme Court, Sandra Day O'Connor. Bill Clinton appointed Ruth Bader Ginsburg to the Supreme Court. Barack Obama selected Sonia Sotomayor for the Court in 2009 and Elena Kagan in 2010.

5-3d Women in the Workplace

An ongoing challenge for American women is to obtain equal pay and equal opportunity in the workplace. In spite of federal legislation and programs to promote equal treatment of women in the workplace, women continue to face various forms of discrimination.

Wage Discrimination In 1963, Congress passed the Equal Pay Act. The act requires employers to pay an equal wage for substantially equal work—males cannot be paid more than females who perform essentially the same job. The following year, Congress passed the Civil Rights Act of 1964, Title VII of which prohibits employment discrimination on the basis of race, color, national origin, gender, and religion. Still, women continue to face wage discrimination.

The Lilly Ledbetter Fair Pay Act of 2009. In 2007, however, the Supreme Court ruled that employers could not be sued under Title VII if the decision to discriminate in pay was made more than 180 days before the claim was made.[13] The plaintiff in this case was Lilly Ledbetter. In 2009, President Obama signed a law that negated the Court's decision. Under the new law, the 180-day statute of limitations resets with each new discriminatory paycheck.

Pay Equity Today. It is estimated that for every dollar earned by men, women earn about 77 cents. Although the wage gap has narrowed significantly since 1963, it still remains. This is particularly true for women in management positions and older women. Notably, when the workers in a particular occupation include a disproportionately high number of women, the wages that are paid in that occupation tend to be relatively low.

Recent research suggests that wage inequality is concentrated in fields in which staff members are expected to put in very long hours. Finance, where long hours are expected, may have the most unequal pay structure of any industry. In contrast, pay differentials are zero among dental hygienists and advertising salespeople. In effect, women may be penalized because child-care responsibilities make it hard for them to work far more than forty hours a week.[14]

The Glass Ceiling Even though an increasing number of women now hold business and professional jobs once held only by men, relatively few of these women are able to rise to the top of the career ladder in their firms. They are held back by the so-called **glass ceiling**—an invisible but real discriminatory barrier that prevents women and minorities from rising to top positions of power or responsibility. Today, less than one-sixth of the top executive positions in the largest American corporations are held by women.

Sexual Harassment Title VII's prohibition of gender discrimination has also been extended to prohibit sexual harassment. **Sexual harassment** occurs

---

glass ceiling
An invisible but real discriminatory barrier that prevents women and minorities from rising to top positions of power or responsibility.

sexual harassment
Unwanted physical contact, verbal conduct, or abuse of a sexual nature that interferes with a recipient's job performance, creates a hostile environment, or carries with it an implicit or explicit threat of adverse employment consequences.

when job opportunities, promotions, salary increases, or even the ability to retain a job depends on whether an employee complies with demands for sexual favors. A special form of sexual harassment, called *hostile environment harassment,* occurs when an employee is subjected to sexual conduct or comments in the workplace that interfere with the employee's job performance or that create an intimidating, hostile, or offensive environment.

On a number of occasions, the Supreme Court has upheld the right of persons to be free from sexual harassment on the job. In 1998, the Court made it clear that sexual harassment includes harassment by members of the same sex.[15] In the same year, the Court held that employers are liable for the harassment of employees by supervisors unless the employers can show that (1) they exercised reasonable care in preventing such problems (by implementing antiharassment policies and procedures, for example), and (2) the employees failed to take advantage of any corrective opportunities provided by the employers.[16]

The Civil Rights Act of 1991 greatly expanded the remedies available for victims of sexual harassment. Under the act, victims can seek damages as well as back pay, job reinstatement, and other compensation.

Sexual Assault on Campus Title IX of the Education Amendments of 1972 prohibits gender-based discrimination in schools that receive federal money. Title IX is best known for requiring equal opportunities in sports for men and women. Sexual assault is also considered discrimination under Title IX, however.

Sexual assault on campus, ranging from unwanted touching to acts of violence, is a long-standing problem. Use of alcohol is a major contributing factor. Under the broadest definition, about one in five college women has experienced sexual assault. Yet few women report assault to school authorities, and those who do often receive little help. In some cases, victims have actually been penalized for making complaints.

Beginning in 2011, the Obama administration began cracking down on the problem. By 2015, 106 colleges and universities were under investigation for mishandling complaints. Many were also under investigation for retaliating against persons reporting an assault. Schools that fail to improve their procedures are at risk of losing federal funds.

Today, many students are unwilling to accept policies or language that they consider discriminatory, whether the target is women or minority group members. Criticisms of *language* that is alleged to be discriminatory or hostile, however, have led to a reaction. Many observers, especially conservatives, reject attempts to "police" such language. They claim that such responses, which they call *political correctness,* violate free speech rights. We look at this issue more closely in this chapter's *Join the Debate* feature.

CRITICAL THINKING

▶ *In recent years, the percentage of young women who have received college diplomas has exceeded the percentage for young men. In the future, how might this development change the social and economic roles of women and men?*

5–4 SECURING RIGHTS FOR OTHER GROUPS

LO Summarize the struggles for equality that other groups in America have experienced.

In addition to African Americans and women, a number of other groups in U.S. society have faced discriminatory treatment. One lingering result of past discrimination can be that a group suffers from below-average incomes and relatively high rates of poverty. Figure 5–1 shows the

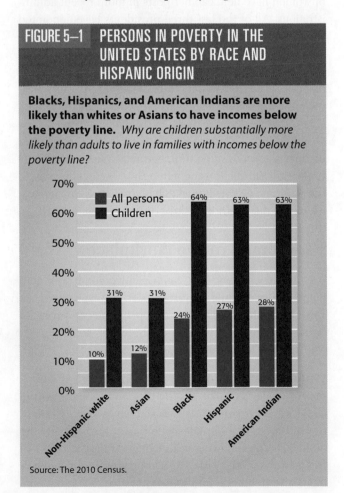

FIGURE 5–1 PERSONS IN POVERTY IN THE UNITED STATES BY RACE AND HISPANIC ORIGIN

Blacks, Hispanics, and American Indians are more likely than whites or Asians to have incomes below the poverty line. *Why are children substantially more likely than adults to live in families with incomes below the poverty line?*

	All persons	Children
Non-Hispanic white	10%	31%
Asian	12%	31%
Black	24%	64%
Hispanic	27%	63%
American Indian	28%	63%

Source: The 2010 Census.

JOIN THE DEBATE

Is "Political Correctness" a Real Problem?

Political correctness has been much in the news of late. Republican presidential candidate Donald Trump, for example, after insulting Fox News reporter Megyn Kelly, dismissed criticism of his language, saying that such criticism was "politically correct." Ben Carson, another candidate, was criticized for saying that no Muslim should be president. His response was that the "culture of political correctness" is "destroying this nation." A much wider group of commentators, including some liberals as well as conservatives, argues that political correctness (or PC) has created a "reign of terror" on college and university campuses. Are these people right? Is political correctness a real problem?

The Language Police Are Perverting Liberalism

New York Magazine columnist Jonathan Chait certainly believes that PC is a major problem. Chait contends that PC leftists threaten the very foundations of liberalism by rejecting free speech as a universal value. "Political correctness is a style of politics in which the more radical members of the left attempt to regulate political discourse by defining opposing views as bigoted and illegitimate," he writes.

Chait's examples of PC behavior go beyond verbal criticism of alleged racism or sexism. One example is a University of Michigan student who lost a job with the student newspaper and was subjected to vandalism. The student had written an article in a conservative publication making fun of political correctness. Other examples include student campaigns to disinvite commencement speakers such as Bill Maher and Ayaan Hirsi Ali. These proposed speakers had called Islam an illegitimate religion. Chait concludes that the new political correctness "has bludgeoned even many of its own supporters into despondent silence." Yet politics is "based on getting people to agree with you, not making them afraid to disagree."

Political Correctness Doesn't Hinder Free Speech—It Expands It

Those who do not think that political correctness is a real problem make a distinction. Acts of hooliganism—such as the vandalism experienced by the Michigan student—are violations of the law and should be treated as such. Also, schools invite commencement speakers in part to honor them, but no one has the *right* to be honored. Typically, however, PC means calling people out on their offensiveness. When Trump calls a reporter a "bimbo," in what universe is that anything other than colossal rudeness?

As to "defining opposing views as bigoted and illegitimate," journalist Lindsay Beyerstein notes that "some views are bigoted and illegitimate." The so-called N-word, once constantly applied to African Americans, is today largely unprintable. That is PC in action. It is also not a problem.

PC's defenders say that it expands free speech rather than hindering it. You may have the right to make offensive comments, but others have the right to respond. Lindy West writes that "a bunch of college students, on the cusp of finding their voices, [are] being publicly berated by high-profile writers . . . because they don't like what [the students] have to say. Are you sure you know who's silencing whom?"

Critical Analysis

President Obama refuses to use the term "radical Islamic terrorism" (he is fine with "Islamist"). Is this an example of PC run amok—or a legitimate attempt to avoid blaming all Muslims for the crimes of a few?

percentage of persons with incomes below the poverty line for five major racial or ethnic groups. The chart provides statistics for children as well as the overall population. Note that in all groups, children are much more likely than adults to live in poverty. This reality makes poverty that much more damaging.

Next, we look at three groups that have had to struggle for equal treatment—Latinos, Asian Americans, and American Indians (or Native Americans). Then we examine the struggles of several other groups of Americans—persons with disabilities and gay men and lesbians.

5–4a Latinos

Latinos, or Hispanics, constitute the largest ethnic minority in the United States. Whereas African Americans represent 13.2 percent of the U.S. population, Latinos now constitute 17.4 percent. Each year, the Hispanic population grows by more than 1 million people, one-third of whom are newly arrived legal immigrants. By 2050, Latinos are expected to constitute almost 30 percent of the U.S. population. Still, Hispanic immigration has declined in recent years. For example, the number of persons returning to Mexico every year now exceeds the number of new arrivals.

Who Are the Hispanics? According to the U.S. Census Bureau definition, Hispanics can be of any race. Note that while *Hispanic* is official U.S. government terminology, some members of this group prefer the term *Latino*—or *Latina* in the feminine case. Opinion polls report that among Hispanics, the two terms are roughly equal in popularity. Actually, though, most Latinos prefer to identify with their country of origin rather than be categorized as either Hispanics or Latinos.

Countries of Origin. As you can see in Figure 5–2, the largest Hispanic group consists of Mexican Americans, who constitute 64.1 percent of the Latino population living in the United States. Some 9.5 percent of Latinos are Puerto Ricans. Persons from El Salvador make up 3.7 percent, and 3.7 percent are Cuban Americans. Most of the remaining Hispanics are from Central and South American countries.

Low Incomes. Economically, Hispanic households are often members of this country's working poor. As

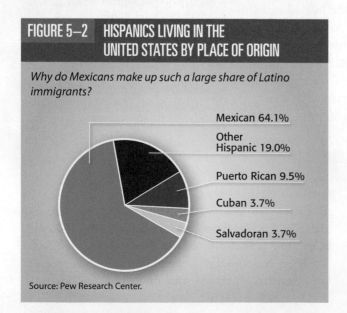

FIGURE 5–2   HISPANICS LIVING IN THE UNITED STATES BY PLACE OF ORIGIN

Why do Mexicans make up such a large share of Latino immigrants?

Mexican 64.1%
Other Hispanic 19.0%
Puerto Rican 9.5%
Cuban 3.7%
Salvadoran 3.7%

Source: Pew Research Center.

Figure 5–1 shows, many have incomes below the government's official poverty line. Latino leaders tend to attribute the low income levels to language problems, lack of job training, and continuing immigration. Immigration disguises statistical progress because language problems and lack of job training are usually more notable among new immigrants than among those who have lived in the United States for many years.

Party Identification In their party identification, Latinos tend to follow some fairly well-established patterns. Traditionally, Mexican Americans and Puerto Ricans identify with the Democratic Party, which has favored more government assistance and support programs for disadvantaged groups.

The Cuban Exception. Cubans, in contrast, tend to identify with the Republican Party. This is largely because of a different history. Cuban émigrés fled from Cuba during and after the Communist revolution led by Fidel Castro. The strong anti-Communist sentiments of the Cubans propelled them toward the more conservative party—the Republicans. Today, relations with Communist Cuba continue to be a key political issue for Cuban Americans. Cubans of the younger generation, however, are much more open to voting for Democrats than their parents were.

The Immigration Issue. A problem for the Hispanic community is that many of its members arrived in this country illegally. (It is almost impossible for a poorly educated Mexican or Central American to gain legal admission.) Demand for the labor of such persons has been high, however, and in fact most unauthorized immigrants came to the United States to work. Others are small children. Many families have members who are U.S. citizens, often children born in this country, while other family members are unauthorized. As a result, deporting illegal immigrants can split up families—or force U.S. citizens into exile.

It follows that immigration reform has been an important issue for many Latinos. In recent years, the Republican Party has taken a stand against any reform that would let unauthorized immigrants regularize their status. This stand has pushed many Latinos toward the Democrats. We discuss immigration in more depth in Chapter 15.

Latinos in American Politics Today Generally, Latinos in the United States have had a comparatively low level of political participation. This is understandable, given that more than one-third of Hispanics are below voting age and also that more than one-fourth are not citizens and thus cannot vote. Although voter turnout among Latinos is generally low compared with the population at large, the Latino voting rate is rising as more immigrants become citizens and as more Hispanics reach voting age. Indeed, when comparing citizens of equal incomes and educational backgrounds, Latino citizens' participation rate is higher than average. In the 2012 elections, Latinos made up 10 percent of the electorate, up from 9 percent in 2008 and 8 percent in 2004. In the midterm elections of 2014, however, when voter turnout was depressed, Latino participation fell back to 8 percent.

Latinos increasingly hold political office, particularly in states with large Hispanic populations. Today, more than 5 percent of the state legislators in Arizona, California, Colorado, Florida, New Mexico, and Texas are of Hispanic ancestry. Cuban Americans have been notably successful in gaining local political power, particularly in Dade County, Florida. Latinos are also increasing their presence in Congress, albeit slowly. Following the 2014 elections, Hispanic representation in Congress was at a new high, with thirty-two members. After the 2016 elections, Latino representation in Congress reached thirty-eight members. Two senators of Cuban heritage—Ted Cruz (R., Tex.) and Marco Rubio (R., Fla.)—were candidates for president in 2016.

5-4b Asian Americans

Asian Americans have also suffered, at times severely, from discriminatory treatment. The Chinese Exclusion Act of 1882 prevented people from China and Japan from coming to the United States to prospect for gold or to work on the railroads or in factories in the West. After 1900, immigration continued to be restricted—only limited numbers of Chinese or Japanese individuals were allowed to enter the United States. Those who were allowed into the country faced racial prejudice from Americans who had little respect for their customs and culture. In 1906, after the San Francisco earthquake, Japanese American students were segregated into special schools so that white children could use their buildings.

Internment of Japanese Americans   The Japanese bombing of Pearl Harbor in 1941, which launched the entry of the United States into World War II (1939–1945), intensified Americans' fear of the Japanese.

Some Asian Americans argue that they face discrimination in Ivy League admissions. *How important is it to get into a top college?*

Actions taken under an executive order issued by President Franklin D. Roosevelt in 1942 subjected many Japanese Americans to curfews, excluded them from certain "military areas," and evacuated most of the West Coast Japanese American population to internment camps (also called "relocation centers").[17] In 1988, Congress provided funds to compensate former camp inhabitants—$1.25 billion for approximately 60,000 people.

A "Model Minority"?   Today, Asian Americans lead other minority groups in median income and median education. Indeed, Asians who have immigrated to the United States since 1965 (including immigrants from India) represent the most highly skilled immigrant groups in American history. Nearly 40 percent of Asian Americans over the age of twenty-five have college degrees.

Recently, Asians have replaced Hispanics as the group with the greatest number of immigrants entering the United States each year.

The image of Asian Americans as a "model minority" has created certain problems for its members, however. Some argue that top private colleges and universities have discriminated against Asian Americans in admissions because so many of them apply. By one estimate, Asian Americans make up as many as 30 percent of the top college candidates as determined by SAT scores. In the Ivy League, however, Asian admissions have consistently run below 20 percent. Still, many good schools below the Ivy level admit Asian Americans freely.

More than a million Indochinese war refugees, most from Vietnam, have immigrated to the United States since the 1970s. Many came with relatives and were sponsored by American families or organizations. Thus, they had support systems to help them get started. Some immigrants from other parts of Indochina, however, have experienced difficulties because they come from cultures that have had very little contact with the practices of developed industrial societies.

5-4c American Indians

When we consider population figures since 1492, we see that American Indians experienced one catastrophe after another. We cannot know exactly how many people lived in the New World when Columbus arrived. Current research estimates the population of what is now the continental United States to have been anywhere from 3 million to 8 million. The Europeans brought with them diseases to which these Native Americans had no immunity. As a result, after a series of terrifying epidemics, the population of the continental United States was reduced to perhaps eight hundred thousand people by 1600. Death rates elsewhere in the New World were comparable. When the Pilgrims arrived at Plymouth, the Massachusetts coast was lined with abandoned village sites due to a recent epidemic.[18]

In subsequent centuries, the American Indian population continued to decline, bottoming out at about half a million in 1925. These were centuries in which the European American and African American populations experienced explosive growth. By 2016, the Native American population had recovered to almost 3 million, or more than 5 million if we count individuals who are only part Indian.

In 1789, Congress designated the native tribes as foreign nations so that the government could sign land and boundary treaties with them. As members of foreign nations, Native Americans had no civil rights under U.S. laws. This situation continued until 1924, when the citizenship rights spelled out in the Fourteenth Amendment to the Constitution were finally extended to American Indians.

Early Policies toward Native Americans
The Northwest Ordinance, passed by Congress under the Articles of Confederation in 1787, stated that "the utmost good faith shall always be observed towards the Indians; their lands and property shall never be taken from them without their consent." Over the next hundred years, these principles were violated more often than they were observed.

In 1830, Congress instructed the Bureau of Indian Affairs (BIA), which Congress had established in 1824 as part of the War Department, to remove all tribes to reservations west of the Mississippi River in order to

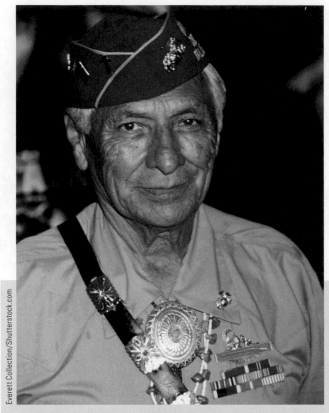

This member of the Navajo Code Talkers is proud of his heritage. His native language was an unbreakable code for transmitting information on the battlefields during World War II. *Why might many Americans be sympathetic to the Indian rights movement?*

free land east of the Mississippi for white settlement. The resettlement was a catastrophe for Indians in the eastern states.

In the late 1880s, the U.S. government changed its policy. The goal became the "assimilation" of American Indians into American society. Each family was given a parcel of land within the reservation to farm. The remaining acreage was sold to whites, thus reducing the number of acres in reservation status from 140 million to about 47 million. Tribes that would not cooperate with this plan lost their reservations altogether.

American Indian Activism   Native Americans have always found it difficult to obtain political power. In part, this is because the tribes are small and scattered, making organized political movements difficult. Today, American Indians remain fragmented politically because large numbers of their population live off the reservations. Nonetheless, beginning in the 1960s, some Indians formed organizations to strike back at the U.S. government and to reclaim their heritage, including their lands.

Compensation for Injustices of the Past   As more Americans became aware of the sufferings of Native Americans, Congress began to compensate them for past injustices. In 1990, Congress passed the Native American Languages Act, which declared that American Indian languages are unique and serve an important role in maintaining Indian culture and continuity. Courts, too, have shown a greater willingness to recognize Native American treaty rights. For example, in 1985, the Supreme Court ruled that three tribes of Oneida Indians could claim damages for the use of tribal land that had been unlawfully transferred in 1795.[19]

The Indian Gaming Regulatory Act of 1988 allows American Indians to have gambling operations on their reservations. Although the profits from casinos have helped to improve the economic and social status of many Native Americans, poverty and unemployment remain widespread on the reservations.

5-4d Obtaining Rights for Persons with Disabilities

Discrimination based on disability crosses the boundaries of race, ethnicity, gender, and religion. Persons with disabilities, especially those with facial deformities or severe mental impairments, face social bias. Although attitudes toward persons with disabilities have changed considerably in the last several decades, such persons continue to suffer from discrimination.

Persons with disabilities first became a political force in the 1970s, and in 1973 Congress passed the initial legislation protecting this group—the Rehabilitation Act. This act prohibited discrimination against persons with disabilities in programs receiving federal aid. The Individuals with Disabilities Education Act (formerly called the Education for All Handicapped Children Act of 1975) requires public schools to provide children with disabilities with free, appropriate, and individualized education in the least restrictive environment appropriate to their needs. The Americans with Disabilities Act (ADA) of 1990, however, is by far the most significant legislation protecting the rights of this group of Americans.

The Americans with Disabilities Act   The ADA requires that all public buildings and public services be accessible to persons with disabilities. The act also mandates that employers "reasonably accommodate" the needs of workers or job applicants with disabilities who are otherwise qualified for particular jobs unless to do so would cause the employer to suffer an "undue hardship."

The ADA defines persons with disabilities as persons who have physical or mental impairments that "substantially limit" their everyday activities. Health conditions that have been considered disabilities under federal law include blindness, a history of alcoholism, heart disease, cancer, muscular dystrophy, cerebral palsy, paraplegia, diabetes, and acquired immune deficiency syndrome (AIDS). The ADA, however, does not require employers to hire or retain workers who, because of their disabilities, pose a "direct threat to the health or safety" of their co-workers.

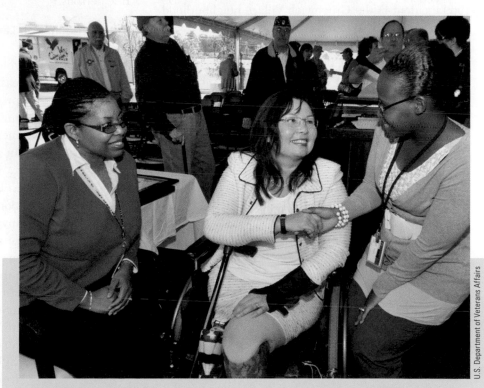

U.S. Department of Veterans Affairs

Tammy Duckworth (D., Ill.), center, greets staff members at a Georgia Vet Center. Representative Duckworth lost both legs after her helicopter was shot down in Iraq in 2004.

Limiting the Scope of the ADA From 1999 to 2002, the Supreme Court handed down a series of rulings that substantially limited the scope of the ADA. The Court found that any limitation that could be remedied by medication or by corrective devices such as eyeglasses did not qualify as a protected disability. According to the Court, even carpal tunnel syndrome was not a disability.[20] In 2008, however, the ADA Amendments Act overturned most of these limits. Carpal tunnel syndrome and other ailments may again qualify as disabilities. (The need for eyeglasses was not, however, covered by the new law.)

In 2001, the Supreme Court reviewed a case raising the question of whether suits under the ADA could be brought against state government employers. The Court concluded that states are immune from lawsuits brought to enforce rights under this federal law.[21]

5-4e Gay Men and Lesbians

Today, many Americans—including six members of Congress—are openly gay, lesbian, or bisexual. Until the late 1960s and early 1970s, though, gay men and lesbians tended to keep quiet about their sexual orientation because exposure usually meant facing harsh consequences. This attitude began to change after a 1969 incident in the Greenwich Village neighborhood of New York City. When the police raided the Stonewall Inn—a bar popular with gay men and lesbians—on June 27 of that year, the bar's patrons responded by throwing beer cans and bottles at the police. The riot

Supporters of same-sex marriage celebrate at the United States Supreme Court after it legalized same-sex marriage in all fifty states in June 2015. *Why has same-sex marriage been an issue for our federal system?*

continued for two days. The Stonewall Inn uprising launched the "gay power" movement. By the end of the year, gay men and lesbians had formed fifty organizations, including the Gay Activist Alliance and the Gay Liberation Front.

A Changing Legal Landscape The number of gay and lesbian organizations has grown from fifty in 1969 to several thousand today. These groups have exerted significant political pressure on legislatures, the media, schools, and churches. In the decades following Stonewall, more than half of the forty-nine states that had sodomy laws repealed them. (*Sodomy laws* prohibit intimate homosexual conduct and certain other forms of sexual activity.) In seven other states, the courts invalidated such laws. Then, in 2003, the United States Supreme Court issued a ruling that effectively invalidated all remaining sodomy laws in the country.

Gaining Legal Status. In *Lawrence v. Texas*,[22] the Court ruled that sodomy laws violated the Fourteenth Amendment's due process clause. According to the Court, "The liberty protected by the Constitution allows homosexual persons the right to choose to enter upon relationships in the confines of their homes and their own private lives and still retain their dignity as free persons."

Antidiscrimination Laws. Today, twenty-one states and more than 170 cities and counties in the United States have laws prohibiting discrimination against homosexuals in at least some contexts. The laws may prohibit discrimination in housing, education, banking, employment, or public accommodations. In a landmark case in 1996, *Romer v. Evans*,[23] the Supreme Court held that a Colorado constitutional amendment that would have invalidated all state and local laws protecting homosexuals from discrimination violated the equal protection clause of the U.S. Constitution. The Court stated that the amendment would have denied to homosexuals in Colorado—but to no other Colorado residents—"the right to seek specific protection from the law."

Changing Attitudes Laws and court decisions protecting the rights of gay men and lesbians reflect social attitudes that are much changed from the 1960s. Liberal political leaders began supporting gay rights starting at least two decades ago. Also, conservative politicians have increasingly softened their stance on the issue. For example, Republican U.S. senators from Alaska, Illinois, and Ohio have supported same-sex marriage.

Public support for same-sex marriage, which was endorsed by only 27 percent of Americans in 1996, has risen ever since. In a striking development, several polling organizations reported in mid-2011 that for the first time ever, an absolute majority of those questioned supported same-sex marriage. Support today is at an all-time high. In May 2015, for example, Gallup reported 60 percent support among those polled.

Same-sex Marriage   By 2015, supporters of same-sex marriage outnumbered opponents in all but fourteen states. On June 26, 2015, in *Obergefell v. Hodges*, the Supreme Court ruled by a five-to-four margin that the Constitution guarantees a right to same-sex marriage in every state.[24] At the time of the ruling, gay marriage was still illegal in thirteen Midwestern and Southern states. The speed with which same-sex marriage became established was striking. As of 2003, the number of states recognizing the right was zero.

We described the progress and success of the same-sex marriage campaign in Chapter 3. As noted, Massachusetts became the first state to recognize same-sex marriage in 2003.[25] In 2013, the Supreme Court granted a major victory to the cause of marriage equality in *United States v. Windsor*. That decision overturned the section of the national Defense of Marriage Act (DOMA) that banned the federal government from recognizing same-sex marriages performed under state law.[26] Finally, *Obergefell v. Hodges* settled the issue nationwide.

In many states, legalization of same-sex marriage was preceded by laws establishing same-sex domestic partnerships. Vermont pioneered this institution in 2000. These partnerships provided many, if not all, of the benefits of marriage under state law, but denied couples the dignity of the marriage title. *Obergefell v. Hodges* did not automatically eliminate this status or convert domestic partnerships into marriages. The ruling did, however, make the institution of domestic partnership a minor part of the legal landscape.

Gays and Lesbians in the Military   Gay men and lesbians who wish to join the military have faced a number of obstacles. Until recently, one was the "don't ask, don't tell" policy. This policy, which banned openly gay men and lesbians from the military, was implemented in 1993 by President Bill Clinton when it became clear that more liberal alternatives would not be accepted. During his presidential campaign, Barack Obama pledged to abolish the policy. Later, gay and lesbian rights activists accused him of "putting the issue on a back burner."

The courts forced the issue, however.[27] The possibility that "don't ask, don't tell" might be thrown out by the courts led Congress to take action. In the "lame duck" session between the November 2010 elections and the swearing-in of new members in January 2011, Congress repealed the policy. As a result, gay men and lesbians may now serve openly in the nation's armed forces.

CRITICAL THINKING

▶ *The number of Latinos in the United States continues to grow. What impact do you think this will have on American culture and politics?*

5-5   BEYOND EQUAL PROTECTION —AFFIRMATIVE ACTION

LO Explain what affirmative action is and why it has been so controversial.

One provision of the Civil Rights Act of 1964 called for prohibiting discrimination in employment. Soon after the act was passed, the federal government began to legislate programs promoting *equal employment opportunity*.

Such programs require that employers' hiring and promotion practices guarantee the same opportunities to all individuals. Experience soon showed that minorities often had fewer opportunities to obtain education and relevant work experience than did whites. Because of this, minorities were still excluded from many jobs. Even though discriminatory practices were made illegal, the change in the law did not make up for the results of years of discrimination. Consequently, under President Lyndon B. Johnson (1963–1969), a new policy was developed.

Called **affirmative action**, this policy required employers to take positive steps to remedy *past* discrimination. Affirmative action programs involved giving special consideration, in jobs and college admissions, to

> **affirmative action**
> A policy that gives special consideration, in jobs and college admissions, to members of groups that have been discriminated against in the past.

members of groups that were discriminated against in the past.

5–5a Affirmative Action Tested

The Supreme Court first addressed the issue of affirmative action in 1978 in *Regents of the University of California v. Bakke*.[28] Allan Bakke, a white male, had been denied admission to the University of California's medical school at Davis. The school had set aside sixteen of the one hundred seats in each year's entering class for applicants who wished to be considered as members of designated minority groups. Many of the students admitted through this special program had lower test scores than Bakke.

Bakke sued the university, claiming that he was a victim of **reverse discrimination**—discrimination against whites. Bakke argued that the use of a **quota system**, in which a specific number of seats were reserved for minority applicants only, violated the equal protection clause. A majority on the Supreme Court concluded that although both the Constitution and the Civil Rights Act of 1964 allow race to be used as a factor in making admissions decisions, race cannot be the *sole* factor. Because the university's quota system was based solely on race, it was unconstitutional.

5–5b Strict Scrutiny Applied

In 1995, the Supreme Court issued a landmark decision in *Adarand Constructors, Inc. v. Peña*.[29] The Court held that any federal, state, or local affirmative action program that uses racial classifications as the basis for making decisions is subject to "strict scrutiny" by the courts. As discussed earlier in this chapter, this means that, to be constitutional, a discriminatory law or action must be narrowly tailored to meet a *compelling* government interest.

In effect, the *Adarand* decision narrowed the application of affirmative action programs. An affirmative action program can no longer make use of quotas or preferences and cannot be maintained simply to remedy past discrimination by society in general. It must be narrowly tailored to remedy actual discrimination that has occurred, and once the program has succeeded, it must be changed or dropped.

reverse discrimination
Discrimination against those who have no minority status.

quota system A policy under which a specific number of jobs, promotions, or other types of placements, such as university admissions, are given to members of selected groups.

5–5c The Diversity Issue

Following the *Adarand* decision, several lower courts faced cases raising the question of whether affirmative action programs designed to achieve diversity on college campuses were constitutional.

The University of Michigan Cases In 2003, the Supreme Court reviewed two cases involving such issues. Both cases involved admissions programs at the University of Michigan.

In *Gratz v. Bollinger*,[30] two white applicants who were denied undergraduate admission to the university alleged reverse discrimination. The university's system automatically awarded every minority applicant one-fifth of the points needed to guarantee admission. The Court held that this policy violated the equal protection clause.

In contrast, in *Grutter v. Bollinger*,[31] the Court held that the University of Michigan Law School's admissions policy was constitutional. The difference between the two admissions policies was that the law school's approach did not apply a mechanical formula giving "diversity bonuses." The Court concluded that diversity on college campuses was a legitimate goal and that limited affirmative action programs could be used to attain this goal.

The Supreme Court Revisits the Issue In 2007, another case involving affirmative action in education came before the Court. The case concerned the policies of two school districts—one in Louisville, Kentucky, and one in Seattle, Washington. Both schools were trying to achieve a more diversified student body by giving preference to minority students if space in the schools was limited and a choice among applicants had to be made. Parents of white children who were turned away from schools because of these policies sued the school districts, claiming that the policies violated the equal protection clause. Ultimately, the Supreme Court held in favor of the parents.[32] The Court's decision did not overrule the 2003 case involving the University of Michigan Law School, however.

The Court's most recent rulings on affirmative action came in two cases, both named *Fisher v. University of Texas*. The Court sent the first case back to the lower courts for further argument in 2013. In the second case, in 2016, the Court found that diversity was a legitimate goal, and that the university's policies were "narrowly tailored" to reach that goal, as the law requires.[33]

5–5d State Actions

Beginning in the mid-1990s, some states have taken actions to ban affirmative action programs or replace them with alternative policies.

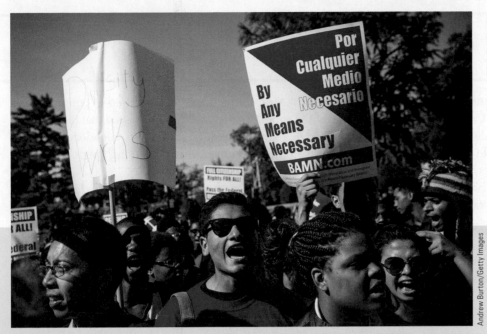

Supporters of affirmative action outside the United States Supreme Court building. The Court was hearing arguments as to whether voters in Michigan have the right to end affirmative action in that state. *Is diversity a legitimate argument in favor of affirmative action? Why or why not?*

Andrew Burton/Getty Images

ways to attract more minority students to their campuses. For example, Texas has established a program under which the top students at every high school in the state are guaranteed admission to the University of Texas, Austin. Originally, the guarantee applied to students who were in the top 10 percent of their graduating class. Today, the percentage varies from year to year. Beginning in 2005, the university reinstated an affirmative action plan, but it was limited to students who were not admitted as part of the top-student guarantee.

The guarantee ensures that the top students at minority-dominated inner-city schools can attend the state's leading public university. It also assures admission to the best white students from rural, often poor, communities. Previously, many of these students could not have hoped to attend the University of Texas. The losers are students from upscale metropolitan neighborhoods or suburbs who have high test scores but are not the top students at their schools. One result is that more students with high test scores enroll in less famous schools, such as Texas Tech University and the University of Texas, Dallas—to the benefit of these schools' reputations.

Bans on Affirmative Action In 1996, by a ballot initiative, California amended its state constitution to prohibit any "preferential treatment to any individual or group on the basis of race, sex, color, ethnicity, or national origin in the operation of public employment, public education, or public contracting." Seven other states have also ended affirmative action.

In 2006, a ballot initiative in Michigan banned affirmative action in that state just three years after the Supreme Court decisions discussed above. In 2012, a federal appeals court overturned the voter-approved ban. In April 2014, however, the Supreme Court reversed the appeals court ruling, arguing that state voters had the right to eliminate affirmative action programs.[34] This decision gave support to bans on affirmative action in other states.

"Race-Blind" Admissions In the meantime, many public universities are trying to find "race-blind"

▶ *Is the Texas plan to admit the top students from each high school to the University of Texas fair? Why or why not?*

AMERICA AT ODDS | Civil Rights

During the first part of the twentieth century, discrimination against African Americans and members of other minority groups was a social norm in the United States. Indeed, much of the nation's white population believed that the ability to discriminate was a constitutionally protected right. Today, the "right to discriminate" has very few defenders. America's laws—and its culture—now hold that discrimination on the basis of race, gender, religion, national origin, and many other characteristics is flatly unacceptable.

Even if civil rights are now broadly supported and protected by law, however, questions remain as to how far these protections should extend. Americans are at odds over a number of civil rights issues, including the following:

- *Is police misconduct directed against minorities— especially black men—a burning issue, or is its importance overrated?*

- *When the Department of Defense decided to allow women soldiers to serve in combat roles, was that a positive development—or a mistake?*

- *Was the Supreme Court right to legalize same-sex marriages nationwide—or was that a step too far?*

- *Is affirmative action still a necessary policy—or should it be abandoned?*

- *When colleges and universities consider admissions, is it legitimate to promote racial, ethnic, gender, or socio-economic diversity—or are such considerations just new forms of discrimination?*

STUDY TOOLS 5

READY TO STUDY? IN THE BOOK, YOU CAN:

☐ Review what you've read with the following chapter quiz.

☐ Check your answers in Appendix D at the back of the book.

☐ Rip out the Chapter Review Card, which includes key terms and chapter summaries.

ONLINE AT WWW.CENGAGEBRAIN.COM, YOU CAN:

☐ Learn about the evolution of same-sex marriage in a few short videos.

☐ Explore various online webpages of the NAACP and the League of United Latin American Citizens, Internet Resource tools.

☐ Interact with figures from the text, and watch quick animation clips.

☐ Prepare for tests with quizzes.

☐ Review the key terms with Flash Cards.

FILL-IN

Learning Outcome 5–1

1. A law based on a _____, such as race, is subject to strict scrutiny by the courts.

Learning Outcome 5–2

2. In *Plessy v. Ferguson* (1896), the Supreme Court established the _____ doctrine, which was used to justify racial segregation in many areas of life for nearly sixty years.

3. The Civil Rights Act of 1964 forbade discrimination on the basis of _____.

Learning Outcome 5–3

4. The feminist movement that began in the 1960s sought _____ for women.

5. It is estimated that for every dollar earned by men, women earn about _____.

Learning Outcome 5–4

6. _____ constitute the largest ethnic minority in the United States.

7. Actions taken under an executive order issued by President Franklin D. Roosevelt in 1942 subjected many

_____ Americans to curfews and evacuated those on the West Coast to "relocation centers."

8. The major legislative act protecting the rights of disabled persons is the _____.

Learning Outcome 5–5

9. Affirmative action is best defined as a policy _____.

10. In *Adarand Constructors, Inc. v. Peña* (1995), the Supreme Court held that any federal, state, or local affirmative action program that uses racial classifications as the basis for making decisions is subject to _____ scrutiny by the courts.

MULTIPLE CHOICE

Learning Outcome 5–1

11. The equal protection clause of the _____ Amendment reads: "No State shall . . . deny to any person within its jurisdiction the equal protection of the laws."
    a. Fifth   **b.** Fourteenth   **c.** Nineteenth

Learning Outcome 5–2

12. "Jim Crow" laws
    a. separated the white community from the black community.
    b. were justified by the Supreme Court's decision in *Brown v. Board of Education of Topeka* (1954).
    c. required an end to segregation.

Learning Outcome 5–3

13. _____ appointed the first woman to serve as a justice of the Supreme Court.
    a. Ronald Reagan   **c.** Barack Obama
    b. George W. Bush

Learning Outcome 5–4

14. In 1789, Congress designated the Native American tribes as _____ so that the government could sign land and boundary treaties with them.
    a. enemies
    b. sovereign states composed of American citizens
    c. foreign nations

15. The Supreme Court ruling that guaranteed same-sex couples the right to marry was
    a. *Lawrence v. Texas* (2003).
    b. *Obergefell v. Hodges* (2015).
    c. *University of California v. Bakke* (1978).

Learning Outcome 5–5

16. The Supreme Court has ruled that states
    a. may ban affirmative action by state universities.
    b. cannot ban affirmative action programs that are used to meet diversity goals.
    c. can ban affirmative action for university admissions but not state government employment.

6

INTEREST GROUPS

LEARNING OUTCOMES *After reading this chapter, you should be able to:*

6-1 Explain what an interest group is, why interest groups form, and how interest groups function in American politics.

6-2 Identify the various types of interest groups.

6-3 Discuss how the activities of interest groups help to shape government policymaking.

6-4 Describe how interest groups are regulated by government.

After finishing this chapter, go to **PAGE 142** for **STUDY TOOLS**.

Brocreative/Shutterstock.com

AMERICA AT ODDS | Are Farmers Getting a Deal That's Too Good?

Many people, including those who live in large cities, have a romantic view of farming and farmers. This view is one of many reasons why interest groups representing farmers are so successful in winning support from the federal government. Over the last five years, about 2 million farmers received subsidies. The federal government's farm program is authorized by five-year farm bills. Farm bills have traditionally passed with bipartisan support because farm programs were in the same bill as the Supplemental Nutrition Assistance Program (SNAP, or food stamps). That ensured that liberals would join with rural legislators to support the bill.

When the last farm bill expired in 2012, however, Congress had become highly polarized, and no new farm bill passed until 2014. The 2014 bill provides $4.4 billion per year for commodity programs, $5.6 billion per year for conservation, and $9.0 billion per year for crop insurance. *Direct payments* were abolished. These payments used to go to growers of corn, cotton, rice, soybeans, and wheat regardless of whether they actually planted the crops. Almost all of the funds saved were added back as crop insurance subsidies, however. Are farmers getting too good a deal? Should farm subsidies be cut?

Agriculture Works—Don't Mess with Success

Farming is one of the riskiest businesses around. Farmers are ten times as likely to be killed on the job as the average worker. The weather is a constant worry. Every year, thousands of farmers lose their crops to floods or drought. Further, unlike many businesses, farmers can't set their own prices for what they sell. If you manufacture dishwashers, you expect that you can set a price for them that will cover your costs. Not so in agriculture. Prices are set by world commodity markets, where prices can swing wildly from month to month.

Despite the dangers, agriculture is a success story. Farm exports are booming as poor countries become richer and their people demand better diets—and the United Nations predicts that farmers will need to produce 70 percent more food by 2050 to keep up with population increases. Farm programs are an important safety net that helps keep our farmers in business. At less than half a percent of the federal budget, these programs are also a bargain.

Wealthy Farmers Don't Need These Subsidies

Everybody loves small farmers, but most of the subsidies don't go to these farmers. Under the previous farm bill, large commercial farms amassed 62 percent of all federal payments. The average family income for these farmers exceeded $200,000 per year. Their subsidies averaged about $30,000 per year. These numbers are unlikely to change under the new bill. Why are we giving so much federal aid to people who are that well off?

There's no doubt that farming is risky. That's why the great majority of farmers carry crop insurance, which—as noted above—is subsidized. Typically, two-thirds of the cost of the insurance is covered by the government. Further, the 2014 bill contains an extra provision to cover policy deductibles. How can you lose? Some may claim that we need disaster assistance and conservation programs. But commodity programs and excessive insurance subsidies need to be cut back dramatically. American food consumers and taxpayers have paid too much for too long.

Where do you stand?

1. What effect might farm programs have on rural residents who are not farmers?

2. Soybeans are the nation's second-largest crop, after corn. Half of all U.S. soybeans are exported, many of them to feed Chinese pigs. What benefits might we gain from this trade?

Explore this Issue online:

- You can find the site of the Environmental Working Group (EWG), a critic of farm subsidies, at www.ewg.org. The EWG has a database that contains a complete record of farm program recipients and what they were paid.

- To find arguments in support of the farm programs, visit the website of the Farm Bureau at www.fb.org.

INTRODUCTION

The groups supporting and opposing farm programs provide but one example of how Americans form groups to pursue or protect their interests. All of us have interests that we would like to have represented in government. Labor unionists would like it to be easier to organize unions, for example. Young people want good educational opportunities. Environmentalists want cleaner air and water.

The old saying that there is strength in numbers is certainly true in American politics. Special interests significantly influence American government and politics. Indeed, some Americans think that this influence is so great that it jeopardizes representative democracy. Others maintain that interest groups are a natural consequence of democracy. After all, throughout our nation's history, people have organized into groups to protect special interests. Because of the important role played by interest groups in the American system of government, we examine such groups in this chapter. We look at what they are, why they are formed, and how they influence policymaking.

6-1 INTEREST GROUPS AND AMERICAN GOVERNMENT

LO Explain what an interest group is, why interest groups form, and how interest groups function in American politics.

An **interest group** is an organized group of people sharing common objectives who actively attempt to influence government policymakers through direct and indirect methods. Whatever their goals—more or fewer social services, higher or lower prices—interest groups pursue these goals on every level and in every branch of government.

On any given day in Washington, D.C., you can see national interest groups in action. If you eat breakfast in the Senate dining room, you might see congressional committee staffers reviewing testimony with representatives from women's groups. Later that morning, you might visit the United States Supreme Court and watch a civil rights lawyer arguing on behalf of a client in a discrimination suit. Lunch in a popular Washington restaurant might find you listening in on a conversation between an agricultural lobbyist and a congressional representative.

That afternoon you might visit an executive department, such as the Department of Labor, and watch bureaucrats working out rules and regulations with representatives from a business interest group. Then you might stroll past the headquarters of the National Rifle Association (NRA), AARP (formerly the American Association of Retired Persons), or the National Wildlife Federation.

6-1a The Constitutional Right to Petition the Government

The right to form interest groups and to lobby the government is protected by the Bill of Rights. The First Amendment guarantees the right of the people "to petition the Government for a redress of grievances." This important right sometimes gets lost among the other, more well-known First Amendment guarantees, such as the freedoms of religion, speech, and the press. Nonetheless, the right to petition the government is as important and fundamental to our democracy as the other First Amendment rights.

The right to petition the government allows citizens and groups of citizens to lobby members of Congress and other government officials, to sue the government, and to submit petitions to the government. Whenever someone e-mails her or his congressional representative for help with a problem, such as not receiving a Social Security payment, that person is petitioning the government.

The existence of strong interest groups is one mark of a free nation. In undemocratic countries, organizing an interest group that is independent of the government is often treated as a serious crime. We look at examples in this chapter's *The Rest of the World* feature.

6-1b Why Interest Groups Form

The United States is a vast country of many regions, scores of ethnic groups, and a huge variety of businesses and occupations. The number of potential interests that can be represented is therefore very large. Beyond the sheer size of the country, however, there are a number of specific reasons why the United States has as many interest groups as it does.

Becoming an Interest Group It is worth remembering that not all groups are interest groups. A group becomes an interest group when it seeks to affect the policies or practices of the government. Many groups do not meet this standard. A social group, for example, may be formed to entertain or educate its members, with no broader purpose. Churches, organized to facilitate

interest group
An organized group of individuals sharing common objectives who actively attempt to influence policymakers.

THE REST OF THE WORLD

Land Seizures in China and India

China and India are the two most populous countries in the world. Some commentators lump the two together simply on that basis. Both are also developing nations that only a few decades ago experienced some of the worst poverty in human history. More recently, both have experienced high rates of economic growth—but that is where the similarities end.

India is a democracy, whereas China is a dictatorship governed by the Chinese Communist Party. Consequently, India has many active and powerful interest groups that can block government actions that are harmful to them. In India, for example, it is very difficult for the national government or a state government to take farmland so it can be used for a highway or to put up a factory. In contrast, interest groups are illegal in China. When a Chinese government body wishes to seize farmland for economic development, there is not much anyone can do to stop it.

Building Roads and Dams

China is currently building a system of limited-access highways that will be substantially larger than the U.S. Interstate system. To build one of these highways, the government simply bulldozes its way past any villages in its path. In India, even a simple project to widen a two-lane road can be tied up in court for years.

In 2012, China completed the Three Gorges Dam on the Yangtze River. The dam powers the largest electricity-generating plant in the world. Two million people were displaced to build it. The process took a decade and a half. Many Chinese were horrified by the project, but nothing was allowed to slow it down. For more than three decades, India has also tried to build a major dam system on the Narmada River in Gujarat state. The dam would bring drinking water, irrigation, and electricity to millions. The project is far from complete, however. Human rights activists and environmental groups have battled it all the way to the Supreme Court of India.

Seizing Farmland

Officially, both China and India agree that anyone with a property interest in seized land should be compensated. In China, however, this principle is regularly violated. In the past few decades, local governments in China have taken land from about 40 million farmers. A quarter of these farmers did not receive any compensation at all. Those who were compensated received, on average, less than 3 percent of the value of the land.[1]

In India, compensation questions can halt projects altogether. Farmers may be poor in India, but they form a powerful lobby within India's democratic system. The farmers' lobby has enjoyed great success in stopping governments from taking farmland to build factories or other projects. In 2015, the national government introduced a bill in Parliament to speed up land acquisition. The bill failed.

Critical Analysis

Why would a nation such as China ban interest groups?

---

worship and community, frequently have no political aims. (Indeed, certain political activities, such as campaigning for or against candidates for office, could cost a church its tax-exempt status.)

A group founded with little or no desire to influence the government can become an interest group, however, if its members decide that the government's policies are important to them. Alternatively, lobbying the government may initially be only one of several activities pursued by a group and may then grow to become the group's primary purpose.

The National Rifle Association (NRA) provides an example of this process. From its establishment in 1871 until the 1930s, the group took little part in politics. As late as the 1970s, a large share of the NRA's members joined for reasons that had nothing to do with politics. Many joined solely to participate in firearms training programs or to win marksman certifications. The NRA continues to provide such services today, but it is now so heavily politicized that anyone likely to take out a membership is certain to broadly agree with the NRA's political positions.

More Government, More Interest Groups

Interest groups may form—and existing groups may become more politically active—when the government expands its scope of activities. More government, in other words, means more interest groups. Prior to the 1970s, for example, the various levels of government were not nearly as active in attempting to regulate the use of firearms as they were thereafter. This change provides one explanation of why the NRA is much more politically active today than it was years ago.

Consider another example—AARP, formerly the American Association of Retired Persons. AARP is a major lobbying force that seeks to preserve or enhance Social Security and Medicare benefits for citizens sixty-five years of age and older. Before the creation of Social Security in the 1930s, however, the federal government did not provide income support to the elderly, and there would have been little reason for an organization such as AARP to exist.

Defending the Group's Interests Interest groups also may come into existence in response to a perceived threat to a group's interests. In the example of the NRA, the threat was an increase in the frequency of attempts to regulate or even ban firearms. This increase threatened the interests of gun owners. As another example, the National Right to Life Committee formed in response to *Roe v. Wade*, the Supreme Court's decision that legalized abortion. Interest groups can also form in reaction to the creation of other interest groups, thus pitting two groups against each other. Political scientist David B. Truman coined the term *disturbance theory* for his description of this kind of defensive formation of interest groups.[2]

purposive incentive
A reason to join an interest group—satisfaction resulting from working for a cause in which one believes.

solidary incentive
A reason to join an interest group—pleasure in associating with like-minded individuals.

material incentive
A reason to join an interest group—practical benefits such as discounts, subscriptions, or group insurance.

The Importance of Leaders Political scientist Robert H. Salisbury provided another analysis of the organization of interest groups that he dubbed *entrepreneurial theory*. This line of thought focuses on the importance of the leaders who establish the organization. The desire of such individuals to guarantee a viable organization is important

to the group's survival.[3] AARP is an example of a group with a committed founder—Dr. Ethel Percy Andrus, a retired high school principal. Andrus organized the group in 1958 to let older Americans purchase health-care insurance collectively. Like the NRA, AARP did not develop into a lobbying powerhouse until years after it was founded.

Incentives to Join a Group The French political observer and traveler Alexis de Tocqueville wrote in 1835 that Americans have a tendency to form "associations" and have perfected "the art of pursuing in common the object of their common desires. . . . In no other country of the world, has the principle of association been more successfully used or applied to a greater multitude of objectives than in America."[4] Of course, Tocqueville could not have foreseen the thousands of associations that now exist in this country. Surveys show that more than 85 percent of Americans belong to at least one group. Table 6–1 shows the percentage of Americans who belong to various types of groups today.

Political scientists have identified various reasons why people join interest groups. Often, people have one or more incentives to join such organizations.

▶ If a group stands for something that you believe is very important, you can gain considerable satisfaction in taking action from within that group. Such satisfaction is referred to as a **purposive incentive**.

▶ Some people enjoy the camaraderie and sense of belonging that come from associating with other people who share their interests and goals. That enjoyment can be called a **solidary incentive**.

▶ Some groups offer their members material incentives for joining, such as discounts on products, subscriptions, or group insurance programs. Each of these could be characterized as a **material incentive**.

> ## "POLITICS IS ABOUT *PEOPLE,* NOT POLITICIANS."
> ~ SCOTT SIMMS, CANADIAN POLITICIAN, BORN 1969

TABLE 6–1 PERCENTAGE OF AMERICANS BELONGING TO VARIOUS GROUPS

Social clubs	17%
Neighborhood groups	18
Hobby, garden, and technology clubs	19
PTA and school groups	21
Professional and trade associations	27
Health, sport, and country clubs	30
Religious groups	61

Source: AARP.

Sometimes, though, none of these incentives is enough to persuade people to join a group.

The Free Rider Problem The world in which we live is one of scarce resources that can be used to create *private goods* and *public goods*. Most of the goods and services that you use are private goods. If you consume them, no one else can consume them at the same time. If you eat a sandwich, no one else can have it.

With public goods, however, your use of a good does not diminish its use by someone else. National defense is a good example. If this country is protected through its national defense system, your protection from enemy invasion does not reduce any other person's protection.

People cannot be excluded from enjoying a public good, such as national defense, just because they did not pay for it. As a result, public goods are often provided by the government, which can force people to pay for the public good through taxation.

The existence of persons who benefit but do not contribute is called the **free rider problem**. Much of what we know about the free rider problem comes from Mancur Olson's classic work of political science, *The Logic of Collective Action.*[5]

Interest Groups and Public Goods. Lobbying, collective bargaining by labor unions, and other forms of representation can also be public goods. If an interest group is successful in lobbying for laws that will improve air quality, for example, everyone who breathes that air will benefit, whether they paid for the lobbying effort or not.

Addressing the Problem. In some instances, the free rider problem can be overcome. For example, social pressure may persuade some people to join or donate to a group for fear of being ostracized. This motivation is more likely to be effective for small, localized groups than for large, widely dispersed groups like AARP, however.

The government can also step in to ensure that the burden of lobbying for the public good is shared by all. When the government classifies interest groups as nonprofit organizations, it confers on them tax-exempt status. The groups' operating costs are reduced because they do not have to pay taxes, and the impact of the government's lost revenue is absorbed by all taxpayers.

6–1c How Interest Groups Function in American Politics

Despite the bad press that interest groups tend to get in the United States, they do serve several purposes in American politics:

Alexis de Tocqueville (1805–1859) a French writer, took a keen interest in America. He toured the United States and collected his observations in *Democracy in America*, published in 1835. *What U.S. institution would he have seen that was undemocratic?*

Everett Historical/Shutterstock.com

▶ Interest groups help bridge the gap between citizens and government—and enable citizens to explain their views on policies to public officials.

▶ Interest groups help raise public awareness and inspire action on various issues.

▶ Interest groups often provide public officials with specialized and detailed information that might be difficult to obtain otherwise. This information may be useful in making policy choices.

▶ Interest groups serve as another check on public officials to make sure that they are carrying out their duties responsibly.

Access to Government In a sense, the American system of government invites the participation of interest groups by offering many points of access for groups wishing to influence policy. Consider the possibilities at just the federal level.

An interest group can lobby members of Congress to act in the interests of the group. If the Senate passes a bill opposed by the group, the group's lobbying efforts can shift to the House of Representatives. If the House passes the bill and the president signs it, the group can try to influence the new law's application by lobbying the executive agency that is responsible for implementing the law. The group might even challenge the law in court. This can happen directly—by filing a lawsuit—or indirectly—by filing a brief as an *amicus curiae*, or "friend of the court." (The phrase is pronounced ah-*mee*-kus kure-ee-eye.)

Interest groups can seek a variety of different benefits when lobbying the government. A frequent goal is favorable treatment under federal or state regulations. Groups may also seek outright subsidies that benefit their members. An increasingly popular objective is special treatment in the tax code. Tax breaks for a special interest can be easier to obtain than subsidies because the breaks don't look like government spending.

Pluralist Theory   The **pluralist theory** of American democracy focuses on the participation of groups in a decentralized government structure that offers many points of access to policymakers. According to the pluralist theory, politics is a contest among various interest groups. These groups vie with one another—at all levels of government—to gain benefits for their members.

Pluralists maintain that the influence of interest groups on government is not undemocratic because individual interests are indirectly represented in the policymaking process through these groups. Although not every American belongs to an interest group, inevitably some group will represent at least some of the interests of each individual. Thus, each interest is satisfied to some extent through the compromises made in settling conflicts among competing interest groups.

Pluralists also contend that because of the extensive number of interest groups vying for political benefits, no one group can dominate the political process. Additionally, because most people have more than one interest, conflicts among groups do not divide the nation into hostile camps. Not all scholars agree that this is how American democracy functions, however.

Majoritarianism and Elite Theory   Political scientists have two other theories to describe American democracy: majoritarianism and elite theory. **Majoritarianism** is the belief that public policy should be set in accordance with the opinions of a majority of the people. Majoritarianism is highly popular, but political scientists find it to be a startlingly poor description of how politics actually works. **Elite theory** contends that, as a practical matter, the government is controlled by one or more elite groups, typically drawn from the wealthiest members of society. One version of elite theory posits that multiple elites compete for power. It is worth noting that many interest groups are largely funded—or even controlled—by wealthy individuals, so pluralism (described previously) and elite theory may overlap.

Evaluating the Theories   How valid are these three theories as explanations of how policy is made? Many political scientists have long believed that both pluralism and elite theory contain elements of truth and that majoritarianism is only an ideal. Political scientists Martin Gilens and Benjamin Page recently tried to find evidence for this belief through a major study. They found that the preferences of interest groups and of economic elites did indeed have a strong influence on policy. The influence of average citizens, however, when separated from the preferences of interest groups or elites, was effectively zero.[6] It follows that ordinary citizens have a good reason to join interest groups. Only by doing so will they be heard.

6-1d How Do Interest Groups Differ from Political Parties?

Although both interest groups and political parties are groups of people joined together for political purposes, they differ in several important ways. As you will read in Chapter 7, a political party is a group of individuals who organize to win elections, operate the government, and determine policy. Interest groups, in contrast, do not seek to win elections or operate the government, although they do seek to influence policy. Interest groups differ from political parties in the following ways:

▶ **Interest groups are often policy *specialists,* whereas political parties are policy *generalists.* Political parties are broad-based organizations that must attract the support of many opposing groups and consider a large number of issues. Interest groups, in contrast, may have only a handful of key policies to promote. An environmental group, obviously, will not be as concerned about the economic status of Hispanics as it is about polluters. A manufacturing group is more involved with pushing for fewer regulations than it is with inner-city poverty.**

▶ **Interest groups are usually more tightly organized than political parties. They are often financed through contributions or dues-paying memberships. Organizers**

pluralist theory
A theory that views politics as a contest among various interest groups—at all levels of government—to gain benefits for their members.

majoritarianism   The belief that public policy is or should be set in accordance with the opinions of a majority of the people.

elite theory   The belief that the government is controlled by one or more elite groups.

of interest groups communicate with members and potential members through conferences, mailings, newsletters, and electronic formats such as e-mail, Facebook, and Twitter.

▶ A political party's main sphere of influence is the electoral system. Parties run candidates for political office. Interest groups may try to influence the outcome of elections, but unlike parties, they do not compete for public office. Although a candidate for office may be sympathetic to—or even be a member of—a certain group, he or she does not run for election as a candidate of that group.

▶ *Identify some public goods other than national defense. Are any of these public goods associated with a significant free rider problem? Why or why not?*

6-2 DIFFERENT TYPES OF INTEREST GROUPS

LO Identify the various types of interest groups.

American democracy embraces almost every conceivable type of interest group, and the number is increasing rapidly. No one has ever compiled a *Who's Who* of interest groups, but you can get an idea of the number and variety by looking through the annually published *Encyclopedia of Associations.*

Some interest groups have large memberships. AARP, for example, has more than 37 million members. Others, such as the Colorado Auctioneers Association, have barely 150 members. Some, such as the U.S. Chamber of Commerce, are household names and have been in existence for many years, while others crop up overnight. Some are highly structured and are run by full-time professionals, while others are loosely structured and informal.

The most common interest groups are those that promote private interests. These groups seek public policies that benefit the economic interests of their members and work against policies that threaten those interests.

6-2a Business Interest Groups

Business has long been well organized for effective action. Hundreds of business groups are now operating in Washington, D.C., in the fifty state capitals, and at the local level across the country. Table 6–2 lists some top business interests and their campaign contributions through the 2016 elections.

TABLE 6–2 TOP BUSINESS CAMPAIGN DONORS, 1990–2016 ELECTION CYCLES	
Firm or Group	**Total, 1990–2016**
1. The Fahr Group (executive recruitment)	$132,108,403
2. Las Vegas Sands (casinos)	$95,732,516
3. National Association of Realtors	$83,682,742
4. Renaissance Technologies (hedge fund)	$80,725,496
5. AT&T	$72,408,685
6. Soros Fund Management	$66,361,031
7. Adelson Drug Clinic (casinos)	$63,742,618
8. Newsweb Corp. (media)	$62,521,412
9. Goldman Sachs (bank)	$56,807,705
10. Perry Homes (construction)	$55,590,174

Source: Center for Responsive Politics

© 2018 Cengage Learning

Two umbrella organizations that include small and large corporations and businesses are the U.S. Chamber of Commerce and the National Association of Manufacturers (NAM). In addition to representing more than 3 million individual businesses, the Chamber has more than three thousand local, state, and regional affiliates. It has become a major voice for millions of small businesses.

Trade Organizations The hundreds of **trade organizations** are far less visible than the Chamber of Commerce and the NAM, but they are also important in seeking policies that assist their members. Trade organizations usually support policies that benefit specific industries. For example, people in the oil industry work for policies that favor the development of oil as an energy resource. Other business groups work for policies that favor the development of coal, solar power, or nuclear power. Trucking companies work for policies that would lower their taxes. Railroad companies would, of course, not want other forms of transportation to receive special tax breaks, because that would hurt their business.

How Business Interest Groups Support Both Parties Traditionally, business interest groups have been viewed as staunch supporters of the Republican Party. This is because Republicans are more likely to promote government policies friendly toward business. Since 2000, however, donations

trade organization
An association formed by members of a particular industry, such as oil or trucking industries, to develop common standards and goals for the industry. Trade organizations, as interest groups, lobby government for legislation or regulations that specifically benefit their members.

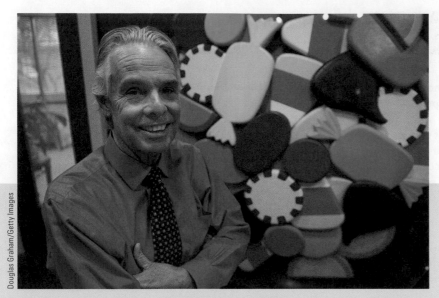

Larry Graham is president of the National Confectioners Association. His group would like sugar to cost less. *Which interest group would want it to cost more?*

from corporations to the Democratic National Committee have more than doubled.

Why would business groups make contributions to the Democratic National Committee? One reason is that in some fields, business leaders are more likely to be Democrats than in the past. Financial industry leaders were once almost entirely Republican, but today some of them support the Democrats. Information technology, a relatively new industry, contains both Republicans and Democrats. An additional reason why many business interests support both parties is to ensure that they will benefit regardless of who wins elections. There is another possible motivation: campaign contributions may be made not to gain political favors but rather to avoid political disfavor that could damage the interests of a business.

Agricultural Interest Groups In our capitalist society, farms clearly are businesses. They are a particular kind of business, however, and deserve special attention.

Producers of various specific farm commodities, such as dairy products, soybeans, grain, fruit, corn, cotton, beef, and sugar beets, have formed their own organizations to promote their interests. In addition, many groups work for general agricultural interests. Three broad-based agricultural groups represent millions of American farmers, from peanut farmers to dairy producers to tobacco growers. They are the American Farm Bureau Federation (Farm Bureau), the National Grange, and the National Farmers Union.

The Farm Bureau, representing more than 5.5 million families (a majority of whom are not actually farm families), is the largest and generally the most effective of the three. Founded in 1919, the Farm Bureau achieved one of its greatest early successes when it helped to obtain government guarantees of "fair" prices during the Great Depression of the 1930s.

Interest groups representing farmers have been spectacularly successful in winning subsidies from the federal government, as we explained in the chapter-opening *America at Odds* feature. Subsidies are not the only way in which the federal government can benefit growers of a particular crop. The government can also restrict imports of a specific commodity, such as sugar. The restrictions raise the price of sugar, which benefits sugar beet growers at the expense of consumers.

6–2b Labor and Professional Interest Groups

Interest groups representing labor have been some of the most influential groups in our country's history. They date back to at least 1886, when the American Federation of Labor (AFL) was formed. The largest and most powerful labor interest group today is the AFL-CIO (the American Federation of Labor–Congress of Industrial Organizations), a confederation of fifty-six unions representing 9 million organized workers and 3.2 million members of community affiliates (affiliates are community groups that are not unions).

Unions not affiliated with the AFL-CIO also represent millions of members. The Change to Win federation consists of four unions and 4.2 million workers. Dozens of other unions are independent. Examples include the National Education Association, the United Electrical Workers (UE), and the Major League Baseball Players Association. We list some top labor campaign donors in Table 6–3.

Union Goals Like labor unions everywhere, American unions press for policies to improve working conditions and ensure better pay for their members. Unions may compete for new members. In many states, for example, the National Education Association and the AFL-CIO's American Federation of Teachers compete fiercely for members.

TABLE 6–3 TOP LABOR AND PROFESSIONAL CAMPAIGN DONORS, 1990–2016 ELECTION CYCLES

Union or Group	Total, 1990–2016
1. Service Employees International Union	$236,375,639
2. National Education Association	$108,099,795
3. Amer. Fed. of State, County, and Municipal Employees	$100,224,969
4. Carpenters & Joiners Union	$83,327,528
5. American Federation of Teachers	$78,624,615
6. Laborers Union (construction)	$75,718,181
7. Int'l. Brotherhood of Electrical Workers	$75,374,397
8. United Food & Commercial Workers Union	$67,329,637
9. AFL-CIO	$57,287,458
10. Amer. Association for Justice (trial lawyers)	$51,339,676

Source: Center for Responsive Politics

© 2018 Cengage Learning

The goals of unions, however, are not necessarily limited to measures that directly benefit their own members. An example is the national campaign for a $15 minimum wage, which has received heavy union support. Very few of those who would benefit from a higher minimum wage are union members or likely to join in the future. Still, some argue that a higher minimum wage would tend to push up wages generally, which would benefit all workers, including union members.

The Decline of Unions   Although unions were highly influential in the 1930s, 1940s, and 1950s, their strength and political power have waned in the last several decades, as you can see in Figure 6–1. Today, members of organized labor make up only 11.1 percent of all wage and salary workers.

FIGURE 6–1   UNION MEMBERSHIP, 1952 TO PRESENT

This figure shows the percentage of wage and salary workers who have been union members from 1952 to the present. Unions represent many workers who are not members, so the percentage of workers represented by a union would be larger. *Why has the share of union members in the labor force fallen?*

© 2018 Cengage Learning

Reasons for Labor's Decline.   There are several reasons why the power of organized labor has declined in the United States. One is the continuing fall in the proportion of the nation's workforce employed in such blue-collar activities as manufacturing and transportation. These sectors have always been among the most heavily unionized.

Another important factor in labor's decline, however, is the general political environment. Forming and maintaining unions is more difficult in the United States than in most other industrial nations. Among the world's wealthy democracies, the United States is one of the most politically conservative, at least on economic issues. Economic conservatives are traditionally hostile to labor unions. Further, many business owners in the United States do not accept unions as legitimate institutions and will make strong efforts to ensure that their own businesses remain nonunionized.

Differing State Laws.   The impact of the political environment on labor's organizing ability can be easily seen by comparing rates of unionization in various states. These rates are especially low in conservative southern states. Georgia and South Carolina are both major manufacturing states, but unions represent only 5.1 percent of those employed in Georgia and only 2.9 percent in South Carolina.

Compare these figures with rates in more liberal states, such as California and New York: unions represent 17.2 percent of the workforce in California and 26.0 percent in New York. One factor that depresses unionization rates is that many states in the South and West have so-called **right-to-work laws**. These laws ban unions from collecting dues or other fees from workers whom they represent but who have not actually joined the union. Such laws create a significant free rider problem for unions. Twenty-five states have right-to-work laws. The most recent states to adopt such laws are in the Midwest. They are Indiana and Michigan (laws passed in 2012) and Wisconsin (2015).

Public-Sector Unions   While organized labor has suffered from declining numbers and a resulting loss in lobbying power, labor has held the line in one industry—government. In the 1960s and 1970s, public-sector unions enjoyed rapid growth. The percentage of government workers who are union members then leveled off, but it remains high. More than one-third of all public-sector workers are union members today.

In contrast to unions in the private sector, public-sector unions do not have

right-to-work laws
Laws that ban unions from collecting dues or other fees from workers whom they represent but who have not actually joined the union.

Unionized hotel workers cheer New York governor Andrew Cuomo's plan to raise the wages of fast-food workers. *Why would labor unions support a higher minimum wage for workers who are not union members?*

the right to strike over wages and working conditions. Still, they are influential. Unlike workers in private industry, public-sector employees—in their role as citizens—have the right to vote for their own bosses. As a result, elected officials are often reluctant to antagonize public-sector unions. One consequence of the influence of these unions is that government workers typically enjoy pension benefits that are substantially more generous than those received by comparable employees in the private sector.

Following the 2010 elections, several Republican governors in the Midwest attempted to curtail the bargaining rights of state and local government employee unions. These governors argued that pension benefits and other perks won by the unions threatened the financial stability of state and local governments. The role and status of public sector unions, therefore, have become important political issues.

Professional Interest Groups Employees are not the only members of the labor force who find a need to organize interest groups. Most professions that require advanced education or specialized training have organizations to protect and promote their interests. These groups are concerned mainly with the standards of their professions, but they also work to influence government policy.

Major professional groups include the American Medical Association (AMA), representing phy-

> **public-interest group**
> An interest group formed for the purpose of working for the "public good." Examples are the American Civil Liberties Union and Common Cause.

sicians; the American Bar Association, representing lawyers; and the American Association for Justice, representing trial lawyers. In addition, there are dozens of less well-known and less politically active professional groups, such as the National Association of Social Workers and the American Political Science Association.

Competing interests sometimes divide professional interest groups from one another. For example, medical groups contend that it is too easy for lawyers to sue physicians, insurance companies, and other businesses, and that generous settlements drive up the cost of health care and other goods. The AMA generally favors restrictions on such lawsuits. The American Association for Justice, naturally, opposes such changes.

6–2c Public-Interest and Other Types of Groups

Some interest groups have aims other than benefiting narrow economic interests. These include so-called **public-interest groups**, which are formed with the broader goal of working for the "public good." The American Civil Liberties Union and Common Cause are examples.

Let there be no mistake, though, about the name *public interest*. There is no such thing as a clear public interest in a nation of 325 million diverse people. The two public-interest groups just mentioned do not represent all American people but only a relatively small part of the American population. In reality, all lobbying groups, organizations, and other political entities represent special interests.

Consumer Interest Groups Groups organized for the protection of consumer rights were very active in the 1960s and 1970s. Some are still active today. One well-known group is Consumers Union, a nonprofit organization started in 1936. In addition to publishing *Consumer Reports* magazine, Consumers Union has been influential in pushing for the removal of phosphates from detergents, lead from gasoline, and pesticides from food. Consumers Union strongly criticizes government agencies when they appear to act against consumer interests. Other major groups include Consumer Action, the

Consumer Federation of America, and Public Citizen.

Consumer groups have been organized in many cities as well. They deal with such problems as substandard housing, discrimination against minorities and women, discrimination in the granting of credit, and business inaction on consumer complaints.

Identity Interest Groups

Americans who share the same race, ethnicity, gender, or other characteristics often have important common interests. African Americans, for example, have a powerful interest in combating the racism and racial discrimination that have marked American history from the beginning. Slaves, of course, were not able to form interest groups. For many years after the abolition of slavery, organizing African American interest groups remained impossibly dangerous. Such groups did not come into existence until the twentieth century.

The National Association for the Advancement of Colored People (NAACP) was founded in 1909, and the National Urban League was created in 1910. During the civil rights movement of the 1950s and 1960s, African Americans organized a number of new groups, some of which lasted (the Southern Christian Leadership Conference, founded in 1957) and some of which did not (the Student Nonviolent Coordinating Committee, organized in 1960). Among the most recent interest groups formed to defend African Americans is the loosely organized Black Lives Matter movement. This movement seeks to end alleged police violence toward African Americans and other minority group members.

The campaigns for dignity and equality of Native Americans, Latinos, women, lesbians and gay men, Americans with disabilities, and many other groups have all resulted in important interest groups. You learned about many of these organizations in Chapter 5. One identity-based group not discussed in that chapter is older Americans. Senior citizens are numerous, are politically active, and have a great deal at stake in debates over certain programs, such as Social Security and Medicare. As a result, groups representing them, such as AARP, can be a potent political force.

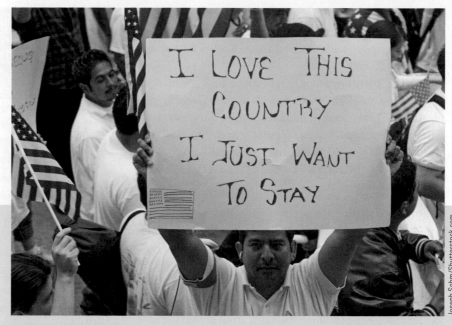

A man at an immigrants' rights rally in Los Angeles. *Why might the Chamber of Commerce—unlike other conservative groups—support increased immigration?*

Ideological Interest Groups Some interest groups are organized to promote not an economic interest or a collective identity but a shared political perspective or ideology. Examples include MoveOn, an Internet-oriented liberal group, and the Club for Growth, a conservative antitax organization.

The Tea Party Movement. The highly decentralized Tea Party movement, which sprang into life in 2009, has been described as an ideological interest group. The activities of the Tea Party movement, however, raise the question of whether it really is an interest group at all. The point is that interest groups, while they are often very concerned about who wins an election and may endorse candidates, do not themselves attempt to gain control of the machinery of government.

In the beginning, most Tea Party leaders claimed that the movement was nonpartisan. Still, some Tea Party groups have attempted to gain control of local Republican Party organizations. It may be only a matter of terminology, but political scientists refer to groups that compete for control of a political party as *factions,* not interest groups.

Environmental Groups. Environmental groups have supported pollution controls, wilderness protection, and clean-air legislation. They have opposed strip mining, nuclear power plants, logging activities, chemical waste dumps, and many other potential environmental hazards. Environmental interest groups range from traditional organizations, such as the National Wildlife Federation with more than 4 million members, to more radical groups, such as Greenpeace USA with a membership of 250,000.

In the past, environmental groups have been characterized as single-interest groups, not ideological organizations. Issues such as climate change, however, have led many modern environmental groups to advocate sweeping changes to the entire economy. Groups with such broad agendas could be considered a type of ideological interest group.

Religious Groups. Religious organizations are another type of group that could be included in the ideological category. Many religious groups work on behalf of conservative social causes. Others take a strong interest in the well-being of those suffering from poverty. Indeed, for decades, many mainstream religious groups have lobbied on behalf of those suffering from poverty. These include Catholic organizations, Lutherans, the National Council of Churches, the Friends (Quakers), and many others. Liberal groups have also played a major role in such lobbying. We list some top ideological and miscellaneous interest groups in Table 6–4.

Single-Issue Interest Groups Numerous interest groups focus on a single issue. For example, Mothers Against Drunk Driving (MADD) lobbies for stiffer penalties for drunk driving. Formed in 1980, MADD now boasts more than 3 million members and supporters. The abortion debate has created various single-issue groups, such as the National Right to Life organization (which opposes abortion) and NARAL Pro-Choice America (founded as the National Association for the Repeal of Abortion Laws in 1969, when abortion was widely illegal). Other examples of single-issue groups are the NRA and the American Israel Public Affairs Committee (a pro-Israel group).

Government Interest Groups Efforts by state and local governments to lobby the federal government have escalated in recent years. When states experience budget shortfalls, these governments often lobby in Washington, D.C., for additional federal funds. The federal government has sometimes lobbied in individual states, too. Until 2009, for example, the U.S. Attorney General's office lobbied against medical marijuana use in states that were considering ballot measures on the issue.

> **direct technique** Any method used by an interest group to interact with government officials directly to further the group's goals.

The Unrepresented Poor As we have noted, liberal and religious interests have done for the poor what the poor cannot do for themselves. As a result,

TABLE 6–4 TOP IDEOLOGICAL AND MISCELLANEOUS CAMPAIGN DONORS, 1990–2016 ELECTION CYCLES	
Group	**Total, 1990–2016**
1. EMILY's List (Democratic)	$42,135,639
2. NextGen Climate Action	$33,103,749
3. Victory Campaign 2004 (Democratic)	$33,038,925
4. Republican Governors Association	$30,664,719
5. Democratic Governors Association	$26,315,817

Source: Center for Responsive Politics

© 2018 Cengage Learning

low-income taxpayers are largely exempt from income taxes. They pay only payroll taxes, and in many cases, they can get rebates on these. Now consider the spending side. The Brookings Institution has estimated that all federal low-income programs together cost more than $800 billion a year. These programs include food stamps (now called the Supplemental Nutrition Assistance Program, or SNAP), Medicaid, and the Earned-Income Tax Credit.

If there were no federal tax and spending programs aimed at low-income persons, as many as 25 percent of U.S. families would have incomes below the official poverty line. If you take into account all benefits that low-income families obtain, that number drops to about 10 percent.

CRITICAL THINKING

▶ *Are you a member of any interest groups? If so, why? If not, which existing groups might best serve your interests? Again, why?*

6–3 HOW INTEREST GROUPS SHAPE POLICY

LO Discuss how the activities of interest groups help to shape government policymaking.

Interest groups operate at all levels of government and use a variety of strategies to steer policies in ways beneficial to their interests. Sometimes, they attempt to influence policymakers directly, but at other times they try to exert indirect influence on policymakers by shaping public opinion. The extent and nature of the groups' activities depend on their goals and their resources.

6–3a Direct Techniques

Lobbying and providing election support are two important **direct techniques** used by interest groups to influence government policy.

Lobbying Today, lobbying refers to all of the attempts by organizations or by individuals to influence the passage, defeat, or contents of legislation or to influence the administrative decisions of government. (The term *lobbying* arose because, traditionally, individuals and groups interested in influencing government policy would gather in the foyer, or lobby, of the legislature to corner legislators and express their concerns.) A **lobbyist** is an individual who handles a particular interest group's lobbying efforts. Most of the larger interest groups have lobbyists in Washington, D.C. These lobbyists often include former members of Congress or former employees of executive bureaucracies who are experienced in the methods of political influence and who "know people." Table 6–5 summarizes some of the basic methods by which lobbyists directly influence legislators and government officials.

Lobbying can be directed at the legislative branch of government or at administrative agencies. As mentioned earlier, lobbying can also be directed at the courts, by filing a lawsuit or an *amicus curiae* brief. Many lobbyists also work at state and local levels. In fact, lobbying at the state level has increased in recent years as states have begun to play a more significant role in policymaking.

Providing Election Support Interest groups often become directly involved in the election process. Many group members join and work with political parties to influence party platforms and the nomination of candidates. Interest groups provide campaign support for legislators who favor their policies and sometimes encourage their own members to try to win posts in party organizations.

Most important, interest groups urge their members to vote for candidates who support the views of the group. They can also threaten legislators with the withdrawal of votes. No candidate can expect to have support from all interest groups, but if the candidate is to win, she or he must have support from many of the strongest ones.

Political Action Committees (PACs). Since the 1970s, federal laws governing campaign financing have allowed corporations, labor unions, and special interest groups to raise funds and make campaign contributions through **political action committees (PACs)**. Both the number of PACs and the amount of money PACs spend on elections have grown astronomically in recent years. There were about 1,000 PACs in 1976. Today, there are more than 4,500 PACs. In 1973, total spending by PACs amounted to $19 million. In the 2015–2016 election cycle, contributions to federal candidates by PACs totaled about $441 million.

Even with their impressive growth, PACs provided a smaller share of campaign spending in the years after 1988, principally because of the development of other funding sources, such as "soft money" and issue ads. (We discuss these sources shortly.)

Note that although campaign contributions do not guarantee that officials will vote the way the groups wish, contributions usually do ensure that the groups will have the ear of the public officials they have helped to elect. (We will discuss election finances in greater detail in Chapter 9.)

lobbying All of the attempts by organizations or by individuals to influence the passage, defeat, or contents of legislation or to influence the administrative decisions of government.

lobbyist An individual who handles a particular interest group's lobbying efforts.

political action committee (PAC) A committee that is established by a corporation, labor union, or special interest group to raise funds and make campaign contributions on the establishing organization's behalf.

TABLE 6–5 DIRECT LOBBYING TECHNIQUES	
Technique	**Description**
Making Personal Contacts with Key Legislators	A lobbyist's personal contacts with key legislators or other government officials—in their offices, in the halls of Congress, or on social occasions such as dinners, boating expeditions, and the like—comprise one of the most effective direct lobbying techniques.
Providing Expertise and Research Results for Legislators	Lobbyists often have knowledge and expertise that are useful in drafting legislation, and this expertise can be a major strength for an interest group. Harried members of Congress cannot possibly be experts on everything they vote on and therefore eagerly seek information to help them make up their minds.
Offering "Expert" Testimony before Congressional Committees	Lobbyists often provide "expert" testimony before congressional committees for or against proposed legislation. Each expert offers as much evidence as possible to support her or his position.
Providing Legal Advice to Legislators	Many lobbyists assist legislators in drafting legislation or prospective regulations. Lobbyists are a source of ideas and sometimes offer legal advice on specific details.
Following Up on Legislation	Because executive agencies responsible for carrying out legislation can often change the scope of the new law, lobbyists may also try to influence the bureaucrats who implement the policy.

© 2018 Cengage Learning

Mega-lobbyist Heather Podesta (center) greets a government official at a Washington, D.C., reception. *Why do former members of Congress often become lobbyists?*

officials are often more impressed by contacts from voters than from lobbyists.

Shaping Public Opinion Public opinion weighs significantly in the policymaking process, so interest groups cultivate their public images carefully. If public opinion favors a certain group's interests, then public officials will be more ready to listen and more willing to pass legislation favoring that group. An interest group's efforts to cultivate public opinion may include online campaigns, television publicity, newspaper and magazine advertisements, and mass mailings. In general, groups use public relations techniques to improve the group's image.

For example, environmental groups often run television ads to dramatize threats to the environment. Oil companies may respond to criticism about gasoline prices with advertising that shows how hard they are working to develop new sources of energy. The goal of all these activities is to influence public opinion.

Rating Systems Some interest groups also try to influence legislators through **rating systems**. A group selects legislative issues that it believes are important to its goals and rates legislators according to the percentage of times they vote favorably on that legislation. For example, a score of 90 percent on the Americans for Democratic Action (ADA) rating scale means that the legislator supported that liberal group's position to a high degree.

Other groups use telling labels to tag members of Congress who support (or fail to support) their interests to a significant extent. For instance, the Communications Workers of America refers to policymakers who take a position consistent with its views as "Heroes" and those who take the opposite position as "Zeroes." Needless to say, such tactics can be an effective form of indirect lobbying, particularly with legislators who do not want to earn a low ADA score or be placed on the "Zeroes" list.

Issue Ads One of the most powerful indirect techniques used by interest groups is the "issue ad"—a television or radio ad taking a position on a particular issue. The Supreme Court has made it clear that the First Amendment's guarantee of free speech protects interest groups' rights to set forth their positions on issues when they fund such activities through independent expenditures that are not coordinated with a candidate's campaign or a political party. Nevertheless, issue

Super PACs. In 2010, the Supreme Court upended the world of campaign finance in *Citizens United v. Federal Election Commission.*[7] The Court ruled that PACs could accept unlimited contributions from individuals, unions, and corporations for the purpose of making **independent expenditures**. These are expenditures that are not coordinated with a candidate's campaign or a political party. This ruling led, in short order, to the creation of super PACs, which channeled more than $1.5 billion into election spending in the 2016 election cycle. Many super PACs were funded by wealthy individuals, and many of them concentrated on negative ads.

6–3b Indirect Techniques

Interest groups also try to influence public policy indirectly through the general public. The effects of such **indirect techniques** may appear to be spontaneous, but indirect techniques are generally as well planned as the direct lobbying techniques just discussed. Indirect techniques can be particularly effective because public

independent expenditure An expenditure for activities that are independent from (not coordinated with) those of a political candidate or a political party.

indirect technique Any method used by interest groups to influence government officials through third parties, such as voters.

rating system A system by which a particular interest group evaluates (rates) the performance of legislators based on how often the legislators have voted with the group's position on particular issues.

advocacy is controversial because the funds spent to air issue ads have had a clear effect on the outcome of elections. Both political parties have benefited from such interest group spending.

527 and 501(c)4 Organizations As you will read in Chapter 9, the Bipartisan Campaign Reform Act of 2002 banned unlimited donations to campaigns and political parties, called *soft money.* In subsequent years, interest groups that had previously given soft money to parties set up new groups called "527s" (after the provision of the tax code that covers them). The 527s engaged in such practices as voter registration, but they also began making large expenditures on issue ads—which were legal so long as the 527s did not coordinate their activities with candidates' campaigns.

In the run-up to the 2008 presidential elections, clever campaign finance lawyers hit upon a new type of group, the 501(c)4 organization, also named after a section of the tax code. Groups such as the Sierra Club and Citizens Against Government Waste have set up special 501(c)4 organizations.

Lawyers argued that a 501(c)4 group could spend some of its funds on direct campaign contributions as long as most of the group's spending was on issue advocacy. Further, a 501(c)4 group could conceal the identity of its contributors. Federal agencies and the courts have not yet determined the legality of these claims. We will discuss this issue in greater depth in Chapter 9.

Mobilizing Constituents Interest groups sometimes urge members and other constituents to contact government officials—by e-mail, Facebook, Twitter, text message, or telephone—to show their support for or opposition to a certain policy. Such efforts are known as *grassroots organizing.*

Large interest groups can generate hundreds of thousands of letters, e-mail messages, texts, tweets, and phone calls. Interest groups often provide pre-written form messages for constituents to use. The NRA has successfully used this tactic to fight strict federal gun control legislation by delivering half a million letters to Congress within a few weeks. Policymakers recognize that such communications are initiated by interest groups, however, and are impressed only when the volume of communications is very large.

In some cases, interest groups are not membership organizations. Instead, they are established by political fund-raisers or wealthy individuals. Sometimes, such groups try to disguise their efforts as grassroots campaigns. Campaigns that masquerade as grassroots mobilizations, but are not, have been given the apt label

Astroturf lobbying. An Astroturf lobbyist might, for example, make anonymous postings online that appear to be from concerned citizens but that actually come from the sponsoring organization.

Going to Court The legal system offers another avenue for interest groups to influence the political process. In the 1950s and 1960s, civil rights groups paved the way for interest group litigation with major victories in cases concerning equal housing, school desegregation, and employment discrimination. Environmental groups, such as the Sierra Club, have also successfully used litigation to press their concerns. For example, an environmental group might challenge in court an activity that threatens to pollute the environment or that will destroy the natural habitat of an endangered species. The legal challenge forces those engaging in the activity to defend their actions and may delay the project. In fact, much of the success of environmental groups has been linked to their use of lawsuits.

***Amicus Curiae* Briefs** An interest group can also influence the outcome of litigation without being a party to a lawsuit. Frequently, an interest group files an *amicus curiae* brief. The brief states the group's legal argument in support of its desired outcome in a case.

For example, the case *Arizona v. United States,* heard by the Supreme Court in 2012, turned on whether a state government could enact immigration laws tougher than those adopted by the federal government. The Court ruled that part, but not all, of the Arizona legislation was unconstitutional.[8] Dozens of organizations filed *amicus* briefs on one side or the other of the issue. Conservative and anti-immigration groups supported the state. Naturally, so did Arizona elected officials, including the state legislature. Those backing the federal government, which had challenged the Arizona law, included the Catholic bishops, labor unions, and the American Bar Association. A variety of civil rights and civil liberties groups, plus the government of Mexico, also opposed the Arizona law.

Often, in such briefs, interest groups cite statistics and research that support their position on a certain issue. This research can have considerable influence on the judges deciding the case.

Demonstrations Some interest groups stage protests to make a statement in a dramatic way. The Boston Tea Party of 1773, in which American colonists dressed as Native Americans and threw tea into Boston Harbor to protest British taxes, is testimony to how long this tactic has been around. Over the years, many groups have organized protest marches and rallies to support or oppose legalized abortion, gay and lesbian rights, and the treatment of Native Americans. Other issues raised by demonstrators have included restrictions on the use of federally owned lands in the West and the power of the richest "1 percent."

Not all demonstration techniques are peaceful. Some environmental groups, for example, have used such dangerous tactics as spiking trees and setting traps on logging roads to puncture truck tires. "Pro-life" groups have bombed abortion clinics, and members of the Animal Liberation Front have broken into laboratories and freed animals being used for experimentation. Some evidence suggests that violent demonstrations can be counterproductive—that is, that they can hurt the demonstrators' cause by angering the public. Historians

continue to debate whether violent demonstrations against the Vietnam War (1965–1975) helped or hurt the antiwar cause.

CRITICAL THINKING

▶ *Why might some lawmakers pay more attention to contacts by ordinary people than contacts by lobbyists?*

6–4 TODAY'S LOBBYING ESTABLISHMENT

LO Describe how interest groups are regulated by government.

Without a doubt, interest groups and their lobbyists have become a permanent feature in the landscape of American government. All the major interest groups have headquarters in Washington, D.C., close to the center of government. Professional lobbyists and staff members of various interest groups move freely between their groups' headquarters and congressional offices and committee rooms. Interest group representatives are routinely consulted when Congress drafts new legislation. As already mentioned, interest group representatives are frequently asked to testify before congressional committees or subcommittees on the effect or potential effect of particular legislation or regulations. In sum, interest groups are an integral part of the American government system.

As interest groups have become a permanent feature of American government, lobbying has developed into a profession. A professional lobbyist—one who has mastered the techniques of lobbying discussed earlier in this chapter—is a valuable ally to any interest group seeking to influence government. Professional lobbyists can and often do represent a number of different interest groups over the course of their careers.

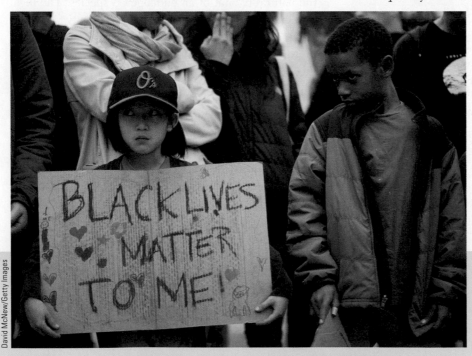

David McNew/Getty Images

Young Los Angeles protesters condemn the killing of unarmed black men by police officers. Such demonstrations were widespread in 2014 and 2015. *Are such demonstrations likely to be effective?*

In recent years, it has become increasingly common for those who leave positions with the federal government to become lobbyists or consultants for the private-interest groups they helped to regulate. In spite of legislation and regulations designed to reduce this "revolving door" syndrome, it is still functioning quite well.

6–4a Why Do Interest Groups Get Bad Press?

Despite their importance to democratic government, interest groups, like political parties, are often criticized by both the public and the press. Our image of interest groups and their special interests is not very favorable. You may have run across political cartoons depicting lobbyists standing in the hallways of Congress with briefcases stuffed with money. These cartoons are not entirely factual, but they are not entirely fictitious either.

Examples of Questionable Activities Consider a few examples. In 2004, the chief executive officer of a coal company donated $3 million to the election campaign of a candidate for the West Virginia Supreme Court. That sum amounted to most of what was spent in the race. At that time, the coal company had a $50 million case pending before the court, which eventually found in the coal company's favor. (In 2009, the United States Supreme Court ruled that the recipient of the largesse should not have participated in the court proceedings.)[9]

In 2015, Republicans alleged that foreign interests had benefited from donations to the Clinton Foundation. The foundation is a charity organized by former secretary of state Hillary Clinton and her husband, former president Bill Clinton. Critics were unable to show, however, that the secretary of state had participated in approving the trade benefits supposedly enjoyed by the foreign interests.

Concentrated Benefits, Dispersed Costs A major complaint by critics of interest groups is that the benefits these groups obtain are not in the general public interest. One reason for this situation is the so-called enthusiasm gap between supporters and opponents of any given subsidy. Sugar producers, for example, benefit greatly from restrictions on sugar imports. They work hard to ensure that these restrictions continue. Yet for sugar consumers—all the rest of us—the price of sugar is a trivial matter. Candy-makers aside, end users of sugar

> **"AN HONEST POLITICIAN IS ONE WHO, WHEN HE IS BOUGHT, *WILL STAY BOUGHT.*"**
>
> ~SIMON CAMERON,
> U.S. FINANCIER AND POLITICIAN,
> 1799–1889

have little incentive to organize. This enthusiasm gap is referred to as "concentrated benefits, dispersed costs."

We tend to think of restrictions on economic activity that provide concentrated benefits as resulting from federal regulation. Many of the restrictions that can hobble economic activity, however, are imposed at the state and local level. For example, Florida requires an individual to obtain an expensive license to work as an interior decorator. This law resulted from lobbying by those already working as interior decorators. We describe a recent dispute over economic restrictions in this chapter's *Join the Debate* feature.

6–4b The Regulation of Interest Groups

In an attempt to control lobbying, Congress passed the Federal Regulation of Lobbying Act in 1946. The major provisions of the act are as follows:

▶ Any person or organization that receives money to influence legislation must register with the clerk of the House and the secretary of the Senate.

▶ Any groups or persons registering must identify their employer, salary, amount and purpose of expenses, and duration of employment.

▶ Every registered lobbyist must make quarterly reports on his or her activities.

▶ Anyone violating this act can be fined up to $10,000 and be imprisoned for up to five years.

The act did not succeed in regulating lobbying to any great degree for several reasons. First, the Supreme Court restricted the application of the law to only those lobbyists who sought to influence federal legislation directly.[10] Any lobbyist seeking to influence legislation indirectly through public opinion did not fall within the scope of the law.

Second, only persons or organizations whose principal purpose was to influence legislation were required to register. Many groups avoided registration by claiming that their principal function was something else. Third, the act did not cover those whose lobbying was directed at agencies in the executive branch or lobbyists who testified before congressional committees. Fourth, the public was almost totally unaware of the information in the quarterly reports filed by lobbyists. Not until 1995 did Congress finally address those loopholes by enacting new legislation.

JOIN THE DEBATE

Should We Let Uber and Lyft Pick Up Passengers?

Until recently, taxis and, to an extent, limousines were the only services that would pick you up and take you from one point to another in a car. Today, depending on where you live, you may have other choices—specifically, Uber or Lyft. These "transportation network" companies directly compete with taxis. These services are built around the Internet. All you need to summon a car is a smartphone app. You use the app to locate the nearest Lyft or Uber driver. You talk directly with that driver. You must already have a credit card number on file with the company—no cash changes hands. The driver picks you up, and your credit card is automatically charged at the end of your ride. Transportation network companies use both full-time and part-time drivers, all of whom own their own cars.

These competitors to taxis are a completely new service and are therefore unregulated. This fact has provoked controversy. Some city councils have banned the services outright. Others are trying to regulate them. (In 2015, for example, California determined that Uber and Lyft drivers are employees, not independent contractors.) Should they just be left alone instead?

Public Safety Is at Issue, and It's Also Unfair Competition

Opponents of Uber, Lyft, and other such services point out that taxi services are heavily regulated in most cities. The goal of the regulations is two-fold: to ensure public safety and to allow taxi drivers to make a living wage. In many cities, you must pay for a license to own a cab. Drivers for Uber and similar companies do not pay anything. Taxis must also carry expensive vehicle-for-hire insurance. They are regularly inspected to protect public safety. Another point— because you must have a credit card to use Uber or Lyft, these companies discriminate against poor people who don't have credit cards or smartphones. In sum, these new services do not compete fairly with licensed, regulated taxi drivers.

It's All about the Taxi Lobby

Supporters of the new "ride-share" systems say that talk of unfair competition and public safety is a smoke-screen. Taxi lobbies simply want to eliminate competition. Uber, Lyft, and the others perform background checks on their drivers. Passengers have the names and mobile phone numbers of their drivers. They rate the drivers, and those who receive low ratings get fewer and fewer calls. Localities that regulate the new services, such as the state of California, require extra insurance. The ride-share market works just as well as any other market. Banning these services simply guarantees that current taxi owners—not necessarily drivers—make high profits and passengers have fewer choices.

Critical Analysis

What might motivate a city council to ban Uber or Lyft services?

6–4c The Lobbying Disclosure Act of 1995

In 1995, Congress passed new, expanded lobbying legislation—the Lobbying Disclosure Act—that reformed the 1946 act in the following ways:

▸ Strict definitions now apply to determine who must register with the clerk of the House and the secretary of the Senate as a lobbyist. A lobbyist is anyone who either spends at least 20 percent of his or her time lobbying members of Congress, their staffs, or executive-branch officials, or is paid more than $5,000 in a six-month period for such work. Any organization that spends more than $20,000 in a six-month period conducting such lobbying activity must also register. These amounts have since been altered to $2,500 and $10,000 per quarter, respectively.

▸ Lobbyists must report their clients, the issues on which they lobbied, and the agency or chamber of Congress they contacted, although they do not need to disclose the names of those they contacted.

Tax-exempt organizations, such as religious groups, were exempted from these provisions, as were organizations that engage in grassroots lobbying, such as a media campaign that asks people to write or call their congressional representative. Nonetheless, the number of registered lobbyists nearly doubled in the first few years after the new legislation took effect.

6-4d Recent Reform Efforts

In 2005, a number of lobbying scandals in Washington, D.C., came to light. As a result, following the midterm elections of 2006, the new Democratic majority in the Senate and House of Representatives undertook a lobbying reform effort. This involved changes to the rules that the two chambers impose on their own members.

Bundled campaign contributions, in which a lobbyist arranges

Uber is now worldwide—this is what its app looks like in Malaysia. The San Francisco Cab Drivers Association reports that nearly one-third of the city's licensed taxi drivers have stopped driving taxis and have begun driving for ride-sharing services. *Why would they switch?*

for contributions from a variety of sources, would have to be reported. Expenditures on the sometimes lavish parties to benefit candidates would have to be reported as well. (Of course, partygoers were expected to pay for their food and drink with a check written out to the candidate.) The new rules covered PACs as well as registered lobbyists, which led one lobbyist to observe sourly that this wasn't lobbying reform but campaign-finance reform.

President George W. Bush signed the Honest Leadership and Open Government Act in 2007. The new law increased lobbying disclosure requirements and placed further restrictions on the receipt of gifts and travel by members of Congress paid for by lobbyists and the organizations they represent. The act also included provisions requiring the disclosure of lawmakers' requests for earmarks in legislation. Earmarks—that is, special provisions benefiting a lawmaker's constituents—are also known as "pork barrel legislation," or simply *pork*.

In March 2010, the Republican-led House Appropriations Committee banned earmarks that benefit profit-making corporations. About a thousand such earmarks had been authorized in the previous year, to the value of $1.7 billion. The ban was renewed in 2012. As it turned out, legislators proved remarkably creative in finding ways around the ban on pork, though the ban did at least limit its prevalence.

CRITICAL THINKING

▶ *As noted at the beginning of this chapter, the right to lobby is protected by the Constitution. If that weren't so, would it be a good idea to ban lobbying? Why or why not?*

AMERICA AT ODDS | Interest Groups

Interest groups are one of the most controversial features of our democratic system. The right to lobby may be protected by the First Amendment, but many people consider lobbying by interest groups to be a source of corruption within the political system. Of course, people can readily see the problems with lobbying when it is done for a cause that they oppose. In contrast, it is easy to support political action for something you believe in, regardless of what others might think of it. Some of the controversies surrounding interest group lobbying include the following:

- *Should labor unions be allowed to organize workplaces by obtaining signed cards—or are secret-ballot elections an essential safeguard?*

- *Are farm subsidies a valid protection for an important industry—or just another giveaway to the politically powerful?*

- *Does lobbying always harm legislation—or can lobbying improve it?*

- *Free riders benefit from a particular activity without paying their share of its costs. Is free riding inherently unfair—or is it only a problem when it is so pervasive that it makes the activity in question (for example, lobbying by consumer groups) unaffordable?*

- *Are there too many lobbyists—or is the real problem that there aren't enough lobbyists for ordinary people?*

STUDY TOOLS 6

READY TO STUDY? IN THE BOOK, YOU CAN:

- ☐ Review what you've read with the following chapter quiz.
- ☐ Check your answers in Appendix D at the back of the book.
- ☐ Rip out the Chapter Review Card, which includes key terms and chapter summaries.

ONLINE AT WWW.CENGAGEBRAIN.COM, YOU CAN:

- ☐ Learn about Wisconsin governor Scott Walker's interactions with interest groups in a short video.
- ☐ Explore various online resources in the NRA and AARP websites via the Internet Resources tool.
- ☐ Interact with figures from the text, and watch quick animation clips.
- ☐ Prepare for tests with quizzes.
- ☐ Review the key terms with Flash Cards.

FILL-IN

Learning Outcome 6–1

1. The right to form interest groups and to lobby the government is protected by the _____ Amendment to the U.S. Constitution.

2. _____ theory describes the defensive formation of interest groups.

Learning Outcome 6–2

3. Today, members of organized labor make up only _____ percent of the labor force.

4. _____ laws ban unions from collecting dues or other fees from workers whom they represent but who have not actually joined the union.

5. An interest group that unites persons who share the same race, ethnicity, gender, or age can be called a/an _____.

Learning Outcome 6–3

6. Lobbying refers to _____.

7. Interest groups can influence the outcome of litigation without being a party to a lawsuit by filing _____.

Learning Outcome 6–4

8. The Supreme Court has guaranteed the rights of interest groups to set forth their position on issues when they fund such activities through independent expenditures that _____.

9. It has become increasingly common for those who leave positions with the federal government to become lobbyists or consultants for the private-interest groups they helped to regulate. This is called the _____ syndrome.

MULTIPLE CHOICE

Learning Outcome 6–1

10. There are various reasons why people join interest groups. Some people find that they gain considerable satisfaction from supporting causes that they agree with. Such satisfaction is referred to as a _____ incentive.
    a. free rider **b.** purposive **c.** material

11. Interest groups
    a. are often policy generalists.
    b. compete for public office.
    c. help bridge the gap between citizens and government.

Learning Outcome 6–2

12. The American Association for Justice represents the interests of
    a. trial lawyers. **b.** children. **c.** senior citizens.

13. MoveOn and the Club for Growth are _____ interest groups.
    a. business **b.** consumer **c.** ideological

Learning Outcome 6–3

14. _____ is a direct technique used by interest groups to influence public policy.
    a. The use of rating systems
    b. Providing election support
    c. Staging demonstrations

15. Lobbying campaigns that masquerade as grassroots mobilizations have been labeled _____ lobbying.
    a. Bluegrass **b.** Turfgrass **c.** Astroturf

Learning Outcome 6–4

16. When a benefit is provided to a limited number of people, the enthusiasm gap between recipients of the benefit and everyone else is called:
    a. concentrated costs and dispersed benefits.
    b. the free rider problem.
    c. concentrated benefits and dispersed costs.

Joe Belanger/Shutterstock.com

7

POLITICAL PARTIES

LEARNING OUTCOMES *After reading this chapter, you should be able to:*

7-1 Summarize the origins and development of the two-party system in the United States.

7-2 Describe the current status of the two major parties.

7-3 Explain how political parties function in our democratic system.

7-4 Discuss the structure of American political parties.

7-5 Describe the different types of third parties and how they function in the American political system.

After finishing this chapter, go to **PAGE 166** for **STUDY TOOLS**.

AMERICA AT ODDS

How Should the Republicans Respond to Trump Voters?

Joseph Sohm/Shutterstock.com

The midterm elections of 2010 and 2014 were good ones for the Republicans. After 2014, the party was stronger at the state level and in the U.S. Congress than it had been for more than half a century. Still, there were signs of trouble. From 1992 through 2012, the Republicans lost the popular vote for president in five out of six elections. In 2012, the Republicans won a 33-vote majority in the U.S. House—but Democratic House candidates actually secured about 1.4 million more votes than the Republicans. Victories based on favorable district boundaries will not last indefinitely. This is especially true given the growing number of Latino and Asian American voters, who usually favor the Democrats.

After the 2012 elections, the Republican National Committee released a report arguing that the party needed to increase its levels of support among Latino and Asian voters, in part by supporting immigration reform. It did not take long to learn that a majority of Republican voters had other ideas. Republican leaders who had not gotten the message by 2016 received a wake-up call in the form of businessman Donald Trump. Despite his obvious flaws as a candidate, Trump won popularity and votes running on a platform hostile to immigration and foreign trade. Should the Republican Party establishment listen to Trump voters—or would that be a mistake?

Trump's Style of Nationalism Spells Disaster in the Long Run

The face of America is changing. Support for gay rights has risen dramatically. The number of Hispanic voters rises year by year, and by 2050, non-Hispanic whites will be a minority of the U.S. population. Despite these changes, some Republicans seem intent on ensuring that they are seen as the "mean party"—the party that hates gay men, lesbians, and immigrants. Yet if Republicans view large numbers of their fellow Americans as "the enemy," the party will lose future elections, no matter how well it does today. Republicans require young voters, but hostility toward gay marriage is poison to that constituency. If the Republicans cannot gain Hispanic votes, eventually the party will even fail to carry Texas.

True, Trump voters have reason to be angry. Low-income conservatives were hit hard by the 2008 economic catastrophe. Millions are still out of the workforce. An epidemic of drug abuse among less-educated whites has actually driven up their mortality rates, even as death rates for other groups are falling. Yet Trump's version of nationalism provides no real solution to these problems.

Trump Has Exposed the Establishment's Political Bankruptcy

Trump's victories reveal a Republican electorate in open revolt against the party's establishment. What is the establishment? It is the politicians supported by what has been called the "donor class." For members of the ultra-wealthy donor class, nothing is more important than reducing the tax rates imposed on the nation's wealthiest citizens. To fund these cuts, it will be necessary to reduce Social Security and Medicare benefits, which together make up more than 40 percent of the federal budget. Immigration is not a problem because corporations owned by these donors can hire the immigrants at low wages. Imports from China may hurt U.S. factory workers, but they help fatten corporate profits.

Trump was the only Republican candidate in 2016 who vowed to protect Social Security and Medicare. His radical policy proposals and personal insults were music to the ears of desperate low-income conservatives. If the Republican Party is to have a future, it must find a way to address the problems of these people—without demonizing Latinos and Muslims. To do so, it must break free from the control of the donor class.

Where do you stand?

1. Would a presidential candidate who is a political "outsider," such as Trump or Senator Bernie Sanders (D., Vt.), help us deal with our problems? Why or why not?

2. Among other measures, Senator Mike Lee (R., Utah) advocates tax breaks for the working class. Search for his program at "conservative reform agenda." Do his ideas have merit? Again, why or why not?

Explore this issue online:

- Columnist Ross Douthat argues for conservative reform while supporting the Republican Party. Follow him at twitter.com/douthatnyt.

- For full-throttle conservatism, visit Rush Limbaugh's site at www.rushlimbaugh.com.

INTRODUCTION

Political ideology can spark heated debates among Americans, as you read in the chapter-opening *America at Odds* feature. Today, political ideologies are typically embodied in political parties. A **political party** can be defined as a group of individuals who organize to win elections, operate the government, and determine policy.

Political parties were an unforeseen development in American political history. The founders defined many other important institutions, such as the presidency and Congress, and described their functions in the Constitution. Political parties, however, are not even mentioned in the Constitution. In fact, the founders decried factions and parties. Thomas Jefferson probably best expressed the founders' anti-party sentiments when he declared, "If I could not go to heaven but with a party, I would not go there at all."[1]

If the founders did not want political parties, though, who was supposed to organize political campaigns and mobilize supporters of political candidates? Clearly, there was a practical need for some kind of organizing group to form a link between citizens and their government. Even our early national leaders, for all their antiparty feelings, soon realized this. Several of them were active in establishing or organizing the first political parties.

7-1 A SHORT HISTORY OF AMERICAN POLITICAL PARTIES

LO Summarize the origins and development of the two-party system in the United States.

Throughout the course of our history, several parties have formed, and some have disappeared. Even today, although we have only two major political parties, a few others always exist at any one time, as will be discussed later in this chapter.

political party A group of individuals who organize to win elections, operate the government, and determine policy.

"BOTH OF OUR POLITICAL PARTIES . . . AGREE CONSCIENTIOUSLY IN THE SAME OBJECT: THE *PUBLIC GOOD;* BUT THEY DIFFER ESSENTIALLY IN WHAT THEY DEEM THE MEANS OF PROMOTING THAT GOOD."

~ THOMAS JEFFERSON, IN A LETTER TO ABIGAIL ADAMS, 1804

7-1a The First Political Parties

The founders rejected the idea of political parties because they believed, as George Washington said in his Farewell Address, that the "spirit of party . . . agitates the community with ill-founded jealousies and false alarms, kindles the animosity of one part against another, foments occasionally riot and insurrection."[2] At some point in the future, the founders feared, a party leader might even seize power as a dictator.

Federalists and Anti-Federalists In spite of the founders' fears, two major political factions—the Federalists and the Anti-Federalists—were formed even before the Constitution was ratified. Remember from Chapter 2 that the Federalists pushed for the ratification of the Constitution because they wanted a stronger national government than the one that had existed under the Articles of Confederation. The

Library of Congress

John Adams (1735–1826) was the Federalists' candidate to succeed George Washington. Adams defeated Thomas Jefferson in 1796 but lost to him in 1800. *What did the Federalists stand for?*

Thomas Jefferson (1743–1826) became our third president and served two terms. Jefferson's Republicans (not to be confused with the later Republican Party of Abraham Lincoln) dominated American politics for more than two decades. *What kinds of people supported this party?*

Library of Congress

Andrew Jackson (1767–1845) led the newly formed Democratic Party. Jackson won the presidential election in 1828, defeating the candidate of the National Republicans (soon to be known as the Whigs). *Which of these two parties was more like the Federalists?*

Library of Congress

Anti-Federalists argued against ratification. They supported states' rights and feared a too-powerful central government.

Federalists and Republicans The Federalist and Anti-Federalist factions continued, in somewhat altered form, after the Constitution was ratified. Alexander Hamilton, the first secretary of the Treasury, became the leader of the Federalist Party, which Vice President John Adams also joined. The Federalists supported a strong central government that would encourage the development of commerce and manufacturing. The Federalists generally thought that a republic should be ruled by its wealthiest and best-educated citizens.

Opponents of the Federalists and Hamilton's policies referred to themselves as Republicans. Today, they are often referred to as Jeffersonian Republicans or Democratic Republicans (names never used at the time), to distinguish this group from the later-established Republican Party. Jefferson's Republicans favored a more limited role for government. They believed that the nation's welfare would be best served if the states had more power than the central government. In their view, Congress should dominate the government, and government policies should serve farming interests rather than promote commerce and manufacturing.

7-1b From 1796 to 1860

The nation's first two parties clashed openly in the elections of 1796, in which John Adams, the Federalists' candidate to succeed George Washington as president, defeated Thomas Jefferson. Over the next four years, Jefferson and James Madison worked to extend the influence of their Republican Party. In the presidential elections of 1800 and 1804, Jefferson won the presidency, and his party also won control of Congress.

Triumph of the Jeffersonians The transition of political power from the Federalists to Jefferson's party is the first example in American history of what political scientists have called a **realignment**. In a realignment, a substantial number of voters change their political allegiance, which usually also changes the balance of power between the two major parties. In fact, the Federalists never returned to power and thus became the first (but not the last) American party to go out of existence. (See the time line of American political parties in Figure 7–1.)

> **realignment** A process in which the popular support for and relative strength of the parties shift and the parties are reestablished with different coalitions of supporters.

FIGURE 7–1 A TIME LINE OF U.S. POLITICAL PARTIES

Many of these parties—including the Constitutional Union Party, Henry Wallace's Progressive Party, and the States' Rights Democrats—were important during only one presidential election.

ANTI-FEDERALISTS
Nonparty faction formed to prevent ratification of the Constitution.

FEDERALIST PARTY
Formed to promote ratification of the Constitution.

JEFFERSON'S REPUBLICAN PARTY
Formed to oppose Federalist policies. Initially led by Thomas Jefferson.

NATIONAL REPUBLICAN PARTY
Split off from Jefferson's Republican Party. Formed by John Quincy Adams and Henry Clay to promote a strong national government. The National Republicans later became the Whig Party.

DEMOCRATIC PARTY
Emerged when Andrew Jackson ran against John Quincy Adams, presidential nominee of the National Republican Party.

WHIG PARTY
Stood for national unity, public works, and limited presidential power. Essentially a reorganized version of the National Republican Party.

REPUBLICAN PARTY
Formed to oppose slavery. Took the name of Jefferson's old party.

CONSTITUTIONAL UNION PARTY
Formed to save the Union from the Civil War. Mostly former southern Whigs.

PEOPLE'S PARTY
Appealed to farmers. Wanted to create inflation to help debtors pay off their obligations.

SOCIALIST PARTY
Labor oriented. Sought to replace capitalism with a system based on government or worker control of corporations.

BULL MOOSE PROGRESSIVE PARTY
Formed by Theodore Roosevelt. Prevented President Taft's reelection for president by splitting the Republican Party.

STATES' RIGHTS DEMOCRATS
Organized by dissident southern Democrats to promote segregation and states' rights.

HENRY WALLACE'S PROGRESSIVE PARTY
Formed to elect Wallace to the presidency and end segregation. Was seen as too sympathetic to Communists.

AMERICAN INDEPENDENT PARTY
Formed by Alabama governor George Wallace. Opposed the civil rights movement.

LIBERTARIAN PARTY
Advocates the least possible intervention by the government in economic and social matters.

REFORM PARTY
Formed by H. Ross Perot to seek the presidency. Opposed federal budget deficits.

GREEN PARTY
Supports environmentalism and opposes corporate influence.

Time line dates: 1787, 1790, 1792, 1800, 1810, 1820, 1828, 1830, 1836, 1840, 1850, 1854, 1860, 1870, 1880, 1887, 1890, 1900, 1901, 1910, 1912, 1920, 1930, 1940, 1948, 1950, 1960, 1968, 1970, 1971, 1980, 1990, 1996, 2000, 2010

© 2018 Cengage Learning

Jefferson's Republicans dominated American politics for the next twenty years. Jefferson was succeeded in the White House by two other members of the party—James Madison and James Monroe. In the mid-1820s, however, Jefferson's Republicans split into two groups. This was the second realignment in American history. Supporters of Andrew Jackson, who was elected president in 1828, called themselves Democrats. The Democrats appealed to small farmers and the growing class of urbanized workers. The other group, the National Republicans (later the Whig Party), was led by John Quincy Adams, Henry Clay, and the great orator Daniel

Webster. It had the support of bankers, business owners, and many southern planters.

The Impending Crisis As the Whigs and Democrats competed for the White House throughout the 1840s and 1850s, the two-party system as we know it today emerged. Both parties were large, with well-known leaders and supporters across the nation. Both had grassroots organizations of party workers committed to winning as many political offices (at all levels of government) for the party as possible. Both the Whigs and the Democrats tried to avoid the issue of slavery.

PART THREE: The Politics of Democracy

148

By the mid-1850s, the Whig coalition had fallen apart. Most northern Whigs were absorbed into the new Republican Party, which opposed the extension of slavery into new territories. Campaigning on this platform in 1860, the Republicans succeeded in electing Abraham Lincoln—the first president elected under the banner of the new Republican Party.

7-1c From the Civil War to the Great Depression

When the former Confederate states rejoined the Union after the Civil War, the Republicans and Democrats were roughly even in strength. The Republicans, though, were more successful in presidential contests. It was in this period that the Republicans picked up the nickname **GOP**, for "grand old party."

In the 1890s, however, the Republicans gained a decisive advantage. In that decade, the Democrats allied themselves with the Populist movement, which consisted largely of indebted farmers in the West and South. The Populists—the People's Party—advocated inflation as a way of lessening their debts. Urban workers in the Midwest and East strongly opposed this program, which would erode the value of their paychecks. After the realigning election of 1896, the Republicans established themselves in the minds of many Americans as the party that knew how to manage the nation's economy. We illustrate the results of the 1896 presidential elections in Figure 7–2.

As a result of a Republican split, the Democrats under Woodrow Wilson won power from 1912 to 1920. Otherwise, the Republicans remained dominant in national politics until the onset of the Great Depression.

7-1d After the Great Depression

The Great Depression of the 1930s destroyed the belief that the GOP could better manage the economy and contributed to another realignment in the two-party system. In a realignment, the minority (opposition) party may emerge as the majority party, and this is certainly what happened in 1932. The election of 1932 brought Franklin D. Roosevelt to the presidency and the Democrats back to power at the national level.

A Civil Rights Plank Roosevelt's programs to fight the Depression were called the *New Deal*. Those who joined the Democrats during Roosevelt's New Deal included a substantial share of African Americans—Roosevelt's relief programs were open to people of all races. (Until the 1930s, African Americans had been overwhelmingly Republican.) In 1948, for the first time ever, the Democrats adopted a civil rights plank as part of the party platform at their national convention. A number of southern Democrats revolted and ran a separate States' Rights ticket for president.

> **GOP** A nickname for the Republican Party—"grand old party."

Library of Congress

From the election of Abraham Lincoln in 1860 until 1932, the Republican Party was the more successful party in presidential politics. *In what areas were the Republicans strong?*

Library of Congress

The realigning election of 1932 brought Franklin Delano Roosevelt to the presidency and the Democrats back to power at the national level. *Why did the Democrats win in 1932?*

FIGURE 7-2 THE 1896 PRESIDENTIAL ELECTION RESULTS

This map shows the 1896 presidential election results by state. This pattern held in subsequent elections. Note that it is almost a complete reverse of the modern political pattern, reflecting the change in the Democrats from a party of segregation and small government to a party of civil rights and government activism.

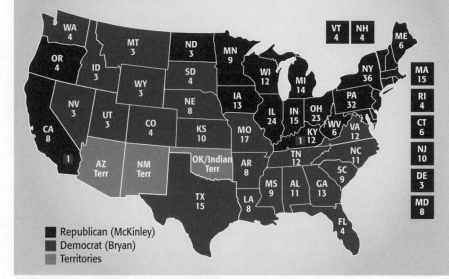

■ Republican (McKinley)
■ Democrat (Bryan)
■ Territories

In 1964, the Democrats, under incumbent president Lyndon Johnson, won a landslide victory, and liberals held a majority in Congress. In the political environment that produced this election result, a coalition of northern Democrats and Republicans crafted the major civil rights legislation that you read about in Chapter 5. The subsequent years were turbulent, with riots and marches in major cities and student protests against the Vietnam War (1965–1975).

A "Rolling Realignment" Conservative Democrats did not like the direction in which their party seemed to be taking them. Under President Richard Nixon, the Republican Party was receptive to these conservative Democrats, and over a period of years, most of them became GOP voters. This was a major alteration in the political landscape, although it was not exclusively associated with a single election. Republican president Ronald Reagan helped cement the new Republican coalition.

Turnover in Congress. The Democrats continued to hold majorities in the House and Senate until 1994, but partisan labels were somewhat misleading. During the 1970s and 1980s, a large bloc of Democrats in Congress, mostly from the South, sided with the Republicans on almost all issues. In time, these conservative Democrats were replaced by conservative Republicans.

A Closely Divided Nation. The result of this "rolling realignment" was that the two major parties were fairly evenly matched. The elections of 2000 were a striking demonstration of how closely the electorate was now divided. Republican George W. Bush won the presidency in that year by carrying Florida with a margin of 537 votes. Democrat Al Gore actually received about half a million more popular votes than Bush. Following the elections, the Senate was made up of 50 Republicans and 50 Democrats. The GOP controlled the House by a razor-thin margin of seven seats. We show the changing levels of support for the major parties in Figure 7–3.

CRITICAL THINKING

▶ *If you could create a new party, what would be its most important principles?*

7-2 AMERICA'S POLITICAL PARTIES TODAY

LO Describe the current status of the two major parties.

Historically, political parties drew together like-minded individuals. Today, too, individuals with similar characteristics tend to align themselves more often with one or the other major party. Such factors as race, age, income, education, marital status, and geography all influence party identification.

7-2a Red States versus Blue States

Geography is one of the many factors that can determine party identification. Examine the national electoral map shown in Figure 7–4. Like past Republicans, Donald Trump did well in the South, the Great Plains, and parts of the Mountain West. He also carried most of the Midwest, a new development. Democrat Hillary Clinton did well in the Northeast, the West Coast, and in certain other states such as Illinois. Beginning with the presidential elections of 2000, the press has made much of the supposed cultural differences between the

FIGURE 7–3 PARTY IDENTIFICATION OVER THE YEARS

This chart shows the levels of popular identification with the two major parties and with the *independent* label. In practice, most independents almost always support one of the major parties. The number of true independents may be as low as 10 percent.

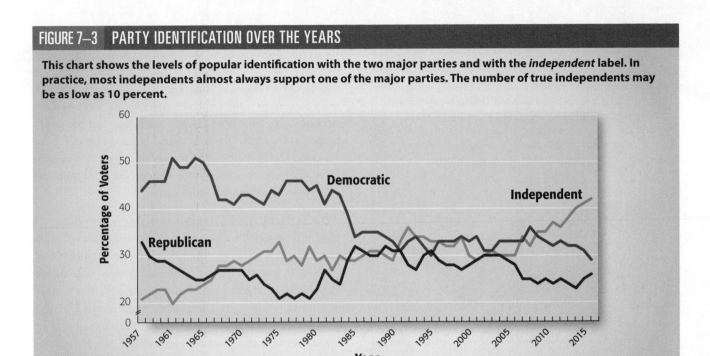

Sources: 1957–1989 and 2015–2016, the Gallup Organization; 1990–2014, the Pew Research Center.

"blue" states that vote for the Democratic candidate and the "red" states that vote for the Republican.[3] In reality, though, many states could better be described as "purple"—that is, a mixture of red and blue. These states could give their electoral votes to either party.

FIGURE 7–4 THE 2016 PRESIDENTIAL ELECTION RESULTS

Donald Trump made major gains in the Midwest. Maine awards two of its electoral votes by congressional district, and the pink dot reflects Trump's victory in one of them.

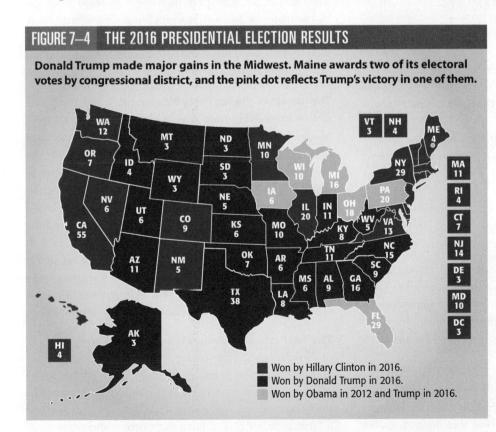

■ Won by Hillary Clinton in 2016.
■ Won by Donald Trump in 2016.
■ Won by Obama in 2012 and Trump in 2016.

For another way to consider the influence of geography, see the map of Minnesota in Figure 7–5.

Most of Minnesota is red, and a quick glance might lead you to think that Trump carried the state. In fact, Clinton carried Minnesota by 2 percentage points. Minnesota looks red because Trump carried almost all of the rural parts of the state. The Clinton counties had larger populations.

This pattern was seen all over the country: the more urban the county, the more likely it was to vote Democratic.

7-2b Shifting Political Fortunes

As noted earlier, by 2000 the two major parties were very closely matched in terms of support. But that situation soon began to shift.

Troubles for Both Parties During 2005, the seemingly endless war in Iraq began to cut into support for the Republicans. In 2006, the Democrats regained control of

FIGURE 7–5 THE 2016 PRESIDENTIAL ELECTION RESULTS IN MINNESOTA

This map displays the Minnesota counties carried by Hillary Clinton (blue) and Donald Trump (red) in the 2016 presidential elections. Clinton took the state by winning the three largest metro areas—the Twin Cities, Rochester, and Duluth. (She also carried two small industrial counties in the far northeast.)

the House and Senate. In 2008, in the shadow of a global financial crisis, Americans elected Democrat Barack Obama as president.

Within one year of Obama's inauguration, the Democratic advantage had vanished. Continued high rates of unemployment were one major reason. Also, a sharp increase in government activity during Obama's first two years in office appeared to bother many voters. In November 2010, the voters handed the U.S. House to the Republicans. (The Democrats still controlled the Senate.)

Recent Elections   By 2012, some were beginning to wonder whether the strong conservatism of the newly elected Republicans might be alienating independent voters. In fact, in the 2012 elections, Democratic presidential candidate Barack Obama prevailed by almost 4 percentage points.

In 2014, however, Republicans won control of the U.S. Senate and did well in state-level races. At least one cause of that party's success is that America has two very different electorates, one for the midterms and

one when presidential candidates are on the ballot. The midterm electorate now is significantly more Republican than the presidential one. In recent years, younger voters have become more Democratic, even as older ones have moved toward the Republicans. Voter turnout declines across the board in the midterms, but the falloff among younger voters (and minority group members) is especially large. This helps to explain why, since at least 2010, Republicans have done much better in midterm elections than in presidential ones.

The Triumph of Partisanship   A key characteristic of recent politics has been the extreme partisanship of party activists and members of Congress. In the 1960s, party coalitions included a variety of factions with differing politics. The rolling realignment after the elections of 1968 resulted in parties that were much more homogeneous. Political scientists have concluded that already by 2009, the most conservative Democrat in the House was to the left of the most moderate Republican.

Making the Other Party Look Weak.   Ideological uniformity has made it easier for the parties to maintain discipline in Congress. Personal friendships across party lines, once common in Congress, have become rare. The belief has grown that compromise with the other party is a form of betrayal. According to this view, the minority party should not attempt to improve legislation proposed by the majority. Instead, it should oppose majority-party measures in an effort to make the majority appear ineffective. The Republican Party has employed such tactics throughout Obama's term of office.

The Impact of the Tea Party Movement.   Political polarization grew even more severe after the 2010 elections. Many of the new Republican members of Congress were pledged to the Tea Party philosophy of no-compromise conservatism. These members were fully prepared to revolt if the GOP leadership presented them with legislation that Democrats could support. Given that the Democrats still controlled the Senate (through 2014) and the presidency, political deadlock seemed inevitable. In fact, the 112th Congress, which convened in January 2011, produced less legislation than any other session since records were first kept. The 113th Congress, which was seated in January 2013, was only slightly more productive.

The Tea Party and Donald Trump.   Tea Party members of Congress espouse conventional small-government conservatism, which has given many a misleading sense of what Tea Party voters actually believe. Political scientists Theda Skocpol and Vanessa Williamson interviewed a large number of Tea Party supporters and came away

The 2016 elections revealed a continuing shift in sources of support for the two major political parties. You can see signs of these changes in Figure 7–4. Trump picked up a swath of states in the industrial heartland that had not gone Republican in twelve years and in some cases much longer than that: Iowa, Wisconsin, Michigan, Ohio, and Pennsylvania. (He also carried Florida.) These are states with above-average numbers of less-well-educated white working class voters, precisely the demographic group most drawn to Trump. College-educated voters narrowly broke for Clinton—in 2012, a majority of this group voted for Republican Mitt Romney. These developments tended to move the country away from the red-blue map of earlier years. The Democrats were becoming a coalition of minority groups, plus Northern white progressives of all socioeconomic classes. The Republicans were continuing to shed minority voters as they became more and more the party of self-conscious whites. The heart of the Trump vote did not lie in the most hard-pressed members of the working class, who tended not to vote at all. Rather, by one analysis, Trump's strongest supporters were better-off whites who believed their communities were crumbling around them. Jobs were lost to competition from Chinese imports. Drug addiction was growing rapidly among rural whites. Behind everything lay the growing recognition that the United States would be a majority-minority nation by 2050. In one sense it already was—as of 2016, minorities were already in the majority among Americans age three and under.

with a more nuanced understanding.[4] Often, Tea Party advocates are not opposed to government benefits as such. Rather, they are opposed to benefits that, in their opinion, go to undeserving recipients. Immigrants are the number-one "undeserving" group. Other groups can include members of racial and ethnic minorities—and even young people. In contrast, most Social Security and Medicare recipients are seen as deserving.

The belief by Tea Party activists that the government supports the undeserving is combined with the sense that they are losing control of their country to new groups that are culturally, morally, and politically alien. A comparison of these beliefs with the rhetoric of Republican presidential contender Donald Trump suggests that he may have been the true representative of Tea Party ideology in 2016. We took another look at Trump's supporters in the chapter-opening *America at Odds* feature.

7–2c Realignment, Dealignment, and Tipping

Despite the narrowness of the Republican margin after 2000, Republican strategists dreamed of a new realignment that would force the Democrats into the minority. These hopes were not fulfilled. After 2006, many Democrats anticipated a realignment that would benefit the Democrats. These dreams were shattered as well. For a major realignment to take place, a large number of voters must conclude that their party is no longer capable of representing their interests and ideals, and that another party can do better. It is hard to identify large groups of voters who could be swayed to support a different party today.

Dealignment One political development that may rule out realignment is the growth in the number of independent voters. By 2016, fully 42 percent of the electorate claimed to be independent. True, many of these voters admitted to leaning toward the Republicans or the Democrats. Still, anyone claiming to be an independent has a weakened attachment to the parties.

Some political scientists argue that with so many independent voters, the concept of realignment becomes irrelevant. Realignment has been replaced by **dealignment**. In such an environment, politics would be unusually volatile, because

> **dealignment** Among voters, a growing detachment from both major political parties.

independents could swing from one party to another. The dramatic changes in fortune experienced by the two major parties in recent years provide some evidence to support the dealignment theory. Both parties have recently experienced record-high unfavorable scores in public opinion polls.

Tipping Realignment is not the only process that can alter the political landscape. What if the various types of voters maintain their political identifications—but one type of voter becomes substantially more numerous? This can happen due to migration between states or between nations, or even due to changes in education levels and occupations. The result could tip a state from one party to another. Many Democratic strategists believe that such *tipping* will benefit their party greatly in the future. How likely is it that this could happen? We look at that question in this chapter's *Perception vs. Reality* feature.

Democratic presidential candidate Hillary Clinton campaigns in Texas before that state's primary. *What kinds of voters supported her?*

CRITICAL THINKING

▶ *Demographers expect that minority group members will be a majority of the U.S. population by 2050. How might this affect the two major parties?*

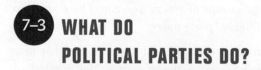

7–3 WHAT DO POLITICAL PARTIES DO?

LO Explain how political parties function in our democratic system.

As noted earlier, the Constitution does not mention political parties. Historically, though, political parties have played a vital role in our democratic system. Their main function has been to link the people's policy preferences to actual government policies. Political parties also perform many other functions.

primary A preliminary election held for the purpose of choosing a party's final candidate.

7–3a Selecting Candidates and Running Campaigns

One of the most important functions of the two political parties is to recruit and nominate candidates for political office. This function simplifies voting choices for the electorate. Political parties take the large number of people who want to run for office and narrow the field. They accomplish this by the use of the **primary**, which is a preliminary election to choose a party's final candidate. This candidate then runs against the opposing party's candidate in the general election.

Primary Elections Voter turnout for primaries is lower than it is for general elections. The voters who do go to the polls are often strong supporters of their party. Indeed, in many states, independents cannot participate in primary elections, even if they lean toward one or the other of the two major parties. As a result, the Republican primary electorate is very conservative, and Democratic primary voters are quite liberal. Candidates often find that they must run to the political right or left during the primaries. Traditionally, candidates then often moved to the center during the general election campaign. Chapter 9 provides much more detail on primary and general elections.

Running Campaigns Through their national, state, and local organizations, parties coordinate campaigns. Political parties take care of a large number of

PERCEPTION VS. REALITY

Demography Favors the Democrats

In 2002, John Judis and Ruy Teixeira published *The Emerging Democratic Majority*.[5] Judis and Teixeira argued that in the future, a growing number of Latinos and young urban professionals would give the Democratic Party an edge. In the following years, the Republicans did well in elections, and the authors' thesis was met with a certain amount of scorn. Beginning in 2008, however, Mexican American voters appeared to be drawing Colorado and Nevada away from the Republicans. Also, urban professionals, many from the north, were turning Republican Virginia into a swing state. Could it be that Judis and Teixeira were onto something?

The Perception

Hispanics and Asian Americans are a growing share of the population. Since 2013, a majority of American first-grade students have been minority group members. By 2050, non-Hispanic whites are expected to make up less than half of the population. If Latinos and Asians continue to favor the Democrats, the Republicans are in serious long-term demographic trouble.

The Reality

The reality is more complicated. Indeed, Judis himself has repudiated his earlier analysis. He now argues that the Republicans will gain an edge. True, various Democratic-leaning parts of the electorate are growing in numbers. At the same time, however, an ever-larger number of white voters have swung to the Republicans. The process is especially notable in a band of states ranging from West Virginia in the east, through Kentucky and Tennessee, and on to Missouri, Arkansas, and Oklahoma. In recent elections, growing white support for the Republicans has effectively counteracted the growth in the Democratic immigrant and urban professional vote. Consider: If whites dominated the electorate today the way that they did back in the 1990s, Democrat Barack Obama would not have been elected president in 2008 and 2012. Obama simply failed to win as many white votes as Democratic president Bill Clinton (1993–2001). But the increase in the minority vote balanced out the growing number of Republican whites.

A further problem in congressional elections is that the Democratic vote is increasingly piled up in big-city districts. The Democrats win these by large margins, but their extra votes are wasted. (It doesn't help Democrats that the Republicans were able to create many safe seats for themselves after the 2010 census, as you will read in Chapter 11.)

Still, the Republicans face a potential problem. The new Democratic voters are already here as children, and they will begin voting when they grow up. Will the Republicans run out of newly conservative whites before the Democrats run out of new minority voters? The hope for Republicans is that, in time, Hispanic voters will grow more conservative. After all, many Irish and Italian American Democrats eventually became Republicans.

Blog On

*The **National Journal** has published a series of articles on the demographic difficulties faced by the Democratic Party. You can find these articles by searching for "demography democrats national journal."*

---

small and routine tasks that are essential to the smooth functioning of the electoral process. For example, they work at getting party members registered and at conducting drives to recruit new voters. Sometimes, party volunteers staff the polling places.

7–3b Informing the Public

Political parties help educate the public about important political issues. In recent years, these issues have included environmental policies, health-care reform, the tax system, immigration, and ways to stimulate the economy. Each party presents its views on these issues through television announcements, newspaper articles or ads, website materials, campaign speeches, and debates. These activities help citizens learn about the issues, form opinions, and consider proposed solutions.

7–3c Coordinating Policymaking

In our complex government, parties are essential for coordinating policy among the various branches of the government. The political party is usually the major institution through which the executive and legislative branches cooperate with each other. Each president, cabinet head, and member of Congress is normally a member of the Democratic Party or the Republican Party. The president works through party leaders in Congress to promote the administration's legislative program.

Ideally, the parties work together to fashion compromises—legislation that is acceptable to both parties and that serves the national interest. Yet in recent years, as we noted earlier, there has been little bipartisanship in Congress. (For a more detailed discussion of the role played by political parties in Congress, see Chapter 11.) Parties also act as the glue of our federal structure by connecting the various levels of government—state and national—with a common bond.

7-3d Checking the Power of the Governing Party

The party with fewer members in the legislature is the **minority party**. The party with more members is the **majority party**. Whether we're considering control of the legislature or of the executive branch, the party that is not in control plays a vital function in American politics. The "out" party does what it can to influence the "in" party and its policies, and to check the actions of the party in power.

For example, depending on how evenly Congress is divided, the out party, or minority party, may be able to attract to its side some of the members of the majority party to pass or defeat certain legislation. The minority party will also work to inform voters of the shortcomings of the majority party's agenda and to plan strategies for winning the next election.

7-3e Balancing Competing Interests

minority party The political party that has fewer members in the legislature than the opposing party.

majority party The political party that has more members in the legislature than the opposing party.

coalition An alliance of individuals or groups with a variety of interests and opinions who join together to support all or part of a political party's platform.

electorate All of the citizens eligible to vote in a given election.

Political parties are often described as vast umbrellas under which Americans with diverse interests can gather. Political parties are essentially **coalitions**—alliances of individuals and groups with a variety of interests and opinions who join together to support the party's platform, or parts of it.

The Democratic Party, for example, includes a number of groups with different views on such issues as health care, immigration, and climate change. The role of party leaders in this situation is to adopt a view broad enough on these issues that no group will be alienated. In this way, different groups can hold their individual views and still come together under the umbrella of the Democratic Party.

Like the Democrats, the Republicans are a coalition. The Republican coalition, however, rests on different principles than the Democratic one. Much more than the Democrats, the Republicans are held together by a shared set of ideas. In a recent study, political scientists Matt Grossmann and David Hopkins found evidence that "the Republican Party is primarily the agent of an ideological movement whose supporters prize doctrinal purity, while the Democratic Party is better understood as a coalition of social groups seeking concrete government action."[6]

This asymmetry reflects an essential truth about the American electorate. Time and again, observers have noted that Americans express ideological support for a smaller, less active government. At the same time, they also support almost every program undertaken by the federal government. It makes sense, then, that a conservative party would benefit from an ideological appeal to voters. The Democrats, in turn, would benefit when they highlight actual programs, such as Social Security or minimum wage laws. Regardless of whether a party is oriented toward small-government ideology or positive government action, however, it still needs to promote unity among diverse party factions.

CRITICAL THINKING

▶ *Presidents often have political goals that are different from those of senators and representatives from the president's own party. What might these presidential goals be?*

7–4 HOW AMERICAN POLITICAL PARTIES ARE STRUCTURED

LO Discuss the structure of American political parties.

Each of the two major American political parties consists of three components: the party in the electorate, the party organization, and the party in government.

1. The party in the **electorate** is the largest component, consisting of all of those people who describe themselves as Democrats or Republicans. In most

states, a voter can register as a Democrat or a Republican, but registration can be changed at will.

2. Each major party has a nationwide organization with national, state, and local offices. As will be discussed later in this section, the party organizations include several levels of people who maintain the party's strength between elections, make its rules, raise money, organize conventions, help with elections, and recruit candidates.

3. The party in government consists of all of the party's candidates who have won elections and now hold public office.

Like sports teams, the parties have mascots. The Republican elephant and the Democratic donkey date to the nineteenth century. Both were first drawn by a Republican cartoonist. The elephant was supposed to illustrate the large size of the GOP in the northern states. *Given that the donkey was drawn by a Republican, what do you think it was meant to represent?*

7–4a The Party in the Electorate

Let's look more closely at the largest component of each party—the party in the electorate. What does it mean to belong to a political party? In many European countries, being a party member means that you actually join a political party. You get a membership card to carry in your wallet, you pay dues, and you vote to select your local and national party leaders. In the United States, becoming a member of a political party is far less involved.

In most states, voters may declare a party preference when they register to vote. This declaration allows them to participate in party primaries. Some states do not register party preferences, however. In short, to be a member of a political party, an American citizen has only to think of herself or himself as a Democrat or a Republican (or a member of a third party, such as the Green Party or the Libertarian Party). Members of parties do not have to work for the party or attend party meetings. Nor must they support the party platform.

Identifiers and Activists Generally, the party in the electorate consists of **party identifiers** (those who identify themselves as being members of the party) and **party activists**—party members who choose to work for the party and may even become candidates for office. Political parties need year-round support from the latter group to survive. During election campaigns in particular, candidates depend on active party members and volunteers to answer phones, conduct door-to-door canvasses, participate in Web campaigns, organize speeches and appearances, and, of course, donate money.

Between elections, parties also need active members to plan the upcoming elections, organize fund-raisers, and stay in touch with party leaders in other communities to keep the party strong. The major functions of American political parties are carried out by the party activists.

Elite Groups Most members of the party in the electorate are ordinary citizens. Even party activists are generally not known outside their own circles. Yet the party in the electorate is not limited to those who lack fortune or fame. It is also made up of elites of various kinds—opinion leaders, media personalities, and prominent persons in all walks of life. It includes fund-raisers, former politicians, and nationally famous political operatives.

Consider talk radio personality Rush Limbaugh and deep-pocket campaign contributors Charles and David Koch. These people have no official position in government or in the Republican Party. They may be members of the party in the electorate, but their influence on the

party identifier
A person who identifies himself or herself as being a supporter of a particular political party.

party activist A party member who helps to organize and oversee party functions and planning during and between campaigns, and may even become a candidate for office.

GOP is considerable. Likewise, comedian Jon Stewart and Arianna Huffington of the *Huffington Post* are influential among Democrats. A large number of entertainment celebrities are ardent Democrats, though some are Republicans.

Various interest groups are also considered to be part of the party coalitions. Labor unions are almost always seen as a base of support for the Democrats. Business groups such as the U.S. Chamber of Commerce are likewise viewed as key Republican players.

Why People Join Political Parties

In a few countries, such as the People's Republic of China, people belong to a political party because doing so will help them to get ahead in life, regardless of whether they agree with the party's ideas and candidates. In the United States, though, people generally belong to a political party because they agree with many of its main ideas and support some of its candidates. Just as with interest groups, people's reasons for choosing one party over another may include solidarity, material, and purposive incentives.

Solidarity Incentives. Some people join a particular party to express their **solidarity**, or mutual agreement, with the views of friends, loved ones, and other like-minded people. People also join parties because they enjoy the excitement of engaging in politics with like-minded others.

Material Incentives. Many believe that by joining a party, they will benefit materially through better employment or personal career advancement. The traditional institution of **patronage**—rewarding the party faithful with government jobs or contracts—lives on, even though it has been limited to prevent abuses.[7] Back in the nineteenth century, when almost all government employees got their jobs through patronage, people spoke of it as the "spoils system," as in "the spoils of war."

solidarity Mutual agreement among the members of a particular group.

patronage A system of rewarding the party faithful and workers with government jobs or contracts.

Purposive Incentives. Finally, some join political parties because they wish to actively promote a set of ideals and principles that they feel are important to American politics and society. As a rule, people join political

Donald Trump accepts the presidential nomination at the 2016 Republican convention in Cleveland, Ohio, on July 21. *Who attends such conventions?*

parties because of their overall agreement with what a particular party stands for.

Thus, when asked why they support the Democratic Party, people may make such remarks as the following: "The economy is better when the Democrats are in control." "The Democrats are for the working people." People might say about the Republican Party: "The Republicans favor a smaller government." "The Republicans are stronger on national defense."

7–4b The Party Organization

In theory, each of the major American political parties has a standard, pyramid-shaped organization. This theoretical structure is much like that of a large company, in which the bosses are at the top and the employees are at various lower levels.

Actually, neither major party is a closely knit or highly organized structure. Both parties are fragmented and *decentralized*, which means there is no central power with a direct chain of command. If there were, the national chairperson of the party, along with the national committee, could simply dictate how the organization would be run, just as if it were Apple or Google. In reality, state party organizations are all very different and are only loosely tied to the party's national structure. Local party organizations are often quite independent from the state organization.

In short, no single individual or group directs all party members. Instead, a number of personalities, frequently at odds with one another, form loosely identifiable leadership groups.

State Organizations The powers and duties of state party organizations differ from state to state. In general, the state party organization is built around a central committee and a chairperson. The committee works to raise funds, recruit new party members, maintain a strong party organization, and help members running for state offices.

The state chairperson is usually a powerful party member chosen by the committee. In some instances, however, the chairperson is selected by the governor or a senator from that state.

Local Organizations Local party organizations differ greatly, but generally there is a party unit for each district in which elective offices are to be filled. These districts include congressional and legislative districts, counties, cities and towns, wards, and precincts.

A **ward** is a political division or district within a city. A **precinct** can be either a political district within a city, such as a block or a neighborhood, or a rural portion of a county. Polling places are located within the precincts. The local, grassroots foundations of politics are formed within voting precincts.

The National Party Organization On the national level, the party's presidential candidate is considered to be the leader of the party. Well-known

> "UNDER DEMOCRACY ONE PARTY ALWAYS DEVOTES ITS CHIEF ENERGIES TO TRYING TO PROVE THAT THE OTHER PARTY IS *UNFIT TO RULE*—AND BOTH COMMONLY SUCCEED."
>
> ~ H. L. MENCKEN,
> AMERICAN JOURNALIST, 1880–1956

members of Congress may also be viewed as national party leaders. In addition to the party leaders, the structure of each party includes four major elements: the national convention, the national committee, the national chairperson, and the congressional campaign committees.

The National Convention. Much of the public attention that the party receives comes at the **national convention**, which is held every four years during the summer before the presidential elections. The news media always cover the conventions, and as a result, these gatherings have become quite extravagant. Lobbyists, big business, and interest groups provide millions of dollars to put on these events. Such organizations have an interest in government subsidies, tax breaks, and regulatory favors.

The conventions inspire and mobilize party members throughout the nation. They provide the voters with an opportunity to see and hear the candidates directly, rather than through a media filter or characterizations provided by supporters and opponents. Candidates' speeches at conventions draw huge audiences.

For example, in 2016 more than 30 million people watched the acceptance speeches of Donald Trump and Hillary Clinton. President Obama's speech was even more widely viewed.

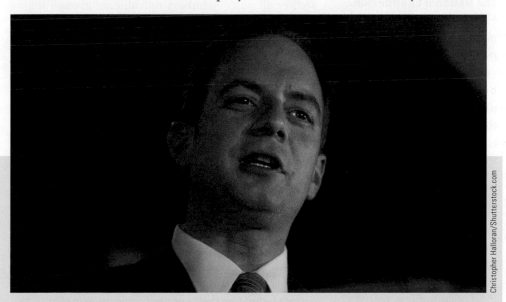

Reince Priebus is chair of the Republican National Committee. *How much control does he have over state party organizations?*

Christopher Halloran/Shutterstock.com

ward A local unit of a political party's organization, consisting of a division or district within a city.

precinct A political district within a city, such as a block or a neighborhood, or a rural portion of a county; the smallest voting district at the local level.

national convention The meeting held by each major party every four years to nominate presidential and vice-presidential candidates, write a party platform, and conduct other party business.

The national conventions are attended by delegates chosen by the states in various ways, which we describe in Chapter 9. The delegates' most important job is to nominate the party's presidential and vice-presidential candidates, who together make up the **party ticket**. A select group of key delegates also writes the **party platform**, which sets forth the party's positions on national issues. Essentially, through its platform, the party promises to initiate certain policies if it wins the presidency. Despite the widespread perception that candidates can and do ignore these promises once they are in office, in fact, many of the promises become law.

The National Committee. Each state elects a number of delegates to the **national party committee**. The Republican National Committee and the Democratic National Committee direct the business of their respective parties during the four years between national conventions. The committees' most important duties, however, are to organize the next national convention and to plan how to support the party's candidate in the next presidential election.

The National Chairperson. Each party's national committee elects a **national party chairperson** to serve as administrative head of the national party. The main duty of the national chairperson is to direct the work of the national committee from party headquarters in Washington, D.C. The chairperson is involved in raising funds, providing for publicity, promoting party unity, encouraging the development of state and local organizations, recruiting new voters, and other activities. In presidential

> **"I AM NOT A MEMBER OF ANY ORGANIZED POLITICAL PARTY. I AM A DEMOCRAT."**
>
> ~ WILL ROGERS, AMERICAN HUMORIST, 1879–1935

party ticket A list of a political party's candidates for various offices. In national elections, the party ticket consists of the presidential and vice-presidential candidates.

party platform The document drawn up by each party at its national convention that outlines the policies and positions of the party.

national party committee The political party leaders who direct party business during the four years between the national party conventions, organize the next national convention, and plan how to support the party's candidate in the next presidential election.

national party chairperson An individual who serves as a political party's administrative head at the national level and directs the work of the party's national committee.

election years, the chairperson's attention is focused on the national convention and the presidential campaign.

The Congressional Campaign Committees. Each party has a campaign committee in each chamber of Congress. In each chamber, members are chosen by their colleagues and serve for two-year terms. The committees work to help elect party members to Congress.

7-4c The Party in Government: Developing Issues

Even though candidates above the local level almost always run for office as either Democrats or Republicans, members of a given party do not always agree with one another on government policy. The party in government helps to organize the government's agenda by coaxing and convincing its own party members in office to vote for its policies. If the party is to translate its promises into public policies, the job must be done by the party in government.

A political party succeeds at the national level when it wins the presidency or control of one or more chambers of Congress. It then has the opportunity to carry out the party platform it developed at its national convention. The platform represents the official party position on various issues. As noted, though, neither all party members nor all candidates running on the party's ticket are likely to share these positions exactly.

A dispute among Democrats during the development of the Affordable Care Act—Obamacare—can serve as an example. A minority of the Democrats in the House strongly opposed abortion. The votes of this group were essential to passing the new legislation. The Democratic leadership therefore had to devote considerable attention to the way the reforms dealt with abortion to win the group's support. The leadership was successful, and in the end almost all Democrats supported the legislation.

CRITICAL THINKING

▶ *The parties often hope they can win additional votes in a state by holding their national convention in that state. Do you think this strategy is likely to be effective? Why or why not?*

7-5 THE DOMINANCE OF OUR TWO-PARTY SYSTEM

LO Describe the different types of third parties and how they function in the American political system.

In the United States, as noted, we have a **two-party system**. This means that the two major parties—the Democrats and the Republicans—dominate national politics. Why has the two-party system become so firmly entrenched in the United States? According to some scholars, the first major political division between the Federalists and the Anti-Federalists established a precedent that continued over time and ultimately resulted in the domination of the two-party system.

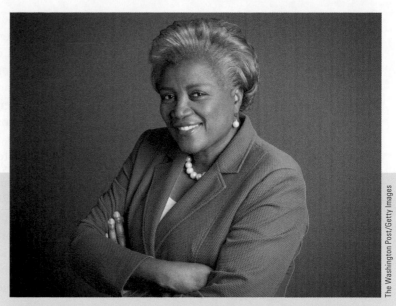

Donna Brazile, interim chair of the Democratic National Committee (DNC) from July 2016. *On the eve of the July 2016 Democratic National Convention, Russian hackers released DNC emails showing bias against Bernie Sanders. The DNC's chair at the time, Debbie Wasserman Schultz, was forced to resign.*

The Washington Post/Getty Images

7-5a The Self-Perpetuation of the Two-Party System

One of the major reasons for the perpetuation of the two-party system is simply that there is no alternative. Minor parties, called **third parties**,[8] have found it extremely difficult to compete with the major parties for votes. There are many reasons for this, some of which are described in the following subsections.

Political Socialization When young people or new immigrants learn about U.S. politics, they tend to absorb the political views of those who are providing them with information. Parents find it easy to pass their political beliefs on to their children, often without even trying. Those beliefs frequently involve support for one of the two major parties.

To be sure, about two-fifths of voters today regard themselves as independents (although they may lean

toward one party or another). These voters apparently believe that neither major party fully represents their views. Such attitudes, however, do not mean that independents are looking for a third party. Typically, true independents are content to swing between the Democrats and the Republicans.

Election Laws Favoring Two Parties American election laws tend to favor the major parties. In many states, for example, the established major parties need relatively few signatures to place their candidates on the ballot, whereas a third party must get many more signatures. The number of signatures required is often based on the total party vote in the last election, which penalizes a new party that is competing for the first time. The rules governing campaign financing also favor the major parties.

Institutional Barriers to a Multiparty System The structure of many of our institutions prevents third parties from enjoying electoral success. The nature of the election process works against third-party candidates, as does the nature of single-member districts.

The Election Process. One of the major institutional barriers to third parties is the election, by the people,

> "Let us not seek the Republican answer or the Democratic answer, but the right answer."
>
> ~ JOHN FITZGERALD KENNEDY,
> THIRTY-FIFTH PRESIDENT OF THE UNITED STATES,
> 1961–1963

two-party system A political system in which two strong and established parties compete for political offices.

third party In the United States, any party other than the two major parties (Republican and Democratic).

CHAPTER 7: Political Parties   161

of governors and (through the electoral college) the president. Voting for governors and members of the electoral college takes place on a statewide, winner-take-all basis. (Maine and Nebraska are exceptions—they can, under certain circumstances, split their electoral votes.) Third-party candidates find it hard to win when they must campaign statewide instead of appealing to voters in a smaller district that might be more receptive to their political positions.

The popular election of executive officers contrasts with the parliamentary system described in *The Rest of the World* feature in Chapter 2. In that system, parliament—not the voters—chooses the nation's executive officers. Third-party voters therefore have a greater chance of affecting the outcome by electing a few members of parliament. Even if the party's delegation is small, it may be able to participate in a coalition government with other parties.

Single-Member Districts versus Proportional Systems. Another institutional barrier to a multiparty system is the single-member district. Today, all federal and most state legislative districts are single-member districts—that is, voters elect one member from their district to the House of Representatives and to their state legislature.[9] In some countries, by contrast, districts are drawn as multimember districts and are represented by multiple elected officials from different parties, according to the proportion of the vote each party received.

In many democracies that use single-member districts to choose members of parliament, additional members are chosen from statewide or nationwide party lists. The number of additional members elected from the party lists is calculated to guarantee that the election results are *proportional*. Under a proportional election system, one party might receive 40 percent of the national vote, another party 35 percent, and a third party 25 percent. Each party can expect to obtain a share of seats in the national parliament that closely reflects its percentage of the vote.

Nonpartisan Elections. While third parties are rarely successful in the United States, the two major parties do not compete in all elections. Some state offices and many local offices are filled by *nonpartisan elections,* in which party identification never appears on the ballot. Are there benefits to the nonpartisan system? We examine that question in this chapter's *Join the Debate* feature.

7-5b Third Parties in American Politics

Despite difficulties, throughout American history third parties have competed for influence in the nation's two-party system. Indeed, as mentioned earlier, third parties have been represented in most of our national elections. These parties are as varied as the causes they represent, but all have one thing in common: their members and leaders want to challenge the major parties because they believe that certain needs and values are not being properly addressed. Table 7–1 lists the most successful American third parties since the Civil War (1861–1865).

TABLE 7–1	THE MOST SUCCESSFUL THIRD-PARTY PRESIDENTIAL CAMPAIGNS SINCE 1865				
This table includes all third-party candidates winning more than 5 percent of the popular vote or any electoral votes since 1865. It does not count "unfaithful electors" in the electoral college who did not vote for the candidate to whom they were pledged.					
Year	**Third Party**	**Third-Party Presidential Candidate**	**Percent of the Popular Vote**	**Electoral Votes**	**Winning Presidential Candidate and Party**
1892	Populist	James Weaver	8.5%	22	Grover Cleveland (D)
1912	Progressive Socialist	Theodore Roosevelt Eugene Debs	27.4 6.0	88 —	Woodrow Wilson (D)
1924	Progressive	Robert LaFollette	16.6	13	Calvin Coolidge (R)
1948	States' Rights	Strom Thurmond	2.4	39	Harry Truman (D)
1960	Independent Democrat	Harry Byrd	0.4	15*	John F. Kennedy (D)
1968	American Independent	George Wallace	13.5	46	Richard Nixon (R)
1980	National Union	John Anderson	6.6	—	Ronald Reagan (R)
1992	Independent	Ross Perot	18.9	—	Bill Clinton (D)
1996	Reform	Ross Perot	8.4	—	Bill Clinton (D)

*Byrd received fifteen electoral votes from unpledged electors in Alabama and Mississippi.
Source: Dave Leip's Atlas of U.S. Presidential Elections at www.uselectionatlas.org.

JOIN THE DEBATE

Are Nonpartisan Elections a Good Idea?

It's hard to miss the partisan battles in Washington, D.C. To a lesser extent, nasty fights also occur in state legislatures and even city councils. As you've learned, the framers of the U.S. Constitution never mentioned political parties. They thought that the nation would be better off without them. Dream on. We will never eliminate partisan elections at the federal level. But what about the state and, particularly, the local levels? Would the states be better off with nonpartisan elections?

Take the Nastiness Out of Elections— Go Nonpartisan

Advocates of nonpartisan elections believe that the two major political parties are the reason that many states are "ungovernable." Political deadlock would be eliminated if state senators and representatives were voted into office without a party label.

Currently, ideological activists— Republicans and Democrats—largely determine the identity of state legislative candidates. Where does that leave independents and moderates? The answer is: underrepresented.

More than two-thirds of American cities have embraced nonpartisan voting. After all, local issues are very different from national ones, and knowing that a candidate is a Republican or a Democrat tells you little about that candidate's policy positions on local issues. It's time to extend nonpartisan elections to state legislatures as well. Nebraska, for one, has such a legislature already.

Nonpartisan Elections Lead to Less-Informed Voters

While enticing in theory, nonpartisan elections do not result in better government, according to their opponents. In some nonpartisan systems, candidates are still affiliated with political parties. Even so, without party labels on the ballot, citizens find it more difficult to cast an informed vote. Ordinary citizens cannot take the time to analyze in any detail the political positions of legislative candidates. Take the example of nonpartisan state elections in Minnesota before 1973. There, prominent local figures were able to win elections even when their politics were unrepresentative of their districts. After partisan labels were introduced in 1973, the state legislature was transformed.

According to law professor David Schleicher, nonpartisan balloting at the city level also leaves voters poorly informed and reduces turnout in elections. True, party labels provide less information in municipal contests than in national elections. They provide at least some information, however, and without them, citizens often know nothing at all. As a result, Schleicher says, voters tend to rely on racial or ethnic clues in candidates' names.

Critical Analysis

If you were independently wealthy and could finance an expensive campaign, would you prefer partisan or nonpartisan elections? Why?

Some third parties have tried to appeal to the entire nation. Others have focused on particular regions, states, or local areas. Most third parties have been short lived. A few, however, such as the Socialist Party (founded in 1901 and disbanded in 1972), lasted for a long time. The number and variety of third parties make them difficult to classify, but most fall into one of the general categories discussed in the following subsections.

Issue-Oriented Parties An issue-oriented third party is formed to promote a particular cause or timely issue. For example, the Free Soil Party was organized in 1848 to oppose the expansion of slavery into the western territories. The Prohibition Party was formed in 1869 to advocate banning the manufacture and use of alcoholic beverages.

Most issue-oriented parties fade into history as the issue that brought them into existence fades from public attention, is taken up by a major party, or is resolved. Some issue-oriented parties endure, however, when they expand their focus beyond a single area of concern. For example, the Green Party was founded in 1972 to raise awareness of environmental issues, but it is no longer a single-issue party. Today, the Green Party campaigns against alleged corporate greed and the major parties' ostensible indifference to a number of issues, including poverty, the excesses of globalism, and the failure of the war on drugs.

Ideological Parties As discussed in Chapter 1, a *political ideology* is a system of political ideas rooted in beliefs about human nature, society, and government. An ideological party supports a particular political doctrine or a set of beliefs.

For example, the Socialist Labor Party believes that our free enterprise system should be replaced by one in which workers control all of the large businesses in the economy. The party's members believe that competition should be replaced by cooperation and social responsibility so as to achieve an equitable distribution of income. In contrast, the Libertarian Party opposes almost all forms of government interference with personal liberties and private enterprise.

Splinter or Personality Parties A splinter party develops out of a split within a major party. This split may be part of an attempt to elect a specific person. For example, when Theodore Roosevelt did not receive the GOP nomination for president in 1912, he created the Bull Moose Party (also called the Progressive Party) to promote his candidacy. From the Democrats have come Henry Wallace's Progressive Party and the States' Rights (Dixiecrat) Party, both formed in 1948. In 1968, the American Independent Party was formed to support George Wallace's campaign for president.

Most splinter parties have been formed around a leader with a strong personality, which is why they are sometimes called *personality parties*. When that person steps aside, the party usually collapses. An example of a personality party is the Reform Party, which was formed in 1996 mainly to provide a campaign vehicle for H. Ross Perot. (The party was later taken over by others and adopted a platform of conservative nationalism.)

7–5c The Effects of Third Parties

Although most Americans do not support third parties or vote for their candidates, third parties have influenced American politics in several ways.

Third Parties Bring Issues to the Public's Attention Third parties have brought many political issues to the public's attention. They have exposed and focused on unpopular or highly debated issues that major parties have preferred to ignore. Third parties are in a position to take bold stands on issues that major parties avoid because third parties are not trying to be all things to all people.

Some people have argued that third parties are often the unsung heroes of American politics, bringing new issues to the forefront of public debate. Progressive social reforms such as the minimum wage, women's right to vote, railroad and banking legislation, and old-age pensions were first proposed by third parties. The Free Soilers of the 1850s were the first true antislavery party, and the Populists and Progressives put many social reforms on the political agenda. Although some of the ideas proposed by third parties were never accepted, others were taken up by the major parties as those ideas became increasingly popular.

Third Parties Can Affect the Vote Third parties can also influence election outcomes. On occasion, they have taken victory from one major party and given it to another, thus playing the "spoiler" role.

For example, in 1912, when the Progressive Party split from the Republican Party, the result was three major contenders for the presidency: Woodrow Wilson, the Democratic candidate; William Howard Taft, the regular Republican candidate; and Theodore Roosevelt, the Progressive candidate. The presence of the

Eugene V. Debs was the Socialist Party candidate for president in five elections. *Why would a self-identified socialist—such as Vermont senator Bernie Sanders—be more successful running as a Democrat?*

Progressive Party "spoiled" the Republicans' chances for victory and gave the election to Wilson, the Democrat. Without Roosevelt's third party, Taft might have won. Similarly, some commentators contended that Green Party candidate Ralph Nader "spoiled" the chances of Democratic candidate Al Gore in the 2000 elections, because many of those who voted for Nader would have voted Democratic had Nader not been on the ballot.

Third Parties Provide a Voice for Dissatisfied Americans   Third parties also provide a voice for voters who are frustrated with and alienated from the Republican and Democratic parties. Americans who are unhappy with the two major political parties can still participate in American politics through third parties that reflect their opinions on political issues. For example, many new Minnesota voters turned out during the 1998 elections to vote for Jesse Ventura, a Reform Party candidate for governor in that state. Ventura won.

Ultimately, third parties in national elections find it difficult to break through in an electoral system that perpetuates their failure. Because third parties normally do not win elections, Americans tend not to vote for them or to contribute to their campaigns, so they continue not to win. As long as Americans hold on to the perception that third parties can never win an election, the current two-party system is likely to persist.

CRITICAL THINKING

▸ *Some have argued that, given the polarization of the two major parties, Americans should organize a new party based on moderate politics. Why might such an initiative fail—or succeed?*

AMERICA AT ODDS | Political Parties

By their very nature, arguments about the parties are some of the most divisive conflicts in politics. We can list only a sampling of the disputes:

- *Is the Republican Party, through excessive conservatism, driving off voters that it needs—or can it win by upholding basic conservative values? For that matter, are the Democrats too liberal—or not liberal enough?*

- *Is it better when the two chambers of Congress and the presidency are held by the same party, thus guaranteeing effective government—or is it better when Congress and the presidency are held by different parties, so that the two parties can check each other?*

- *Is the increasing importance of political independents a positive development—or is it a sign that citizens are becoming dangerously detached from our political system?*

- *Are political parties desirable and inevitable—or should elections be nonpartisan whenever possible?*

- *Is it better to support a third party when you are in greater agreement with its positions than with those of either major party—or should you avoid wasting your vote and always support the major party that is closer to your politics?*

- *Finally, looking forward, do the Republicans or the Democrats offer the best solutions for our problems?*

STUDY TOOLS 7

READY TO STUDY? IN THE BOOK, YOU CAN:

☐ Review what you've read with the following chapter quiz.

☐ Check your answers in Appendix D at the back of the book.

☐ Rip out the Chapter Review Card, which includes key terms, chapter summaries, and answers to the following quiz.

ONLINE AT WWW.CENGAGEBRAIN.COM, YOU CAN:

☐ Learn about Ronald Reagan's political legacy in a video.

☐ Explore various online resources in the GOP and Democratic party websites via the Internet Resources tool.

☐ Interact with figures from the text, and watch quick animation clips.

☐ Prepare for tests with quizzes.

☐ Review the key terms with Flash Cards.

FILL-IN

Learning Outcome 7–1

1. The nation's first two political parties, the _____, clashed openly in the elections of 1796.

2. In 1860, Abraham Lincoln became the first president elected under the banner of the new _____ Party.

3. After the election of 1896, the _____ Party established itself in the minds of many Americans as the party that knew how to manage the economy.

Learning Outcome 7–2

4. Since 1957, the number of independents has gone up and the number of _____ has gone down.

5. Dealignment among voters refers to _____.

Learning Outcome 7–3

6. A _____ is a preliminary election held for the purpose of choosing a party's final candidate.

Learning Outcome 7–4

7. The Republican and Democratic candidates for president and vice president are nominated at each party's _____.

Learning Outcome 7–5

8. The third-party presidential campaign of _____ resulted in the election of Democrat Woodrow Wilson as president in 1912.

MULTIPLE CHOICE

Learning Outcome 7–1

9. A process in which a substantial number of voters change their political allegiance is called
   a. realignment.   b. dealignment.   c. tipping.

Learning Outcome 7–2

10. After the 2010 elections, many of the new Republican members of Congress were pledged to the Tea Party philosophy of
    a. moving the Republican Party toward the center.
    b. breaking political deadlock in Washington.
    c. no-compromise conservatism.

Learning Outcome 7–3

11. Functions of the political parties include
    a. conducting elections, articulating an ideology, and coordinating policymaking among those elected to various offices.
    b. selecting candidates, coordinating policymaking, and balancing competing interests within the party.
    c. managing membership, selecting candidates, and balancing competing interests.

Learning Outcome 7–4

12. To be a member of a political party in the United States
    a. you must join the party and pay membership dues.
    b. you must support the party platform.
    c. you need only think of yourself as a member of the party—as a Democrat or a Republican (or a member of a third party).

Learning Outcome 7–5

13. An issue-oriented third party
    a. supports a particular political doctrine or set of beliefs.
    b. is formed to promote a particular cause.
    c. is also referred to as a splinter party.

GOVT
ONLINE

PREPARE FOR TESTS ON
THE STUDYBOARD!

○ CORRECT

○ INCORRECT

○ INCORRECT

○ INCORRECT

**Personalize Quizzes
from Your StudyBits**

**Take Practice
Quizzes by Chapter**

CHAPTER QUIZZES

▶ Chapter 1

Chapter 2

Chapter 3

Chapter 4

4LTR
PRESS

8

PUBLIC OPINION AND VOTING

LEARNING OUTCOMES *After reading this chapter, you should be able to:*

8-1 Describe the political socialization process.

8-2 Discuss the different factors that affect voter choices.

8-3 Explain how public opinion polls are conducted, problems with polls, and how they are used in the political process.

8-4 Indicate some of the factors that affect voter turnout, and discuss what has been done to improve voter turnout and voting procedures.

After finishing this chapter, go to **PAGE 190** for **STUDY TOOLS**.

AMERICA AT ODDS | How Important Is It to Target Independents?

The share of the electorate that claims to be independent—not supporting any political party—now hovers around 40 percent. That simple fact would suggest that independent voters are important in elections, especially presidential ones. It may be true that many "independents" are really Democrats or Republicans in disguise, but other independents—about 10 percent of the total electorate—are true swing voters. It seems to make sense, therefore, that any candidate, particularly one running for president, should try to win independents to her or his side.

But not everyone agrees that this is an effective strategy. Some claim that presidential candidates are better off catering to the "base" of their party. The goal is to get the largest number of faithful party supporters to the ballot box. After all, in the presidential election year of 2012, voter turnout was 58 percent. In 2014, an off-year with just senators and representatives on the national ballot, turnout was only 36 percent. That's a difference of 22 percent. In any swing state, the turnout gap will be substantially larger than the percentage of true swing voters. In 2000 and 2004, Republican presidential candidate George W. Bush attempted to mobilize Republican turnout at the expense of appealing to moderate voters—and he won.

If You Don't Win Swing Votes, You Won't Be Elected

Those who argue that independents are crucial say the numbers tell it all. Winning over independents is the key to winning a presidential election. Look at Gallup's figures for early 2016. Of those polled, 26 percent were Republicans and 16 percent were independents leaning Republican, for a total of 42 percent. Democrats were at 30 percent and Democratic leaners 15 percent, for a total of 45 percent. With those numbers, how on earth can you win without swing voters?

According to many political scientists, swing voters are capable of responding to either liberal or conservative arguments. That is because they carry both liberal and conservative value systems in their heads. As long as there are independents who can be attracted to both conservative and progressive beliefs, they will swing between the parties. Therefore, politicians should moderate their positions to appeal to the center.

But You Will Also Lose If You Abandon Your Values

Other political scientists argue that the moderate swing voter is largely a myth. Many "moderate" voters seem moderate because they hold some conservative positions and some liberal ones. Many of these opinions are actually quite radical. A voter might, for example, endorse large increases in Social Security benefits, a liberal position. That same voter might favor the deportation of all 11 million unauthorized immigrants, a decidedly conservative stand. Typically, these voters are uninterested in politics and may have little political information. That is why they can hold opinions that appear to be inconsistent.

Because such voters swing from party to party, politicians still want to appeal to them. Attempting to take moderate positions will not necessarily help, however, because many of these voters are not really moderate. Instead, a conservative candidate is better off presenting himself or herself as the most attractive possible conservative. Progressives should follow this strategy as well. It's not just ideas that win elections, but qualities such as optimism, empathy, and a consistent set of values.

Where do you stand?

1. If you were a candidate for the presidency, what "moderate" positions would you take?
2. Is there any way for any candidate to appeal to all voters? Why or why not?

Explore this issue online:

- Ezra Klein argues that moderates are mostly a statistical artifact. Find his article at "klein moderate myth."
- Linda Killian contends that the moderate middle is real enough. Search for "killian independent real."

INTRODUCTION

For a democracy to be effective, members of the public must form opinions and openly express them to their elected officials. Only when the opinions of Americans are communicated effectively to elected representatives can those opinions form the basis of government action.

Citizens use many methods to communicate with elected officials, including tweets, e-mail, texting, telephone calls, and attendance at rallies or "town hall" meetings with representatives. The most accurate way of gauging overall public opinion between elections, however, is through public opinion polls, which we describe in this chapter.

The ultimate way that citizens communicate their views, of course, is by casting ballots for their preferred candidates. Many factors affect the political beliefs that motivate voters, and we discuss these factors in this chapter. We also look at the mechanics of voting, which can have a definite impact on election results.

8-1 HOW DO PEOPLE FORM POLITICAL OPINIONS?

> **LO** Describe the political socialization process.

What exactly is **public opinion**? We define it as the sum total of a complex collection of opinions held by many people on issues in the public arena, such as taxes, health care, Social Security, clean-air legislation, and unemployment. When asked, most Americans are willing to express an opinion on such issues. Not one of us, however, was born with these opinions. Most people acquire their political attitudes, opinions, beliefs, and knowledge through a complex learning process called **political socialization**. This process begins in childhood and continues throughout life.

public opinion The views of the citizenry about politics, public issues, and public policies; a complex collection of opinions held by many people on issues in the public arena.

political socialization The learning process through which most people acquire their political attitudes, opinions, beliefs, and knowledge.

agents of political socialization People and institutions that influence the political views of others.

> **"A GOVERNMENT CAN BE NO BETTER THAN THE PUBLIC OPINION THAT SUSTAINS IT."**
>
> ~ FRANKLIN DELANO ROOSEVELT, THIRTY-SECOND PRESIDENT OF THE UNITED STATES, 1933–1945

Most political socialization is informal, and it usually begins during early childhood, when the dominant influence on a child is the family. Although parents normally do not sit down and say to their children, "Let us explain to you the virtues of becoming a Republican," their children nevertheless come to know the parents' feelings, beliefs, and attitudes. The strong early influence of the family later gives way to the multiple influences of school, church, peers, television, co-workers, and other groups. People and institutions that influence the political views of others are called **agents of political socialization**.

8-1a The Importance of Family

As just suggested, most parents or caregivers do not deliberately set out to form their children's political ideas and beliefs. They are usually more concerned with the moral, religious, and ethical values of their offspring. Yet a child first sees the political world through the eyes of his or her family, which is perhaps the most important force in political socialization. Children do not "learn" political attitudes the same way they learn to master in-line skating. Rather, they learn by hearing their parents' everyday conversations about politicians and issues and by observing their parents' actions and reactions.

The family's influence is strongest when children can clearly perceive their parents' attitudes, and most can. In one study, more high school students could identify their parents' political party affiliation than their parents' other attitudes or beliefs. The political party of the parents often becomes the political party of the children, particularly if both parents support the same party.

8-1b Schools and Churches

Education also strongly influences an individual's political attitudes. From their earliest days in school, children learn about the American political system. They say the Pledge of Allegiance and sing patriotic songs. They celebrate national holidays, such as Presidents' Day and Veterans' Day, and learn about the history and symbols associated with them. In the upper grades, young people acquire more knowledge about government and democratic procedures through civics classes and participation in student government and various clubs. They also learn citizenship skills through school rules and regulations. Generally, those with more education have more knowledge about politics and policy than those with less education. The

Family support for going to college often matters. *Why might it be important to encourage youth from low-income families to attend college?*

level of education also influences a person's political values, as will be discussed later in this chapter.

A majority of Americans hold strong religious beliefs, and these attitudes can also contribute significantly to political socialization. For example, if a family's church emphasizes that society has a collective obligation to care for the poor, the children in that family may be influenced in a liberal direction. If the church instead depicts the government as irreligious and morally threatening, children will receive a conservative message.

8-1c The Media

The **media**—newspapers, magazines, television, radio, and the Internet—also have an impact on political socialization. The most influential of these media is television, which continues to be a leading source of political information for older voters. As explained later in this chapter, older citizens turn out to vote significantly more often than younger ones.

Still, the Internet—and social media in particular—is an extremely important source of information for younger citizens. Social media are also important for politicians. Consider that President Obama has 70.4 million followers on Twitter, placing him fourth worldwide.

Some contend that the media's role in shaping public opinion has increased to the point that the media are as influential as the family, particularly among high school students. For example, in her analysis of the media's role

in American politics, media scholar Doris A. Graber points out that high school students, when asked where they obtain the information on which they base their attitudes, mention the Internet and social media far more than they mention their families, friends, and teachers.[1]

Other studies have shown that the media's influence on people's opinions may not be as great as some have thought. Typically, people go online, watch television, or read articles with preconceived ideas about the issues. These preconceived ideas act as a kind of perceptual screen that blocks out information that is not consistent with the ideas. Generally, the media tend to wield the most influence over the views of persons who have not yet formed opinions about various issues or candidates. (See Chapter 10 for a more detailed discussion of the media's role in American politics.)

8-1d Opinion Leaders

Every city or community has well-known citizens who are able to influence the opinions of their fellow citizens. These people may be public officials, religious leaders, teachers, or celebrities. They are the people to whom others listen and from whom others draw ideas and convictions about various issues of public concern. These *opinion leaders* play a significant role in the formation of public opinion.

Opinion leaders often include politicians and former politicians. Opinion leaders are not limited to political figures, however. In different ways, both Lady Gaga and Kate Middleton, Duchess of Cambridge, are opinion leaders (though British royals are required to stay out of politics). Media figures such as actress Angelina Jolie and pastor Rick Warren are opinion leaders as well.

8-1e Major Life Events

Often, the political attitudes of an entire generation of Americans are influenced

> **media** Newspapers, magazines, television, radio, the Internet, and any other printed or electronic means of communication.

by a major event. For example, consider the Great Depression (1929–1939), the most severe economic depression in modern U.S. history. This event persuaded many Americans who lived through it that the federal government should step in when the economy is in decline. A substantial number of voters came to believe that the New Deal programs and policies of President Franklin Roosevelt showed that the Democratic Party was concerned about the fate of ordinary people. As a result, they became supporters of that party.

The generation that lived through World War II (1939–1945) tends to believe that American intervention in foreign affairs is good. In contrast, the generation that came of age during the Vietnam War (1965–1975) is more skeptical of American interventionism. A national tragedy, such as the terrorist attacks of September 11, 2001, is also likely to influence the political attitudes of a generation. The recent Great Recession and the financial crisis that struck in September 2008 will surely affect popular attitudes in years to come.

8-1f Peer Groups

Once children enter school, the views of friends begin to influence their attitudes and beliefs. From junior high school on, the **peer group**—friends, classmates, co-workers, club members, or religious group members—becomes a significant factor in the political socialization process.

Most of this socialization occurs when the peer group is involved with political activities or other causes. For example, your political beliefs might be influenced by a peer group with which you are working on a common cause, such as cleaning up a local river bank or campaigning for a favorite candidate. Your political beliefs probably are not as strongly influenced by peers with whom you, say, snowboard regularly or attend concerts.

8-1g Economic Status and Occupation

A person's economic status may influence her or his political views. For example, poorer people are more likely to favor government assistance programs. On an issue such as abortion, lower-income people are more likely to be conservative—that is, to be against abortion—than are higher-income groups (of course, there are many exceptions).

Where a person works also affects her or his opinions. Co-workers who spend a great deal of time working together tend to influence one another. For example, labor union members working together for a company may have similar political opinions, at least on issues of government involvement in the economy. Individuals working for a nonprofit agency that depends on government funds will tend to support government spending in that area. Business managers are more likely to favor tax laws helpful to businesses than are factory workers.

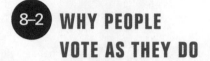

CRITICAL THINKING

▶ *Thinking about your own life, what sources of political socialization were most important to you? How did they influence your beliefs?*

8-2 WHY PEOPLE VOTE AS THEY DO

LO Discuss the different factors that affect voter choices.

What prompts some citizens to vote Republican and others to vote Democratic? What persuades voters to choose certain kinds of candidates? Researchers have collected more information on voting than on any other form of political participation in the United States. These data shed some light on why people decide to vote for particular candidates.

8-2a Party Identification

Many voters have a standing allegiance to a political party, or a *party identification*, although the proportion of the population that does so has fallen in recent decades. For established voters, party identification is one of the most important and lasting predictors of how a person will vote. Party identification is an emotional attachment to a party that is influenced by family, age, peer groups, and other factors that play a role in the political socialization process discussed earlier.

A large number of voters call themselves independents. Despite this label, many independents actually support one or the other of the two major parties quite regularly.

8-2b Perception of the Candidates

Voters often base their decisions on the perceived character of the candidates rather than on their qualifications or policy positions. Such perceptions were important in 2010 and 2012. Following each of these elections, many political analysts concluded that the Republican Party

peer group Associates, often close in age to one another; may include friends, classmates, co-workers, club members, or religious group members.

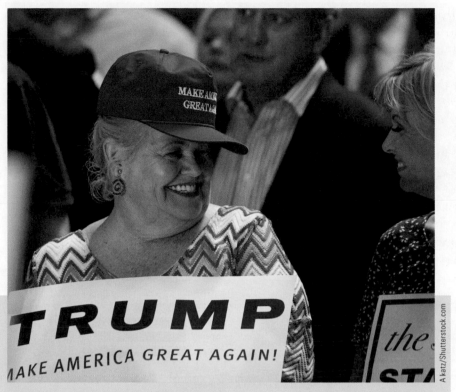

A supporter of Republican presidential candidate Donald Trump. *Why does the Republican Party enjoy greater support in the South?*

had forfeited two to three U.S. Senate races by nominating Tea Party–supported candidates that were regarded by many voters as "too extreme." This perception was, to a large extent, based not on the political positions taken by the candidates, but on personal attitudes.

In 2012, for example, Tea Party–backed Republicans in Missouri and Indiana looked like sure bets to gain Senate seats. Missouri's Todd Akin, however, made the mistake of claiming that women cannot become pregnant as a result of "legitimate rape." In Indiana, Richard Mourdock stated that pregnancies resulting from rape were "intended by God." The perception that these two men were hostile toward women's rights sank both of their candidacies.

In 2014, Republican leaders made a major effort to ensure that the party's candidates were not the kinds of people who would make such mistakes. By and large, the party succeeded.

Of course, the kind of candidate-vetting that Republicans engaged in during 2014 only works if voters are willing to listen to the "party elders." What if major sections of a party are in open rebellion against the leadership? If that is so, the primary candidates who win may be ones perceived as sharing that rebellious spirit. In 2016, Donald Trump benefitted from just such circumstances.

When members of the Republican establishment attacked Trump, his supporters actually saw the attacks as a validation of his candidacy.

8-2c Policy Choices

When people vote for candidates who share their positions on particular issues, they are engaging in policy voting. If a candidate for senator in your state opposes gun control laws, for example, and you decide to vote for him or her for that reason, you have engaged in policy voting.

Historically, economic issues have had the strongest influence on voters' choices. When the economy is doing well, it is very difficult for a challenger, particularly at the presidential level, to defeat the incumbent. In contrast, when the country is experiencing inflation, rising unemployment, or high interest rates, the incumbent may be at a disadvantage. A main issue in elections since 2008 has been the financial crisis facing Americans.

One factor that limits the impact of the issues on voting decisions is that party identification can define policy choices for voters. For example, a Republican who believes that global warming is a serious problem is likely to be uncomfortable in a party that rejects that opinion. Rather than adjust their partisan identification, many people find themselves adjusting their position on the issues instead.

8-2d Socioeconomic Factors

Some factors that influence how people vote can be described as socioeconomic. These factors include educational attainment, occupation and income, age, gender, religion and ethnicity, and geographic location. Some of these factors have to do with the circumstances into which individuals are born. Others have to do with personal choices. Figure 8–1 shows how various groups voted in the 2016 presidential elections.

Educational Attainment As a general rule, people with more education are more likely to vote Republican, although, in recent years, voters with postgraduate degrees have tended to vote Democratic. Educational

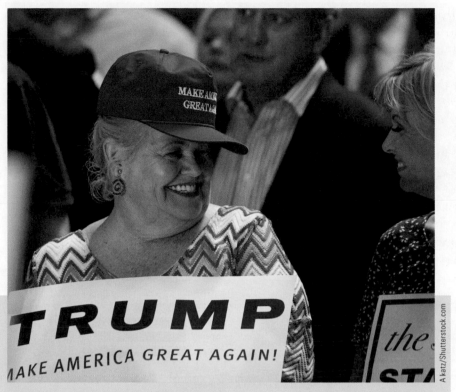 *A katz/Shutterstock.com*

FIGURE 8-1 VOTING BY GROUPS IN THE 2016 PRESIDENTIAL ELECTIONS

Joseph Sohm/Shutterstock.com

Joseph Sohm/Shutterstock.com

PERCENTAGE VOTING FOR TRUMP

Gender
Male	53
Female	41

Race
Non-Hispanic White	58
Black	8
Hispanic	29
Asian	29

Educational Attainment
High school or less	51
Some college	52
College graduate	45
Postgraduate education	37

Family Income
Under $30,000	41
$30,000–49,999	42
$50,000–99,999	50
$100,000 and above	48

Age
18–29	37
30–44	42
45–64	53
65 or over	53

Religion
White Evangelical	81
Catholic	52
Jewish	24
No religion	26

Gay, Lesbian, or Bisexual?
Yes	14
No	48

NATIONAL TOTAL FOR TRUMP AS OF NOVEMBER 11: 46.99%

PERCENTAGE VOTING FOR CLINTON

Gender
Male	41
Female	54

Race
Non-Hispanic White	37
Black	88
Hispanic	65
Asian	65

Educational Attainment
High school or less	45
Some college	43
College graduate	49
Postgraduate education	58

Family Income
Under $30,000	53
$30,000–49,999	51
$50,000–99,999	46
$100,000 and above	47

Age
18–29	65
30–44	50
45–64	44
65 or over	45

Religion
White Evangelical	16
Catholic	45
Jewish	71
No religion	68

Gay, Lesbian, or Bisexual?
Yes	78
No	47

NATIONAL TOTAL FOR CLINTON AS OF NOVEMBER 11: 47.54%

Source: The National Election Pool, as reported by the *New York Times*, CNN, and Fox News.

attainment, of course, can be linked to income level. Recent studies show that among students from families with income in the bottom fifth of the population, only 12 percent earn a bachelor's degree by the age of twenty-four. In the top fifth, the figure is 73 percent.

Occupation and Income Businesspersons tend to vote Republican and have done so for many years. This is understandable, given the pro-business stand traditionally adopted by that party. Recently, professionals (such as attorneys, professors, and physicians) have been more likely to vote Democratic than in earlier years. It appears that institutional and social changes have made it less likely that professionals will see themselves as small businesspersons or identify with business interests. Manual laborers, factory workers, and especially union members are more likely to vote for the Democrats, who have a history of pro-labor positions.

In the past, the higher the income, the more likely it was that a person would vote Republican. Conversely, a much larger percentage of low-income individuals voted Democratic. But this pattern is also breaking down.

Age The conventional wisdom is that the young are liberal and the old are conservative. Certainly, younger voters were unusually supportive of Barack Obama in the 2008 and 2012 elections. Yet in years past, age differences in support for the parties have often been quite small.

One age-related effect is that people's attitudes are shaped by the events that unfolded as they grew up. As we observed earlier, many voters who came of age during Franklin Roosevelt's New Deal held on to a preference for the Democrats. Voters who were young when Ronald Reagan was president have had a tendency to prefer the Republicans. Younger voters are noticeably more liberal on one set of issues, however—those dealing with the rights of minorities, women, and gay males and lesbians.

Gender In the 1960s and 1970s, there seemed to be no fixed pattern of voter preferences by gender in presidential elections. Women and men tended to vote for the various candidates in roughly equal numbers. Some political analysts believe that a **gender gap** became a major determinant of voter decision making in the 1980 presidential elections, however. In that year, Ronald Reagan outdrew Jimmy Carter by 16 percentage points among male voters, whereas women gave about an equal number of votes to each candidate. In the years since, the gender gap has been a continuing phenomenon. For example, in 2012 Barack Obama carried the female vote by 55 to 44 percentage points, while losing the male vote by a 45 to 52 point margin.

In 2016, Clinton carried the women's vote by 54 to 41 percentage points, while losing men by a 41 to 53 point margin. Of course, Clinton was female, and Trump was famous for rudeness toward women.

The modern feminist movement and the recognition that women have suffered from various types of discrimination doubtless have something to do with the gender gap. It also appears, however, that compared with men, women on average have a stronger commitment to the liberal value of community and a weaker belief in the conservative value of self-reliance.

Religion and Ethnic Background A century ago, at least in the northern states, white Catholic voters were likely to be Democrats, and white Protestant voters were probably Republicans. There are a few places around the country where this pattern continues to hold, but for the most part, non-Hispanic white Catholics are now almost as likely as their Protestant neighbors to support the Republicans.

Regular Church Attendance. In recent years, a different religious variable has become important in determining voting behavior. Regardless of their denomination, white Christian voters who attend church regularly have favored the Republicans by substantial margins. White Christian voters who attend church rarely or who find religion less important in their lives are more likely to vote Democratic.

Although some churches do promote liberal ways of thinking, the number of churches that promote conservative values is much larger. Note, too, that most Jewish voters are strongly Democratic, regardless of whether they attend services.

Minority Group Members. Most African Americans are Protestants, but African Americans are one of the most solidly Democratic constituencies in the United States. This is a complete reversal of the circumstances that existed a century ago. As noted in

> ## "IN POLITICS, AN ORGANIZED MINORITY IS A POLITICAL MAJORITY."
>
> ~ REV. JESSE JACKSON, CIVIL RIGHTS ACTIVIST, 1941–PRESENT

gender gap The difference between the percentage of votes cast for a particular candidate by women and the percentage of votes cast for the same candidate by men.

Chapter 7, for many years after the Civil War, those African Americans who could vote were overwhelmingly Republican. Not until President Franklin Roosevelt's New Deal did black voters begin to turn to the Democrats. While we would predict that today's African American voters would trend Democratic based on their low average income, black support for the Democrats far exceeds the levels that could be deduced from economics alone.

Latino voters have supported the Democrats by margins of about two to one, with some exceptions: older Cuban Americans are strongly Republican. In contrast to support from African Americans, Hispanic support for the Democrats is only modestly greater than what we would predict based on low average income. This fact might encourage the minority of Republicans who have sought to win Latino votes by such measures as immigration reform.

Most Asian Americans favor the Democrats. Vietnamese Americans, however, are strongly Republican.

Muslim Americans. Muslim Americans are an interesting example of changing preferences. In 2000, a majority of Muslims of Middle Eastern background voted for Republican presidential candidate

> **Solid South** A term used to describe the tendency of the southern states to vote Democratic after the Civil War.

> "WHENEVER A FELLOW TELLS ME HE IS BIPARTISAN, *I KNOW HE IS GOING TO VOTE AGAINST ME.*"
>
> ~ HARRY TRUMAN,
> THIRTY-THIRD PRESIDENT OF THE
> UNITED STATES, 1945–1953

George W. Bush because of Islamic cultural conservatism. Today, Muslims are the most Democratic religious group in the nation. Anti-Muslim campaigns by certain conservative groups appear to be a major cause of this transformation.

Geographic Region In today's presidential contests, states in the South, the Great Plains, and parts of the Rocky Mountains are strongly Republican. The Northeast, the West Coast, and Illinois are firmly Democratic. Many of the swing states that decide elections are located in the Midwest, although several Rocky Mountain states swing between the parties as well.

The Solid South. A very different pattern existed a century ago. In those years, most white southerners were Democrats, and people spoke of the **Solid South**—solidly Democratic, that is. The Solid South lasted for a century after the Civil War. In large part, it resulted from southern resentment of the Republicans for their role in the "War between the States" and their support of African Americans in the postwar era. At the end of the nineteenth century, the Republicans were strong in the Northeast and much of the Midwest, while the Democrats were able to find support outside the South in the Great Plains and the Far West.

The ideologies of the two parties have likewise undergone something of a reversal. One hundred years ago, the Democrats were seen as *less* likely than the Republicans to support government intervention in the economy. The Democrats were also the party that opposed civil rights. Today, the Democrats are often regarded as the party that supports "big government" and affirmative action programs.

Southern Conservatism. One consequence of the distinctive conservatism of southern white voters is that the concept of a "white vote" is misleading. It is better to think of a southern white vote and a northern white vote. In the run-up to the 2012 elections, some observers claimed that Obama had a "white working-class problem" because Republican

Muslim Americans are a growing minority group. *Who do they tend to support politically, and why?*

Mitt Romney was winning this group. In fact, polls showed white working-class voters breaking evenly between the parties in the West and the Northeast. Obama was narrowly ahead in the Midwest. Only in the South were white working-class voters solidly for Romney—just like every other class of whites in the South.

Southern white support for the Republicans greatly exceeds what could be predicted from average incomes. In this, southern whites are a mirror image of African Americans. The contrast between these groups has deep historical roots. Southern white support has led some Republicans to reject the strategy of attempting to appeal to Latinos and to "double-down" on the white vote instead. Liberal economist Paul Krugman describes this strategy as "an attempt to persuade Ohio whites to start voting like Alabama whites, which I guess could happen. But what if the effect is, instead, to persuade Hispanics to start voting like African Americans?"

8-2e Ideology

Ideology is another indicator of voting behavior. A significant percentage of Americans today identify themselves as conservatives. Recent polls indicate that 37 percent of Americans consider themselves to be conservatives, 24 percent consider themselves liberals, and 35 percent identify themselves as moderates.

For many Americans, where they fall in the political spectrum is a strong indicator of how they will vote: liberals and some moderates vote for Democrats, and conservatives vote for Republicans. The large numbers of Americans who fall in the political center do not adhere strictly to an ideology. (We looked at the political beliefs of so-called moderates in the chapter-opening *America at Odds* feature.)

Recent splits in the Republican Party between traditional small-government conservatives and Trump's nationalist supporters have complicated the ideological picture. Europe, however, has had parties that reflect Trump-style politics for many years. We describe them in this chapter's *The Rest of the World* feature. In the United States, this particular point of view has had trouble gaining expression within our two-party system. The attitudes are not new, however—they have been seen in politics since at least the 1840s.

CRITICAL THINKING

▶ *For what reasons might Cuban Americans and Vietnamese Americans be more conservative than members of other minority groups?*

8–3 PUBLIC OPINION POLLS

LO Explain how public opinion polls are conducted, problems with polls, and how they are used in the political process.

You may hear a news report or read a magazine article stating that "a significant number of Americans" feel a certain way about an issue. Such reports most often come from polls of public opinion.

A **public opinion poll** is a survey of the public's opinion on a particular topic at a particular moment. The results of opinion polls are most often cast in terms of percentages: 62 percent feel this way, 31 percent do not, and 7 percent have no opinion.

Of course, a poll cannot survey the entire U.S. population. Therefore, public opinion pollsters have devised scientific polling techniques for measuring public opinion through the use of **samples**—groups of people who are typical of the general population.

8-3a Early Polling Efforts

Since the 1800s, magazines and newspapers have often spiced up their

public opinion poll A survey of the public's opinion on a particular topic at a particular moment.

sample In the context of opinion polling, a group of people selected to represent the population being studied.

"Grab the suitcases, dear, there's been a shift in public opinion!"

Cartoonresource/Shutterstock.com

THE REST OF THE WORLD

Anti-Immigration Politics in Europe

In the United States, the most remarkable development in the 2016 presidential primaries was the rise of Donald Trump within the Republican Party. In 2015, Trump's first major policy proposal was to build a wall between the United States and Mexico and have the government of Mexico pay for it. How to make Mexico pay was left to the imagination. Trump later extended his anti-immigrant rhetoric to Muslims.

Commentators debated the nature of "Trumpism" and what other political movements it resembled. It did not take long to hit upon an answer. Movements with similar politics have been active in Europe for years. Given the parliamentary systems typical of Europe, these movements have organized as political parties. Variously characterized as "populist," "nationalist," or part of the "extreme right wing," these parties have gained strength in countries throughout the continent. They are particularly significant in Denmark, Finland, France, the Netherlands, and Sweden, just to name a few.

France Took the Lead Years Ago

Since 1972, France has been home to the National Front, a socially conservative, nationalist political party. When first founded, the party was suspected of fascist tendencies. Under leader Marine Le Pen, daughter of the party's founder, the National Front has moved toward the center and tried to gain a degree of respectability. It remains hostile to immigration, foreign trade, and French participation in the European Union. Its domestic policies include strong support for "law and order." Its economic policies, however, are quite liberal by American standards. The National Front has no problem with social welfare or deficit spending so long as the beneficiaries are native French.

Europe's Immigration Crisis

By 2015, the Middle Eastern nation of Syria was four years into a horrifying civil war that had killed up to 500,000 Syrians and driven half the nation's people from their homes. In that year,

hundreds of thousands of Syrians gave up on their homeland—and set out for Europe, the nearest bloc of wealthy nations. One million refugees entered Germany in 2015 alone.

European anti-immigration sentiment exploded. In France, the National Front became one of the nation's three major parties, along with the Republicans and the Socialists. In Sweden, second only to Germany as a refugee destination, the nationalist Sweden Democrats became the second-largest party. In Hungary and Poland, parties with some nationalist and populist tendencies now control the government. Greece and Hungary have small, explicitly fascist parties as well.

Critical Analysis

How should Europe respond to the vast wave of asylum-seekers crossing its shores?

articles by conducting **straw polls** of readers' opinions. Straw polls simply ask a large number of people the same question. The problem with straw polls is that the opinions expressed usually represent an atypical subgroup of the population, or a **biased sample**. A survey of those who read *People* will most likely produce different results than a survey of those who read *Sports Illustrated*, for example.

straw poll A nonscientific poll in which there is no way to ensure that the opinions expressed are representative of the larger population.

biased sample A poll sample that does not accurately represent the population.

The *Literary Digest* Fiasco The most famous of all straw-polling errors was committed by the *Literary Digest* in 1936 when it tried to predict the outcome of that year's presidential elections. The *Digest* forecast that Republican Alfred Landon would easily defeat Democratic incumbent Franklin D. Roosevelt. Instead, Roosevelt won by a landslide. The editors of the *Digest* had sent mail-in cards to names in telephone directories, to its own subscribers, and to automobile owners—a staggering 2,376,000 people. In the Depression year of 1936, however, people who owned a car or a telephone or who subscribed to the *Digest* were not representative of most Americans. The vast majority of

Americans could not afford such luxuries. The sample turned out to be unrepresentative and consequently inaccurate.

The First Scientific Poll Takers Several newcomers to the public opinion poll industry, however, did predict Roosevelt's victory. Two of these organizations are still at the forefront of the polling industry today: the Gallup Organization, started by George Gallup, and Roper Associates, founded by Elmo Roper and now known as the Roper Center.

8-3b How Polling Has Developed

Today, polling is used extensively by political candidates and policymakers. Politicians and the news media generally place a great deal of faith in the accuracy of poll results. Polls can be quite accurate when they are conducted properly. In the twenty presidential elections in which Gallup has participated, its polls conducted in late October correctly predicted the winner in sixteen of the races.[2] Even polls taken several months in advance have been able to predict the eventual winner.

Types of Polls In the earliest days of scientific polling, interviewers typically went door to door locating respondents. Such in-person surveys were essential in the mid-twentieth century, when a surprisingly large number of homes did not have telephones.

Telephone Polls. In time, the number of homes without phones dwindled, and polling organizations determined that they could obtain satisfactory samples of voters through telephone interviews alone. In recent years, poll takers have even replaced human interviewers with prerecorded messages that solicit responses. Such methods allow companies to conduct very large numbers of polls at little cost. Questions have arisen as to whether automated polling is as accurate as polling that uses live interviewers, however.

Further complications for telephone poll takers include the increase in the use of cell phones—which not all pollsters bother to call. Today, many cell phone users no longer have a landline number. An additional problem is the public's growing use of Skype and other Internet-based telephone systems. Poll takers have not yet determined a way to integrate such users into their polls. Finally, a growing number of people simply refuse to participate in telephone surveys.

Internet Polls. Technological advances have opened up a new possibility—the Internet survey. The Harris

> ## "A popular government without popular information, or the means of acquiring it, is but a prologue to a farce or a tragedy, or perhaps both."
>
> ~ JAMES MADISON, FOURTH PRESIDENT OF THE UNITED STATES, 1809–1817

Poll now specializes in this type of research. As when telephone interviews were introduced, serious questions exist as to whether the samples obtained by Harris and other Internet polling firms can be representative. Internet usage has become extremely widespread, but it is still not universal.

Sampling Today, the most reputable polls sample between 1,000 and 1,500 people. How can interviewing such a small group possibly indicate what millions of voters think? To be successful, a sample must consist of people who are typical of the population. If the sample is not properly chosen, then the results of the poll may not reflect the beliefs of the general population.

The most important principle in sampling is randomness. A **random sample** means that each person within the entire population being polled has an equal chance of being chosen. For example, if a poll is trying to measure how women feel about an issue, the sample should include respondents from all groups within the female population in proportion to their percentage in the entire population. A properly drawn random sample would include appropriate numbers of women in terms of age, race and ethnicity, geography, income, and religious affiliation.

What Polls Really Tell Us As noted earlier, poll results are almost always publicized using exact numbers. A typical result would be that 80 percent of those polled are partly or completely dissatisfied with the actions of the U.S. Congress, 12 percent are partly or completely satisfied, and 8 percent have no opinion. Figures such as these, though, can provide

> **random sample** In the context of opinion polling, a sample in which each person within the entire population being polled has an equal chance of being chosen.

a misleading picture of what the poll is actually saying. Public opinion polls are fundamentally *statistical*. The true result of a poll is not a single figure, but a range of probabilities. In the example just given, the figure 80 percent is merely the midpoint of all the possible results.

Sampling Error. An important concept in understanding polls is **sampling error**—the difference between what the poll shows and what the results would have been if *everyone* in the relevant population had been interviewed. A professional polling firm might state of a given poll that it has "95 percent confidence that the maximum margin of sampling error is plus or minus four percentage points."

To claim "95 percent confidence" means that there is a 5 percent chance that this poll is off by four points or more. The 95 percent figure is an industry standard. That means that out of the thousands of polls released every year, 5 percent are expected to yield results that are outside their own margin of error.

Statistical Noise. It follows that there is not much point in paying attention to small, short-lived changes in polling results. Consider a polling firm's report that President Barack Obama's popularity rating was, in five consecutive weeks, 45 percent, 43 percent, 44 percent, 47 percent, and 45 percent. Do these figures mean that Obama was less popular in week two and more popular in week four? Almost certainly not. The fluctuation in the figures is most likely due to random error—it is statistical "noise."

Arianna Huffington, founder of the Huffington Post. This online news and opinion site aggregates polling results in an attempt to make better predictions. *How useful are such sites?*

Albert H. Teich/Shutterstock.com

8-3c Problems with Opinion Polls

Today, more than ever before, Americans are bombarded with the results of public opinion polls. As it happens, however, accurate polls can be difficult and expensive to conduct. Professional poll takers confront a variety of problems that can interfere with the validity of a poll, which we describe in this section.

In some cases, firms may not even try to prepare a valid poll. In recent years, two polling firms were accused of simply making up their results without conducting any actual surveys. Statistical evidence also exists that some firms conducting low-quality polls quietly adjust their results to be more in line with the findings of more reputable pollsters.

Statistical Modeling and House Effects
One source of error follows from the fact that it is almost impossible to obtain a body of respondents that truly reflects the population at large. Many people refuse to be interviewed. Some kinds of people—including poor people and students—are hard to reach. In addition, it happens that women answer the telephone more frequently than do men.

Weighting. Polling firms respond to these difficulties by *weighting* the responses of various groups. If the survey did not locate enough evangelical Christians, for example, the responses of the evangelicals who were contacted will be weighted more heavily. Thus, a pollster might double the numerical value of the answers provided by the evangelicals before adding the results back into the total sample. A pollster would do this if, in the initial sample, the number of evangelicals interviewed was half what it should have been. If the model that the pollster uses to weight the responses is flawed, however, the poll results will be off as well.

Weighting for purely demographic variables is a small part of the modeling problem. Errors are much

sampling error In the context of opinion polling, the difference between what the sample results show and what the true results would have been had everybody in the relevant population been interviewed.

more common when pollsters attempt to adjust for the number of Republicans, Democrats, and independents in their samples. Perhaps the greatest difficulty is determining who is likely to turn out and vote. In the months leading up to the 2016 elections, each major polling firm had its own model for weighting groups of respondents and determining who was a likely voter. Most of these models were trade secrets. One result of the differing models was a substantial variation in predicted results.

House Effects. Based on their differing models, some polling firms consistently published results more favorable to one or the other of the two major parties than the results released by other pollsters. When a pollster's results appear to consistently favor one of the parties, polling experts refer to the phenomenon as a **house effect**. Not surprisingly, firms that exhibited house effects in 2016 frequently had ties to the political party favored by their results.

The connection was not exact, however. Some partisan firms did not exhibit a house effect, and some pollsters who were well known for nonpartisanship did have one. Also, a firm with a house effect is not always wrong. It may be noticing something that most of its competitors have missed.

Bias in Framing Questions To obtain accurate results, professional poll takers must ensure that there is no bias in their polling questions. How a question is phrased can significantly affect how people answer it.

Poorly Worded or Misleading Questions. The number of ways in which survey questions can be poorly worded is vast. Questions can contain loaded terms: "How would you rate the career of golf legend Tiger Woods?" To call Woods a "legend" biases the question in his favor. A question can combine two or more queries that ought to be kept separate: "Which of the following companies provides the fastest and most economical Internet service?" The most economical service is unlikely to be the fastest.

Surveys concerning the Affordable Care Act ("Obamacare") provide another example of troublesome wording. A typical survey might show that 55 percent of respondents oppose the act, 40 percent support it, and 5 percent aren't sure. These results do not tell us *why* respondents oppose the reform. A recent CNN poll asked those opposing the law whether it was too liberal or not liberal enough. The answers were: support the reform, 40 percent; oppose because it is too liberal, 38 percent; oppose because it is not liberal enough, 17 percent. Presumably, those opposing the legislation

because it is insufficiently liberal do not support the conservative view of Obamacare.

Poll respondents are under no obligation to be consistent. A famous example is that in every poll, a majority of Americans favors cuts to federal spending. When asked whether we should cut the budget of any particular program, however, the answer is almost always "no." This raises questions as to whether politicians should—or even can—respond to survey results. For more on this topic, see this chapter's *Perception vs. Reality* feature.

Yes and No Questions. Polling questions also sometimes reduce complex issues to questions that simply call for "yes" or "no" answers. For example, a survey question might ask respondents whether they favor giving aid to foreign countries. A respondent's opinion on the issue might vary depending on the recipient country or the purpose of the aid. The poll would nonetheless force the respondent to give a "yes" or "no" answer that does not fully reflect his or her opinion.

Inadequate Information. Respondents sometimes answer "I don't know" or "I don't have enough information to answer," even when the poll does not offer such options. Interestingly, a study of how polling is conducted on the complex issue of school vouchers (school vouchers were discussed in Chapter 4) found that about 4 percent volunteered the answer "I don't know" when asked if they favored or opposed vouchers. When respondents were offered the option of answering "I haven't heard or read enough to answer," however, the proportion choosing that answer jumped to about 30 percent.[3]

Other Problems. In addition to potential bias in framing questions, poll takers must also be concerned about other issues that affect the reliability of their polls. For example, respondents interviewed may be influenced by the interviewer's personality or tone of voice. They may give the answer that they think will please the interviewer.

Timing of Polls Opinion polls of voter preferences cannot reflect rapid shifts in public opinion unless they are taken frequently. One example of this problem was the polls taken during the presidential elections of 1980. The candidates in that year were incumbent Democratic president Jimmy Carter and Republican Ronald Reagan. Almost to the end of the campaign, polls showed Carter in the

> **house effect** In the case of a polling firm, a consistent tendency to report results more favorable to one of the political parties than the results reported by other pollsters.

Do Politicians Always Follow the Polls?

During every election campaign, major candidates conduct their own polling. At the presidential level, they do so almost daily. The number of opinion polls released is enormous, not just before elections, but all year. The question is, once in office, do politicians continue to "follow the polls"? Do polls affect the kinds of legislation they support?

The Perception

Many critics of politicians argue that all they do is follow public opinion. Any personal convictions that they may have are less important than the need for political survival. These politicians rely on polls to help them vote for whatever will get them reelected.

The Reality

If politicians simply followed public opinion, our country's laws would be quite different. Take the example of religion. Polls indicate that 65 percent of Americans believe "liberals have gone too far in keeping religion out of schools and government."

According to 76 percent, public high schools should be allowed to sponsor prayer before football games. "Voluntary prayer" in the public schools (that is, prayer led by teachers from which students could "voluntarily" opt out) is favored by three-fourths of respondents. Of course, as you learned in Chapter 4, the Supreme Court has ruled that such steps would violate the First Amendment of the Constitution.

Consider also evolution versus creationism, another topic discussed in Chapter 4. One poll found that almost half of respondents believed that God created human beings more or less in their present form within the last 10,000 years. Not surprisingly, a majority of Americans also want creationism to be taught alongside evolution in the public schools. Both school-sponsored prayer and the teaching of creationism in public schools would require amending the Constitution. Members of Congress never seem to propose such an amendment, however.

If the public appears to be conservative on various cultural issues, it also gives stronger support than political elites do to programs such as Social Security and Medicare. Much of political Washington believes that the benefits provided by these programs need to be trimmed. In polls, however, only one American in ten agrees with this idea. A majority may prefer to see Social Security benefits increased. This group, however, is not getting its way. We might conclude from this that the "economic progressives, social conservatives" we described in Chapter 1 have little political clout.

Blog On

Pollingreport.com has a large collection of public opinion polls. At its home page, try searching for "evolution." For details on the public's reluctance to cut most federal programs, search the Web for "pew cutting programs."

lead. Only the most capable analysts took note of the very large number of undecided voters. In the last week before the elections, these voters broke sharply for Reagan. Few polls were conducted late enough to detect this development.

Polling Problems in 2012 and 2014 As a whole, public opinion polls did a good job of predicting the 2012 election results, despite a bias toward the Republicans shown by a handful of pollsters. These pollsters, however, included some of the biggest names in the field. Gallup, for example, overestimated turnout among Republican voters and underestimated turnout among Democrats. Rasmussen, a top Republican poll taker,

made the mistake of weighting Republican responses more heavily than independent ones. Figure 8–2 shows the predictions of leading poll takers in 2016.

In 2014, the biggest problem pollsters faced was the very low voter turnout in that year. Because many citizens who did not vote leaned Democratic, a majority of the polls overestimated the Democratic vote.

Misuse of Polls Today, a frequently heard complaint is that, instead of measuring public opinion, polls can end up creating it. For example, to gain popularity, a candidate might claim that all the polls show that he or she is ahead in the race. People who want to support the winner may back this candidate despite their true

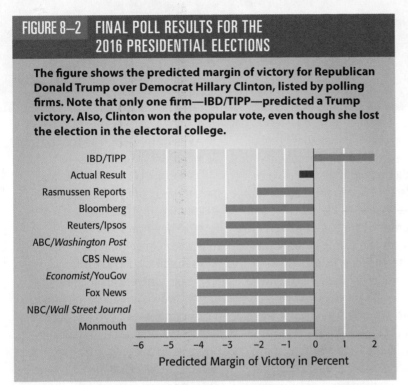

FIGURE 8–2 FINAL POLL RESULTS FOR THE 2016 PRESIDENTIAL ELECTIONS

The figure shows the predicted margin of victory for Republican Donald Trump over Democrat Hillary Clinton, listed by polling firms. Note that only one firm—IBD/TIPP—predicted a Trump victory. Also, Clinton won the popular vote, even though she lost the election in the electoral college.

Source: Real Clear Politics blog. Popular vote as of November 13, 2016.

feelings. This is often called the "bandwagon" effect. Presidential approval ratings lend themselves to the bandwagon effect.

The media also sometimes misuse polls. Many journalists take the easy route during campaigns and base their political coverage almost exclusively on poll findings. Media companies often report only the polls conducted by their affiliated pollsters, announcing the results as the absolute truth regardless of whether the results are typical or are at serious variance with polls taken by other organizations.

Indeed, given the diversity of results among different polling organizations, savvy political analysts look at as many different polls as they can. Experts often average the results of polls that ask a particular question. Some of them even weight these polls based on how reliable they believe each firm to be.

The Problem of Push Polls One tactic in political campaigns is to use **push polls**, which ask "fake" polling questions that are actually designed to "push" voters toward one candidate or another. The National Council on Public Polls describes push polls as outright political manipulation—the spreading of rumors and lies by one candidate about another. Push pollsters usually do not give their name or identify the poll's sponsor. The interviews last less than a minute, whereas legitimate

pollsters typically interview a respondent for five to thirty minutes.

Some researchers argue that identifying a push poll is not always straightforward. Political analyst Charlie Cook points out that "there are legitimate polls that can ask push questions, which test potential arguments against a rival to ascertain how effective those arguments might be in future advertising. . . . These are not only legitimate tools of survey research, but any political pollster who did not use them would be doing her or his clients a real disservice."[4]

Distinguishing between push polls and push questions, then, can be challenging—which is usually the intent of the push pollsters. A candidate does not want to be accused of conducting push polls, because the public considers them a "dirty trick" and may turn against the candidate who uses them.

CRITICAL THINKING

▶ *Suggest some poll questions that most respondents would probably answer in the same way. Think of some others that would divide those who are being interviewed into two distinct camps.*

8-4 VOTING AND VOTER TURNOUT

LO Indicate some of the factors that affect voter turnout, and discuss what has been done to improve voter turnout and voting procedures.

Voting is arguably the most important way in which citizens participate in the political process. Because we do not live in a direct democracy, Americans use the vote to elect politicians to represent their interests, values, and opinions in government. In many states, public-policy decisions—for example, access to medical marijuana—are also decided by voters through referendums and initiatives. Our right to vote also

push poll A campaign tactic used to feed false or misleading information to potential voters, under the guise of taking an opinion poll, with the intent to "push" voters away from one candidate and toward another.

Donald Trump's victory came as a surprise to everyone except his own supporters. As you can see in Figure 8–2, most poll takers thought that Hillary Clinton had an edge of 3 or 4 percentage points. In fact, Clinton barely won the popular vote and lost in the electoral college. When pollsters cluster in this way, it raises suspicions that some of them are "herding," that is, altering their assumptions to bring their results closer to what everyone else is reporting. Whether or not this happened, there was clearly a degree of industry-wide polling error in Clinton's favor. Analysis of the election results suggests that this error was due to assumptions about voter turnout.

Based on preliminary results, turnout appeared to be down compared with 2012. Clinton got many fewer votes than Barack Obama did in 2012—but Trump also received fewer votes than Mitt Romney. One exception was the turnout among Trump's most loyal supporters. Clearly, Trump had mobilized members of the electorate who had not voted previously. One way in which poll takers try to improve their accuracy is by using "likely voter" screens. In the 2016 elections, these screens may have resulted in greater error, rather than less. Some Trump voters were screened out because they had not voted in the past. Among polling experts, Nate Silver was almost alone in warning about

this possibility, though he too thought a Clinton victory probable.

A second group that seems to have turned out in record numbers is Hispanics, mobilized by a fear of Trump. They, however, had the misfortune to be concentrated in strongly partisan states such as California and Texas, where enhanced Latino turnout would not affect the results. It is important to know that exit polls, such as the ones used to generate Figure 8–1, have always been subject to substantial error. In particular, Hispanic leaders considered the estimate that 29 percent of Latinos voted for Trump to be absurdly high. Exit polls in the past have had trouble reaching Spanish-speaking voters.

---

helps keep elected officials accountable because they must face reelection.

8-4a Factors Affecting Voter Turnout

If voting is so important, then why do so many Americans fail to exercise their right to vote? Why is *voter turnout*—the percentage of those who actually turn out to vote from among those eligible to vote—relatively low? In many foreign countries, voter turnout is greater than in the United States. In a few nations, such as Australia and Brazil, citizens may be fined if they do not vote. Naturally, such policies enhance turnout.

As you will read shortly, in the past, legal restrictions based on income, gender, race, and other factors kept a number of people from voting. In the last decades of the twentieth century, these restrictions were almost completely eliminated, and yet voter turnout in presidential elections still hovered around 55 percent, as shown in Figure 8–3.

According to a Pew Research Center survey, one of the reasons for low voter turnout is that many nonvoters (close to 40 percent) do not feel that they have a duty to vote. The survey also found that nearly 70 percent of nonvoters said that they did not vote because they lacked information about the candidates.[5] Finally, some people believe that their vote will not make any difference, so they do not bother to become informed about the candidates and issues or go to the polls. We compare voter turnout rates around the world in Figure 8–4.

8-4b The Legal Right to Vote

In the United States today, citizens who are at least eighteen years of age and who are not felons have the right to vote. This was not always true. Recall from Chapter 5 that restrictions on *suffrage*, the legal right to vote, have existed since the founding of our nation. Expanding the right to vote has been an important part of the gradual democratization of the American electoral process.

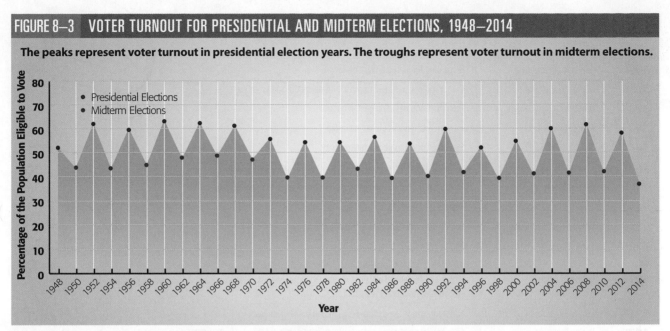

FIGURE 8–3 VOTER TURNOUT FOR PRESIDENTIAL AND MIDTERM ELECTIONS, 1948–2014

The peaks represent voter turnout in presidential election years. The troughs represent voter turnout in midterm elections.

Sources: Historical Data Archive, Inter-university Consortium for Political and Social Research; Michael P. McDonald and Samuel L. Popkin, "The Myth of the Vanishing Voter," *American Political Science Review*, Vol. 95, No. 4 (December 2001), p. 966; and the United States Elections Project.

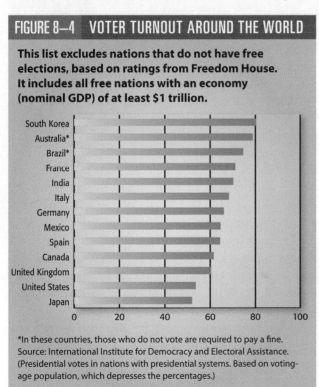

FIGURE 8–4 VOTER TURNOUT AROUND THE WORLD

This list excludes nations that do not have free elections, based on ratings from Freedom House. It includes all free nations with an economy (nominal GDP) of at least $1 trillion.

*In these countries, those who do not vote are required to pay a fine.
Source: International Institute for Democracy and Electoral Assistance. (Presidential votes in nations with presidential systems. Based on voting-age population, which depresses the percentages.)

Table 8–1 summarizes the major amendments, Supreme Court decisions, and laws that extended the right to vote to various American groups.

Historical Restrictions on Voting   Those who drafted the Constitution left the power to set suffrage qualifications to the individual states. Most states limited suffrage to adult white males who owned a specified amount of property, but these restrictions were challenged early on in the history of the republic. By 1828, laws restricting the right to vote to Christians were abolished in all states, and property ownership and tax-payment requirements gradually began to disappear as well. By 1850, all white males were allowed to vote. Restrictions based on race and gender continued, however.

Preventing African Americans from Voting.   The Fifteenth Amendment, ratified in 1870, guaranteed suffrage to African American males. Yet, for many decades, African Americans were effectively denied the ability to exercise their voting rights. Using methods ranging from mob violence to economic pressure, groups of white southerners kept black Americans from voting. We briefly listed some of these techniques in Chapter 5.

Some states required citizens to pass **literacy tests** and to answer complicated questions about government and history before they could register to vote. Registrars made sure that African Americans would almost always fail such tests. The **poll tax**, a fee of several dollars, was another device used to discourage African Americans from voting. At the time, this tax was a sizable burden, not only for most blacks but also for poor whites.

literacy test A test given to voters to ensure that they could read and write and thus evaluate political information. This technique was used in many southern states to restrict African American participation in elections.

poll tax A fee of several dollars that had to be paid before a person could vote. This device was used in some southern states to discourage African Americans and low-income whites from voting.

TABLE 8–1 EXTENSION OF THE RIGHT TO VOTE

Year	Action	Impact
1870	Fifteenth Amendment	Discrimination based on race outlawed.
1915	*Guinn v. United States*	Grandfather clause ruled unconstitutional by the Supreme Court.
1920	Nineteenth Amendment	Discrimination based on gender outlawed.
1924	Congressional act	All Native Americans given citizenship.
1944	*Smith v. Allwright*	Supreme Court prohibits white primary.
1957	Civil Rights Act of 1957	Justice Department can sue to protect voting rights in various states.
1960	Civil Rights Act of 1960	Courts authorized to appoint referees to assist voter-registration procedures.
1961	Twenty-third Amendment	Residents of District of Columbia given right to vote for president and vice president.
1964	Twenty-fourth Amendment	Poll tax in national elections outlawed.
1965	Voting Rights Act of 1965	Literacy tests prohibited; federal voter registrars authorized in seven southern states; voting rules in most southern states subject to federal oversight.
1970	Voting Rights Act Amendments of 1970	Voting age for federal elections reduced to eighteen years; maximum thirty-day residency required for presidential elections; state literacy tests abolished.
1971	Twenty-sixth Amendment	Minimum voting age reduced to eighteen for all elections.
1975	Voting Rights Act Amendments of 1975	Federal voter registrars authorized in ten more states; bilingual ballots to be used in certain circumstances.
1982	Voting Rights Act Amendments of 1982	Extended provisions of Voting Rights Act Amendments of 1970 and 1975; private parties allowed to sue for violations.
2006	Voting Rights Act extension	Extended Voting Rights Act for another twenty-five years.

Another restriction was the **grandfather clause**, which had the effect of restricting voting rights to those whose ancestors had voted before the 1860s. This technique was prohibited by the United States Supreme Court in 1915.[6]

The White Primary. Still another voting barrier was the **white primary**—African Americans were prohibited from voting in Democratic primary elections. (In southern states at that time, winning the Democratic primary almost always guaranteed victory in the general election.) The Supreme Court initially upheld this practice on the grounds that the political parties were private entities, not public, and thus could do as they wished. Eventually, in 1944, the Court banned the use of white primaries.[7]

Voting Rights Today

Today, these four devices just discussed for restricting voting rights are explicitly outlawed by constitutional amendments and by the Voting Rights Act of 1965, as discussed in Chapter 5.

Furthermore, the Nineteenth Amendment gave women the right to vote in 1920. In 1971, the Twenty-sixth Amendment reduced the minimum voting age to eighteen.

Some restrictions on voting rights still exist. Every state except North Dakota requires voters to register with the appropriate state or local officials before voting. In eleven states and the District of Columbia, however, voters can register up to or even on voting day. California and Oregon do not require citizens to actively register. All citizens of these states who are nineteen or over and who have a driver's license or state ID card are automatically registered. In 2016, dozens of states were considering similar bills.

Residency requirements are also usually imposed for voting. Since 1970, however, no state can impose a residency requirement of more than thirty days. Twenty-five states require that length of time, while the other twenty-five states require fewer or no days.

Another voting requirement is citizenship. Noncitizens may not vote in any public election held anywhere in the United States. (Until the early twentieth century, several states allowed noncitizens to cast ballots.) Most states also do not permit prison inmates, people with mental illness, or election-law violators to vote. Should former prison inmates regain the right to vote? We discuss that issue in this chapter's *Join the Debate* feature.

grandfather clause
A clause in a state law that had the effect of restricting voting rights to those whose ancestors had voted before the 1860s. It was one of the techniques used in the South to prevent African Americans from exercising their right to vote.

white primary
A primary election in which African Americans were prohibited from voting. The practice was banned by the Supreme Court in 1944.

8-4c Attempts to Improve Voter Turnout

Various attempts have been made to improve voter turnout. Typically, these attempts have a partisan dimension, because the kinds of people who find it difficult to register to vote tend to be disproportionately Democratic in their sympathies. Many, for example, are African Americans, a reliably Democratic voting bloc. As a result, Republicans are generally wary of efforts to make registration easier.

The Motor Voter Law   The National Voter Registration Act (the "Motor Voter Law") of 1993 simplified the voter-registration process. The act requires states to provide all eligible citizens with the opportunity to register to vote when they apply for or renew a driver's license. The law also requires that states allow mail-in registration. Forms are available at public assistance agencies. The law, which took effect in 1995, has facilitated millions of registrations.

Mail-in Voting   In 1998, Oregon voters approved a ballot initiative requiring that all elections in that state, including presidential elections, be conducted exclusively by mail.

Washington State has required all counties to use postal ballots beginning with the 2012 elections, and Colorado began using postal ballots exclusively in 2014. Voter turnout in these states is well above the national average, especially in midterm elections, when many voters stay home. Many states have recently made such ballots an option for all voters. In the past, *absentee ballots* were often available only to those who clearly could not make it to a polling place on Election Day. Reasons for an absentee ballot might include military service, business travel, or ill health.

Other Attempts to Make Voting Easier
Many states have recently passed laws to make voting more convenient. California, Hawaii, and Vermont plan to join other states in allowing Election Day registration. As of 2016, thirty-seven states and the District of Columbia permit early voting. Thirty-two states and D.C. now offer online registration.

8-4d Laws That May Discourage Voting

Not all new laws have tried to make voting easier. As you read in Chapter 5, Congress passed the Voting Rights Act in 1965 to ensure that state and local governments, particularly in the South, would not interfere with the voting rights of African Americans. One provision of the act was that state and local governments with a history of violating voters' rights must obtain "preclearance" from the federal government before making changes to voting rules and district boundaries. In 2013, however, the Supreme Court threw out the formula in the act that determined which states and localities must obtain preclearance, claiming that the rules were obsolete.

New Restrictive Laws   A number of state governments quickly implemented new voting laws. Laws that require voters to show photo identification at the polls have been common for some years, but after 2013, they were adopted more widely. As of 2016, thirty-three states have such laws. Three other such state laws have been struck down in the courts. Other new laws were passed as well. For example, Arizona and Kansas now require proof of citizenship, such as a birth certificate or a passport, to vote in state elections. Many poorer citizens—especially minority group members—do not have these documents.

Burlingham/Shutterstock.com

These voters participated in early voting in 2016. *Does early voting enhance turnout?*

JOIN THE DEBATE

Should Felons Be Allowed to Vote?

Suppose that you commit a crime that is punishable by a prison term. You serve your time and are released. You are now a felon—someone who has been convicted of a serious crime. You may believe that you have "repaid your debt to society" by going to prison, but in quite a few states, felons do not have the right to vote. Many people agree that those who are actually serving time in prison should not vote. But what about those who have rejoined society?

Because America puts a larger share of its people behind bars than any other nation, the number of ex-cons is staggering. At least 13 percent of the nation's African American male population is disenfranchised (can't vote). The United States takes a much harder line on this issue than most countries. A substantial number of our allies, in fact, allow people to vote while they are still in prison. Among our European allies, only Belgium and Iceland permanently disenfranchise felons. Should such people have the right to vote?

No One Should Be Denied the Right to Vote

Felony disenfranchisement affects almost 6 million persons in the United States. One negative result of this exclusion is racial discrimination. The percentage of African Americans who are felons is much greater than their share of the total population. Compared with whites, a disproportionate number of blacks are excluded from the democratic process because of state laws that prevent felons from voting.

Regardless of race, those who are convicted of felonies are disproportionately poor. By excluding many poor persons and minority group members from the voting rolls, we bias the vote. Some question how we can call ourselves a fully democratic country if we disenfranchise so many people.

When You Break the Rules, You Lose Some Rights

No one questions the need for punishment when individuals violate our accepted rules of behavior. Therefore, why should anyone question each state's right to prevent former convicts from exercising all of the rights enjoyed by law-abiding citizens? Felons are not the kind of people we want to choose our leaders.

When voters are asked whether felons should have the right to vote, the answer is almost always "no." This is true even in liberal states such as Massachusetts.

Further, only ten states automatically ban felons from voting, and in these states felons can appeal to have their rights restored. Perhaps Florida could relax its laws—in that state, only the state's governor and cabinet can restore a felon's voting rights. But other states should be allowed to do as they please.

Critical Analysis

If the millions of former convicts in America could register to vote, would it make any difference? Why or why not?

Other states have eliminated same-day registration on Election Day. In some states, young citizens lost the right to "preregister" to vote before they turned eighteen. Some states decided to restrict early voting—a practice that minorities have used more than others. North Carolina, for example, eliminated Sunday early voting. In that state, African American church congregations had adopted the practice of marching as a group to polling places at the conclusion of Sunday services.

Voter Fraud versus Voting Rights The goal of these new state voting laws, according to state officials, is to reduce voter fraud. Supporters of the laws argue that photo ID requirements do not restrict anyone's rights. After all, Americans have to show their IDs when they cash a check or board an airplane.

Some have contended, however, that Republicans have raised the specter of voter fraud to pass laws that make it harder for disadvantaged persons (mostly Democrats) to vote. In July 2016, a U.S. appeals court struck down a series of voting restrictions in Texas on the basis of racial discrimination. The ruling may affect other states as well.[8]

8–4e Attempts to Improve Voting Procedures

Because of serious problems in achieving accurate vote counts in recent elections, steps have been taken to attempt to ensure more accuracy in the voting process. In 2002, Congress passed the Help America Vote Act, which, among other things, provided funds to the states to help them purchase new electronic voting equipment. Concerns about the possibility of fraudulent manipulation of electronic voting machines then replaced the worries over inaccurate vote counts caused by the previous equipment.

In the 2006 elections, about half of the states that were using new electronic voting systems reported problems. Because of these problems fewer polling places used electronic systems in 2008 and 2010. Indeed, more than half of all votes cast in these years used old-fashioned paper ballots. As a result, vote counting was slow.

In 2012, the development of voter-verified paper audit trail (VVPAT) printers led to the reintroduction of electronic machines in many states. In seventeen states, however, some or all of the votes were cast through electronic devices that lacked a paper audit trail. A full quarter of all votes were cast using these questionable systems.[9] The trend toward the reintroduction of electronic systems continued with the 2014 elections.

One feature of the 2012 elections was the large number of states that allowed early voting at polling places that opened weeks before Election Day. A benefit of early voting was that it allowed election workers time to ensure that all systems were working properly by Election Day. As just noted, however, since 2012 some states have attempted to cut back on early voting.

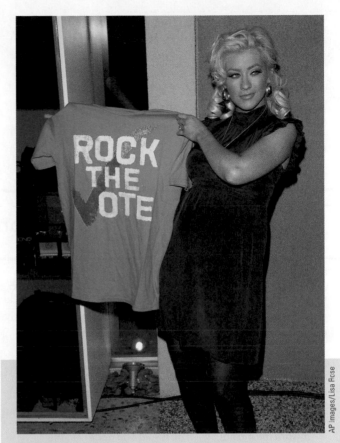

Singer Christina Aguilera appears in a Rock the Vote poster. *Why do young people need extra encouragement to vote?*

8-4f Who Actually Votes

Just because an individual is eligible to vote does not necessarily mean that the person will cast a ballot. Why do some eligible voters go to the polls while others do not? Although nobody can answer this question with absolute conviction, certain factors appear to affect voter turnout.

Educational Attainment Among the factors affecting voter turnout, education appears to be the most important. The more education a person has, the more likely it is that she or he will be a regular voter. People who graduated from high school vote more regularly than those who dropped out, and college graduates vote more often than high school graduates.

Income Level and Age Differences in income also lead to differences in voter turnout. Wealthy people tend to be overrepresented among regular voters. Generally, older voters turn out to vote more regularly than younger voters do, although participation tends to decline among the very elderly. Participation likely increases with age because older people tend to be more

settled, are already registered, and have had more experience with voting.

Minority Status Racial and ethnic minorities traditionally have been underrepresented among the ranks of voters. In several recent elections, however, participation by these groups, particularly African Americans and Hispanics, has increased. In part because the number of Latino citizens has grown rapidly, the increase in the Hispanic vote has been even larger than the increase in the black vote.

Immigration and Voter Turnout The United States has experienced high rates of immigration in recent decades, and that has had an effect on voter-turnout figures. In the past, voter turnout was often expressed as a percentage of the **voting-age population**, the number of people residing in the United States who are at least eighteen years old. Due to legal and illegal immigration, however, many people of voting age are not eligible to vote because they are not citizens. Millions

> **voting-age population** The number of people residing in the United States who are at least eighteen years old.

more cannot vote because they are felons. Additionally, the voting-age population excludes Americans abroad, who are eligible to cast absentee ballots.

vote-eligible population The number of people who are actually eligible to vote in an American election.

Today, political scientists calculate the **vote-eligible population**, the number of people who are actually entitled to vote in American elections. They have found that there may be 20 million fewer eligible voters than the voting-age population suggests. Therefore, voter turnout is actually greater than the percentages sometimes cited.

Some experts have argued that the relatively low levels of voter turnout often reported for the years between 1972 and 2000 were largely due to immigration.[10] Beginning in 2004, however, presidential voter turnout improved by any calculation method.

AMERICA AT ODDS | Public Opinion and Voting

Public opinion polls reveal that Americans are in broad agreement on many issues, such as the basic political structure of our nation. Nevertheless, polls also report that Americans are at odds with one another on many other issues. After all, the questions posed by poll takers are typically divisive ones. Issues surrounding who votes and why can also be contentious. Some examples include the following:

- *Is the disenfranchisement of felons a form of racial discrimination—or a rational part of the punishment process?*

- *Given that historical events shape popular attitudes toward the parties, when all is said and done, will the impact of the Great Recession benefit one of the major parties—or will the effects of the recession prove trivial?*

- *Should legislators follow public opinion as faithfully as they can—or, as the Democrats did on health-care reform,*

- *should lawmakers do what they think is best for the country regardless of the polls?*

- *We discussed push polls earlier in this chapter. Should push polls be banned—or would that violate First Amendment guarantees of free speech?*

- *Should voters be more concerned with the policy positions of the presidential candidates—or are the presidential candidates' personalities and personal characteristics of equal or greater concern?*

STUDY TOOLS 8

READY TO STUDY? IN THE BOOK, YOU CAN:

- ☐ Review what you've read with the following chapter quiz.
- ☐ Check your answers in Appendix D at the back of the book.
- ☐ Rip out the Chapter Review Card, which includes key terms and chapter summaries.

ONLINE AT WWW.CENGAGEBRAIN.COM, YOU CAN:

- ☐ Learn about public opinion and tweeting in a short video.
- ☐ Explore various online resources in the Gallup and PollingReport.com websites in the Internet Resources tool.
- ☐ Interact with figures from the text, and watch quick animation clips.
- ☐ Prepare for tests with quizzes.
- ☐ Review the key terms with Flash Cards.

FILL-IN

Learning Outcome 8–1

1. Agents of political socialization include
   _____.

Learning Outcome 8–2

2. For established voters, _____ is one of the most important and lasting predictors of how a person will vote.

3. When people vote for candidates who share their positions on particular issues, they are engaging in
   _____.

4. Socioeconomic factors that influence how people vote include _____.

5. The difference between the percentage of votes cast for a candidate by women and the percentage cast by men is called _____.

Learning Outcome 8–3

6. A random sample means that _____.

7. When a pollster's results appear to consistently favor a particular political party, polling experts refer to the phenomenon as a _____.

8. A _____ is a campaign tactic used to feed false or misleading information to potential voters, under the guise of conducting an opinion poll.

9. In the years immediately following the adoption of the Constitution, most states limited the right to vote to adult white men who _____.

Learning Outcome 8–4

10. Methods used to keep African Americans from voting even after the Fifteenth Amendment to the U.S. Constitution was ratified included _____.

MULTIPLE CHOICE

Learning Outcome 8–1

11. Most political socialization is informal, and it usually begins
    a. in college.
    b. in high school.
    c. during early childhood.

12. The family is an important agent of political socialization because
    a. most families deliberately set out to form their children's political ideas and beliefs.
    b. a child first sees the political world through the eyes of his or her family.
    c. parents are responsible for registering their children to vote.

Learning Outcome 8–2

13. Historically, _____ issues have had the strongest influence on voters' choices.
    a. foreign policy   b. social   c. economic

Learning Outcome 8–3

14. A Literary Digest poll incorrectly predicted that Alfred Landon would win the presidential election in 1936 because the
    a. pollsters used an unrepresentative sample.
    b. pollsters used a random sample.
    c. sample size was too small.

Learning Outcome 8–4

15. In 1971, the Twenty-sixth Amendment reduced the minimum voting age to
    a. sixteen.   b. eighteen.   c. twenty-one.

16. Among the factors affecting voter turnout, _____ appears to be the most important.
    a. educational attainment
    b. race
    c. income level

9 CAMPAIGNS AND ELECTIONS

LEARNING OUTCOMES *After reading this chapter, you should be able to:*

9-1 Explain how elections are held and how the electoral college functions in presidential elections.

9-2 Discuss how candidates are nominated.

9-3 Indicate what is involved in launching a political campaign today, and describe the structure and functions of a campaign organization.

9-4 Describe how the Internet has transformed political campaigns.

9-5 Summarize the current laws that regulate campaign financing and the role of money in modern political campaigns.

After finishing this chapter, go to **PAGE 213** for **STUDY TOOLS**

AMERICA AT ODDS | Does Money Really Buy Elections?

David Carillet/Shutterstock.com

Money and politics. Those words go together like bacon and eggs. Of course, we are no longer in an era when politicians could be bought off with bags of hundred-dollar bills. But campaigns are expensive, and candidates can always use extra funds. In 2010, the United States Supreme Court loosened the campaign finance laws considerably. In effect, the Court blessed essentially unlimited campaign spending by corporations, unions, nonprofit groups, and individuals. The only restriction the courts have imposed is that these unlimited funds cannot go directly to a candidate's campaign but must be spent independently.

As expected, the hue and cry went out that now, more than ever, the wealthy would determine the outcome of elections. Yet not everyone is sure that the facts support this assumption.

Big Money Cannot and Does Not Buy Elections

Consider former Florida governor Jeb Bush. He raised $100 million in his quest to become the 2016 Republican presidential candidate. Yet Bush dropped out of the race after the first four state contests. Indeed, in the 2016 presidential race, there seemed to be an inverse relationship between campaign spending and winning votes. Frontrunner Donald Trump, after all, spent almost nothing in the early part of his campaign.

In the 2012 presidential contest, Mitt Romney and Barack Obama each spent more than a billion dollars. These "big bucks" do not appear to have benefited either candidate. After all, the presidential race was the biggest news story in the nation. Millions watched the candidates debate, first during the Republican primaries and then in the general elections. The audiences for these debates rivaled the audiences for NFL football games. In such circumstances, how much can a candidate really gain by spending another million dollars on TV ads?

In some state-level races, the picture was even clearer. Consider Meg Whitman, the former eBay CEO who ran as a Republican for governor of California in 2010. She spent $140 million. Democrat Jerry Brown spent less than a fifth of that, but it was enough to get his message across. Whitman lost. Californians reported that they were sick and tired of Whitman's endless ads. True, candidates rarely succeed when they have almost no money. Beyond a certain level, however, spending ceases to help.

Money Matters—But Mostly Below the Presidential Level

True, the voting public pays close attention to presidential elections. Therefore, a candidate's personality, image, agenda, trustworthiness, and even physical appearance may be more important than how much money she or he has raised. As the Brown–Whitman contest illustrates, people may also give a governor's race the same level of scrutiny as a presidential contest.

In races further down the ballot, however, it's a different story. Voters are paying less attention, and money matters a lot more. In recent years, conservative groups have outspent liberal ones in state legislative races by a ratio of three to two. In 2010, such spending helped Republicans gain a net total of 675 seats in state legislatures. Because Republicans controlled about two-thirds of these legislative bodies, they were usually the ones to set district boundaries after the 2010 census. These boundaries were useful to the Republicans in strengthening their position in the U.S. House of Representatives.

Campaign contributions have consequences. As a member of Congress once said, "If politicians were immune to the effect of campaign contributions, they would be the only people in the history of the world who . . . took money from perfect strangers and made sure it had no effect on them." Big contributors expect something in return.

Where do you stand?

1. Some argue that we should eliminate campaign contributions and pay for campaigns through public funds, with equal sums given to each candidate. Would you favor such a program? Why or why not?

2. If you were a member of Congress running for reelection against a weak opponent, would you still accept large campaign contributions? Why or why not?

Explore this issue online

- Jonathan Soros argues that money can't buy votes, but it can buy influence. Find his argument by searching for "jon soros big money."

- In the *New Republic*, David Dayen argues that money still matters. To learn more, search for "dayen billionaires."

INTRODUCTION

During campaigns, candidates vie to become representatives of the people in both national and state offices. Campaigning for election has become an arduous task for every politician. As you will see in this chapter, American campaigns are long and expensive undertakings. Still, America's campaigns are an important part of our political process, because it is through campaigns that citizens learn about the candidates and decide how they will cast their votes.

American democracy would be impossible without campaigns and elections. For freedom to thrive, however, elections are not enough. Democracy requires the kind of shared political culture that we described in Chapter 1. It also requires that all candidates be able to present their views to the public, regardless of whether they have wealthy backers. We looked at that question in the chapter-opening *America at Odds* feature.

9-1 HOW WE ELECT CANDIDATES

LO Explain how elections are held and how the electoral college functions in presidential elections.

The ultimate goal of a political campaign and the associated fund-raising efforts is, of course, winning the election. The most familiar kind of election is the **general election**, which is a regularly scheduled election held in even-numbered years on the Tuesday after the first Monday in November. During general elections, the voters decide who will be the U.S. president, vice president, and senators and representatives in Congress. The president and vice president are elected every four years, senators every six years, and representatives every two years.

General elections are also held to choose state and local government officials, often at the same time as those for national offices. A **special election** is held at the state or local level when the voters must decide an issue before the next general election or when vacancies occur by reason of death or resignation.

9-1a Conducting Elections and Counting the Votes

Since 1888, all states in the United States have used the **Australian ballot**—a secret ballot that is prepared, distributed, and counted by government officials at public expense. As its name implies, this ballot was first developed in Australia.

Recall from Chapter 8 that local units of government, such as cities, are divided into smaller voting districts, or precincts. Within each precinct, voters cast their ballots at a designated polling place. (An exception is the few states that conduct elections entirely by mail.)

An election board supervises the polling place and the voting process in each precinct. The board sets hours for the polls to be open according to the laws of the state and sees that ballots or voting machines are available.

In most states, the board provides the list of registered voters and makes certain that only qualified voters cast ballots in each precinct. When the polls close, staff members count the votes and report the results, usually to the county clerk or the board of elections.

Representatives from each party, called **poll watchers**, are allowed at each polling place. Their job is to make sure the election is run fairly and that fraud doesn't occur.

9-1b Presidential Elections and the Electoral College

When citizens vote for president and vice president, they are not voting directly for the candidates. Instead, they are voting for **electors** who will cast their ballots in the **electoral college**. The electors are selected during each presidential election year by the states' political parties, subject to the laws of the state. Each state has as many electoral votes as it has U.S. senators and representatives (see Figure 9–1). In addition, there are three electors from the District of Columbia, even though it is not a state.

---

general election A regularly scheduled election to choose the U.S. president, vice president, and senators and representatives in Congress. General elections are held in even-numbered years on the Tuesday after the first Monday in November.

special election An election that is held at the state or local level when the voters must decide an issue before the next general election or when vacancies occur by reason of death or resignation.

Australian ballot A secret ballot that is prepared, distributed, and counted by government officials at public expense; used by all states in the United States since 1888.

poll watcher A representative from one of the political parties who is allowed to monitor a polling place to make sure that the election is run fairly and that fraud doesn't occur.

elector In American politics, a member of the electoral college.

electoral college The group of electors who are selected by the voters in each state to officially elect the president and vice president. The number of electors in each state is equal to the number of that state's representatives in both chambers of Congress.

FIGURE 9-1 STATE ELECTORAL VOTES IN 2016

The size of each state reflects the number of electoral votes that state has, following the changes required by the 2010 census. The colors show which party the state voted for in the 2016 presidential elections: red for Republican, blue for Democratic. A candidate must win 270 electoral votes to be elected president. Maine awards two of its electoral votes by congressional district, and the red dot reflects that the Republicans carried one of them.

AK 3
WA 12
OR 7
CA 55
NV 6
ID 4
UT 6
MT 3
WY 3
CO 9
NM 5
AZ 11
HI 4
ND 3
SD 3
NE 5
KS 6
OK 7
TX 38
MN 10
IA 6
MO 10
AR 6
LA 8
WI 10
IL 20
IN 11
KY 8
TN 11
MS 6
AL 9
GA 16
MI 16
OH 18
WV 5
VA 13
NC 15
SC 9
FL 29
PA 20
NY 29
VT 3
NH 4
ME 4
MA 11
RI 4
CT 7
NJ 14
DE 3
MD 10
DC 3

The Winner-Take-All System The electoral college system is primarily a **winner-take-all system**, in which the candidate who receives the largest popular vote in a state is credited with all that state's electoral votes. The only exceptions are Maine and Nebraska.[1]

In December, after the general election, electors (either Republicans or Democrats, depending on which candidate has won the state's popular vote) meet in their state capitals to cast their votes for president and vice president. When the Constitution was drafted, the framers intended that the electors would use their own discretion in deciding who would make the best president. Beginning as early as 1796, however, electors have usually voted for the candidates to whom they are pledged. The electoral college ballots are then sent to the U.S. Senate, which counts and certifies them before a joint session of Congress held early in January. The candidates who receive a majority of the electoral votes are officially declared president and vice president.

What It Takes to Win To be elected, a candidate must receive more than half of the 538 electoral votes available. Thus, a candidate needs 270 votes to win. If no presidential candidate gets an electoral college majority (which has happened twice—in 1800 and 1824), the House of Representatives chooses among the top three candidates, with each state delegation casting only a single vote. If no candidate for vice president gets a majority of electoral votes, the vice president is chosen by the Senate, with each senator casting one vote.

CRITICAL THINKING

▶ *Should the District of Columbia be admitted as a state—and therefore elect members to the U.S. House and Senate in addition to participating in the electoral college?*

9-2 HOW WE NOMINATE CANDIDATES

LO Discuss how candidates are nominated.

The first step on the long road to winning an election is the nomination process. Nominations narrow the field of possible candidates and limit each political party's choice to one person.

For many local government posts, which are often nonpartisan, self-nomination is the most common way to become a candidate. A self-proclaimed candidate usually files a petition to be listed

winner-take-all system A system in which the candidate who receives the most votes wins. In contrast, proportional systems allocate votes to multiple winners.

on the ballot. Each state has laws that specify how many signatures a candidate must obtain to show that he or she has some public support. An alternative is to be a *write-in candidate*—voters write the candidate's name on the ballot on Election Day.

Candidates for major offices are rarely nominated in these ways, however. As you read in Chapter 7, most candidates for high office are nominated by a political party and receive considerable support from party activists throughout their campaigns.

9–2a Party Control over Nominations

The methods used by political parties to nominate candidates have changed during the course of American history. Broadly speaking, the process has grown more open over the years, with the involvement of ever-greater numbers of local leaders and ordinary citizens. Today, any voter can participate in choosing party candidates. This was not true as recently as 1968, however, and was certainly not possible during the first years of the republic.

The Caucus System George Washington was essentially unopposed in the first U.S. presidential elections in 1789—no other candidate was seriously considered in any state. By the end of Washington's eight years in office, however, political divisions among the nation's leaders had solidified into political parties, the Federalists and Jefferson's Republicans (see Chapter 7). These early parties were organized by gatherings of important persons, who often met in secret. The meetings came to be called **caucuses**.[2]

Beginning in 1800, members of Congress who belonged to the two parties held caucuses to nominate candidates for president and vice president. The Republican caucus chose Thomas Jefferson in 1800, as expected, and the Federalist caucus nominated the incumbent president, John Adams. By 1816, the Federalist Party had ceased to exist, and the Republican congressional caucus was in complete control of selecting the president of the United States.

The Death of "King Caucus" The congressional caucus system collapsed in 1824.[3] It was widely seen as undemocratic—opponents derided it as "King Caucus." A much-diminished caucus nominated a presidential candidate who then came in third in the electoral vote. The other three major candidates were essentially self-nominated.[4] The four candidates split the electoral vote so completely that the House of Representatives had to decide the contest. It picked John Quincy Adams, even though Andrew Jackson had won more popular and electoral votes.

In the run-up to the 1828 elections, two new parties grew up around the major candidates. Adams's supporters called themselves the National Republicans (later known as the Whigs). Jackson's supporters organized as the Democratic Party, which won the election.

9–2b A New Method: The Nominating Convention

In 1832, both parties settled on a new method of choosing candidates for president and vice president—the national nominating convention. A number of state parties had already adopted the convention system for choosing state-level candidates. New Jersey held conventions as early as 1800.

Nominating Conventions A **nominating convention** is an official meeting of a political party to choose its candidates. Those who attend the convention are called **delegates**, and they are chosen to represent the people of a particular geographic area. Conventions can take place at multiple levels. A county convention might choose delegates to attend a state convention. The state convention, in turn, might select delegates to the national convention. By 1840, the convention system was the most common method of nominating political party candidates at the state and national levels.

Limits of the Convention System While the convention system drew in a much broader range of leaders than had the caucus, it was not a particularly democratic institution. Convention delegates were rarely chosen by a vote of the party's local members. Typically, they were appointed by local party officials, who were usually, with good reason, called bosses. These local leaders often gained their positions in ways that were far from democratic. Not until 1972 did ordinary voters in all states gain the right to select delegates to the national presidential nominating conventions.

9–2c Primary Elections and the Loss of Party Control

The corruption that so often accompanied the convention system led reformers to call for a new way to

caucus A meeting held to choose political candidates or delegates.

nominating convention An official meeting of a political party to choose its candidates. Nominating conventions at the state and local levels also select delegates to represent the citizens of their geographic areas at a higher-level party convention.

delegate A person selected to represent the people of one geographic area at a party convention.

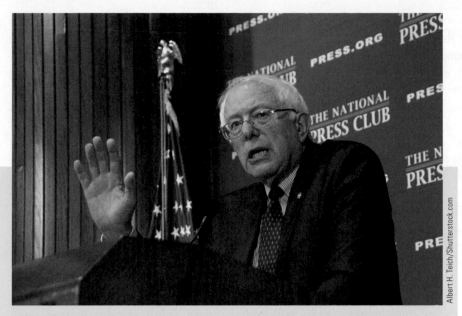

Vermont senator Bernie Sanders ran for the Democratic presidential nomination in 2016. *How successful was he?*

choose candidates—the **primary election**, in which voters go to the polls to decide among candidates who seek the nomination of their party. Candidates who win a primary election then go on to compete against the candidates from other parties in the general election.

The first primary election may have been held in 1842 by Democrats in Crawford County, Pennsylvania. The technique was not widely used, however, until the end of the nineteenth century and the beginning of the twentieth. These were years in which reform was a popular cause.

Direct and Indirect Primaries The rules for conducting primary elections are highly variable, and a number of different types of primaries exist. One major distinction is between a direct primary and an indirect primary.

In a **direct primary**, voters cast their ballots directly for candidates. The elections that nominate candidates for Congress and for state or local offices are almost always direct primaries.

In an *indirect primary,* voters choose delegates, who in turn choose the candidates. The delegates may be pledged to a particular candidate but sometimes run as *unpledged delegates.* The major parties use indirect primaries to elect delegates to the national nominating conventions that choose candidates for president and vice president.

The Role of the States Primary elections are normally conducted by state governments. States set the dates and conduct the elections. They provide polling places, election officials, and registration lists, and they then count the votes. By sponsoring the primaries, state governments have obtained considerable influence over the rules by which the primaries are conducted. The power of the states is limited, however, by the parties' First Amendment right to freedom of association, a right that has been repeatedly confirmed by the United States Supreme Court.[5]

On occasion, parties that object to the rules imposed by state governments have opted out of the state-sponsored primary system altogether.[6] Note that third parties typically do not participate in state-sponsored primaries but hold nominating conventions instead. The major parties rarely opt out of state elections, however, because the financial—and political—costs of going it alone are high. (When primary elections are used to choose candidates for local *nonpartisan* positions, state control is uncontested.)

Primary Voters Voter turnout for primaries is lower than it is in general elections. The voters who do go to the polls are often strong supporters of their party. Indeed, as you will learn shortly, independents cannot participate in primary elections in some states, even if they lean toward one of the two major parties. As a result, the Republican primary electorate is very conservative, and Democratic primary voters are quite liberal. Candidates often find that they must run to the political right or left during the primaries. They may then move to the center during the general election campaign.

Insurgent Candidates Primary elections were designed to take nominations out of the hands of the party bosses. Indeed, the most important result of the primary system has been to reduce dramatically the power of elected and party officials over the nominating process.

> **primary election** An election in which voters choose the candidates of their party, who will then run in the general election.
>
> **direct primary** An election held within each of the two major parties—Democratic and Republican—to choose the party's candidates for the general election. Voters choose the candidate directly, rather than through delegates.

Ever since primary elections were established, the insurgent candidate who runs against the party "establishment" has been a common phenomenon. Running against the "powers that be" is often a very effective campaign strategy, and many insurgents have won victories at the local, state, and national levels.

Occasionally, an insurgent's platform is strikingly different from that of the party as a whole. Yet even when an insurgent's politics are abhorrent to the rest of the party—for example, an insurgent might make an outright appeal to racism—the party has no way of denying the insurgent the right to the party label in the general election.

Closed and Open Primaries

Primaries can be classified as closed or open.

Closed Primaries. In a **closed primary**, only party members can vote to choose that party's candidates, and they may vote only in the primary of their own party. Thus, only registered Democrats can vote in the Democratic primary, and only registered Republicans can vote for the Republican candidates. A person usually establishes party membership when she or he registers to vote. Some states have a *semiclosed* primary, which allows voters to register with a party or change their party affiliations on Election Day.

Regular party workers favor the closed primary because it promotes party loyalty. Independent voters usually oppose it because it forces them to select a party if they wish to participate in the nominating process.

Open Primaries. In an **open primary**, voters can vote for a party's candidates regardless of whether they belong to the party. In most open primaries, all voters receive both a Republican ballot and a Democratic ballot. Voters then choose either the Democratic or the Republican ballot in the privacy of the voting booth. In a *semiopen* primary, voters request the ballot for the party of their choice.

Mixed Forms. The fifty states have developed dozens of variations on the open and closed primary plans. In some states, primaries are closed only to

> "THERE IS NO EXCITEMENT ANYWHERE IN THE WORLD . . . TO MATCH THE EXCITEMENT OF AN AMERICAN PRESIDENTIAL CAMPAIGN."
>
> ~ THEODORE H. WHITE, AMERICAN JOURNALIST AND HISTORIAN, 1915–1986

persons registered to another party, and independents can vote in either primary. In several states, an independent who votes in a party primary is automatically enrolled in that party. In other states, the voter remains an independent. The two major parties often have different rules. For example, in five states, Democrats allow independent voters to participate in primaries or caucuses, but Republicans do not. In one state, Alabama, the reverse is the case.

Blanket and "Top Two" Primaries Until 2000, California and a few other states employed a *blanket primary,* in which voters could choose the candidates of more than one party. A voter might participate in choosing the Republican candidate for governor, for example, and at the same time vote to pick the Democratic candidate for the U.S. Senate. In that year, however, the Supreme Court ruled that the blanket primary violated the parties' right to freedom of association.[7] Similar primary systems in Washington and Alaska were struck down in later cases.

The Louisiana Model. Beginning in 1977, Louisiana had a unique system in which all candidates participated in the same primary, regardless of party. The two candidates receiving the most votes then proceeded on to the general election. In 2008, Louisiana abandoned this "jungle primary" for the U.S. House and Senate, but kept it for state and local offices. In 2010, however, Louisiana restored the jungle system for all offices.

The "Top Two" Primary. Even as Louisiana was questioning its system, other states began picking it up. Washington adopted the Louisiana system in 2004, and in 2008 the Supreme Court ruled that it was constitutional.[8] In June 2010, California voters adopted a system known as the *"top two" primary* that was patterned on the one in Washington. The California system went into effect in 2011, and in the 2014 general elections, seven U.S. House contests featured two members of the same party facing off against each other. The 2016 elections featured seven such races for the House and one for the Senate.

In such systems, political parties continue to have the right to designate preferred candidates, using conventions or other means, but their endorsements do not appear on the ballot. An insurgent Republican and a "regular" Republican, for example, would both be labeled simply "Republican."

closed primary A primary in which only party members can vote to choose that party's candidates.

open primary A primary in which voters can vote for a party's candidates regardless of whether they belong to the party.

9-2d Nominating Presidential Candidates

In some respects, being nominated for president is more difficult than being elected. The nominating process often narrows a very large number of hopefuls down to a single candidate from each party. Choosing a presidential candidate is unlike nominating candidates for any other office. One reason for this is that the nomination process combines several different methods.

The "Invisible Primary" Well before the official primary season begins in the year of the election, candidates for president are busy garnering as much support as possible. In recent years, unofficial presidential campaigns have often begun as much as three years before Election Day. In this period, candidates attempt not only to enhance their public images, but also to gain the support of their party's elected officials, fund-raisers, and other leaders. This effort has been called the "invisible primary," and it can have a major impact on the primary election outcomes.[9] Historically, this was particularly true for Republicans. The 2016 primary season, however, proved to be a dramatic counterexample. In that year, many Republican voters were in open revolt against the party's leaders. Establishment support for former Florida governor Jeb Bush, the initial frontrunner, appeared to hurt, rather than help him. Donald Trump, the victorious candidate, made a point of his contempt for party leaders. The second-ranking candidate, Ted Cruz (R., Tex.), gloried in his unpopularity among his Senate colleagues.

Presidential Primaries Most of the states hold presidential primaries, beginning early in the election year. For a candidate, a good showing in the early primaries results in plenty of media attention as television networks and newspaper reporters play up the results. Subsequent primaries tend to eliminate candidates unlikely to be successful.

The presidential primaries do not necessarily follow the same rules the states use for nominating candidates for the U.S. Congress or for state and local offices. Often, the presidential primaries are not held on the same date as the other primaries. States frequently hold the presidential primaries early in hope of exercising greater influence on the outcome.

The top three Republican presidential candidates as of early 2016: businessman Donald Trump, Texas senator Ted Cruz, and Florida senator Marco Rubio. *What are the advantages of choosing presidential candidates through primaries?*

Caucuses The caucus system is an alternative to primary elections. Strictly speaking, the caucus system is a convention system. The caucuses are party conventions held at the local level that elect delegates to conventions at the county or congressional district level. These mid-level conventions then choose the delegates to the state convention, which finally elects the delegates to the national party convention.

Unlike the caucuses of two centuries ago, modern caucuses are open to all party members. It is not hard to join a party. At the famous Iowa caucuses, you become a party member simply by attending a local caucus.

While some states, such as Iowa and Minnesota, rely on the caucus/convention system to nominate candidates for state and local positions, the system is more frequently used only to choose delegates to the Democratic and Republican national conventions. Most states with presidential caucuses use primaries to nominate state and local candidates. Thirteen states choose Democratic national convention delegates through caucuses. Republicans use caucuses in fourteen states.

Primaries—The Rush to Be First

Traditionally, states have held their presidential primaries at various times over the first six months of a presidential election year. In an effort to make their primaries prominent in the media and influential in the political process, however, many states moved the date of their primary to earlier in the year—a practice known as *front-loading*. In 1988, a group of southern states created a "Super Tuesday" by holding their primaries on the same day in early March. Then, other states moved their primaries to an earlier date, too.

The practice of front-loading primaries has gained momentum over the last decade. The states with later primary dates found that most nominations were decided early in the season, leaving their voters "out of the action." Many states, to compete, moved up their primaries. This rush to be first was particularly notable in the year or so preceding the 2008 presidential primaries.

The Impact of Front-Loading

Many Americans worried that with a shortened primary season, long-shot candidates would no longer be able to propel themselves into serious contention by doing well in small early-voting states, such as New Hampshire and Iowa.

The practice of front-loading reached its limits in the 2008 Democratic primaries. The Democrats allocated delegates on a proportional basis, so that each candidate received delegates based on his or her share of the vote. That rule made an early decision impossible, and Barack Obama did not obtain a majority of the Democratic delegates until June 3. As a result, many of the most important Democratic primaries took place late in the season. States that had moved their primaries to Super Tuesday on February 5 discovered that they were lost in the crowd of early contests. Front-loading, in other words, had become counterproductive. In an attempt to reduce front-loading, in 2012 the Republican National Committee ruled that only four traditionally early states, including Iowa, New Hampshire, South Carolina, and Nevada, could choose delegates in February. In 2016, states other than these four could not vote until March 1. Super Tuesday, as a result, fell on March 1. Eleven largely Southern states chose delegates on that date. States choosing delegates before March 15 had to allocate them proportionally. From March 15 on, delegates could be selected on a winner-take-all basis.

The Republicans had adopted similar rules in 2012, although in that year, several states violated the rules and were penalized. By 2016, the new rules were more widely accepted. The Democratic Party generally fell in line with these decisions, although the Democrats did not allow winner-take-all voting in the later primaries.

The 2016 Republican Primaries

During 2015, the most striking feature of the Republican primary contest was the number of candidates—the largest in any primary season in U.S. history. The field included at least five current or former senators, nine current or former governors, and many people who had never held public office. Of the nonpoliticians, only a handful—including neurosurgeon Ben Carson, businesswoman Carly Fiorina, and businessman Donald Trump—had any national reputation at all. The others were clearly headed nowhere, and the same was true of a majority of the governors and senators in the contest.

The Republican Presidential Debates. As in the 2011–2012 election cycle, a key characteristic of the race was the importance of the debates among the candidates. Debates among presidential primary candidates are not new. Beginning in 2011, however, the debates assumed an importance never before seen. Millions of Republicans and others tuned in to watch them. The 2015–2016 debates were more popular still. Debates in 2015 allowed the Republicans to winnow the field of candidates even before the voting began. In the first debate, Fox News allowed only the top ten contenders, as measured by polling, onto the main stage. Other networks followed similar rules in later debates. By late February, the Republicans were down to five major contenders. Only three were viewed as realistic possibilities—Texas senator Ted Cruz, Florida senator Marco Rubio, and businessman Donald Trump.

The Republican Primaries. As soon as actual voters began expressing their opinions in Iowa and New Hampshire, Donald Trump became the clear Republican frontrunner. Trump's campaign was significantly different from the campaigns of other recent Republican candidates. (We described Trump's nationalist, populist appeal earlier in this text.) Because Trump was uniquely antiestablishment, the race soon became Trump versus everyone else.

While in principle there were probably enough Republican anti-Trump votes to defeat the businessman, that vote was split among multiple candidates. No single traditional small-government conservative had the support needed to stop him. Even after Super Tuesday, the anti-Trump field was split between Cruz and Rubio (and also Ohio governor John Kasich). That split made it impossible to stop Trump. As March progressed, Trump won support in large, winner-take-all states. The result was that increasingly frantic efforts by party leaders to derail his candidacy all failed.

In May, however, Trump accumulated enough delegates to guarantee his nomination at the Republican National Convention. In the following months, most, though not all, Republicans rallied behind their nominee. Some did so with obvious reluctance. A few, such as 2012 Republican presidential candidate Mitt Romney, refused to support him.

The 2016 Democratic Primaries Like Republican Jeb Bush, Democrat Hillary Clinton sought to win enough early support to dissuade other candidates from running against her. Clinton was considerably more successful at that than Bush. Still, Clinton faced a major opponent. Vermont senator Bernie Sanders challenged Clinton from the left, running as a democratic socialist. He soon won strong support from younger voters and, to an extent, from older liberals and hard-pressed white, working-class Democrats. Sanders' appeal was largely idealistic. He championed liberal causes that were widely viewed as impossible to implement given Republican strength in Congress. These included a universal health-care insurance program entirely run by the government, as seen in many European countries. Tuition at state colleges and universities was to be abolished—another European practice. Large banks were to be broken up. Inevitably, taxes would rise.

In contrast, Clinton emphasized her experience as first lady, as a U.S. senator from New York, and as secretary of state during Obama's first term as president. Clinton's supporters argued that her depth of knowledge and policy expertise would translate into greater progress toward liberal goals than Sanders' ideological passion.

Although Sanders did well in early states such as Iowa and New Hampshire, he found the limits of his potential support in the South Carolina primary. In that state, black voters make up more than half of the Democratic primary electorate. While African Americans are a liberal force within the Democratic Party, that liberalism did not translate into support for Sanders. Clinton beat Sanders 84 to 16 percent among black voters in South Carolina. African Americans recognized Clinton as a politician who had been their friend for decades. Sanders hurt himself because, at least in the

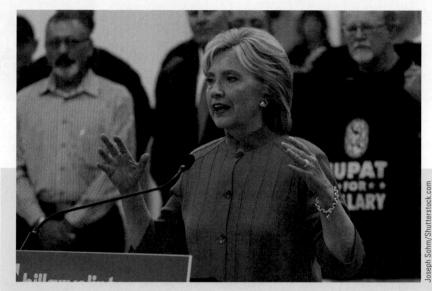

Hillary Clinton speaks to union members before the Nevada caucuses. *Would many Americans like to see a woman as president? Why or why not?*

earlier part of the contest, he emphasized economic class to such an extent that he appeared to neglect racial issues. By the end of Super Tuesday, Clinton's march to the Democratic nomination was unstoppable. To what extent did Sanders hurt himself by adopting the socialist label? We examine that question in this chapter's *Perception versus Reality* feature.

Clinton wrapped up enough delegates for a nomination in June. Many of Sanders' supporters rallied around the slogan "Bernie or bust." In July, however, on the eve of the Democratic National Convention, Sanders strongly endorsed Clinton.

National Party Conventions Created in the 1830s, the American national political convention is unique in Western democracies. Elsewhere, candidates for prime minister or chancellor are chosen within the confines of party councils. That is actually closer to the way the framers of the Constitution wanted it done.

Giant Pep Rallies. At one time, national conventions were often giant free-for-alls. It wasn't always clear who the winning presidential and vice-presidential candidates would be until the delegates voted.

As more states opted to hold presidential primaries, however, the drama of national conventions diminished. Today, the conventions have been described as massive pep rallies. Nonetheless, each convention's task remains a serious one. In late summer, two thousand to three thousand delegates gather at each convention to represent the wishes of the voters and political leaders of their home states.

PERCEPTION VS. REALITY

Is the Word *Socialism* Still Poison in U.S. Political Campaigns?

In the early twentieth century, America had a major socialist movement. Still, the Socialist Party won very few elections. After World War II (1939–1945), the United States entered a decades-long confrontation with the Soviet Union, a Communist Party–led empire centered on what is now Russia. The Soviets described their system as *socialism* (*communism* was an ideal for the distant future). For millions of Americans, socialism became a very unpopular label. Yet Vermont senator Bernie Sanders has always called himself a "democratic socialist." In 2016, he ran for president on the Democratic ticket. He lost, but he did carry many states in the Democratic primaries. This leads to a question: Is socialism still a dirty word in U.S. politics?

The Perception

For many older Americans, the word *socialism* is still political poison. Many are astonished that a major politician could embrace it.

The Reality

Informed of Sanders' considerable appeal to American youth, one resident of Cuba plaintively asked: "Don't they know that socialism is a bad thing?" Well, if you live in Cuba, where socialism can be defined as whatever the Castro brothers are doing, it surely is a "bad thing." It was bad in the Soviet Union, and it has been an economic catastrophe in today's Venezuela. For many young Americans, however, the word means something else. Often, *capitalism* now appears to mean "the worst excesses of private enterprise." Socialism, as "anticapitalism," thus becomes "opposition to the worst excesses of private enterprise." What's not to like?

What Sanders means by socialism is something else again. He means Denmark. Unlike Cuba or the Soviet Union, Denmark and the other Nordic countries are among the most successful societies on earth. In international comparisons, they regularly rank as among the wealthiest, freest, and happiest countries anywhere.

But as the prime minister of Denmark firmly says, Denmark is not a socialist country. It has a thriving capitalist system and adheres to free-market economic principles. What Denmark also has is a system of social benefits that is vastly more generous than what we have. (Of necessity, taxes are also much higher.) In large part, it owes these benefits to the influence of the Social Democratic Party, the largest single party in all the Nordic nations. The Social Democrats are heirs to the socialist movement, but unlike the Communists, they gave up on abolishing capitalism generations ago.

Therefore, the Nordic lands are often called social democracies. They have none of the ruthless authoritarianism and tight government control of the economy seen in a country such as Cuba. But if social democracy and socialism are not the same, is Bernie really a socialist? Many political scientists would argue that he is not.

Blog On

The worldwide organization that unites social democratic parties retains the historical name "Socialist International." Find out about these parties by visiting www.socialistinternational.org.

The Convention Schedule. On the first day of the convention, delegates hear the reports of the **Credentials Committee**, which inspects each prospective delegate's claim to be seated as a legitimate representative of her or his state. When the eligibility of delegates is in question, the committee decides who will be seated. Then, a carefully chosen keynote speaker whips up enthusiasm among the delegates. Later, the convention deals with committee reports and debates on the party platform. Finally, it turns to nominations and voting.

Balloting takes place with an alphabetical roll call in which states and territories announce their votes. The vice-presidential nomination takes place later. Acceptance speeches by the presidential and vice-presidential candidates are timed to take place during prime-time television hours. We provided more details on the national party conventions in Chapter 7.

Credentials Committee A committee of each national political party that evaluates the claims of national party convention delegates to be the legitimate representatives of their states.

CRITICAL THINKING

▶ *Is the caucus system undemocratic? Why or why not?*

9–3 THE MODERN POLITICAL CAMPAIGN

LO Indicate what is involved in launching a political campaign today, and describe the structure and functions of a campaign organization.

Once nominated, candidates focus on their campaigns. The term *campaign* originated in the military context. Generals mounted campaigns, using their scarce resources (soldiers and materials) to achieve military objectives. Using the term in a political context is apt. In a political campaign, candidates also use scarce resources (time and funds) in an attempt to defeat their adversaries in the battle for votes.

9–3a Responsibilities of the Campaign Staff

To run a successful campaign, a candidate's campaign staff must be able to raise funds, get media coverage, produce and pay for political ads, schedule the candidate's time effectively with constituent groups and potential supporters, convey the candidate's position on the issues, conduct research on the opposing candidate, and persuade the voters to go to the polls.

When party identification was firmer and TV campaigning was still in its infancy, a strong party organization on the local, state, or national level could furnish most of the services and expertise that the candidate needed. Today, party organizations are no longer as important as they once were in providing campaign services. Instead of relying so extensively on political parties, candidates now turn to professionals to manage their campaigns.

The fact that party organizations no longer provide large quantities of campaign services, however, should not lead anyone to believe that the parties are unimportant in campaigns. Because of the intense political polarization that has taken place in recent years, the parties are in some ways more important than ever. Political experts know that today, the party label allows them to predict how a senator or representative will vote on almost all issues. Many voters are also aware of this reality.

9–3b The Professional Campaign Organization

As mentioned, the role of the political party in managing campaigns has declined, although the party continues to play an important role in recruiting volunteers and getting out the vote. Professional **political consultants** now manage nearly all aspects of a presidential candidate's campaign. Most candidates for governor, the House, and the Senate also rely on consultants. Political consultants generally specialize in a particular area of the campaign, such as researching the opposition, conducting polls, developing the candidate's advertising, or organizing "get-out-the-vote" efforts. Nonetheless, most candidates have a campaign manager who coordinates and plans the **campaign strategy**. Figure 9–2 shows a typical presidential campaign organization.

A major development in contemporary American politics is the focus on reaching voters through effective use of the media, particularly television. At least half of the budget for a major political campaign is consumed by television advertising. Media consultants are therefore pivotal members of the campaign staff. The nature of political advertising is discussed in more detail in Chapter 10.

9–3c Opposition Research

Major campaigns, such as those for governor, senator, and U.S. president, typically make use of **opposition research**. A staff member—or even an entire team—spends time discovering as much negative information about opposing candidates as possible. Journalists often rely on opposition researchers for their stories.

In 2012, Barack Obama was already so well researched that there was little point to making any further efforts. Rather, the many Republican candidates focused on researching each other, sometimes with devastating results.

Researching Hillary Clinton Beginning in 2015, however, Democratic candidate Hillary Clinton became the target of intense opposition research—even though she had been in the public eye since 1992, when her husband, Bill Clinton, first ran for president. Republicans recognized that any claims of improper behavior during Clinton's time as first lady (1993–2001) or as U.S. senator from New York (2001–2009) would be old news. The hope was to find something damaging that took place when she was secretary of state (2009–2013).

political consultant
A professional political adviser who, for a fee, works on an area of a candidate's campaign. Political consultants include campaign managers, pollsters, media advisers, and "get-out-the-vote" organizers.

campaign strategy
The comprehensive plan developed by a candidate and his or her advisers for winning an election.

opposition research
The attempt to learn damaging information about an opponent in a political campaign.

FIGURE 9–2   A TYPICAL PRESIDENTIAL CAMPAIGN ORGANIZATION

Most aspects of a candidate's campaign are managed by professional political consultants, as this figure illustrates.

CANDIDATE

Campaign Manager
Develops overall campaign strategy, manages finances, oversees staff

Campaign Staff
Undertakes the various tasks associated with campaigning

MEDIA CONSULTANTS
Help to shape the candidate's image and manage campaign advertising

FUND-RAISERS
Raise money to pay for the campaign

LAWYERS AND ACCOUNTANTS
Monitor legal and financial aspects of the campaign

PRIVATE POLLSTER
Gathers up-to-the-minute data on public opinion

SPEECHWRITERS
Prepare speeches for the candidate's public appearances

PRESS SECRETARY
Maintains press contacts, is responsible for disseminating campaign news

RESEARCHERS
Investigate opponents' records and personal history

TRAVEL PLANNER
Arranges for the candidate's transportation and accommodations

POLICY EXPERTS
Provide input on foreign and domestic policy issues

WEB CONSULTANT
Oversees the candidate's Internet presence

State Campaign Chairpersons
Monitor state and local campaigns

Local Committees
Direct efforts of local volunteers

Volunteers
Publicize the candidate at the local level through personal visits, phone calls, direct mailings, and online activities

© Cengage Learning

Researchers hoped to find problems in Clinton's handling of the 2012 attack on the U.S. diplomatic mission in Benghazi, Libya. Her use of a private e-mail account was criticized by the FBI. Some researchers examined contributions to the Clinton Foundation, a charity. As of Election Day, no one had managed to find a "smoking gun." Still, the constant drumbeat of accusations did cut heavily into Clinton's reputation for honesty.

Researching the Republicans   Donald Trump, the Republican primary winner, seemed to be vulnerable to opposition research. He had engineered four corporate bankruptcies, freezing out hundreds of creditors, many of them small businesses. Former students of Trump University sued, claiming that the defunct, non-accredited real estate school was a scam. Still, most of Trump's followers apparently believed that anything said against him in the "mainstream media" was a lie. In the general election, however, where Trump faced a wider audience, he lost support when he seemed to attack ordinary citizens. An example was his remarks on the parents of U.S. Army captain Humayun Khan, a Muslim war hero killed in Iraq. Trump was also damaged by a videotape in which he bragged of his power to physically molest women.

CRITICAL THINKING

▶ *Some people have accused political consultants of "managing the candidate" too well, making the candidate appear stilted and unnatural. How could a candidate prevent that from happening?*

9-4   THE INTERNET CAMPAIGN

LO Describe how the Internet has transformed political campaigns.

Over the years, political leaders have benefited from understanding and using new communications technologies. In the 1930s, command of a new medium—radio—gave President Franklin D. Roosevelt an edge. In 1960, Democratic presidential candidate John F. Kennedy gained an advantage over Republican Richard Nixon because Kennedy had a better understanding of the visual requirements of television.

Today, the ability to make effective use of social media and the Internet is essential to a candidate. In the 2008 presidential elections, Barack Obama gained an edge on his rivals in part because of his superior use of the new

The 2016 presidential elections provided a unique opportunity to test theories about how elections are won. In particular, what effect do campaign advertisements have on the outcome? How important is the "ground game," that is, the get-out-the-vote effort? With only about $250 million, Trump was able to air a mere fraction of the number of TV ads bought in 2012 by Barack Obama and Mitt Romney. As we suggested in the chapter-opening *America at Odds* feature, at the presidential level at least, spending on TV ads does not appear to be that important. Few viewers could be ignorant of the claims made by the two major campaigns or of the denunciations directed at the candidates. Many experts thought that Trump's lack of a ground game would hurt him. The Republican National Committee, however, had a very effective ground game in place. Conservative Super PACs also devoted considerable resources to the effort, even though many of them never spoke the word "Trump," campaigning instead for Republican House and Senate candidates. It appears that the Republican get-out-the-vote effort was sufficient.

The 2016 presidential race was marked by the sheer volume of negativity directed at the major candidates. Trump's scandalous business career, prickly temperament, and ever-changing policy positions provided endless opportunities for the Democrats to dump opprobrium on his head. Clinton's thirty-plus years in politics gave Republicans a vast range of opportunities to search for scandal. In Clinton's case, many of the supposed scandals were fiction. These included the claim that she was somehow responsible for the attacks on U.S. personnel at Benghazi, Libya, in 2012, when she was secretary of state. Just days before the elections, FBI director James Comey raised new questions about her use of a private e-mail server while at the State Department. A week later, Comey confirmed that the new allegations were baseless, but by then the damage was done. Clinton herself blamed Comey for her defeat.

technologies. His team relied on the Internet for fund-raising, targeting potential supporters, and creating local political organizations. His 2012 campaign was even more sophisticated. By 2016, every major presidential candidate understood the need for an effective online operation.

9–4a Fund-Raising on the Internet

Internet fund-raising grew out of an earlier technique: the direct-mail campaign. In direct mailings, campaigns send solicitations to large numbers of likely prospects, typically seeking contributions. Developing good lists of prospects is central to an effective direct-mail operation, because postage, printing, and the rental of address lists make the costs of each mailing high. In many direct-mail campaigns, most of the funds raised are used up by the costs of the campaign itself. In contrast to the costs, response rates are low—a 1 percent response rate is a tremendous success. From the 1970s on, conservative organizations became especially adept at managing direct-mail campaigns. For a time, this expertise gave conservative causes and candidates an advantage over liberals.

To understand the old system is to recognize the superiority of the new one. The cost of e-mailing is very low. Lists of prospects need not be prepared as carefully, because e-mail sent to unlikely prospects does not waste resources. E-mail fund-raising did face one problem when it was new—many people were not yet online. Today, the extent of online participation is no longer a concern.

The new technology brought with it a change in the groups that benefited the most. Conservatives were no longer the most effective fund-raisers. Instead, liberal and libertarian organizations enjoyed some of the greatest successes.

Democrats Online As noted, Barack Obama took Internet fund-raising to a new level. One of the defining characteristics of his fund-raising was its decentralization. The Obama campaign attempted to recruit as many supporters as possible to act as fund-raisers who would solicit contributions from their friends and neighbors. As a result, Obama was spared much personal fund-raising effort during campaigns. (As president, however, he has raised large sums for other Democrats). In 2015 and 2016, Hillary Clinton sought to emulate Obama's online success. Her chief opponent, Senator Bernie Sanders, was also very popular on the Internet, however. That popularity let Sanders raise more money in small donations than Clinton.

Republicans Online Already in 2008, one Republican candidate was able to use the Internet with great success—Texas representative Ron Paul, who espoused a libertarian philosophy that was highly appealing to many high-tech enthusiasts. Paul pioneered the online *moneybomb* technique, described by the San José *Mercury News* as "a one-day fund-raising frenzy." Despite Paul's fund-raising prowess, his libertarian politics were sufficiently far from the conservative Republican mainstream that he was able to win only a handful of national convention delegates. Later Republican candidates, such as 2012 nominee Mitt Romney, had more limited Internet operations. Most of these candidates raised more of their funds from wealthy donors than from small online contributions. (Billionaire Donald Trump was largely self-funded.)

9–4b Targeting Supporters

In 2004, President George W. Bush's chief political adviser, Karl Rove, pioneered a new campaign technique known as *microtargeting*. The process involves collecting as much information as possible about voters in a gigantic database and then filtering out various groups for special attention.

Through microtargeting, for example, the Bush campaign could identify Republican prospects living in heavily Democratic neighborhoods—potential supporters whom the campaign might otherwise have neglected because the neighborhood as a whole seemed so unpromising. In 2004, the Democrats had nothing to

match Republican efforts. In 2012, however, Obama's microtargeting operation vastly outperformed Romney's.

9–4c Support for Local Organizing

Perhaps the most effective use of the Internet has been as an organizing tool. One of the earliest Internet techniques was to use the site Meetup.com to organize real-world meetings. In this way, campaigns were able to gather supporters without relying on the existing party and activist infrastructure.

The 2012 and 2016 Campaigns As with fundraising, Barack Obama took Web-based organizing to a new level. In 2012, Obama had seven times as many Facebook supporters as Romney (28 million versus 4 million).

For 2015–2016, we can use Twitter followers as a measure of online presence. As of Super Tuesday, Clinton was well in the lead with 4.3 million followers. Sanders had a respectable 1.3 million. On the Republican side, Trump led with 2.9 million followers. Rubio had 865,000 followers, Cruz had 715,000, and Kasich a mere 146,000.[10]

The Ground Game A modern campaign collects as much data as it can—in part, through use of Internet resources—to identify the people whose votes it wants. The data are used to make human contact more efficient by directing volunteers toward the voters they most need to reach. Such get-out-the-vote drives have been called the *ground game* (as opposed to advertising, called the *air game*).

President Obama's Twitter page. *How important was the Internet to Obama's reelection?*

By 2012, Obama had had years to perfect his ground game, and it showed. The Obama campaign was able to create active local support groups in towns and counties across the country—many in areas that had traditionally supported Republicans. By comparison, Romney's ground game sometimes looked like a comedy of errors. In 2016, both Clinton and Sanders attempted to perfect their ground games. Sanders enjoyed relative success in caucus states, where turnout is lower than in primary states. That spoke well for the enthusiasm of his supporters, but it was not enough to overcome Clinton's advantages. On the Republican side, political novice Donald Trump was slow in setting up his ground game, but that did not stop him from the nomination.

Tom Steyer is a hedge fund manager, philanthropist, and environmentalist. He is also one of the largest individual contributors to Democratic candidates and has his own super PAC. *Is removing money from politics a realistic goal? Why or why not?*

CRITICAL THINKING

▶ *Some candidates are more successful than others in using the Internet. Do such candidates have any traits in common? If so, what might these be?*

9-5 WHAT IT COSTS TO WIN

LO Summarize the current laws that regulate campaign financing and the role of money in modern political campaigns.

The modern political campaign is an expensive undertaking. Candidates must spend huge sums for professional campaign managers and consultants, television and radio ads, the printing of campaign literature, travel, office rent, equipment, and other necessities.

The cost of campaigning has grown considerably. The Center for Responsive Politics has estimated that the total cost of the 2016 elections would reach $6.6 billion, up somewhat from 2012. This includes the primary and general elections, and races at all levels from president on down. It is true that in 2016, the Trump and Clinton candidate committees—the committees directly under candidate control—spent less than in 2012. Trump in particular spent much less. Yet spending by losing presidential candidates, congressional campaigns, the major parties, and outside groups rose substantially. Consider that by October 2016, the Senate race in Pennsylvania cost $139 million and the New Hampshire Senate race cost $102 million.

9-5a Presidential Spending

Presidential campaigns are even more expensive than congressional campaigns. In the 2015–2016 presidential election cycle, spending on behalf of the two major candidates exceeded $1.6 billion.

In today's campaign-finance environment, the sums spent by the candidates themselves and by the parties are only part of the story. Independent expenditures by outside groups nominally unconnected with the campaigns have become as important as spending by the candidates themselves.

The groups responsible for much of this spending, known as *super PACs,* are a new development. They became prominent only in the 2011–2012 campaign cycle. Super PACs followed from recent court decisions, especially the Supreme Court's ruling in *Citizens United v. Federal Election Commission.* We discuss that decision later in this section. First, however, we examine the development of our campaign-finance system.

9-5b The Federal Election Campaign Act

The high cost of campaigns gives rise to the fear that campaign contributors and special interest groups will try to buy favored treatment from those who are elected to office. In an attempt to prevent these abuses, the government has tried to regulate campaign financing.

Legislation to regulate campaign finance was passed in 1925 and 1939, but these early efforts were almost completely ineffective. The first reform that actually had teeth was the Federal Election Campaign Act (FECA) of 1971.[11] The act was amended in 1974. As amended, the new law did the following:

▶ Restricted the amount that could be spent on mass media advertising, including television.

▶ Limited how much individuals and groups could contribute to candidates.

▶ Limited the amount that candidates and their families could contribute to their own campaigns.

▶ Prevented corporations and labor unions from participating directly in political campaigns, but allowed them to set up political action committees (discussed shortly).

▶ Required disclosure of all contributions and expenditures of more than $100.

▶ Created the Federal Election Commission (FEC) to administer and enforce the act's provisions.

In addition, the act provided public financing for presidential primaries and general elections, funded by a check-off on federal income tax returns. From 1976 through 2000, presidential campaigns were largely funded by the public purse. Beginning in 2004, however, leading Democratic and Republican presidential candidates were refusing public funding for the primaries because they could raise much more money without it. By 2012, the public financing of presidential campaigns was effectively over.

Freeing Up Self-Financing In 1976, the United States Supreme Court declared unconstitutional the provision in the 1971 act that limited the amount each individual could spend on his or her own campaign. The Court held that a "candidate, no less than any other person, has a First Amendment right to engage in the discussion of public issues and vigorously and tirelessly to advocate his own election."[12]

The Rise of PACs The FECA allowed corporations, labor unions, and special interest groups to set up national *political action committees (PACs)* to raise money for candidates. PACs can contribute up to $5,000 per candidate in each election, but there is no limit on the total amount of PAC contributions during an election cycle.

As discussed in Chapter 6, the number of PACs grew significantly for several decades, as did their campaign contributions. In the 2004 election cycle, about 36 percent of campaign funds spent on House races came from PACs.[13] Since 2004, however, other methods of raising campaign funds have reduced the relative importance of traditional PACs.

9–5c Skirting the Campaign-Financing Rules

The FECA was designed to regulate funds given to the campaign organizations of candidates for office. There are ways, however, to influence the political process without giving money directly to a candidate's campaign. Individuals and corporations soon developed such practices. One way to skirt the rules was to contribute to the political parties instead of the candidates. A second was to make independent expenditures not coordinated with a candidate's campaign or a political party.

Soft Money The FECA and its amendments did not prohibit individuals or corporations from contributing to political parties. Contributors could make donations to the parties to cover the costs of registering voters, printing flyers, advertising, developing campaigns to get out the vote, and holding fund-raising events. Contributions to political parties were called **soft money**.

By 2000, the parties were raising nearly $463 million per election season through soft money contributions. Soft dollars became the main source of campaign money in the presidential race until after the 2002 elections, when soft money was banned, as you will read shortly.

Independent Expenditures The campaign-financing laws did not prohibit corporations, labor unions, and special interest groups from making **independent expenditures** in an election campaign. Independent expenditures, as the term implies, are expenditures for activities that are independent of (not coordinated with) those of a candidate or a political party.

> **"A PROMISING YOUNG MAN SHOULD GO INTO POLITICS SO THAT HE CAN GO ON PROMISING FOR THE REST OF HIS LIFE."**
>
> ~ ROBERT BYRNE, AMERICAN AUTHOR, BORN 1930

soft money Campaign contributions not regulated by federal law, such as some contributions that are made to political parties instead of to particular candidates.

independent expenditure An expenditure for activities that are independent from (not coordinated with) those of a political candidate or a political party.

Decisions by the courts have distinguished two types of independent expenditures. In the first type, an interest group or other contributor wages an "issue campaign" without going so far as to say "Vote for Candidate X." An issue campaign might, however, go so far as to publish voter guides informing voters of candidates' positions. The courts have repeatedly upheld the right of groups to advocate their positions in this way.

Alternatively, a group might explicitly campaign for particular candidates. The Supreme Court has held that an issue-oriented group has a First Amendment right to advocate the election of its preferred candidates as long as it acts independently of the candidates' campaigns. In 1996, the Court held that these guidelines apply to expenditures by political parties as well.[14]

Charles Koch (pronounced "coke") is the CEO of Koch Industries, the second-largest privately held company by revenue in the United States. With his brother David, he is known for massive donations to libertarian and conservative causes. *Should such donations be limited?*

9-5d The Bipartisan Campaign Reform Act of 2002

The increasing use of soft money and independent expenditures led to a demand for further campaign-finance reform. In 2002, Congress passed, and the president signed, the Bipartisan Campaign Reform Act. The measure is also known as the McCain-Feingold Act after its chief sponsors, Senators John McCain (R., Ariz.) and Russell Feingold (D., Wisc.).

The new law banned soft money at the national level. It also regulated campaign ads paid for by interest groups and prohibited any such issue-advocacy commercials within thirty days of a primary election or sixty days of a general election.

The 2002 act set the amount that an individual could contribute to a federal candidate at $2,000 and the amount that an individual could give to all federal candidates at $95,000 over a two-year election cycle. (Under the law, some individual contribution limits are indexed for inflation and thus may change slightly with every election cycle.) Individuals could still contribute to state and local parties, so long as the contributions

did not exceed $10,000 per year per individual. The new law went into effect the day after the 2002 general elections.

The Supreme Court Upholds McCain-Feingold Several groups immediately filed lawsuits challenging the constitutionality of the new law. Supporters of the restrictions on campaign ads by special interest groups argued that the large amounts of funds spent on these ads create an appearance of corruption in the political process. In contrast, an attorney for the National Rifle Association (NRA) argued that because the NRA represents "millions of Americans speaking in unison . . . [it] is not a *corruption* of the democratic political process; it *is* the democratic political process."[15] In December 2003, the Supreme Court upheld nearly all of the clauses of the act in *McConnell v. Federal Election Commission.*[16]

The Supreme Court Changes Its Mind Beginning in 2007, however, the Supreme Court began to chip away at the limits on independent expenditures contained in McCain-Feingold. In that year, in *Federal Election Commission v. Wisconsin Right to Life, Inc.*, the Court invalidated a major part of the 2002 law and overruled a portion of its own 2003 decision upholding the act. In the four years since the earlier ruling, Chief Justice John Roberts, Jr., and Associate Justice Samuel Alito, Jr., had been appointed, and both were conservatives.

In a five-to-four decision, the Court held that issue ads could not be prohibited in the time period preceding elections (thirty days before primary elections and sixty days before general elections) *unless* they were "susceptible of no reasonable interpretation other than as an appeal to vote for or against a specific candidate."[17] The Court concluded that restricting *all* television ads paid for by corporate or labor union treasuries in the weeks before an election amounted to censorship of political speech.

Citizens United v. Federal Election Commission (FEC) A January 2010 Supreme Court ruling helped establish our current wide-open campaign-finance system. This decision, *Citizens United v. FEC*, was initially seen as fostering a vast new wave of corporate spending on elections. The actual results were somewhat different, as you will read shortly.

In the *Wisconsin Right to Life* case described earlier, the Court ruled out bans on issue ads placed by corporations and other organizations in the run-up to an election. In *Citizens United v. FEC*, the Court extended this protection to ads that attack or praise specific candidates, including ads that suggest voting for particular candidates.[18] Two months later, in *Speechnow v. FEC*, a federal court of appeals held that it was not possible to limit contributions to independent-expenditure groups based on the size or source of the contribution.[19]

As a result of these two decisions, *Citizens United* and *Speechnow*, there is now no limit on the ability of corporations, unions, nonprofit groups, or individuals to fund advertising, provided that they do not contribute directly to a candidate's campaign. While Republican leaders applauded the *Citizens United* ruling as a victory for free speech, most Democrats were appalled. They feared that the ruling would result in a massive tilting of the political landscape toward corporate wealth.

McCutcheon v. FEC The Supreme Court handed down yet another ruling that freed up campaign financing in April 2014. In *McCutcheon v. FEC*, the Court struck down a decades-old cap on the total amount that any individual can contribute to federal candidates in a two-year election cycle.[20] The overall limit had been $48,600. As a result of this ruling, to give one example, a wealthy individual could now make the maximum legal contribution to every single House candidate of a particular party.

9-5e The Current Campaign-Finance Environment

Because the *Citizens United* decision was issued less than a year before the 2010 elections, its impact in that year was modest. By 2012, however, the new rules had changed the shape of the campaign-finance environment. Individuals and PACs still faced limits on what they could contribute directly to candidates' campaigns and to the parties. Despite these limits, the campaigns and parties were still able to raise huge sums. Meanwhile, independent organizations stood out as the wildcard in American politics. We list the largest independent expenditures in the 2016 election cycle in Table 9–1.

Super PACs A new type of organization came into existence to take advantage of the new rules. Known officially as "independent expenditure–only committees," the new bodies were soon dubbed super PACs.

The Myth of Independence. The super PACs' supposed independence from campaigns turned out to be a convenient fiction. By 2011, every major presidential candidate had one or more affiliated super PACs, usually run by former members of the candidate's own campaign. A division of labor soon developed. Super PACs would run negative ads to damage a candidate's opponents, while candidate committees accentuated the positive about the candidate.

The Role of the Individual Donor. When the *Citizens United* decision was handed down, a flood of corporate cash was expected to enter the political system. The ruling did result in more corporate (and union) spending, but far less than anticipated. Apparently, many companies were reluctant to take stands that might alienate a large number of customers. What caught everyone by surprise was the huge sums poured into super PACs by individuals, notably individuals of great wealth.

For example, Charles and David Koch, two brothers with a long-standing commitment to libertarian politics, soon became some of the largest political donors ever. In 2015, it was reported that a network of Koch organizations planned to spend almost $890 million during the 2015–2016 election cycle. By 2016, however, the Koch brothers faced a problem in Donald Trump, a candidate who was repugnant to the brothers' libertarian beliefs. In the end, Koch fundraising was limited to $250 million. Much of this money went to get-out-the-vote drives for Senate and House candidates. Such drives are potentially more effective than television advertisements.

In 2012, casino magnate Sheldon Adelson and his wife made total donations to Republican candidates that may have exceeded $100 million. In 2016, their donations were about half that sum. Adelson is particularly interested in supporting Israel.

TABLE 9-1 THE TWENTY TOP GROUPS MAKING INDEPENDENT EXPENDITURES DURING THE 2015–2016 CYCLE

This table lists independent expenditures only. Some groups have designated only a part of their total fund-raising as independent expenditures.

Committee	Affiliation	Raised in 2015–2016	Type	Disclosure of Contributors
Priorities USA Action	Hillary Clinton	$117,047,422	Super PAC	full
Right to Rise USA	Jeb Bush	$86,817,138	Super PAC	full
Senate Leadership Fund	Republican	$60,834,460	Super PAC	full
Senate Majority PAC	Democratic	$60,629,235	Super PAC	full
Democratic Congressional Campaign Committee	Democratic	$59,877,326	Party committee	full
National Republican Congressional Committee	Republican	$58,848,634	Party committee	full
Conservative Solutions PAC	Marco Rubio	$55,443,483	Super PAC	full
Get Our Jobs Back	Donald Trump	$50,010,166	Super PAC	full
NRA & NRA Institute for Legislative Action	gun rights	$49,719,389	501c, Super PAC	partial
Democratic Senatorial Campaign Committee	Democratic	$46,290,452	Party committee	full
National Republican Senatorial Committee	Republican	$35,254,013	Party committee	full
House Majority PAC	Democratic	$33,412,267	Super PAC	partial
Congressional Leadership Fund	Republican	$29,984,123	Super PAC	partial
Freedom Partners Action Fund	Koch brothers (libertarian)	$29,718,852	Super PAC	full
US Chamber of Commerce	business	$28,021,319	501c	none
Women Vote!	Democratic	$26,388,017	Super PAC	partial
Club for Growth & Club for Growth Action	anti-tax	$21,623,133	Super PAC, 501c	partial
NextGen Climate Action & NextGen California Action Committee	Tom Steyer (environmental)	$21,309,977	Super PACs	partial
Granite State Solutions	Sen. Kelly Ayotte	$18,799,608	Super PAC	full
America Leads	Chris Christie	$18,578,852	Super PAC	full

Source: Center for Responsive Politics

While conservative donors gained much attention, some billionaires also backed Democrats. Tom Steyer, a California hedge fund billionaire and environmentalist, donated more than $65 million to progressive candidates in 2012. In 2016, his contributions reached $57 million. Another major Democratic billionaire was financier and philanthropist Donald Sussman, who gave almost $35 million, including $11 million to Hillary Clinton's Super PAC.

527 and 501c Committees In addition to super PACs, another type of independent committee is the *527 committee,* named after the provision of the tax code that covers it. Spending by 527s rose rapidly after 2002, and in the 2004 election cycle, the committees spent about $612 million to "advocate positions," as they were not allowed to "expressly advocate" voting for

specific candidates. By 2008, the 527 committees began to decline in importance, and by 2012 they had been replaced almost completely by super PACs, which were allowed to campaign for and against candidates.

One reason for the decline of the 527 in 2008 was the creation of a new kind of body, the *501(c)4 organization,* known as the *501c.* Like the the 527, this type of committee was named after a provision in the tax code. According to some lawyers, a 501c could make limited contributions directly to campaigns and—perhaps more importantly—could conceal the identities of its donors. So far, the FEC has refused to rule on the legality of this technique. Table 9–1 indicates which major independent committees are super PACs and which are 501c organizations. Some groups have organized both types.

The 501c's ability to hide its contributors created a new campaign-finance issue. Republicans argued that donors needed the right to remain anonymous so that they would not have to fear retribution. Democrats contended that anonymous contributions were simply a further corruption of the political process. Attempts to end donor anonymity through legislation failed. We discuss the issue of anonymous donations in this chapter's *Join the Debate* feature.

JOIN THE DEBATE

Should We Let Political Contributors Conceal Their Identities?

In the run-up to every November general election, television watchers can be certain that they will be bombarded with negative political ads. Such ads must identify their sponsors. But if you see an ad by the Committee for the Advancement of Everything Good, how can you tell who actually funded it?

Many such ads are put together by super PACs or 501c organizations. If you go to the websites of these organizations, you are not likely to learn who provided the funds. In some cases, you might be able to find the answer at the website of the Federal Election Commission or of a watchdog organization such as the one at opensecrets.org. Yet in 2016 all of the $28 million in donations made through the U.S. Chamber of Commerce were anonymous, and so were $32 million in contributions made through the NRA.

Full Disclosure, Please

Polls show that a strong majority of voters are concerned about the role of money in politics. No one believes that special interest money is going to disappear, but most voters from both parties say that we should know who is making the contributions.

Opponents of anonymous contributions point to a number of reasons

why they should have no place in our democracy. When voters evaluate a candidate, they have the right to know who stands behind that person. Which unions, corporations, trade associations, or individual billionaires are supporting him or her? How can we battle undue influence on the part of special interests if we don't know which interests are supporting which candidates? Also, those who fund misleading advertisements or even flat-out lies should take responsibility for their messages.

Furthermore, small campaign contributors lose out when they are up against well-funded super PACs with anonymous donors. Candidates can compete fairly for public office only when we eliminate secret funding of political campaigns.

Political Privacy Should Be a Civil Right

Not everyone is in favor of forcing secret donors to political campaigns out into the open. Consider that in 1958, the United States Supreme Court ruled that Alabama could not require the NAACP to disclose its membership rolls. Why? Because if segregationists in Alabama were able to identify NAACP members, they could retaliate against the most

vulnerable ones. Some members might lose their jobs or be threatened with violence. Publicizing the membership list of an organization such as the NAACP would make a mockery of the constitutional rights to free association and free speech. According to the Court, the privacy of group membership is critical to "effective advocacy of both public and private points of view, particularly controversial ones."[21]

If all political contributions were exposed, what could happen to a supporter of a liberal cause such as gay rights if he or she worked for a conservative employer? In California, supporters of same-sex marriage picketed and boycotted various groups that funded opposition to gay marriage. Banning anonymous donations harms free speech—not the other way around.

Critical Analysis

Which kind of donor might be more interested in identity protection—an individual billionaire or a corporation that sells products to the public? Why?

Some observers believe that if the founders could see how presidential campaigns are conducted today, they would be shocked at how candidates "pander to the masses." Whether they would be shocked at the costliness of modern campaigns is not as clear. After all, the founders themselves were an elitist, wealthy group, as are many of today's successful candidates for high political office. In any event, Americans today are certainly stunned by how much it takes to win an election. Some of the specific controversies that divide Americans concerning campaigns are the following:

- *Is the electoral college a dangerous anachronism—or a force for stability within our political system?*

- *Should all voters be free to participate in any party primary—or does such a step make it too difficult for the parties to present a coherent group of candidates and policies?*

- *Should states retain their treasured right to set the dates of their presidential primaries—or should the national parties assume responsibility for establishing a rational primary schedule?*

- *Are campaign contributions a constitutionally protected form of free speech—or are they too often a source of corruption within the political system?*

- *Should all politically active groups be required to furnish the identities of their major contributors—or should we allow contributors to remain anonymous because they might suffer reprisals due to their contributions?*

STUDY TOOLS 9

READY TO STUDY? IN THE BOOK, YOU CAN:

- ☐ Review what you've read with the following chapter quiz.
- ☐ Check your answers in Appendix D at the back of the book.
- ☐ Rip out the Chapter Review Card, which includes key terms and chapter summaries.

ONLINE AT WWW.CENGAGEBRAIN.COM, YOU CAN:

- ☐ Learn about the drama of elections in a short video.
- ☐ Explore various online resources in the Political Moneyline and Frontloading Headquarters websites in the Internet Resources tool.
- ☐ Interact with figures from the text, and watch quick animation clips.
- ☐ Prepare for tests with quizzes.
- ☐ Review the key terms with Flash Cards.

FILL-IN

Learning Outcome 9–1

1. The electoral college system is primarily a winner-take-all system, in which the candidate _____.

2. A candidate must win at least _____ electoral votes, cast by the electors, to become president through the electoral college system.

Learning Outcome 9–2

3. In a/an _____ primary, voters cast their ballots directly for candidates.

4. In the context of presidential primaries, the practice known as front-loading refers to _____.

5. In late summer of a presidential election year, _____ gather at their party's national convention to adopt the party platform and to nominate the party's presidential and vice-presidential candidates.

Learning Outcome 9–3

6. The attempt to learn damaging information about an opponent in a political campaign is called _____ research.

Learning Outcome 9–4

7. A campaign technique known as microtargeting involves _____.

Learning Outcome 9–5

8. The Federal Election Campaign Act of 1971 and its amendments provided public financing for presidential primaries and general elections, funded by a checkoff on _____.

9. After the Supreme Court's decision in *Citizens United v. Federal Election Commission* (2010), a new type of organization came into existence. Known officially as "independent expenditure–only committees," the new bodies were soon dubbed _____.

MULTIPLE CHOICE

Learning Outcome 9–1

10. The total number of electoral votes available is
    a. 538.
    b. 535.
    c. 435.

11. If no presidential candidate receives the required number of electoral votes,
    a. a runoff election is held in January.
    b. the House of Representatives votes on the top three candidates, with each state delegation casting only a single vote.
    c. the Senate votes on the candidates, with each senator casting one vote.

Learning Outcome 9–2

12. In a/an _____ primary, only party members can vote to choose that party's candidates, and they may vote only in the primary of their own party.
    a. closed   **b.** open   **c.** indirect

Learning Outcome 9–3

13. With the rise of candidate-centered campaigns in the past several decades, the role of the political party in managing campaigns has
    a. increased.
    b. stayed about the same.
    c. declined.

Learning Outcome 9–4

14. Barack Obama gained an edge on his rivals in part because of his superior use of
    a. radio.
    b. television.
    c. social media and the Internet.

Learning Outcome 9–5

15. The Federal Election Campaign Act allows corporations, labor unions, and interest groups to set up PACs to raise money for candidates. PACs can contribute up to _____ per candidate in each election, but there is no limit on the total amount of PAC contributions during an election cycle.
    a. $2,000   **b.** $5,000   **c.** $95,000

GOVT
ONLINE

REVIEW FLASHCARDS
ANYTIME, ANYWHERE!

**Create Flashcards
from Your StudyBits**

**Review Key Term
Flashcards Already
Loaded on the
StudyBoard**

4LTR
PRESS

Access GOVT ONLINE at www.cengagebrain.com

10 POLITICS AND THE MEDIA

LEARNING OUTCOMES *After reading this chapter, you should be able to:*

10-1 Explain the role of the media in a democracy.

10-2 Summarize how television influences the conduct of political campaigns.

10-3 Explain why talk radio has been described as the Wild West of the media.

10-4 Describe types of media bias and explain how such bias affects the political process.

10-5 Indicate the extent to which the Internet is reshaping news and political campaigns.

After finishing this chapter, go to **PAGE 234** for **STUDY TOOLS**.

AMERICA AT ODDS

In a Digital World, Do We Still Need Print Media?

Helder Almeida/Shutterstock.com

When we say "print media," people immediately think of the *New York Times, Time* magazine, the *Wall Street Journal,* or the *Washington Post.* These and other publications generated and disseminated the nation's news for more than a hundred years. That's all changing, though, because of the online revolution. For newspapers, classified ads were always a major revenue source. But Internet sites such as Craigslist have taken over this function in recent years. Newspapers and news magazines have tried to make up for ad revenue losses through advertising revenues from their websites. They have had limited success.

For online news, the mobile world is now where the action is. More readers are using mobile devices to access the top fifty digital news sites than are using computers. In 2016 alone, mobile ad spending rose more than 70 percent. It now accounts for 40 percent of all digital ad spending. Meanwhile, spending on ads in print media has seen a slow but steady decline.

Does it matter? Some Americans don't think that we will miss much if print media were to disappear altogether.

Who Needs Print Media?

There are those—particularly in the younger generation—who do not mourn the loss of newspapers and news magazines. After all, we have more access to news than ever before. Online news sources remain current twenty-four hours a day and are usually free. An army of citizen bloggers can tell you what is happening anywhere in the world anytime you wish. So who needs print media?

In the "good old days," local newspapers were usually monopolies. Today, in contrast, journalists must deal with competition just like everyone else, and that's for the best. Even if your hometown newspaper shuts down, "hyperlocal" websites are increasingly available to deliver local news. Much of that news can be "pushed" to you any time of day if you so choose.

In the past, most Americans have had to put up with the opinions of their local newspaper whether they agreed with that publication or not. That is no longer necessary. You can find the news presented in whatever way you wish on hundreds of Internet news sites and thousands of blogs. Print media are dying. Long live the news.

There Will Always Be a Role for Real Reporters and Thus Print Media

Print may have declined in importance, but defenders of the press can argue that it is far from dead. Fifty-six percent of all newspaper readers still rely on printed editions. Newspapers still earn almost $17 billion a year in ads.

But let's get to the heart of the matter. People have to be paid to do a good job, no matter what that job is. Journalists have families to feed—and most of the free content on the Web can be traced back to journalists working for print media. This is even true for hyperlocal sites. Newspapers continue to employ the overwhelming majority of paid journalists. How many bloggers attend city council meetings and report what happens? Precious few.

A reporter summed it up: "The real value of what newspapers (and magazines) provide . . . is organization, editing, and reputation." The issue is not the survival of print media, but the survival of an informed citizenry. The news industry needs to learn how online editions can earn enough to support the job of reporting. If this is done, traditional media will retain their central role in gathering and disseminating the news.

Where do you stand?

1. Is it possible to verify the truthfulness of statements by online bloggers? If so, how?
2. If all print media disappeared, would that inconvenience you? Why or why not?

Explore this issue online:

- Search for "state of the news media" to see a comprehensive report by the Pew Research Center.
- Ann Arbor is now the largest city in the nation without a for-profit daily newspaper. (The University of Michigan still supports a daily.) See what replaced the *Ann Arbor News* at www.mlive.com/ann-arbor.

INTRODUCTION

The debate over the decline of print media, described in the chapter-opening *America at Odds* feature, is just one aspect of an important topic: the role of the media in American politics. Strictly defined, the term *media* means communication channels. It is the plural form of *medium,* as in a medium, or means, of communication. In this strict sense, any method used by people to communicate—including the telephone—is a communication medium.

In this chapter, though, we look at the **mass media**—channels through which people can communicate to large audiences. These channels include the **print media** (newspapers and magazines) and the **electronic media** (radio, television, and the Internet).

10–1 THE ROLE OF THE MEDIA IN A DEMOCRACY

LO Explain the role of the media in a democracy.

What the media say and do has an impact on what Americans think about political issues. But just as clearly, the media also *reflect* what Americans think about politics. Some scholars argue that the media are the fourth "check" in our political system—checking and balancing the power of the president, the Congress, and the courts. The power of the media today is enormous, but how the media use their power is an issue about which Americans are often at odds.

10–1a Media Characteristics

mass media
Communication channels, such as newspapers and radio and television broadcasts, through which people can communicate to large audiences.

print media
Communication channels that consist of printed materials, such as newspapers and magazines.

electronic media
Communication channels that involve electronic transmissions, such as radio, television, and the Internet.

The media are a dominant presence in our lives largely because they provide entertainment. Americans today enjoy more leisure than at any time in history, and we fill it up with e-books, movies, Web surfing, texting, and television—a huge amount of television. But the media play a vital role in our political lives as well, particularly during campaigns and elections. Politicians and political candidates have learned—often the hard way—that positive media exposure and news coverage are essential to winning votes.

As you read in Chapter 4, one of the most important civil liberties protected in the Bill of Rights is freedom of the press. Like free speech, a free press is considered a vital tool of the democratic process. If people are to cast informed votes, they must have access to a forum in which they can discuss public affairs fully and assess the conduct and competency of their officials. The media provide this forum.

In contrast, government censorship of the press is common in many nations around the globe. One example is China, where the Web is heavily censored, even though China now has more Internet users than any other country on earth.

10–1b The New Media and the Old

From the founding of the nation through the early years of the twentieth century, all media were print media—newspapers, magazines, and books. Beginning in the twentieth century, however, new media forms were introduced. Radio and motion pictures were the first new media, and they became important in the first half of the twentieth century.

Following World War II (1939–1945), broadcast television became the dominant form of communication. Cable television networks arrived in the 1970s. The Internet, including e-mail and the World Wide Web, came into widespread use by the general public in the 1990s.

The Decline of the Old Media   Film and radio did not displace print media in the early twentieth century. Television, though, had a much greater effect. Beginning about 1950, the number of adults reading a daily paper began to decline, although circulation remained steady due to population growth.

Later, the Internet proved to be even more devastating to newspapers. Newspaper circulation fell modestly in the 1990s. In 2006, however, circulation began to collapse, declining more than 5 percent each year. We will return to these problems later in the chapter.

Youth and the New Media   Today, millions of Americans have developed unprecedented habits of media consumption. Leaders of the movement include the wealthy and "early adopters" of new technology. Above all, the new consumers include the young. As one might expect, the upcoming generation of media users rarely read newspapers. But even television is now of lesser importance.

True, young people still watch a variety of television programs. Many of them, however, primarily view such

Comedians John Oliver and Aasif Mandvi at the White House Correspondents' Dinner. Oliver's show *Last Week Tonight* on HBO combines crude humor with investigative journalism. *Why do young people like his performance?*

Fena Schild/Shutterstock.com

composed of middle-aged white men—to be irrelevant to their lives. Limbaugh is not irrelevant to American politics, however. His millions of listeners vote, and they can influence the outcome of Republican presidential primaries.

In short, considering the electorate as a whole, television remains a key medium in terms of political influence. Much of this chapter, therefore, deals with the impact of television.

10–1c The Media and the First Amendment

As noted earlier, freedom of the press is essential if the media are to play their role in supporting the democratic process. The concept of freedom of the press has been applied to print media since the adoption of the Bill of Rights. Such freedoms were not, however, immediately extended to other types of media as they came into existence.

Film was one of the first types of new media to be considered under the First Amendment, and in 1915 the United States Supreme Court ruled that "as a matter of common sense," freedom of the press did not apply to the movies.[1] Radio received no protection upon its development, and neither did television. The Court did not extend First Amendment protections to the cinema until 1952.[2] Although the Court has stated that the First Amendment is relevant to broadcast media such as radio and television, to this day it has not granted these media complete protection.

In contrast, the Court extended First Amendment protections to the Internet in 1997, in its first opportunity to rule on the issue.[3] Cable TV received substantial protections in 2000.[4]

Although First Amendment protections now clearly prohibit the U.S. government from restricting speech on the Internet, other threats exist. We examine one of them in this chapter's *The Rest of the World* feature.

shows online, as streaming video. Often, youth and other early adopters of new technology have "cut the cord" and abandoned cable TV service altogether in favor of online streaming. Even e-mail has been abandoned by many of today's youth. Instead, messages are transmitted via Facebook, Twitter, Tumblr, Google+, and the smartphone. For such persons, old-media personalities such as television news anchors and radio talk-show hosts are completely obsolete.

New Media versus Old Voters Yet radio, television, and print media remain important to American politics and government. Older Americans largely rely on these more traditional media outlets, and older voters outnumber the young. As of 2016, approximately 113 million Americans were age fifty or older. The number of U.S. residents age eighteen through twenty-nine was less than half that figure. Older voters are also much more likely to turn out to vote than younger ones. Finally, some of the most enthusiastic adopters of new media are not yet eighteen and cannot vote even if they want to.

To give an example, many young people may find radio host Rush Limbaugh—with his audience largely

THE REST OF THE WORLD

Who Controls the Internet?

The Internet was created by the U.S. military through the Defense Advanced Research Projects Agency—DARPA (formerly ARPA). Soon it was opened to university researchers and later to the public at large. Censoring it was almost impossible. "The Internet interprets censorship as damage," one early administrator exalted. "We will route around you!"

The Internet Goes Global

In time, the Internet became an international—not just an American—institution. Every nation with a modern economy has embraced the Internet. Poorer countries that want to develop must do so as well. A worldwide Internet, however, means participation by unfree nations. Leaders of these nations have no interest in free speech. Given this, how can the Internet remain both free and worldwide?

Threats from Abroad

No other nation can prevent a country such as China from censoring the Internet within its own borders. But could unfree nations export their controls to the rest of the world? An Obama administration plan in 2014 fueled fear of such a development. Under the plan, the U.S. Commerce Department would give up control of the Internet Corporation for Assigned Names and Numbers (ICANN). This organization is in charge of Internet names and addresses—it is the group that decided, say, that Google would own www.google.com. Many people feared that this function would pass to a United Nations body controlled by world governments.

That would bring in China, Iran, Russia, and other repressive regimes. Power over addresses could be leveraged to support censorship. New financial rules could be crippling. Russia has proposed, for example, that Facebook, Google, and other sites

pay cable companies a fee every time someone accesses them. No one has the power to impose such rules on the United States, but the Internet could become fragmented between free and unfree nations. As a result of these concerns, ICANN independence was delayed until 2016. The rules adopted in that year gave governments almost no input into ICANN decisions. Ninety governments endorsed the new system, but sixteen objected. (The minority was overruled.)

Critical Analysis

Sites such as The Pirate Bay specialize in copyright violation. Does Internet freedom mean that a nation such as Armenia or Sweden should be allowed to permit such sites? Why or why not?

10–1d The Agenda-Setting Function of the Media

One of the criticisms often levied against the media is that they play too large a role in determining the issues, events, and personalities that are in the public eye. When people take in the day's top news stories, they usually assume that these stories concern the most important issues facing the nation. In actuality, the media decide the relative importance of issues by publicizing some issues and ignoring others, and by giving some stories high priority and others low priority.

agenda setting The ability to determine which issues are considered important by the public and by politicians.

By helping to determine what people will talk and think about, the media set the *political agenda*—the issues that politicians will address. In other words, the media are engaged in **agenda setting**. To borrow from Bernard Cohen's classic statement on the media and public opinion, the press (media) may not be successful in telling people what to think, but it is "stunningly successful in telling its readers what to think about."[5]

For example, television played a significant role in shaping public opinion about the Vietnam War (1965–1975), which has been called the first "television war." Part of the public opposition to the war in the late 1960s came about as a result of the daily portrayal of the war's horrors on TV news programs. Film footage and narrative accounts of the destruction, death, and suffering in

Vietnam brought the war into living rooms across the United States.

Priming and Framing   Two additional concepts related to agenda setting are *priming* and *framing*.

Priming.   In **priming**, a television show or an Internet blogger publicizes facts or ideas that may influence how the public thinks about a particular issue. As an example of priming, if the public is informed that the general rate of taxation in the United States is lower than it has been at any time since the 1950s, people are likely to be more receptive to the idea of raising tax rates on upper-income individuals.

In contrast, if the media point out that compared with other wealthy nations, the United States collects a much larger share of its tax revenue from the upper classes, then popular responses to proposals to tax our richer citizens may be quite different.

Framing.   **Framing** an issue involves establishing the context in which it is understood. Frames are stories about how the world works. As an example, consider the different stories that can be told about someone who is experiencing poverty. A TV news show might cover a man whose condition was, to all appearances, due primarily to bad luck. Perhaps he suffered from a life-threatening disease, could not work, lost his job, and then became homeless. This description would set up a particular frame, encouraging viewers to take a positive attitude toward social spending that would provide aid to such an individual.

Another TV report might show a woman who became addicted to alcohol or drugs at an early age, dropped out of high school, and became pregnant without a partner to help support her. Such an account could lead to an entirely different frame, which could lead to a much more skeptical attitude toward spending that benefits the poor.

Limits of Agenda Setting   The degree to which the media influence public opinion is not always that clear, however. As you read in Chapter 8, some studies show that people filter the information they receive from the media through their own preconceived ideas about issues. People bring their own frames to political stories, in other words, and these frames can be very powerful.

Scholars who try to analyze the relationship between American politics and the media inevitably confront the chicken-and-egg conundrum: Do the media cause the public to hold certain views, or do the media merely reflect the public's views?

> "THE PRESS MAY NOT BE SUCCESSFUL MUCH OF THE TIME IN TELLING PEOPLE WHAT TO THINK, *BUT IT IS STUNNINGLY SUCCESSFUL IN TELLING ITS READERS WHAT TO THINK ABOUT.*"
>
> ~ BERNARD C. COHEN, AMERICAN POLITICAL SCIENTIST, BORN 1926

10–1e The Medium Does Affect the Message

Of all the media, television still has the greatest impact on most Americans, especially older ones. Television reaches almost every home in the United States. Even outside their homes, Americans can watch television—in airports, shopping malls, golf clubhouses, and medical offices. People can view television shows on their computers, and they can download TV programs to their smartphones and tablet devices and view the programs whenever and wherever they want.

The Nature of Television Coverage   Today, Americans watch more television than ever, and it is the primary news source for more than 65 percent of the citizenry. As you will read shortly, politicians take maximum advantage of the power and influence of television. But does the television medium alter the presentation of political information in any way? Compare the coverage given to an important political issue by the print media—including the online sites of major newspapers and magazines—with the coverage provided by broadcast and cable TV networks. You will note some striking differences.

For one thing, the print media (particularly leading newspapers such as the *Washington Post,* the *New York Times,* and the *Wall Street Journal*) treat an important issue in much more detail than television does. In addition to news stories based on reporters' research, you will find editorials taking positions on the issue and

priming An agenda-setting technique in which a media outlet promotes specific facts or ideas that may affect the public's thinking on related topics.

framing An agenda-setting technique that establishes the context of a media report. Framing can mean fitting events into a familiar story or filtering information through preconceived ideas.

arguments supporting those positions. Television news, in contrast, is often criticized as being too brief and too superficial.

Time Constraints The medium of television necessarily imposes constraints on how political issues are presented. Time is limited. News stories must be reported quickly, in only a few minutes or occasionally in only a **sound bite**, a televised comment lasting for just a few seconds that captures a thought or a perspective and has an immediate impact on the viewers.

A Visual Medium Television reporting also relies extensively on visual elements, rather than words, to capture the viewers' attention. Inevitably, the photos or videos selected to depict a particular political event have exaggerated importance to viewers. The visual aspect of television contributes to its power, but it also creates a potential bias. Those watching the news presentation do not know what portions of a video being shown have been deleted, what other photos may have been taken, or whether other records of the event exist.

Television Is Big Business Today's TV networks compete aggressively with one another to air "breaking news" and to produce interesting news programs. Competition in the television industry understandably has had an effect on how the news is presented. To make profits, or even stay in business, TV stations need viewers. And to attract viewers, the news industry has turned to "infotainment"—programs that inform and entertain at the same time. Slick sets, attractive reporters, and animated graphics that dance across the television screen are commonplace on most news programs, particularly on the cable news channels.

TV networks also compete with one another for advertising income. Although the media in the United States are among the freest in the world, their programming nonetheless remains vulnerable to the influence of their advertising sponsors.

10-1f Ownership of the Media

Concentrated ownership of media is another issue. Many mainstream media outlets are owned by giant corporations, such as Time Warner, Rupert Murdoch's News Corporation, and Disney. An often-expressed concern is that these giant corporations will influence news coverage to benefit their interests.

sound bite A televised comment, lasting for only a few seconds, that captures a thought or a perspective and has an immediate impact on viewers.

There is little evidence, however, that these corporations significantly influence reporting. Their media outlets do show a generalized support of the capitalist economic system, but capitalism is so widely accepted in this country that the press would probably endorse it under any form of media ownership.

In some circumstances, it may benefit a media outlet to have owners with deep pockets. Consider the *Washington Post,* one of the nation's most important publications. Like many other newspapers, the *Post* has faced serious financial difficulties. Its previous owners, aware that they did not have the means to ensure the paper's quality, sold it to Jeff Bezos, founder and chief executive officer of Amazon.com. Bezos has a record of innovation and a deep understanding of the Internet. He bought the *Post* as an individual—Amazon does not own it. Still, his wealth may allow the paper the time and resources it needs to establish a new, viable business model.

Local Monopolies Concentrated ownership may be a more serious problem at the local level than at the national level. If only one or two companies own a city's newspaper and its TV stations, these outlets may not present a diversity of opinion. Further, the owners are unlikely to air information that could be damaging either

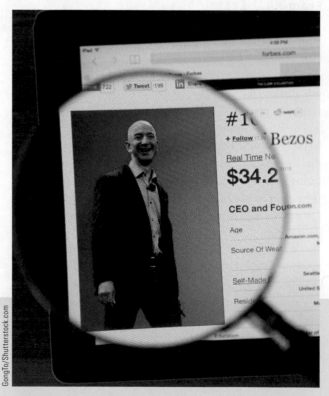

GongTo/Shutterstock.com

Jeff Bezos, CEO of Amazon. *If Amazon instead of Bezos had bought the* Washington Post, *would the public reaction have been as positive?*

to their advertisers or to themselves, or even to publicize views that they disagree with politically. For example, TV networks have refused to run antiwar commercials created by religious groups. Still, some media observers are not particularly concerned about concentrated ownership of traditional outlets, because the Internet has generated a massive diversification of media.

The Murdoch Empire A possible exception to the claim that major corporations do not influence reporting is the Murdoch media conglomerate. Murdoch's holdings in the United States, which include the Fox television networks, the *Wall Street Journal,* and the *New York Post,* are famous for promoting conservative politics. Still, Fox News is only one voice among many in America.

CRITICAL THINKING

▶ *How do you typically obtain information about political events? Does your method differ from how your parents obtain information? Your grandparents?*

10-2 THE CANDIDATES AND TELEVISION

LO Summarize how television influences the conduct of political campaigns.

Given the TV-saturated environment in which we live, it should come as no surprise that candidates spend a great deal of time—and money—cultivating a TV presence through political ads, debates, and general news coverage. Candidates and their campaign managers realize that the time and money are well spent because television has an important impact on the way people see the candidates, understand the issues, and cast their votes.

10-2a Political Advertising

Today, televised **political advertising** consumes at least half of the total budget for a major political campaign. For the 2012 election cycle, the Sunlight Foundation has estimated that total spending on political advertisements reached $9.8 billion. When the numbers for the 2016 cycle are added up, they are expected to be larger still.

Negative Advertising Political advertising first appeared on television during the 1952 presidential campaign. At that time, there were only about 15 million television sets. Today, there are as many TV sets as people. Initially, political TV commercials were more or less

like any other type of advertising. Instead of focusing on the positive qualities of a product, thirty-second or sixty-second ads focused on the positive qualities of a political candidate. Within the decade, however, **negative political advertising** began to appear on TV.

Personal Attacks Go Way Back. Despite the barrage of criticism levied against the candidates' use of negative political ads during recent election cycles, such ads are not new. Indeed, **personal attack ads**—advertising that attacks the character of a candidate—have a long tradition. In 1800, an article in the *Federalist Gazette of the United States* described Thomas Jefferson as having a "weakness of nerves, want of fortitude, and total imbecility of character."

Recent personal attacks on opponents have been so ferocious that they make old-fashioned name-calling almost quaint. Consider the 2004 campaign by Swift Boat Veterans for Truth against John Kerry, the Democratic presidential candidate. With no evidence, the group accused Kerry, a decorated Vietnam War veteran, of lying to obtain his medals. In 2016, Hillary Clinton's ads highlighted Donald Trump's habit of making contemptuous and lewd statements about women. For his part, Trump joined other Republicans in calling Clinton a criminal for maintaining a non-governmental e-mail server while secretary of state. (This action could have made it easier for foreign hackers to obtain classified material.) The FBI criticized Clinton but refused to bring charges. The attacks were effective. Media Matters reported that in 2016, major networks gave the e-mails almost seven times as much coverage as all policy issues put together.

Issue Ads Candidates use negative **issue ads** to focus on flaws in their opponents' positions on various issues, such as immigration and terrorism. Candidates also try to undermine their opponents' credibility by pointing to discrepancies between what the opponents

> **political advertising**
> Advertising undertaken by or on behalf of a political candidate to familiarize voters with the candidate and his or her views on campaign issues; advertising for or against policy issues.

> **negative political advertising** Political advertising undertaken for the purpose of discrediting a candidate in voters' eyes. Attack ads are one form of negative political advertising.

> **personal attack ad** A negative political advertisement that attacks a candidate's character.

> **issue ad** A political advertisement that focuses on a particular issue. Issue ads can be used to support or attack a candidate's position or credibility.

An advertisement for the "Journalism Is Not a Crime" campaign in Times Square, New York City. The campaign seeks the release of three journalists imprisoned in Egypt who worked for Al Jazeera, an Arabic television news channel. *In what places around the world can it be dangerous to be a reporter?*

say in their campaign speeches, on the one hand, and their political records, such as their voting records, on the other hand. Their records are available to the public and thus can be easily verified.

Issue ads can be even more devastating than personal attacks—as Barry Goldwater learned in 1964 when his opponent in the presidential race, President Lyndon Johnson, aired the "daisy girl" ad. This ad, a new departure in negative advertising, showed a little girl standing quietly in a field of daisies. She held a daisy and pulled off the petals, counting to herself. Suddenly, a deep voice was heard counting: "10, 9, 8, 7, 6, ..." When the countdown hit zero, the unmistakable mushroom cloud of an atomic explosion filled the screen. Then President Johnson's voice was heard saying, "These are the stakes: to make a world in which all of God's children can live, or to go into the dark. We must either love each other or we must die." A message on the screen then read: "Vote for President Johnson on November 3." The implication, of course, was that Goldwater would lead the country into a nuclear war.

Negative Advertising—Is It Good or Bad for Our Democracy? The debate over the effect of negative advertising on our political system is ongoing. Some observers argue that negative ads can backfire. Extreme ads may create sympathy for the candidate being attacked rather than support for the attacker, particularly when the charges against the candidate being attacked are not credible. Many people fear that attack ads and "dirty tricks" used by both parties during a campaign may alienate citizens from the political process itself and thus lower voter turnout in elections.

Yet candidates and their campaign managers typically assert that they use negative advertising simply because it works. Negative TV ads are more likely than positive ads to grab the viewers' attention and make an impression. Also, according to media expert Shanto Iyengar, "the more negative the ad, the more likely it is to get free media coverage. So there's a big incentive to go to extremes."[6]

Others believe that negative advertising is a force for good because it sharpens public debate, thereby enriching the democratic process. This is the position taken by Vanderbilt University political science professor John Geer. He contends that negative ads are likely to focus on substantive political issues instead of candidates' personal characteristics. Thus, negative ads do a better job of informing the voters about important campaign issues than positive ads do.[7]

10-2b Television Debates

Televised debates have been a feature of presidential campaigns since 1960, when Republican Richard M. Nixon and Democrat John F. Kennedy squared off in four famous TV debates. Television debates provide an opportunity for voters to find out how candidates differ on issues. They also allow candidates to capitalize on the power of television to improve their images or point out the failings of their opponents.

It is widely believed that Kennedy won the first of the 1960 debates in large part because of Nixon's haggard appearance and poor makeup—many people who heard the debate on the radio thought that Nixon had done well. No presidential debates were held during the general election campaigns of 1964, 1968, or 1972, but the debates have been a part of every election since 1976.

The 1992 debates, which starred Republican George H. W. Bush and Democrat Bill Clinton, also included a third-party candidate, H. Ross Perot. Since 1996, however, the Commission on Presidential Debates, which now organizes the events, has limited the participants to candidates of the two major parties.[8] The commission also organizes debates between the vice-presidential candidates.

TV Debates and Election Outcomes   Many contend that the presidential debates help shape the outcome of the elections. Others doubt that the debates—or the postdebate "spin" applied by campaign operatives and political commentators—have changed many votes. Evidence on this question is mixed.

Gallup polling figures suggest that in 1960 the debates helped Kennedy to victory. In 1980, Republican Ronald Reagan did well in a final debate with Democratic incumbent Jimmy Carter. Reagan impressed many voters with his sunny temperament, which helped dispel fears that he was a right-wing radical. In Gallup's opinion, however, Reagan would have won the election even without the debate.

Later presidential debates were less conclusive, though in 2000 Democrat Al Gore may have hurt himself with a condescending attitude toward Republican George W. Bush. In the first 2012 debate, Democrat Barack Obama turned in a surprisingly poor performance compared to Republican Mitt Romney, but Obama still won reelection easily. In contrast, the 2016 debates were important. Going into the first debate—with more than 80 million viewers—Hillary Clinton had only a narrow lead over Donald Trump in the polls. Right after the debates, she led by seven percentage points. Clinton was disciplined and focused, while Trump (who refused to prepare) was at times almost incoherent. Clinton also recognized that Trump reacted poorly to criticism. She therefore brought up an incident in which Trump had humiliated a Miss Universe winner by calling her fat. Trump took the bait, and spent days denouncing the beauty queen—a disastrous course of action.

10-2c News Coverage

Whereas political ads are expensive, coverage by the news media is free. Accordingly, the candidates try to take advantage of the media's interest in campaigns to increase the quantity and quality of news coverage. This is not always easy. Often, the media devote the lion's share of their coverage to polls and other indicators of which candidate is ahead in the race.

> ## "FOR A POLITICIAN TO COMPLAIN ABOUT THE PRESS IS LIKE *A SHIP'S CAPTAIN COMPLAINING ABOUT THE SEA.*"
>
> ~ ENOCH POWELL, BRITISH POLITICIAN, 1912–1998

Managed News Coverage   In recent years, candidates' campaigns have shown increasing sophistication in creating newsworthy events for journalists and TV camera crews to cover. This effort is commonly referred to as **managed news coverage**. For example, typically one of the jobs of the campaign manager is to create newsworthy events that demonstrate the candidate's strong points so that the media can capture this image of the candidate.[9]

In 2015, however, one candidate was such a master at winning press attention that he hardly needed the services of a campaign manager to gain coverage. That candidate was Donald Trump, who had spent many years as a TV reality show host. As a result of Trump's sometimes outrageous comments, he won more news coverage from the top three TV networks in 2015 than any other story except the weather. According to the Tyndall Report, ABC News devoted eighty-one times as much coverage to Trump as it did to Bernie Sanders.

Spinning the Story   Many aspects of a campaign focus on potential news coverage. Political consultants plan political events to accommodate the press. The campaign staff attempts to make what the candidate is doing appear interesting. The staff also knows that journalists and political reporters compete for stories and that these individuals can be manipulated. Hence, they frequently are granted favors, such as exclusive personal interviews with the candidate. Each candidate also has press advisers, often called **spin doctors**, who try to convince reporters to give the story or event a **spin**, or interpretation, that is favorable to the candidate.[10]

10-2d "Popular" Television

Although not normally regarded as a forum for political debate, television programs such as dramas, sitcoms, and late-night comedy shows often use political themes. For

> **managed news coverage**   News coverage that is manipulated (managed) by a campaign manager or political consultant to gain media exposure for a political candidate.
>
> **spin doctor**   A political candidate's press adviser who tries to convince reporters to give a story or event concerning the candidate a particular "spin" (interpretation, or slant).
>
> **spin**   A reporter's slant on, or interpretation of, a particular event or action.

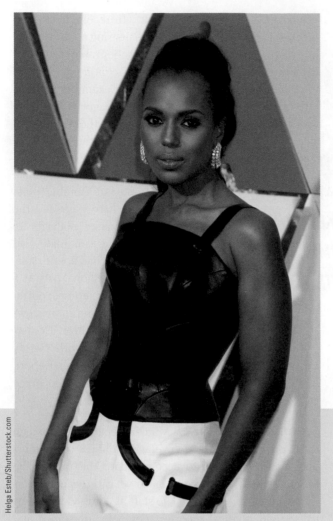

Kerry Washington plays the lead role in the ABC series *Scandal*. TV shows that fictionalize politics have become popular recently. *Why might that be so?*

example, the popular Netflix drama *House of Cards* depicts the successes of a sleazy politician played by Kevin Spacey. *Scandal* is an ABC drama focusing on a Washington crisis management firm, with Kerry Washington as the firm's head. In the CBS show *Madam Secretary*, Téa Leoni stars as the secretary of state. Late-night shows and programs such as *The Daily Show* on Comedy Central and *The Late Show* on CBS provide a forum for politicians to demonstrate their lighter sides.

CRITICAL THINKING

▶ *Media experts believe that negative political advertisements often include statements that are flatly untrue. What, if anything, should the media do when that happens?*

10–3 TALK RADIO—THE WILD WEST OF THE MEDIA

LO Explain why talk radio has been described as the Wild West of the media.

Ever since Franklin D. Roosevelt held his first "fireside chats" on radio, politicians have realized the power of that medium. From the beginning, radio has been a favorite outlet for the political right.

During the 1930s, for example, the nation's most successful radio commentator was Father Charles Edward Coughlin, a Roman Catholic priest based at the National Shrine of the Little Flower church in Royal Oak, Michigan. Coughlin's audience numbered more than 40 million listeners—in a nation that had only 123 million inhabitants in 1930. Coughlin started out as a Roosevelt supporter, but he soon moved to the far right, advocating anti-Semitism and expressing sympathy for Adolf Hitler. Coughlin's fascist connections eventually destroyed his popularity.

Modern talk radio took off in the United States during the 1990s. In 1988, there were 200 talk-show radio stations. Today, there are more than 1,200. The growth of talk radio was made possible by the Federal Communications Commission's repeal of the fairness doctrine in 1987.

Introduced in 1949, the *fairness doctrine* required the holders of broadcast licenses to present controversial issues of public importance in a manner that was (in the commission's view) honest, equitable, and balanced. That doctrine would have made it difficult for radio stations to broadcast conservative talk shows exclusively, as many now do.

Today, five of the top six talk-radio shows, as measured by Arbitron ratings, are politically conservative. No liberal commentator ranks higher than fourteenth place in the ratings. (Several of the shows ranked higher than fourteenth are not political but deal with subjects such as personal finance and paranormal activities.)

10–3a Audiences and Hosts

The Pew Research Center for the People and the Press reports that 17 percent of the public regularly listen to talk radio. This audience is predominantly male, middle-aged, and conservative. Among those who regularly listen to talk radio, 45 percent consider themselves conservatives.

Talk radio is sometimes characterized as the Wild West of the media. Talk-show hosts do not attempt to hide their political biases. If anything, they exaggerate them for effect. No journalistic conventions are observed. Leading shows, such as those of Rush Limbaugh, Sean Hannity, Andrew Wilkow, and Michael Savage, espouse a brand of conservatism that is robust, even radical. Opponents are regularly characterized as Nazis, Communists, or both at the same time. Limbaugh, for example, consistently refers to feminists as "feminazis."

Talk-show hosts sometimes appear to care more about the entertainment value of their statements than whether they are, strictly speaking, true. Hosts have often publicized fringe beliefs, such as the contention that President Barack Obama was not really born in the United States. The government of Britain actually banned Michael Savage from entry into that country based on his remarks about Muslims.

10-3b The Impact of Talk Radio

The overwhelming dominance of strong conservative voices on talk radio is justified by supporters as a good way to counter what they perceive as the liberal bias in the mainstream print and TV media. (We discuss the question of bias in the media in the following section.) Supporters say that such shows are simply a response to consumer demand. Those who think that talk radio is good for the country argue that talk shows, taken together, provide a great populist forum. Others are

> "A NATION THAT IS AFRAID TO LET ITS PEOPLE *JUDGE TRUTH AND FALSEHOOD IN AN OPEN MARKET* IS A NATION THAT IS AFRAID OF ITS PEOPLE."
>
> ~ JOHN FITZGERALD KENNEDY, THIRTY-FIFTH PRESIDENT OF THE UNITED STATES, 1961–1963

uneasy because they fear that talk shows empower fringe groups, perhaps magnifying their rage.

Those who claim that talk-show hosts go too far ultimately have to deal with the constitutional issue of free speech. While the courts have always given broad support to freedom of expression, broadcast media have been something of an exception, as mentioned earlier. The Supreme Court, for example, upheld the fairness doctrine in a 1969 ruling.[11]

Presumably, the doctrine could be reinstated. In 2009, after the Democratic victories in the 2008 elections, a few liberals advocated doing just that. President Obama and the Democratic leadership in Congress, however, quickly put an end to this notion. Americans have come to accept talk radio as part of the political environment, and any attempt to curtail it would be extremely unpopular.

CRITICAL THINKING

▶ **Why, in your opinion, have liberal commentators found it so difficult to develop successful talk-radio shows?**

10-4 THE QUESTION OF MEDIA BIAS

LO Describe types of media bias and explain how such bias affects the political process.

The question of media bias is important in any democracy. After all, for our political system to work, citizens must be well informed. And they can be well informed only if the news media, the source of much of their information, do not slant the news. Today, however, relatively few Americans believe that the news media are unbiased in their reporting. Accompanying this perception is a notable decline in the public's confidence in the news media in recent years.

In a 2015 Gallup poll measuring the public's confidence in various institutions, only 24 percent of the respondents stated that they had "a

A talk radio host at a college radio station. *Is this host likely to have the same politics as leading commercial radio talk hosts? Why or why not?*

Wavebreakmedia/Shutterstock.com

great deal" or "quite a lot" of confidence in newspapers. Among these respondents, 21 percent had the same degree of confidence in television news. Also, 19 percent of respondents in a 2014 poll reported a similar level of confidence in Internet news sources. Because of these low percentages, some analysts believe that the media are facing a crisis of confidence.

Despite these low figures, however, the public does believe that the press is successful in fulfilling its role as a watchdog. In a recent poll by the Pew Research Center, 68 percent of respondents agreed that "press criticism of political leaders keeps them from doing things that should not be done." Republicans, Democrats, and independents were equally likely to agree with this statement.

10-4a Partisan Bias

For years, conservatives have argued that there is a liberal bias in the media, and liberals have complained that the media reflect a conservative bias. The majority of Americans think that the media reflect a bias in one direction or another. According to a recent poll, 46 percent of the respondents believed that the news media leaned left, whereas only 26 percent thought that the news media had a conservative bias.

The Attitudes of Journalists   Surveys and analyses of the attitudes and voting habits of reporters have suggested that journalists do indeed hold liberal views. The website CampaignMoney.com has calculated that from 1999 to 2016, campaign contributors who listed their occupation as journalist or reporter gave 73 percent of their donations to Democrats. Only 14 percent of the donations went to Republicans. Among journalists working for national outlets, 22 percent described themselves as liberal and only 5 percent as conservative. In contrast, 14 percent of local reporters called themselves liberals, and 18 percent adopted the conservative label.

There is substantial evidence that top journalists working for the nation's most famous newspapers and networks do tend to be liberal. Many journalists themselves perceive the *New York Times* as liberal (although an even larger number view Fox News as conservative).

Still, members of the press are likely to view themselves as moderates. In a recent study, the Pew Research Center for the People and the Press found that 64 percent of reporters in both national and local media applied the term *moderate* to themselves.

The Impact on Reporting   A number of media scholars, including Kathleen Hall Jamieson, suggest that even if many reporters hold liberal views, these views are not reflected in their reporting.[12] Media analysts Debra Reddin van Tuyll and Hubert P. van Tuyll have similarly concluded that left-leaning reporters do not automatically equate to left-leaning news coverage. They point out that reporters are only the starting point for news stories. Before any story goes to print or is aired on television, it has to go through a progression of editors and perhaps even the publisher. Because employees at the top of the corporate ladder in news organizations are more right leaning than left leaning, the end result of the editorial and oversight process is more balanced coverage.[13]

Perhaps the most important protection against bias in reporting is a commitment to professionalism on the part of most journalists. Professional ethics dictate a commitment to "objectivity" and truthfulness. Reporters may sometimes violate this code, but it does have an impact.

Helga Esteb/Shutterstock.com

Megyn Kelly hosts *The Kelly File* on the Fox News Channel. Although a conservative, in 2015 Kelly took part in a feud with Republican presidential candidate Donald Trump. *Was the press unfair to Trump---or did they propel his rise with vast amounts of free publicity?*

In addition, a recent, helpful development is the growing number of fact-checking operations such as PolitiFact and FactCheck. FactCheck, for example, is a project of the Annenberg Public Policy Center of the University of Pennsylvania. Services such as these enable journalists to be more objective in identifying and cracking down on political lies and misrepresentations.

10-4b The Bias against Losers

Kathleen Hall Jamieson believes that media bias does play a significant role in shaping presidential campaigns and elections, but she argues that it is not a partisan bias. Rather, it is a bias against losers. A candidate who falls behind in the race is immediately labeled a "loser," making it even more difficult for the candidate to regain favor in the voters' eyes.[14]

Jamieson says that the media use the winner–loser framework to describe events throughout the campaigns. Even a presidential debate is regarded as a "sporting match" that results in a winner and a loser. In the days leading up to the 2016 debates, reporters focused on what each candidate had to do to "win" the debate. When the debate was over, reporters immediately speculated about who had "won" as they waited for post-debate polls to answer that question. According to Jamieson, this approach "squanders the opportunity to reinforce learning." The debates are an important source of political information for the voters, and this fact is eclipsed by the media's win–lose focus.

10-4c A Changing News Culture

Today's news culture is in the midst of change. News organizations are redefining their purpose and increasingly looking for special niches in which to build their audiences. For some, the niche is *hyperlocalism*—that is, narrowing the focus of news to the local area. For others, it is personal commentary, revolving around highly

ABC anchor George Stephanopoulos and wife Alexandra Wentworth arrive at the White House Correspondents' Association Dinner. Stephanopoulos was formerly White House Communications Director under President Bill Clinton and has donated to a Clinton-run charity. *Is such a background appropriate for a news anchor?*

politicized TV figures such as Bill O'Reilly (conservative) and Rachel Maddow (liberal). In a sense, news organizations have begun to base their appeal more on *how* they cover the news and less on *what* they cover. Traditional journalism—fact-based reporting instead of opinion and punditry—is becoming a smaller part of this mix.

Another development is the move toward highly specific subject matter that appeals strongly to a limited number of viewers. Magazines have always done this—consider the many magazine titles on topics such as model railroading or home decorating. With the large number of cable channels, *narrowcasting* has become important on television as well. Networks now appeal to members of particular ethnic groups (BET—Black Entertainment Television), hobbyists (Cooking Channel), or history buffs (History Channel).

Online streaming services also provide niche programming. True, users who rely only on streaming video may have trouble accessing the most up-to-the-minute network television news shows. Overall, however, there is no shortage of late-breaking news sources online.

CRITICAL THINKING

▶ *Often, media consumers prefer outlets that confirm their own personal biases. What problems might this create for American democracy?*

10–5 POLITICAL NEWS AND CAMPAIGNS ON THE WEB

LO Indicate the extent to which the Internet is reshaping news and political campaigns.

Cyberspace is getting bigger every day. More than 46 percent of the world's inhabitants currently use the Internet, a total of about 3.4 billion people. About half of all users live in Asia. Worldwide, more than 2 million people access the Internet using mobile phones. In the United States, 87 percent of the population are Internet users. In addition, popular social media sites have enormous numbers of personalized pages—Twitter has about 320 million active accounts, and Facebook has about 1.6 billion.

Not surprisingly, the Internet is a major source of information. All major newspapers are online, as are transcripts of major television news programs. About two-thirds of Internet users consider the Internet to be an important source of news. In addition, having an Internet strategy has become an integral part of political campaigning.

10–5a News Organizations Online

Almost every major news organization, both print and broadcast, delivers news via the Web. Indeed, an online presence is required to compete effectively with other traditional news companies for revenues. The online share of newspaper company revenues has increased over the years. Still, only 15 percent of U.S. newspaper revenues come from online sources.

Characteristics of Newspaper Sites Some newspaper sites simply copy articles from their printed versions. The websites for major newspapers, however, including those for the *Washington Post* and the *New York Times,* offer a different array of coverage and options than their printed editions. Websites have a notable advantage over their printed counterparts. They can add breaking news, informing readers of events that occurred just minutes ago. They can also link readers to more extensive reports on particular topics. (Many papers shy away from in-text linking, though, perhaps fearing that if readers leave the news organization's site, they might not return.)

Inadequate Revenues A major problem facing news organizations is that readers or viewers of online newspapers and news programs are typically the same people who read the printed news editions and view the news programs on TV. Web-only readers of a particular newspaper make up a relatively small percentage of those going online for their news. Therefore, investing heavily in online news delivery may not be a solution for news companies seeking to increase readership and revenues.

In fact, the additional revenues that newspapers have gained from their online editions do not come close to making up for the massive losses in advertising revenue suffered by their print editions. In many instances, publications have not sold enough advertising in their online editions even to make up for the additional expense of publishing on the Web.

Google's Dominance of Online Ad Revenue The problem is not that there is an absolute shortage of online advertising revenue. In fact, by 2012, the advertising industry was spending more on Internet advertising than it spent on all print newspapers and magazines put together.

The real problem is that *content providers*—such as newspaper sites that hire journalists and create new material—receive a very small share of the online advertising revenue. Most of the revenue goes to *aggregators,* including search engine sites that develop little new content but mostly direct users elsewhere. Google, by far the largest of these aggregators, collects one-third of all online ad revenues.

By 2016, at $25 billion, Google's U.S. ad revenues exceeded the revenues of the entire U.S. newspaper industry. Figure 10–1 shows U.S. newspaper and online ad revenues. Of course, if the business of journalism were to collapse, Google would have little to aggregate. As of now, the cybersphere is nowhere close to resolving this issue.

10–5b Blogs and the Emergence of Citizen Journalism

As mentioned earlier, the news culture is changing, and at the heart of this change—and of much innovation in news delivery today—is the blogosphere. There has been

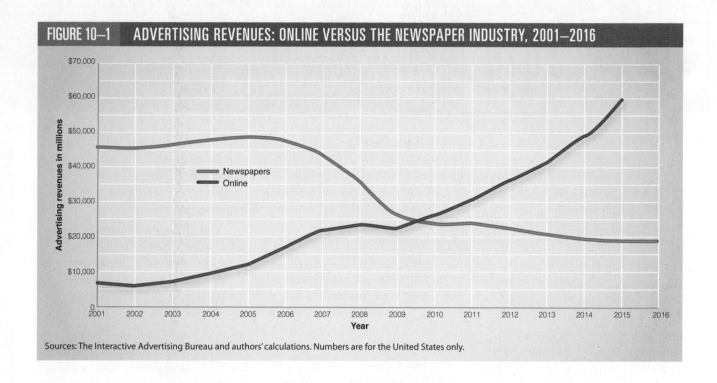

FIGURE 10–1   ADVERTISING REVENUES: ONLINE VERSUS THE NEWSPAPER INDUSTRY, 2001–2016

Sources: The Interactive Advertising Bureau and authors' calculations. Numbers are for the United States only.

a veritable explosion of blogs in recent years. Mainstream news organizations want to make their websites more competitive and appealing and counter the influence of blogs run by private citizens and those not in the news business. As a result, they have been adding blogs to their own websites.

Blogs are offered by independent journalists, various scholars, political activists, and the citizenry at large. Anyone who wants to can create a blog and post news or information, including videos, to share with others. Many blogs are political in nature, both reporting political developments and discussing politics. Taken as a whole, the collection, analysis, and dissemination of information online by the citizenry can be called **citizen journalism**. Other terms that have been used to describe the news blogosphere include *people journalism* and *participatory journalism*. When blogs focus on news and developments in a specific community, the term *community journalism* is often applied.

The increase in news blogs and do-it-yourself journalism on the Web clearly poses a threat to mainstream news sources. Compared with the operational costs faced by a major news organization, the cost of creating and maintaining blogs is trivial. Moreover, the most successful blogs are able to sell advertising. Because of their low costs, it does not take much advertising to keep such sites in business. How can major news sources adhere to their traditional standards and still compete with this new world of news generated by citizens?

10-5c Podcasting the News

Another nontraditional form of news distribution is **podcasting**—the distribution of audio or video files to personal computers or mobile devices such as smartphones.[15] Though still a relatively small portion of the overall news-delivery system, podcasts are becoming increasingly popular. Almost anyone can create a podcast and make it available for downloading onto computers or mobile devices, and like blogging, podcasting is inexpensive. As you will read next, political candidates are using both blogging and podcasting as part of their Internet campaign strategies.

While podcasting, streaming video, and similar services are not expensive to offer, they do consume substantial Internet bandwidth. Is this a problem? We discuss that issue in this chapter's *Join the Debate* feature.

10-5d Cyberspace and Political Campaigns

Today's political parties and candidates realize the benefits of using the Internet to conduct online campaigns and raise funds. Voters also

citizen journalism
The collection, analysis, and dissemination of information online by independent journalists, scholars, politicians, and the general citizenry.

podcasting
The distribution of audio or video files to personal computers or mobile devices such as smartphones.

JOIN
THE DEBATE

Could We Lose Our High-Speed Internet?

Most students take it for granted that they have access to high-speed Internet not only at their colleges and universities, but also in their homes. They expect to find Wi-Fi hot spots at coffee shops and other places. One of the underpinnings of Internet access is a principle known as network neutrality, or net neutrality. Under this principle, Internet service providers (ISPs) such as cable and telephone companies are to treat all Internet traffic equally, without discrimination.

For example, if your ISP is a phone company, it can't keep you from using a competing phone-over-Internet service, such as Skype. Even more to the point, Netflix should not have to pay more for Internet access than anyone else just because it accounts for 30 percent of broadband traffic during peak hours every day. Also, no ISP should set aside a "fast lane" that allows content from favored services to load more quickly—and content from other services more slowly. Recently, the Federal Communications Commission (FCC) issued new rules to guarantee net neutrality. Not everyone, however, thinks that FCC regulations are a good idea. Major ISPs have sued to overturn the new rules, and the case is being heard by a U.S. appeals court.

Just Say No to Government Interference

Opponents of regulation point out that the Internet may have been created by the government, but it has been substantially free of regulation for decades. Now is not the time to change this system. Under the new FCC rules, ISPs will be public utilities just like companies that sell electricity or voice telephone services. ISPs such as Verizon and Comcast will not be able to charge extra for higher-speed access.

In effect, the government will be telling ISPs how much they can charge for their services. Investment in Internet infrastructure will be discouraged. ISPs will lose the incentive to innovate in other ways as well. The Internet is complex. It changes all the time. No government regulator will be able to keep up with that change. Enforced net neutrality will mean less change, less innovation, and perhaps less high-speed Internet access. In fact, major ISPs contend that broadband investment has dropped 8 percent since the FCC ruling.

Net Neutrality Means More Innovation, Not Less

Advocates of regulation contend that net neutrality has been under threat by giant, monopolistic ISPs. Years ago, the number of ISPs a user could contract with was vast. No longer. A few cable and telephone companies dominate the landscape. We need regulation to keep these giants from abusing their power.

Net neutrality has lowered barriers to entry online. Entrepreneurs have been encouraged to create new services, such as Facebook, Netflix, Twitter, and YouTube. Without net neutrality rules, in the future some Internet content will get priority treatment in exchange for a fee. Other traffic will slow down. Imagine if large ISPs had been able to make video-streaming sites pay extra. YouTube would have been strangled in the crib. The Internet has always been funded by fees paid by users. These sums have paid for huge investments in infrastructure, and they will continue to do so. Major ISPs may have told the appeals court that broadband investment is falling, but at the same time they are telling their own shareholders that investment is increasing.

Critical Analysis

Would you be willing to pay a little more for each streaming movie you watch to guarantee no interruptions? Why or why not?

are increasingly using the Web to access information about parties and candidates, promote political goals, and obtain political news. Generally, the use of the Internet is an inexpensive way for candidates to contact, recruit, and mobilize supporters, as well as to disseminate information about their positions on issues. In effect, the Internet can replace brochures, letters, and position papers. Individual voters or political party supporters can use the Internet to avoid having to go to special meetings or to a campaign site to do volunteer work or obtain information on a candidate's positions.

That the Internet is now a viable medium for communicating political information and interacting with voters was made clear in the campaigns preceding the

A group of business people crowd around a smartphone. *In what ways do Americans use smart phones differently than they use computers?*

candidate's views and arranges for podcasting of campaign information and updates to supporters. The manager hires staff to monitor the Web for news about the candidates and to track the online publications of *netroots groups*. (These are online activists who support the candidate but are not controlled by the candidate's organization.)

Controlling the Netroots One of the challenges facing candidates today is delivering a consistent campaign message to voters. Netroots groups may make this task more difficult. Such a group may publish online promotional ads or other materials that do not represent a candidate's position, for example, or attack the candidate's opponent in ways that the candidate does not approve. Yet no candidate wants to alienate these groups, because they can raise significant sums of money and garner votes for the candidate.

2012 presidential elections. According to a Pew Research Center survey following the 2012 presidential elections, 47 percent of Americans said that they had gone online for election news—up from 36 percent who had done so in the 2008 campaign. Among Internet users, 18 percent had posted political comments in a blog or on a social networking site. Fully 45 percent of users had watched online videos related to the campaigns. One in three had forwarded political content to someone else.

Online Fund-Raising The Internet can be an effective—and inexpensive—way to raise campaign funds. Fund-raising on the Internet by presidential candidates became widespread after the Federal Election Commission decided, in June 1999, that the federal government could distribute matching funds for credit-card donations received by candidates via the Internet. We discussed Internet fund-raising in depth in Chapter 9—see the section titled *Fund-Raising on the Internet.*

The Rise of the Internet Campaign An increasingly important part of political campaigning today is the Internet campaign. Candidates typically hire Web managers to manage their Internet campaigns. The job of the Web manager, or Web strategist, is to create a well-designed, informative, and user-friendly campaign website to attract viewers, hold their attention, manage their e-mails, and track their credit-card contributions. The Web manager also hires bloggers to promote the

Candidates' 24/7 Exposure Just as citizen journalism has altered the news culture, so have citizen videos changed the traditional campaign. For example, a candidate can never know when a comment that she or he makes may be caught on camera by someone with a cell phone or digital camera and published on the Internet for all to see.

A candidate's opponents may post a compilation of video clips showing the candidate's inconsistent comments over time on a specific topic, such as abortion or the health-care reform legislation. The effect can be very damaging, because it makes the candidate's "flip-flopping" on the issue apparent.

Recent Political Gaffes Political scientists have argued over the importance of political gaffes. Awkward comments by Mitt Romney and Barack Obama in 2012 didn't seem to have much effect on the polls. In 2016, Donald Trump constantly made statements that, based on past assumptions, should have been fatal. In reality, nothing that Trump said about politicians, journalists, Latinos and African Americans, or for that matter policy issues seemed to disturb loyal Republican voters. His comments about women, however, did hurt him. These included the tape, mentioned earlier, in which Trump boasted of his power to molest women. Thereafter, more than a dozen women stepped forward to allege that he had groped them without their consent.

Hillary Clinton was a disciplined candidate, and her list of misstatements was relatively short. Her real problem was that she disliked reporters, and they disliked her. Clinton's attitude was shaped by the decades-long effort by her opponents to find some scandal they could pin on her. Most of these scandals were bogus. Clinton's supporters were also convinced that more troublesome issues, such as her private e-mail server, had been blown out of proportion. Still, the constant barrage of bad press seriously damaged her reputation.

CRITICAL THINKING

▶ *To what extent do the media—in particular, the new media—encourage political participation? To what extent might they discourage participation by providing non-political entertainment?*

Politics and the Media

Americans love to hate the media, possibly because we spend so much time watching and reading them. Without a doubt, the media are undergoing a revolution today. With the loss of classified ads to the Internet, newspapers are in serious financial jeopardy. Online news sources, meanwhile, have yet to hit upon a reliable method of generating adequate income. In this changing environment, Americans are at odds over a number of media topics:

- *Do the difficulties faced by print media threaten the existence of competent journalism—or is this not an important problem?*

- *Is the media's agenda-setting function a vital contribution to the democratic process—or an improper attempt to manipulate viewers?*

- *Should protection of the First Amendment be extended to broadcast media without exception—or would such a move threaten the morals of the country and make it impossible for viewers to avoid sexual content?*

- *Are negative advertisements an inevitable and unremarkable aspect of political campaigns—or should the voters punish politicians who employ them?*

- *Does talk radio add to the vigor of our political discourse—or is it a corrupting influence that divides the nation?*

- *Do the mainstream media have a liberal bias—or do they merely publicize facts that do not square with conservative beliefs?*

STUDY TOOLS 10

READY TO STUDY? IN THE BOOK, YOU CAN:

☐ Review what you've read with the following chapter quiz.

☐ Check your answers in Appendix D at the back of the book.

☐ Rip out the Chapter Review Card, which includes key terms and chapter summaries.

ONLINE AT WWW.CENGAGEBRAIN.COM, YOU CAN:

☐ Learn about YouTube's effect on the Middle East in a short video.

☐ Explore various online resources in the Politifact and FAIR.org websites in the Internet Resources tool.

☐ Interact with figures from the text, and watch quick animation clips.

☐ Prepare for tests with quizzes.

☐ Review the key terms with Flash Cards.

FILL-IN

Learning Outcome 10–1

1. _____ is an agenda-setting technique in which a media outlet promotes specific facts or ideas that may affect the public's thinking on related topics.

2. Of all the media, _____ still has the greatest impact on most Americans.

3. A sound bite is _____.

4. Newspapers today are in financial difficulty because _____.

Learning Outcome 10–2

5. The first televised presidential debate, between _____, took place in 1960.

6. Spin doctors are _____.

Learning Outcome 10–3

7. The talk-radio audience is predominantly _____.

8. Talk radio is sometimes characterized as the Wild West of the media because _____.

Learning Outcome 10–4

9. It has been suggested that the media use the winner–loser framework to describe events throughout the campaigns, contributing to a bias against _____.

Learning Outcome 10–5

10. Citizen journalism refers to _____.

11. The principle that Internet service providers should treat all traffic equally is called _____.

12. When a politician uses poorly chosen words, we refer to this as a/an _____.

MULTIPLE CHOICE

Learning Outcome 10–1

13. In the news business, framing refers to
   a. fitting events into a familiar story or filtering information through preconceived ideas.
   b. news coverage that is managed by a political consultant to gain media exposure for a political candidate.
   c. narrowing the focus of news to the local area.

Learning Outcome 10–2

14. The 1964 "daisy girl" ad is an example of
   a. a personal attack ad.
   b. citizen journalism.
   c. a negative issue ad.

Learning Outcome 10–3

15. Modern talk radio took off in the United States during the
   a. 1930s, after Franklin Roosevelt's first "fireside chat."
   b. 1950s, after political advertising first appeared on television.
   c. 1990s, after the repeal of the fairness doctrine.

Learning Outcome 10–4

16. In a 2015 Gallup poll measuring the public's confidence in various institutions, _____ percent of the respondents stated that they had a "great deal" or "quite a lot" of confidence in television news.
   a. 67
   b. 42
   c. 21

Learning Outcome 10–5

17. _____ refers to the distribution of audio or video files to personal computers or mobile devices such as smartphones.
   a. Blogging
   b. Podcasting
   c. Narrowcasting

11

THE CONGRESS

LEARNING OUTCOMES *After reading this chapter, you should be able to:*

11-1 Explain how seats in the House of Representatives are apportioned among the states.

11-2 Describe the power of incumbency.

11-3 Identify the key leadership positions in Congress, describe the committee system, and indicate some important differences between the House of Representatives and the Senate.

11-4 Summarize the specific steps in the lawmaking process.

11-5 Identify Congress's oversight functions, and explain how Congress fulfills them.

11-6 Indicate what is involved in the congressional budgeting process.

After finishing this chapter, go to **PAGE 259** for **STUDY TOOLS**.

AMERICA AT ODDS | Should It Take Sixty Senators to Pass Important Legislation?

Denis Kuvaev/Shutterstock.com

The number of Senate votes required to force an end to a *filibuster* is sixty. A filibuster takes place when senators use the chamber's tradition of unlimited debate to block legislation. In years past, filibustering senators would speak for hours on a proposed bill. In recent decades, however, Senate rules have permitted filibusters in which actual continuous floor speeches are not required. Senators merely announce that they are filibustering.

The threat of a filibuster has created an *ad hoc* rule that important legislation needs the support of sixty senators. (There are exceptions. Budget bills can be handled using a special *reconciliation* rule that does not permit filibusters.) If one party can elect sixty or more U.S. senators, and if they all follow the party line, they can force through any legislation they want. The Democrats, in fact, enjoyed a supermajority in the Senate for seven months, from July 7, 2009, until February 4, 2010, when they lost a seat in a special election.

Are sixty votes an appropriate requirement for passing important legislation in the Senate?

Don't Let the Majority Trample on the Minority

In the course of our history, the filibuster in the U.S. Senate has served us well. Filibusters provide the minority with an effective means of preventing the majority from ramming legislation down the throats of American voters.

A simple majority does not signify an adequate degree of consensus. It takes two-thirds of both chambers of Congress to override a veto by the president. That's another supermajority. Changing the Constitution requires three-quarters of the state legislatures. If these supermajority rules were good enough for the founders, then the principle still is good enough for the Senate.

In the past, the American public has supported the filibuster in public opinion polls—for good reason. One of the most important characteristics of our political system is that it is not easy to create new laws. The existence of two chambers of Congress—and the president's veto power—ensures this. The Senate was always meant to be a body that could delay legislation. Further, in 2013, the Senate changed the rules so that filibusters don't apply to votes on whether to approve most presidential appointees. That should be more than enough reform.

Don't Let Obstructionists Determine Legislation

Supermajority rules allow a minority to block the preference of the majority. Even James Madison, who worried about the tyranny of the majority over the minority, recognized the opposite possibility. He said that "the fundamental principle of free government" might be reversed by requiring supermajorities. "It would be no longer majority that would rule: the power would be transferred to the minority."

Madison's warning has been amply justified. At one time, the filibuster was reserved for the defense of major principles. Not all of these principles were laudable—the filibuster was used to defend Jim Crow laws and to prevent African Americans from voting in much of the South. Still, the procedure was rare. Today, it is used for most legislation.

In recent years, the major parties have become politically unified and monolithic. Members of the minority are prepared to cast party-line votes to frustrate the will of the majority on most legislation. Such votes make governance almost impossible. Congress has never passed so few bills in each session as it does under current circumstances.

The Senate should reduce the votes required to end a filibuster to a majority of those present.

Where do you stand?

1. Why might it be appropriate to require supermajority voting for important legislation?

2. Under what circumstances do supermajority voting rules prevent democracy from being fully realized?

Explore this issue online:

- You can find out more about the filibuster by entering "filibuster" into a search engine.

- For debates on the merits of the tradition, search on "filibuster pro con."

INTRODUCTION

Congress is the lawmaking branch of government. When someone says, "There ought to be a law," at the federal level it is Congress that will make that law. The framers had a strong mistrust of powerful executive authority. Consequently, they made Congress—not the executive branch (the presidency)—the central institution of American government. Yet, as noted in Chapter 2, the founders created a system of checks and balances to ensure that no branch of the federal government, including Congress, could exercise too much power.

Many Americans view Congress as a largely faceless, anonymous legislative body that is quite distant and removed from their everyday lives. Yet the people you elect to Congress represent and advocate for your interests at the very highest level of power.

Furthermore, the laws created by the men and women in the U.S. Congress affect the daily lives of every American in one way or another. Learning about your congressional representatives and how they are voting in Congress on issues that concern you is an important step toward becoming an informed voter. Even the details of how Congress makes law—such as the Senate rules described in the chapter-opening *America at Odds* feature—should be of interest to the savvy voter.

11–1 THE STRUCTURE AND MAKEUP OF CONGRESS

> **LO** Explain how seats in the House of Representatives are apportioned among the states.

The framers agreed that the Congress should be the "first branch of the government," as James Madison said, but they did not immediately agree on its organization. Ultimately, they decided on a *bicameral legislature*—a Congress consisting of two chambers. This was part of the Great Compromise, which you read about in Chapter 2.

The framers favored a bicameral legislature so that the two chambers, the House and the Senate, might serve as checks on each other's power and activity. The House was to represent the people. The Senate was to represent the states and would protect the interests of small states by giving them the same number of senators (two per state) as the larger states.

apportionment The distribution of House seats among the states on the basis of their respective populations.

congressional district The geographic area that is served by one member in the House of Representatives.

11–1a Apportionment of House Seats

The Constitution provides for the **apportionment** (distribution) of House seats among the states on the basis of their respective populations. States with larger populations, such as California, have many more representatives than states with smaller populations, such as Wyoming. California, for example, currently has fifty-three representatives in the House. Wyoming has only one.

Every ten years, House seats are reapportioned based on the outcome of the decennial (ten-year) census conducted by the U.S. Census Bureau. Each state is guaranteed at least one House seat, no matter what its population. Today, seven states have only one representative.[1] The District of Columbia, American Samoa, Guam, the Northern Mariana Islands, and the U.S. Virgin Islands all send nonvoting delegates to the House. Puerto Rico, a self-governing possession of the United States, is represented by a nonvoting resident commissioner.

11–1b Congressional Districts

Whereas senators are elected to represent all of the people in a state, representatives are elected by the voters of a particular area known as a **congressional district**. The Constitution makes no provisions for congressional districts. In the early 1800s, each state was given the right to decide whether to have districts at all.

Most states set up single-member districts, in which voters in each district elected one of the state's representatives. In states that chose not to have districts, representatives were chosen at large, from the state as a whole. In 1842, however, Congress passed an act that required all states to send representatives to Congress from single-member districts.

The Size of the House For many years, the number of House members increased as the population expanded. In 1929, however, a federal law fixed House membership at 435. Thus, today the 435 members of the House are chosen by the voters in 435 separate congressional districts across the country. If a state's population allows it to have only one representative, the entire state is one congressional district. In contrast, states with large populations have many districts. California's population, for example, entitles it to send fifty-three representatives to the House, so it has fifty-three congressional districts. As a result of the rule limiting the size of the House to 435 members, U.S. congressional districts on average now have very substantial populations—about 750,000 people. We compare the size of the U.S. House to the size of parliamentary bodies of other nations in this chapter's *The Rest of the World* feature.

The Requirement of Equal Representation By default, the lines of the congressional districts are drawn by the state legislatures. Alternatively, the task may be handed off to a designated body such as an independent commission.[2] States must meet certain requirements in drawing district boundaries. To ensure equal representation in the House, districts in a given state must contain, as nearly as possible, equal numbers of people. Additionally, each district must have contiguous boundaries and must be "geographically compact," although this last requirement is not enforced very strictly.

If congressional districts are not made up of equal populations, people's votes are not equally valuable. In the past, state legislators often used this fact to their advantage. For example, traditionally, many state legislatures were controlled by rural areas. By drawing districts that were not equal in population, rural leaders attempted to curb the number of representatives from growing urban centers. At one point in the 1960s, in many states the largest district had twice the population of the smallest district. In effect, this meant that a person's vote in the largest district had only half the value of a person's vote in the smallest district.

For some time, the United States Supreme Court refused to address this problem. In 1962, however, the Court ruled that the Tennessee state legislature's **malapportionment** was an issue that could be heard in the federal courts because it affected the constitutional requirement of equal protection under the law.[3] Two years later, the Supreme Court held that congressional districts must have equal populations.[4] This principle has come to be known as the **"one person, one vote" rule**. In other words, one person's vote has to count as much as another's vote.

Representative Cheri Bustos (D., Illinois) plays in the annual Congressional Women's Softball Game. Bustos is a former reporter and editor. *Is it a good idea for a journalist to seek elected office?*

Kris Connor/Getty Images

Gerrymandering Although in the 1960s the Supreme Court ruled that congressional districts must be equal in population, it continued to be silent on the issue of gerrymandered districts. **Gerrymandering** occurs when a district's boundaries are drawn to maximize the influence of a certain group or political party.

Where a party's voters are scarce, the boundaries of a district can be drawn to include as many of the party's voters as possible. Where the party is strong, the lines are drawn so that the opponent's supporters are spread across two or more districts, thus diluting the opponent's strength. (The term *gerrymandering* was originally used to describe the district lines drawn to favor the party of Governor Elbridge Gerry of Massachusetts prior to the 1812 elections—see Figure 11–1.)

Although there have been constitutional challenges to political gerrymandering,[5] the practice

---

malapportionment
A condition in which the voting power of citizens in one district is greater than the voting power of citizens in another district.

"one person, one vote" rule A rule, or principle, requiring that congressional districts have equal populations so that one person's vote counts as much as another's vote.

gerrymandering
The drawing of a legislative district's boundaries in such a way as to maximize the influence of a certain group or political party.

FIGURE 11–1 THE FIRST "GERRYMANDER"

Prior to the 1812 elections, the Massachusetts legislature divided up Essex County in a way that favored Governor Elbridge Gerry's party. The result was a district that looked something like a salamander. A newspaper editor of the time referred to it as a "gerrymander," and the name stuck.

Source: *Congressional Quarterly's Guide to Congress*, 3d ed. (Washington, D.C.: Congressional Quarterly Press, 1982), p. 695.

FIGURE 11–2 EXAMPLES OF VOTER DISTRIBUTION

Example 1: A bipartisan gerrymander that protects incumbents of both parties.

Example 2: An unstable system. All districts have the same number of voters from each party.

Example 3: A classic partisan gerrymander. The X Party should carry three districts.

© Cengage Learning

continues. It was certainly evident following the 2010 census. Sophisticated computer programs were now able to analyze the partisan leanings of individual neighborhoods and city blocks. District lines were drawn to "pack" the opposing party's voters into the smallest number of districts or "crack" the opposing party's voters into several different districts. Packing and cracking make congressional races less competitive.

How Gerrymandering Works. For a better understanding of how gerrymandering works, look at the examples in Figure 11–2. In the examples, sixty-four voters must be distributed among four districts, each of which will have a population of sixteen. The two political parties are the O Party and the X Party.

In Example 1, each district contains only one kind of voter. This type of gerrymander is sometimes created when a state legislature is more interested in preserving the seats of incumbents than in benefiting a particular party. In this case, it would be almost impossible for a sitting member to lose in a general election.

In Example 2, every district is divided evenly between the parties. The slightest swing toward one of the parties could give that party all four seats. A legislature would almost never come up with these boundaries, but an independent redistricting board might do so.

Example 3 is a partisan gerrymander favoring the X Party. The district in the lower right is an example of packing—the maximum possible number of O voters is packed into the district. In the other three districts, O Party supporters are cracked apart so that they do not have a majority in any of the districts. In these districts, the X Party has majorities of eleven to five, ten to six, and eleven to five.

Gerrymandering after the 2010 Census. The 2010 elections were a Republican triumph, and the party won control of state legislatures across the country. These victories occurred just before the states were required to redraw the boundaries of congressional districts following the 2010 census. The result was a large number

The U.S. House of Representatives is the "lower" chamber of our Congress. (In international terminology, it is the lower house.) The U.S. House consists of 435 members, a number established in 1929. That means, today, the average member of the House represents about 750,000 Americans. In other democracies, members of the lower house represent a far smaller number of people.

Almost all large nations—and even many of the smaller ones—have lower houses that are larger than the U.S. House. Britain's House of Commons has 650 members, each of whom represents 100,000 inhabitants. The French National Assembly has 577 members, each representing about 115,000 people.

Only one nation in the entire world has a lower house with members who represent more people than House representatives do in America. That nation is India. Each of the 552 members of the House of the People represents more than 2.3 million citizens. This makes a certain amount of sense—India has a total population of almost 1.3 billion.

Build a Bigger House?

New York University professor of sociology Dalton Conley argues that as the third most populous nation on earth, the United States should have a larger House of Representatives. The average House member spoke for only 200,000 citizens in 1913. If that ratio were kept today, we would have more than 1,600 representatives. Because districts would be smaller, campaigns would be cheaper. We might have more citizen-legislators and fewer lifetime politicians. We would be more likely to see our representatives more often. Members of the House would do more of the work of the House, and there would be less reliance on staff members.

Critical Analysis

To create a larger House of Representatives, Congress itself would have to pass the necessary legislation. Why might current members of Congress be reluctant to do this?

of Republican gerrymanders, which had a substantial effect on the 2012 elections. In these elections, Democratic candidates for the U.S. House actually collected more votes than Republican candidates. The Democrats picked up only eight seats, however. In the end, the partisan breakdown was 200 Democrats and 235 Republicans.

Consider Pennsylvania, which went for Barack Obama by 5.4 percentage points in 2012. Pennsylvania voters cast 2.72 million votes for Democratic House candidates and 2.65 million votes for Republicans. These votes elected five Democratic representatives and thirteen Republicans—even though more votes were cast for Democrats. The Republicans look set to enjoy the fruits of their 2010 redistricting for years to come.

As you might expect, the Democrats also engaged in gerrymandering when they had a chance. Illinois is one example. The geography of that state, however, limited the effects of the Democratic gerrymander. So many Democrats are concentrated in Chicago that it was impossible to draw district boundaries that would let the city elect any more Democrats than it was already

electing. The concentration of Democrats in large cities was a problem for the party in many other states as well.

Racial Gerrymandering. Although political gerrymandering has a long history, gerrymandering to empower minority groups is a relatively new phenomenon. In the early 1990s, the U.S. Department of Justice instructed state legislatures to draw district lines to maximize the voting power of minority groups. As a result, several **minority-majority districts** were created. Many of these districts took on bizarre shapes. For example, North Carolina's newly drawn Twelfth Congressional District was 165 miles long—a narrow strip that, for the most part, followed Interstate 85.

Limits on Racial Gerrymandering. The practice of racial gerrymandering has generated heated arguments on both sides of the issue. Some groups contend that minority-majority districts are necessary to ensure equal representation of minority groups, as mandated by the Voting Rights

> **minority-majority district** A district in which minority groups make up a majority of the population.

Act of 1965. They further contend that these districts have been instrumental in increasing the number of African Americans holding political office. Before 1990, redistricting plans in the South often created only white-majority districts.[6]

Opponents of racial gerrymandering argue that such race-based districting is unconstitutional because it violates the equal protection clause. In a series of cases in the 1990s, the Supreme Court agreed and held that when race is the dominant factor in the drawing of congressional district lines, the districts are unconstitutional and must be redrawn.[7]

In 2001, however, the Supreme Court issued a ruling that seemed to suggest that it would not police racial gerrymandering very closely. North Carolina's Twelfth District, which had been redrawn in 1997, was again challenged in court as unconstitutional, and a lower court agreed. Yet when the case reached the Supreme Court, the justices concluded that there was insufficient evidence that race had been the dominant factor in redrawing the district's boundaries.[8]

11-1c The Representation Function of Congress

Of the three branches of government, Congress has the closest ties to the American people. Members of Congress represent the interests and wishes of the constituents in their home states. At the same time, they must also consider larger national issues, such as the economy and the environment. Often, legislators find that the interests of their constituents are at odds with the demands of national policy.

For example, limits on emissions of carbon dioxide may help reduce climate change, to the benefit of all Americans and the people of the world generally. Yet consider members of Congress who come from states where most electricity comes from coal-burning power plants. These legislators may fear that new laws would hurt the local economy and cause companies to lay off workers.

trustee A representative who tries to serve the broad interests of the entire society and not just the narrow interests of his or her constituents.

instructed delegate A representative who deliberately mirrors the views of the majority of his or her constituents.

earmark Spending provision inserted into legislation that benefits only a small number of people.

All members of Congress face difficult votes that set representational interests against lawmaking realities. There are several views on how legislators should decide such issues.

The Trustee View of Representation Some believe that representatives should act as **trustees** of the broad interests of the entire society, rather than serving only the narrow interests of their constituents. Under the trustee view, a legislator should act according to her or his conscience and perception of national needs. For example, a senator from North Carolina might support laws regulating the tobacco industry, even though the state's economy could be negatively affected.

The Instructed-Delegate View of Representation In contrast, others believe that members of Congress should behave as **instructed delegates**. The instructed-delegate view requires representatives to mirror the views of their constituents, regardless of their opinions. Under this view, a senator from Nebraska would strive to obtain subsidies for corn growers, and a representative from the Detroit area would seek to protect the automobile industry.

Legislators who are acting as instructed delegates are particularly likely to try to insert language into various bills that would benefit special interests back home. Such provisions are called **earmarks**, or pork-barrel legislation. We provide greater detail on earmarks in this chapter's *Join the Debate* feature.

The Partisan View of Representation Because the political parties often take different positions on legislative issues, there are times when members of Congress are very attentive to the wishes of the party leadership. Especially on matters that are controversial, the Democratic members of Congress will be more likely to vote in favor of policies endorsed by a Democratic president, while Republicans will be more likely to oppose them.

Typically, members of Congress combine these three approaches to representation. Legislators may take a trustee approach on some issues, adhere to the instructed-delegate view on other matters, and follow the party line on still others.

CRITICAL THINKING

▶ *Some states have tried to prevent gerrymandering by establishing independent redistricting commissions. What kinds of individuals should serve on such commissions? Why?*

In recent years, Congress voted to fund a "bridge to nowhere" in Alaska, a program to combat wild hogs in Missouri, and payment of storage fees for Georgia peanut farmers. Such special interest legislation is called pork-barrel spending—members of Congress "bring home the bacon" this way to benefit local businesses and workers.

Formally, an item of pork is called an earmark. The Congressional Research Service defines earmarks as spending provisions that apply to a very limited number of individuals or entities. The Office of Management and Budget defines earmarks as direct allocations of funds that bypass merit-based or competitive allocation processes of the executive branch. In 2010, immediately after the elections that gave them control of the U.S. House, Republicans announced that they would ban earmarks that benefited specific individuals or corporations. (Earmarks that benefit local governments are still allowed.) This ban was widely applauded at the time. Since then, however, some people have had second thoughts.

Pork Is a Necessary Part of a Democratic System

Those who defend earmarks contend that Congress has a right to determine who benefits from government spending. After all, directing money to particular purposes is a core constitutional function of Congress. Senators and members of the House know their states and districts. Why shouldn't they play a role in funding local projects?

Another argument for pork is that it can help heal a broken Congress. The institution today is paralyzed. Political polarization between Republicans and Democrats is not the only problem. The Republicans themselves are divided between mainstream conservatives and Tea Party radicals. The Tea Party group is large enough that a Republican Speaker cannot pass legislation with mainstream conservatives alone. As former Speaker John Boehner said, "It's not like the old days. Without earmarks to offer, it's hard to herd the cats." Earmarks used to be the lubricant that allowed Congress to do its work. We need them back.

No Thanks— Pork Is Corruption

Opponents of earmarks reject a system in which legislators can be bribed to vote with the leadership. Laws should stand or fall on their own merits. Further, pork is a key component of excessive government spending. The cost of the earmarks themselves may not seem that large. But as Senator Tom Coburn (R., Okla.) has put it, earmarks are "the gateway drug to spending addiction in Washington."

Advocates of pork forget that the pork ban wasn't imposed on a reluctant Congress by outside reformers. Republicans in the House are responsible for the ban. These Republicans are typically elected from safe seats and don't need to bribe the voters back home. Rather, they worry about primary challenges from more conservative opponents. What better way to show that you are a conservative purist than by refusing pork? Further, the restrictions are not even that strict—many legislators have found ways around the pork ban.

Critical Analysis

If the president inserts special requests into executive funding proposals, is that also pork? Why or why not?

11-2 CONGRESSIONAL ELECTIONS

LO Describe the power of incumbency.

The U.S. Constitution requires that representatives to Congress be elected every second year by popular vote. Senators are elected every six years, also by popular vote (since the ratification of the Seventeenth Amendment). Under Article I, Section 4, of the Constitution, state legislatures control the "Times, Places and Manner of holding Elections for Senators and Representatives." Congress, however, "may at any time by Law make or alter such Regulations." You can see the results of the 2016 House elections in Figure 11–3.

Each dot represents one congressional district. Red dots show a Republican representative, and blue dots show a Democrat. In three metropolitan areas—Chicago, Los Angeles, and New York—the dots on the main map overlap so much that many of them are hidden. That is the reason for the three metro area close-ups.

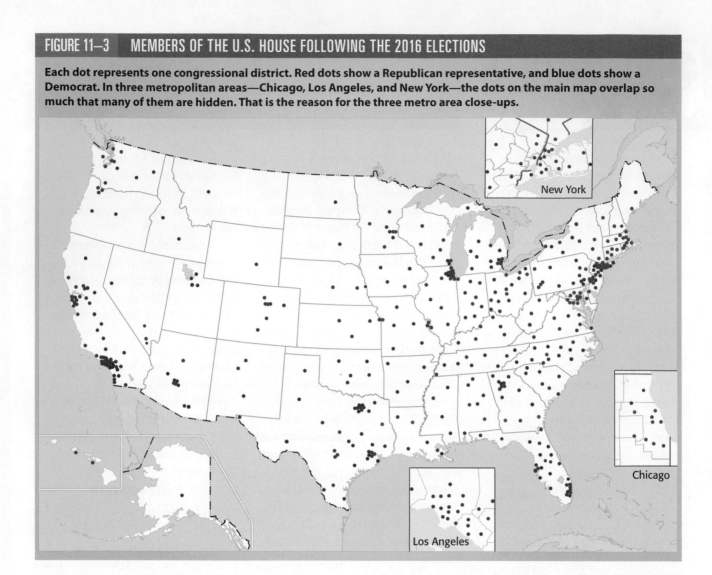

11–2a Who Can Be a Member of Congress?

The Constitution sets forth only a few qualifications that those running for Congress must meet. To be a member of the House, a person must have been a citizen of the United States for at least seven years before his or her election, must be a legal resident of the state from which he or she is to be elected, and must be at least twenty-five years of age.

To be elected to the Senate, a person must have been a citizen for at least nine years, must be a legal resident of the state from which she or he is to be elected, and must be at least thirty years of age. The Supreme Court has ruled that neither the Congress nor the states can add to these three qualifications.[9]

Once elected to Congress, a senator or representative receives an annual salary from the government—$174,000 for rank-and-file members as of 2016. He or she also enjoys certain perks and privileges. Additionally, if a member of Congress wants to run for reelection in the next congressional elections, that person's chances are greatly enhanced by the power that incumbency brings to a reelection campaign.

11–2b The Power of Incumbency

An *incumbent* is someone who is already in office. The power of incumbency has long been noted in American politics. Typically, incumbents win so often and by such large margins that some observers have claimed that our electoral system involves something similar to a hereditary entitlement. As you can see in Figure 11–4, most incumbents in Congress are reelected if they run.

Incumbent politicians enjoy several advantages over their opponents. A key advantage is their fund-raising ability. Most incumbent members of Congress have a much larger network of contacts, donors, and lobbyists

FIGURE 11–4   THE POWER OF INCUMBENCY

While incumbents who run are usually reelected, this chart reveals occasional periods of some turbulence when fewer incumbents than usual won reelection. *In what years did that turbulence occur?*

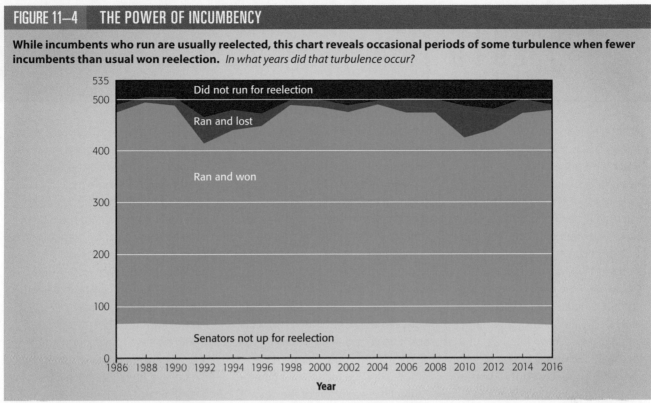

Sources: Norman Ornstein, Thomas E. Mann, and Michael J. Malbin, *Vital Statistics on Congress, 2001–2002* (Washington, D.C.: The AEI Press, 2002); and authors' updates.

than their opponents have. Incumbents raise, on average, twice as much in campaign funds as their challengers. Other advantages that incumbents can put to work to aid their reelection include:

▶ *Professional staffs*—members have large administrative staffs both in Washington, D.C., and in their home districts.

▶ *Lawmaking power*—members can back legislation that will benefit their states or districts and then campaign on that legislative record in the next election.

▶ *Access to the media*—because they are elected officials, members have many opportunities to stage events for the press and thereby obtain free publicity.

▶ *Name recognition*—incumbent members are usually far better known to the voters than are challengers.

Critics argue that the advantages enjoyed by incumbents reduce the competition necessary for a healthy democracy. These incumbency advantages also serve to suppress voter turnout. Voters are less likely to turn out when an incumbent candidate is practically guaranteed reelection.

11–2c Congressional Terms

As noted earlier, members of the House of Representatives serve two-year terms, and senators serve six-year terms. This means that every two years we hold congressional elections: the entire House of Representatives and a third of the Senate are up for election. In January of every odd-numbered year, a "new" Congress convenes (of course, two-thirds of the senators are not new, and most House incumbents are reelected, so they are not new to Congress either). Each Congress has been numbered consecutively, dating back to 1789. The Congress that convened in 2017 was the 115th.

Congressional Sessions Each congressional term is divided into two regular sessions, one for each year. Until about 1940, Congress remained in session for only four or five months, but the complicated rush of legislation and the public's increased demand for services in recent years have forced Congress to remain in session through most of each year.[10] Both chambers, however, schedule short recesses, or breaks, for holidays and vacations. The president may call a *special session* during a recess, but because Congress now meets on nearly a year-round basis, such sessions are rare.

Term Limits As you will read in Chapter 12, the president can serve for no more than two terms in office, due to the Twenty-second Amendment. There is no limit on the number of terms a senator or representative can serve, however. For example, Robert Byrd (D., W.V.) served more than fifty-two years in the U.S. Senate,

2016 ELECTION

Going into the 2016 election season, the Democrats had high hopes that they could at least retake the U.S. Senate. After all, twenty-four Republican seats were up for reelection, compared to only ten Democratic seats. Many of the Republican seats were in states that Barack Obama carried handily in 2012. In the end, however, the Democrats had a net pickup of only two seats, in Illinois and New Hampshire. If Hillary Clinton had eked out a victory in 2016, Democratic Senate candidates probably could have also won at least in Pennsylvania and Wisconsin. That would have given

the Democrats fifty seats instead of forty-eight. With the Senate tied, vice president Tim Kaine could have broken the tie and let the Democrats organize the Senate. It was not to be. With the Republicans in control of both chambers plus the presidency, it appeared as if they would be able to pass almost any legislation they wanted.

One institutional barrier stood between the Republicans and such absolute control—the filibuster, which we described in the chapter-opening *America at Odds* feature. The fifty-two Republican members of the new Senate would not be able to stop a

filibuster. That takes sixty votes. As we explain later in this chapter, however, it is possible to rewrite the Senate rules through a simple majority vote. Doing so is called the *nuclear option*, because it is considered the ultimate parliamentary weapon. Republicans were quite likely to employ the nuclear option if Democrats tried to filibuster Donald Trump's expected Supreme Court nomination. Abolishing the right to filibuster legislation would be a weightier step, but the Republicans may take it. If they do, their power to legislate really will be unlimited.

---

from 1959 until he died in June 2010, at the age of ninety-two. Some observers favor term limits for members of Congress. The Supreme Court, however, has ruled that state-level attempts to impose term limits on members of the U.S. House or Senate are unconstitutional.[11]

CRITICAL THINKING

▸ *What benefits could a state hope to gain from representation by a long-serving legislator?*

 11–3 ## CONGRESSIONAL LEADERSHIP, THE COMMITTEE SYSTEM, AND BICAMERALISM

Speaker of the House The presiding officer in the House of Representatives. The Speaker is a member of the majority party and is the most powerful member of the House.

LO Identify the key leadership positions in Congress, describe the committee system, and indicate some important differences between the House of Representatives and the Senate.

The Constitution provides for the presiding officers of both the House and the Senate, and each chamber has added other leadership positions as it has seen fit. Leadership and organization in both chambers are based on membership in the two major political parties. The majority party in each chamber chooses the major officers of that chamber, controls debate on the floor, selects all committee chairpersons, and has a majority on all committees.

11–3a House Leadership

The Constitution states that members of the House are to choose their Speaker and other officers but says nothing more about these positions. Today, important "other officers" include the majority and minority leaders and whips.

Speaker of the House Chief among the leaders in the House of Representatives is the **Speaker of the House**. This office is filled by a vote taken at the beginning of each congressional term. The Speaker has traditionally been a member of the majority party who has risen in rank and influence through years of service in the House. The candidate for Speaker is selected by the majority-party caucus. The House as a whole then approves the selection.

Powers of the Speaker. As the presiding officer of the House and the leader of the majority party, the Speaker has a great deal of power. In the nineteenth century, the Speaker had even more authority. Speakers known by such names as "Uncle Joe Cannon" and "Czar Reed" ruled the House with a firm hand. A revolt in 1910 reduced the Speaker's powers and gave some of them to various committees. Nevertheless, the Speaker still has many important powers, including the following:

▶ The Speaker has substantial control over what bills are assigned to which committees.

▶ The Speaker may preside over the sessions of the House, recognizing or ignoring members who wish to speak.

▶ The Speaker votes in the event of a tie, interprets and applies House rules, rules on points of order (questions about procedures asked by members), puts questions to a vote, and interprets the outcome of most of the votes taken.

▶ The Speaker plays a major role in making important committee member assignments.

▶ The Speaker schedules bills for action.

When the Speaker Votes. The Speaker may choose whether to vote on any measure. If the Speaker chooses to vote, he or she appoints a temporary presiding officer (called a Speaker *pro tempore*), who then occupies the Speaker's chair. The Speaker does not often vote. Under the House rules, the only time the Speaker *must* vote is to break a tie. Otherwise, a tie automatically defeats a bill. On rare occasions, this rule creates an opportunity for the Speaker. If, by choosing to vote, the Speaker actually *creates* a tie, the proposal will be defeated.

From John Boehner to Paul Ryan. The powers of the Speaker are considerable, and they come with responsibilities for the effective management of the House. Such management is not always easy. For example, members of the Tea Party–oriented Freedom Caucus have tried to pass legislation that President Obama—or even the Senate—would never accept. To accomplish its goals, the Freedom Caucus was willing to disrupt the normal functions of government. This tactic created major problems for Speaker John Boehner of Ohio, who resigned in frustration in October 2015. To replace Boehner, Republican leaders prevailed upon Paul Ryan of Wisconsin to become Speaker—a job he did not want. Ryan, the Republican vice-presidential candidate in 2012, had won respect as a policy leader during his time as chair of the House Budget Committee.

Majority Leader The **majority leader** of the House is elected by the majority-party caucus to act as spokesperson for the party and to keep the party together. The majority leader's job is to help plan the party's legislative program, organize other party members to support legislation favored by the party, and make sure the chairpersons on the many committees finish work on bills that are important to the party. The majority leader makes speeches on important bills, stating the majority party's position.

Minority Leader The House **minority leader** is the leader of the minority party. Although not as

> **majority leader** The party leader elected by the majority party in the House or in the Senate.

> **minority leader** The party leader elected by the minority party in the House or in the Senate.

Following the resignation of Speaker John Boehner in October 2015, Paul Ryan (R., Wisc.), left, was elected Speaker of the House. In 2014, Kevin McCarthy (R., Calif.), center, was elected House majority leader. Nancy Pelosi (D., Calif.), right, was the House minority leader. Pelosi had been the first woman to hold the Speaker position. *How much power do these individuals have?*

powerful as the majority leader, the minority leader has similar responsibilities. The primary duty of the minority leader is to maintain solidarity within the minority party. The minority leader persuades influential members of the party to follow the party's position and organizes fellow party members in criticism of the majority party's policies and programs.

Whips The leadership of each party includes assistants to the majority and minority leaders known as **whips**. Whips originated in the British House of Commons, where they were named after the "whipper in," the rider who keeps the hounds together in a fox hunt. The term is applied to assistant party leaders because of the pressure that they place on party members to uphold the party's positions.

© McConnell.Senate.gov/Official_Photos.cfm

www.schumer.senate.gov

As a result of the 2016 elections, Mitch McConnell (R., Ky.), left, was reelected as the Senate majority leader. Charles (Chuck) Schumer (D., N.Y.), right, was expected to become the Senate minority leader in 2017 after Harry Reid (D., Nev.) retired. *What would happen if a leader disagreed with a majority of his or her caucus on an important issue?*

Whips try to determine how each member is going to vote on an issue and then advise the party leaders on the strength of party support. Whips also try to see that members are present when important votes are to be taken and that they vote with the party leadership. For example, if the Republican Party strongly supports a tax-cut bill, the Republican Party whip might meet with other Republican Party members in the House to try to ensure that they will show up and vote with the party.

11-3b Senate Leadership

The Constitution makes the vice president of the United States the president of the Senate. As presiding officer, the vice president may call on members to speak and put questions to a vote. The vice president is not an elected member of the Senate, however, and may not take part in Senate debates. The vice president may cast a vote in the Senate only in the event of a tie.

whip A member of Congress who assists the majority or minority leader in the House or in the Senate in managing the party's legislative program.

President Pro Tempore Because vice presidents are rarely available—and do not often desire—to preside

over the Senate, senators elect another presiding officer, the *president pro tempore* ("pro tem"), who serves in the absence of the vice president. The president pro tem is elected by the whole Senate and is ordinarily the member of the majority party with the longest continuous term of service in the Senate. The current president pro tem is Orrin Hatch (R., Utah). In the absence of both the president pro tem and the vice president, a temporary presiding officer is selected from the ranks of the Senate, usually a junior member of the majority party.

Party Leaders The real power in the Senate is held by the majority leader, the minority leader, and their whips. The majority leader is the most powerful individual and chief spokesperson of the majority party. The majority leader directs the legislative program and party strategy. The minority leader commands the minority party's opposition to the policies of the majority party and directs the legislative strategy of the minority party.

11-3c Congressional Committees

Thousands of bills are introduced during every session of Congress, and no single member can possibly be adequately informed on all the issues that arise. The committee system is a way to provide for specialization, or a division of the legislative labor. Members of a committee concentrate on just one area or topic—such as agriculture or transportation—and develop sufficient expertise to draft appropriate legislation when needed. The flow of legislation through both the House and the Senate is determined largely by the speed with which these committees act on bills and resolutions.

Standing Committees The permanent and most powerful committees of Congress are called **standing committees**. Their names are listed in Table 11–1. Normally, before any bill can be considered by the entire House or Senate, it must be approved by a majority vote in the standing committee to which it was assigned.

As mentioned, standing committees are controlled by the majority party in each chamber. Committee membership is generally divided between the parties according to the number of members in each chamber. In both the House and the Senate, committee *seniority*—the length of continuous service on a particular committee—typically plays a role in determining the committee chairpersons.

Subcommittees and Other Committees Most House and Senate committees also have **subcommittees**

with limited areas of jurisdiction. Today, there are more than two hundred subcommittees.

Select Committees and Joint Committees. Congress also has other types of committees. Special, or select, committees are formed to study specific problems or issues. These committees may be either permanent or temporary.

Joint committees are created by the concurrent action of both chambers of Congress and consist of members from each chamber. Joint committees have dealt with the economy, taxation, and the Library of Congress.

Conference Committees. A **conference committee**, which also includes members from both chambers, is formed for the purpose of achieving agreement between the House and the Senate on the exact wording of a legislative act when the two chambers pass legislative proposals in different forms. No bill can be sent to the White House to be signed into law unless it first passes both chambers in identical form.

If the leadership in either chamber believes that an acceptable compromise with the other chamber is impossible, it can block legislation simply by refusing

TABLE 11–1 STANDING COMMITTEES IN THE 115TH CONGRESS, 2017–2019	
House Committees	**Senate Committees**
Agriculture	Agriculture, Nutrition, and Forestry
Appropriations	Appropriations
Armed Services	Armed Services
Budget	Banking, Housing, and Urban Affairs
Education and the Workforce	Budget
Energy and Commerce	Commerce, Science, and Transportation
Ethics	Energy and Natural Resources
Financial Services	Environment and Public Works
Foreign Affairs	Finance
Homeland Security	Foreign Relations
House Administration	Health, Education, Labor, and Pensions
Judiciary	Homeland Security and Governmental Affairs
Natural Resources	Judiciary
Oversight and Government Reform	Rules and Administration
Rules	Small Business and Entrepreneurship
Science, Space, and Technology	Veterans' Affairs
Small Business	
Transportation and Infrastructure	
Veterans' Affairs	
Ways and Means	

© 2018 Cengage Learning

standing committee
A permanent committee in Congress that deals with legislation concerning a particular area, such as agriculture or foreign relations.

subcommittee
A division of a larger committee that deals with a particular part of the committee's policy area. Most standing committees have several subcommittees.

conference committee
A temporary committee that is formed when the two chambers of Congress pass differing versions of the same bill. The conference committee consists of members from the House and the Senate who work out a compromise bill.

to appoint members to a conference committee. In 2013, the Republicans employed this technique on several bills, beginning with the 2014 federal budget resolution.

Little Legislatures Most of the actual work of legislating is performed by the committees and subcommittees (the "little legislatures"[12]) within Congress. In creating or amending laws, committee members work closely with relevant interest groups and administrative agency personnel. (For more details on the interaction among these groups, see the discussion of "issue networks" and "iron triangles" in Chapter 13.)

11-3d The Differences between the House and the Senate

To understand what goes on in the chambers of Congress, we need to look at the effects of bicameralism. Each chamber has developed certain distinct features. The major differences between the House and the Senate are listed in Table 11–2.

Size Matters Obviously, with 435 voting members, the House cannot operate the same way as the Senate, which has only 100 members. With its larger size, the House needs both more rules and more formality—otherwise, no work would ever get done. The most obvious formal rules have to do with debate on the floor.

The Senate normally permits extended debate on all issues that arise before it. In contrast, the House uses an elaborate system: The House **Rules Committee** normally proposes time limits on debate for any bill. The rules are then accepted or modified by the House. Despite its greater size, as a consequence of its stricter time

Rules Committee A standing committee in the House of Representatives that provides special rules governing how particular bills will be considered and debated by the House. The Rules Committee normally proposes time limits on debate for any bill.

filibustering The Senate tradition of unlimited debate undertaken for the purpose of preventing action on a bill.

TABLE 11–2 MAJOR DIFFERENCES BETWEEN THE HOUSE AND THE SENATE	
House*	Senate*
Members chosen from local districts	Members chosen from entire state
Two-year term	Six-year term
Always elected by voters	Originally (until 1913) elected by state legislatures
May impeach (accuse, indict) federal officials	May convict federal officials of impeachable offenses
Larger (435 voting members)	Smaller (100 members)
More formal rules	Fewer rules and restrictions
Debate limited	Debate extended
Floor action controlled	Unanimous consent rules
Less prestige and less individual notice	More prestige and media attention
Originates bills for raising revenues	Has power of "advice and consent" on presidential appointments and treaties
Local or narrow leadership	National leadership

*Some of these differences, such as term of office, are provided for in the Constitution, while others, such as debate rules, are not.

© Cengage Learning

limits on debate, the House is often able to act on legislation more quickly than the Senate.

The "Hastert Rule" in the House One informal rule affecting only House Republicans can prevent consideration of legislation even if it has passed in the Senate. That is the *Hastert Rule*, named after a former Republican Speaker. Under the rule, when the Republicans have a majority in the House, the Speaker will not allow any measure to reach the floor unless it has the support of a majority of the Republican members of the House. Democratic Speakers also have the power to block legislation in this way, but they have not turned this procedure into an informal rule.

The Hastert Rule came under considerable pressure in late 2012 and 2013, when Republican Speaker John Boehner felt compelled to violate it repeatedly. Legislation in December 2012 prevented large-scale tax increases at the cost of allowing taxes to rise for the wealthiest citizens. It passed without the support of most Republicans. Boehner also waived the rule to end the government shutdown that took place in October 2013. As we noted earlier, divisions in the Republican ranks led Boehner to resign from the Speaker position in 2015.

In the Senate, Debate Can Just Keep Going and Going At one time, both the House and the Senate allowed unlimited debate, but the House ended this practice in 1811. The use of unlimited debate in the Senate to obstruct legislation is called **filibustering** (as discussed in the chapter-opening *America at Odds* feature). Until 2013, the filibuster could also be used to hold up presidential nominations for judicial or executive positions, as we explain later in this chapter.

Today, under Senate Rule 22, filibusters may be ended by invoking **cloture**—a procedure for closing debate and bringing the matter under consideration to a vote in the Senate. Sixteen senators must sign a petition requesting cloture. Then, after two days have elapsed, three-fifths of the entire membership must vote for cloture. Normally, that means sixty senators. Once cloture is invoked, each senator may speak on a bill for no more than one hour before a vote is taken. Additionally, a final vote must take place within one hundred hours after cloture has been invoked.

The Senatorial Hold Senators have an additional tool they can use to delay legislation. Individual senators may place a *hold* on a particular bill. A senator simply informs the leader of his or her party of the hold. Party leaders do not announce who has placed a hold, so holds are often anonymous. Recent rule changes designed to curb anonymous holds have been ineffective. Cloture can be used to lift a hold.

Senators often place holds on nominees for executive or judicial positions in an attempt to win concessions from the executive branch. For example, in 2010, Senator Richard Shelby (R., Ala.) placed holds on at least seventy of President Obama's nominations in an attempt to force the administration to support two military spending programs in Alabama.

The Senate Wins the Prestige Race, Hands Down Because of the large number of representatives, few can garner the prestige that a senator enjoys. Senators have relatively little difficulty gaining access to the media. Members of the House, who run for reelection every two years, have to survive many reelection campaigns before they can obtain such recognition. Usually, a representative must become an important committee leader to enjoy the consistent attention of the national news media.

One consequence of the prestige difference is that it has been very difficult for a member of the House to win a presidential nomination. In contrast, the parties have often nominated senators, and a number of senators have gone on to become president.

Clearly, the Senate is the more powerful of the two chambers, given its control over presidential appointments and treaties. The right of the House to originate revenue bills does not, in practice, give that chamber an advantage. The Senate can effectively initiate a revenue bill by taking a House-passed spending measure, stripping

out the language, and inserting entirely different text. (Such a step is uncommon, but it has happened from time to time.) In most other nations, however, it is the "lower house"—equivalent to our House of Representatives—that has most of the power.

11-4 THE LEGISLATIVE PROCESS

LO Summarize the specific steps in the lawmaking process.

Look at Figure 11–5. It shows the basic process through which a bill becomes law at the national level. Not all of the complexities of the process are shown, to be sure. For example, the figure does not indicate the extensive lobbying and media politics that are often involved in the legislative process, nor does it mention the informal negotiations and "horse trading" that occur to get a bill passed.

The basic steps in the process are as follows:

1. *Introduction of legislation.* Although individual members of Congress or their staffs—as well as private citizens and lobbying groups—may come up with ideas for new legislation, most bills are proposed by the executive branch. Only a member of Congress can formally introduce legislation, however. In reality, many bills are proposed, developed, and even written by the White House or an executive agency. Then a "friendly" senator or representative introduces the bill in Congress. Such bills are rarely ignored entirely, although they are often amended or defeated.

   To a degree not seen for some decades, the Obama administration during Obama's first term let Congress take the lead on writing important new legislation dealing with issues such as health-care reform and financial regulation. Even under Obama, however, a majority of the legislation considered by Congress came from the executive branch.

2. *Referral to committees.* As soon as a bill is introduced and assigned a number, it is sent to the appropriate standing committee. In the House, the Speaker assigns the bill to the

cloture A procedure for ending filibusters in the Senate and bringing the matter under consideration to a vote.

FIGURE 11–5   HOW A BILL BECOMES A LAW

This illustration shows the most typical way in which proposed legislation is enacted into law. It follows two hypothetical bills, House bill No. 100 (HR 100) and Senate bill No. 200 (S 200). The path of HR 100 is traced by an orange line, and that of S 200 by a teal line. In practice, most bills begin as similar proposals in both chambers. Bills must be passed by both chambers in identical form before they can be sent to the president.

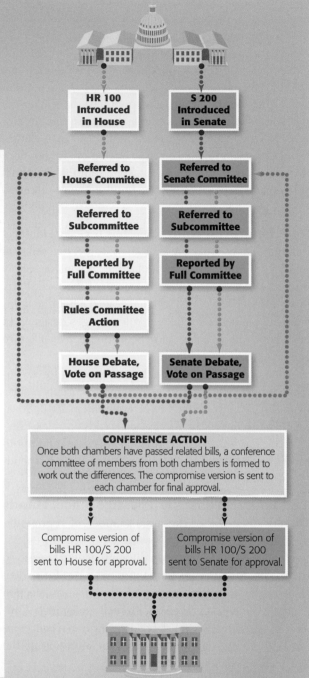

HR 100 Introduced in House

S 200 Introduced in Senate

Referred to House Committee   **Referred to Senate Committee**

Referred to Subcommittee   **Referred to Subcommittee**

Reported by Full Committee   **Reported by Full Committee**

Rules Committee Action

House Debate, Vote on Passage   **Senate Debate, Vote on Passage**

CONFERENCE ACTION
Once both chambers have passed related bills, a conference committee of members from both chambers is formed to work out the differences. The compromise version is sent to each chamber for final approval.

Compromise version of bills HR 100/S 200 sent to House for approval.

Compromise version of bills HR 100/S 200 sent to Senate for approval.

committee. In the Senate, the presiding officer does so. For example, a farm bill in the House would be sent to the Agriculture Committee, and a gun control bill would be sent to the Judiciary Committee.

A committee chairperson will typically send the bill on to a subcommittee. For example, a Senate bill concerning NATO (the North Atlantic Treaty Organization) in Europe would be sent to the subcommittee dealing with European affairs. Alternatively, the chairperson may decide to put the bill aside and ignore it. Most bills that are pigeonholed in this manner receive no further action.

If a bill is not pigeonholed, committee staff members go to work researching it. The subcommittee may hold public hearings during which people who support or oppose the bill can express their views. Subcommittees also have the power to order witnesses to testify at public hearings. Witnesses may be executive agency officials, experts on the subject, or representatives of interest groups concerned about the bill.

The subcommittee must meet to approve the bill as it is, add new amendments, or draft a new bill. This meeting is known as the **markup session**. If members cannot reach a consensus on changes, a vote on the changes is taken.

When a subcommittee completes its work, the bill goes to the full standing committee, which then meets for its own markup session. The committee may hold its own hearings, amend the subcommittee's version, or simply approve the subcommittee's recommendations.

A bill goes to full committee, then usually to a specialized subcommittee for study, hearings, revisions, and approval. Next, the bill goes back to full committee, where more hearings and revisions may occur. The full committee may approve the bill and recommend passage. Committees rarely give an unfavorable report. Instead, the bill may "die" in committee. In the House, many bills go before the Rules Committee for a "rule" expediting floor action, setting conditions for debate and amendments on the floor. Some bills are "privileged" and go directly to the floor. In the Senate, no special rules are used—the leadership normally schedules action. A bill is debated, usually amended, and then passed or defeated. If passed, it goes to the other chamber to follow the same route through the committee and floor stages. (If the other chamber has already passed a related bill, both versions go straight to conference.) A compromise bill approved by both chambers is sent to the president, who can sign it, veto it, or let it become law without a signature. Congress may override a veto by a two-thirds majority vote in each chamber.

© Cengage Learning

markup session
A meeting held by a congressional committee or subcommittee to approve, amend, or redraft a bill.

3. **Reports on a bill.** Finally, the committee will report the bill back to the full chamber. It can report the bill favorably, report the bill with amendments, or report a newly written bill. It can also report a bill unfavorably, but usually such a bill will have been pigeonholed earlier instead. Along with the bill, the committee will send to the House or Senate a written report that explains the committee's actions, describes the bill, lists the major changes made by the committee, and gives opinions on the bill.

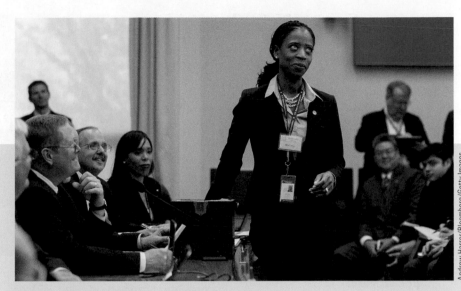

Newly elected representative Mia Love (R., Utah) picks a lottery number that will determine where her new office will be located. Love's parents were born in Haiti, and she is the first Republican African American woman to sit in Congress. *Why would some African Americans be conservatives?*

Andrew Harrer/Bloomberg/Getty Images

4. **The Rules Committee and scheduling.** Scheduling is an extremely important part of getting a bill enacted into law. A bill must be put on a calendar. Typically, in the House the Rules Committee plays a major role in the scheduling process. This committee, along with the House leaders, regulates the flow of the bills through the House. The Rules Committee will also specify how much time can be spent on debate and whether amendments can be made by a floor vote.

   In the Senate, a few leading members control the flow of bills. The Senate brings a bill to the floor by "unanimous consent," a motion by which all members present on the floor set aside the formal Senate rules and consider a bill. In contrast to the procedure in the House, individual senators have the power to disrupt work on legislation—refusing to agree to unanimous consent is the way in which a senatorial hold is enforced.

5. **Floor debate.** Because of its large size, the House imposes severe limits on floor debate. The Speaker recognizes those who may speak and can force any member who does not "stick to the subject" to give up the floor. Normally, the chairperson of the standing committee reporting the bill will take charge of the session during which it is debated. You can often watch such debates on C-SPAN.

   Only on rare occasions does a floor debate change anybody's mind. The written record of the floor debate completes the legislative history of the proposed bill in the event that the courts have to interpret it later on. Floor debates also give the full House or Senate the opportunity to consider amendments to the original version of the bill.

6. **Vote.** In both the House and the Senate, the members present generally vote for or against the bill. There are several methods of voting, including voice votes, standing votes, and recorded votes (also called roll-call votes). Since 1973, the House has had electronic voting. The Senate does not have such a system, however.

7. **Conference committee.** To become a law, a bill must be passed in identical form by both chambers. When the two chambers pass differing versions of the same bill, the measure is turned over to a conference committee—a temporary committee with members from the two chambers, as mentioned earlier.

   Most members of the committee are drawn from the standing committees that handled the bill in both chambers. In theory, the conference committee can consider only those points in a bill on which the two chambers disagree. No proposals are supposed to be added. In reality, however, the conference committee sometimes makes important changes in the bill or adds new provisions. Traditionally, these included "pork-barrel" provisions.

   Once the conference committee members agree on the final compromise bill, a **conference report** is submitted to each chamber. The bill must be accepted or rejected by both chambers as it was written by the committee, with no

conference report
A report submitted by a conference committee after it has drafted a single version of a bill.

further amendments made. If the bill is approved by both chambers, it is ready for action by the president.

8. *Presidential action.* All bills passed by Congress must be submitted to the president for approval. The president has ten days to decide whether to sign the bill or veto it. If the president does nothing, the bill goes into effect unless Congress has adjourned before the ten-day period expires. In that case, the bill dies in what is called a **pocket veto**.

9. *Overriding a veto.* If the president decides to veto a bill, Congress can still get the bill enacted into law. With a two-thirds majority vote in both chambers, Congress can override the president's veto.

Michigan residents line up to attend a House Oversight and Government Reform Committee hearing on the Flint, Michigan, water crisis in March 2016. As a result of a state government blunder that was not intercepted by the EPA, Flint's water was contaminated with lead. *Should a governor resign following a scandal such as this?*

CRITICAL THINKING

▶ *Why do debates on the floor of the House or the Senate almost never change anyone's mind?*

11–5 INVESTIGATION AND OVERSIGHT

LO Identify Congress's oversight functions, and explain how Congress fulfills them.

Steps 8 and 9 of the legislative process just described illustrate the interlocking roles that the executive and the legislative branches play in making laws. The relationship between Congress and the president is at the core of our system of government, although, to be sure, the judicial branch plays a vital role as well (see Chapter 14).

One of the most important functions of Congress is its oversight (supervision) of the executive branch and its many federal departments and agencies. The executive bureaucracy, which includes the president's cabinet departments, wields tremendous power, as you will read in Chapters 12 and 13. Congress can rein in that power by choosing not

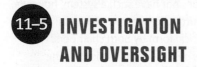

pocket veto A special type of veto power used by the chief executive after the legislature has adjourned. Bills that are not signed die after a specified period of time.

to provide the money necessary for the bureaucracy to function. (The budgeting process will be discussed later in this chapter.)

11–5a The Investigative Function

Congress also has the authority to investigate the actions of the executive branch, the need for certain legislation, and even the actions of its own members. The numerous congressional committees and subcommittees regularly hold hearings to investigate the actions of the executive branch. Congressional committees receive opinions, reports, and assessments on a broad range of issues.

Neglecting Oversight A widely held belief is that between 2001 and 2007, when Republicans controlled both chambers of Congress and the presidency, Congress neglected its oversight function out of deference to President Bush. Many also believe that Congress neglected its oversight function from 2009 to 2011, when the Democrats controlled both chambers of Congress and the presidency.

Going Overboard Likewise, many people believe that Congress may go overboard in its investigations when Congress and the White House are controlled by different parties. Republicans made such accusations during the Bush administration, after the Democrats gained control of Congress in the 2006 elections. When Republicans took control of both chambers in 2014, it was the Democrats' turn to complain. For example, in 2015 a House committee grilled former Secretary of State Hillary Clinton about the death of four Americans in Benghazi, Libya, in 2012. The efforts of the committee were undermined when House majority leader Kevin McCarthy admitted that one goal of the investigation was to reduce Clinton's public opinion poll numbers.

The Congressional Budget Office   One way in which Congress has "kept itself honest" is by establishing oversight bodies separate from—but responsible to—Congress. One such body is the Congressional Budget Office (CBO), which evaluates the impact of proposed legislation on the federal budget and the budget deficit. The CBO has frequently been in the news in recent years due to its "scoring" of various proposals considered by the House and the Senate. Members of Congress have found themselves tailoring measures to earn a better score from the CBO.

11-5b Impeachment Power

Congress has the power to impeach and remove from office the president, vice president, and other "civil officers," such as federal judges. To *impeach* means to accuse a public official of—or charge him or her with—improper conduct in office. The House of Representatives is vested with this power. After a vote to impeach in the full House, the accused official is then tried in the Senate. If convicted by a two-thirds vote, the official is removed from office.

Impeaching Presidents   The House has twice exercised its impeachment power against a president. It voted to impeach Andrew Johnson in 1868 and Bill Clinton in 1998. Both Johnson and Clinton were acquitted by the Senate. A vote to impeach President Richard Nixon was pending before the full House of Representatives in 1974 when Nixon chose to resign. Nixon is the only president ever to resign from office.

Impeaching Other Officers   Congress has taken action to remove officials other than the president. For example, the House of Representatives voted to impeach district court judge Thomas Porteous in March 2010 on charges of bribery and perjury. In December of that year, the Senate convicted Porteous and disqualified him from ever holding any "office of honor or profit under the United States," as the formal language puts it. Only one United States Supreme Court justice has ever been impeached. The House impeached Samuel Chase in 1804, but he was later acquitted by the Senate.

> **"LAWS ARE LIKE SAUSAGES. *IT IS BETTER IF THE PUBLIC DOES NOT SEE HOW THEY ARE MADE."***
>
> – JOHN GODFREY SAXE, AMERICAN POET, 1816–1887 (MISATTRIBUTED TO OTTO VON BISMARCK, CHANCELLOR OF GERMANY, 1871–1890)

11-5c Senate Confirmation

Article II, Section 2, of the Constitution states that the president may appoint ambassadors, justices of the Supreme Court, and other officers of the United States "with the Advice and Consent of the Senate." The Constitution leaves the precise nature of how the Senate will give this "advice and consent" up to the lawmakers.

The Traditional Confirmation Process   Traditionally, the Senate either confirms or fails to confirm the president's nominees for the Supreme Court, other federal judgeships, members of the president's cabinet, and other top executive branch officers. Nominees appear first before the appropriate Senate committee—the Judiciary Committee for federal judges or the Foreign Relations Committee for the secretary of state, for example. If the individual committee approves the nominee, the full Senate will vote on the nomination.

As you will read further in Chapters 12 and 14, Senate confirmation hearings have been very politicized at times. Judicial appointments often receive the most intense scrutiny by the Senate, because federal judges serve for life.

The president has a somewhat freer hand with cabinet appointments, because the heads of executive departments (unlike federal judges) are expected to be loyal to the president. Nonetheless, Senate confirmation has always been an important check on the president's power. We will discuss the relationship between Congress and the president in more detail in Chapter 12.

Appointment Delays and the "Nuclear Option"   Throughout American history, the Senate has often rejected nominees for executive and judicial positions. In recent decades, however, a new pattern has taken hold. Senators from one party have begun delaying nominations as part of an ideological struggle with a president from the other party. Given Senate traditions, such tactics have been available to both the minority and the majority party. The filibuster has often been the tool used in delaying nominations. This practice was first employed in the 1990s by the Republicans in their battles with President Bill Clinton. Democrats then adopted it against George W. Bush. Under Obama, the Republicans resumed the practice. In 2013, however, the use of the filibuster to delay appointments was substantially curbed when the Senate exercised what has been called the *nuclear option.*

Supreme Court nominee Merrick Garland, left, meets with Senator Mark Kirk (R., Illinois). Senate majority leader Mitch McConnell earlier announced that the Senate would not hold hearings on Garland's nomination. *If, like Kirk, you were a Republican elected in a majority-Democratic state, what would you do to enhance your chances of reelection?*

use of the filibuster against all executive and judicial nominees other than those to the Supreme Court. While this step made it easier to approve candidates, the Republicans continued to use other Senate rules to delay nominations.

Of course, when the Republicans took control of the Senate after the 2014 elections, they no longer needed the filibuster to block nominations. Following the death of conservative Supreme Court justice Antonin Scalia in February 2016, Senate Republicans announced that they would refuse to hold confirmation hearings on any nominee that Obama might submit. Filling the empty seat might be delayed for at least a year, until after a new president took office in January 2017.

The Nuclear Option. Senate rules that require supermajority votes for such steps as ending a filibuster have no basis in the Constitution. That document allows senators to pass legislation and approve nominees by a majority vote of those present. The filibuster—and the senatorial hold discussed earlier—exist because a Senate majority has approved these rules. It follows that a majority can repeal them. In the past, such a violation of tradition would have been unthinkable. Given current political polarization, however, the unthinkable has become possible. Changing Senate rules through a simple majority vote has been called the *constitutional option*. It is also known as the **nuclear option**, an analogy to the ultimate weapon.

The Option Is Employed. In 2005, after Senate Democrats filibustered many Bush nominees, Republicans threatened to use the nuclear option to move the nominations forward. At the last minute, a bipartisan group called the "gang of fourteen" engineered a compromise under which the filibuster would be reserved for "extraordinary circumstances." In 2013, with a large number of Obama nominees blocked, the Democrats claimed that the Republicans had violated this agreement. No settlement was reached, and in November the Senate voted to eliminate the

nuclear option
Changing Senate rules—in particular, rules that require a supermajority—by simple majority vote. Also known as the *constitutional option*.

11–6 THE BUDGETING PROCESS

LO Indicate what is involved in the congressional budgeting process.

The Constitution makes it very clear that Congress has the power of the purse, and this power is significant. Only Congress can impose taxes, and only Congress can authorize expenditures. To be sure, the president submits a budget, but all final decisions are up to Congress.

The congressional budget is, of course, one of the most important determinants of what policies will or will not be implemented. For example, the president might order executive agencies under presidential control to undertake specific programs, but these orders are meaningless if there is no money to pay for their execution. For any program that receives an annual appropriation, Congress can nullify a president's ambitious plans simply by refusing to allocate the necessary money to executive agencies to implement the program.

FIGURE 11–6   THE BUDGETING PROCESS

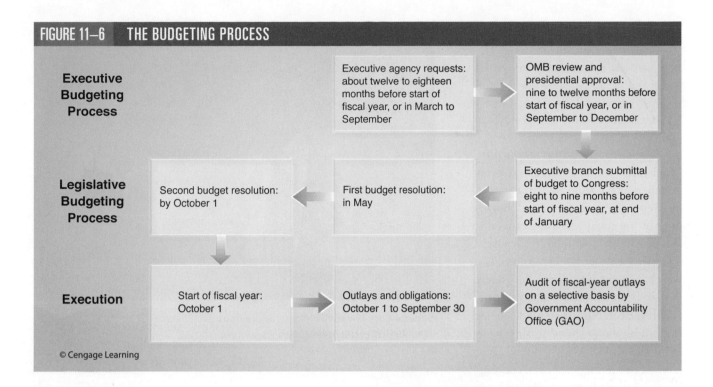

11–6a Authorization and Appropriation

The budgeting process is a two-part procedure. **Authorization** is the first part. It involves the creation of the legal basis for government programs. In this phase, Congress passes authorization bills outlining the rules governing the expenditure of funds. Limits may be placed on how much money can be spent and for what period of time.

Appropriation is the second part of the budgeting process. In this phase, Congress determines how many dollars will actually be spent in a given year on a particular government activity. Appropriations must never exceed the authorized amounts, but they can be less.

An exception to this process involves **entitlement programs**, which require the government to provide benefits, such as Social Security benefits or veterans' benefits, to persons who qualify under entitlement laws. Many such programs operate under open-ended authorizations that, in effect, place no limits on how much can be spent (although it is usually possible to estimate the cost of a particular entitlement program fairly accurately). The Affordable Care Act, also known as Obamacare, is, for the most part, an entitlement program. For this reason, repeated votes by the Republican-led house to "defund" Obamacare have had no practical effect.

The remaining federal programs fall into the category of discretionary spending, and so they can be altered at will by Congress. National defense is the most important item in the discretionary-spending part of the budget. Discretionary spending also includes earmarks, or pork, which we described earlier in this chapter in the *Join the Debate* feature.

11–6b The Actual Budgeting Process

Figure 11–6 outlines the lengthy budgeting process. The process runs from January, when the president submits a proposed federal budget for the next **fiscal year**, to the start of that fiscal year on October 1. In actuality, about eighteen months prior to October 1, the executive agencies submit their requests to the Office of Management and Budget (OMB), and the OMB outlines a proposed budget. If the president approves it, the budget is officially submitted to Congress.

The legislative budgeting process begins

authorization A part of the congressional budgeting process—the creation of the legal basis for government programs.

appropriation A part of the congressional budgeting process—the determination of how many dollars will be spent in a given year on a particular government activity.

entitlement program A government program (such as Social Security) that allows, or entitles, a certain class of people (such as elderly persons) to receive benefits.

fiscal year A twelve-month period that is established for bookkeeping or accounting purposes. The government's fiscal year runs from October 1 through September 30.

eight to nine months before the start of the fiscal year. The **first budget resolution** is supposed to be passed in May. It sets overall revenue goals and spending targets and, by definition, the size of the federal budget deficit or surplus.

The **second budget resolution**, which sets "binding" limits on taxes and spending, is supposed to be passed in September, before the beginning of the fiscal year on October 1. When Congress is unable to pass a complete budget by October 1—which is very common—it usually passes **continuing resolutions**, which enable the executive agencies to keep on doing whatever they were doing the previous year with the same amount of funding. But even continuing resolutions have not always been passed on time.

Budget Projections The budget process involves making predictions about the state of the U.S. economy for years to come. This process is necessarily very imprecise. Since 1996, both Congress and the president have attempted to make ten-year projections for income (from taxes) and spending, but no one can really know what the financial picture of the United States will look like in ten years. While one- or two-year predictions are often fairly realistic, long-term projections have never come close to being accurate.

The Debt Ceiling Issue
In any year in which the federal government spends more than it takes in, the resulting deficit adds to the national debt. U.S. law sets a ceiling on the size of the national debt. It is popularly believed that votes to raise the debt ceiling, which take place regularly, are ways of authorizing additional, future spending. This belief is incorrect. Congress has traditionally appropriated

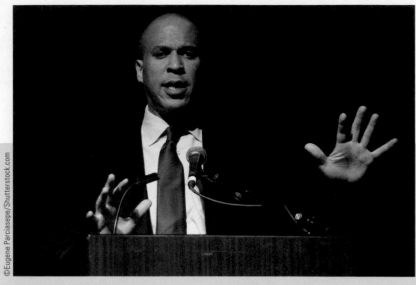

Senator Cory Booker (D., N.J.) was previously the mayor of Newark, N.J. *What kinds of positions best prepare a person for the U.S. Senate?*

sums that would force the government to breach the ceiling and has then raised the ceiling at a later date.

In the past, members of Congress often took advantage of the vote to raise the ceiling to "grandstand," to show off their opposition to federal spending. They did so knowing that in the end, the ceiling would inevitably be raised. In 2011, however, Republicans in the House threatened to refuse to raise the debt ceiling unless the Obama administration made major spending concessions. If the debt ceiling was not raised, the government would not be able to pay out on already-established obligations. Bankers and economists warned that such a default would result in disaster. In the end, the Republicans were at least partially successful. A deal with the Obama administration led to a variety of restraints on spending.

---

first budget resolution A budget resolution, which is supposed to be passed in May, that sets overall revenue goals and spending targets for the next fiscal year, beginning on October 1.

second budget resolution A budget resolution, which is supposed to be passed in September, that sets "binding" limits on taxes and spending for the next fiscal year.

continuing resolution A temporary resolution passed by Congress that enables executive agencies to continue working with the same funding that they had in the previous fiscal year.

"You've got to work things out in the cloakroom, and when you've got them worked out, you can debate a little before you vote."

—LYNDON B. JOHNSON,
SENATE MAJOIRTY LEADER, 1955–1961
PRESIDENT OF THE UNITED STATES,
1963–1969

House Republicans attempted to repeat the tactic in 2013, with the added pressure of refusing to pass a continuing resolution to fund the government. Democrats, believing they had been taken advantage of in 2011, refused to budge. The House tactics were very unpopular, and Republicans were forced to abandon them. Still, the danger exists that such tactics might be revived at some point in the future.

CRITICAL THINKI

▶ *Why do you think C grams that operate instead of reauth*

5. Filibusters
Learning O
6. A mark
7. In t

AMERICA AT ODDS | The Congress

The founders thought that Congress would be the branch of government that was closest to the people. Yet Congress is one of the least popular institutions in America. It seems that anything that Congress does annoys a substantial share of the electorate. Needless to say, Americans are at odds over Congress on a variety of issues:

- *Is the Senate's filibuster rule a legitimate safeguard of minority rights—or a disastrous handicap on Congress's ability to address the nation's problems?*

- *Is political gerrymandering just a normal part of the political game—or does it deprive voters of their rights?*

- *Does racial gerrymandering allow the voices of minority groups to be heard—or is it an unconstitutional violation of the equal protection clause?*

- *When voting on legislation, should members of Congress faithfully represent the views of their constituents—or should they stay true to their own beliefs about what is good for the nation?*

- *Should legislative earmarks, or "pork," be banned as a waste of taxpayers' resources—or is it appropriate for members of Congress to support specific projects in their own districts?*

STUDY TOOLS 11

READY TO STUDY? IN THE BOOK, YOU CAN:

☐ Review what you've read with the following chapter quiz.

☐ Check your answers in Appendix D at the back of the book.

☐ Rip out the Chapter Review Card, which includes key terms and chapter summaries.

ONLINE AT WWW.CENGAGEBRAIN.COM, YOU CAN:

☐ Learn in a short video how Congress is managed.

☐ Explore various online resources in the Roll Call and U.S. House of Representatives websites in the Internet Resources tool.

☐ Interact with figures from the text, and watch quick animation clips.

☐ Prepare for tests with quizzes.

☐ Review the key terms with Flash Cards.

FILL-IN

Learning Outcome 11–1

1. Every _____ years, seats in the House of Representatives are reapportioned based on the outcome of the census.

2. Under the trustee view of representation, a legislator should try to _____.

Learning Outcome 11–2

3. Incumbent members of Congress enjoy several advantages over their challengers in elections, including

_____.

Learning Outcome 11–3

4. The Speaker of the House has the power to

_____.

...ay be ended by invoking _____.

...up session is _____.

...e House, the _____ Committee plays a
...ajor role in the scheduling process and will also specify
the amount of time to be spent on debate.

Learning Outcome 11–5

8. In practice, the Senate's power of "advice and consent" means that the Senate confirms or fails to confirm the president's nominees to _____.

Learning Outcome 11–6

9. The budgeting process is a two-part procedure that includes _____.

MULTIPLE CHOICE

Learning Outcome 11–1

10. Congressional districts in a given state must contain, as nearly as possible, equal numbers of
    a. men and women.
    b. Republicans and Democrats.
    c. people.

Learning Outcome 11–2

11. The U.S. Constitution requires that members of the House of Representatives be elected every
    a. second year by popular vote.
    b. six years by popular vote.
    c. second year by state legislatures.

Learning Outcome 11–3

12. In the Senate, the _____ is typically the most powerful individual and directs the legislative program and strategy of his or her party.
    a. vice president
    b. majority leader
    c. president pro tempore

Learning Outcome 11–4

13. As soon as a bill is introduced in either the House or the Senate, it is sent to
    a. the floor of the chamber.
    b. the appropriate standing committee.
    c. a conference committee.

Learning Outcome 11–5

14. The Senate
    a. voted to impeach Richard Nixon.
    b. convicted Bill Clinton of impeachable offenses by a two-thirds vote.
    c. tries officials who have been impeached in the House.

Learning Outcome 11–6

15. When Congress is unable to pass a budget by the beginning of the fiscal year, it usually passes _____, which let executive agencies keep on doing whatever they were doing the previous year with the same funding.
    a. continuing resolutions
    b. entitlement programs
    c. earmarks

12 THE PRESIDENCY

LEARNING OUTCOMES *After reading this chapter, you should be able to:*

12–1 List the constitutional requirements for becoming president.

12–2 Explain the roles that a president adopts while in office.

12–3 Indicate the scope of presidential powers.

12–4 Describe advantages enjoyed by Congress and by the president in their institutional relationship.

12–5 Discuss the organization of the executive branch and the role of cabinet members in presidential administrations.

After finishing this chapter, go to **PAGE 285** for **STUDY TOOLS**.

AMERICA AT ODDS

Should the New President Get Tough on the Middle East?

RobertChlopas/Shutterstock.com

As long as most young people can remember, Middle East headlines have involved wars and other armed conflicts. ISIS (also called the Islamic State, ISIL, or Daesh) has conquered territory in Iraq and Syria. It has released videos in which its terrorists behead Westerners, plus Middle Eastern Christians, Jews, and Muslims. Iran continues to sponsor terrorist groups throughout the region. Presumably, Iran has suspended work on nuclear weapons, but it is developing long-range missiles. Libya has become a "failed state" after years of bloodshed between opposing groups.

Given all this, what is the role of the United States in the Middle East? Should the next president attempt to limit our involvement with such a troubled region? Or should the next president seek to reassert American influence in the Middle East, perhaps by deploying U.S. infantry—"boots on the ground"—to stop ISIS?

The decisions of the new president will be influenced by two great traditions in American foreign policy: idealism and realism. Within the Republican establishment, a hawkish idealism prevails, often promoted by a faction known as the neoconservatives. These people strongly believe that U.S. military power can be a force for good in the world. In contrast, so-called realists seek to avoid military commitments that are not clearly and directly connected to the security of the homeland. Realism is popular among Democrats, though some of its advocates are Republicans.

The New President Should Be More Interventionist

Many people do not want the Middle East to be America's problem. Yet idealist hawks argue that when we do not intervene in the Middle East, it becomes an even greater problem for us. When Obama pulled out of Iraq, he left a power vacuum that was filled by Iran—and ISIS. A few years ago, Obama said that if Syrian President Bashar al-Assad used chemical weapons against his people, there would be serious consequences. But when Assad crossed the "red line," Obama backed off from bombing. He was saved from complete embarrassment by Russian president Vladimir Putin, of all people. (Putin persuaded Assad to surrender his chemical weapons. U.S. forces then decommissioned them.)

By now at least a quarter of a million Syrians are dead, and almost half the nation's people have been forced to flee their homes. When our president engages in inaction in the Middle East, Russia and Iran step in and push us aside. Had we stepped into the Syrian civil war and really supported the rebels, ISIS would never have been allowed to establish its own state within a state. We would not see ISIS warriors beheading Americans and others.

We Don't Have a Stake in This Fight

Opponents of intervention ask: Don't the war hawks get it yet? We cannot be the world's policemen. Americans have gained nothing from sending U.S. troops to the Middle East. We went into Afghanistan to save its people from a tyranny imposed by the Taliban. True, the Taliban were driven from the capital, Kabul, but the civil war there is endless. In Iraq, what did we get for thousands of American deaths and injuries? Hawks may say Iraq fell apart because we withdrew, but the same thing probably would have happened if we left in, say, the year 2020.

As to Syria, we could easily conquer the entire country if we went in with guns blazing. And then we would own the place—"you break it, you buy it." Before long, everyone in Syria would hate us as foreign occupiers. In Libya, we helped bring down a dictator, Muammar Gaddafi. Where did that get us? The nation is a total mess, torn apart by armed factions.

The new president should not waste American lives and treasure in the Middle East. The region will not know peace until its own people are willing to struggle for it.

Where do you stand?

1. Recent polls suggest that a majority of Americans want to send ground troops to fight ISIS in Iraq and Syria. Do you agree with this idea? Why or why not?

2. Why have all recent presidents been concerned with events in the Middle East?

Explore this issue online:

- *Commentary* magazine is home to many of the idealist hawks known as neoconservatives. Find it at www.commentarymagazine.com.

- You can find libertarian anti-interventionists at www.antiwar.com and progressive ones at www.theglobalist.com.

INTRODUCTION

President Lyndon B. Johnson (1963–1969) stated in his autobiography that "of all the 1,886 nights I was President, there were not many when I got to sleep before 1 or 2 A.M., and there were few mornings when I didn't wake up by 6 or 6:30."[1] President Harry Truman (1945–1953) once observed that no one can really understand what it is like to be president: there is no end to "the chain of responsibility that binds him," and he is "never allowed to forget that he is president." These responsibilities are, for the most part, unremitting. Unlike Congress, the president never adjourns.

At the apex of the political ladder, the presidency is the most powerful and influential political office that any one individual can hold. Presidents can help to shape not only domestic policy but also global developments.

Since the demise of the Soviet Union and the Communist-controlled governments in eastern Europe

Promotional poster for the feature film *Hellcats of the Navy*, starring future president Ronald Reagan and his wife, Nancy Davis. *How might Reagan's career as an actor have helped him in politics?*

in the early 1990s, the president of the United States has been the leader of the most powerful nation on earth. The president heads the greatest military force anywhere. Presidents have more power to reach their political objectives than any other players in the American political system. (We discussed the president's foreign policy in this chapter's opening *America at Odds* feature.) It is not surprising, therefore, that many Americans aspire to attain this office.

12–1 WHO CAN BECOME PRESIDENT?

LO List the constitutional requirements for becoming president.

The notion that anybody can become president of this country has always been a part of the American mythology. Certainly, the requirements for becoming president set forth in Article II, Section 1, of the Constitution are not difficult to meet:

> No Person except a natural born Citizen, or a Citizen of the United States, at the time of the Adoption of this Constitution, shall be eligible to the Office of President; neither shall any Person be eligible to that Office who shall not have attained to the Age of thirty-five Years, and been fourteen Years a Resident within the United States.

This language does make it impossible for a foreign-born naturalized citizen to become president, even if that person came to this country as an infant. For more on that issue, see this chapter's *Join the Debate* feature.

12–1a Perks of the President

Given the demands of the presidency, why would anyone seek the office? There are some very special perks associated with the presidency. The president enjoys, among other things, the use of the White House. The White House has 132 rooms located on 18.3 acres of land in the heart of the nation's capital. At the White House, the president in residence has a staff of more than eighty persons, including chefs, gardeners, maids, butlers, and a personal tailor.

Amenities also include a tennis court, a swimming pool, bowling lanes, and a private movie theater. Additionally, the president has at his or her disposal a fleet of automobiles, helicopters, and jets (including *Air Force One,* which costs about $230,000 an hour to run). For relaxation, the presidential family can go to Camp David, a resort hideaway in the Catoctin Mountains of Maryland. Other perks include free dental and medical care.

JOIN
THE DEBATE

A Foreign-Born President?

As you just read, Article II of the Constitution states that "[n]o Person except a natural born Citizen . . . shall be eligible to the Office of President." This restriction has long been controversial, for it has kept many otherwise qualified Americans from running for president. These persons have included former California governor Arnold Schwarzenegger, who was born in Austria. In all, some 20 million Americans born outside the United States are excluded by this provision.

The requirement of native birth has come up most recently because of claims by conspiracy theorists known as "birthers" that President Obama was not born in the United States. These individuals claim that Obama's Hawaiian birth certificate was forged, and they are undeterred by the fact that Obama's birth was also announced in two Honolulu newspapers.

In 2015, Republican presidential candidate Donald Trump, a prominent birther, claimed that a rival candidate, Texas senator Ted Cruz, was ineligible for the presidency because he was born in Alberta, Canada, to a citizen mother and a noncitizen father. Trump's claim was rejected by legal experts.

An Obsolete Provision

America is a nation of immigrants, so it strikes some as odd that a foreign-born person would be barred from aspiring to the presidency. Naturalized U.S. citizens are allowed to vote, to serve on juries, and to serve in the military. They are also allowed to serve as secretary of state and represent the nation in foreign affairs. Why can't they run for president? Critics of the Constitution's citizenship requirement think that the requirement should be abolished by a constitutional amendment. They point out that the clause was initially included in the Constitution to prevent European princes from attempting to force the young republic back under monarchical rule in the late 1700s. Clearly, the clause is now obsolete and should no longer apply.

A Requirement Still Valid Today

Other Americans believe that the constitutional ban should remain. They argue that national security could be compromised by a foreign-born president. With the immense power that the president wields, especially in foreign policy, loyalty is of the utmost concern.

In addition, the Constitution is difficult to amend, requiring support from two-thirds of both chambers of Congress and ratification by three-fourths of the states. Opponents argue that the need for an amendment that would allow immigrants to run for president is hardly as pressing as the prior need for antidiscrimination amendments, such as the ones that abolished slavery and gave women the right to vote.

Critical Analysis

Do you see a problem with someone born in a foreign country serving as president? Why or why not?

12–1b Presidential Age and Occupation

Modern presidents have included a haberdasher (Harry Truman), the owner of a peanut warehouse (Jimmy Carter), and an actor (Ronald Reagan), although all of these men also had significant political experience before assuming the presidency. The most common previous occupation of U.S. presidents, however, has been the legal profession. Out of forty-four presidents, twenty-six have been lawyers. Many presidents have also been wealthy.

Although the Constitution states that anyone who is thirty-five years of age or older can become president, the average age at inauguration has been fifty-five. The youngest person elected president was John F. Kennedy (1961–1963), who assumed the presidency at the age of forty-three (the youngest person to hold the office was Theodore Roosevelt, who was forty-two when he became president after the assassination of William McKinley). The oldest was Donald Trump, who was seventy years old when he became president.

12-1c Race, Gender, and Religion

For most of American history, all presidential candidates, even those of minor parties, were white, male, and of the Protestant religious tradition.[2] In recent years, however, the pool of talent has expanded. In 1928, Democrat Al Smith became the first Roman Catholic to run for president on a major-party ticket, and in 1960 Democrat John F. Kennedy was elected as the first Catholic president. Among recent unsuccessful Democratic presidential candidates, Michael Dukakis was Greek Orthodox and John Kerry was Roman Catholic.

President Woodrow Wilson throwing out the first pitch on the opening day of the Major League Baseball season in 1916. *Why might a president wish to perform this task?*

In 2008, the doors swung wide in the presidential primaries as the Democrats chose between a white woman, Hillary Clinton, and an African American man, Barack Obama. By that time, about 90 percent of Americans told pollsters that they would be willing to support an African American for president, and the same number would support a woman.

In 2012, none of the top three finishers in the Republican primaries was Protestant. Among the 2016 finalists, however, Democrat Hillary Clinton and Republicans Ted Cruz, John Kasich, and Donald Trump are all Protestant. Republican Marco Rubio is Catholic, and Democrat Bernie Sanders is Jewish. As Cuban Americans, Cruz and Rubio are also Hispanic.

CRITICAL THINKING

▶ *Why do some people believe so strongly that Barack Obama must have been born in a foreign country?*

12-2 THE PRESIDENT'S MANY ROLES

LO Explain the roles that a president adopts while in office.

The president has the authority to exercise a variety of powers. Some of these are explicitly outlined in the Constitution, and some are simply required by the office—such as the power to persuade. In the course of

exercising these powers, the president performs a variety of roles. For example, as commander in chief of the armed services, the president can exercise significant military powers.

Which roles a president executes successfully usually depends on what is happening domestically and internationally, as well as on the president's personality. Some presidents, including Bill Clinton (1993–2001) during his first term, have shown much more interest in domestic policy than in foreign policy. Others, such as George H. W. Bush (1989–1993), were more interested in foreign affairs than in domestic ones.

Table 12–1 summarizes the major roles of the president. An important role is, of course, that of chief executive. Other roles include those of commander in chief, head of state, chief diplomat, chief legislator, and political party leader.

12-2a Chief Executive

According to Article II of the Constitution,

> The executive Power shall be vested in a President of the United States of America. . . . [H]e may require the Opinion, in writing, of the principal Officer in each of the executive Departments, upon any Subject relating to the Duties of their respective Offices . . . and he shall nominate, and by and with the Advice and Consent of the Senate, shall appoint . . . Officers of the United States . . . . [H]e shall take Care that the Laws be faithfully executed.

TABLE 12–1 ROLES OF THE PRESIDENT

Chief executive   Enforces laws and federal court decisions, along with treaties approved by the United States.

- Appoints, with Senate approval, and removes high-ranking officers of the federal government.
- Grants reprieves, pardons, and amnesties.
- Handles national emergencies during peacetime, such as riots or natural disasters.

Vacclav/Shutterstock.com

Commander in chief   Leads the nation's armed forces.

- Can commit troops for up to ninety days in response to a military threat (War Powers Resolution).
- Can make secret agreements with other countries.
- Can set up military governments in conquered lands.
- Can end fighting by calling a cease-fire (armistice).

Rafal Oikis/Shutterstock.com

Head of state   Performs ceremonial activities as a personal symbol of the nation.

- Decorates war heroes.
- Dedicates parks and museums.
- Throws out first pitch of baseball season.
- Lights national Christmas tree and pardons the national Thanksgiving turkey.
- Receives foreign heads of state.

R Carner/Shutterstock.com

Chief diplomat   Directs U.S. foreign policy and is the nation's most important representative in dealing with foreign countries.

- Negotiates and signs treaties with other nations, which go into effect with Senate approval.
- Makes pacts (executive agreements) with other heads of state, without Senate approval.
- Can accept the legitimacy of another country's government (power of recognition).

1000 Words/Shutterstock.com

Chief legislator   Informs Congress about the condition of the country and recommends legislative measures.

- Proposes legislative program to Congress in traditional State of the Union address.
- Suggests budget to Congress, and submits annual economic report.
- Can veto a bill passed by Congress.
- Can call special sessions of Congress.

Brandon Bourdages/Shutterstock.com

Political party leader   Heads political party.

- Chooses a vice president.
- Makes several thousand top government appointments, often to party faithful (patronage).
- Tries to execute the party's platform.
- Attends party fund-raisers.
- May help reelect party members running for office as mayors, governors, or members of Congress.

Gary Hathaway/Shutterstock.com

This constitutional provision makes the president of the United States the nation's **chief executive**, or the head of the executive branch of the federal government.

When the framers created the office of the president, they created a uniquely American institution. Nowhere else in the world at that time was there a democratically chosen chief executive. The executive branch is also unique among the branches of government because it is headed by a single individual—the president.

12–2b Commander in Chief

The Constitution states that the president "shall be Commander in Chief of the Army and Navy of the United States, and of the Militia of the several States, when called into the actual Service of the United States." As **commander in chief** of the nation's armed forces, the president exercises tremendous power.

Under the Constitution, war powers are divided between Congress and the president. Congress was given the power to declare war and the power to raise and maintain the country's armed forces. The president, as commander in chief, was given the power to deploy the armed forces.

12–2c Head of State

Traditionally, a country's monarch has performed the function of **head of state**—the country's representative to the rest of the world. The United States, of course, has no king or queen to act as head of state. Thus, the president of the United States fulfills this role.

The president engages in many symbolic or ceremonial activities, such as throwing out the first pitch to open the baseball season and turning on the lights of the national Christmas tree. The president also decorates war heroes, dedicates parks and museums, receives visiting heads of state at the White House, and goes on official state visits to other countries.

Some argue that presidents should not perform such ceremonial duties because they take time that the president should be spending on "real work." Most presidents, however, have found the role of head of state to be politically useful.

> **chief executive** The head of the executive branch of government; in the United States, the president.
>
> **commander in chief** The supreme commander of a nation's military force.
>
> **head of state** The person who serves as the ceremonial head of a country's government and represents that country to the rest of the world.

Donald Trump's differences with his own party may be greater on foreign policy than on any other topic. This matters, because in no area of government does the president have more power than in foreign relations. The president is rarely limited by the need to seek legislation from Congress. Presidents have become accustomed to using military force without waiting for congressional backing. Indeed, there are no institutional barriers that prevent the president from initiating a nuclear war.

When it comes to foreign policy, Trump has principles, even if he has few worked-out policies. The trade deficit, under which the United States imports more goods and services than it exports, must be cut severely. Relations with allies are to be put on a "transactional" basis—that is, allies are expected to pay handsomely for any military defense provided by the United States. Perhaps most troubling of all, Trump seems fond of Russian president Vladimir Putin, whereas all past presidents have considered

Russia to be a foe. This appalls the neoconservatives, the Republican hawks mentioned in the chapter-opening *America at Odds* feature. Many of them broke ranks to support Hillary Clinton, who endorsed a much more conventional foreign policy. Trump's Republican colleagues are sure to pressure him toward more traditional policies. They may or may not succeed.

12–2d Chief Diplomat

A **diplomat** is a person who represents one country in dealing with representatives of another country. In the United States, the president is the nation's **chief diplomat**. The Constitution did not explicitly reserve this role to the president, but since the beginning of this nation, presidents have assumed the role based on their explicit constitutional powers to "receive [foreign] Ambassadors" and, with the advice and consent of the Senate, to appoint U.S. ambassadors and make treaties. As chief diplomat, the president directs the foreign policy of the United States and is our nation's most important representative.

12–2e Chief Legislator

Nowhere in the Constitution do the words *chief legislator* appear. The Constitution, however, does require that the president "from time to time give to the Congress Information of the State of the Union, and recommend to their Consideration such

Measures as he shall judge necessary and expedient." The president has, in fact, become a major player in shaping the congressional agenda—the set of measures that actually get discussed and acted on.

Presidential Activism This was not always the case. In the nineteenth century, some presidents preferred to let Congress lead the way in proposing and implementing policy. Since the administration of Theodore Roosevelt (1901–1909), however, presidents have taken an activist approach. Presidents are now expected to develop a legislative program and propose a budget to Congress every year.

In the past, this shared power has often put Congress and the president at odds. President Bill Clinton's administration, for example, drew up a health-care reform package in 1993 and presented it to Congress almost on a take-it-or-leave-it basis. Congress left it.

Legislation under Obama To avoid such confrontations, President Obama frequently let Congress determine much of the content of important new legislation, such as the health-care reform bills. In the example of health-care reform, President Obama's deference to Congress had several negative consequences. These included an unusually large number of earmarks,

diplomat A person who represents one country in dealing with representatives of another country.

chief diplomat The role of the president of the United States in recognizing and interacting with foreign governments.

a protracted and unpopular legislative process, and opportunities for conservatives to mobilize against the reforms. Still, in the end, Obama succeeded where Clinton had failed.

12–2f Political Party Leader

The president of the United States is also the *de facto* leader of his or her political party. The Constitution, of course, does not mention this role because, in the eyes of the founders, parties should have no place in the American political system.

As party leader, the president exercises substantial powers. For example, the president chooses the chairperson of the party's national committee. The president can also exert political power within the party by using presidential appointment and removal powers.

Naturally, presidents are beholden to the party members who put them in office. Thus, usually they indulge in the practice of **patronage**—appointing individuals to government or public jobs to reward those who helped them win the presidential contest.

The president may also reward party members with fund-raising assistance. (Campaign financing was discussed in Chapter 9.) The president is, in a sense, "fund-raiser in chief" for his or her party, and recent presidents, including Bill Clinton, George W. Bush, and

Barack Obama, have proved themselves to be prodigious fund-raisers.

CRITICAL THINKING

▶ *Does our president have too many roles to fill?*

12–3 PRESIDENTIAL POWERS

LO Indicate the scope of presidential powers.

The president exercises numerous powers. Some of these powers are set forth in the Constitution. Others, known as *inherent powers,* are those that are necessary to carry out the president's constitutional duties. We look next at these powers, as well as at the expansion of presidential powers over time.

12–3a The President's Constitutional Powers

As you have read, the constitutional source for the president's authority is found in Article II of the Constitution, which states, "The executive Power shall be vested in a President of the United States of America." The Constitution then sets forth the president's relatively limited constitutional responsibilities.

The Specified Powers Article II grants the president broad but vaguely described powers. From the very beginning, there were different views as to what exactly the "executive Power" clause enabled the president to do. Nonetheless, Sections 2 and 3 of Article II list the following specific presidential powers. These powers parallel the roles of the president discussed in the previous section:

Paul J. Richards/Getty Images

President Obama with Japan's prime minister, Shinzo Abe. *How can the president benefit by meeting foreign leaders?*

patronage The practice by which elected officials give government jobs to individuals who helped them gain office.

- To serve as commander in chief of the armed forces and the state militias.

- To appoint, with the Senate's consent, the heads of the executive departments, ambassadors, justices of the Supreme Court, and other top officials.

- To make treaties, with the advice and consent of the Senate.

- To grant reprieves and pardons, except in cases of impeachment.

- To deliver the annual State of the Union address to Congress and to send other messages to Congress from time to time.

- To call either house or both houses of Congress into special sessions.

- To receive ambassadors and other representatives from foreign countries.

- To commission all officers of the United States.

- To ensure that the laws passed by Congress "be faithfully executed."

In addition, Article I, Section 7, gives the president the power to veto legislation. We will now discuss some of these powers in more detail. As you will see, many of the president's powers are balanced by the powers of Congress. We return to the complex relationship between the president and Congress later in this chapter.

Proposal and Ratification of Treaties A **treaty** is a formal agreement between two or more countries. The president has the sole power to negotiate and sign treaties with other countries. The Senate, however, must approve a treaty by a two-thirds vote of the members present before it becomes effective. If the treaty is approved by the Senate and signed by the president, it becomes law.

Nuclear Weapons Agreements. Presidents have not always succeeded in winning the Senate's approval for treaties. In 1999, Bill Clinton was unable to persuade the Senate to approve the Comprehensive Test Ban Treaty, which would have prohibited all signers from testing nuclear weapons. Clinton argued that the United States no longer needed to test its nuclear weapons and that the treaty's restrictions on other countries would enhance our national security. The treaty was defeated largely on a party-line vote, with the Republicans opposed.

In contrast, Barack Obama convinced the Senate to approve the New Strategic Arms Reduction

treaty A formal agreement between the governments of two or more countries.

Treaty (New START) with Russia in December 2010. The treaty reduced by half the number of nuclear missiles in both countries and provided for inspections. New START was supported by all of the Democrats and by many Republicans.

Trade Agreements. Obama was less successful as a treaty maker in his second term, especially after the 2014 elections, which produced a Republican Senate. In 2015, he narrowly won support for the power to negotiate the Trans-Pacific Partnership (TPP), a proposed agreement between the United States and various nations that lie on the Pacific rim. These include Australia, Canada, Japan, Mexico, Vietnam, and six others. The proposed treaty would cover issues of trade, intellectual property, and dispute resolution. The power to negotiate depended on *fast-track authority*, under which Congress agreed that it would vote the entire deal up or down without amendments. Given how narrowly fast-track authority passed, it was questionable whether Obama would win support for the eventual package. Presidential candidates Bernie Sanders and Donald Trump opposed it vehemently, while candidates Hillary Clinton and Ted Cruz demanded that it be renegotiated.

The Power to Grant Reprieves and Pardons
The president's power to grant a pardon serves as a check on judicial power. A *pardon* is a release from punishment or the legal consequences of a crime. It restores a person to the full rights and privileges of citizenship.

In 1925, the United States Supreme Court upheld an expansive interpretation of the president's pardon power in a case involving an individual convicted for contempt of court. The Court held that the power covers all offenses "either before trial, during trial, or after trial, by individuals, or by classes, conditionally or absolutely, and this without modification or regulation by Congress."[3] The president can grant a pardon for any federal offense, except in cases of impeachment.

One of the most controversial pardons was that granted by President Gerald Ford (1974–1977) to former president Richard Nixon (1969–1974) after the Watergate affair (to be discussed later in the chapter) before any formal charges were brought in court.

Sometimes pardons are granted to a class of individuals as a general amnesty. For example, President Jimmy Carter granted amnesty to tens of thousands of people who had resisted the draft during the Vietnam War by failing to register for the draft or by moving abroad.

President Gerald Ford appearing at a House Judiciary Committee hearing on his decision to pardon former President Richard Nixon. A presidential appearance before a congressional committee is highly unusual. *Should it happen more often? Why or why not?*

The President's Veto Power   As noted in Chapter 11, the president can **veto** a bill passed by Congress. Congress can override the veto with a two-thirds vote by the members present in each chamber. The result of a veto override is that the bill becomes law against the wishes of the president.

If the president does not send a bill back to Congress after ten congressional working days, the bill becomes law without the president's signature. If the president refuses to sign the bill and Congress adjourns within ten working days after the bill has been submitted to the president, however, the bill is killed for that session of Congress. As mentioned in Chapter 11, this is called a *pocket veto*.

Presidents used the veto power sparingly until the administration of Andrew Johnson (1865–1869). Johnson vetoed twenty-one bills. Franklin D. Roosevelt (1933–1945) vetoed more bills by far than any of his predecessors or successors in the presidency. During his administration, there were 372 regular vetoes, 9 of which were overridden by Congress, and 263 pocket vetoes.

The Veto in Recent Administrations.   President George W. Bush (2001–2009) used his veto power very sparingly. Indeed, during the first six years of his presidency, Bush vetoed only one bill—a proposal to expand the scope of stem-cell research. Bush vetoed so few bills largely because the Republican-led Congress during those years strongly supported his agenda. After the Democrats took control of Congress in 2007, Bush vetoed eleven bills. Congress overrode four of the vetoes.

With a Congress led by his own party during the first two years of his presidency, President Obama faced circumstances similar to those enjoyed by George W. Bush. Consequently, in his first two years in office, Obama exercised the veto power only twice. Surprisingly, Obama issued no vetoes during the next four years even though the Republicans were in control of the House. Apparently, no measure that Obama would have opposed was able to make its way through the Democratic-controlled Senate. By mid-2016, however, with Republicans in control of the Senate, Obama had issued seven additional vetoes and was threatening more.

The Line-Item Veto.   Many presidents have complained that they cannot control "pork-barrel" legislation—federal expenditures tacked onto bills to "bring home the bacon" to a particular congressional member's district. For example, expenditures on a specific sports stadium might be added to a bill involving crime. The reason is simple: the president would have to veto the entire bill to eliminate the pork—and that might not be feasible politically. Presidents have often argued in favor of a *line-item veto* that would enable them to veto just one (or several) items in a bill. In 1996, Congress passed and President Clinton signed a line-item veto bill. In 1998, though, the Supreme Court concluded that the bill was unconstitutional.[4]

12-3b The President's Inherent Powers

In addition to the powers explicitly granted by the Constitution, the president also has *inherent powers*—powers that are necessary to carry out the specific responsibilities of the president as set forth in the Constitution.

The presidency is, of course, an institution of

> **veto** A Latin word meaning "I forbid"; the refusal by an official, such as the president of the United States or a state governor, to sign a bill into law.

President Jimmy Carter (center) with Egyptian president Anwar Sadat (left) and Israeli prime minister Menachem Begin (right) at the signing of the Camp David Accords in 1978. Since then, Egypt and Israel have remained at peace with each other. *Would negotiating such agreements help a president politically? Why or why not?*

12-3c The Expansion of Presidential Powers

The Constitution defines presidential powers in very general language, and even the founders were uncertain just how the president would perform the various functions. George Washington (1789–1797) set many of the precedents that have defined presidential power. For example, he removed officials from office, interpreting the constitutional power to appoint officials as implying power to remove them as well.[6]

Washington established the practice of meeting regularly with the heads of the three departments that then existed (plus the attorney general) and of turning to them for political advice. He set a precedent for the president to act as chief legislator by submitting proposed legislation to Congress.

Expansion under Later Presidents Abraham Lincoln (1861–1865), confronting the problems of the Civil War during the 1860s, took several important actions while Congress was not in session. He suspended certain constitutional liberties, spent funds that Congress had not appropriated, blockaded southern ports, and banned "treasonable correspondence" from the U.S. mail. Lincoln carried out all of these actions in the name of his power as commander in chief and his constitutional responsibility to "take Care that the Laws be faithfully executed."[7]

Other presidents, including Thomas Jefferson, Andrew Jackson, Woodrow Wilson, Franklin D. Roosevelt, and George W. Bush, also greatly expanded the powers of the president. The power of the president continues to evolve, depending on the person holding the office, the relative power of Congress, and events at home and abroad.

The President's Expanded Legislative Powers Congress has come to expect the president to develop a legislative program. From time to time, the president

government, but it is also an institution that consists, at any one moment in time, of one individual. That means the lines between the presidential office and the person who holds that office often become blurred. Certain presidential powers that are generally recognized today were simply assumed by strong presidents to be inherent powers of the presidency, and their successors then continued to exercise these powers.

President Woodrow Wilson clearly indicated this interplay between presidential personality and presidential powers in the following observation:

> The President is at liberty, both in law and conscience, to be as big a man as he can. His capacity will set the limit; and if Congress be overborne by him, it will be no fault of the makers of the Constitution—it will be from no lack of constitutional powers on his part, but only because the President has the nation behind him, and Congress has not.[5]

In other words, because the Constitution is vague as to the actual carrying out of presidential powers, presidents are left to define the limits of their authority—subject, of course, to obstacles raised by the other branches of government.

submits special messages on certain subjects. These messages call on Congress to enact laws that the president thinks are necessary. The president also works closely with members of Congress to persuade them to support particular programs. The president writes, telephones, and meets with various congressional leaders to discuss pending bills. The president also sends aides to lobby on Capitol Hill.

One study of the legislative process found that "no other single actor in the political system has quite the capability of the president to set agendas in given policy areas." As one lobbyist told a researcher, "Obviously, when a president sends up a bill [to Congress], it takes first place in the queue. All other bills take second place."

Outgoing President Bill Clinton addresses the troops during an awards ceremony at Fort Myer, Virginia, in January 2001. *Why do presidents enjoy visiting the troops?*

Helene C. Stikkel/U.S.Department of Defense

The Power to Persuade. The president's political skills and ability to persuade others play a large role in determining the administration's success. According to Richard Neustadt in his classic work *Presidential Power,* "Presidential power is the power to persuade."[8] For all of the resources at the president's disposal, the president still must rely on the cooperation of others if the administration's goals are to be accomplished. After three years in office, President Harry Truman made this remark about the powers of the president:

> The president may have a great many powers given to him in the Constitution and may have certain powers under certain laws which are given to him by the Congress of the United States; but the principal power that the president has is to bring people in and try to persuade them to do what they ought to do without persuasion. That's what the powers of the president amount to.[9]

Persuasive powers are particularly important when divided government exists. If a president from one political party faces a Congress dominated by the other party, the president must overcome more opposition than usual to get legislation passed.

Going Public. The president may also use a strategy known as "going public"[10]—that is, using press conferences, public appearances, and televised events to arouse public opinion in favor of certain legislative programs. The public may then pressure legislators to support the administration's programs. A president who has the support of the public can wield significant persuasive power over Congress. Presidents who are voted into office through "landslide" elections have increased bargaining power because of their widespread popularity. Those with less popular support have less bargaining leverage.

The ability of the president to "go public" effectively is dependent on popular attitudes toward the president. It is also dependent on the political climate in Washington, D.C. In periods of severe political polarization—such as the last several years—going public can actually be counterproductive. Simply by endorsing a proposal that might have had bipartisan support, the president can turn the question into a partisan issue. Without support from at least some members of both parties, the proposal then fails to pass.

The Power to Influence the Economy. Some of the greatest expansions of presidential power occurred during Franklin Roosevelt's administration. Roosevelt claimed the presidential power to regulate the economy during the Great Depression in the 1930s. Since that time, Americans have expected the president to be actively involved in economic matters and social programs. That expectation becomes especially potent during a major economic downturn, such as the Great Recession that began in December 2007.

Each year, the president sends Congress a suggested budget and the *Economic Report of the President*. The budget message proposes what amounts of money the government will need for its programs. The *Economic Report of the President* presents the state of the nation's economy and recommends ways to improve it.

Voters may rate a president based on the state of the economy. Experts have observed that the president's ability to control the level of economic activity is subject to severe limits. From the public's point of view, however, evaluating its leaders based on results makes good sense. If a president is under constant political pressure to improve the economy, he or she is likely to do whatever is possible to reach that goal. How much can a president actually do to affect the economy? We examine that question in this chapter's *Perception vs. Reality* feature.

Legislative Success. Presidents' legislative success is defined as how often they get their way on roll-call votes on which they have taken a clear position. Typically, a president's success record is very high upon first taking office and then gradually declines. This is sometimes attributed to the president's "honeymoon period," when Congress may be most likely to work with the president to achieve the president's legislative agenda.

The media often put a great deal of emphasis on how successful a president is during the "first hundred days" in office. Ironically, this is also the period when the president is least experienced in the ways of the White House, particularly if the president was a Washington outsider, such as a state governor, before becoming president.

Library of Congress

As chief diplomat, George Washington made foreign policy decisions without consulting Congress. This action laid the groundwork for an active presidential role in foreign policy.

Library of Congress

By the time Abraham Lincoln gave his Inauguration Day speech, seven southern states had already seceded from the Union. Some scholars believe that Lincoln's skillful and vigorous handling of the Civil War increased the power and prestige of the presidency.

Library of Congress

In its attempts to counter the effects of the Great Depression, Franklin D. Roosevelt's administration not only extended the role of the national government in regulating the nation's economic life, but also further increased the power of the president.

Can the President Really Fix the Economy?

Recovery from the international economic crisis that struck in 2008 has been relatively slow. Many Americans are still out of the workforce. As political scientists know, a president running for reelection often won't be reelected if the state of the economy is not improving. There is clearly a public perception that the president can engage in numerous actions to "fix the economy." So, if the economy isn't growing, it's the president's fault.

The Perception

What the president wants, the president gets. If the president has the right ideas about how to improve the economy, he or she just has to make sure that those ideas become public policy. Therefore, when millions are still out of work and wages are stagnant, clearly the president is responsible.

The Reality

What presidents say and what happens are not necessarily related. When it comes to the economy, that statement is especially true. Consider *monetary policy*—changing the amount of money in circulation to warm up or cool down the economy. Presidents have almost no control over monetary policy because the independent Federal Reserve System (Fed) carries it out. Presidents can, to be sure, "jawbone" the current head of the Fed—try to exert influence—but that is about the extent of presidential power over monetary policy.

Fiscal policy—tax rates, subsidies, decreases and increases in government spending levels—is another policy lever. People often believe that the president can control such variables. The reality is often quite the opposite.

Only Congress can pass laws that change our tax code and that change the amount of taxpayer dollars spent. This is not to say that a president is incapable of influencing tax rates and the level of government spending, but such influence does not usually go very far if one or both chambers of Congress are in the hands of the other party. This is especially true today, given high levels of political polarization. President Ronald Reagan could dramatically lower tax rates when Democrats controlled Congress, but that was another era.

President Obama was able to get an economic stimulus bill passed in 2009 because the Democrats controlled both chambers of Congress. In 2011, however, Republicans took control of the House. As a result, Obama had little influence on taxing and spending decisions. The economic recovery was strong enough to ensure Obama's reelection in 2012, but jobs, wages, and economic inequality remained powerful issues in the 2016 elections.

Blog On

To learn more about economic policy, try consulting two talented bloggers. Greg Mankiw, a Harvard economics professor, is a moderate Republican. Find him at gregmankiw.blogspot.com. Matt Yglesias is a pro-market progressive, and you can find his contributions to the Vox blog at www.vox.com/authors/matthew-yglesias.

In 2009, President Obama had the most successful legislative year of any president in half a century. Large Democratic majorities in both chambers of Congress were surely important in explaining Obama's ability to obtain the legislation that he sought. Obama was also successful in 2010. After the Democrats lost control of the U.S. House in November 2010, however, Obama's success rate fell considerably.

The Increasing Use of Executive Orders

As the nation's chief executive, the president is considered to have the inherent power to issue **executive orders**, which are presidential orders to carry out policies described in laws that have been passed by Congress. These orders have the force of law.

The Purpose of Executive Orders. Presidents have issued executive orders for a variety of purposes, including to establish procedures for appointing non-career administrators, to restructure the White House bureaucracy, and to ration consumer goods and administer wage and price controls under emergency conditions. Other goals have included classifying

executive order
A presidential order to carry out a policy or policies described in a law passed by Congress.

government information as secret, implementing affirmative action policies, and regulating the export of certain items. Presidents issue executive orders frequently, sometimes as many as one hundred a year.

Obama's Executive Orders. Obama issued fewer executive orders than other recent presidents, but he also issued more *executive memorandums* than any president in history. In practice, memorandums and orders are indistinguishable. Compared to other recent presidents, Obama's total number of executive actions—orders and memorandums—was above average. (Some earlier presidents, including Carter, Kennedy, and Truman, issued many more.) Republicans contended that some of Obama's actions exceeded his constitutional authority. They were especially critical of orders that sought to limit the deportation of unauthorized immigrants. Two such orders in late 2014 would have protected more than 4 million individuals. In 2015, a U.S. appeals court blocked these orders. Ultimately, the Supreme Court will address the issue.

Signing Statements A signing statement is a written statement issued by a president at the time he or she signs a bill into law. James Monroe (1817–1825) was the first president to issue such a statement. For many years, signing statements were rare—before the presidency of Ronald Reagan, only seventy-five were issued. Most were "rhetorical" in character. They might praise the legislation or the Congress that passed it, or criticize the opposition. On occasion, however, the statements noted constitutional problems with one or more clauses of a bill or provided details as to how the executive branch would interpret legislative language.

Reagan and Signing Statements. Reagan issued a grand total of 249 signing statements. For the first time, each statement was published in the *U.S. Code Congressional and Administrative News*, along with the text of the bill in question. A substantial share of the statements addressed constitutional issues. Reagan staff member Samuel Alito, Jr.—who now sits on the

President George W. Bush (center) looks over a brief with Vice President Dick Cheney and National Security Adviser Condoleezza Rice (later to be secretary of state). *What are some of the tools a president can use to carry out foreign policy?*

Photo Courtesy Office of White House Management

United States Supreme Court—issued a memo in favor of using signing statements to "increase the power of the Executive to shape the law."

Signing Statements under Bush. George W. Bush took the use of signing statements to an entirely new level. Bush's 161 statements challenged more than 1,100 clauses of federal law—more legal provisions than were challenged by all previous presidents put together.[11] The powers that the statements claimed for the president alarmed some people. One statement rejected Congress's authority to ban torture. Another affirmed that the president could have anyone's mail opened without a warrant. Obama reduced the number of signing statements substantially.

Evolving Presidential Power in Foreign Affairs The precise extent of the president's power in foreign affairs is constantly evolving. The president is commander in chief and chief diplomat, but only Congress has the power to formally declare war, and the Senate must ratify any treaty that the president has negotiated with other nations. Nevertheless, from the beginning, our country has been led by the president in foreign affairs.

George Washington laid the groundwork for our long history of the president's active role in foreign policy. For example, when war broke out between Britain and

signing statement
A written statement, appended to a bill at the time the president signs it into law, indicating how the president interprets that legislation.

France in 1793, Washington chose to disregard a treaty of alliance with France and to pursue a course of strict neutrality. Since that time, on many occasions presidents have taken military actions and made foreign policy without consulting Congress.

Executive Agreements. In foreign affairs, presidential power is enhanced by the ability to make **executive agreements**, which are pacts between the president and other heads of state. Executive agreements do not require Senate approval (even though Congress may refuse to appropriate the necessary money to carry out the agreements), but they have the same legal status as treaties.

Presidents form executive agreements for a wide range of purposes. Some involve routine matters, such as promises of assistance to other countries. Others concern matters of great importance. In 1940, for example, President Franklin Roosevelt formed an important executive agreement with British prime minister Winston Churchill. The agreement provided that the United States would lend American destroyers to Britain to help protect that nation and its shipping during World War II. In return, the British allowed the United States to use military and naval bases on British territories in the Western Hemisphere.

To prevent presidential abuse of the power to make executive agreements, Congress passed a law in 1972 that requires the president to inform Congress within sixty days of making any executive agreement. The law did not limit the president's power to make executive agreements, however, and they continue to be used far more than treaties in making foreign policy. For example, in 2015, the United States and five other world powers approved a deal with Iran to limit that country's ability to obtain nuclear weapons. President Obama treated the pact as an executive agreement rather than a treaty, in part because there were not enough votes in the Senate to pass it as a treaty. Needless to say, Republicans (and a few Democrats) strongly opposed this step.

Military Actions. The U.S. Constitution gives Congress the power to declare war. Consider, however, that although Congress has declared war in only five different conflicts during our nation's history,[12] the United States has engaged in more than two hundred activities involving the armed services.

> "IF ONE MORNING I WALKED ON TOP OF THE WATER ACROSS THE POTOMAC RIVER, THE HEADLINE THAT AFTERNOON WOULD READ: 'PRESIDENT CAN'T SWIM.'"
>
> ~ LYNDON B. JOHNSON, THIRTY-SIXTH PRESIDENT OF THE UNITED STATES, 1963–1969

Without a congressional declaration of war, President Truman sent U.S. armed forces to Korea in 1950, thus involving American troops in the conflict between North and South Korea. The United States also entered the Vietnam War (1965–1975) without a declaration of war. George H. W. Bush did, however, obtain congressional approval to use American troops to force Iraq to withdraw from Kuwait in 1991.

The War Powers Resolution. As commander in chief, the president can respond quickly to a military threat without waiting for congressional action. This power to involve the nation in a war upset many members of Congress as the undeclared war in Vietnam dragged on for years into the 1970s. Criticism of the president's role in the Vietnam conflict led to the passage of the War Powers Resolution of 1973.

The law, which was passed over President Nixon's veto, requires the president to notify Congress within forty-eight hours of deploying troops. It also prevents the president from keeping troops abroad for more than sixty days (or ninety days, if more time is needed for a successful withdrawal). If Congress does not authorize a longer period, the troops must be removed.

The War on Terrorism. President George W. Bush did not obtain a declaration of war from Congress for the war against terrorism that began on September 11, 2001. Instead, Congress passed a joint resolution authorizing the president to use "all necessary and appropriate force against those nations, organizations, or persons he determines planned, authorized, committed, or aided the terrorist attacks that occurred on September 11, 2001."

This resolution was the basis for America's subsequent involvement in Afghanistan. Also, in October 2002, Congress passed a joint resolution authorizing the use of U.S. armed forces against Iraq.

Obama at War. President Obama inherited conflicts in Afghanistan and Iraq, and he was more interested in winding these conflicts down than expanding them. No requests for congressional authority were

executive agreement
A binding international agreement, or pact, that is made between the president and another head of state and that does not require Senate approval.

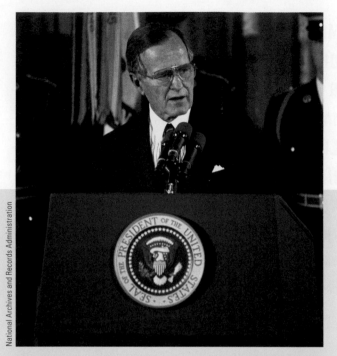

President George H. W. Bush presents a posthumous Medal of Honor. *Why did Bush order U.S. forces into combat with Iraq in 1991?*

and when to use nuclear weapons. In 1945, President Truman made the extraordinary decision to drop atomic bombs on the Japanese cities of Hiroshima and Nagasaki. "The final decision," he said, "on where and when to use the atomic bomb was up to me. Let there be no mistake about it." Today, the president travels at all times with the "football"—the briefcase containing the codes used to launch a nuclear attack.

CRITICAL THINKING

▶ *Some observers believe that it is almost impossible for the president to change the nation's policies simply by delivering a speech, no matter how important the topic. Do you think this is true? Why or why not?*

12-4 CONGRESSIONAL AND PRESIDENTIAL RELATIONS

LO Describe advantages enjoyed by Congress and by the president in their institutional relationship.

Despite the seemingly immense powers at the president's disposal, the president is limited in what he or she can accomplish, or even attempt. In our system of checks and balances, the president must share some powers with the legislative and judicial branches of government. The president's power is checked not only by these institutions, but also by the media, public opinion, and the voters. The founders hoped that this system of shared power would lessen the chance of tyranny.

Some scholars believe the relationship between Congress and the president is the most important one in the American system of government. Congress traditionally has had the upper hand in some areas, primarily in passing legislation. In some other areas, though, particularly in foreign affairs, the president can exert tremendous power that Congress has almost no ability to check.

necessary. In 2011, however, Obama used air power in Libya without congressional authorization.

In 2013, with clear reluctance, Obama asked for authority to bomb the forces of dictator Bashar al-Assad in Syria. The reason was that Assad was using poison gas against his own people. Assad later agreed to turn over his chemical weapons for destruction. This settlement was fortunate for Obama, in part because it appeared likely that Congress would refuse to give him support for military action.

Obama did not request authority to attack the terrorist group ISIS in Iraq and Syria in 2014. Some observers, contemplating Obama's request for a vote over Syria's chemical weapons and his failure to make such a request over Libya and ISIS, thought they saw a pattern. Obama was willing to seek authority for steps that he was not eager to take. For actions on which he was dead-set, he preferred to ignore Congress as much as possible.

Nuclear Weapons. Since 1945, the president, as commander in chief, has been responsible for the most difficult of all military decisions—if

"AS TO THE PRESIDENCY, THE TWO HAPPIEST DAYS OF MY LIFE WERE THOSE OF MY ENTRANCE UPON THE OFFICE AND MY SURRENDER OF IT."

~ MARTIN VAN BUREN, EIGHTH PRESIDENT OF THE UNITED STATES, 1837–1841

12-4a Advantage: Congress

Congress has the advantage over the president in the areas of legislative authorization, the regulation of foreign and interstate commerce, and some budgetary matters. Of course, as you have already read, the president today proposes a legislative agenda and a budget to Congress every year. Nonetheless, only Congress has the power to pass the legislation and appropriate the money. The most the president can do constitutionally is veto an entire bill if it contains something that she or he does not like. (As noted, however, recent presidents have frequently used signing statements in an attempt to nullify portions of bills that they did not approve.)

Presidential popularity is a source of power for the president in dealings with Congress. Presidents spend a great deal of time courting public opinion, eyeing their "presidential approval ratings," and meeting with the press. Much of this activity is for the purpose of gaining leverage with Congress. Yet even when the president puts all of his or her persuasive powers to work in achieving a legislative agenda, Congress still retains the ultimate lawmaking authority.

Divided Government When government is divided—with at least one house of Congress controlled by a different party than the White House—the president can have difficulty even getting a legislative agenda to the floor for a vote. President Barack Obama faced such a problem in 2011, when the Republicans gained a majority in the House of Representatives. During his

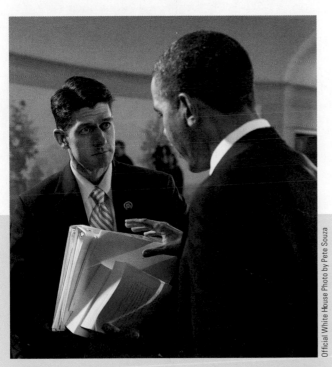

President Obama talks with Representative Paul Ryan (R., Wisc.) during a meeting on health-care reform in 2010. Ryan, later Speaker of the House, was then chair of the House Budget Committee. *What are the relative powers of Congress and the president over the budget?*

Official White House Photo by Pete Souza

first two years as president, Obama had worked with a very cooperative Democrat-led Congress. After the Republicans became the majority party in the House, however, divided government existed again. Indeed, few people in public life could remember a time when partisan hostilities had been so intense.

Different Constituencies Congress and the president have different constituencies, and this fact influences their relationship. Members of Congress represent a state or a local district, and this gives them a regional focus. As we discussed in Chapter 11, members of Congress like to have legislative successes of their own to bring home to their constituents—military bases that remain operative, public-works projects that create local jobs, or trade rules that benefit a big local employer. Ideally, the president's focus should be on the nation as a whole: national defense, homeland security, the national economy. At times, this can put the president at odds even with members of his or her own party in Congress.

Furthermore, members of Congress and the president face different election cycles (every two years in the House, every six years in the Senate, and every four years for the president), and the president is limited to two terms in office. Consequently, the president and Congress sometimes feel a different sense of urgency about implementing legislation. For example, the president often senses the need to demonstrate legislative success during the first year in office, when the excitement over the elections is still fresh in the minds of politicians and the public.

12-4b Advantage: The President

The president has the advantage over Congress in dealing with a national crisis, in setting foreign policy, and in influencing public opinion. In times of crisis, the presidency is arguably the most crucial institution in government because, when necessary, the president can act quickly, speak with one voice, and represent the nation to the world.

Some scholars have argued that recent presidents have abused the powers of the presidency by taking advantage of crises. Others have argued that there is an unwritten "doctrine of necessity" under which presidential powers can and should be expanded during a crisis. When this has happened in the past, however, Congress has always retaken some control when the crisis was over, in a natural process of institutional give-and-take.

A president is in a much stronger bargaining position if he or she has just won office in a "landslide election." Presidents elected in landslides include Reagan in 1984

President Nixon meets Chinese leader Mao Zedong. Nixon's opening to China was a foreign policy success, but his domestic abuses of power led to his resignation in 1974. *What is the mechanism by which Congress can remove a sitting president?*

(59 percent of the vote), Nixon in 1972 (61 percent), and Johnson in 1964 (also 61 percent). Given low voter turnout, however, no president has ever received the votes of a majority of all eligible adults. Johnson came closest, but even he won the votes of fewer than 40 percent of the electorate. As a result, it is questionable whether even presidents elected by a landslide can claim to have a "mandate from the people."

executive privilege
An inherent executive power claimed by presidents to withhold information from, or to refuse to appear before, Congress or the courts. The president can also accord the privilege to other executive officials.

Watergate scandal
A scandal involving an illegal break-in at the Democratic National Committee offices in 1972 by members of President Richard Nixon's reelection campaign staff.

cabinet An advisory group selected by the president to assist with decision making. Traditionally, the cabinet has consisted of the heads of the executive departments and other officers whom the president may choose to appoint.

The War on Terrorism
A problem faced during the George W. Bush administration was that the "war on terrorism" had no obvious end or conclusion. It was not clear when the crisis would be over and the nation could return to normal government relations and procedures. Many supporters of Barack Obama believed that upon election, he would restore civil liberties lost during Bush's war on terrorism. As it turned out, the Obama administration has kept most of Bush's policies in place.

Executive Privilege
As you read in Chapter 11, Congress has the authority to investigate and oversee the activities of other branches of government. Nonetheless, both Congress and the public have accepted that a certain degree of secrecy by the executive branch is necessary to protect national security. Some presidents have claimed an inherent executive power to withhold information from, or to refuse to appear before, Congress or the courts. This is called **executive privilege**, and it has been invoked by presidents from the time of George Washington to the present.

Abuses of Executive Privilege   One of the problems with executive privilege is that it has been used for more purposes than simply to safeguard national security. President Nixon invoked executive privilege in an attempt to avoid handing over taped White House conversations to Congress during the **Watergate scandal**. President Clinton invoked the privilege in an attempt to keep details of his sexual relationship with White House intern Monica Lewinsky a secret.

CRITICAL THINKING

▶ *Would we be better off if executive privilege didn't exist, or are there some matters a president must be able to keep private? Discuss.*

12–5 THE ORGANIZATION OF THE EXECUTIVE BRANCH

LO Discuss the organization of the executive branch and the role of cabinet members in presidential administrations.

In the early days of this nation, presidents answered their own mail. Only in 1857 did Congress authorize a private secretary for the president, to be paid by the federal government. Even Woodrow Wilson typed most of his correspondence, although by that time several secretaries were assigned to the president. When Franklin Roosevelt became president in 1933, the entire staff consisted of thirty-seven employees. Not until Roosevelt's New Deal and World War II did the presidential staff become a sizable organization.

12–5a The President's Cabinet

The Constitution does not specifically mention presidential assistants and advisers. The Constitution states only that the president "may require the Opinion, in writing, of the principal Officer in each of the executive Departments." Since the time of our first president, however, presidents have had an advisory group, or **cabinet**, to turn to for counsel. Originally, the cabinet consisted of only four officials—the secretaries of state, treasury, and war, plus the attorney general.

Today, the cabinet includes fourteen department secretaries, the attorney general, and a number of other officials. (See Table 12–2 for the names of the major executive departments represented in the cabinet.) Additional cabinet members vary from one presidency to the next. Typically, the vice president is a member. President Clinton added ten officials to the cabinet, and George W. Bush added five. Barack Obama added the following members, in addition to the vice president:

▶ **The administrator of the Environmental Protection Agency.**

▶ **The administrator of the Small Business Administration.**

▶ **The chair of the Council of Economic Advisers.**

▶ **The director of the Office of Management and Budget.**

▶ **The United States ambassador to the United Nations.**

TABLE 12–2   THE MAJOR EXECUTIVE DEPARTMENTS

The heads of all of these departments are members of the president's cabinet.

Department	Year of First Establishment
Department of State	1789
Department of the Treasury	1789
Department of Defense*	1789
Department of Justice (headed by the attorney general)†	1789
Department of the Interior	1849
Department of Agriculture	1889
Department of Commerce‡	1903
Department of Labor‡	1903
Department of Health and Human Services§	1953
Department of Housing and Urban Development	1965
Department of Transportation	1967
Department of Energy	1977
Department of Education	1979
Department of Veterans Affairs	1989
Department of Homeland Security	2002

*Established in 1947 by merging the Department of War, created in 1789, and the Department of the Navy, created in 1798.

†Formerly the Office of the Attorney General; renamed and reorganized in 1870.

‡Formed in 1913 by splitting the Department of Commerce and Labor, which was created in 1903.

§Formerly the Department of Health, Education, and Welfare; renamed when the Department of Education was spun off in 1979.

▶ **The United States trade representative.**

▶ **The White House chief of staff.**

Use of the Cabinet   Because the Constitution does not require the president to consult with the cabinet, the use of this body is purely discretionary. Some presidents have relied on the counsel of their cabinets more than others. After a cabinet meeting in which a vote was seven nays against his one aye, President Lincoln supposedly said, "Seven nays and one aye, the ayes have it."[13]

Still other presidents have sought counsel from so-called **kitchen cabinets**, informal groups of unofficial advisers. The term *kitchen cabinet* originated during the presidency of Andrew Jackson, who relied on the counsel of close friends who allegedly met with him in the kitchen of the White House.

In general, presidents usually don't rely heavily on the advice of the formal cabinet. They are aware that department heads are often more responsive to the wishes of their own staffs, to their own political ambitions, or to obtaining resources for their departments than they are to the presidents they serve.

Obama's "Czars"   President Obama's response to the need to seek advice was to centralize the advisory function within the White House Office (discussed below) by appointing a large number of in-house "czars." Each of these White House czars has responsibility for a certain policy area.

Critics of the Obama administration believe that the czar system tends to undercut the authority of cabinet members. Congress also loses leverage, because cabinet members must be confirmed by the Senate, whereas czars are responsible only to the president.

12–5b The Executive Office of the President

In 1939, President Franklin Roosevelt set up the **Executive Office of the President (EOP)** to cope with the increased responsibilities brought on by the Great Depression. Since then, the EOP has grown significantly to accommodate the increasingly expansive role played by the national government, including the executive branch, in the nation's economic and social life.

The EOP is made up of the top advisers and

kitchen cabinet The name given to a president's unofficial advisers. The term was coined during Andrew Jackson's presidency.

Executive Office of the President (EOP) A group of staff agencies that assist the president in carrying out major duties.

assistants who help the president carry out major duties. Over the years, the EOP has changed according to the needs and leadership style of each president. It has become an increasingly influential and important part of the executive branch.

Table 12–3 lists various offices within the EOP as of 2016. Note that the organization of the EOP is subject to change. Presidents have frequently added new bodies to its membership and subtracted others. President Obama made a number of changes to the EOP's table of organization during his years in office.

The White House Office Of all of the executive staff agencies, the White House Office has the most direct contact with the president. The White House Office is headed by the **chief of staff**, who advises the president on important matters and directs the operations of the presidential staff. A number of other top officials, assistants, and special assistants to the president also provide aid in such areas as national security, the economy, and political affairs. The **press secretary** meets with reporters and makes public statements for the president. The counsel to the president serves as the White House lawyer and handles the president's legal matters.

The White House staff also includes speechwriters, researchers, the president's physician, and a correspondence secretary. Altogether, the White House Office has more than four hundred employees.

TABLE 12–3	THE EXECUTIVE OFFICE OF THE PRESIDENT AS OF 2016
Agency	
Council of Economic Advisers	
Council on Environmental Quality	
Executive Residence	
National Security Council	
Office of Administration	
Office of Management and Budget	
Office of National Drug Control Policy	
Office of Science and Technology Policy	
Office of the U.S. Trade Representative	
Office of the Vice President	
White House Office	

Source: www.whitehouse.gov.

The White House staff has several duties. First, the staff investigates and analyzes problems that require the president's attention. Staff members who are specialists in certain areas, such as diplomatic relations or foreign trade, gather information for the president and suggest solutions. White House staff members also screen the questions, issues, and problems that people present to the president, so matters that can be handled by other officials do not reach the president's desk.

White House Office
The personal office of the president. White House Office personnel handle the president's political needs and manage the media, among other duties.

chief of staff The person who directs the operations of the White House Office and advises the president on important matters.

press secretary
A member of the White House staff who holds news conferences for reporters and makes public statements for the president.

© Official White House Photo by Pete Souza

President Barack Obama, Vice President Joe Biden, then–Secretary of State Hillary Clinton, and members of the national security team receive an update on the mission against Osama bin Laden in the Situation Room of the White House on May 1, 2011. *What happened to bin Laden?*

Additionally, the staff provides public relations support. For example, the press staff handles the president's relations with the White House press corps and schedules news conferences. Finally, the White House staff ensures that the president's initiatives are effectively transmitted to the relevant government personnel. Several staff members are usually assigned to work directly with members of Congress for this purpose.

The First Lady The White House Office also includes the staff of the president's spouse. First Ladies have at times taken important roles within the White House. For example, Franklin Roosevelt's wife, Eleanor, advocated the rights of women, labor, and African Americans. As First Lady, Hillary Clinton helped develop an unsuccessful plan for a national health-care system. If she had won the 2016 elections, Bill Clinton would have become the nation's First Gentleman.

The Office of Management and Budget The **Office of Management and Budget (OMB)** was originally the Bureau of the Budget. Under recent presidents, the OMB has become an important and influential unit of the Executive Office of the President. The main function of the OMB is to assist the president in preparing the proposed annual budget, which the president must submit to Congress in January of each year (see Chapter 11 for details).

The federal budget lists the revenues and expenditures expected for the coming year. It indicates which programs the federal government will pay for and how much they will cost. Thus, the budget is an annual statement of the public policies of the United States translated into dollars and cents. Making changes in the budget is a key way for presidents to influence the direction and policies of the federal government.

The president appoints the director of the OMB with the consent of the Senate. The director oversees the OMB's work and argues the administration's positions before Congress. The director also lobbies members of Congress to support the president's budget or to accept key features of it. Once the budget is approved by Congress, the OMB has the responsibility of putting it into practice. The OMB oversees the execution of the budget, checking on federal agencies to ensure that they use funds efficiently.

Beyond its budget duties, the OMB also reviews new bills prepared by the executive branch. It checks all legislative matters to be certain that they agree with the president's own positions.

The National Security Council The **National Security Council (NSC)** was established in 1947 to manage the domestic and foreign policies regarding the defense of the United States. Its members are the

Vice President Mike Pence speaks to supporters at a rally in Chesterfield, Missouri. *What powers does he have under the Constitution?*

president, the vice president, and the secretaries of state and defense. It also includes several informal advisers. The NSC is the president's link to his or her key foreign and military advisers. The president's special assistant for national security affairs (commonly called the national security adviser) heads the NSC staff.

12–5c The Vice Presidency and Presidential Succession

As a rule, presidential nominees choose running mates who balance the ticket or whose appointment rewards or appeases party factions. For example, to balance the ticket geographically, a presidential candidate from the South may solicit a running mate from the West.

In 2008, Barack Obama picked Delaware senator Joe Biden, who had thirty-five years of experience in Congress. Obama wished

Office of Management and Budget (OMB) An agency in the Executive Office of the President that has the primary duty of assisting the president in preparing and supervising the administration of the federal budget.

National Security Council (NSC) A council that advises the president on domestic and foreign matters concerning the safety and defense of the nation.

to counter detractors who claimed that he was too inexperienced.

In 2012, Republican presidential candidate Mitt Romney chose Representative Paul Ryan of Wisconsin to join his ticket. Ryan helped Romney appeal to the party's conservative wing. Ryan had gained recognition as chair of the House Budget Committee when he authored a series of proposed budgets that won near-universal Republican support.

In July 2016, on the eve of the national party conventions, Donald Trump named Indiana governor Mike Pence as his running mate. Pence was as conventional as it is possible for a Republican to be, and he was clearly meant to balance the very unconventional Trump. One week later, Hillary Clinton named Virginia senator and former governor Tim Kaine to complete her ticket. Fluent in Spanish, Kaine began his legal career by representing African Americans in housing discrimination cases.

The Role of Vice Presidents For much of our history, the vice president has had almost no responsibilities. Still, the vice president is in a position to become the nation's chief executive should the president die, be impeached and convicted, or resign the presidential office. Nine vice presidents have become president because of the death or resignation of the president.

In recent years, the responsibilities of the vice president have grown immensely. The vice president has become one of the most—if not *the* most—important of the president's advisers. The first modern vice president to act as a major adviser was Walter Mondale, who served under Jimmy Carter. Later, Bill Clinton relied heavily on Vice President Al Gore, who shared many of Clinton's values and beliefs.

Without question, however, the most powerful vice president in American history was Dick Cheney, who served under George W. Bush. The unprecedented delegation of power that Cheney enjoyed would not have been possible without the president's agreement, and Bush clearly approved of it. Vice President Joe Biden has been one of President Barack Obama's most important advisers, but not at the level of Cheney.

Presidential Succession One of the questions left unanswered by the Constitution was what the vice president should do if the president becomes incapable of carrying out necessary duties while in office. The Twenty-fifth Amendment to the Constitution, ratified in 1967, filled this gap.

The Twenty-fifth Amendment. The amendment states that when the president believes that he or she is

Lyndon B. Johnson is sworn in as U.S. president aboard Air Force One on November 22, 1963, shortly after the assassination of President John F. Kennedy in Dallas, Texas. Standing to the right is Kennedy's widow, Jacqueline Kennedy. To the left, behind Johnson, is his wife, Lady Bird Johnson. *How often have U.S. presidents been assassinated?*

White House Photo Office, LBJ Library photo by Cecil Stoughton incapable of performing the duties of the office, he or she must inform Congress in writing of this fact. When the president is unable to communicate, a majority of the cabinet, including the vice president, can declare that fact to Congress.

In either case, the vice president then serves as acting president until the president resumes normal duties. If a dispute arises over the return of the president's ability to discharge the normal functions of the presidential office, a two-thirds vote of both chambers of Congress is required if the vice president is to remain acting president. Otherwise, the president resumes these duties.

Vice-Presidential Vacancies. The Twenty-fifth Amendment also addresses the question of how the president should fill a vacant vice presidency. Section 2 of the amendment states, "Whenever there is a vacancy in the office of the Vice President, the President shall nominate a Vice President who shall take office upon confirmation by a majority vote of both Houses of Congress."

In 1973, Gerald Ford became the first appointed vice president of the United States after Spiro Agnew was forced to resign. One year later, President Richard Nixon resigned, and Ford advanced to the office of president. President Ford named Nelson Rockefeller as his vice president. For the first time in U.S. history, neither the president nor the vice president had been elected to his position.

What if both the president and the vice president die, resign, or are disabled? According to the Succession Act of 1947, the Speaker of the House of Representatives will then act as president on her or his resignation as Speaker and as representative. If the Speaker is unavailable, next in line is the president pro tem of the Senate, followed by the permanent members of the president's cabinet in the order of the creation of their departments (see Table 12–2 earlier in this chapter).

CRITICAL THINKING

▶ *Members of the Washington political community often harbor a degree of resentment toward those who work in the White House Office. What might cause these feelings?*

AMERICA AT ODDS | The Presidency

The president is the most conspicuous figure in our political system. Everyone has opinions about what the president should do—and in a presidential election year, who the president should be. To an extent not seen in regard to other offices, the public also has a serious interest in the president's personality and character. The president, after all, represents all of us. Americans are at odds over a variety of questions relating to the presidency. These include the following:

- *Should the president try, whenever possible, to compromise with other political players, such as the Congress—or should the president generally stand on principle?*

- *Should the president seek to expand his or her authority so as to deal more effectively with the nation's problems—or should the president try to adhere to a strict constitutional understanding of the powers of the office?*

- *Is it appropriate for the president to rely primarily on staff members within the White House Office when determining*

- *policy—or should the president offer the cabinet a substantial policymaking role?*

- *Should voters evaluate presidential candidates primarily on the positions they take on the issues—or are the president's character, personality, and decision-making style more important considerations?*

- *Should the president be the "moral leader" of the country in the sense of basing policies on religious values—or should the president avoid any intermingling of religion and policy?*

STUDY TOOLS 12

READY TO STUDY? IN THE BOOK, YOU CAN:

☐ Review what you've read with the following chapter quiz.

☐ Check your answers in Appendix D at the back of the book.

☐ Rip out the Chapter Review Card, which includes key terms and chapter summaries.

ONLINE AT WWW.CENGAGEBRAIN.COM, YOU CAN:

☐ Learn about presidential responsibilities in a short video.

☐ Explore various online resources in the National Archives and Gallup poll websites in the Internet Resources tool.

☐ Interact with figures from the text, and watch quick animation clips.

☐ Prepare for tests with quizzes.

☐ Review the key terms with Flash Cards.

FILL-IN

Learning Outcome 12–1

1. The most common previous occupation of U.S. presidents has been _____.

Learning Outcome 12–2

2. The president leads the nation's armed forces in his or her role as _____.

3. In his or her role as _____, the president delivers the traditional State of the Union address and has the power to veto bills passed by Congress.

Learning Outcome 12–3

4. The president has the power to issue executive orders, which are _____.

5. The _____ requires the president to notify Congress within forty-eight hours of deploying troops.

Learning Outcome 12–4

6. Executive privilege is _____.

Learning Outcome 12–5

7. Traditionally, the cabinet has consisted of _____.

8. The Executive Office of the President (EOP) is made up of a number of executive staff agencies, including the _____.

MULTIPLE CHOICE

Learning Outcome 12–1

9. Which of the following is a constitutional requirement for becoming president of the United States?
   a. Must be at least thirty years old.
   b. Must be of sound moral character.
   c. Must be a natural born citizen of the United States.

Learning Outcome 12–2

10. When the president _____, he or she is performing the role of head of state.
    a. attends party fund-raisers
    b. makes executive agreements
    c. receives foreign dignitaries

11. When the president negotiates and signs treaties with other nations, he or she is performing the role of
    a. chief diplomat.
    b. chief executive.
    c. commander in chief.

Learning Outcome 12–3

12. The presidential strategy known as "going public" refers to
    a. using press conferences, public appearances, and televised events to arouse public opinion in favor of certain legislative programs.
    b. publicly acknowledging mistakes or misconduct.
    c. appearing on talk shows.

Learning Outcome 12–4

13. The term *divided government* refers to the
    a. cultural and political differences between the red states and the blue states.
    b. case when at least one chamber of Congress is held by a different party than the White House.
    c. separation of powers.

Learning Outcome 12–5

14. If a vacancy occurs in the vice presidency,
    a. there is currently no provision for filling the office.
    b. the Speaker of the House acts as vice president.
    c. a vice president is nominated by the president and confirmed by a majority vote in both chambers of Congress.

13 THE BUREAUCRACY

LEARNING OUTCOMES *After reading this chapter, you should be able to:*

13-1 Describe the size and functions of the U.S. bureaucracy and the major components of federal spending.

13-2 Discuss the structure and basic components of the federal bureaucracy.

13-3 Describe how the federal civil service was established and how bureaucrats get their jobs.

13-4 Explain how regulatory agencies make rules and how issue networks affect policymaking in government.

13-5 Identify some of the ways in which the government has attempted to curb waste and improve efficiency in the bureaucracy.

After finishing this chapter, go to **PAGE 308** for **STUDY TOOLS.**

AMERICA AT ODDS | Is Federal Regulation Excessive?

dizain/Shutterstock

Many people believe that the financial crisis of 2008 and 2009 was caused by inadequate regulation of financial enterprises. As a result, these businesses took on far too much risk. It's not surprising, therefore, that Congress later imposed a large number of new regulations on the financial industry. Compliance has been costly.

In the distant past, there was very little government regulation of American business. Take the health-care industry, for example. A hundred years ago, drugs were not tested before they were put on the market. Physicians were licensed by the states, but that was about it.

Today, regulation is widespread. Estimates of its costs vary dramatically. According to the Office of Management and Budget (OMB), the annual cost of federal regulations lies between $68 billion and $103 billion, with total benefits of $261 billion to $981 billion. Others argue that the OMB's sums are not comprehensive. One study quoted by conservatives puts total costs at $2.03 trillion per year. Liberals do not find this figure credible—it puts the costs at 11 percent of the entire economy. Whatever the true costs are, the question remains: Are current levels of regulation appropriate?

Unbridled Capitalism Is Dead

The law of the capitalist jungle is what got us into the biggest financial crisis since the Great Depression. Investment banking firms created ever-riskier financial assets, which they sold to naive individuals and even to local governments as solid, gold-plated investments. In the mortgage industry, unethical salespeople who earned big commissions tricked unsuspecting families into buying homes that were too expensive for their modest means. These problems were largely due to an absence of proper regulation.

Even with something as important as the prescription drugs that we take, the government is not giving us enough protection. Recently, despite its staff members' misgivings, the Food and Drug Administration (FDA) allowed a drug named Avandia to hit the market. That drug turned out to have potential cardiac side effects, and no safety statement on the drug's label warned of them. We need more regulation to protect our lives and our pocketbooks.

Too Much of Anything Is Bad

Many believe that regulation today is too costly relative to the benefits received. The Consumer Product Safety Commission requires that warning labels appear even on common products. A standard ladder has six hundred words of warning pasted on it, including a warning not to place it in front of a swinging door. What are we—idiots?

Excessive regulation can have harmful effects other than the costs of compliance. One is slower economic growth. Big businesses have more resources to respond to complicated regulations than small ones do. But jobs are created when new, small businesses can grow. If the costs of regulation cripple small businesses, consumers won't be able to enjoy their products—and big businesses can avoid competition that might drive down prices. Regulation also opens the door to abuses. Consider LabMD, a small medical data firm that spent vast sums fighting off an FDA investigation. An administrative law judge eventually found LabMD blameless, but by then it was out of business.

Where do you stand?

1. How much do you think you benefit from regulation in our economy? Give some examples.

2. Are there any circumstances under which warning labels on consumer products could help you? Give some examples.

Explore this issue online:

• Type "approving drugs quickly" into any search engine. The results will include arguments for and against the FDA's "Fast Track Development Program" for drugs.

• ProcCon.org provides arguments on both sides of many issues, including regulatory questions. The section "Health and Medicine" is especially relevant to regulation.

INTRODUCTION

Did you eat breakfast this morning? If you did, **bureaucrats**—individuals who work in the offices of the government bureaucracy—had a lot to do with that breakfast.

If you had bacon, the meat was inspected by federal agents. If you drank milk, the price was affected by rules and regulations of the Department of Agriculture. If you looked at a cereal box, you saw fine print about fat and vitamins, which was the result of regulations made by several other federal agencies, including the Food and Drug Administration. If you ate leftover pizza for breakfast, state or local inspectors made sure that the kitchen of the pizza eatery was sanitary and safe. Other bureaucrats ensured that the employees who put together (and perhaps delivered) the pizza were protected against discrimination in the workplace.

Government employees deliver our mail, clean our streets, teach in our public schools, run our national parks, and attempt to ensure the safety of our food and the prescription drugs that we take. Life as we know it would be quite different without the bureaucrats who keep our governments—federal, state, and local—in operation. Still, Americans differ about the positive and negative aspects of various federal bureaucracies, as discussed in the chapter-opening *America at Odds* feature.

13-1 THE NATURE AND SIZE OF THE BUREAUCRACY

LO Describe the size and functions of the U.S. bureaucracy and the major components of federal spending.

Today, the word *bureaucracy* often evokes a negative reaction. For some, it conjures up visions of depersonalized automatons performing chores without any sensitivity toward the needs of those they serve. For others, it is synonymous with government "red tape." A **bureaucracy**, however, is simply a large, complex administrative organization that is structured hierarchically in a pyramid-like fashion.[1] Government bureaucrats carry out the policies of elected government officials.

bureaucrat An individual who works in a bureaucracy. As generally used, the term refers to a government employee.

bureaucracy A large, complex, hierarchically structured administrative organization that carries out specific functions.

The concept of a bureaucracy is not confined to the federal government. Any large organization must have a bureaucracy. In each bureaucracy, everybody (except the head of the bureaucracy) reports to at least one other person. In the federal government, the head of the bureaucracy is the president of the United States, and the bureaucracy is part of the executive branch.[2]

13-1a The Uses of Bureaucracy

A bureaucratic form of organization allows each person to concentrate on her or his area of knowledge and expertise. In your college or university, for example, you do not expect the basketball coach to solve the problems of the finance office. The reason the federal government bureaucracy exists is that Congress, over time, has delegated certain tasks to specialists.

For example, in 1914 Congress passed the Federal Trade Commission Act, which established the Federal Trade Commission to regulate deceptive and unfair trade practices. Those appointed to the commission were specialists in that area. Similarly, Congress passed the Consumer Product Safety Act in 1972, which established the Consumer Product Safety Commission to investigate the safety of consumer products. The commission is one of many federal administrative agencies.

Another key aspect of any bureaucracy is that the power to act resides in the *position* rather than in the *person.* In your college or university, the person who is president now has more or less the same authority as any previous president. Additionally, bureaucracies usually entail *standard operating procedures*—directives on what procedures should be followed in specific circumstances. Bureaucracies normally also have a merit system, meaning that people are hired and promoted on the basis of demonstrated skills and achievements.

13-1b The Growth of Bureaucracy

The federal government that existed in 1789 was small. It had three departments, each with only a few employees: (1) the Department of State (nine employees), (2) the Department of War (two employees), and (3) the Department of the Treasury (thirty-nine employees). By 1798, nine years later, the federal bureaucracy was still quite small. The secretary of state had seven clerks. His total expenditures on stationery and printing amounted to $500, or about $10,240 in 2017 dollars. The Department of War spent, on average, a grand total of $1.4 million each year, or about $28.6 million in 2017 dollars.

Growing Government Employment Times have changed. Figure 13–1 shows the number of government employees at the local, state, and national levels from 1959 to 2016 as a percentage of the total U.S. population. Most growth has been at the state and local levels. All in all, the three levels of government employ about 16 percent of the civilian labor force. Today, more Americans are employed by government (at all three levels) than by the entire manufacturing sector of the U.S. economy.

As you examine Figure 13–1, you will notice a substantial increase in government employment relative to the population from 1959 up to about 1980. During those years, the absolute number of government workers nearly doubled. Government employment has been more stable since 1980, when Republican Ronald Reagan was elected president.

The Impact of President Reagan Indeed, during Reagan's first four years in office, government employment fell. Most of this decrease was at the local level. The drop was caused in part by the recession of 1980–1982 and in part by the elimination of revenue sharing. This program had transferred large sums from the federal government to state and especially local governments. The loss of government jobs was made up in Reagan's second term, but the rapid rise in government employment relative to population seen before 1980 did not return.

Recently, government employment has once again dropped, in absolute as well as relative terms. President Obama's 2009 stimulus program, which transferred large sums to local governments, helped stabilize government employment through 2010. By 2016, however, almost 750,000 fewer people worked for the various levels of government. Most of those who lost their jobs had worked at the local level. It is also notable that the United States Postal Service shed more than 200,000 jobs between 2006 and 2016.

13-1c The Costs of Maintaining the Government

The costs of maintaining the government are high and growing. In 1929, government at all levels accounted for about 11 percent of the nation's gross domestic product (GDP). Today, that figure is about 36 percent. Average

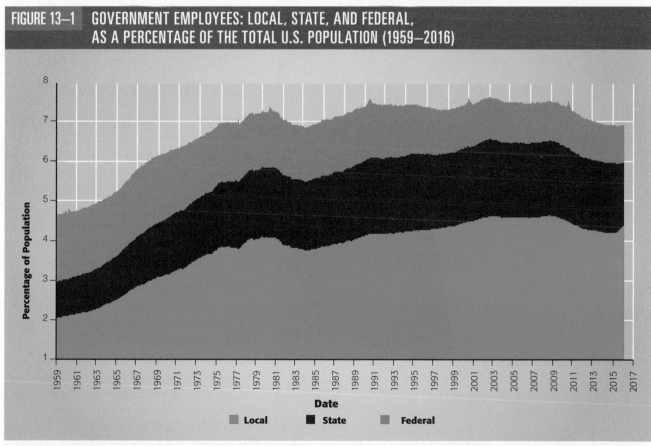

FIGURE 13–1 GOVERNMENT EMPLOYEES: LOCAL, STATE, AND FEDERAL, AS A PERCENTAGE OF THE TOTAL U.S. POPULATION (1959–2016)

The number of local government employees has the greatest effect on total government employment. The brief spikes in 1980, 1990, 2000, and 2010 represent temporary federal census workers.

Source: The Federal Reserve Economic Data (FRED) service of the St. Louis Federal Reserve.

citizens pay a significant portion of their income to federal, state, and local governments. They do this by paying income taxes, sales taxes, property taxes, and many other types of taxes and fees.

As of 2017, the individual income tax—and taxes that are collected along with it, such as the capital gains tax—make up 43 percent of the federal government's revenues. The corporate income tax adds another 10 percent. Income from the Social Security and Medicare taxes contributes about 26 percent. All other taxes and revenue sources come to 9 percent. That leaves 12 percent of the budget to be funded by borrowing. That amount is down considerably from the depths of the latest recession, but is still high by historical standards. Figure 13–2 illustrates major sources of federal revenue.

The government is costly, to be sure, but it also provides numerous services for Americans. Cutting back on the size of government inevitably means a reduction in those services. The trade-off between government spending and popular services has been central to American politics throughout our history.

13-1d Where Does All the Money Go?

It is worth examining where federal spending actually goes. If you ask people on the street, you will get varied responses—from too much spent on welfare to too much spent on foreign aid. As it turns out, neither of those categories makes up a very large percentage of federal government spending. Consider Figure 13–3.

Social Spending   As you can see in Figure 13–3, over half of the federal budget consists of various social programs. Some of these programs, such as Social Security and Medicare, are funded by payroll taxes and paid out to all qualifying persons, regardless of income. Together, these two programs make up 40 percent of the federal budget.

Other programs, including Medicaid and the Supplemental Nutrition Assistance Program (SNAP, formerly "food stamps"), are available only to low-income individuals. Medicaid, the Children's Health Insurance Program (CHIP), and miscellaneous low-income and disability support programs account for 22 percent of spending. Temporary Assistance for Needy Families (TANF)—traditional cash welfare—accounts for only 0.4 percent of the federal budget—$17 billion. It is completely overshadowed within the "miscellaneous" pie slice by disability payments, SNAP, and the Earned Income Tax Credit (EITC) program.

Defense   Defense spending is a big number—with veterans' benefits, it amounts to about a fifth of the whole. The wars in Iraq and Afghanistan were obviously expensive. One recent estimate of their cost was $170 billion a year, or 4.6 percent of the total. That is serious money, but it's not really "busting the bank." Furthermore, spending on wars has fallen.

Everything Else   At 12 percent of the total, "everything else" includes a vast range of programs. One example is military and economic foreign aid, at 1.4 percent of the total, or $56 billion. That's a substantial sum, but it is less than many people imagine it to be. One item that bears watching is the interest on the national debt—the interest currently is about $303 billion per year. Federal budget deficits will cause this figure to grow in future years.

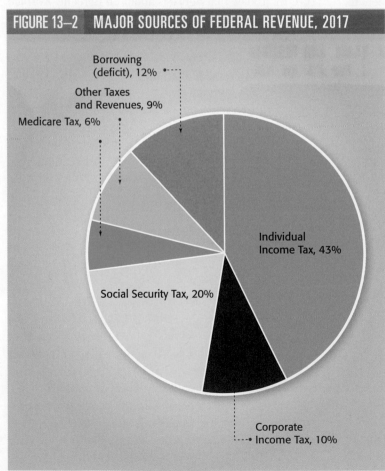

FIGURE 13–2   MAJOR SOURCES OF FEDERAL REVENUE, 2017

Borrowing (deficit), 12%
Other Taxes and Revenues, 9%
Medicare Tax, 6%
Individual Income Tax, 43%
Social Security Tax, 20%
Corporate Income Tax, 10%

Source: www.usgovernmentrevenue.com

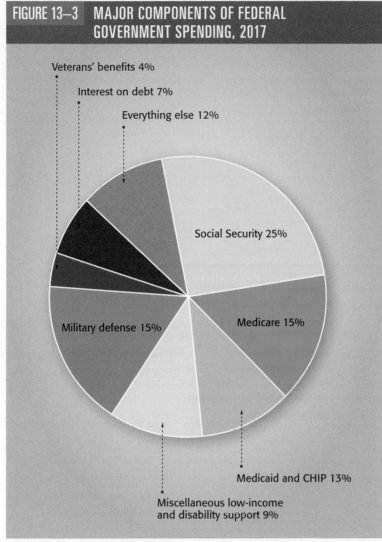

FIGURE 13–3 MAJOR COMPONENTS OF FEDERAL GOVERNMENT SPENDING, 2017

Veterans' benefits 4%

Interest on debt 7%

Everything else 12%

Social Security 25%

Military defense 15%

Medicare 15%

Medicaid and CHIP 13%

Miscellaneous low-income and disability support 9%

Source: www.usgovernmentdebt.us

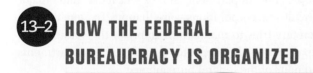

CRITICAL THINKING

▶ *Does your college or university have a bureaucracy? What does it do?*

13–2 HOW THE FEDERAL BUREAUCRACY IS ORGANIZED

LO Discuss the structure and basic components of the federal bureaucracy.

A complete organization chart of the federal government would cover an entire wall. A simplified version is provided in Figure 13–4. The executive branch consists of a number of bureaucracies that provide services to Congress, to the federal courts, and to the president directly.

The executive branch of the federal government includes four major types of structures:

▶ **Executive departments.**

▶ **Independent executive agencies.**

▶ **Independent regulatory agencies.**

▶ **Government corporations.**

Each type of structure has its own relationship to the president and its own internal workings.

13–2a The Executive Departments

You were introduced to the various executive departments in Chapter 12, when you read about how the president works with the cabinet and other close advisers. The fifteen executive departments, which are directly accountable to the president, are the major service organizations of the federal government. They are responsible for performing government functions such as training troops (Department of Defense), printing currency (Department of the Treasury), and enforcing federal laws setting minimum safety and health standards for workers (Department of Labor).

Table 13–1 provides an overview of each of the departments within the executive branch. The table lists a few of the many activities undertaken by each department. Because the president appoints the department heads, they are expected to help carry out the president's policy objectives. Often, they attempt to maximize the president's political successes as well.

Each executive department was created by Congress as the perceived need for it arose, and each department manages a specific policy area. In 2002, for example, Congress created the Department of Homeland Security to deal with terrorism and other threats. The head of each department is known as the secretary, except for the Department of Justice, which is headed by the attorney general. Each department head is appointed by the president and confirmed by the Senate.

FIGURE 13–4　THE ORGANIZATION OF THE FEDERAL GOVERNMENT

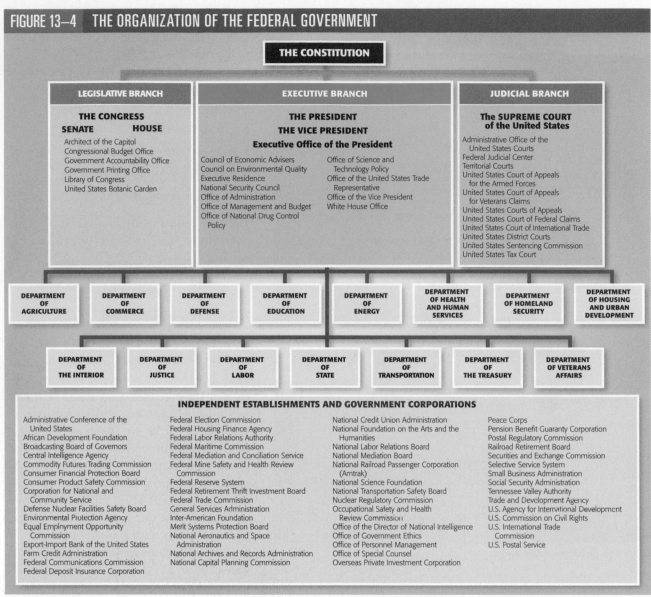

THE CONSTITUTION

LEGISLATIVE BRANCH

THE CONGRESS
SENATE　　HOUSE

Architect of the Capitol
Congressional Budget Office
Government Accountability Office
Government Printing Office
Library of Congress
United States Botanic Garden

EXECUTIVE BRANCH

THE PRESIDENT
THE VICE PRESIDENT
Executive Office of the President

Council of Economic Advisers
Council on Environmental Quality
Executive Residence
National Security Council
Office of Administration
Office of Management and Budget
Office of National Drug Control
　Policy

Office of Science and
　Technology Policy
Office of the United States Trade
　Representative
Office of the Vice President
White House Office

JUDICIAL BRANCH

The SUPREME COURT
of the United States

Administrative Office of the
　United States Courts
Federal Judicial Center
Territorial Courts
United States Court of Appeals
　for the Armed Forces
United States Court of Appeals
　for Veterans Claims
United States Courts of Appeals
United States Court of Federal Claims
United States Court of International Trade
United States District Courts
United States Sentencing Commission
United States Tax Court

DEPARTMENT OF AGRICULTURE | DEPARTMENT OF COMMERCE | DEPARTMENT OF DEFENSE | DEPARTMENT OF EDUCATION | DEPARTMENT OF ENERGY | DEPARTMENT OF HEALTH AND HUMAN SERVICES | DEPARTMENT OF HOMELAND SECURITY | DEPARTMENT OF HOUSING AND URBAN DEVELOPMENT

DEPARTMENT OF THE INTERIOR | DEPARTMENT OF JUSTICE | DEPARTMENT OF LABOR | DEPARTMENT OF STATE | DEPARTMENT OF TRANSPORTATION | DEPARTMENT OF THE TREASURY | DEPARTMENT OF VETERANS AFFAIRS

INDEPENDENT ESTABLISHMENTS AND GOVERNMENT CORPORATIONS

Administrative Conference of the
　United States
African Development Foundation
Broadcasting Board of Governors
Central Intelligence Agency
Commodity Futures Trading Commission
Consumer Financial Protection Board
Consumer Product Safety Commission
Corporation for National and
　Community Service
Defense Nuclear Facilities Safety Board
Environmental Protection Agency
Equal Employment Opportunity
　Commission
Export-Import Bank of the United States
Farm Credit Administration
Federal Communications Commission
Federal Deposit Insurance Corporation

Federal Election Commission
Federal Housing Finance Agency
Federal Labor Relations Authority
Federal Maritime Commission
Federal Mediation and Conciliation Service
Federal Mine Safety and Health Review
　Commission
Federal Reserve System
Federal Retirement Thrift Investment Board
Federal Trade Commission
General Services Administration
Inter-American Foundation
Merit Systems Protection Board
National Aeronautics and Space
　Administration
National Archives and Records Administration
National Capital Planning Commission

National Credit Union Administration
National Foundation on the Arts and the
　Humanities
National Labor Relations Board
National Mediation Board
National Railroad Passenger Corporation
　(Amtrak)
National Science Foundation
National Transportation Safety Board
Nuclear Regulatory Commission
Occupational Safety and Health
　Review Commission
Office of the Director of National Intelligence
Office of Government Ethics
Office of Personnel Management
Office of Special Counsel
Overseas Private Investment Corporation

Peace Corps
Pension Benefit Guaranty Corporation
Postal Regulatory Commission
Railroad Retirement Board
Securities and Exchange Commission
Selective Service System
Small Business Administration
Social Security Administration
Tennessee Valley Authority
Trade and Development Agency
U.S. Agency for International Development
U.S. Commission on Civil Rights
U.S. International Trade
　Commission
U.S. Postal Service

Sources: *United States Government Manual 2016* (www.usgovernmentmanual.gov); and www.whitehouse.gov.

13–2b A Typical Departmental Structure

Each cabinet department consists of the department's top administrators (the secretary of the department, deputy secretary, undersecretaries, and the like), plus a number of subagencies. For example, the National Park Service is a subagency within the Department of the Interior. The Drug Enforcement Administration is a subagency within the Department of Justice.

Although there are organizational differences among the departments, each department generally follows a typical hierarchical bureaucratic structure.

One aspect of the secretary of agriculture's job is to carry out the president's agricultural policies. Another aspect is to promote and protect the department. The secretary spends time ensuring that Congress allocates enough money for the department to work effectively. The secretary also makes sure that constituents, or the people the department serves—farmers and major agricultural corporations—are happy. In general, the secretary tries to maintain or improve the status of the department with respect to all of the other departments and units of the federal bureaucracy.

The secretary of agriculture is assisted by a deputy secretary and several assistant secretaries and undersecretaries, all of whom are nominated by the president and put into office with Senate approval. The secretary and assistant secretaries have staffs that help with all sorts of jobs, such as hiring new people and generating positive public relations for the Department of Agriculture.

TABLE 13–1 EXECUTIVE DEPARTMENTS

Department (Year of Original Establishment)	Principal Duties	Selected Subagencies
State (1789)	Negotiates treaties; develops our foreign policy; protects citizens abroad.	Bureau of Consular Affairs (passports).
Treasury (1789)	Pays all federal bills; borrows money; collects federal taxes; mints coins and prints paper currency; supervises national banks.	Internal Revenue Service; U.S. Mint.
Defense (1789)*	Manages the armed forces (Army, Navy, Air Force, Marines); operates military bases.	National Security Agency; Departments of the Air Force, Navy, Army; Defense Intelligence Agency.
Justice (1789)†	Gives legal advice to the president; enforces federal criminal laws; supervises federal prisons.	Federal Bureau of Investigation; Drug Enforcement Administration; Bureau of Prisons; U.S. Marshals.
Interior (1849)	Supervises federally owned lands and parks; operates federal hydroelectric power facilities; supervises Native American affairs.	U.S. Fish and Wildlife Service; National Park Service; Bureau of Indian Affairs; Bureau of Land Management.
Agriculture (1889)	Provides assistance to farmers and ranchers; conducts research to improve agriculture; works to protect forests.	Agricultural Research Service; Food Safety and Inspection Service; Federal Crop Insurance Corporation; Forest Service.
Commerce (1903)‡	Grants patents and trademarks; conducts national census; monitors the weather; protects the interests of businesses.	Bureau of the Census; Bureau of Economic Analysis; Patent and Trademark Office; National Oceanic and Atmospheric Administration.
Labor (1903)‡	Administers federal labor laws; promotes the interests of workers.	Occupational Safety and Health Administration; Bureau of Labor Statistics; Wage and Hour Division.
Health and Human Services (1953)§	Promotes public health; enforces pure food and drug laws; sponsors health-related research.	Food and Drug Administration; Centers for Disease Control and Prevention; Centers for Medicare and Medicaid Services.
Housing and Urban Development (1965)	Deals with the nation's housing needs; develops and rehabilitates urban communities; oversees resale of mortgages.	Government National Mortgage Association; Office of Fair Housing and Equal Opportunity.
Transportation (1967)	Finances improvements in mass transit; develops and administers programs for highways, railroads, and aviation.	Federal Aviation Administration; Federal Highway Administration; National Highway Traffic Safety Administration.
Energy (1977)	Promotes the conservation of energy and resources; analyzes energy data; conducts research and development.	Office of Civilian Radioactive Waste Management; National Nuclear Security Administration.
Education (1979)	Coordinates federal programs and policies for education; administers aid to education; promotes educational research.	Office of Special Education; Office of Elementary and Secondary Education; Office of Postsecondary Education.
Veterans Affairs (1989)	Promotes the welfare of veterans of the U.S. armed forces.	Veterans Health Administration; Veterans Benefits Administration.
Homeland Security (2002)	Works to prevent terrorist attacks within the United States, control America's borders, and handle attacks and natural disasters.	U.S. Customs and Border Protection; U.S. Coast Guard; Secret Service; Federal Emergency Management Agency.

*Established in 1947 by merging the Department of War, created in 1789, and the Department of the Navy, created in 1798.
†Formerly the Office of the Attorney General; renamed and reorganized in 1870.
‡Formed in 1913 by splitting the Department of Commerce and Labor, which was created in 1903.
§Formerly the Department of Health, Education, and Welfare; renamed when the Department of Education was spun off in 1979.

13–2c Independent Executive Agencies

Independent executive agencies are federal bureaucratic organizations that have a single function. They are independent in the sense that they are not located within a cabinet department. Rather, independent executive agency heads report directly to the president. A new federal independent executive agency can be created only through cooperation between the president and Congress.

The Creation of Independent Agencies

Before the twentieth century, the federal government did almost all of its work through the executive departments. In the twentieth century, in contrast, presidents began to ask for certain executive agencies to be kept separate, or independent, from existing departments. Today, there are more than two hundred independent executive agencies.

The Danger of Partisan Politics
Sometimes, agencies are kept independent because of the sensitive nature of their functions. But at other times, Congress creates independent agencies to protect them from

independent executive agency
A federal agency that is not located within a cabinet department.

partisan politics—politics in support of a particular party. The U.S. Commission on Civil Rights, which was created in 1957, is a case in point. Congress wanted to protect the work of the commission from the influences not only of Congress's own political interests, but also those of the president.

The Central Intelligence Agency (CIA), which was formed in 1947, is another good example. Both Congress and the president know that the intelligence activities of the CIA could be abused if the agency were not independent. Finally, the General Services Administration (GSA) was created as an independent executive agency in 1949 to provide services and office space for most federal agencies. To serve all parts of the government, the GSA has to be an independent agency.

Among the more than two hundred independent executive agencies, a few stand out in importance either because of the mission they were established to accomplish or because of their large size. We list selected independent executive agencies in Table 13–2.

13–2d Independent Regulatory Agencies

An **independent regulatory agency** is responsible for a specific type of public policy. Its function is to create and implement rules that regulate private activity and protect the public interest in a particular sector of the economy.

One of the earliest independent regulatory agencies was the Interstate Commerce Commission (ICC), established in 1887. (This agency was abolished in 1995.) After the ICC was formed, other agencies were created to regulate aviation (the Civil Aeronautics Board, or CAB, which was abolished in 1985), communications (the Federal Communications Commission, or FCC), the stock market (the Securities and Exchange Commission, or SEC), and many other areas of business. Table 13–3 lists some major independent regulatory agencies.

13–2e Government Corporations

Another form of federal bureaucratic organization is the **government corporation**, a business that is owned by the government. Government corporations are not exactly like corporations in which you buy stock and become a shareholder. The U.S. Postal Service (USPS) is a government corporation, for example, but it does not sell shares.

Government corporations are like private corporations in that they provide a service that could be handled by the private sector. They are also like private corporations in that they charge for their services, though sometimes they charge less than private-sector corporations do for similar services. Table 13–4 lists selected government corporations.

Facing Losses When a private business fails to make a profit, its shareholders have a problem. The value of the company may drop, in some instances to zero. If a small business loses money, its owners must either raise more capital or shut down the firm. If a government corporation runs at a loss, taxpayers may be forced to foot the bill.

TABLE 13–2	SELECTED INDEPENDENT EXECUTIVE AGENCIES	
Name	**Date Formed**	**Principal Duties**
Central Intelligence Agency (CIA)	1947	Gathers and analyzes political and military information about foreign countries; conducts covert operations outside the United States.
General Services Administration (GSA)	1949	Purchases and manages property of the federal government; oversees federal government spending projects; discovers overcharges in government programs.
Small Business Administration (SBA)	1953	Promotes the interests of small businesses; provides low-cost loans to small businesses.
National Aeronautics and Space Administration (NASA)	1958	Is responsible for the U.S. space program, including building, testing, and operating space vehicles.
Environmental Protection Agency (EPA)	1970	Undertakes programs aimed at reducing air and water pollution; works with state and local agencies to fight environmental hazards.
Social Security Administration (SSA)*	1994	Manages the government's Social Security programs, including Retirement and Survivors Insurance, Disability Insurance, and Supplemental Security Income.

*Separated from the Department of Health and Human Services in 1994; originally established in 1946.

TABLE 13–3 SELECTED INDEPENDENT REGULATORY AGENCIES

Name	Date Formed	Principal Duties
Federal Reserve System (Fed)	1913	Determines policy on interest rates, credit availability, and the money supply.
Federal Trade Commission (FTC)	1914	Works to prevent businesses from engaging in unfair trade practices and forming business monopolies.
Securities and Exchange Commission (SEC)	1934	Regulates the nation's stock exchanges; requires financial disclosure by companies that wish to sell stocks and bonds to the public.
Federal Communications Commission (FCC)	1934	Regulates interstate and international communications by radio, television, wire, satellite, and cable.
National Labor Relations Board (NLRB)	1935	Protects employees' rights to join unions and to bargain collectively with employers; attempts to prevent unfair labor practices by both employers and unions.
Equal Employment Opportunity Commission (EEOC)	1964	Works to eliminate discrimination that is based on religion, gender, race, color, national origin, age, or disability; examines claims of discrimination.

The U.S. Postal Service is an example of this problem. In recent years, as Americans have increasingly relied on the Internet for communications, the volume of first-class mail had dropped considerably. As a result, the USPS has been losing money (this in spite of the fact that parcel deliveries have gone up, also because of the Internet—specifically, as a result of online shopping). Losses in 2012 amounted to $16 billion. In August 2012, the service defaulted on a monthly $5.5 billion payment due to the U.S. Treasury to finance retirees' health-care expenses. It has defaulted on this payment every year since. The USPS has cut costs dramatically, spending $4 billion less in 2013 than it did in 2012. Still, it lost $5 billion in 2013. It lost $5.5 billion in 2014 and $5.1 billion in 2015. Some observers claim that the service's real problem is that Congress has forced it to prefund retiree benefits in a way that no other business or government agency must do.

To solve the problem permanently, the USPS proposed to lay off additional employees, close rural post offices, reduce pension benefits, and even end Saturday delivery. Many of these steps require congressional approval, which was not forthcoming. The alternative would be direct federal subsidies to the service, which has been self-supporting since the early 1980s.

Intermediate Forms of Organization A number of intermediate forms of organization exist that fall between a government corporation and a private one. In some circumstances, the government can take control of a private corporation. When a company goes bankrupt, for example, it is subject to the supervision of a federal judge until it exits from bankruptcy or is liquidated. The government can also purchase stock in a private corporation. The government used this technique to funnel funds into major banks during the financial crisis that began in September 2008. In addition, the government can set up a corporation and sell stock to the public.

The Federal Home Loan Mortgage Corporation (Freddie Mac) and the Federal National Mortgage Association (Fannie Mae) are examples of stockholder-owned government-sponsored enterprises. Fannie Mae (founded in 1938) and Freddie Mac (created in 1970) buy, resell, and guarantee home mortgages. In September 2008, the government placed the two businesses into a conservatorship—effectively a bankruptcy overseen

TABLE 13–4 SELECTED GOVERNMENT CORPORATIONS

Name	Date Formed	Principal Duties
Tennessee Valley Authority (TVA)	1933	Operates a Tennessee River control system and generates power for a seven-state region; controls floods and promotes the navigability of the Tennessee River.
Federal Deposit Insurance Corporation (FDIC)	1933	Insures individuals' bank deposits up to $250,000 and oversees the business activities of banks.
National Railroad Passenger Corporation (Amtrak)	1970	Provides a national and intercity rail passenger service network; controls more than 23,000 miles of track with about 505 stations.
U.S. Postal Service (formed from the old U.S. Post Office department—the Post Office itself is older than the Constitution)	1971	Delivers mail throughout the United States and its territories; is the largest government corporation.

by the Federal Housing Finance Agency instead of a federal judge. The government also took an 80 percent share of the stock of each firm. Today, Fannie Mae and Freddie Mac are making money again, and their profits go into the U.S. Treasury.

CRITICAL THINKING

▶ *Some people have advocated selling off government corporations, such as the U.S. Postal Service, and turning them into truly private enterprises. Would it be a good idea to "privatize" the U.S. Postal Service? Why or why not?*

13–3 HOW BUREAUCRATS GET THEIR JOBS

LO Describe how the federal civil service was established and how bureaucrats get their jobs.

As already noted, federal bureaucrats holding top-level positions are appointed by the president and confirmed by the Senate. These bureaucrats include department and agency heads, their deputy and assistant secretaries, and the like. The list of positions that are filled by appointments is published after each presidential election in a document called *Policy and Supporting Positions.* The volume is more commonly known as the *Plum Book,* because the eight thousand jobs it summarizes are known as "political plums." Normally, these jobs go to those who supported the winning presidential candidate.

13–3a The Civil Service

The rank-and-file bureaucrats—the rest of the federal bureaucracy—are part of the **civil service** (nonmilitary employees of the government). They obtain their jobs through the Office of Personnel Management (OPM), an agency established by the Civil Service Reform Act of 1978. The OPM recruits, interviews, and tests potential government workers and determines who should be hired. The OPM makes recommendations to individual agencies as to which persons meet relevant standards (typically, the top three applicants for a position), and the agencies then generally decide which of the recommended individuals they will hire.

The 1978 act also created the Merit Systems Protection Board (MSPB) to oversee promotions,

civil service Nonmilitary government employees.

employees' rights, and other employment matters. The MSPB evaluates charges of wrongdoing, hears employee appeals from agency decisions, and can order corrective action against agencies and employees.

13–3b Origins of the Merit System

The idea that the civil service should be based on a merit system dates back more than a century. The Civil Service Reform Act of 1883 established the principle of government employment on the basis of merit through open, competitive examinations.

Initially, only about 10 percent of federal employees were covered by the merit system. Today, more than 90 percent of the federal civil service is recruited on the basis of merit. Are public employees paid too much? For a discussion of this question, see this chapter's *Join the Debate* feature.

Monkey Business Images/Shutterstock.com

A U.S. Postal Service letter carrier. *How do postal employees get their jobs?*

JOIN THE DEBATE

Are Government Workers Paid Too Much?

Popular beliefs about the pay of government workers vary dramatically. Many people believe that only individuals working in private business can hope to receive large paychecks. Others, however, see government workers as an elite group whose members enjoy secure and high-paid jobs, unlike average American workers who are competing in the global economy.

Are government workers paid too much? That can be a difficult question to answer. Those arguing about this issue do not even agree on how public-sector pay compares with pay in the private sector.

Yes, They're Overpaid

Conservatives who believe that government workers are a new elite point to generous retirement benefits. Government workers typically have "defined benefit" plans that guarantee their retirement income. Private-sector employees who are lucky enough to have any kind of pension now generally have "defined contribution" plans under which benefits rise and fall with the stock market.

Government wages aren't bad, either. An article by two U.S. Bureau of Labor Statistics (BLS) economists found that, on average, workers in state government have total compensation 3 to 10 percent greater than workers in the private sector, while in local government the gap is 10 to 19 percent.[3] A 2015 study by the libertarian Cato Institute claimed that federal employees made an average of $119,934 in wages and benefits, while total compensation for private-sector workers was only $67,246. Cato based its findings on figures from the Bureau of Economic Analysis (BEA).[4] It's not fair that government workers get a better deal than the rest of us.

No, They're Not

Other studies yield different results. A paper by a Boston College team concluded that state and local workers are paid 9.5 percent less than comparable workers in the private sector, although generous benefits reduce the gap to 4 percent.[5] It's worth remembering that many government workers don't do the same kind of work as employees in the private sector. On average,

federal workers are much better educated and more likely to be employed in jobs that are also well paid in the private sector. At the local level, for example, teachers and police officers need to be well educated. At the state level, the same is true for college professors and judges, among others. Most teachers could make more money if they did something else.

At the federal level, the real point may not be that pay is high, but that pay scales are more egalitarian than in private business. The Congressional Budget Office has found that federal workers with only a high school education are paid 36 percent more than in the private sector. Employees with professional degrees, however, earn 18 percent less.[6]

Critical Analysis

Is it important for government to try to attract high-quality employees? Why or why not?

13-3c The OPM Hacking Scandal

In June 2015, federal cybersecurity experts discovered that hackers had downloaded personal information on millions of Americans from computers at the OPM. The database in question, EPIC, contains information from background checks that the government undertakes before issuing security clearances. EPIC includes a 127-page form that asks about past addresses and jobs, friends and relatives, and foreign contacts. It also contains data about problems with drugs, drinking, gambling, and

mental health, criminal records, and bankruptcies. EPIC even contains 1.1 million fingerprint files. In July, experts discovered that hackers had accessed a second OPM database containing Social Security numbers and employment information on 21.5 million Americans.

Officials privately blamed a group called Deep Panda that is sponsored by the Chinese government. What the Chinese obtained may be the best database for recruiting spies in world history. EPIC also contains information on foreign contacts of those seeking security clearances. Chinese intelligence officials are doubtless scouring the database to locate Chinese citizens who may have been in contact with Americans. Officials may be asking persons on that list some uncomfortable questions. If any of them actually provided help or information to Americans, they could be facing espionage charges.

CRITICAL THINKING

▶ *When most private companies hire new employees, they don't use systems similar to those of the civil service. Why is this so?*

13–4 REGULATORY AGENCIES: ARE THEY THE FOURTH BRANCH OF GOVERNMENT?

LO Explain how regulatory agencies make rules and how issue networks affect policymaking in government.

In Chapter 2, we considered the system of checks and balances among the three branches of the U.S. government—executive, legislative, and judicial. Recent history, however, shows that it may be time to regard the regulatory agencies as a fourth branch of the government. Although the U.S. Constitution does not mention regulatory agencies, these agencies can and do make **legislative rules** that are as legally binding as laws passed by Congress. With such powers, regulatory agencies have an influence that rivals that of the president, Congress, and the courts. Indeed, most Americans do not realize how much of our "law" is created by regulatory agencies.

Regulatory agencies have been on the American political scene since the nineteenth century, but their golden age came during the regulatory explosion of the 1960s and 1970s. Congress itself could not have overseen the actual implementation of all of the laws that it was enacting at that time to control pollution and deal with other social problems. It therefore chose (and still chooses) to delegate to administrative agencies the tasks involved in implementing its laws. By delegating some of its authority to an administrative agency, Congress can indirectly monitor a particular area in which it has passed legislation without becoming bogged down in the details relating to the enforcement of that legislation—details that are often best left to specialists.

13–4a Agency Creation

To create a federal administrative agency, Congress passes **enabling legislation**, which specifies the name, purpose, composition, and powers of the agency being created.

An Example: The FTC The Federal Trade Commission (FTC), for example, was created in 1914 by the Federal Trade Commission Act, as mentioned earlier. The act prohibits unfair and deceptive trade practices. The act also describes the procedures that the agency must follow to charge persons or organizations with violations of the act, and it provides for judicial review of agency orders.

Other portions of the act grant the agency powers to "make rules and regulations for the purpose of carrying out the Act," to conduct investigations of business practices, to obtain reports on business practices from interstate corporations, to investigate possible violations of federal antitrust statutes, to publish findings of its investigations, and to recommend new legislation.

Finally, the act empowers the FTC to hold trial-like hearings and to **adjudicate** (formally resolve) certain kinds of disputes that involve FTC regulations or federal antitrust laws. When adjudication takes place, within the FTC or any other regulatory agency, an administrative law judge (ALJ) conducts the hearing and, after weighing the evidence presented, issues an *order*. The ALJ's order may be appealed to a federal court. Unless it is overturned on appeal, the order becomes final.

The Power of Regulatory Agencies Enabling legislation makes the regulatory agency a potent organization. For example, the Securities and Exchange Commission (SEC) imposes rules regarding the disclosures a company must make to those who purchase its new stock. Under its enforcement authority, the SEC also investigates and prosecutes alleged violations of these regulations. Finally, SEC judges decide whether its rules have been violated and, if so, what punishment should

legislative rule An administrative agency rule that carries the same weight as a statute enacted by a legislature.

enabling legislation A law enacted by a legislature to establish an administrative agency. Enabling legislation normally specifies the name, purpose, composition, and powers of the agency being created.

adjudicate To render a judicial decision. In administrative law, it is the process in which an administrative law judge hears and decides issues that arise when an agency charges a person or firm with violating a law or regulation enforced by the agency.

A farmer works the land. *What interest groups represent farmers?*

Joseph Sohm/Shutterstock

A Cost-Benefit Analysis As an example of cost-benefit analysis in rulemaking, consider the Clean Air Fine Particle Implementation Rule, issued by the Environmental Protection Agency (EPA) in 2007. The EPA estimated the costs of the regulation as $7.3 billion per year, with benefits ranging from $19 billion to $167 billion per year. The benefits largely consist of reductions in health-care costs and premature deaths—and, as these figures suggest, such calculations can be highly uncertain. Does the United States suffer from excessive regulation, as some have claimed? We examined that question in the chapter-opening *America at Odds* feature.

be imposed on the offender (although, as noted, the judgment may be appealed to a federal court).

13–4b Rulemaking

A major function of a regulatory agency is **rulemaking**—the formulation of new regulations. The power that an agency has to make rules is conferred on it by Congress in the agency's enabling legislation.

For example, the Occupational Safety and Health Administration (OSHA) was authorized by the Occupational Safety and Health Act of 1970 to develop and issue rules governing safety in the workplace. Under this authority, OSHA has issued various safety standards, including rules to prevent the spread of certain diseases, such as acquired immune deficiency syndrome (AIDS). The rules specify various standards—on how contaminated needles should be handled, for instance—with which health-care workers must comply.

Requirements for Making Rules Agencies cannot just make a rule whenever they wish. Rather, they must follow certain procedural requirements, particularly those set forth in the Administrative Procedure Act of 1946. Agencies must also make sure that their rules are based on substantial evidence and are not "arbitrary and capricious." Therefore, before proposing a new rule, an agency may engage in extensive investigation to obtain data on the problem to be addressed by the rule. Based on this information, the agency may undertake a cost-benefit analysis of a new rule to determine whether its benefits outweigh its costs.

13–4c Policymaking

Bureaucrats in federal agencies are expected to exhibit **neutral competency**, which means that they are supposed to apply their technical skills to their jobs without regard to political issues. In principle, they should not be swayed by the thought of personal or political gain. In reality, each independent agency and each executive department is interested in its own survival and expansion. All agencies and departments wish to retain or expand their functions and staffs. To do this, they must gain the goodwill of both the White House and Congress.

Support from Congress While the administrative agencies of the federal government are prohibited from directly lobbying Congress, departments and agencies have developed techniques to help them gain congressional support. Each organization maintains a congressional information office, which specializes in helping members of Congress by supplying any requested information and solving casework problems.

For example, if a member of the House of Representatives receives a complaint from a constituent that his Social Security payments are not arriving on time, that member of Congress may contact the Social Security Administration and ask that something be done. Typically, requests from members of Congress receive immediate attention.

> **rulemaking** The process undertaken by an administrative agency when formally proposing, evaluating, and adopting a new regulation.
>
> **neutral competency** The application of technical skills to jobs without regard to political issues.

Iron Triangles Analysts have determined that one way to understand the bureaucracy's role in policymaking is to examine the **iron triangle**, which is a three-way alliance among legislators (members of Congress), bureaucrats, and interest groups. Presumably, the laws that are passed and the policies that are established benefit the interests of all three corners of the iron triangle, as shown in Figure 13–5. Iron triangles are well established in almost every part of the bureaucracy.

Who Belongs to an Iron Triangle? As an example, consider agricultural policy. The Department of Agriculture consists of almost 100,000 individuals working directly for the federal government and thousands of other individuals who work indirectly for the department as contractors, subcontractors, and consultants. Now think about the various interest groups and client groups that are concerned with what the bureaus and agencies in the Agriculture Department can do for them. These groups include the American Farm Bureau Federation, the National Milk Producers Federation, various regional citrus growers associations, and many others. Finally, in Congress two major committees are concerned with agriculture: the House Committee on Agriculture and the Senate Committee on Agriculture, Nutrition, and Forestry.

The bureaucrats, interest groups, and legislators who make up this iron triangle cooperate to create mutually beneficial regulations and legislation. Because of the connections between agricultural interest groups and policymakers within the government, the agricultural industry has benefited greatly over the years from significant farm subsidies.

Congress's Role. The Department of Agriculture is headed by the secretary of agriculture, who is nominated by the president (and confirmed by the Senate). But that secretary cannot even buy a desk lamp if Congress does not approve the appropriations for the department's budget.

Within Congress, the responsibility for considering the Department of Agriculture's request for funding belongs first to the House and Senate appropriations committees and then to the agriculture subcommittees of the appropriations committees. The members of those committees, most of whom represent agricultural states, have been around a long time and have their own ideas about what is appropriate for the Agriculture Department's budget. They carefully scrutinize the ideas of the president and the secretary of agriculture.

The Influence of Interest Groups. The various interest groups—including producers of farm chemicals and farm machinery, agricultural cooperatives, grain dealers, and exporters—have vested interests in what the Department of Agriculture does and in what Congress lets the department do. Those interests are well represented by the lobbyists who crowd the halls of Congress. Many lobbyists have been working for agricultural interest groups for decades. They know the congressional committee members and Agriculture Department staff very well and meet with them routinely.

Issue Networks The iron triangle relationship does not apply to all policy domains. When making policy decisions on environmental and welfare issues, for example, many members of Congress and agency officials rely heavily on "experts." Legislators and agency heads tend to depend on their staff members for specialized knowledge of rules, regulations, and legislation.

iron triangle A three-way alliance among legislators, bureaucrats, and interest groups to make or preserve policies that benefit their respective interests.

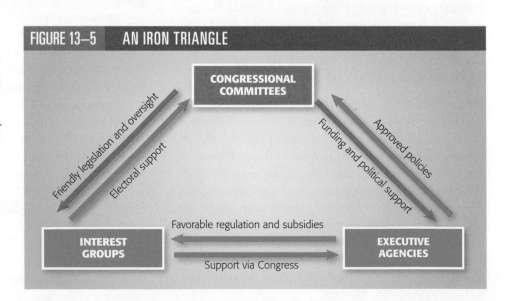

FIGURE 13–5   AN IRON TRIANGLE

CONGRESSIONAL COMMITTEES

Friendly legislation and oversight

Electoral support

Funding and political support

Approved policies

Favorable regulation and subsidies

Support via Congress

INTEREST GROUPS

EXECUTIVE AGENCIES

These experts have frequently served variously as interest group lobbyists and as public-sector staff members during their careers, creating a revolving-door effect. They often have strong opinions and interests regarding the direction of policy and are thus able to exert a great deal of influence on legislators and bureaucratic agencies.

The relationships among these experts, which are less structured than iron triangles, are often referred to as **issue networks**. Like iron triangles, issue networks are made up of people with similar policy concerns. Issue networks are less interdependent and unified than iron triangles, however, and often include more players, such as media outlets.[7] (See Figure 13–6.)

A key characteristic of issue networks is that there can be more than one network in a given policy area. To take the example of the environment, one issue network tends to advocate greater environmental regulation, while another network opposes such regulations as undue burdens on businesses and landowners. In other words, competing interests often form rival issue networks that tend to limit each other's power.

CRITICAL THINKING

▶ *Who—or what—can stop an iron triangle from absorbing ever-greater amounts of government resources?*

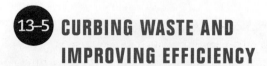

13–5 CURBING WASTE AND IMPROVING EFFICIENCY

LO Identify some of the ways in which the government has attempted to curb waste and improve efficiency in the bureaucracy.

There is no doubt that our bureaucracy is costly. There is also little doubt that at times it can be wasteful and inefficient. The government has made many attempts to reduce waste, inefficiency, and wrongdoing. For example, federal and state governments have passed laws requiring more openness in government. Other laws encourage employees to report any waste and wrongdoing that they observe.

13–5a Helping Out the Whistleblowers

The term **whistleblower**, as applied to the federal bureaucracy, has a special meaning: it is someone who blows the whistle, or reports, on gross governmental inefficiency, illegal activities, or other wrongdoing. Whistleblowers often take their complaints to the press.

Laws Protecting Whistleblowers Federal employees may be reluctant to blow the whistle on their superiors for fear of reprisals. To encourage federal employees to report government wrongdoing, Congress has passed laws to protect whistleblowers.

FIGURE 13–6 ISSUE NETWORK: THE ENVIRONMENT

Executive Departments and Agencies
- Environmental Protection Agency
- Agriculture Department
- Energy Department
- Department of the Interior
- National Oceanic and Atmospheric Admin.
- Bureau of Land Management
- Army Corps of Engineers

Key Congressional Committees
- **Senate**
  Appropriations, Energy and Natural Resources, Environment and Public Works, Finance, Commerce, Science, and Transportation
- **House of Representatives**
  Agriculture, Appropriations, Natural Resources, Transportation and Infrastructure

Selected Interest Groups
- **Environmental Groups**
  Environmental Defense, Friends of the Earth, National Audubon Society, Clean Water Action, National Wildlife Federation, The Ocean Conservancy, American Forests
- **Industry Groups**
  Citizens for a Sound Economy, Edison Electric Institute, U.S. Chamber of Commerce, National Food Processors Association, International Wood Products Association, National Mining Association, American Resort Development Association

issue networks
Groups of individuals or organizations—which consist of legislators and legislative staff members, interest group leaders, bureaucrats, the media, scholars, and other experts—that support particular policy positions on a given issue.

whistleblower
In the context of government employment, someone who "blows the whistle" (reports to authorities or the press) on gross governmental inefficiency, illegal action, or other wrongdoing.

The home page of the FBI on an Apple iPhone. *Was Apple right or wrong to resist the FBI's demand for help in cracking the iPhone of a suspected terrorist?*

The Whistleblower Protection Act of 1989 authorized the Office of Special Counsel (OSC), an independent agency, to investigate complaints of reprisals against whistleblowers. Many federal agencies also have toll-free hotlines that employees can use to anonymously report bureaucratic waste and inappropriate behavior.

One set of laws encourages reports by making cash rewards to whistleblowers. Under four different programs, if the government saves or retrieves a significant sum as a result of a tip-off, a percentage of the government's gain can be paid to the whistleblower. Under the False Claims Act, a private individual can even pursue a claim in court if the Justice Department fails to proceed.

Many such cases involve tax fraud by corporations and individuals, not government malfeasance. In September 2012, the government paid out the largest such reward ever—$104 million. The money went to a banker who blew the whistle on a Swiss bank that was helping U.S. citizens defraud the Internal Revenue Service. The whistleblower, however, also had to serve forty months in prison for his part in the fraud.

Whistleblowers Continue to Face Problems
In spite of these laws, there is little evidence that whistleblowers are adequately protected against retaliation. According to a study conducted by the Government Accountability Office, 41 percent of the whistleblowers who turned to the OSC for protection during a recent three-year period reported that they were no longer employed by the agencies on which they blew the whistle. Indeed, given how difficult it is to fire a federal employee under normal circumstances, it is amazing how quickly most whistleblowers are "shown the door."

Many federal employees who have blown the whistle say that they would not do so again because it was so difficult to get help. Even when they did get help, they faced a stressful ordeal.

Whistleblowers under Obama. Barack Obama's supporters expected that, as president, he would protect whistleblowers. Many of them were disappointed, however, when the new administration took an unusually harsh line regarding information disclosures. Indeed, some believe that Obama's record on whistleblowers is the worst of any president's.

The Obama administration has charged seven individuals who leaked information to the press with violations of the Espionage Act of 1917. Before Obama took office, only three persons had ever been charged under that act for talking to the press. Some of those charged may have endangered national security. In other cases, though, the true crime may simply have been embarrassing the government.

Whistleblowers and National Security. It is, of course, possible that leaking information can simultaneously endanger national security and also expose government actions that are unethical and possibly illegal or unconstitutional. Some of the revelations provided by Edward Snowden concerning activities of the National Security Agency (discussed in Chapter 4) may have fallen into such a category. The news that the government had spied on various foreign leaders created substantial problems for the U.S. government. Reports of spying on American citizens, however, generated outrage in many quarters.

13–5b Improving Efficiency and Getting Results

The Government Performance and Results Act, which went into effect in 1997, has forced the federal government to change the way it does business. Since 1997, almost every agency (except the intelligence agencies) has had to describe its goals and identify methods for evaluating how well those goals are met. A goal can be as broad as lowering the number of highway traffic deaths or as narrow as reducing the number of times an agency's phone rings before it is answered.

As one example, consider the National Oceanic and Atmospheric Administration (NOAA). It has improved the effectiveness of its short-term forecasting services, particularly in issuing warnings of tornadoes. The warning time has increased from seven to fifteen minutes. This may not seem significant, but it provides additional critical time for those in the path of a tornado.

President Obama's contribution to the attempt to improve government effectiveness was to create a chief performance officer. This individual reports directly to the president and works with other economic officials in an attempt to increase efficiency and eliminate waste in government.

13-5c Another Approach— Pay-for-Performance Plans

For some time, the private sector has used pay-for-performance plans as a means to increase employee productivity and efficiency. About one-third of the major firms in this country use some kind of alternative pay system, such as team-based pay, skill-based pay, profit-sharing plans, or individual bonuses. In contrast, workers for the federal government traditionally have received fixed salaries. Promotions and salary increases are given on the basis of seniority, not output.

The federal government has been experimenting with pay-for-performance systems. For example, the U.S. Postal Service has implemented the Economic Value Added Variable Pay Program, which ties bonuses to performance. As part of a five-year test of a new pay system, three thousand scientists working in Air Force laboratories received salaries based on results.

13-5d Privatization

Another idea for reforming government bureaucracies is **privatization**, which means turning over certain types of government work to the private sector. Privatization can take place by contracting out (outsourcing) work to the private sector or by *managed competition*, in which the task of providing public services is opened up to competition. In managed competition, both the relevant government agency and private firms can compete for the work.

> *"THE ONLY THING THAT SAVES US FROM THE BUREAUCRACY IS ITS INEFFICIENCY."*
>
> ~ EUGENE J. MCCARTHY, U.S. SENATOR FROM MINNESOTA, 1959–1971

State and local governments have been experimenting with privatization for some time. Almost all of the states have privatized at least a few of their services, and some states, including California, Colorado, and Florida, have privatized more than one hundred activities formerly undertaken by government. In Scottsdale, Arizona, the city contracts for fire protection. In Baltimore, Maryland, nine of the city's schools are outsourced to private entities.

13-5e Government in the Sunshine

The last four decades of the twentieth century saw a trend toward more openness in government. The theory was that because Americans pay for the government, they own it—and they have a right to know what the government is doing with the taxpayers' dollars.

The Freedom of Information Act. In response to pressure for more government openness and disclosure, Congress passed the Freedom of Information Act in 1966. This act requires federal agencies to disclose any information in agency files, with some exceptions, to any persons requesting it. Since the 1970s, *sunshine laws*, which require government meetings to be open to the public, have been enacted at all levels of American government.

Government Openness after 9/11. The trend toward greater openness in government came to an abrupt halt on September 11, 2001. In the wake of the terrorist attacks on the World Trade Center and the Pentagon, the government began tightening its grip on information. In the months following the attacks, hundreds of thousands of documents were removed from government websites. No longer can the public access plans of nuclear power plants, descriptions of airline security violations, or maps of pipeline routes. Agencies were instructed to be more cautious about releasing information in their files and were given new guidelines on what should be considered public information.

13-5f Government Online

Increasingly, government agencies have attempted to improve their effectiveness and efficiency by making

privatization
The transfer of the task of providing services traditionally provided by government to the private sector.

The home page of USA.gov, the federal government's online "front door." *In what ways have you personally interacted with the federal government?*

use of the Internet. One method has been to make information available to the public online. This may appear to run counter to the information restrictions imposed following 9/11, but much government information is not relevant to national security issues.

Under the Obama administration, for example, it is possible to get annual data on immigration, on airline flight delays, and on job-related deaths that name the employer of the deceased. The *Federal Register,* a record of government notices, can now be read online.

Local governments have posted such information as real estate records, restaurant health inspection scores, and the geographic locations of crimes. Some parts of the government have resisted the trend toward openness, however. Lawyers and other interested parties must often pay to obtain information held by the courts.

Filing Forms Online Another way that government agencies are using the Internet to improve services is to let citizens file forms and apply for services online. For example, if you change your address, you may be able to request an update sticker for your driver's license by visiting a state website. Also, you may be able to apply for unemployment benefits without visiting an unemployment office and receive payments through a government-issued debit card. The federal government

distributes payments for Medicare, tax refunds, and a variety of other programs automatically and electronically.

E-Fraud One danger of automatic payments is the possibility of fraud. This problem is not new. Criminals have long attempted to defraud the government—and the taxpayer—by filing false income tax forms or by making improper claims following natural disasters. The Internet, however, has made it possible for crooks to "game the system" more easily. Claims can be processed without examination by an actual person. Such faulty payment systems demonstrate that bureaucrats still have a role to play, even in the high-tech era.

Law Enforcement versus Online Privacy A major recent issue concerning the government's online presence has been the extent to which the government can require cooperation from Internet service providers and technology companies. Law enforcement agencies such as the Federal Bureau of Investigation (FBI) naturally want the widest possible powers to demand cooperation. Such demands, however, run the danger of infringing on the privacy rights of Americans (and foreigners as well). In 2014, as we explained in Chapter 4, the United States Supreme Court ruled unanimously that law enforcement personnel cannot search cell phones without a search warrant. It remains an open question, however, as to what kinds of demands law enforcement agencies can make even if they have a search warrant. Can the government demand that a technology corporation actually write new software to assist in a search? We discuss a recent case involving Apple Inc. and the FBI in this chapter's *Perception vs. Reality* feature.

CRITICAL THINKING

▶ *In the name of security, some states have gone so far as to bar access to emergency evacuation plans. Why might these states have done this? What problems could result if citizens lack access to this information?*

Must Apple Help the FBI Hack a Terrorist's iPhone?

Following the terrorist attack in San Bernardino, California, in December 2015, the FBI recovered an Apple iPhone that had been used by one of the perpetrators. The FBI was not immediately able to access the information stored on the phone, however, because the data were encrypted. The encryption was relatively simple, involving a four-digit password. Such a password could be bypassed by simply trying all possible options—not that hard with only four digits. The phone in question, however, was set up to erase all data if anyone entered ten invalid passwords in a row.

The FBI therefore demanded that Apple write a new operating system that would bypass the phone's security features. Apple refused, citing security risks that such a "backdoor" would pose for its customers. In February 2016, the FBI obtained a court order requiring Apple to cooperate. In March, however, the FBI announced that it had found a way to crack the iPhone without Apple's help. The court order was lifted, but the underlying issue remains.

The Perception

For many Americans, this issue is a "no brainer." Everyone should be prepared to help law enforcement authorities. President Obama said that Apple's position amounted to "fetishizing our phones above every other value. That can't be the right answer."

The Reality

Apple, however, was supported in this matter by most of the high-tech industry. Indeed, the FBI's legal position was weaker than many realize. The court order was based on a 1789 law that obviously was never meant to apply to smartphones. Congress has passed legislation that explicitly requires the financial industry to cooperate with such requests from law enforcement. It has never adopted legislation that would impose such requirements on communications firms. The laws it has passed tend to strengthen privacy rights, rather than the reverse.

It's common to argue against some action by claiming it puts us on a "slippery slope" to disaster. Usually such arguments are bogus, but in this example, thousands of cases are already stacked up behind this one FBI request. Police agencies are transparently eager to crack phones in an attempt to address the most trivial offenses. And it's not just American agencies that want this power. Standing next in line to the FBI is the government of China. It would love to have another way to track down and punish advocates of free speech and democratic elections.

Nor is Apple standing still. Newer iPhone operating systems are much harder to crack than older ones. Future iPhones may be impossible to crack no matter how much help Apple may provide. Congress could ban such phones, of course. U.S. public opinion is likely to provide the ultimate resolution of this dispute.

Blog On

The Atlantic *magazine has run several articles on this issue. Locate them by searching for "apple fbi atlantic."*

Although the story is often told about red tape and wasteful spending generated by our bureaucracy, all in all, the U.S. bureaucracy compares favorably with bureaucracies in other countries. Citizens typically overestimate the amount of "government waste" by very large margins. Still, the U.S. government faces the same problems with its bureaucracy—sluggishness, inefficiency, and even incompetence—that large businesses and organizations throughout the country face. Americans are at odds over a number of issues relating to the bureaucracy, including the following:

- *Can new financial regulations eliminate the danger of a catastrophe such as the one we experienced in September 2008—or will clever financiers find ways around any new regulations?*

- *Do the recent health-care reforms provide vital protection to the citizenry—or are they an example of excessive government meddling in the private sector?*

- *Are government employees overpaid—or is their pay appropriate, given their responsibilities?*

- *Is the outsourcing of government services a way to improve efficiency—or does it mostly serve to hide the true cost and scope of government?*

- *Should our leaders focus on openness and transparency in government—or are such measures dangerous during the war on terrorism?*

STUDY TOOLS 13

READY TO STUDY? IN THE BOOK, YOU CAN:

☐ Review what you've read with the following chapter quiz.

☐ Check your answers in Appendix D at the back of the book.

☐ Rip out the Chapter Review Card, which includes key terms and chapter summaries.

ONLINE AT WWW.CENGAGEBRAIN.COM, YOU CAN:

☐ Learn about federal regulations for deep water oil drilling in a short video.

☐ Explore various online resources in the NASA and U.S. General Services Administration websites in the Internet Resources tool.

☐ Interact with figures from the text, and watch quick animation clips.

☐ Prepare for tests with quizzes.

☐ Review the key terms with Flash Cards.

FILL-IN

Learning Outcome 13–1

1. All in all, the three levels of government employ about _____ percent of the civilian labor force.

Learning Outcome 13–2

2. The head of each executive department is known as the _____, except for the Department of Justice, which is headed by the attorney general.

3. The _____ Department grants patents and trademarks, conducts the national census, and monitors the weather.

Learning Outcome 13–3

4. Federal bureaucrats holding top-level positions are appointed by the _____ and confirmed by the _____.

5. The Civil Service Reform Act of 1883 established the principle of government employment on the basis of _____.

Learning Outcome 13–4

6. To create a federal administrative agency, Congress passes _____, which specifies the name, purpose, composition, and powers of the agency being created.

7. An iron triangle is _____.

Learning Outcome 13–5

8. A whistleblower is someone who _____.

MULTIPLE CHOICE

Learning Outcome 13–1

9. The amount spent on defense, together with veterans' benefits, accounts for about ____ percent of federal spending.

   a. 5   **b.** 19   **c.** 49

Learning Outcome 13–2

10. The principal duties of the ____ Department include negotiating treaties, developing foreign policy, and protecting citizens abroad.

    a. State

    b. Homeland Security

    c. Defense

11. The independent executive agencies

    a. are businesses owned by the government.

    b. create and implement rules that regulate private activity and protect the public interest in a particular sector of the economy.

    c. are federal bureaucratic organizations that have a single function.

12. The ____ is a government corporation.

    a. General Services Administration

    b. U.S. Postal Service

    c. Securities and Exchange Commission

Learning Outcome 13–3

13. The document called *Policy and Supporting Positions* (the *Plum Book*) summarizes about ____ jobs that are filled by appointments after each presidential election.

    a. six hundred

    b. one thousand

    c. eight thousand

Learning Outcome 13–4

14. The process undertaken by an administrative agency when formally proposing, evaluating, and adopting a new regulation is called

    a. adjudication.

    b. rulemaking.

    c. neutral competency.

Learning Outcome 13–5

15. "Sunshine laws" require government

    a. meetings to be open to the public.

    b. agencies to outsource work to the private sector.

    c. agencies to let citizens file forms and apply for services online.

14 THE JUDICIARY

LEARNING OUTCOMES *After reading this chapter, you should be able to:*

14-1 Summarize the origins of the American legal system and the basic sources of American law.

14-2 Delineate the structure of the federal court system.

14-3 Say how federal judges are appointed.

14-4 Explain how the federal courts make policy, and describe the role of ideology and judicial philosophies in judicial decision making.

14-5 Identify some of the criticisms of the federal courts and some of the checks on the power of the courts.

After finishing this chapter, go to **PAGE 331** for **STUDY TOOLS**.

AMERICA AT ODDS | Should the People Elect Judges?

Martin Dallaire/Shutterstock.com

The founders of the American republic were concerned that too great a degree of popular control over the government could lead to "mob rule," and so they sought to insulate various institutions from direct popular elections. Federal judges, in particular, were to be appointed and serve for life. In contrast, in many states, all judges are popularly elected.

From time to time, judges are defeated at the polls. The most common way to defeat a judge is to accuse that official of being "soft on crime." Some people believe that despite the long prison sentences common in recent years, the judicial system is still too friendly to criminals. Others believe that elections tempt judges to cut corners on civil liberties. (In general, voters are not sympathetic to the civil liberties of alleged criminals.) So, should state judges be named through appointment? Or should the states rely on popular election?

The People Should Rule

Those who favor electing judges do not believe that judges can be insulated from politics. Governors, who often do the appointing when judges aren't elected, are highly political creatures. They tend to appoint supporters of their own party. If politics is going to play a role in judicial selection, then the people ought to have their say directly. Let the voters decide whether a judge is tough enough on crime or too tough on business. We admit ordinary people into the judicial process through juries, and judges should respond to public opinion as well. Officials who do not have to win a popular election may become remote from the people. Living in upscale neighborhoods, they will never experience what it is like to walk home at night fearing for their safety. Instead, they can end up living in a legal never-never land where abstractions matter more than the real world. It takes elections to give us the kinds of judges that we really want.

The Courts Must Be Insulated from Popular Pressure

Many opponents of judicial elections believe that they allow too much opportunity for popular panics and prejudices to influence the process. Popular "lock 'em up" attitudes toward criminals do not lead to an optimum strategy for crime reduction. Rather, we need to study what works and what doesn't. In some states, "get tough" policies have led to absurd cases of individuals serving life sentences for trivial offenses. Indeed, in states such as Texas, even conservative Republicans have recently concluded that we are imprisoning too many people at too great an expense. The last thing we need is to place additional pressure on judges by threatening them with removal.

Any move toward greater use of elections would bring with it a further problem—the corrupting influence of campaign contributions. Several states that use judicial elections are famous for their harsh sentences and enthusiasm for the death penalty. Judges in these states are also conspicuously friendly toward the moneyed interests that helped get them elected.

Where do you stand?

1. How much information do voters typically have about judicial candidates?
2. If judges had to raise campaign contributions, what kinds of people would be most likely to contribute? Why?

Explore this issue online:

- Justice at Stake is a national organization that supports appointing, not electing, judges. Its website is at www.justiceatstake.org.
- Randolph Hammock, a Los Angeles County Superior Court judge, has written an article defending the election of judges. Find it by searching on "hammock judicial elections."

INTRODUCTION

As you read in this chapter's opening *America at Odds* feature, the question of whether judges should be elected has elicited controversy. Also controversial is the policymaking function of the United States Supreme Court. After all, when the Court renders an opinion on how the Constitution is to be interpreted, it is, necessarily, making policy on a national level.

To examine the nature of this controversy, we first need to explain how the **judiciary** (the courts) functions in this country. We begin by looking at the origins and sources of American law. We then describe the federal court system, at the apex of which is the United States Supreme Court, and consider various issues relating to the courts.

> ## "IT IS CONFIDENCE *IN THE MEN AND WOMEN WHO ADMINISTER THE JUDICIAL SYSTEM* THAT IS THE TRUE BACKBONE OF THE RULE OF LAW."
>
> ~ JOHN PAUL STEVENS, ASSOCIATE JUSTICE OF THE UNITED STATES SUPREME COURT, 1975–2010

14-1 THE ORIGINS AND SOURCES OF AMERICAN LAW

LO Summarize the origins of the American legal system and the basic sources of American law.

judiciary The courts, one of the three branches of government in the United States.

common law The body of law developed from judicial decisions in English and U.S. courts, not attributable to a legislature.

precedent A court decision that furnishes an example or authority for deciding subsequent cases involving identical or similar facts and legal issues.

stare decisis A common law doctrine under which judges normally are obligated to follow the precedents established by prior court decisions. Pronounced *ster*-ay dih-*si*-sis.

The American colonists brought with them the legal system that had developed in England over hundreds of years. Thus, to understand how the American legal system operates, we need to go back in time to the early English courts and the traditions they established.

14-1a The Common Law Tradition

After the Normans conquered England in 1066, William the Conqueror and his successors began the process of unifying the country under their rule. One of the methods they used was the establishment of the "king's courts," or *curiae regis*. Before the Norman Conquest, disputes had been settled according to the local legal customs in various regions of the country. The law developed in the king's courts, however, applied to the country as a whole. What evolved in these courts was the beginning of the **common law**—the body of general rules that was applied throughout the entire English realm.

The Rule of Precedent The early English courts developed the common law rules from the principles underlying judges' decisions in actual legal controversies. Judges attempted to be consistent, and whenever possible, they based their decisions on the principles applied in earlier cases. They also considered new kinds of cases with the awareness that their decisions would make new law. Each interpretation became part of the law on the subject and served as a legal **precedent**—that is, a decision that furnished an example or authority for deciding subsequent cases involving identical or similar legal issues and facts.

Stare Decisis The practice of deciding new cases with reference to former decisions, or precedents, eventually became a cornerstone of the English and American judicial systems. The practice formed a doctrine called ***stare decisis*** ("to stand on decided cases").

Under this doctrine, judges are obligated to follow the precedents established in their jurisdictions. For example, if the Supreme Court of Georgia holds that a state law requiring candidates for state office to pass drug tests is unconstitutional, that decision will control the outcome of future cases on that issue brought before the state courts in Georgia.

Similarly, a decision made on a given issue by the United States Supreme Court (the nation's highest court) is binding on all inferior (lower) courts. For example, the Georgia case on drug testing might be appealed to the United States Supreme Court. If the Court agrees that the Georgia law is unconstitutional, the high court's ruling will be binding on *all* courts in the United States. In other words, similar drug-testing laws in other states will be invalid and unenforceable.

Departures from Precedent Sometimes a court will depart from the rule of precedent if it decides that a precedent is simply incorrect or that technological or social changes have rendered the precedent inapplicable. Cases that overturn precedent often receive a great deal of publicity.

An Example: *Brown v. Board of Education.* For example, in 1954, in *Brown v. Board of Education of Topeka*,[1] the United States Supreme Court expressly overturned precedent. It concluded that separate educational facilities for African Americans, which had been upheld as constitutional in many earlier cases under the "separate-but-equal" doctrine[2] (see Chapter 5), were inherently unequal and violated the equal protection clause. The Supreme Court's departure from precedent in *Brown* received a tremendous amount of publicity as people began to realize the political and social ramifications of this change in the law.

Another Example: *Citizens United v. FEC.* More recently, the Supreme Court departed from precedent in its 2010 ruling *Citizens United v. Federal Election Commission*.[3] In this decision, the Court determined that the government may not ban political spending by corporations in elections when the spending is undertaken independently of the campaigns of individual candidates. (The ruling implicitly covers unions and nonprofit groups as well.) The Court's decision overturned two precedents that had upheld restrictions on corporate spending.[4]

14-1b Primary Sources of American Law

In any governmental system, the main function of the courts is to interpret and apply the law. In the United States, the courts interpret and apply several sources of law when deciding cases. We look here only at the **primary sources of law**—that is, sources that *establish* the law—and the relative priority of these sources when particular laws come into conflict.

Constitutional Law The U.S. government and each of the fifty states have separate written constitutions that set forth the general organization, powers, and limits of their respective governments. **Constitutional law** consists of the rights and duties set forth in these constitutions.

The U.S. Constitution is the supreme law of the land. As such, it is the basis of all law in the United States. Any law that violates the Constitution is invalid and unenforceable. Because of the paramount importance of the U.S. Constitution in the American legal system, the complete text of the Constitution is found in Appendix B.

> "It is better, so the Fourth Amendment teaches, that the guilty sometimes go free than that citizens be subject to easy arrest."
>
> ~ WILLIAM O. DOUGLAS, ASSOCIATE JUSTICE OF THE UNITED STATES SUPREME COURT, 1939–1975

The Tenth Amendment to the U.S. Constitution reserves to the states and to the people all powers not granted to the federal government. Each state in the union has its own constitution. Unless they conflict with the U.S. Constitution or a federal law, state constitutions are supreme within the borders of their respective states.

Statutory Law Statutes enacted by legislative bodies at any level of government make up another source of law, which is generally referred to as **statutory law**. Federal statutes—laws enacted by the U.S. Congress—apply to all of the states. State statutes—laws enacted by state legislatures—apply only within the state that enacted the laws. Any state statute that conflicts with the U.S. Constitution, with federal laws enacted by Congress, or with the state's constitution will be deemed invalid if challenged in court and will not be enforced.

Statutory law also includes the ordinances (such as local zoning or housing-construction laws) passed by cities and counties. None of these may violate the U.S. Constitution, the relevant state constitution, or any existing federal or state laws.

Administrative Law Another important source of American law consists of **administrative law**—the rules, regulations, orders, and decisions of administrative agencies. As you read in Chapter 13, at the federal level Congress creates executive agencies, such as the Food and

---

primary source of law A source of law that establishes the law. Primary sources of law include constitutions, statutes, administrative agency rules and regulations, and decisions rendered by the courts.

constitutional law Law based on the U.S. Constitution and the constitutions of the various states.

statutory law The body of law enacted by legislatures (as opposed to constitutional law, administrative law, or case law).

administrative law The body of law created by administrative agencies (in the form of rules, regulations, orders, and decisions) in order to carry out their duties and responsibilities.

Drug Administration and the Environmental Protection Agency, to perform specific functions. Typically, when Congress establishes an agency, it authorizes the agency to create rules that have the force of law and to enforce those rules by bringing legal actions against violators.

Rules issued by various government agencies now affect nearly every aspect of our lives. For example, almost all of a business's operations are subject to government regulation. These include the firm's capital structure and financing, its hiring and firing practices, its relations with employees and unions, and the way it manufactures and markets its products.

Government agencies exist at the state and local levels as well. States commonly create agencies that parallel federal agencies. Just as federal statutes take precedence over conflicting state statutes, federal agency regulations take precedence over conflicting state regulations.

Case Law As is evident from the earlier discussion of the common law tradition, another basic source of American law consists of the rules of law announced in court decisions, or **case law**. These rules of law include interpretations of constitutional provisions, of statutes enacted by legislatures, and of regulations issued by administrative agencies.

Thus, even though a legislature passes a law to govern a certain area, how that law is interpreted and applied depends on the courts. The importance of case law, or *judge-made law*, is one of the distinguishing characteristics of the common law tradition.

14-1c Civil Law and Criminal Law

All of the sources of law just discussed can be classified in other ways as well. One of the most significant classification systems divides all law into two categories: civil law and criminal law.

Civil law spells out the duties that individuals in society owe to other persons or to their governments, excluding the duty not to commit crimes. Typically, in a civil case, a private party sues another private party (although the government can also sue a party for a civil law violation). The object of a civil lawsuit is to make the defendant—the person being sued—comply with a legal duty (such as a contractual promise) or pay money damages for failing to comply with that duty.

Criminal law, in contrast, has to do with wrongs committed against the public as a whole. Criminal acts are prohibited by local, state, and federal government statutes. Thus, criminal defendants are prosecuted by public officials, such as a district attorney (D.A.), on behalf of the government, not by their victims or other private parties.

In a criminal case, the government seeks to impose a penalty (usually a fine and/or imprisonment) on a person who has violated a criminal law. For example, when someone robs a convenience store, that person has committed a crime and, if caught and proved guilty, will usually spend time in prison.

14-1d Basic Judicial Requirements

A court cannot decide just any issue at any time. Before a court can hear and decide a case, specific requirements must be met. To a certain extent, these requirements act as restraints on the judiciary because they limit the types of cases that courts can hear and decide. Courts also have procedural requirements that judges must follow.

Jurisdiction In Latin, *juris* means "law," and *diction* means "to speak." Therefore, **jurisdiction** literally refers to the power "to speak the law." Jurisdiction applies either to the geographic area in which a court has the right and power to decide cases, or to the right and power of a court to decide matters concerning certain persons, types of property, or subjects. Before any court can hear a case, it must have jurisdiction over the person against whom the suit is brought, the property involved in the suit, and the subject matter.

The Jurisdiction of State Courts. A state trial court usually has jurisdictional authority over the residents of a particular area of the state, such as a county or district.

> "OUR CONSTITUTION IS COLORBLIND, *AND NEITHER KNOWS NOR TOLERATES CLASSES AMONG CITIZENS.*"
>
> ~ JOHN MARSHALL HARLAN, ASSOCIATE JUSTICE OF THE UNITED STATES SUPREME COURT, 1877–1911

case law The rules of law announced in court decisions. Case law includes the aggregate of reported cases that interpret judicial precedents, statutes, regulations, and constitutional provisions.

civil law The branch of law that spells out the duties that individuals in society owe to other persons or to their governments, excluding the duty not to commit crimes.

criminal law The branch of law that defines and governs actions that constitute crimes. Generally, criminal law has to do with wrongful actions committed against society for which society demands redress.

jurisdiction The authority of a court to hear and decide a particular case.

(A **trial court** is, as the term implies, a court in which trials are held and testimony is taken.) A state's highest court (often called the *state supreme court*)[5] has jurisdictional authority over all residents within the state. In some cases, if an individual has committed an offense such as injuring someone in an automobile accident or selling defective goods within the state, the court can exercise jurisdiction even if the individual is a resident of another state.

State courts can also exercise jurisdiction over those who do business within the state. A New York company that distributes its products in California, for example, can be sued by a California resident in a California state court.

An attorney addressing a jury. If a criminal case goes to trial, a jury of ordinary citizens typically determines guilt or innocence. *How might trials by jury help protect our rights?*

Federal Court Jurisdiction. Because the federal government is a government of limited powers, the jurisdiction of the federal courts is limited. Article III, Section 2, of the Constitution states that the federal courts can exercise jurisdiction over all cases "arising under this Constitution, the Laws of the United States, and Treaties made, or which shall be made, under their Authority." Whenever a case involves a claim based, at least in part, on the U.S. Constitution, a treaty, or a federal law, a **federal question** arises. Any lawsuit involving a federal question can originate in a federal court.

Federal courts can also exercise jurisdiction over cases involving **diversity of citizenship**. Such cases may arise when the parties in a lawsuit live in different states or when one of the parties is a foreign government or a foreign citizen. Before a federal court can take jurisdiction in a diversity case, the amount in controversy must be more than $75,000. (Congress raised the limit to $75,000 in 1996. In 1789, the sum was $500, which is $14,320 in 2017 dollars.)

Standing to Sue To bring a lawsuit before a court, a person must have **standing to sue**, or a sufficient "stake" in the matter to justify bringing a suit. Thus, the party bringing the suit must have suffered a harm or been threatened with a harm by the action at issue, and the issue must be justiciable. A **justiciable controversy** is one that is real and substantial, as opposed to hypothetical or academic.

The requirement of standing to sue clearly limits the issues that can be decided by the courts. Furthermore, both state and federal governments can specify

by law when an individual or group has standing to sue. For example, the federal government will not allow a taxpayer to sue the Department of Defense for spending tax dollars wastefully.

Court Procedures Both the federal and the state courts have established procedural rules that apply in all cases. These procedures are designed to protect the rights and interests of the parties, ensure that the litigation proceeds in a fair and orderly manner, and identify the issues that must be decided by the court—thus saving court time and costs. Different procedural rules apply in criminal and civil cases. Generally, criminal procedural rules attempt to ensure that defendants are not deprived of their constitutional rights.

Parties involved in civil or criminal cases must comply with court

trial court A court in which trials are held and testimony is taken.

federal question A question that pertains to the U.S. Constitution, acts of Congress, or treaties. A federal question provides a basis for federal court jurisdiction.

diversity of citizenship A basis for federal court jurisdiction over a lawsuit that arises when (1) the parties in the lawsuit live in different states or when one of the parties is a foreign government or a foreign citizen, and (2) the amount in controversy is more than $75,000.

standing to sue The requirement that an individual must have a sufficient stake in a controversy before he or she can bring a lawsuit. The party bringing the suit must demonstrate that he or she has either been harmed or been threatened with a harm.

justiciable controversy A controversy that is not hypothetical or academic but real and substantial; a requirement that must be satisfied before a court will hear a case. *Justiciable* is pronounced jus-*tish*-a-bul.

procedural rules or risk being held in **contempt of court**. A party who is held in contempt of court can be fined, taken into custody, or both. A court must take care to ensure that the parties—and the court itself—comply with procedural requirements. Procedural errors often serve as grounds for a mistrial or for appealing the court's decision to a higher tribunal.

CRITICAL THINKING

▶ *Why does national law—even administrative law established by a federal agency—overrule conflicting state law, even when a state law is based on the state constitution?*

14–2 THE FEDERAL COURT SYSTEM

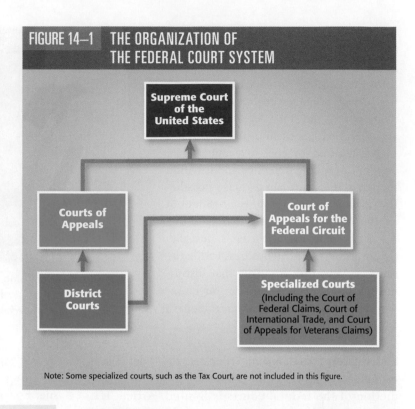

FIGURE 14–1 THE ORGANIZATION OF THE FEDERAL COURT SYSTEM

Supreme Court of the United States

Courts of Appeals

Court of Appeals for the Federal Circuit

District Courts

Specialized Courts (Including the Court of Federal Claims, Court of International Trade, and Court of Appeals for Veterans Claims)

Note: Some specialized courts, such as the Tax Court, are not included in this figure.

LO Delineate the structure of the federal court system.

The federal court system is a three-tiered model consisting of U.S. district courts (trial courts), U.S. courts of appeals, and the United States Supreme Court. Figure 14–1 shows the organization of the federal court system.

Bear in mind that the federal courts constitute only one of the fifty-two court systems in the United States. Each of the fifty states has its own court system, as does the District of Columbia. No two state court systems are exactly the same. In general, though, the states have different levels, or tiers, of courts, just as the federal system does.

Normally, state courts deal with questions of state law, and the decisions of a state's highest court on matters of state law are normally final. If a federal question is involved, however, a decision of a state supreme court may be appealed to the federal court system. We will discuss the federal court system in the pages that follow.

14–2a U.S. District and Specialized Courts

contempt of court
A ruling that a person has disobeyed a court order or has shown disrespect to the court or to a judicial proceeding.

On the lowest tier of the federal court system are the U.S. district courts, or federal trial courts— the courts in which cases involving federal laws begin. The cases in these courts are decided by a judge or a jury. There is at least one federal district court in every state, and there is one in the District of Columbia. The number of judicial districts has varied historically, but no new district has been created since 1966. Figure 14–2 shows their geographic boundaries. Currently, there are ninety-four judicial districts and 678 district court judgeships. The number of judges per district varies from two in North Dakota to twenty-eight in the Southern District of New York.

The federal system also includes other trial courts, such as the Court of International Trade and others listed in Figure 14–1. These courts have limited, or specialized, subject-matter jurisdiction—that is, they can exercise authority over only certain kinds of cases.

One specialized court has recently received exceptional scrutiny—the Foreign Intelligence Surveillance Court (FISC). This court was initially created to issue search warrants against suspected foreign spies inside the United States. The USA Patriot Act of 2001 greatly expanded its powers. The FISC almost never rejects a warrant request. It meets in secret and releases no information on individual cases.

More controversially, the court does not report the legal interpretations under which it issues its rulings. In 2013, revelations of large-scale surveillance by the National Security Agency (NSA) raised questions about the FISC's practices. (NSA actions must be approved by the FISC.) Some legal experts doubted that the FISC's decisions could be squared with the Fourth Amendment

FIGURE 14–2   U.S. COURTS OF APPEALS AND U.S. DISTRICT COURTS

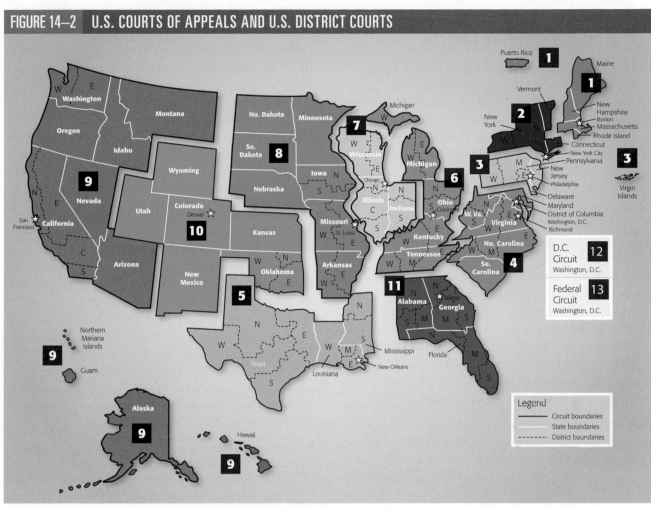

Source: Administrative Office of the United States Courts.

to the U.S. Constitution, which bars unreasonable searches. The USA Freedom Act of June 2015 sought to submit the FISC to greater scrutiny.

14–2b U.S. Courts of Appeals

On the middle tier of the federal court system are the U.S. courts of appeals. Courts of appeals, or **appellate courts**, do not hear evidence or testimony. Rather, an appellate court reviews the transcript of the trial court's proceedings, other records relating to the case, and attorneys' arguments as to why the trial court's decision should or should not stand.

In contrast to a trial court, where normally a single judge presides, an appellate court consists of a panel of three or more judges. The task of the appellate court is to determine whether the trial court erred in applying the law to the facts and issues involved in a particular case.

There are thirteen federal courts of appeals in the United States. The courts of appeals for twelve of the circuits, including the Court of Appeals for the D.C. Circuit, hear appeals from the U.S. district courts located within their respective judicial circuits (see Figure 14–2).

Decisions made by federal administrative agencies may be reviewed by either a district court or the court of appeals, depending on the agency. The Court of Appeals for the Federal Circuit has national jurisdiction over certain types of cases, such as those concerning patent law and some claims against the national government.

The decisions of the federal appellate courts may be appealed to the Supreme Court. If a decision is not appealed, or if the high court declines to review the case, the appellate court's decision is final.

appellate court
A court having appellate jurisdiction. An appellate court normally does not hear evidence or testimony. Instead, it reviews the transcript of the trial court's proceedings, other records relating to the case, and attorneys' arguments as to why the trial court's decision should or should not stand.

14–2c The United States Supreme Court

The highest level of the three-tiered model of the federal court system is the United States Supreme Court. According to Article III of the U.S. Constitution, there is only one national Supreme Court, but Congress is empowered to create additional ("inferior") courts as it deems necessary. The inferior courts that Congress has created include the second tier in our model—the U.S. courts of appeals—as well as the district courts and any other courts of limited, or specialized, jurisdiction.

The United States Supreme Court consists of nine justices—a chief justice and eight associate justices—although that number is not mandated by the Constitution. The Supreme Court has original, or trial, jurisdiction only in unusual instances (set forth in Article III, Section 2). In other words, only rarely does a case originate at the Supreme Court level. Most of the Court's work is as an appellate court. The Supreme Court has appellate authority over cases decided by the U.S. courts of appeals, as well as over some cases decided in the state courts when federal questions are at issue.

The Writ of *Certiorari* To bring a case before the Supreme Court, a party may request that the Court issue a **writ of *certiorari***, often called "cert." The writ of *certiorari* is an order that the Supreme Court issues to a lower court requesting the latter to send it the record of the case in question.

Parties can petition the Supreme Court to issue a writ of *certiorari*, but whether the Court will do so is entirely within its discretion. The Court will not issue a writ unless at least four of the nine justices approve. In no instance is the Court required to issue a writ of *certiorari*.[6]

Most petitions for writs of *certiorari* are denied. A denial is not a decision on the merits of a case, nor does it indicate that the Court agrees with a lower court's opinion. The denial of a writ has no value as a precedent. A denial simply means that the decision of the lower court remains the law within that court's jurisdiction.

Which Cases Reach the Supreme Court? There is no absolute right to appeal to the United States Supreme Court. Although thousands of cases are filed with the Supreme Court each year, on average the Court hears fewer than one hundred. As shown in Figure 14–3, the number of cases heard by the Court each year has declined significantly since the 1980s. In large part, this has occurred because the Court has raised its standards for accepting cases in recent years.

Typically, the Court grants petitions for cases that raise important policy issues that need to be addressed. In its 2015–2016 term, for example, the Court heard cases involving such issues as the following:

▸ **Does the Environmental Protection Agency have the power, under current legislation, to regulate carbon dioxide emissions from existing power plants? The Court temporarily blocked such actions pending final review.[7]**

▸ **Can the president issue an executive order that blocks the deportation of up to 5 million unauthorized immigrants? In a four-to-four split that in effect upheld an appeals court ruling, the Court blocked such an order for at least a year.[8]**

> **writ of *certiorari*** An order from a higher court asking a lower court for the record of a case. *Certiorari* is pronounced sur-shee-uh-*rah*-ree.

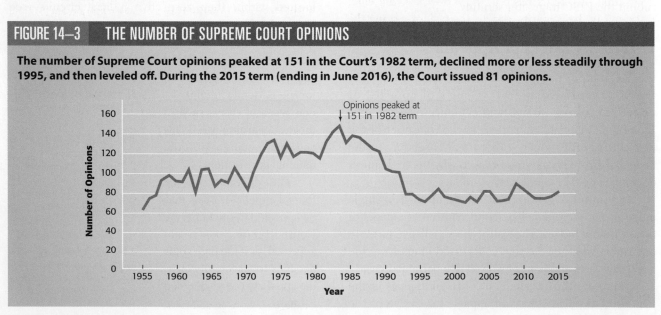

FIGURE 14–3   THE NUMBER OF SUPREME COURT OPINIONS

The number of Supreme Court opinions peaked at 151 in the Court's 1982 term, declined more or less steadily through 1995, and then leveled off. During the 2015 term (ending in June 2016), the Court issued 81 opinions.

- Can government employees be required to pay service fees to a labor union when they are not members? In another four-to-four split, the Court allowed such payments to continue for now in California.[9]

- Can Texas discourage abortions by imposing exceptional requirements on abortion providers? The Court struck down the Texas law decisively.[10]

If the lower courts have rendered conflicting opinions on an important issue, the Supreme Court often reviews one or more cases involving that issue to define the law on the matter. For example, in 2014, four appellate courts ruled that same-sex couples had a constitutional right to marry. The Sixth Circuit Court, however, issued an opinion denying that right. These conflicting judgments forced a somewhat reluctant Supreme Court to take up the issue. The result was *Obergefell v. Hodges* (2015), which established a nationwide right to same-sex marriage.[11]

Supreme Court Opinions Like other appellate courts, the United States Supreme Court normally does not hear any evidence. The Court's decision in a particular case is based on the written record of the case and the written arguments (legal briefs) that the attorneys submit. The attorneys also present **oral arguments**—spoken arguments presented in person rather than on paper—to the Court. Some observers of the Court have advocated that the oral arguments be video-recorded and provided to the public through C-SPAN. The Court does not agree, however, and cameras are banned.

Reaching an Opinion. After considering all this information, the justices discuss the case in **conference**. The conference is strictly private—only the justices are allowed in the room.

When the Court has reached a decision, the chief justice, if in the majority, assigns the task of writing the Court's **opinion** to one of the justices. When the chief justice is not in the majority, the most senior justice voting with the majority assigns the writing of the Court's opinion. The opinion outlines the reasons for the Court's decision, the rules of law that apply, and the judgment. An opinion that commands the support of more than half of the justices is called a *majority opinion*.

Concurring and Dissenting Opinions. Often, one or more justices who agree with the Court's decision do so for reasons different from those outlined in the majority opinion. These justices may write **concurring opinions**, setting forth their own legal reasoning on the issue. Frequently, one or more justices disagree with the Court's conclusion. These justices may write **dissenting opinions**, outlining the reasons they feel the majority erred in arriving at its decision.

Although a dissenting opinion does not affect the outcome of the case before the Court, it may be important later. In a subsequent case concerning the same issue, a jurist or attorney may use the legal reasoning in the dissenting opinion as the basis for an argument to reverse the previous decision and establish a new precedent.

Sometimes, the opinion with the support of the largest number of justices does not command a majority of the Court. Such an opinion is called a *plurality opinion*. It becomes the Court's opinion only if it is supported by enough concurring opinions to form a majority. It is possible, though rare, for a plurality opinion to be a dissent if a large enough collection of alternative opinions agree with each other.

CRITICAL THINKING

- *Some people believe that the Supreme Court should accept more cases and thereby resolve more issues. Others contend that such a move would result in fewer well-thought-out opinions. Who do you think has the better argument, and why?*

 14–3 FEDERAL JUDICIAL APPOINTMENTS

LO Say how federal judges are appointed.

Unlike state court judges, who are often elected, all federal judges are appointed. Article II, Section 2, of the Constitution authorizes the president to appoint the justices of the Supreme Court with the advice and consent of the Senate. Laws enacted by Congress provide that the same procedure is to be used for appointing judges to the lower federal courts as well.

Federal judges receive lifetime appointments (because under Article III of the Constitution they "hold their Offices during good Behaviour"). Federal judges may be removed from office through the impeachment

oral argument A spoken argument presented to a judge in person by an attorney on behalf of her or his client.

conference In regard to the Supreme Court, a private meeting of the justices in which they present their arguments concerning a case under consideration.

opinion A written statement by a court expressing the reasons for its decision in a case.

concurring opinion A statement written by a judge or justice who agrees (concurs) with the court's decision, but for reasons different from those in the majority opinion.

dissenting opinion A statement written by a judge or justice who disagrees with the majority opinion.

process, but such proceedings are extremely rare and are usually undertaken only if a judge engages in blatantly illegal conduct, such as bribery. In the history of this nation, only fifteen federal judges have been impeached, and only eleven left office due to a conviction or resignation. Normally, federal judges serve until they resign, retire, or die.

Although the Constitution sets no specific qualifications for those who serve on the Supreme Court, those who have done so share one characteristic: all have been attorneys. The backgrounds of the Supreme Court justices have been far from typical of the characteristics of the American public as a whole. Table 14–1 summarizes the backgrounds of all of the 112 United States Supreme Court justices to 2016.

14-3a The Nomination Process

The president receives suggestions and recommendations as to potential nominees for judicial positions from various sources, including the Justice Department, senators, other judges, the candidates themselves, state political leaders, bar associations, and other interest groups. After selecting a nominee, the president submits her or his name to the Senate for approval. The Senate Judiciary Committee then holds hearings and makes its recommendation to the Senate, where it takes a majority vote to confirm the nomination.

Senatorial Courtesy When judges are nominated to the district courts (and, to a lesser extent, the U.S. courts of appeals), a senator of the president's political party from the state where there is a vacancy traditionally has been allowed to veto the president's choice. This practice is known as **senatorial courtesy**. At times, senatorial courtesy even permits senators from the opposing party to veto presidential choices. Because of senatorial courtesy, home-state senators of the president's party may be able to influence the choice of the nominee.

Partisanship It should come as no surprise that partisanship plays a significant role in the president's selection of nominees to the federal bench, particularly to the Supreme Court, the crown jewel of the federal judiciary. Traditionally, presidents have attempted to strengthen their legacies by appointing federal judges with political and philosophical views similar to their own. In the history of the Supreme Court, fewer than 13 percent of

senatorial courtesy A practice that allows a senator of the president's party to veto the president's nominee to a federal court judgeship within the senator's state.

TABLE 14-1	BACKGROUNDS OF UNITED STATES SUPREME COURT JUSTICES TO 2016	
		Number of Justices (112 = Total)
Occupational Position before Appointment		
Private legal practice		25
State judgeship		21
Federal judgeship		31
U.S. attorney general		7
Deputy or assistant U.S. attorney general		2
U.S. solicitor general		3
U.S. senator		6
U.S. representative		2
State governor		3
Federal executive post		9
Other		3
Religious Affiliation		
Protestant		83
Roman Catholic		14
Jewish		7
Unitarian		7
No religious affiliation		1
Age on Appointment		
Under 40		5
41–50		33
51–60		60
61–70		14
Political Party Affiliation		
Federalist (to 1835)		13
Jeffersonian Republican (to 1828)		7
Whig (to 1861)		1
Democrat		46
Republican		44
Independent		1
Education		
College graduate		96
Not a college graduate		16
Gender		
Male		108
Female		4
Race		
White (non-Hispanic)		109
African American		2
Hispanic		1

Sources: *Congressional Quarterly's Guide to the U.S. Supreme Court* (Washington, D.C.: Congressional Quarterly Press, 1997); and authors' updates.

Sonia Sotomayor became the first Latina on the Supreme Court when she was confirmed by the Senate in 2009. *Why might President Obama have chosen her?*

For example, consider a decision interpreting the federal Constitution by the U.S. Court of Appeals for the Ninth Circuit. If not overruled by the Supreme Court, it establishes a precedent that will be followed in the states of Alaska, Arizona, California, Hawaii, Idaho, Montana, Nevada, Oregon, and Washington.

14–3b Confirmation or Rejection by the Senate

The president's nominations are not always confirmed. In fact, almost 20 percent of presidential nominations for the Supreme Court have been either rejected or not acted on by the Senate. The process of nominating and confirming federal judges, especially Supreme Court justices, often involves political debate and controversy. Many bitter battles over Supreme Court appointments have ensued when the Senate and the president have disagreed on political issues.

From 1893 until 1968, the Senate rejected only three Court nominees. From 1968 through 1986, however, two presidential nominees to the highest court were rejected, and two more nominations, both by President Ronald Reagan, failed in 1987. The most significant of these nominees was Robert Bork, who faced hostile questioning about his strongly conservative views during the confirmation hearings. The Bork hearings are often considered to be a turning point after which confirmation hearings became much more contentious.

One of President George H. W. Bush's nominees to the Supreme Court—Clarence Thomas—was also the subject of considerable controversy. The nation watched on television as Anita Hill, a former aide, leveled charges of sexual harassment at Thomas, who nevertheless was confirmed.

George W. Bush's Appointments During George W. Bush's second term, Chief Justice William Rehnquist died, and Sandra Day O'Connor, the Court's first woman justice, retired. These events allowed Bush to nominate John G. Roberts, Jr., to replace Rehnquist and Samuel A. Alito, Jr., to replace O'Connor. Both nominations were confirmed by the Senate with relatively little difficulty. The appointment of Alito,

the justices nominated by a president have been from an opposing political party.

That said, presidents have often discovered that the justices they appointed took very different positions than expected. President Dwight D. Eisenhower (1953–1961), for example, had no idea when he appointed Chief Justice Earl Warren that Warren would seek to overturn the system of racial segregation. The Court accomplished this goal through rulings such as *Brown v. Board of Education* (see Chapter 5).[12]

Courts of Appeals Appointments to the U.S. courts of appeals can also have a lasting impact. Recall that these courts occupy the level just below the Supreme Court in the federal court system. Also recall that the decisions rendered by these courts—about 60,000 per year—are final unless overturned by the Supreme Court. Given that the Supreme Court renders opinions in fewer than one hundred cases a year, the decisions of the federal appellate courts have a wide-reaching effect on American society.

> "AS NIGHTFALL DOESN'T COME AT ONCE, NEITHER DOES OPPRESSION. *IN BOTH INSTANCES, . . . WE MUST BE AWARE OF CHANGE IN THE AIR, HOWEVER SLIGHT, LEST WE BECOME UNWITTING VICTIMS OF THE DARKNESS.*"
>
> ~ WILLIAM O. DOUGLAS, ASSOCIATE JUSTICE OF THE UNITED STATES SUPREME COURT, 1939–1975

in particular, changed the character of the Court, because he was distinctly more conservative than O'Connor.

Obama's Nominees   In May 2009, as a result of a judicial retirement, President Barack Obama named Sonia Sotomayor to the Court. Sotomayor had served for more than a decade as a judge of the U.S. Court of Appeals for the Second Circuit and was the first Hispanic American ever nominated to the Supreme Court.

A second retirement gave Obama an additional chance to pick a nominee, in May 2010. He chose Elena Kagan, his solicitor general. It was a sign of the increased political polarization in the Senate that neither Sotomayor nor Kagan received more than a handful of votes from Republican senators.

The Death of Justice Scalia   In February 2016, Justice Antonin Scalia died unexpectedly. Scalia and Justice Clarence Thomas were the two most conservative members of the Court. The chances of Barack Obama—or any Democratic president—nominating a replacement as conservative as Scalia were zero. It appeared possible that the Court was about to take an abrupt lurch to the left. Senate majority leader Mitch McConnell therefore announced that the Republicans would refuse to consider any nominee that Obama might submit. Filling Scalia's seat might have to wait until after January 2017, when a new president would assume office. Republican senators clearly hoped that the new president would be a Republican.

In recent years, the Court has issued a substantial number of five-to-four decisions in which Scalia was part of a five-justice conservative majority. With his seat vacant, there were only eight justices, raising the possibility of frequent four-to-four tie votes. When that happens, the decision of the lower court is sustained. The Court's action does not, however, serve as a precedent. What if two circuit courts have come to different conclusions on an important issue? A Court divided four-to-four would not be able to overrule either of them. Americans could be subject to different federal laws depending on the judicial circuit in which they live.

In March 2016, Obama nominated Merrick Garland, chief judge of the D.C. Circuit Court, as Scalia's replacement. Garland had a moderate reputation, and Republicans had supported him in the past. He was, in fact, about the least liberal candidate that Obama could be expected to pick. His nomination raised a possibility: what if a Democrat won the White House in 2016? Republicans might then be tempted to confirm Garland immediately after the election to prevent the incoming president from naming anyone more liberal. We examine the fight for Scalia's seat in this chapter's *Join the Debate* feature.

▸ *In recent years, senators have increasingly made use of the filibuster to delay or prevent the approval of judicial nominees. Is this a legitimate tactic or an example of partisan excess? Explain.*

 14–4   THE COURTS AS POLICYMAKERS

LO Explain how the federal courts make policy, and describe the role of ideology and judicial philosophies in judicial decision making.

In the United States, judges and justices play a major role in government. Unlike judges in some other countries, U.S. judges have the power to decide on the constitutionality of laws or actions undertaken by the other branches of government.

Clearly, the function of the courts is to interpret and apply the law, not to make law—that is the function of the legislative branch of government. Yet judges can and do "make law." Indeed, they cannot avoid

Courtesy of The White House.

President Obama visits with justices Ruth Bader Ginsburg and Elena Kagan in the White House. *What effects might result from the growing number of women on the Court?*

Should Congress Ever Refuse to Consider a Supreme Court Nominee?

The U.S. Constitution gives the president the power to nominate Supreme Court justices, but they are confirmed only with the "Advice and Consent" of the Senate. Does that mean that the Senate must consider all presidential nominations when there is a vacancy on the Court? Or does the Senate have the right to "wait things out"? This is not a theoretical question, because in 2016 the death of Justice Antonin Scalia created a vacancy on the nine-person court. As we have noted, Senate majority leader Mitch McConnell announced that there would be no hearings on any Obama nomination. Rather, the Senate would wait until the next president made her or his choice. Should the Senate have the option of refusing to act?

It's the Senate's Duty to Consider a President's Nominee

Presidents do not stop working in the final year of their term, and neither does the Supreme Court. The American people deserve a full set of nine justices to decide important constitutional issues. Playing politics with the nomination process is just not

right. Every Supreme Court nominee deserves a fair hearing, even during an election year.

Senate minority leader Harry Reid contended that a refusal by the Senate to hold hearings "would be a shameful abdication of one of the Senate's most essential constitutional responsibilities." Dragging out the nomination process until after the elections puts crass partisan politics before effective governance. Leaving the Court at eight justices—with the inevitable four-to-four ties—will slow down the process of deciding important cases. The American people have a right to a functioning Court.

The Senate Has Refused to Act in the Past and Can Do So Again

During the election year of 1852, Whig president Millard Fillmore tried three times to fill the seat of a recently deceased justice. The Democrat-controlled Senate refused to act on any of the nominations. There have been similar cases since that time. Indeed, in the election year of 1992, then-Senator Joe Biden (later Obama's vice president) argued that the president should follow the example of "a

majority of his predecessors" and delay naming a Supreme Court replacement. "Once the political season is under way," he said, "action on a Supreme Court nomination must be put off until after the election campaign is over."

There simply is no requirement in the Constitution that the Senate hold hearings on any presidential nomination. Suspending the nomination process during a presidential election year lets the voters decide who the next justice will be.

It is true that a Court made up of eight members may break four-to-four on some cases. If the Court is that evenly divided, however, it is even more important that the outcome of the case be determined by a new appointee. That justice will reflect the views of the American people, as reflected in their votes for president and the Senate.

Critical Analysis

Why might Republicans be worried about who is chosen to fill a vacant Supreme Court seat?

making law in some cases, because the law does not always provide clear answers to questions that come before the courts.

14–4a The Issue of Broad Language

The text of the U.S. Constitution is set forth in broad terms. When a court interprets a constitutional provision and applies that interpretation to a specific set of circumstances, the court is essentially "making the

law" on that issue. Examples of how the courts, and especially the United States Supreme Court, make law abound.

The Right to Privacy Consider privacy rights, which we discussed in Chapter 4. Nothing in the Constitution or its amendments specifically states that we have a right to privacy. Yet the Supreme Court, through various decisions, has established such a right by deciding that it is implied by several constitutional amendments.

The Court has also held that this right to privacy includes a number of specific rights, such as the right to have an abortion.

Vague Language and New Technologies

Statutory provisions and other legal rules also tend to be expressed in general terms, and the courts must decide how those general provisions and rules apply to specific cases. The Americans with Disabilities Act of 1990 is an example. The act requires employers to reasonably accommodate the needs of employees with disabilities. But the act does not say exactly what employers must do to "reasonably accommodate" such persons. Thus, the courts must decide, on a case-by-case basis, what this phrase means.

Additionally, in some cases there is no relevant law or precedent to follow. In recent years, for example, courts have been struggling with new kinds of legal issues stemming from new communications technologies, including the Internet. Until legislative bodies enact laws governing these issues, it is up to the courts to fashion the law that will apply—and thus make policy.

14–4b The Power of Judicial Review

Recall from Chapter 2 that the U.S. Constitution divides government powers among the executive, legislative, and judicial branches. This division of powers is part of our system of checks and balances. Essentially, the founders gave each branch of government the constitutional authority to check the other two branches. The federal judiciary can exercise a check on the actions of either of the other branches through its power of **judicial review**.

Marbury v. Madison The Constitution does not actually mention judicial review. Rather, the Supreme Court claimed the power for itself in *Marbury v. Madison*, first discussed in Chapter 3.[13] In that case, which was decided by the Court in 1803, Chief Justice John Marshall held that a provision of a 1789 law affecting the Supreme Court's jurisdiction violated the Constitution and was thus void. Marshall declared, "It is emphatically the province and duty of the judicial department [the courts] to say what the law is. . . . If two laws conflict with each other, the courts must decide on the operation of each. . . . [I]f a law be in opposition to the constitution . . . the court must determine which of these conflicting rules governs the case. This is the very essence of judicial duty."

judicial review The power of the courts to decide on the constitutionality of legislative enactments and of actions taken by the executive branch.

The Views of the Founders Most constitutional scholars believe that the framers intended that the federal courts should have the power of judicial review. In *Federalist Paper* No. 78, Alexander Hamilton clearly espoused the doctrine. Hamilton stressed the importance of the "complete independence" of federal judges and their special duty to "invalidate all acts contrary to the manifest tenor of the Constitution." Without judicial review by impartial courts, there would be nothing to ensure that the other branches of government stayed within constitutional limits when exercising their powers, and "all the reservations of particular rights or privileges would amount to nothing." Chief Justice Marshall shared Hamilton's views and adopted Hamilton's reasoning in *Marbury v. Madison.*

14–4c Judicial Activism versus Judicial Restraint

As already noted, making policy is not the primary function of the federal courts. Yet it is unavoidable that courts do, in fact, influence or even establish policy when they interpret and apply the law. Further, the power of judicial review gives the courts, and particularly the Supreme Court, an important policymaking tool. When the Supreme Court upholds or invalidates a state or federal statute, the consequences for the nation can be profound.

One issue that is often debated is how the federal courts should wield their policymaking power, particularly the power of judicial review. Often, this debate is couched in terms of judicial activism versus judicial restraint.

Activist versus Restraintist Justices The terms *judicial activism* and *judicial restraint* do not have precise meanings. Generally, however, an activist judge or justice believes that the courts should actively use their powers to check the legislative and executive branches to ensure that they do not exceed their authority. A restraintist judge or justice, in contrast, generally assumes that the courts should defer to the decisions of the legislative and executive branches. After all, members of Congress and the president are elected by the people, whereas federal court judges are not. In other words, the courts should not thwart the implementation of legislative acts unless those acts are clearly unconstitutional.

Political Ideology and Judicial Activism/ Restraint One of the Supreme Court's most activist eras occurred during the period from 1953 to 1969 under the leadership of Chief Justice Earl Warren. The Warren Court propelled the civil rights movement

Chief Justice Samuel Alito, Jr., and Chief Justice Stephen Breyer. *How did the appointment of these two justices change the Court?*

forward by holding, among other things, that laws permitting racial segregation violated the equal protection clause (see Chapter 5).

Because of the activism of the Warren Court, the term *judicial activism* has often been linked with liberalism. Neither judicial activism nor judicial restraint is necessarily linked to a particular political ideology, however. In fact, many observers claim that today's Supreme Court is often activist on behalf of a conservative agenda.

14-4d Ideology and the Courts

The policymaking role of the courts gives rise to an important question: To what extent do ideology and personal policy preferences affect judicial decision making? Numerous scholars have attempted to answer this question, especially with respect to Supreme Court justices.

Few doubt that ideology affects judicial decision making, although, of course, other factors play a role as well. Certainly, there are numerous examples of ideology affecting Supreme Court decisions. As new justices replace old ones and new ideological alignments are formed, the Court's decisions are affected. Yet many scholars argue that there is no real evidence that personal preferences influence Supreme Court decisions to an *unacceptable* extent.

Keep in mind that judicial decision making, particularly at the Supreme Court level, can be very complex. When deciding cases, the Supreme Court often must consider any number of sources of law, including constitutions, statutes, and administrative agency regulations—as well as cases interpreting relevant portions of those sources. At times, the Court may also take demographic data, public opinion, foreign laws, and other factors into account. How much weight is given to each of these sources or factors will vary from justice to justice. After all, reasoning of any kind, including judicial reasoning, does not take place in a vacuum.

It is only natural that a justice's life experiences, personal biases, and intellectual abilities and predispositions will influence the reasoning process. Nevertheless, it is expected that when reviewing a case, a Supreme Court justice does not start out with a conclusion (such as "I don't like this particular law that Congress passed") and then look for legal sources to support that conclusion.

14-4e Ideology and Today's Supreme Court

In contrast to the liberal Supreme Court under Earl Warren, today's Court has been generally conservative. The Court began its rightward shift after President Ronald Reagan (1981–1989) appointed conservative William Rehnquist as chief justice in 1986, and the Court moved further to the right as other conservative appointments to the bench were made by Reagan and George H. W. Bush (1989–1993).

The Roberts Court Many Supreme Court scholars believe that the appointments of John Roberts (as chief justice) and especially Samuel Alito (as associate justice) caused the Court to drift even further to the right. Certainly, the five conservative justices on the bench during the Roberts Court's first several terms voted together and cast the deciding votes in numerous cases. The remaining justices held liberal to moderate views and often formed an opposing bloc.

A notable change in the Court occurred when Alito replaced retiring justice Sandra Day O'Connor.

Chief Justice John Roberts. *How has the chief justice handled issues raised by Obamacare?*

O'Connor had often been the "swing" vote on the Court, sometimes voting with the liberal bloc and at other times siding with the conservatives.

On the Roberts Court, the swing voter is usually Justice Anthony Kennedy, who is generally more conservative in his views than O'Connor was. Although Justice Kennedy dislikes being described as a swing voter, he often decides the outcome of a case. From October 2010 through June 2015, Kennedy was in the majority in 84 percent of the cases decided by a narrow five-to-four vote. No other justice came close to this percentage.

President Obama's naming of Justices Elena Kagan and Sonia Sotomayor to the Court did not change its ideological balance. Both women joined the liberal bloc, but the men they replaced had been fairly liberal as well.

The Court's Conservatism In recent years, the nature of the Court's conservatism has come into sharper focus. It is a mistake to equate the ideology of the Court's majority with the conservatism, say, of the Republicans in Congress or with the ideology of the conservative movement. To be sure, there are members of the Court who are unmistakably *movement*

conservatives—that is, members in good standing of the conservative movement. Justice Clarence Thomas is in this camp, and so was the late Justice Antonin Scalia. Yet Justice Kennedy and Chief Justice Roberts—and even Justice Alito—often "march to their own drummer."

Obamacare. A leading example was Chief Justice Roberts's 2015 ruling on Obamacare. In *King v. Burwell,* the question was how to interpret the text of the Affordable Care Act. The case focused on one clause in a long bill (the act is about the length of *Harry Potter and the Order of the Phoenix*). The clause referred to subsidies granted to low-income individuals who used state exchanges to buy health-care insurance. The federal exchange was not mentioned. Opponents of Obamacare argued that subsidies for the federal exchange were contrary to the plain text of the legislation. In a six-to-three majority opinion, Chief Justice Roberts found that it was clear from the language of the bill taken as a whole that Congress meant to grant federal exchange subsidies.[14] The ruling angered many conservatives.

Gay Rights. Another area in which Court conservatives have parted from the conservative movement is that of gay rights. Justice Kennedy, in particular, has favored gay rights ever since *Lawrence v. Texas*, a 2003 ruling that abolished laws against homosexual acts.[15] Kennedy joined with the Court's majority in that case, providing an important vote to decide the issue. Kennedy's vote was also decisive in later gay rights cases, such as *Obergefell v. Hodges,* the 2015 ruling that established a right to same-sex marriage in all fifty states.[16]

Toward a More Liberal Court? Progressives celebrated a number of victories in the Court's 2014–2015 term. The *Obergefell v. Hodges* same-sex marriage ruling was a major example of a liberal decision. Some Court watchers explained the liberal trend by noting that in 2014–2015, conservatives sponsored a large number of cases in an attempt to push the law to the right. Often, the Court resisted. In June 2015, however, the Court announced that it would take up several questions on which it had a conservative record. These included cases on affirmative action and voting rights.

The return to conservatism was clear in February 2016, when the Court, by a five-to-four vote, stayed (blocked) implementation of an EPA attempt to regulate carbon dioxide emissions from power plants. Blocking a proposed regulation pending judicial review was almost unprecedented, and seemed to guarantee that the Court would eventually throw out the plan. Four days after this ruling, Justice Antonin Scalia died. The Court was now split four-to-four between conservatives and progressives. As explained earlier, Republicans in the Senate refused to consider any Obama nominee to replace Scalia. The hope was that a Republican president elected in November 2016 might fill the seat. In fact, Republican Donald Trump was elected president, and he had promised to name a very conservative nominee.

14-4f Approaches to Legal Interpretation

It would be a mistake to look at the judicial philosophy of today's Supreme Court solely in terms of the political ideologies of liberalism and conservatism. In fact, some Supreme Court scholars have suggested that other factors are as important as, or more important than, the justices' political philosophies in determining why they decide as they do. These factors include the justices' attitudes toward legal interpretation and their perceptions of the Supreme Court's role in the federal judiciary. Two important judicial philosophies, both of which are often associated with conservative principles, are *strict construction* and *originalism*.

Strict Construction   The term *strict construction* is widely used in the press and by politicians. Republican presidential candidates routinely promise to appoint justices who will interpret the Constitution strictly and not "legislate from the bench." The opposite of strict construction is *broad construction*. Advocates of strict construction often contend that the government should do nothing that is not specifically mentioned in the Constitution. In 1803, for example, some strict constructionists argued that the national government had no power to double the size of the country by purchasing the Louisiana Territory. Such radical strict constructionism had little support in 1803 and is accepted by few people today.

Despite the wide popularity of strict construction as a concept, members of the Supreme Court generally reject the description.

> "THE CONSTITUTION ITSELF SHOULD BE OUR GUIDE, *NOT OUR OWN CONCEPT OF WHAT IS FAIR, DECENT, AND RIGHT.*"
>
> ~ HUGO L. BLACK, ASSOCIATE JUSTICE OF THE UNITED STATES SUPREME COURT, 1937–1971

Justice Scalia, for example, who is normally considered to have been one of the purest examples of a strict constructionist on the Court, prefered to call himself a *textualist* instead. Scalia wrote, "I am not a strict constructionist, and no one ought to be. . . . A text should not be construed strictly, and it should not be construed leniently; it should be construed reasonably, to contain all that it fairly means."[17]

What Scalia meant by textualism is that when determining the meaning of legislation, he would refuse to consider the legislative debates that took place when the measure was passed, the nature of the problem the legislation was meant to address, or anything other than the actual text of the law.

Original Intent   A second conservative philosophy is called *originalism*. Justice Thomas is a well-known advocate of this approach. Originalists believe that to determine the meaning of a particular constitutional phrase, the Court should look to the intentions of the founders. What did the framers of the Constitution themselves intend when they included the phrase in the document? To discern the intent of the founders, justices might look to sources that shed light on the founders' views. These sources could include writings by the founders, newspaper articles from that period, the

Justice Anthony Kennedy tours the aircraft carrier USS John C. Stennis. Kennedy has typically held the "swing" vote on the closely divided Roberts Court. *On what kinds of cases has Kennedy broken with the conservative movement?*

Andre T. Richard/Mass Communication Specialist/U.S. Navy

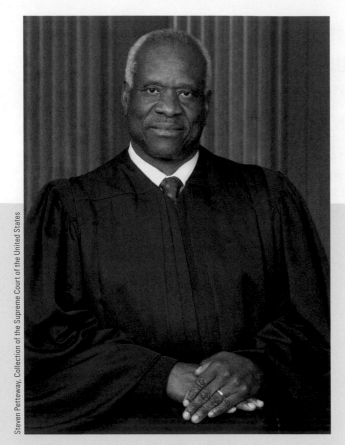

Justice Clarence Thomas is widely seen as a conservative. *How might he approach the text of legislation?*

and Thomas opposed the ruling. In contrast, modernists might argue that discrimination against gays and lesbians is exactly the type of evil that the amendment sought to prevent, even though such an application never occurred to those who wrote it.

 CRITICAL THINKING

▶ *If a Democratic president is able to fill Justice Scalia's seat on the Supreme Court, how might the new Court rule on abortion? On affirmative action?*

14–5 ASSESSING THE ROLE OF THE FEDERAL COURTS

LO Identify some of the criticisms of the federal courts and some of the checks on the power of the courts.

The federal courts have often come under attack, particularly in the last decade or so, for many reasons. This should come as no surprise in view of the policymaking power of the courts. After all, a Supreme Court decision can establish national policy on such issues as abortion, racial segregation, and gay rights. Critics, especially on the political right, frequently accuse the judiciary of "legislating from the bench." We discuss these criticisms in this chapter's *Perception vs. Reality* feature.

14–5a Criticisms of the Federal Courts

Certainly, policymaking by unelected judges and justices in the federal courts has serious implications in a democracy. Some Americans, including many conservatives, contend that making policy from the bench has upset the balance of powers envisioned by the framers of the Constitution. They cite Thomas Jefferson, who once said, "To consider the judges as the ultimate arbiters of all constitutional questions [is] a very dangerous doctrine indeed, and one which would place us under the despotism of an oligarchy."[18] This group believes that we should rein in the power of the federal courts, and particularly judicial activism.

14–5b The Case for the Courts

On the other side of the debate over the courts are those who argue in favor of leaving the courts alone. Several federal court judges have sharply criticized congressional efforts to interfere with their authority. They claim that such efforts violate the Constitution's separation of powers. James M. Jeffords, a former independent

Federalist Papers, and notes taken during the Constitutional Convention.

Originalism, Textualism, and Modernism
Such analysis of source materials is precisely what textualists wish to avoid when it comes to assessing modern-day statutory law. Nevertheless, Justice Scalia considered himself an originalist as well as a textualist. In the 2013–2014 term, Scalia was in agreement with Justice Thomas 91 percent of the time.

Originalism can be contrasted with what has been called *modernism.* Modernists seek to examine the Constitution in the context of today's society and to consider how modern life affects the words in the document. For an example of how originalism and modernism contrast, consider *Lawrence v. Texas,* a case mentioned earlier.

Justice Kennedy's majority opinion in the case held that laws that criminalize same-sex intimate relations are unconstitutional under the Fourteenth Amendment. An originalist could object to this judgment because the legislators who adopted the amendment never considered that it might apply to gay men and lesbians. In fact, both Scalia

PERCEPTION VS. REALITY

The Supreme Court Legislates from the Bench

Our Constitution gives legislative powers to the Congress exclusively. All executive powers are granted to the president. And all judicial powers are given to the judiciary. The United States Supreme Court is the final arbiter and interpreter of what is and is not constitutional. Because of its power of judicial review, it has the ability to "make law," or so it seems.

The Perception

Using the power of judicial review, the Supreme Court creates new laws. In 1954, the Court determined that racial segregation was illegal, a position that is universally accepted today but was hugely controversial back in the 1950s. The Court has also legalized same-sex marriage and, of course, abortion. These decisions, especially the legalization of abortion, remain very divisive today.

Such decisions have had a major impact on the nature of American society. Because citizens elect members of Congress and the president only—and not members of the

Supreme Court—it is undemocratic to allow these nine justices to determine laws for our nation.

The Reality

The Supreme Court cannot actually write new laws. It can only eliminate old ones. When the Court threw out laws that criminalized adult sexual activity by gay men and lesbians, it was abolishing laws, not creating them. The Court does not have the power to legislate—to create new laws.

Consider what would happen if the Court decided that some basic level of health care is a constitutional right—a highly unlikely event. Could the Court establish mechanisms by which such a right could be enforced? It could not. It takes members of Congress months of hard work to craft bills that affect our health-care system. Such legislation fills thousands of pages and can be developed only with the assistance of large numbers of experts and lobbyists. The federal courts could not undertake such projects even if they wanted to.

The courts must decide how they will handle the cases that are brought before them. To do so establishes judicial policy. It does not constitute lawmaking. In any event, we have no alternative to judicial review when it comes to determining what is or is not constitutional. Without the Supreme Court, Congress and the president could make all sorts of laws that violate our Constitution and infringe on our rights, and there would be nothing to stop them. As Chief Justice John Roberts said during his confirmation hearings, "Judges are like umpires. Umpires don't make the rules; they apply them."

Blog On

Plenty of bloggers follow the activities of the Supreme Court. One of the best is SCOTUSblog, at www.scotusblog.com, sponsored by Bloomberg Law.

---

senator from Vermont, likened the federal court system to a referee: "The first lesson we teach children when they enter competitive sports is to respect the referee, even if we think he [or she] might have made the wrong call. If our children can understand this, why can't our political leaders?"[19]

Others argue that there are already sufficient checks on the courts. We look at some of those next.

Judicial Traditions and Doctrines One check on the courts is judicial restraint. Supreme Court justices traditionally have exercised a great deal of self-restraint. Justices sometimes admit to making decisions that fly in

the face of their personal values and policy preferences, simply because they feel obligated to do so in view of existing law.

Self-restraint is also mandated by various established judicial traditions and doctrines, including the doctrine of *stare decisis,* which theoretically obligates the Supreme Court to follow its own precedents. Furthermore, the Supreme Court will not hear a meritless appeal just so it can rule on the issue.

Finally, the justices often narrow their rulings to focus on just one aspect of an issue, even though there may be nothing to stop them from broadening their focus and thus widening the impact of their decisions.

A painting of the late Justice Antonin Scalia by Nelson Shanks is displayed in the Great Hall of the Supreme Court during funeral ceremonies. *What impact did Scalia have on the Court?*

the authority to limit or otherwise alter the jurisdiction of the lower federal courts. Finally, although it is most unlikely, Congress could even change the number of justices on the Supreme Court, in an attempt to change the ideological balance on the Court. (President Franklin D. Roosevelt proposed such a plan in 1937—without success.)

The Public's Regard for the Supreme Court Some have proposed that Congress, not the Supreme Court, be the final arbiter of the Constitution. In debates on this topic, one factor is often overlooked: the American public's high regard for the Supreme Court and the federal courts generally. The Court continues to be respected as a fair arbiter of conflicting interests and the protector of constitutional rights and liberties.

Even when the Court issued its decision to halt the manual recount of votes in Florida following the 2000 elections, which effectively handed the presidency to George W. Bush, Americans respected the Court's decision-making authority—although many disagreed with the Court's decision. Polls continue to show that Americans have much more trust and confidence in the Supreme Court than they do in Congress.

Other Checks The judiciary is subject to other checks as well. Courts may make rulings, but they cannot force federal and state legislatures to appropriate the funds necessary to carry out those rulings. For example, if a state supreme court decides that prison conditions must be improved, the state legislature has to find the funds to carry out the ruling or the improvements will not take place.

Additionally, legislatures can revise old laws or pass new ones in an attempt to negate a court's ruling. This may happen when a court interprets a statute in a way that Congress did not intend. Congress may also propose amendments to the Constitution to reverse Supreme Court rulings, and Congress has

CRITICAL THINKING

▶ *Why do you think that Americans trust the Supreme Court much more than they do Congress?*

AMERICA AT ODDS | The Judiciary

A Supreme Court decision can affect the lives of millions of Americans. For example, in 1973 the Supreme Court, in *Roe v. Wade,* held that the constitutional right to privacy included the right to have an abortion. The influence wielded by the Court today is a far cry from the Court's relative obscurity at the founding of this nation. Initially, the Supreme Court was not even included in the plans for government buildings in the national capital. It did not have its own building until 1935. Over time, however, the Court has established a reputation with the public for dispensing justice in a fair and reasonable manner. Still, Americans are at odds over a number of judicial issues:

- *Should state judges be elected—or does selection by appointment lead to a better court system?*

- *Should the United States Supreme Court accept more cases to provide a greater number of definitive rulings— or should it take on relatively few cases so that it can treat each one thoroughly?*

- *Should senators accept a Supreme Court nomination by a president of the opposing party whenever the nominee appears to have sound judicial temperament—or should senators vote only for those nominees who share their political philosophies?*

- *Should judges defer to the decisions of legislatures and administrative agencies whenever possible—or should they strictly police the constitutionality of legislative and executive decisions?*

- *Is it crucial that the Constitution be interpreted in terms of the beliefs of the founders—or should justices take account of modern circumstances that the founders could not have envisioned?*

STUDY TOOLS 14

READY TO STUDY? IN THE BOOK, YOU CAN:

- ☐ Review what you've read with the following chapter quiz.
- ☐ Check your answers in Appendix D at the back of the book.
- ☐ Rip out the Chapter Review Card, which includes key terms and chapter summaries.

ONLINE AT WWW.CENGAGEBRAIN.COM, YOU CAN:

- ☐ Learn more about Justice Ruth Bader Ginsburg in Major Players in American Government.
- ☐ Explore various online resources in the Supreme Court and Federal Court system websites in the Internet Resources tool.
- ☐ Interact with figures from the text, and watch quick animation clips.
- ☐ Prepare for tests with quizzes.
- ☐ Review the key terms with Flash Cards.

FILL-IN

Learning Outcome 14–1

1. Primary sources of American law include _____.

2. In the context of the courts, *jurisdiction* means _____.

Learning Outcome 14–2

3. To bring a case before the Supreme Court, a party may request a _____, which is an order the Court issues to a lower court asking that court to send it the record of the case in question.

4. The attorneys involved with a case will present _____ to the Supreme Court, after which the justices discuss the case in conference.

5. A/An _____ opinion is a statement written by a justice who agrees with the Court's decision, but for reasons different from those outlined by the majority.

Learning Outcome 14–3

6. Because of a practice known as _____, home-state senators of the president's political party may be able to influence the choice of a nominee for the U.S. district court in that state.

7. Two important judicial philosophies that describe justices' attitudes toward legal interpretation, both of which are often associated with conservative principles, are

_____.

8. In recent years, the "swing vote" on the Supreme Court has been Justice _____.

9. Congress can check the power of the courts in several ways, including _____.

MULTIPLE CHOICE

10. A precedent is best defined as a
    a. controversy that is real and substantial.
    b. court decision that furnishes an example or authority for deciding subsequent cases.
    c. ruling that a person has disobeyed a court order.

11. The U.S. courts of appeals
    a. are the courts in which cases involving federal law begin.
    b. hear appeals from the U.S. district courts located within their respective judicial circuits.
    c. hear testimony and evidence before they make decisions in cases.

12. A nominee for the Supreme Court must be confirmed by a
    a. majority vote in the Senate.
    b. two-thirds vote in the Senate.
    c. majority vote in the House Judiciary Committee.

13. The power of the courts to decide on the constitutionality of legislative enactments and of actions taken by the executive branch is called
    a. judicial review.
    b. *stare decisis.*
    c. jurisdiction.

14. Judicial self-restraint is mandated by various judicial traditions and doctrines, such as _____, which theoretically obligates the Supreme Court to follow its own precedents.
    a. *curiae regis*
    b. *stare decisis*
    c. justiciable controversy

GOVT
ONLINE

ACCESS TEXTBOOK CONTENT ONLINE—
INCLUDING ON SMARTPHONES!

Includes Videos & Other
Interactive Resources!

Access GOVT ONLINE at www.cengagebrain.com

15 DOMESTIC POLICY

LEARNING OUTCOMES *After reading this chapter, you should be able to:*

15-1 Explain what domestic policy is, and summarize the steps in the policymaking process.

15-2 Discuss the issue of health-care funding and recent legislation on universal health insurance.

15-3 Summarize the issues of energy independence, climate change, and alternative energy sources.

15-4 Describe the two major areas of economic policymaking, and discuss the issue of the public debt.

After finishing this chapter, go to **PAGE 353** for **STUDY TOOLS**.

Lou Oates/Shutterstock.com

AMERICA AT ODDS | Do We Send Too Many People to Prison?

Currently, there are about 2.2 million people in U.S. prisons and jails. That's roughly one in every one hundred adults. We are setting records—the share of our population in prison is thirteen times more than in Japan, nine times more than in Germany, and five times more than in Britain.

In 1970, the proportion of Americans behind bars—the *incarceration rate*—was only one-fourth of what it is today. Not surprisingly, the number of drug offenders in prison is responsible for much of this increase. Such lockups have multiplied thirteenfold since 1980.

Defense attorney Jim Felman of Tampa, Florida, said that America is conducting "an experiment in imprisoning first-time nonviolent offenders for periods of time previously reserved only for those who had killed someone." Holding that many prisoners is not cheap. It costs between $20,000 and $60,000 a year to house a convicted criminal in a state prison, depending on the state. Because of these costs, a number of conservative governors have begun to rethink their commitment to high rates of incarceration. Indeed, the massive growth in prison populations that marked the last few decades appears to have come to an end, and the incarceration rate is no longer growing. Given all this, do we still send too many Americans to prison?

Keep Criminals behind Bars—It Works

Supporters of aggressive incarceration policies argue that still more criminals should be behind bars. Putting more people in prison reduces crime rates. After all, incentives matter. If potential criminals know that they will be thrown in jail more readily and stay there longer, they will have less incentive to engage in illegal activities.

Also, the crime rate is strongly determined by the number of criminals at large. When we remove a criminal from the streets and put that person in prison, the prisoner can no longer commit crimes that harm the public. This effect of removal is called *incapacitation*. The evidence shows that during the 1960s, when incarceration rates fell, the crime rate more than doubled. As incarceration rates rose sharply in the 1990s, the crime rate went steadily down. As a comparison, the risk of criminal punishment in England has been falling. In consequence, crime rates have risen in England while they have fallen in the United States.

Tough sentencing is effective. We should not turn career criminals loose on the streets.

Too Many Laws and Too Many Prisoners

Those who argue against our high rates of incarceration point out that many individuals are convicted of nonviolent crimes. The government should not be spending tens of thousands of dollars to keep such people in prison.

Too many acts have been criminalized, particularly at the federal level. Many crimes are so vaguely defined that most Americans would not know if they were breaking the law. Granted, hard-core criminals should be behind bars. But what about the casual pot smoker? (In 2015, more than 600,000 people were arrested for possession of marijuana.) Or someone convicted under a federal statute designed to protect the environment? Lying to a federal official is a felony. Who can say how many people might be imprisoned based on such an act?

In California, until recently, about 7,600 persons were serving life sentences because they were convicted of a third offense—and in almost half of these cases, the third crime was nonserious or nonviolent. In 2012, voters changed the law to allow the release of nonviolent offenders, and about 2,000 have since left prison. California voters recognized the truth: the cost to society of putting drug users and other minor offenders behind bars is much greater than the benefits.

Where do you stand?

1. Could factors other than high incarceration rates be causing our current low crime rates? What might they be?
2. Why do you think federal, state, and local governments arrest so many drug-law violators?

Explore this issue online:

- You can find several articles in *The Economist*, a British magazine, arguing that the United States imprisons too many people. Search on "economist us incarceration."
- The Criminal Justice Legal Foundation is among the few groups that advocate increased rates of incarceration. See its arguments at www.cjlf.org.

INTRODUCTION

Whether we send too many people to prison is just one of the issues that confront our nation's policymakers today. How are questions of national importance, such as this one, decided? Who are the major participants in the decision-making process?

To learn the answers to these questions, we need to delve into the politics of policymaking. *Policy,* or *public policy,* can be defined as a plan or course of action taken by the government to respond to a political issue or to enhance the social or political well-being of society. Public policy is the end result of the policymaking process, which will be described shortly.

In this chapter, after discussing how policy is made through the policymaking process, we look at several aspects of **domestic policy**, which consists of public policy concerning issues *within* a national unit. Specifically, we examine health-care policy, energy policy, and economic policy. We focus on these policy areas because they have been among the federal government's top priorities. Another major issue has been unauthorized immigration. We examine that problem in this chapter's *Join the Debate* feature.

Bear in mind that although the focus here is on policy and policymaking at the national level, state and local governments also engage in policymaking. These governments establish policies to achieve goals relating to activities within their boundaries. This process is clearly at work in the criminal justice issues discussed in this chapter's opening *America at Odds* feature.

domestic policy Public policy concerning issues within a national unit, such as national policy on health care or the economy.

policymaking process The procedures involved in identifying an issue and then getting it on the political agenda; formulating, adopting, and implementing a policy with regard to the issue; and then evaluating the results of the policy.

agenda setting In policymaking, getting an issue on the political agenda to be addressed by Congress; part of the first stage of the policymaking process.

15–1 THE POLICY-MAKING PROCESS

LO Explain what domestic policy is, and summarize the steps in the policymaking process.

A new law does not appear out of the blue. First, the problem addressed by the new law has to become part of the political agenda—that is, the problem must be defined as a political issue to be resolved by government

action. Furthermore, once the issue gets on the political agenda, proposed solutions to the problem have to be formulated and then adopted. Issue identification and agenda setting, policy formulation, and policy adoption are all parts of the **policymaking process**, illustrated in Figure 15–1. The process does not end there, however. Once the law is passed, it has to be implemented and then evaluated.

Each phase of the policymaking process involves interactions among various individuals and groups. The president and members of Congress are obviously important participants in the process. Remember from Chapter 6 that interest groups also play a key role. Groups that may be affected adversely by a new policy will try to convince Congress not to adopt the policy. Groups that will benefit from the policy will exert whatever influence they can on Congress to do the opposite. Congressional committees and subcommittees may investigate the problem to be addressed by the policy and, in so doing, solicit input from members of various groups or industries.

The participants in policymaking and the nature of the debates involved depend on the particular policy being proposed, formed, or implemented. Whatever the policy, however, debate over its pros and cons occurs during each stage of the policymaking process. Additionally, making policy decisions typically involves *trade-offs,* in which policymakers must sacrifice one goal to achieve another because of budget constraints and other factors.

15–1a Issue Identification and Agenda Setting

If no one recognizes a problem, then no matter how important the problem may be, politically it does not yet really exist. Thus, *issue identification* is part of the first stage of the policymaking process. Some group—whether it be the media, the public, politicians, or even foreign commentators—must identify a problem that can be solved politically. The second part of this stage of the policymaking process involves getting the issue on the political agenda to be addressed by Congress. This is called **agenda setting**, or *agenda building*.

A problem in society may be identified as an issue and included on the political agenda when an event or series of events leads to a call for action. For example, the failure of a major bank may lead to the conclusion that the financial industry is in trouble and that the government should take action to rectify the problem. Dramatic increases in health-care costs may cause the media

FIGURE 15–1 THE POLICYMAKING PROCESS

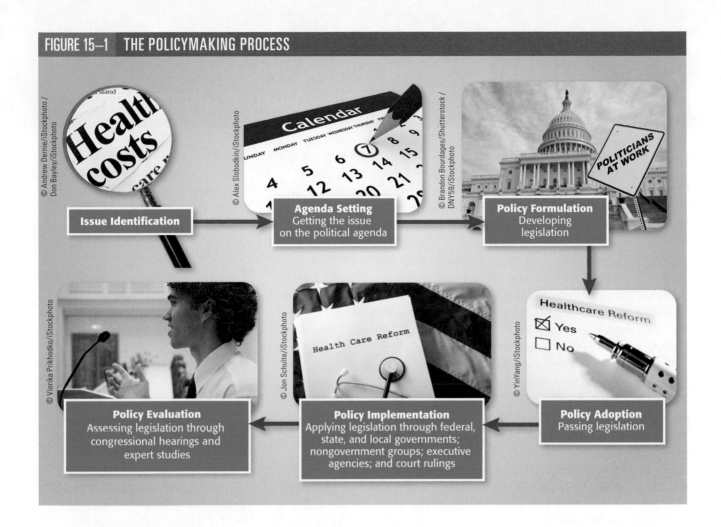

Issue Identification

Agenda Setting
Getting the issue
on the political agenda

Policy Formulation
Developing
legislation

Policy Evaluation
Assessing legislation through
congressional hearings and
expert studies

Policy Implementation
Applying legislation through federal,
state, and local governments;
nongovernment groups; executive
agencies; and court rulings

Policy Adoption
Passing legislation

Healthcare Reform
☒ Yes
☐ No

or other groups to consider health care a priority that should be on the national political agenda. Sometimes, the social or economic effects of a national calamity, such as the Great Depression of the 1930s or the terrorist attacks of September 11, 2001, create a pressing need for government action.

15–1b Policy Formulation and Adoption

The second stage in the policymaking process involves the formulation and adoption of specific plans for achieving a particular goal, such as health-care reform. The president, members of Congress, administrative agencies, and interest group leaders typically are the key participants in developing proposed legislation. Remember from Chapter 13 that iron triangles and issue networks work together in forming mutually beneficial policies. To a certain extent, the courts also establish policies when they interpret statutes passed by legislative bodies or make decisions concerning disputes not yet addressed by any law, such as disputes involving new technology.

Note that some issues may become a part of the political agenda but never proceed beyond that stage of the policymaking process. Usually, this happens when it is impossible to achieve a consensus on what policy should be adopted.

15–1c Policy Implementation

Because of our federal system, the implementation of national policies works most smoothly when there is cooperation among the federal government and the state and local governments. For example, the Affordable Care Act, nicknamed Obamacare, assumed that the states would set up marketplaces where individuals could buy health-care insurance. This example also shows that the federal government can act without the states if it must—in thirty-six states the federal government set up a marketplace because the state government refused to participate.

Successful implementation usually requires the support of groups outside the government. For example, the state health-care insurance marketplaces established under Obamacare are effective only because of the participation of commercial insurance companies.

JOIN
THE DEBATE

What Should We Do about Unauthorized Immigrants?

Illegal immigration became a major issue in 2016, largely because of the dramatic positions of several Republican presidential candidates. Republican finalists Donald Trump and Senator Ted Cruz (R., Tex.) favored total deportation of all illegal immigrants (known as *unauthorized immigrants* by the Department of Homeland Security). Trump's rhetoric was especially harsh. In contrast, most Democratic leaders favored a path to citizenship.

Currently, about 11 million unauthorized immigrants live in the United States. Some crossed the border illegally, and others arrived legally but overstayed their visas. A majority of these persons are from Latin America, particularly Mexico. Because Congress has failed to reform our immigration laws, little has been done about this problem for years. So the debate continues. Should we deport them, or should we offer them a path to citizenship or at least legal status?

Ship Them Home

The greatest applause line in any Trump speech represents one extreme position: deport them all, build a "great wall" on the southern border, and make Mexico pay for it. There's a reason these people are called *illegal*—they are breaking the law. Lawbreakers should not stay. After

we deport them, then they can apply legally to become U.S. residents.

Illegal immigrants are mainly low-skilled, low-wage workers. They compete against our poorest citizens and drive down their wages. They cause overcrowded schools and hospital emergency rooms. If we do not actually deport them all, we must at least prevent those who stay from becoming U.S. citizens. Democrats would like them to become citizens, of course. That would amount to a scheme to add 11 million new Democratic voters. Such a result is not fair to our existing citizens, who were never asked whether they wanted this influx. How would the liberal citizens of Berkeley, California, react to a plan to import thousands of new right-wing voters into town, with the result that the City Council flips from Democrat to Republican?

Do What Is Right— Give Them a Path to Citizenship

Others point out that the costs of total deportation would be staggering. We would need hundreds of thousands of new federal enforcement officers. Such a project would turn us into a police state. What would it be like to be a U.S. citizen of Mexican ancestry living in the middle of such an

operation? Your civil rights would fly out the window.

In fact, as we observed in the *Perception vs. Reality* feature in Chapter 1, deporting unauthorized immigrants would not improve the wages or job prospects of lower-income citizens. Immigrants not only work, but they consume. This additional spending leads to more employment, not less. A UCLA study predicted that mass deportation would reduce California's tax revenues by 8.5 percent and would shrink the state economy by tens of billions of dollars.

We have unauthorized immigrants because it is almost impossible for a low-skilled person to legally enter the United States. Now that they are here, we cannot allow them to remain as second-class residents. America tried that with African Americans, and it was a disaster. A path to citizenship is the only solution.

Critical Analysis

If immigrants who become citizens vote overwhelmingly for Democrats, is that the fault of the Democrats—or the Republicans? In either case, why?

Policy implementation also involves agencies in the executive branch (see Chapter 13). Once Congress establishes a policy by enacting legislation, the executive branch, through its agencies, enforces the new policy. Furthermore, the courts are involved in policy implementation, because the legislation and administrative regulations enunciating the new policy must be interpreted and applied to specific situations by the courts.

15–1d Policy Evaluation

The final stage of policymaking involves evaluating the success of a policy during and following its implementation. Groups both inside and outside the government participate in the evaluation process.

Congress may hold hearings to obtain feedback from different groups on how a statute or regulation has affected them. Scholars and scientists may conduct studies to determine whether a particular law, such as an environmental law designed to reduce air pollution, has actually achieved the desired result—less air pollution. Sometimes, feedback obtained in these or other ways indicates that a policy has failed, and a new policymaking process may be undertaken to modify the policy or create a more effective one.

15-1e Policymaking and Special Interests

The policymaking steps just discussed may seem straightforward, but they are not. Every bill that passes through Congress is a compromise. Every bill that passes through Congress is also an opportunity for individual members of Congress to help constituents, particularly those who were kind enough to contribute financially to the members' reelection campaigns.

The Farm Bill   Consider the Agricultural Act of 2014, commonly known as the 2014 farm bill. The act authorizes about $95 billion per year over the next decade. About $75 billion is actually for the Special Nutrition Assistance Program (SNAP), or food stamps. As we observed in the *America at Odds* feature in Chapter 6, combining food stamp authorization with agricultural subsidies has been a way to get urban liberals to vote for the legislation.

The centerpiece of the farm bill was the abolition of *direct payments* for certain crops—payments made regardless of whether the recipient actually planted the crops in question. Most of the funds saved were transferred to a much-enlarged crop insurance program. Supporters claimed that the new bill would reduce federal expenditures. Critics, pointing to falling prices for corn, soybeans, and wheat, argued that it would in fact be more expensive.

Special Provisions to Help the Bill Along   A polarized Congress meant that the bill would be hard to pass—indeed, it was two years late. Special provisions, not requested by the Department of Agriculture, helped the bill along. A pilot program for industrial hemp production helped secure the support of members from Kentucky. Profit-margin insurance for catfish helped sew up the Mississippi delegation. Newly insured products include biofuels, lamb, peanuts, poultry, sesame, sushi rice, and swine. Various GMO (genetically modified organism) crops now receive special insurance treatment. The bill included livestock disaster relief and funds to combat a disease called citrus greening in Florida.

Some provisions had little to do with agriculture or nutrition. The EPA was prohibited from proceeding with a program against overfishing. Central State University in Ohio, a historically black college, received additional federal aid. Clearly, policymaking is a complicated process.

CRITICAL THINKING

▶ *What role do the media have in the agenda-setting process?*

15-2 HEALTH-CARE POLICY

LO Discuss the issue of health-care funding and recent legislation on universal health insurance.

In March 2010, Congress passed the Patient Protection and Affordable Care Act and a companion bill. The two bills, which President Barack Obama immediately signed, contained health-care reforms that were among the most consequential government initiatives in many years.

Even before the new legislation was adopted, the federal government was paying the health-care costs of more than 100 million Americans. When President Obama took office, the government was picking up the tab for about 50 percent of the nation's health-care costs. Private insurance was responsible for about a third of all health-care payments, and the rest was met either by patients themselves or by charity. Paying for health-care expenses, in other words, was already a major federal responsibility, and questions about how the government should carry out that function in the future were unavoidable.

15-2a Two Problems with U.S. Health Care

Our system for funding health care has suffered from two major problems. One is that health care is expensive. As of 2017, almost 18 percent of national spending in the United States goes to health care, compared with 11 percent in France, 10 percent in Canada, and 8.5 percent in Britain. U.S. health-care costs have been rising for years, as you can see in Figure 15–2.

A second problem has been lack of health-care insurance. About 18 percent of the population had no health-care insurance as of 2013, before the Affordable Care Act was fully implemented. Lack of coverage means that people may put off seeing a physician until it is too late for effective treatment or may be forced into bankruptcy due to large medical bills. One study has estimated that in recent years 20,000 people per year have died prematurely because they lacked health insurance.[1] (Others dispute these findings.) All other economically

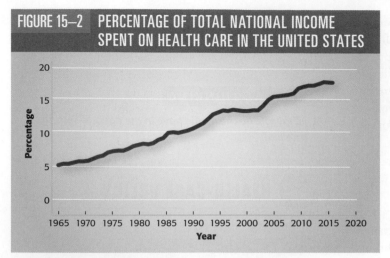

FIGURE 15–2 PERCENTAGE OF TOTAL NATIONAL INCOME SPENT ON HEALTH CARE IN THE UNITED STATES

Source: National Health Expenditure Accounts, Centers for Medicare & Medicaid Services.

advanced nations provide health insurance to everyone, typically through a government program similar to Social Security or Medicare in the United States.

Before discussing the recently passed health-care reforms, let's first look at the programs that were already in place. The most important of these are **Medicare**, which provides health-care insurance to Americans aged sixty-five and over, and **Medicaid**, which funds health-care coverage for low-income persons.

15–2b Medicaid and Medicare

Medicare A federal government program that pays for health-care insurance for Americans aged sixty-five years and over.

Medicaid A joint federal–state program that pays for health-care services for low-income persons.

Children's Health Insurance Program (CHIP) A joint federal–state program that provides health-care insurance for low-income children.

entitlement program A government program that provides benefits to all persons who meet specified requirements.

The federal government pays for health care in a variety of ways. Like many major employers, it buys health-care insurance for its employees. Members of the armed forces, veterans, and Native Americans receive medical services provided directly by the government. Most federal spending on health care, however, is accounted for by Medicare and Medicaid.

Medicaid A joint federal–state program, Medicaid provides health-care subsidies to low-income persons. The federal government provides about 60 percent of the Medicaid budget, and the states provide the rest. More than 60 million people are in the program. Many Medicaid recipients are elderly residents of nursing homes—the Medicare program does not pay for nursing home expenses.

Although recent cost-containment measures have slowed the growth of Medicaid spending, the cost of Medicaid has doubled in the last decade. This increase has put a considerable strain on the budgets of many states. About 17 percent of the average state general fund budget now goes to Medicaid. Another program, the **Children's Health Insurance Program (CHIP)**, covers children in families with incomes that are modest but too high to qualify for Medicaid. By fiscal year 2016, the total cost of Medicaid and CHIP for all levels of government was about $610 billion.

Medicare Medicare is the federal government's health-care program for persons sixty-five years of age and older. Medicare is now the government's second-largest domestic spending program, after Social Security. In 1970, Medicare accounted for only 0.7 percent of total annual U.S. national income (gross domestic product, or GDP). It currently accounts for more than 3 percent of GDP, and costs are expected to rise as millions of "baby boomers" retire over the next two decades.

By 2030, the sixty-five-and-older population is expected to double. Further, technological developments in health care and the advancement of medical science are driving medical costs up every year. There are simply more actions that medical science can take to keep people alive—and Americans naturally want to take advantage of these services.

Entitlement Programs Medicare and Medicaid are examples of federal **entitlement programs**. Social Security and unemployment compensation are two other examples. Entitlement programs pay out benefits to persons who meet specified requirements. In the case of Social Security, for example, the government issues payments based on a recipient's age at retirement and past wage or salary income.

A special characteristic of entitlement programs is that they continue from year to year, regardless of whether Congress passes an annual funding measure.

> ## "IT HELPS TO THINK OF THE GOVERNMENT AS *AN INSURANCE COMPANY WITH AN ARMY.*"
>
> ~ MIKE HOLLAND, OFFICE OF SCIENCE AND TECHNOLOGY POLICY UNDER PRESIDENT GEORGE W. BUSH

An entitlement continues until the government explicitly adopts a new law to change the benefits or otherwise alter the program. Further, Congress has no direct control over how much an entitlement program will cost in any particular year. It is usually possible to estimate the costs, but the actual amount of spending depends on how many eligible persons sign up for the benefits. In understanding the 2010 Affordable Care Act (Obamacare) it is important to realize that the program was primarily designed as an entitlement.

Because entitlements do not need to be explicitly renewed, they are different from *discretionary spending*. In a discretionary program, Congress establishes a binding annual budget for a government agency that the agency cannot exceed. Note that "discretionary" does not mean "unimportant." As an example, the nation's armed forces are funded through discretionary spending.

15-2c The Democrats Propose Universal Coverage

For a long time the United States was the only economically advanced nation that did not provide universal health-insurance coverage to its citizens. Democratic president Bill Clinton (1993–2001) and first lady Hillary Clinton made a serious push for a universal plan during President Clinton's first term, but the project failed to pass Congress.

Many universal health-insurance plans—for example, the systems in Canada and France—involve government monopolies. In these nations, the government is responsible for providing basic health-care insurance to everyone through **national health insurance**. Some wealthy nations, such as the Netherlands and Switzerland, provide universal coverage through private insurance companies instead. The plan that the United States has adopted also relies on private insurance companies.

Congress Addresses the Issue The program developed by Congress in 2009 assumed that employer-provided health insurance would continue to be a major part of the system. Large employers that did not offer a plan would be required to pay a penalty. Medicaid would be available to individuals with incomes up to about 1.5 times the federal poverty level. (In 2016, the poverty level for a family of four was $24,250.) A new health-insurance marketplace, the Health Insurance Exchange, would allow individuals and small employers

to shop for plans. Insurance companies would not be allowed to deny anyone coverage.

Most individuals would be required to obtain coverage or pay an income tax penalty. This requirement is known as the **individual mandate**. Those with low-to-middle incomes would receive help in paying their premiums. Subsidies would be phased out for those earning more than four times the federal poverty level.

To fund the program, Congress adopted various new taxes and fees, such as a new tax on investments for high-income persons, an increased Medicare tax rate, and a new tax on high-end ("Cadillac") health policies that cost more than a specified amount.

Expected Results The bills passed by Congress and signed by President Obama were to become effective over a period of several years. One immediate change was that young people could remain covered by their parents' insurance until they turned twenty-six. Another immediate result was subsidies to small employers that obtained insurance plans for their employees. The most important provisions, however, did not take effect until January 1, 2014. From that day on, subsidies were available to help citizens purchase health-care insurance if they were not covered by Medicare, Medicaid, or an employer's plan.

The Conservative Reaction In 2009, the Democrats were able to win the support—or at least the acquiescence—of groups that had opposed universal health-care plans in the past. That included the American Medical Association, hospitals, insurance companies, and pharmaceutical firms. Nevertheless, opposition to the reforms was widespread and strong. Conservatives saw the Affordable Care Act as a "big government takeover" of health care and a threat to popular freedoms. The individual mandate was at the heart of much of the opposition. After all, it was a way of pressuring people to do something that they might not otherwise do. Supporters of reform could point out that the system

national health insurance A program, found in many of the world's economically advanced nations, under which the central government provides basic health-care insurance coverage to everyone in the country.

individual mandate In the context of health-care reform, a requirement that all persons obtain health-care insurance from one source or another. Those failing to do so must pay a penalty.

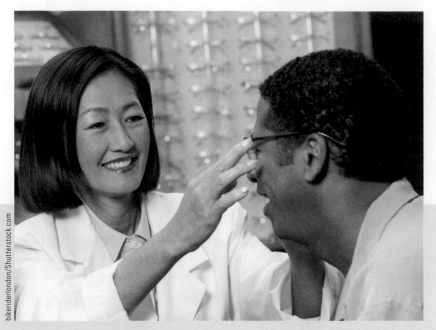

An optometrist helps a patient choose new eyeglasses. Health insurance rarely covers eyeglass lenses and frames. *Why might this be so?*

until the end of the year. Obamacare's troubled roll-out was a political blow to the Democrats.

By the end of the signup period in April 2014, however, 8 million Americans had obtained insurance policies through the state and federal exchanges. This was 2 million more than predicted by the Congressional Budget Office. By 2016, the number enrolled was close to 13 million. Still, the election of a Republican president and Congress in 2016 meant that Obamacare could yet be abolished.

▶ *Is it reasonable for health care to continue to absorb increasingly larger shares of the nation's budget—or will that interfere too much with our country's ability to purchase other goods and services? Explain your reasoning.*

would face financial collapse unless everyone, healthy or unhealthy, bought insurance. This fact did nothing to make the reforms more palatable.

As we explained in Chapter 3, attempts to challenge the constitutionality of the reforms failed, although the United States Supreme Court did allow state governments to opt out of expanding the Medicaid program.[2] Repeated attempts by Republicans in the House to repeal or delay Obamacare were ineffectual. Because most of the program took the form of an entitlement, the Republicans would need control of both chambers of Congress and the presidency to abolish it. In 2012, however, Obama was reelected and the Democrats retained control of the Senate. Repeal of Obamacare was one of the Republican demands during the government shutdown of October 2013, but that campaign eventually collapsed. Most recently, in 2015 the Supreme Court rejected a claim that major parts of the Affordable Care Act should be thrown out due to poorly worded language.[3]

Implementation Begins On October 1, 2013, Americans who were eligible to buy health-care insurance through a state or federal exchange had their first chance to do so. It was expected, though not required, that most of the signups would take place online. Many of the state online exchanges functioned effectively. A few never worked properly, forcing signups to take place off-line. The federal site turned out to be almost completely nonfunctional. The site was not fully operational

15-3 ENERGY AND THE ENVIRONMENT

LO Summarize the issues of energy independence, climate change, and alternative energy sources.

Energy policy was a second major priority for the Obama administration, but its accomplishments in this area were relatively modest. The Democrats did move a major energy bill through the House in 2009, but it died in the Senate. Energy policy is important because of two problems: (1) our reliance on imported oil, and (2) the possibility of global climate change.

15-3a The Problem of Imported Oil

It is estimated that in 2016, our nation imported 45 percent of its petroleum supply. This figure has fallen substantially in recent years. In 2005, imports were more than 60 percent of consumption. Still, oil imports are a potential problem largely because many of the nations that export oil are not particularly friendly to the United States. Some, such as Iran, are outright adversaries. Other oil exporters that could pose difficulties include Iraq, Libya, Nigeria, Russia, and Venezuela.

Fortunately for the United States, the sources of our imported oil are highly diversified, and we are not excessively dependent on any one nation. Canada and Mexico, friendly neighbors, supply 45 percent of our imports. Many of our European and Asian allies, however, are dependent on imports from questionable regimes.

The Price of Oil Rises . . .

Until 2003, the price of oil was low, and the U.S. government was under little pressure to address our dependence on imports. In 1998, the price per barrel fell below $12. In July 2008, however, the price of oil spiked to more than $140 a barrel, forcing U.S. gasoline prices above $4 per gallon.

A Mercedes-Benz plug-in hybrid. Fuel-efficient cars are one way that the United States is curbing its use of petroleum. Another is a reduction in the number of miles driven. *Why are young people driving less than previous generations did?*

. . . and Falls

The most recent change in oil prices has been more encouraging. In July 2014, the price of oil, then at about $110 per barrel, began to fall. By January 2015, the price was below $50 per barrel. After bottoming out close to $30, it appears likely to stay in the $50 range for some time to come. What happened? The answer is that the high prices of the preceding years persuaded the oil industry to make substantial—and successful—efforts to increase the oil supply. We discuss that development later in the "New Energy Sources" section.

15-3b Climate Change

Observations collected by agencies such as the National Aeronautics and Space Administration (NASA) suggest that during the last half century, average global temperatures increased by about 0.74 degree Celsius (1.33 degrees Fahrenheit). Most climatologists believe that this **climate change** is the result of human activities, especially the release of **greenhouse gases** such as carbon dioxide (CO_2) into the atmosphere.

A United Nations body, the Intergovernmental Panel on Climate Change (IPCC), has estimated that during the twenty-first century, global temperatures could rise an additional 1.0 to 4.8 degrees Celsius (1.8 to 8.6 degrees Fahrenheit). Warming may continue in subsequent centuries.

Effects of Climate Change

The predicted outcomes of climate change vary, depending on the climate models on which they are based. If the oceans grow warmer, seawater will expand, and polar ice will melt. (This last event is already under way.) These two developments will cause sea levels to rise, negatively affecting coastal areas. Rainfall patterns are expected to change, turning some areas into deserts but allowing agriculture to expand elsewhere. Other likely effects could include increases in extreme weather.

The Climate Change Debate

Some dispute the consensus view of climate change. They argue that any observed warming is due largely to natural causes and may not continue into the future. Although this position is rare among scientists, it has been common in the broader community of Americans. Recent public opinion polls, for example, reveal that about 40 percent of Americans believe either that global warming is due to natural causes, or it does not exist.

Attitudes toward climate change have become highly politicized. Some commentators on the political right contend that global warming is a giant liberal hoax designed to clear the way for increased government control of the economy and society. At the same time, many on the

climate change
The increase in the average temperature of the Earth's surface over the last half century and its projected continuation; also referred to as *global warming*.

greenhouse gas A gas that, when released into the atmosphere, traps the sun's heat and slows its release into outer space. Carbon dioxide (CO_2) is a major example.

political left believe that the right-wing refusal to accept the existence of climate change threatens the very future of the human race.

The Clean Power Plan Political deadlock meant that Congress would take no action on CO_2 emissions. The Obama administration therefore sought to act on its own. In 2015, the Environmental Protection Agency (EPA) issued the Clean Power Plan (CPP), a program to reduce CO_2 emissions from existing power plants. (The EPA had earlier released a plan covering new power plants.) Each state could develop its own plan, but if a state refused to participate, the EPA would draft a plan for it. If implementation of the CPP began on schedule in 2022, it would be one of the most potent ways of limiting CO_2 emissions ever devised.

Twenty-nine states sued to stop the CPP. (Eighteen states supported it.) In February 2016, the Supreme Court blocked the plan pending a Court ruling. Then, in November of that year, Donald Trump was elected president of the United States. CPP was clearly dead as long as Trump was president.

15–3c New Energy Sources

The issues of U.S. energy security and climate change raise the question of whether we can develop new energy sources. Energy security means finding energy sources that are produced either in this country or by friendly neighbors such as Canada. A reduction in global warming means deploying energy sources that do not release CO_2 and other greenhouse gases into the atmosphere. As explained next, however, new energy sources may be accompanied by problems.

Expanded Supplies of Oil and Natural Gas By 2012, many Americans had begun to realize that they were entering a new era of energy production. U.S. oil production, which declined rapidly after 1985, began to grow again in 2009. This development was based in part on technological improvements and in part on higher prices. For example, production from oil sands in Alberta, Canada, was not profitable when prices for petroleum were low.

With gasoline prices approaching $4 per gallon, however, extraction was economical.

The Natural Gas Boom. An even more dramatic development was the increase in supplies of natural gas. Only a few years ago, experts believed that the United States would soon need to import natural gas. Because gas cannot be transported by ship efficiently unless it is converted to *liquefied natural gas (LNG)*, imports would be costly.

By 2012, however, gas producers were planning to *export* LNG. The nation was running out of facilities to store all the new gas, some of which was simply flamed off into the atmosphere. Low natural gas prices plus new EPA air-pollution regulations made coal uncompetitive as a source of electricity. As a result, about one hundred coal-based power plants were closed or scheduled for retirement, and construction of new coal-based plants was at a standstill. Coal-producing regions such as eastern Kentucky and West Virginia faced serious economic difficulties.

An unexpected consequence of the boom in natural gas production was its environmental impact. Burning natural gas does release some CO_2 into the atmosphere, but less than half as much as coal. By 2009, U.S. emissions of CO_2 were falling. (They leveled off from 2010 on.) More fuel-efficient vehicles on the road added to the reduction.

The Fracking Revolution. Why has it been possible for the United States to ramp up oil and natural gas

An array of dishes used to harvest solar energy in Arizona. This technology has had a hard time competing with photovoltaic panels that can be mounted on roofs. *Why do some people object to renewable energy projects?*

Dennis MacDonald/Getty Images

production so greatly during the last several years? The answer is an extraction technique known as hydraulic fracturing, or **fracking**. This method involves pumping a high-pressure mixture of water, sand, and chemicals into oil- or gas-bearing underground rock, usually shale, to release the oil or gas. Fracking is not actually a new technique. High prices of oil and gas combined with improvements in the process, however, have made fracking cost-effective.

New oilfields in Texas and North Dakota are based on fracking. A growing concern, though, is that the technology could lead to the contamination of underground water sources. Accordingly, various state governments are developing regulations aimed at preventing such contamination.[4]

By 2014, fracking had turned the United States into the number-one oil producer in the world. As we observed earlier, by then increased supplies of petroleum had caused the price of oil to fall dramatically. In the past, Saudi Arabia would have cut its production in an attempt to keep prices up. In 2014, however, the Saudis maintained production in the hopes of driving high-cost U.S. fracking companies out of business. The Saudi move did reduce the number of new wells developed by U.S. oil firms. Vigorous cost-cutting measures by the U.S. industry, however, meant that the United States was able to maintain oil production despite lower prices.

Offshore Drilling   Another method of reducing our reliance on foreign oil is additional exploration and drilling for oil and natural gas in waters off the American coastline. For twenty years, however, the federal government prohibited offshore drilling in much of the ocean. The concern was that oil spills could severely damage the environment.

In March 2010, Obama proposed opening up a number of new areas for drilling. In April 2010, three weeks after Obama's announcement, an offshore drilling platform in the Gulf of Mexico exploded and sank. The drilling platform was leased to BP, formerly known as British Petroleum. By the time the well was permanently plugged, 4.9 million barrels of oil had spilled into the Gulf—the largest oil spill in American history. In reaction to the disaster, President Obama placed a temporary moratorium on new deepwater-drilling projects.

Nuclear Energy   One energy source that cannot contribute to global warming is nuclear power—nuclear reactors do not release greenhouse gases. Still, due to concern over possible dangers and the difficulty of storing spent nuclear fuel, no new nuclear power plants have been built in the United States in more than thirty years. Because nuclear power based on uranium appears to solve the problems of both energy security and greenhouse gas emissions, it has recently attracted renewed interest.

The key obstacle to the construction of new nuclear plants is cost. Nuclear power plants must compete on price with natural gas plants. Currently, nuclear energy simply cannot compete.

Nuclear power also suffered a severe blow in 2011 as a result of a series of disasters. A giant tsunami devastated the northeast coast of Japan, and more than 25,000 people died. Four reactors located on the coast were flooded, and radioactive material was released. Following the disaster, support for new nuclear plants in the United States fell.

Renewable Energy   Not all methods of supplying energy come with potentially hazardous by-products, such as greenhouse gases or nuclear waste. For example, hydroelectric energy, generated by water flowing through dams, is a widely used technology that employs no coal, natural gas, oil, or other fossil fuels.

Energy from such technologies is referred to as **renewable energy**, because it does not rely on extracting resources that can run out, such as oil, coal, and uranium ore. Obviously, renewable energy can reduce our dependence on imported oil, and as noted, it produces no greenhouse gases that may contribute to climate change. The problem has been that most existing renewable technologies, such as solar power cells, were expensive.

In recent years, however, the cost of solar power and wind energy has been falling fast. In some locations, wind power now competes with natural gas in price. As a result, the number of solar- and wind-power installations has grown rapidly. Of course, the wind does not always blow, and the sun does not always shine, so absent large improvements in battery technology, there are practical limits to how much of our electricity can be provided by these technologies.

CRITICAL THINKING

▶ *One possible way to reduce greenhouse gas emissions would be to tax them by imposing a "carbon tax" on fuels that contain carbon. Why hasn't Congress taken such a solution seriously?*

fracking Technique for extracting oil or natural gas from underground rock by the high-power injection of a mixture of water, sand, and chemicals.

renewable energy Energy from technologies that do not rely on extracted resources, such as oil and coal, that can run out.

15-4 ECONOMIC POLICY AND TAXES

LO Describe the two major areas of economic policymaking, and discuss the issue of the public debt.

Under our current troubled economic conditions, policies that affect the economy are more important than any other set of activities the government undertakes. **Economic policy** consists of all actions taken by the government to address the ups and downs in the nation's level of business activity. National economic policy is solely the responsibility of the national government.

15-4a The Goals of Economic Policy

Everyone understands that the nation's economy passes through periods of "boom and bust" and that we recently experienced a major bust. Even in times when the economy has been less turbulent, however, the nation has alternated between periods of strong economic growth and periods of weak or no growth. This rhythm seems to be inherent in the capitalist system, and it is called the *business cycle*.

A period in which the economy stops growing altogether and undergoes a contraction is called a **recession**. The most recent recession began in December 2007 and officially ended in June 2009. We say "officially," because even though economic growth resumed in 2009, the nation's economy is still operating below its potential.

Unemployment The most important sign of an economic downturn is a high rate of **unemployment**. The rate of unemployment is measured by a government survey. People are defined as unemployed if they are without a job and are actively looking for one. An unemployment rate of 7 percent means

economic policy
All actions taken by the national government to address ups and downs in the nation's level of business activity.

recession A period in which the level of economic activity falls; usually defined as two or more quarters of economic decline.

unemployment The state of not having a job when actively seeking one.

inflation A sustained rise in average prices; equivalent to a decline in the value of the dollar.

monetary policy
Actions taken by the Federal Reserve to change the amount of money in circulation to affect interest rates, credit markets, the rate of inflation, the rate of economic growth, and the rate of unemployment.

that there are seven people looking for work for every ninety-three people who have a job. If "discouraged workers," who have given up looking for work, are also counted, the unemployment rate is substantially higher. Figure 15–3 shows an alternative method of examining the problem. Rather than counting the unemployed, this chart counts those who are actually working.

Even in the best of times, there is always a degree of unemployment, because some people are between jobs. Unemployment rates of 8 or 9 percent, however, are clear signs of economic and social distress. Few experiences are more psychologically damaging than extended unemployment. Reducing unemployment is a major policy objective.

Inflation Unemployment and recession go hand in hand. A second economic problem that the government must occasionally address is associated with economic booms. That problem is **inflation**, a sustained rise in average prices. A rise in prices is equivalent to a decline in the value of the dollar. High rates of inflation were a serious problem in the 1970s, but rates have fallen since. Even though the rate of inflation is now relatively low, many people are fearful that high rates could return at some point in the future.

The national government has two main tools to smooth the business cycle and to reduce unemployment and inflation. These tools are monetary policy and fiscal policy, and we describe them in the following sections.

15-4b Monetary Policy

One of the tools used in managing the economy is **monetary policy**, which involves changing the amount of money in circulation to affect interest rates, credit markets, the rate of inflation, the rate of economic growth, and the rate of unemployment. Monetary policy is under the control of the Federal Reserve System, an independent regulatory agency.

The Federal Reserve System (the Fed) was established by Congress as the nation's central banking system in 1913. The Fed is governed by a board of seven governors, including the very influential chairperson. The president appoints the members of the board of governors, and the Senate must approve the nominations. Members of the board serve for fourteen-year terms. In addition to controlling the money supply, the Fed has a number of responsibilities in supervising and regulating the nation's banking system.

FIGURE 15–3 U.S. EMPLOYMENT—ALL PERSONS AGED 25–54

Much of the growth in employment in the 1980s was due to women entering the workforce. Note that the percentage of persons who are working has not yet returned to what it was before the Great Recession of 2007–2009.

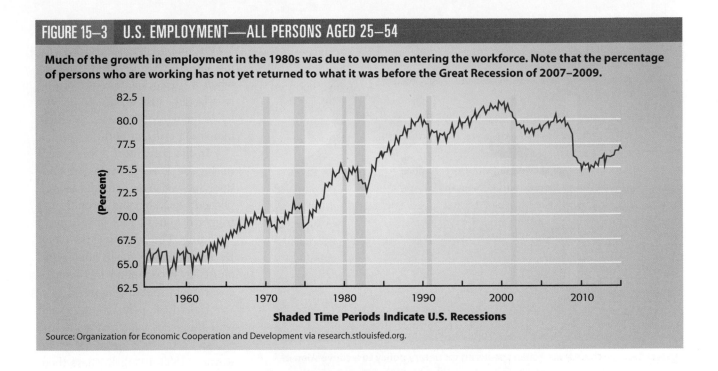

Shaded Time Periods Indicate U.S. Recessions

Source: Organization for Economic Cooperation and Development via research.stlouisfed.org.

Easy Money, Tight Money The Fed and its **Federal Open Market Committee (FOMC)** make decisions about monetary policy several times each year. In theory, monetary policy is relatively straightforward. In periods of recession and high unemployment, the Fed pursues an **easy-money policy** to stimulate the economy by expanding the rate of growth of the money supply. An easy-money policy supposedly will lead to lower interest rates and induce consumers to spend more and producers to invest more.

In periods of rising inflation, the Fed does the reverse: it reduces the rate of growth in the amount of money in circulation. This is called a *tight-money policy*. This policy should cause interest rates to rise, thus inducing consumers to spend less and businesses to invest less.

"Pushing on a String" Although an easy-money policy may sound simple, the reality is not simple at all. To give one example, if times are hard enough, people and businesses may not want to borrow even if interest rates go down to zero. The government cannot force anyone to borrow, after all.

This state of affairs is not hypothetical—it has characterized the economy since 2008. The Fed has managed to keep the interest rate for short-term federal debt almost at zero, but rates of borrowing remain depressed. Instead of percolating into the actual economy, much of the extra money created by the Fed has piled up in excess bank reserves. With some reason, the failure

of easy-money policy to spur the economy has been described as "pushing on a string."

The Fed responded to the failure of its easy-money policy by adopting some unorthodox tactics. Ordinarily, the Fed expands the money supply by using the newly created money to purchase short-term federal government debt. After 2010, however, it undertook programs of buying long-term federal debt in the hope that long-term purchases would be more effective than short-term ones. In addition, it began purchasing private-sector debt obligations, such as securities based on residential mortgages.

Beginning in 2013, the Fed began winding down its unusual policies. In 2014, it stopped its unorthodox bond purchases. In December 2015, for the first time since the Great Recession, the Fed raised its key interest rate by 0.25 percent. Some economists, however, argued that the Fed was moving too fast. These economists recommended hiking interest rates only after the economy was clearly overheating.

Conservative Criticisms

A number of conservatives have expressed alarm at the Fed's recent policies. Some fear that the extra money created by the Fed—which is currently just sitting there—could pass into the

Federal Open Market Committee (FOMC) The most important body within the Federal Reserve System; decides how monetary policy should be carried out.

easy-money policy A monetary policy that involves stimulating the economy by expanding the rate of growth of the money supply.

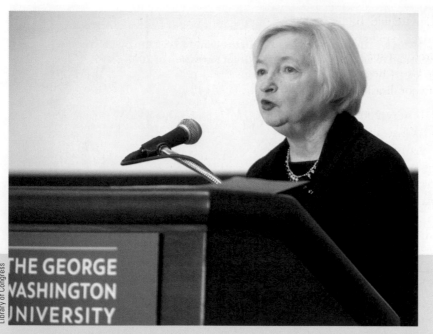

Federal Reserve chair Janet Yellen speaks on monetary policy to a convention of business journalists. *How does the Fed make monetary policy?*

real economy with explosive speed. The result would be increased inflation.

A second response has been the growth in the philosophy of "hard money" among radical conservatives. Hard-money advocates believe that the government should tie the value of the dollar to commodities such as gold. Mainstream economists believe that such a policy would lead to a dramatic contraction in the money supply and a recession of unprecedented severity.

15–4c Fiscal Policy

Prior to the onset of the Great Recession, mainstream economists agreed on one point: under ordinary circumstances, monetary policy would be sufficient to steer the economy. If monetary policy proved to be inadequate, however, many economists also recommended use of a second tool—fiscal policy.

The principle underlying **fiscal policy**, like the one that underlies monetary policy, is relatively simple: when unemployment is rising and the economy is entering a recession, fiscal policy should stimulate economic activity by decreasing taxes, increasing government spending, or both. When unemployment is decreasing and prices are rising (that is, when we have inflation), fiscal policy should curb economic activity by reducing government spending, increasing taxes, or both.

In the past, fiscal policy meant raising or lowering rates of taxation. Such changes could be accomplished quickly and would not trigger disputes about government spending. The severity of the Great Recession, however, led some economists to recommend increases in government spending as well.

U.S. fiscal policy is associated with the economic theories of the British economist John Maynard Keynes (1883–1946). Keynes's theories, which we address next, were the result of his study of the Great Depression of the 1930s.

Keynes and the Great Depression According to **Keynesian economics**, the nation cannot automatically recover from a disaster such as the Great Depression—or for that matter, the Great Recession. In both cases, the shock that initiates the crisis frightens consumers and businesses so much that they, in great numbers, begin to reduce their borrowing and spending.

Unfortunately, if everyone in the economy tries to cut spending at the same time, demand for goods and services drops sharply. That, in turn, reduces the income of everyone selling these goods and services. People become even more reluctant to borrow and spend. The cycle feeds on itself.

The Keynesian solution to this type of impasse is for the government to provide the demand through a huge, if temporary, spending program. The spending should be financed by borrowing. The government, in other words, begins borrowing when the private sector stops. Some economists believe that just such a spending program broke the back of the Great Depression—that is, the "spending program" known as World War II (1939–1945).

Keynes and the Great Recession Until recently, support for Keynesianism was relatively bipartisan. Republican president Richard Nixon once said, "I am now a Keynesian." Even President George W. Bush justified his tax cuts with Keynesian rhetoric. From the years after World War II until the first years of the twenty-first century, it was relatively easy to be

fiscal policy The use of changes in government expenditures and taxes to alter national economic variables.

Keynesian economics An economic theory proposed by British economist John Maynard Keynes that is typically associated with the use of fiscal policy to alter national economic variables.

a Keynesian. After all, Keynesian solutions could be implemented through relatively small changes to rates of taxation. The Bush administration sponsored just such a tax-based stimulus in early 2008, when the Great Recession had already begun but was not yet a major disaster.

Obama versus the Republicans. In February 2009, with the full scope of the recession evident, Obama proposed and Congress passed a stimulus package of roughly $800 billion, made up mostly of spending, not tax cuts. This was a classical Keynesian response to the recession, but it turned out to be a one-time measure. From 2009 on, Republicans in Congress strongly rejected Keynesianism. An important group of economists had long opposed Keynesian theories. They argued that it is not possible to stimulate the economy through federal borrowing. The borrowing just drains funds from some other part of the economy. A few members of Congress turned to these thinkers. Most of the Republicans, however, simply objected to the use of budget deficits as a recession-fighting tool.

The Eclipse of Keynesianism. If it took World War II to eliminate unemployment in the 1940s, Keynesian economics faced a problem in 2009. The increase in the federal budget deficit necessary to end the economic crisis could be very large. Some Keynesians outside the Obama administration calculated that, to have a real impact, stimulus spending would have to be three times the $800 billion already committed.[5] That type of program was politically impossible. Few Americans would accept new government spending programs amounting to trillions of dollars. By the time of his State of the Union address in 2010, Obama himself was employing rhetoric that was substantially anti-Keynesian.

State and local government spending dropped sharply after the expiration of the 2009 stimulus, and more than half a million state and local workers lost their jobs. At the federal level, even though explicitly Keynesian fiscal policies were off the table, the government continued to run trillion-dollar budget deficits through 2012. The size of these deficits became a major political issue. By 2013, however, the deficit had begun to decline noticeably.

15-4d The Federal Tax System

The government raises money to pay its expenses in two ways: through taxes

British economist John Maynard Keynes developed theories of how to pull the world out of the Great Depression in the 1930s. *What policies did Keynes advocate to end a depression?*

levied on business and personal income and through borrowing. The American income tax system is progressive—meaning that as you earn more income, you pay a higher tax rate on the additional income earned.

The 2016 tax rates are shown in Table 15–1. The rates shown are marginal ones. That means that they are the rates imposed on the last dollar you earn. An individual may be a multimillionaire, but he or she will still pay only 10 percent on taxable income up to $9,275. The

TABLE 15–1	TAX RATES FOR SINGLE PERSONS AND MARRIED COUPLES: TAX YEAR 2016, FILED IN APRIL 2017.		
Individuals		**Married Filing Jointly**	
Marginal Tax Bracket	**Marginal Tax Rate**	**Marginal Tax Bracket**	**Marginal Tax Rate**
0–$9,275	10%	0–$18,550	10%
$9,276–$37,650	15%	$18,551–$75,300	15%
$37,651–$91,150	25%	$75,301–$151,900	25%
$91,151–$190,150	28%	$151,901–$231,450	28%
$190,151–$413,350	33%	$231,451–$413,350	33%
$413,351–$415,050	35%	$413,351–$466,950	35%
$415,051 +	39.6%	$466,951 +	39.6%

Source: Internal Revenue Service.

39.6 percent rate is charged only on income in excess of $415,050. (Note that the second-highest income bracket is absurdly narrow—a side effect of a surcharge to pay for the Affordable Care Act.)

More than 40 percent of American families earn so little that they have no income tax liability at all, and this figure temporarily hit 47 percent at the height of the recession. (For a discussion of the amount of taxes paid by the rich versus other groups in American society, see this chapter's *Perception vs. Reality* feature.)

Tax Loopholes Generally, the higher the tax rate, the greater the public's reaction to that tax rate. Individuals and corporations facing high tax rates will react by making concerted attempts to get Congress to add various loopholes to the tax law that will allow them to reduce their taxable incomes.

Years ago, when Congress imposed very high tax rates on high incomes, it also provided for more loopholes. These loopholes enabled many wealthy individuals to decrease their tax bills significantly. For example, special tax provisions allowed investors in oil and gas wells to reduce their taxable income.

Will We Ever Have a Truly Simple Tax System? The Tax Reform Act of 1986 was intended to lower taxes and simplify the tax code—and it did just that for most taxpayers. A few years later, however, large

PERCEPTION VS. REALITY

Tax-Rate Cuts Allow the Rich to Pay Lower Taxes

As the saying goes, only two things are certain—death and taxes. In recent years, though, different presidents have instituted a number of tax-rate cuts. A major reduction occurred in 2003 under the administration of George W. Bush.

The Perception

You may have heard or read that the Bush tax-rate cuts favored the rich. After all, it's the rich who received the lion's share of the benefits from these tax-rate cuts.

The Reality

First, we must distinguish between tax rates and taxes paid. It is true that the Bush tax cuts lowered the top marginal income tax rate from 39.6 percent to 35 percent and that the long-term capital gains tax rate dropped from 20 percent to 15 percent. Also, the rate applied to dividends fell. Therefore, the tax rates on the highest-income individuals did

indeed fall after the tax cuts of 2003 were enacted.

At the same time, though, the percentage of taxes paid by the rich went up, not down. Indeed, the share of individual income taxes paid by the top 1 percent of income earners has been rising for more than thirty-five years.

According to the nonpartisan Congressional Budget Office, the top 45 percent of income earners in the United States pay 99.1 percent of all income taxes. The top 10 percent pay more than 70 percent of all income taxes. At the bottom end of the scale, more than 40 percent of this nation's households pay no income taxes at all (though they do pay Social Security and Medicare taxes). Finally, it is true that the rich have been getting richer in the United States. Nevertheless, their individual tax liabilities have gone up more quickly than their share of income.

These data give us some indication of what may happen since

Congress failed to extend the Bush tax cuts on the upper tax brackets. As a result of changes made in December 2012, the top long-term capital gains tax rate rose to 23.8 percent. The marginal income tax rate for a couple making more than $450,000 per year went up from 35 percent to 39.6 percent. Wealthy individuals are likely to respond to these higher tax rates by adjusting their behavior. The higher rates could actually result in the rich paying less in taxes, not more.

Blog On

Scott Adams, creator of the Dilbert comic strip, makes hilarious and fresh observations about all sorts of things on his blog. Taxing the rich is just one of his topics—try searching on "dilbert blog tax."

federal deficits forced Congress to choose between cutting spending and raising taxes, and Congress opted to do the latter. Tax increases occurred under the administrations of both George H. W. Bush (1989–1993) and Bill Clinton (1993–2001). In fact, the tax rate for the highest income bracket rose from 28 percent in 1986 to 39.6 percent in 1993. Thus, the effective highest marginal tax rate increased significantly.

In response to this sharp increase in taxes, those who were affected lobbied Congress to legislate special exceptions and loopholes so that the full impact of the rate increase would not be felt by the wealthiest Americans. As a result, the tax code is more complicated than it was before the 1986 Tax Reform Act.

While in principle everyone is for a simpler tax code, in practice Congress rarely is able to pass tax-reform legislation. Why? The reason is that those who now benefit from our complicated tax code will not give up their tax breaks without a fight.

These groups include homeowners who deduct interest on their mortgages (and therefore the home-building industry as well), charities that receive tax-deductible contributions, and businesses that get tax breaks for research and development. Those who benefit typically know all about the tax provisions that help them. Those who do not benefit can ignore the added complexity in the tax code when filing their returns—but they will still have to pay higher taxes to make up for the tax breaks enjoyed by special interests.

15-4e The Public Debt

When the government spends more than it receives, it has to finance this shortfall. Typically, it borrows. The U.S. Treasury sells IOUs on behalf of the U.S. government. They are called U.S. Treasury bills, notes, or bonds, depending on how long the funds are borrowed. All are commonly called *treasuries*.

The sale of these obligations to corporations, private individuals, pension plans, foreign governments, foreign companies, and foreign individuals is big business. After all, except for a few years in the late 1990s and early 2000s, federal government expenditures have always exceeded federal government revenues.

Every time there is a federal government deficit, there is an increase in the total accumulated **public debt** (also called the *national debt*), which is defined as the total value of all outstanding federal government borrowing. If the existing public debt is $5 trillion and the government runs a deficit of $100 billion, then at the end of the year the public debt is $5.1 trillion. Figure 15–4 shows what has happened to the *net* public debt over time, in comparison with the overall size of the economy. (The net public debt doesn't count sums that the government owes to itself, although it does include funds held by the Fed.)

public debt The total amount of money that the national government owes as a result of borrowing; also called the *national debt*.

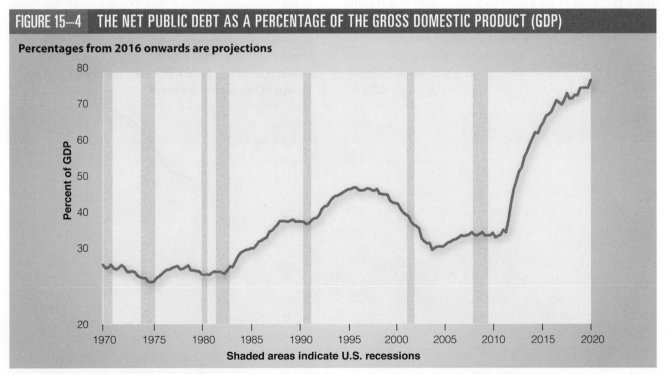

FIGURE 15–4 THE NET PUBLIC DEBT AS A PERCENTAGE OF THE GROSS DOMESTIC PRODUCT (GDP)

Percentages from 2016 onwards are projections

Shaded areas indicate U.S. recessions

Source: research.stlouisfed.org and the Congressional Budget Office.

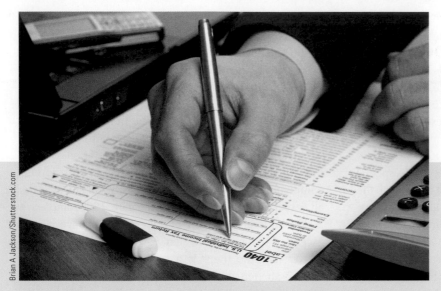

No one likes paying taxes, but they have been called "the dues we pay to live in a civilized society." *What would it be like to live in a society with little or no government?*

The Burden of the Public Debt   We often hear about the burden of the public debt. Some even maintain that the government will eventually go bankrupt. As long as the government can collect taxes to pay interest on its public debt, however, that will never happen. What happens instead is that when treasuries come due, they are simply "rolled over," or refinanced. That is, if a $1 million Treasury bond comes due today and is cashed in, the U.S. Treasury pays it off with the money it gets from selling another $1 million bond.

The interest on treasuries is paid by federal taxes. Even though much of the interest is being paid to American citizens, the more the federal government borrows to meet these payments, the greater the percentage of its budget is committed to making interest payments. This reduces the government's ability to supply funds for anything else, including transportation, education, housing programs, and the military.

Budget Deficit Explosion, 2009–2012   As discussed earlier, the initial response of the federal government to the Great Recession was to increase spending. At the same time, the economy was shrinking, so tax revenues were shrinking, too. Between increased spending and lower revenues, the federal budget deficit shot up. The deficit for 2011 was $1.3 trillion. That was about 8.6 percent of the entire economy. If we look at all levels of government together, for every five dollars of spending, three were backed up by tax receipts. The other two were borrowed.

By 2015, however, the federal budget deficit was down to $439 billion. Given current policies, the deficit should not exceed $750 billion until the 2020s. Some economists contend that so long as the deficit does not cause the public debt to grow faster than the economy as a whole, we have no problem. To meet that standard, however, the deficit would need to fall below $370 billion and stay low thereafter.

CRITICAL THINKING

▶ *Does your family benefit from any tax breaks that you know of? If so, what are they?*

AMERICA AT ODDS | Domestic Policy

The Preamble to the U.S. Constitution states that one of the goals of the new government was to "promote the general Welfare." Domestic policy is certainly the main way in which our government seeks to promote the general welfare. But how should this be done? Americans are at odds over many domestic issues. A few of them are listed here:

- *Do we send too many people to prison—or do our current incarceration policies protect the public?*

- *Should health-care insurance be a right of all citizens—or does such a program sap individual initiative and lead to an over-mighty government?*

- *Is climate change a serious problem that must be addressed now—or are the risks overblown and the proposed solutions a danger to our economy?*

- *Is new offshore drilling essential to our energy independence—or is it an unacceptable threat to the environment?*

- *Is a budgetary stimulus a necessary tool to fight recessions—or does it simply worsen the long-term budget deficit?*

STUDY TOOLS 15

READY TO STUDY? IN THE BOOK, YOU CAN:

- ☐ Review what you've read with the following chapter quiz.
- ☐ Check your answers in Appendix D at the back of the book.
- ☐ Rip out the Chapter Review Card, which includes key terms and chapter summaries.

ONLINE AT WWW.CENGAGEBRAIN.COM, YOU CAN:

- ☐ Learn about health-care reform in a short video.
- ☐ Explore various online resources in the U.S. Treasury and Artists Against Fracking websites with the Internet Resources tool.
- ☐ Interact with figures from the text, and watch quick animation clips.
- ☐ Prepare for tests with quizzes.
- ☐ Review the key terms with Flash Cards.

FILL-IN

Learning Outcome 15–1

1. The stages of the policymaking process are _____.

Learning Outcome 15–2

2. _____ is now the federal government's second-largest domestic spending program, after Social Security.

3. The individual mandate in the 2010 health-care reform legislation is a requirement that _____.

Learning Outcome 15–3

4. The nations of _____ supply 45 percent of our oil imports.

5. The predicted outcomes of climate change include _____.

6. Renewable energy technologies include _____.

Learning Outcome 15–4

7. A period in which the economy stops growing altogether and undergoes a contraction is called a _____.

8. Monetary policy is under the control of the _____, an independent regulatory agency.

MULTIPLE CHOICE

Learning Outcome 15–1

9. A discussion in the media about a problem that might have a political solution is an example of
   a. policy adoption.
   b. policy implementation.
   c. issue identification.

Learning Outcome 15–2

10. About _____ percent of national spending in the United States goes to health care.
    a. 4
    b. 18
    c. 29.5

11. One immediate change brought about by the health-care reform bills that passed in 2010 was that young people can remain covered by their parents' insurance until they turn
    a. 26.
    b. 21.
    c. 18.

Learning Outcome 15–3

12. By mid-2016, the price of a barrel of crude oil, which not long before exceeded $140, was
    a. closer to $175.
    b. averaging between $90 and $100.
    c. about $50.

Learning Outcome 15–4

13. _____ policy uses changes in government expenditures and taxes to alter national economic variables.
    a. Monetary
    b. Fiscal
    c. Domestic

14. According to the nonpartisan Congressional Budget Office, about _____ percent of this nation's households pay no income taxes at all.
    a. 10
    b. 23
    c. 40

GOVT
ONLINE
STUDY YOUR WAY
WITH STUDYBITS!

WEAK

FAIR

STRONG

UNASSIGNED

Rate and Organize StudyBits

Collect What's Important

Create Flashcards From Your StudyBits

85%

Track/Monitor Your Progress

CORRECT

INCORRECT

INCORRECT

INCORRECT

Personalize Your Quizzes

4LTR PRESS

Access GOVT ONLINE at www.cengagebrain.com

U.S. Department of Defense

16 FOREIGN POLICY

LEARNING OUTCOMES *After reading this chapter, you should be able to:*

16-1 Discuss how foreign policy is made, and identify the key players in this process.

16-2 Summarize the history of American foreign policy.

16-3 Identify the foreign policy challenges that our government has sought to meet by using military force.

16-4 Describe issues that the government has handled primarily through diplomacy, including the Israeli-Palestinian conflict, curbing weapons of mass destruction, and the rise of China as a world power.

After finishing this chapter, go to **PAGE 376** for **STUDY TOOLS**.

AMERICA AT ODDS | How Much of a Threat Is Putin's Russia?

Frederic Legrand/Shutterstock

Most students today are too young to remember the Union of Soviet Socialist Republics—the Soviet Union, or USSR. That country broke up into fifteen independent republics in 1991. From the end of World War II until the late 1980s, America and its allies were pitted against the Soviet Union in what was called the "Cold War." (You'll read more about the Cold War in this chapter.)

Millions of Soviet soldiers were under arms during the Cold War. The USSR had a world-class navy and a vast arsenal of nuclear weapons. The heart of the old Soviet Union was the Russian Republic, which contained about half the USSR's population. Today's Russia is much weaker than the Soviet Union. Yet in recent years, Russia's president, Vladimir Putin, has begun to demonstrate an alarming degree of aggressiveness. How much of a threat does Putin's Russia present?

Russia Is a Very Serious Threat

Consider what Putin has done. He has threatened Europe by cutting off natural gas supplies. He has waged war on the small nation of Georgia, detaching portions of Georgian territory. Because Putin opposed Ukraine's new Europe-friendly government, he invaded and annexed Ukraine's Crimean peninsula. He then sponsored an insurrection in Russian-speaking areas of eastern Ukraine. When it seemed that the Ukrainian government would put down the rebellion, Russia moved its own troops into Ukraine to prevent such a result. Putin has initiated a series of provocations aimed at the small Baltic nations. Unlike Ukraine, however, the Baltic states are members of the North Atlantic Treaty Organization (NATO). That means that America and most of Europe are sworn to defend their territory as if it were our own.

Putin has said that the biggest geopolitical disaster of the twentieth century was the fall of the Soviet Union. He wants to restore its former glory. An example is Russia's recent intervention into the Syrian civil war, which involved bombing and even the use of troops. In the long run, economic troubles may limit Russia's capabilities. In the short run, however, they may provoke Putin into distracting his citizens through military adventures.

In the Long Run, Russia Is Weak

There is no question that Putin has begun making trouble for the world. Yet consider the balance of forces. Add the European Union to the United States and you have an economy sixteen times the size of Russia's. The U.S. defense budget is seven times that of Russia. The old Soviet Union drew strength from the ideology of communism, which had supporters around the world. Today's Russia has no ideology that can match the attractions of the West. Indeed, the crisis in Ukraine began because that nation wanted to draw closer to the European Union—an organization that is truly attractive to the peoples of Eastern Europe.

Russia's state-controlled economy is fragile and inefficient. Russia's population is even declining. The United States and our European allies have imposed sanctions (punishments) on Russia due to its Ukraine policy. Sanctions, together with the fall in the price of oil—Russia's chief export—have pushed the Russian economy into recession. As a regional power, Russia can make trouble. It does not, however, threaten the world.

Where do you stand?

1. Does it matter that most of the nations Putin has threatened militarily are former members of the Soviet Union? Why or why not?

2. Why don't people refer to the war on terrorism as a Cold War?

Explore this issue online:

- For an insightful article in the magazine *National Interest,* search on "new cold war will be different."

- The Vox website has a card stack titled "Everything You Need to Know about Ukraine." Find it by searching on "vox cards ukraine."

INTRODUCTION

What we call **foreign policy** is a systematic and general plan that guides a country's attitudes and actions toward the rest of the world. Foreign policy includes all of the economic, military, commercial, and diplomatic positions and actions that a nation takes in its relationships with other countries. Although foreign policy may seem quite removed from the concerns of everyday life, it can and does have a significant impact on the day-to-day lives of Americans.

American foreign policy has been shaped by two principles that are often seen as contradicting each other. One is **moral idealism**, the belief that the most important goal in foreign policy is to do what is right. Moral idealists think that it is possible for nations to relate to each other as part of a rule-based community. Moral idealism appeals to the often-held American belief that our nation is special and should provide an example to the rest of the world.

A contrasting view is **political realism**, the belief that nations are inevitably selfish. In this view, foreign countries are by definition dangerous. The chapter-opening *America at Odds* feature, for example, discusses the dangers posed by Russia. Foreign policy must therefore be based on protecting our national security, regardless of moral arguments. Although there have been times when one or the other of these two principles has dominated, U.S. foreign policy has usually been a mixture of both.

foreign policy A systematic and general plan that guides a country's attitudes and actions toward the rest of the world. Foreign policy includes all of the economic, military, commercial, and diplomatic positions and actions that a nation takes in its relationships with other countries.

moral idealism In foreign policy, the belief that the most important goal is to do what is right. Moral idealists think that it is possible for nations to cooperate as part of a rule-based community.

political realism In foreign policy, the belief that nations are inevitably selfish and that we should seek to protect our national security, regardless of moral arguments.

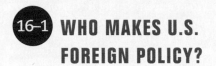

Refugees from Syria, Afghanistan, and other countries at the Munich train station in Germany. *Should the United States accept more Syrian refugees on the basis of moral idealism? Why or why not?*

16–1 WHO MAKES U.S. FOREIGN POLICY?

LO Discuss how foreign policy is made, and identify the key players in this process.

The framers of the Constitution envisioned that the president and Congress would cooperate in developing American foreign policy. The Constitution did not spell out exactly how this was to be done, though. As commander in chief, the president has assumed much of the decision-making power in the area of foreign policy. Nonetheless, members of Congress, a number of officials, and a vast national security bureaucracy help to shape the president's decisions and to limit the president's powers.

16–1a The President's Role

Article II, Section 2, of the Constitution names the president commander in chief of the armed forces. As commander in chief, the president oversees the military and guides defense policies. Presidents have interpreted this role broadly, sending American troops, ships, and weapons to trouble spots at home and around the world.

The Constitution authorizes the president to make treaties, which must be approved by two-thirds of the

Senate. In addition, the president is empowered to form executive agreements—pacts between the president and the heads of other nations. These executive agreements do not require Senate approval.

The president's foreign policy responsibilities have special significance in that the president has ultimate control over the use of nuclear weapons. The president also influences foreign policymaking in the role of head of state. As the symbolic head of our government, the president represents the United States to the rest of the world. When a serious foreign policy issue or international question arises, the nation expects the president to make a statement on the matter.

16–1b The Cabinet

Many members of the president's cabinet concern themselves with international problems and recommend policies to deal with them. As U.S. power in the world has grown and as economic factors have become increasingly important, the departments of Agriculture, Commerce, Energy, and Treasury have become more involved in foreign policy decisions. The secretary of state and the secretary of defense, however, are the only cabinet members who concern themselves with foreign policy matters on a full-time basis.

The Department of State

The Department of State is, in principle, the government agency most directly involved in foreign policy. The department is responsible for diplomatic relations with nearly two hundred independent nations around the globe, as well as with the United Nations and other multilateral organizations, such as the Organization of American States. Most U.S. relations with other countries are maintained through embassies, consulates, and other U.S. offices around the world.

As the head of the State Department, the secretary of state has traditionally played a key role in foreign policymaking, and many presidents have relied heavily on

> **"TO BE PREPARED FOR WAR IS ONE OF THE MOST EFFECTUAL MEANS OF PRESERVING PEACE."**
>
> ~ GEORGE WASHINGTON, COMMANDER OF THE CONTINENTAL ARMY AND FIRST PRESIDENT OF THE UNITED STATES, 1789–1797

the advice of their secretaries of state. Under many presidents since the end of World War II, however, the State Department has taken a back seat in foreign policy to the president's National Security Council, described later. The Obama administration has been an exception to this trend—secretaries of state Hillary Clinton and John Kerry have played the leading role in foreign policy.

The Department of Defense

The Department of Defense is the principal executive department that establishes and carries out defense policy and protects our national security. The secretary of defense advises the president on all aspects of U.S. military and defense policy, supervises all of the military activities of the U.S. government, and works to see that the decisions of the president as commander in chief are carried out. The secretary advises and informs the president on the nation's military forces, weapons, and bases and works closely with the U.S. military, especially the Joint Chiefs of Staff, in gathering and studying defense information.

The Joint Chiefs of Staff (JCS) include the chair and vice chair of the JCS; the military service chiefs of the Army, Navy, Air Force, and Marines; and the chief of the National Guard. All are appointed by the president and confirmed by the Senate.

Secretary of Defense Ash Carter meets with Prince Mohammed bin Salman, deputy crown prince and minister of defense of Saudi Arabia. *Why wouldn't our president be there, too?*

U.S. Department of Defense

The joint chiefs regularly serve as the key military advisers to the president, the secretary of defense, and the National Security Council. They are responsible for handing down the president's orders to the nation's military units, preparing strategic plans, and recommending military actions. They also propose military budgets, new weapons systems, and military regulations.

16–1c Other Agencies

Several other government agencies are also involved in the foreign relations of the United States. Two key agencies in the area of foreign policy are the National Security Council and the Central Intelligence Agency.

The National Security Council The National Security Council (NSC) was established by the National Security Act of 1947. The formal members of the NSC include the president, the vice president, the secretary of state, and the secretary of defense. Meetings are often attended by the chairperson of the Joint Chiefs of Staff, the director of the Central Intelligence Agency, and representatives from other departments.

The national security adviser, who is a member of the president's White House staff, is the director of the NSC. The adviser informs the president, coordinates advice and information on foreign policy, and serves as a liaison with other officials.

The NSC and its members can be as important and powerful as the president wants them to be. Some presidents have made frequent use of the NSC, whereas others have convened it infrequently. Similarly, the importance of the role played by the national security adviser in shaping foreign policy can vary significantly, depending on the administration and the adviser's identity.

The Central Intelligence Agency The Central Intelligence Agency (CIA) was created after World War II to coordinate American intelligence activities abroad. The CIA provides the president and his or her advisers with up-to-date information about the political, military, and economic activities of foreign governments.

The CIA gathers much of its intelligence from overt sources, such as foreign radio broadcasts and newspapers, people who travel abroad, the Internet, and satellite photographs. Other information is gathered from covert activities, such as the CIA's own secret investigations into the economic or political affairs of other nations. Covert operations may involve secretly supplying weapons to a force rebelling against an unfriendly government or seizing suspected terrorists in a clandestine operation and holding them for questioning.

The CIA has tended to operate autonomously, and the details of its work, methods, and operating funds have been kept secret. Intelligence reform passed by Congress in 2004, however, makes the CIA accountable to a national intelligence director. The CIA is now required to cooperate more with other U.S. intelligence agencies and has lost a degree of the autonomy it once enjoyed.

16–1d Powers of Congress

Although the executive branch takes the lead in foreign policy matters, Congress also has some power over foreign policy. Remember that Congress alone has the power to declare war. It also has the power to appropriate funds to build new weapons systems, equip the U.S. armed forces, and provide for foreign aid. The Senate has the power to approve or reject treaties and the appointment of ambassadors.

In 1973, Congress passed the War Powers Resolution, which limits the president's use of troops in military action without congressional approval. Presidents since then, however, have not interpreted the resolution to mean that Congress must be consulted before military action is taken. On several occasions, presidents have ordered military action and then informed Congress after the fact.

A few congressional committees are directly concerned with foreign affairs. The most important are the Armed Services Committee and the Committee on Foreign Affairs in the House, and the Armed Services Committee and the Foreign Relations Committee in the Senate. Other congressional committees deal with matters that indirectly influence foreign policy, such as oil, agriculture, and imports.

CRITICAL THINKING

▶ *Should American citizens know more about what the CIA does, or would such knowledge merely benefit our opponents? In either case, why?*

16–2 A SHORT HISTORY OF AMERICAN FOREIGN POLICY

LO Summarize the history of American foreign policy.

Many U.S. foreign policy initiatives have been rooted in moral idealism. A primary consideration in U.S. foreign policy, though, has always been *national security*—the protection of the independence and political integrity of the nation.

Over the years, the United States has attempted to preserve its national security in many ways. These ways have changed over time and are not always internally consistent. This inconsistency results from the fact that foreign policymaking, like domestic policymaking, reflects the influence of various political groups in the United States. These groups—including the voting public, interest groups, Congress, and the president and relevant agencies of the executive branch—are often at odds over what the U.S. position should be on particular foreign policy issues.

16-2a Isolationism

The nation's founders and the early presidents believed that **isolationism**—avoiding political involvement with other nations—was the best way to protect American interests. The United States was certainly not yet strong enough to directly influence European developments. During the 1700s and 1800s, the United States generally attempted to avoid conflicts and political engagements elsewhere.

In accordance with this isolationist philosophy, President James Monroe in 1823 proclaimed what became known as the **Monroe Doctrine**. Monroe stated that the United States would not tolerate foreign intervention in the Western Hemisphere. In return, Monroe promised that the United States would stay out of European affairs.

16-2b The Beginning of Interventionism

Isolationism gradually gave way to **interventionism** (direct involvement in foreign affairs). The first true step toward interventionism occurred with the Spanish-American War of 1898. The United States fought this war to free Cuba from Spanish rule. Spain lost and subsequently ceded control of several of its possessions, including Guam, Puerto Rico, and the Philippines, to the United States. The United States thus acquired

a **colonial empire** and was acknowledged as a world power.

The growth of the United States as an industrial economy also confirmed the nation's position as a world power. For example, in the early 1900s, President Theodore Roosevelt proposed that the United States could invade Latin American countries when it was necessary to guarantee political or economic stability.

16-2c The World Wars

When World War I broke out in 1914, President Woodrow Wilson initially proclaimed a policy of **neutrality**—the United States would not take sides in the conflict. The United States did not enter the war until 1917, after U.S. ships in international waters were attacked by German submarines that were blockading Britain.

Wilson called the war a way to "make the world safe for democracy." In his eyes, Germany was not merely dangerous but evil. Wilson, in short, was our most famous presidential advocate of moral idealism.

After World War I ended in 1918, the United States returned to a policy of isolationism. Consequently, we refused to join the League of Nations, an international body intended to resolve

Library of Congress Prints and Photographs Division[LC-USZC4-12215]

President James Monroe (1817–1825) said that the United States would not allow foreign intervention in the Western Hemisphere. *What position did Monroe take on U.S. intervention in Europe?*

isolationism
A political policy of noninvolvement in world affairs.

Monroe Doctrine
A U.S. policy, announced in 1823 by President James Monroe, that the United States would not tolerate foreign intervention in the Western Hemisphere, and in return, we would stay out of European affairs.

interventionism
Direct involvement by one country in another country's affairs.

colonial empire
A group of dependent nations that are under the rule of an imperial power.

neutrality The position of not being aligned with either side in a dispute or conflict, such as a war.

peacefully any future conflicts between nations.

But the U.S. policy of isolationism ended when the Japanese attacked Pearl Harbor in 1941. We joined the Allies—Australia, Britain, Canada, China, France, and the Soviet Union—to fight the Axis nations of Germany, Italy, and Japan. One of the most significant foreign policy actions during World War II was the dropping of atomic bombs on the Japanese cities of Hiroshima and Nagasaki in August 1945 in a successful attempt to force Japan to surrender.

16–2d The Cold War

After World War II ended in 1945, the wartime alliance between the United States and the Soviet Union began to deteriorate quickly. The Soviet Union opposed America's political and economic systems. Many Americans considered Soviet attempts to spread communist systems to other countries a major threat to democracy. After the war ended, countries in Eastern Europe—Bulgaria, Czechoslovakia, East Germany, Hungary, Poland, and Romania—fell under Soviet domination, forming what became known as the Soviet bloc.

The United States entered World War II after the surprise Japanese attack on Pearl Harbor, Hawaii, on December 7, 1941. *Which nations were our allies in this conflict?*

Soviet bloc The group of Eastern European nations that fell under the control of the Soviet Union following World War II.

Marshall Plan A plan providing for U.S. economic assistance to European nations following World War II to help those nations recover from the war. The plan was named after George C. Marshall, secretary of state from 1947 to 1949.

containment A U.S. policy designed to contain the spread of communism by offering military and economic aid to threatened nations.

The Marshall Plan and the Policy of Containment
In 1947, when it appeared that local Communist parties, backed by the Soviets, would take over Greece and Turkey, President Harry Truman took action. He convinced Congress to appropriate $400 million ($4.4 billion in 2017 dollars) in aid for those countries to prevent the spread of communism.

The Truman Doctrine and the Marshall Plan. The president also proclaimed what became known as the *Truman Doctrine.* It would be "the policy of the United States to support free peoples who are resisting attempted subjugation by armed minorities or by outside pressures."[1]

The Truman administration also instituted a policy of economic assistance to war-torn Europe, called the **Marshall Plan** after George Marshall, who was then the U.S. secretary of state. During the next five years, Congress appropriated $17 billion (about $172 billion in 2017 dollars) for aid to sixteen European countries. By 1952, the nations of Western Europe, with U.S. help, had recovered and were again prospering.

The Containment Policy and NATO. These actions marked the beginning of a policy of **containment** designed to contain (prevent) the spread of communism by offering threatened nations U.S. military and economic aid.[2] To make the policy of containment effective, the United States initiated a program of collective security involving the formation of mutual defense alliances with other nations.

In 1949, through the North Atlantic Treaty, the United States, Canada, and ten European nations formed a military alliance—the North Atlantic Treaty Organization (NATO). The treaty declared that an attack on any member of the alliance would be considered an attack against all members.

Britain's Winston Churchill was a valuable friend of the United States during World War II. *What did Churchill mean when he referred to the "iron curtain"?*

The Cold War Begins By 1949, almost all illusions of friendship between the Soviet Union and the Western allies had disappeared. The United States became the leader of a bloc of democratic nations in Western Europe, the Pacific, and elsewhere.

The tensions between the Soviet Union and the United States became known as the **Cold War**—a war of words, warnings, and ideologies that lasted from the late 1940s through the late 1980s. Although the Cold War was mainly a war of words and belief systems, "hot" wars in Korea (1950–1953) and Vietnam (1965–1975) grew out of the efforts to contain communism.

The Arms Race and Deterrence The tensions induced by the Cold War led both the Soviet Union and the United States to try to surpass each other militarily. They began competing for more and better weapons, particularly nuclear weapons, with greater destructive power.

This phenomenon, known as the *arms race,* was supported by a policy of **deterrence**—of rendering ourselves and our allies so strong militarily that our very strength would deter (stop or discourage) any attack on us. Out of deterrence came the theory of **mutually assured destruction (MAD)**, which held that if the forces of two nations were capable of destroying each other, neither nation would take a chance on war.

The Cuban Missile Crisis In 1962, the United States and the Soviet Union came close to a nuclear confrontation in what became known as the **Cuban missile crisis**. The United States learned that the Soviet Union had placed nuclear weapons on the island of Cuba, ninety miles from the coast of Florida.

The crisis was defused without military conflict. A U.S. naval blockade of Cuba convinced the Soviet Union to agree to remove the missiles. The United States also agreed to remove some of its missiles near the Soviet border in Turkey. Both sides recognized that a nuclear war between the two superpowers was unthinkable.

Although the United States agreed not to invade Cuba or attempt to overthrow its government, it did institute an embargo against the island. (An *embargo* is a ban on trade.) The United States also refused to recognize the Cuban government. That policy lasted until December 2014, when President Obama and Cuban president Raúl Castro announced plans to normalize relations between the two countries. Diplomatic relations were officially restored in July 2015, and Obama visited the island in March 2016. Only Congress can lift the embargo, however, and as of 2016 Congress has not yet shown an interest in taking such a step.

Détente and Arms Control In 1969, the United States and the Soviet Union began negotiations on a treaty to limit the number of antiballistic missiles (ABMs) and offensive missiles that each country could develop and deploy. In 1972, both sides signed the Strategic Arms Limitation Treaty (SALT I). This event marked the

Cold War The war of words, warnings, and ideologies between the Soviet Union and the United States that lasted from the late 1940s through the late 1980s.

deterrence A policy of building up military strength for the purpose of discouraging (deterring) military attacks by other nations; the policy that supported the arms race between the United States and the Soviet Union during the Cold War.

mutually assured destruction (MAD) A phrase referring to the assumption that if the forces of two nations are capable of destroying each other, neither nation will take a chance on war.

Cuban missile crisis A nuclear standoff that occurred in 1962 when the United States learned that the Soviet Union had placed nuclear warheads in Cuba.

beginning of a period of **détente**, a French word that means a "relaxation of tensions."

In 1983, President Ronald Reagan (1981–1989) nearly reignited the arms race by proposing a missile defense system known as the strategic defense initiative (SDI, or "Star Wars"). Nonetheless, Reagan pursued arms control agreements with Soviet leaders, as did Reagan's successor, President George H. W. Bush (1989–1993).

The Dissolution of the Soviet Union

In the late 1980s, the political situation inside the Soviet Union began to change rapidly. Mikhail Gorbachev, the new leader, had initiated an effort to democratize the Soviet political system and decentralize the economy. The reforms quickly spread to other countries in the Soviet bloc. In 1989, the Berlin Wall, constructed nearly thirty years earlier to separate Soviet-dominated East Berlin from West Berlin, was torn down. East Germany and West Germany were reunited in 1990.

In August 1991, a number of disgruntled Communist Party leaders who wanted to reverse the reforms briefly seized control of the Soviet central government. Russian citizens rose up in revolt and defied those leaders. The democratically elected president of the Russian republic (the largest republic in the Soviet Union), Boris Yeltsin, confronted troops in Moscow that were under the control of the conspirators. The attempted coup collapsed after three days. The Communist Party in the Soviet Union lost almost all of its power.

The fifteen republics constituting the Soviet Union—including the Russian republic—declared their independence. By the end of the year, the Union of Soviet Socialist Republics (USSR) no longer existed. For years following the collapse of the Soviet Union, Russia—the main successor state—posed little or no threat to world peace. Under President Vladimir Putin, however, Russian policy has been much more aggressive. We discussed these developments in the chapter-opening *America at Odds* feature.

16–2e Post–Cold War Foreign Policy

The demise of the Soviet Union altered the framework and goals of U.S. foreign policy. During the Cold War, the moral

détente A French word meaning a "relaxation of tensions." Détente characterized the relationship between the United States and the Soviet Union in the 1970s as they attempted to pursue cooperative dealings and arms control.

> **"SOVIET UNION FOREIGN POLICY IS A PUZZLE, INSIDE A RIDDLE WRAPPED IN AN ENIGMA."**
>
> ~ WINSTON CHURCHILL, BRITISH PRIME MINISTER DURING WORLD WAR II, 1874–1965

underpinnings of American foreign policy were clear to all—the United States was the defender of the "free world" against the Soviet aggressor.

U.S. foreign policymakers have struggled since the end of the Cold War to determine the degree of intervention that is appropriate and prudent for the U.S. military. Should we intervene in a humanitarian crisis, such as a famine? Should the U.S. military participate in peacekeeping missions, such as those instituted after civil or ethnic strife in other countries? Americans have faced these questions in Bosnia, Kosovo, Rwanda, Somalia, and Sudan.

Yet no overriding framework emerged in U.S. foreign policy until September 11, 2001. Since that date, our goal has been to capture and punish the terrorists who planned and perpetrated the events of that day and to prevent future terrorist attacks against Americans. Sometimes, that goal has involved "regime change," one of the objectives of the war against Iraq in 2003.

CRITICAL THINKING

▸ *The Cold War between the United States and the Soviet Union never turned into a shooting war. Why not?*

16–3 PROBLEMS REQUIRING THE USE OF FORCE

LO Identify foreign policy challenges that our government has sought to meet by using military force.

We can divide the main foreign policy problems that confront the United States into two types. One set of issues is dealt with primarily through diplomacy. We discuss these issues later in this chapter. In contrast, some problems must be handled through the use of force. When in foreign lands, the use of force means deployment of the U.S. armed forces. When the problem is terrorism, which can involve attacks on the American homeland, the primary response may sometimes be provided instead by U.S. police agencies such as the FBI. We consider terrorism next.

16–3a The Problem of Terrorism

One of the most difficult challenges faced by governments around the world is how to control terrorism. *Terrorism* is defined as the use of staged violence, often against civilians, to achieve political goals. Terrorism has occurred in almost every region of the world.

The most devastating terrorist attack in U.S. history occurred on September 11, 2001, when radical Islamist terrorists used hijacked airliners as missiles to bring down the World Trade Center towers in New York City and to destroy part of the Pentagon building in Washington, D.C. A fourth airplane crashed in a Pennsylvania field after passengers fought back against the hijackers. In all, almost three thousand innocent civilians were killed as a result of these terrorist acts.

Other examples of terrorist acts include the Palestinian attacks on Israeli Olympic athletes in Munich, Germany, in 1972; the Libyan suitcase bombing of an American airliner over Lockerbie, Scotland, in 1988; the bombing of two U.S. embassies in Africa in 1998; the bombing of the Navy ship USS *Cole* in a Yemeni port in 2000; and coordinated bomb attacks on London's transportation system in 2005.

Terrorists are willing to destroy others' lives and property, and often sacrifice their own lives, for a variety of reasons. Terrorist acts generally fall into one of three broad categories, discussed next.

Local or Regional Terrorism Some terrorist acts have been committed by extremists motivated by the desire to obtain freedom from a nation or government that they regard as an oppressor. Another motivation for terrorism is to disrupt peace talks. In Israel, for example, numerous suicide bombings by Palestinians against Israeli civilians have served to stall efforts to negotiate a peace between Israel and the Palestinians.

Separatist Groups. The Irish Republican Army, which sought to unite British-governed Northern Ireland with the independent Republic of Ireland, conducted bombings and other terrorist acts in Northern Ireland and England over a period of many years. The attacks came to an end in 1997 as part of a peace process that lasted from 1995 until 2005.

Basque separatists in Spain have engaged in terrorism for decades. The separatists were initially—and

An impromptu memorial to the 130 residents of Paris, France, who died in terrorist attacks in November 2015. The Islamic State in Iraq and Syria (ISIS) claimed responsibility. *Why would ISIS attack Western civilians?*

incorrectly—blamed for bombing a commuter train in Madrid, Spain, on March 11, 2004. That terrorist attack, actually perpetrated by Islamic radicals, killed 191 people and injured hundreds of others.

Domestic Terrorism in the United States. In parts of the South, whites used terrorist methods to prevent African Americans from voting all the way from the late nineteenth century until the 1960s. In other words, domestic terrorism in America has a long pedigree. Indeed, attacks on minority group members continue to be a problem to this day.

In the Vietnam War era, antiwar radicals engaged in a series of bombings.[3] In the 1990s, right-wing extremism was an issue. The bombing of the Oklahoma City federal building in 1995, which killed 168 people, was the act of vengeful extremists who claimed to fear an oppressive federal government. Although Timothy McVeigh and Terry Nichols, who were convicted of the crime, were not directly connected to a particular political group, they expressed views characteristic of the extreme right-wing militia movement in the United States.

A more recent problem in the United States has been attacks by domestic Islamists who have been "self-radicalized" through the Internet. While these individuals may communicate with foreign terrorist organizations, they are not under foreign control. An example is the two self-radicalized Muslim brothers who set off bombs at the Boston Marathon in 2013. Three people died in this incident, and many more lost the use of one or both of their legs. The terrorist attack in San Bernardino, California, in 2015 is another example, one that we have discussed several times in this text.

State-Sponsored Terrorism Some terrorist attacks have been planned and sponsored by governments. For example, the bombing of Pan Am Flight 103—which exploded over Lockerbie, Scotland, in 1988, killing all 259 people on board and 11 on the ground—was later proved to be the work of an intelligence officer working for Libya.

The United Nations imposed economic sanctions (punishments) against Libya in an effort to force Libyan dictator Muammar Gaddafi to extradite those who were suspected of being responsible for the bombing. More than a decade after the bombing, Libya agreed to hand the men over for trial.

The case of Pan Am Flight 103 illustrates the difficulty in punishing the perpetrators of state-sponsored terrorism. The victim country must first prove who the terrorists are and for whom they were working. Then it must decide what type of retribution is warranted.

Foreign Terrorist Networks A relatively new phenomenon in the late 1990s and early 2000s was the emergence of nonstate terrorist networks, such as al Qaeda. Al Qaeda is the nongovernmental organization that planned and carried out the terrorist attacks of September 11, 2001. Its leader until his death in 2011 was the Saudi dissident Osama bin Laden.

Throughout the 1990s, al Qaeda conducted training camps in the mountains of Afghanistan, which was ruled by an ultraconservative Islamic faction known as the Taliban. The U.S. government determined that al Qaeda was responsible for terrorist attacks on two U.S. embassies in Africa in 1998 and the bombing of the USS *Cole*

coalition An alliance of nations formed to undertake a foreign policy action, particularly a military action. A coalition is often a temporary alliance that dissolves after the action is concluded.

weapons of mass destruction Chemical, biological, and nuclear weapons that can inflict massive casualties.

"FIGHTING TERRORISM IS LIKE BEING A GOALKEEPER. YOU CAN MAKE A HUNDRED BRILLIANT SAVES BUT THE ONLY SHOT THAT PEOPLE REMEMBER IS THE ONE THAT GETS PAST YOU."

~ PAUL WILKINSON, BRITISH TERRORISM EXPERT, BORN 1937

in 2000. In 1998, President Bill Clinton (1993–2001) ordered the bombing of terrorist camps in Afghanistan in retaliation for the embassy bombings, but with little effect. Al Qaeda cells continued to operate largely unimpeded until the terrorist attacks of September 11.

16–3b The U.S. Response to 9/11— The War in Afghanistan

Immediately after the 9/11 terrorist attacks, Congress passed a joint resolution authorizing President George W. Bush (2001–2009) to use "all necessary and appropriate force" against nations, organizations, and individuals that the president determined had "planned, authorized, committed, or aided the terrorist attacks."

In late 2001, supported by a **coalition** of allies, the U.S. military attacked al Qaeda camps in Afghanistan and the ruling Taliban regime that harbored those terrorists. Once the Taliban had been ousted, the United States helped to establish a government in Afghanistan that did not support terrorism. Instead of continuing the hunt for al Qaeda members in Afghanistan, however, the Bush administration increasingly looked to Iraq as a threat to U.S. security.

16–3c The Focus on Iraq

On March 20, 2003, U.S. and British forces attacked the nation of Iraq. Iraqi military units crumbled quickly. Saddam Hussein, Iraq's dictator, was captured in December 2003 and executed in 2006.

The First Gulf War The attack on Iraq was in fact the second U.S. conflict with that country. In 1990, Hussein had attacked and occupied Kuwait, a small neighboring country. This unprovoked aggression was, at the time, perhaps the most flagrant violation of international law since World War II. U.S. President George H. W. Bush (George W. Bush's father) organized an international coalition to free Kuwait. The coalition forces did not advance into Iraq to unseat Hussein, however.

Reasons for the Second War The cease-fire that ended the first Gulf War required Iraq to submit to inspections for chemical, biological, and nuclear weapons—**weapons of mass destruction**. In 1998, however, Hussein ceased to cooperate with the inspections. The George W. Bush administration believed that Hussein was developing an atomic bomb and that the Iraqi regime was in some way responsible for the 9/11 terrorist attacks. (Both beliefs later proved to be incorrect.) Bush sought United Nations support for the use of military force, but China, France, and Russia blocked the move. In March 2003, Bush told Hussein to leave Iraq or face war. Hussein was defiant, and war followed.

Rise and Fall of the Insurgency Iraq is divided into three main ethnic or religious groups: Kurds, Arabs of the Sunni branch of Islam, and Arabs of the Shiite branch of Islam. The Kurdish-speaking people live in the north. The Sunni Muslims live mostly in central Iraq and had been the group in power under Hussein's rule. The Shiite Muslims, who live mostly in the south, make up the majority of the population, but they had been persecuted by the Sunnis under Hussein.

After the overthrow of Hussein's government, Sunni rebels soon launched an insurrection against the occupation forces. The insurgents, including the newly organized al Qaeda in Iraq, attacked not only U.S. and Iraqi government forces but also Shiite civilians. Shiite radicals responded with attacks on Sunnis, and Iraq appeared to be drifting toward interethnic civil war. American voters began to turn against the war, and in the 2006 elections they handed Congress to the Democrats.

Instead of withdrawing U.S. troops, however, the Bush administration increased troop levels in 2007. The "surge," as it was called, was surprisingly successful. Many Sunnis, who also had been terrorized by al Qaeda, turned against the insurgency and allied with the Americans.

With the insurgency fatally undermined, the United States planned its withdrawal. President Barack Obama announced that U.S. combat forces would leave Iraq by the end of August 2010, and the rest of the troops would be out by the end of 2011. In fact, U.S. forces departed slightly ahead of schedule.

16-3d Again, Afghanistan

The war in Iraq tended to draw the Bush administration's attention away from Afghanistan, which was never completely at peace even after the Taliban had been ousted from Kabul, the capital. By 2006, the Taliban had

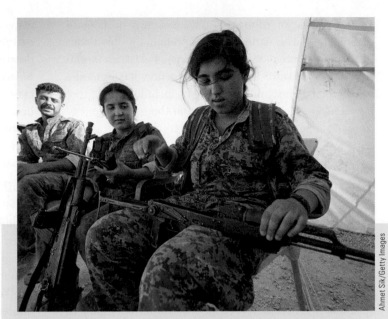

Kurdish fighters at the outskirts of the Syrian town of Kobane in 2015. The town was almost completely destroyed during attacks by ISIS. Kurdish forces were eventually able to drive off the attackers. *What vital interests does the United States have in the Middle East, if any?*

regrouped and were waging a war of insurgency against the new government. The United States and its NATO allies were now the new government's principal military defenders.

The Afghan-Pakistani Border A problem for the coalition forces was that the Taliban were able to take shelter on the far side of the Afghan-Pakistani border, in Pakistan's Federally Administered Tribal Areas. These districts are largely free from central government control.

In 2009, Taliban forces began to take complete control of districts in the Tribal Areas and adjacent districts in the Northwest Frontier Province. Facing a direct challenge to Pakistan's sovereignty, the Pakistani military began to engage the Taliban forces in what soon became a major struggle.

U.S. Attacks in Pakistan Under the George W. Bush administration, the CIA began operating remote-controlled aircraft (drones) known as Predators over Pakistan. Predators are equipped with small missiles, which were used to kill a number of Taliban and al Qaeda leaders. President Obama ramped up the Predator program significantly.

One result was increasing tensions with Pakistan, which could not openly support the Predator campaign.

Pakistan's role in Afghanistan, in fact, has been quite complicated. The nation has been nominally allied with the United States. At the same time, Pakistan's intelligence agency, Inter-Services Intelligence, has funded a variety of Islamist militant groups, including units that have engaged in terrorist attacks on the government of Afghanistan and U.S. forces in that country.

The Death of Bin Laden During the winter of 2010–2011, U.S. intelligence agencies learned that al Qaeda leader Osama bin Laden might be hiding in the Pakistani city of Abbottabad. On May 1, 2011, U.S. Navy Seals entered bin Laden's residential compound and killed him.

The reaction in America was one of relief and satisfaction. The reaction in Pakistan was quite different. Many Pakistanis considered the incident a violation of their country's sovereignty. American commentators speculated that bin Laden could not have hidden in Abbottabad without support from elements of the military, as that city is home to the Pakistan Military Academy.

Obama and Afghanistan In 2009, President Obama increased the number of U.S. troops in Afghanistan by 47,000. At the same time, he indicated that he hoped to withdraw some U.S. forces as early as 2011. In fact, only 10,000 U.S. soldiers left Afghanistan that year. Withdrawals picked up speed in 2012, however, and most U.S. troops were out of Afghanistan by the end of 2014.

16–3e The Civil War in Syria and the Growth of ISIS

In September 2014, the air forces of the United States and five Arab states began a campaign of bombing in Iraq and Syria. The campaign was directed at an organization known as ISIS. President Obama had spent much of his administration attempting to reduce and eventually end United States interventions in Middle Eastern nations, but now we were back at war. What happened?

The Legacy of the "Arab Spring" Beginning in December 2010, the Arab world was swept by a wave of protests against autocratic rulers. With the sole exception of Tunisia, the protesters failed to win their democratic objectives. In Egypt, the dictator Hosni Mubarak was ousted, but a democratic regime was overthrown by the nation's military. A civil war in Libya dislodged the dictator Muammar Gaddafi, but Libyans thereafter were unable to establish an effective national government. (The rebels were greatly aided by international air support organized by President Obama.)

Civil War in Syria Protests in Syria developed into a civil war, as rebels attempted to forcibly overthrow the regime of Bashar al-Assad. By 2015, the fighting had killed more than 400,000 Syrians. More than 11 million out of a total population of 23 million had been driven from their homes. Many people around the world called for Western intervention to assist the rebels, but aid was limited. A problem for the United States and its allies was that only a minority of the rebels could be called pro-democratic. Others were Islamists of varying levels of radicalism. The United States and other powers did

British newspapers showing front-page headlines about the masked ISIS militant dubbed "Jihadi John." This British citizen is believed to be responsible for beheading at least five Western hostages. *Why does ISIS engage in such vicious behavior?*

force al-Assad to give up his chemical weapons, however, as discussed later in this chapter.

The Rise of ISIS The most radical faction fighting in Syria was called ISIS, short for the "Islamic State in Iraq and Greater Syria." An alternative transliteration of the Arabic is ISIL, the "Islamic State in Iraq and the Levant." (Both "Greater Syria" and "the Levant" refer to the lands on the eastern shore of the Mediterranean from the Gaza Strip north to Syria proper.) As the name indicates, ISIS was active in both Syria and Iraq. In fact, ISIS is a reorganized version of the group once known as al Qaeda in Iraq. In February 2014, however, al Qaeda expelled ISIS, citing the group's brutality.

ISIS Attacks Iraq. In June 2014, ISIS swept through northern Iraq, almost to Baghdad. The Iraqi army fled, despite outnumbering ISIS forces greatly. ISIS changed its name to simply "the Islamic State" and set up a government in the Iraqi city of Mosul. When its forces threatened to overrun the autonomous Kurdish region in Northern Iraq, President Obama provided air support to the Kurds.

Obama and the Iraqi Government. The advance of ISIS through Iraq was aided by the hostility felt by Sunnis toward the government of Iraq, which had mistreated them. Initially, Obama held off on direct support for the Iraqi government because he did not want America to provide a "Shiite air force" that protected sectarian interests within Iraq. After the Iraqi government was reorganized in an attempt to conciliate the Sunnis, however, the United States agreed to provide it air support. Obama promised the American people that the United States would not provide "boots on the ground"—infantry forces would need to be organized by the Iraqis themselves. Many Republican presidential candidates and members of Congress, however, called for limited U.S. ground forces that could at least help the U.S. Air Force locate its targets. By 2016, ISIS was losing territory in Iraq and Syria. Possibly in response, the group had also initiated a new strategy—terrorist attacks on Western nations such as France and Belgium.

CRITICAL THINKING

▶ *Sometimes, it is possible to negotiate with certain terrorist groups, such as the Irish Republican Army, and "bring them in from the cold." Why might such a strategy be impossible with ISIS?*

16-4 DIPLOMACY IN AN UNSTABLE WORLD

> **LO** Describe issues that the government has handled through diplomacy, including the Israeli-Palestinian conflict, curbing weapons of mass destruction, and the rise of China as a world power.

Given the death and destruction that result from the use of military force, there is much to be said for resolving problems through diplomacy whenever possible. Diplomacy, however, can involve the use of nonviolent coercive measures, such as sanctions that limit a target nation's ability to participate in the world economy. In the past, sanctions have been used to pressure nations ranging from South Africa under the apartheid system through Hussein's Iraq to Cuba.

Diplomacy can also be important in addressing problems with nations that are friendly or even allied to us. Economic and social problems experienced by our European allies, for example, have been a source of concern. We look at Europe's problems in this chapter's *The Rest of the World* feature. We discuss other diplomatic issues in the following section.

16-4a The Israeli-Palestinian Conflict

The long-running conflict between Israel and its Arab neighbors has poisoned the atmosphere in the Middle East for more than half a century. American presidents dating back at least to Richard Nixon (1969–1974) have attempted to persuade the parties to reach a settlement. Barack Obama is only the latest American leader to address the problem.

The Arab-Israeli Wars For many years after Israel was founded in 1948, the neighboring Arab states did not accept its legitimacy as a nation. The result was a series of wars between Israel and neighboring states, including Egypt, Jordan, and Syria, waged in 1948, 1956, 1967, and 1973. Following the 1948 Arab-Israeli War, a large number of Palestinians—Arab residents of the area, known as Palestine until 1948—were forced into exile, adding to Arab grievances.

> **ISIS** The Islamic State in Iraq and Greater Syria; a terrorist organization that by 2014 had taken over substantial portions of Iraq and Syria. Also known as *ISIL* (the Islamic State in Iraq and the Levant) or the Islamic State.

THE REST OF THE WORLD

Europe under Siege

During presidential election years, you'll hear plenty about our nation's problems—growing inequality, increased abuse of opiates, and so on. But how are other nations doing? Consider the twenty-eight nations of the European Union (EU). They have a level of development comparable to that of the United States. And they have some large problems.

The Refugee Crisis

Currently, the biggest issue in Europe is immigration. Of course, immigration is also an issue in the United States. Still, U.S. illegal immigration has at least stopped growing. In 2015, more than a million refugees entered Europe, the largest number headed for Germany. These refugees had fled their home countries because of war, death threats, and religious persecution. Many are from Syria, but others are from Afghanistan, Iraq, and the nations of Africa. The refugees are often Muslim, and assimilation will not be easy. For example, the newcomers often have beliefs about the role of women that are far from the European norm.

Terrorist Attacks

Terrorist attacks are a concern in America, but the problem is worse in Europe. U.S. Muslims are relatively well assimilated. In contrast, the EU has a large population of impoverished and poorly integrated Muslims, including many alienated young men. They are a natural recruiting ground for the jihadi terrorists who recently struck in Brussels and Paris.

The Wages of Austerity

Nineteen members of the EU share a common currency, the euro. They are members of the *eurozone*. Following the world economic crisis of 2008, however, evidence began to accumulate that the design of the eurozone was catastrophically flawed. Members of the zone had never adopted the common institutions that would have been necessary to make it work. Further, a program of *austerity*—enforced by leading nations such as Germany—made it impossible for individual nations to use monetary or fiscal policy to stimulate their economies. This was a serious problem for the zone's weakest members, such as Ireland, Portugal, Spain, and above all Greece. The United States, in contrast, was much more effective at shaking off the effects of the Great Recession. Notably, the Fed adopted an aggressive monetary policy.

Grexit and Brexit

The financial crisis posed a question: Could Greece even remain in the eurozone? After all, if Greece controlled its own currency, it could lower its value, helping debtors and exporters. In the end, however, Greeks decided that abandoning the euro—"Grexit"—was out of the question. Geographically and economically, Britain lies on the other end of the continent from Greece. Britain never joined the eurozone, and a large share of the British public opposed membership in the EU itself. Certainly, immigration, terrorism, and financial crises made the EU less attractive. In 2016, Britain held a referendum on whether to leave Europe. The vote was close, but departure—"Brexit"—won. The impact of this vote on Britain and Europe were incalculable.

Critical Analysis

The twenty-eight EU countries have a variety of cultures and languages. How hard would it be for the United States to remain a union if it had more than twenty official languages?

Palestine Liberation Organization (PLO)
An organization formed in 1964 to represent the Palestinian people. The PLO has a long history of terrorism but for some years has functioned primarily as a political party.

The failure of the Arab states in the 1967 war led to additional Palestinian refugees and the rise of the **Palestine Liberation Organization (PLO)**, a nonstate body committed to armed struggle against Israel. In the late 1960s and early 1970s, Palestinian groups launched a wave of terrorist attacks against Israeli targets around the world.

Following the 1973 Yom Kippur War, Egyptian president Anwar el-Sadat launched a major peace initiative. He traveled to Israel in 1977 and addressed the Israeli parliament, a major turning point. U.S. president Jimmy Carter (1977–1981) then sponsored intensive negotiations.

Egypt and Israel signed a peace treaty in 1979 that marked the end to an era of major wars between Israel and other states. Lower-level conflicts continued, however. On several occasions, Israel launched attacks against nonstate militias in Lebanon in response to incursions across the Israeli-Lebanon border. Israel and Jordan eventually signed a peace treaty in 1994, but no peace treaty between Israel and Syria has yet been negotiated, and the conflict between Israel and the Palestinians continues.

Israel and the Palestinians Resolving the Israeli-Palestinian dispute has always presented more difficulties than achieving peace between Israel and neighbors such as Egypt. One problem is that the hostilities between the two parties run deeper.

Israeli and Palestinian Grievances. On the Palestinian side, many families lost their homes after the 1948 war. Then, after the 1967 war, the West Bank of the Jordan River and the Gaza Strip fell under Israeli control, and the Palestinians living in these areas became an occupied people.

On the Israeli side, the sheer viciousness of the Palestinian terrorist attacks—which frequently resulted in the deaths of civilians, including children—made negotiations with those responsible hard to imagine. A further complication was the Israeli settlements on the West Bank and the Gaza Strip, which the Palestinians considered their own. Israeli settlers living on the West Bank had an obvious interest in opposing any peace deal that required them to move.

International Principles. Despite the difficulties, the international community, including the United States, was in agreement on several principles for settling the conflict. Lands seized by Israel in the 1967 war should be restored to the Palestinians, who could organize their own independent nation-state there. In turn, the Palestinians would have to recognize Israel's right to exist and take concrete steps to guarantee Israel's security.

The international consensus, however did not address some important issues. These include what compensation, if any, should go to Palestinians who lost homes in what is now Israel. In fact, the Palestinian leadership has never abandoned its demand that the descendants of Palestinians forced out of Israel be allowed to return. Still, it is generally recognized that this demand must be given up as part of a final deal. A second issue is whether Israel could adjust its borders to incorporate some of the Israeli settlement areas, plus part or all of eastern Jerusalem, which had been under Arab control before 1967.

Negotiations In 1993 in Oslo, Norway, Israel and the PLO met officially for the first time. The resulting **Oslo Accords** were signed in Washington under the watchful eye of President Bill Clinton. A major result was the establishment of a Palestinian Authority, under Israeli control, on the West Bank and the Gaza Strip.

> **Oslo Accords** The first agreement signed between Israel and the PLO; led to the establishment of the Palestinian Authority in the occupied territories.

Palestinian and Jewish antiwar activists hug during a peace rally. The gathering was organized following the death of a Palestinian child in an arson attack. *What issues stand in the way of peace between the Israelis and the Palestinians?*

Negotiations Collapse. In 2000, talks between Israel and the Palestinian Authority collapsed in acrimony. After the failure of these talks, an uprising by Palestinian militants led to Israeli military incursions into the West Bank and the temporary collapse of the Palestinian Authority. In 2005, Israeli prime minister Ariel Sharon, concluding that he had no credible peace partner, carried out a plan to unilaterally withdraw from the Gaza Strip and to build an enormous security fence between Israel and the West Bank. The fence came under strong international criticism because it incorporated parts of the West Bank into Israel.

North Koreans view a television screen showing a North Korean long-range rocket launch in February 2016. *Why do you think that North Korea wants nuclear weapons?*

A Divided Palestine. Gaza was taken over in 2007 by Hamas, a radical Islamist party that refuses to recognize Israel. After the imposition of an Israeli blockade, Hamas launched missile attacks on Israel, which in turn briefly occupied the strip in December 2008. The West Bank remained under the control of the PLO-led Palestinian Authority, and so the Palestinians, now politically divided, were in an even worse bargaining position than before.

Attempts by the United States to restart talks between the Israelis and Palestinians collapsed in 2014. In that year, fighting between Israel and Hamas broke out again, resulting in thousands of deaths, most of them Palestinian. The Gaza Strip experienced massive destruction to housing and infrastructure. By 2015, the United States had given up, at least temporarily, on attempts to restart the peace process.

16-4b Weapons of Mass Destruction

The Cold War may be over, but the threat of nuclear warfare—which formed the backdrop of foreign policy during the Cold War—has by no means disappeared. The existence of nuclear weapons in Russia and in other countries around the world continues to challenge U.S. foreign policymakers.

Concerns about nuclear proliferation mounted in 1998 when India and Pakistan detonated nuclear devices within a few weeks of each other—events that took U.S. intelligence agencies by surprise. Increasingly, American officials have focused on the threat of an attack by a rogue nation or a terrorist group that possesses weapons of mass destruction. Of most concern recently have been attempts by North Korea and Iran to develop nuclear capabilities and the use of chemical weapons by the Assad regime in Syria.

North Korea's Nuclear Program North Korea signed the Treaty on the Non-Proliferation of Nuclear Weapons in 1985 and submitted to weapons inspections by the International Atomic Energy Agency (IAEA) in 1992. Throughout the 1990s, however, there were discrepancies between North Korean declarations and IAEA inspection findings. In 2002, North Korea expelled the IAEA inspectors.

Opening Negotiations. The administration of George W. Bush insisted that any talks with North Korea must also include all of North Korea's neighbors—China, Japan, Russia, and South Korea. In 2003, North Korea finally agreed to such talks.

Since that time, it has proved quite difficult to keep North Korea at the bargaining table—its representatives have stormed out of the talks repeatedly, for the most trivial reasons. China is the one power with substantial economic leverage over North Korea, and typically, Chinese leaders have been the ones to lead the North Koreans back to the table.

Tensions heightened in 2006, when North Korea conducted its first nuclear test. In the spring of 2007, North Korea agreed that it would begin to dismantle its nuclear facilities and would allow inspectors from the United Nations (UN) into the country. In return, the other nations agreed to provide various kinds of aid.

The Collapse of Negotiations. In 2009, North Korea tested a long-range missile under the guise of attempting to launch a satellite. The UN Security Council voted unanimously to condemn the test. North Korea then pulled out of the six-party talks and expelled all nuclear inspectors from the country.

After a third missile test in 2013, China for the first time imposed significant economic sanctions on North Korea. The UN Security Council imposed its own sanctions, which led to an explosion of violent rhetoric from the northern regime.

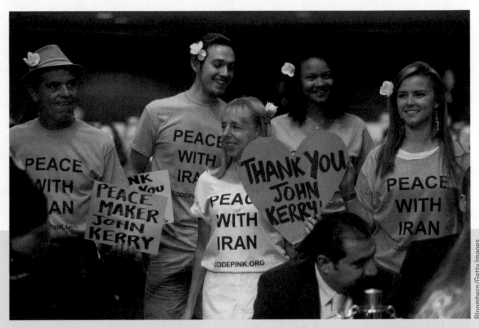

Demonstrators from Code Pink support Secretary of State John Kerry before a Senate hearing on the nuclear agreement with Iran. *What might follow from the fact that the United States and Iran are both enemies of ISIS?*

North Korea's aggressive behavior may have been linked to a succession crisis. In 2011, the dictator Kim Jong-il died and was succeeded by his youngest son, Kim Jong-un. Kim Jong-il himself was the son of North Korea's first Communist dictator. North Korea, therefore, is unique in that it is effectively a Communist monarchy.

Iran: An Emerging Nuclear Threat?

In November 1979, militant students in Tehran, Iran, seized the U.S. embassy and took fifty-two American citizens hostage. The crisis lasted 444 days. Ever since, Iran and the United States have been at odds with each other.

In the years that followed, the rest of the world discovered that Iran was engaged in a covert nuclear program. Investigators for the International Atomic Energy Agency reported that Iran was enriching uranium that could be used in the fabrication of a nuclear bomb.

Iranian leaders have publicly stated that they have no intention of using their nuclear program for destructive purposes. They claim that they are seeking only to develop nuclear energy plants.

Iran as a Security Threat. Like North Korea, Iran has been openly hostile to the United States. In addition, Mahmoud Ahmadinejad, president of Iran from 2005 to 2013, repeatedly called for the complete destruction of Israel. It is no surprise, therefore, that Israel considers Iranian nuclear weapons to be a threat to its existence. Perhaps more surprising is that Iran's Arab neighbors

consider these weapons a threat as well. Leaked U.S. diplomatic cables reveal that Arab leaders have urged the United States to take out the Iranian nuclear program by force.

War or Peace? From 2009 on, the diplomatic team confronting Iran consisted of Britain, China, France, Germany, Russia, and the United States. When negotiations with Iran appeared to be going nowhere, the United States and its allies increasingly turned to coercive measures. These included sanctions, imposed by the United States, the European Union, and the United Nations. The United States was able to persuade or pressure a majority of the world's nations not to buy Iran's oil. The United States was also able to cut Iran off from the international banking system. This step made it extremely difficult for Iran to finance imports and exports. By 2013, the Iranian economy was in serious trouble.

Another coercive measure would be to bomb Iran's nuclear sites. In 2008, Israel began preparations that would allow it to launch such a strike if necessary. After Benjamin Netanyahu became prime minister of Israel in 2009, he called for air strikes with increasing urgency. One type of attack, in fact, was launched immediately. In 2010, a sophisticated U.S. computer "worm" took down about a thousand of the five thousand centrifuges used in Iran's uranium enrichment program. Many were completely destroyed.

Again, Negotiations. In 2013, Iran elected a new president, Hassan Rouhani. In short order, Rouhani initiated a charm offensive aimed at reestablishing diplomatic negotiations. The new leader repudiated the anti-Israel rhetoric of previous Iranian president Ahmadinejad.

At the United Nations, Rouhani called for a diplomatic resolution of the nuclear issue. Shortly thereafter, serious negotiations began between Iran and six other nations: Britain, China, France, Germany, Russia, and the United States. In November 2013, Iran and the multinational team announced a six-month interim deal. Iran would freeze parts of its nuclear program in return for the lifting of some sanctions.

The negotiations that followed were difficult, and deadlines were frequently extended. Finally, in July 2015, Iran and the six world powers came to an agreement. Under the terms of the deal, Iran would be able to hold only about half the uranium needed to make one bomb. Its number of centrifuges would be reduced dramatically. International representatives would have the right to demand inspections of Iranian nuclear facilities. It was estimated that if Iran repudiated the deal in the future, it would be one year away from the ability to make a bomb, as opposed to the current two months. In return for these measures, all sanctions tied to Iran's nuclear program would be lifted. Certain U.S. sanctions not tied to the nuclear program remain in effect, however.

Opposition to the Deal. Given that the agreement was signed by six world powers and the European Union, it clearly had international support. The agreement had its opponents, however. In March 2015, Israeli prime minister Benjamin Netanyahu addressed the U.S. Congress at the invitation of Republican leaders. He ripped into the proposed agreement, calling for additional demands that Iran was sure to reject.

Still, the opponents of the deal had two problems. One was that rejecting the deal would effectively remove all limits on Iran's nuclear program. The second was that "no deal" would lead to the collapse of the sanctions, because nations other than the United States would no longer agree to impose them. The only realistic options for blocking an Iranian bomb would then be military.

Use of Chemical Weapons by Syria Most nations have signed treaties banning the use of chemical weapons—they were, in fact, one of the few instruments of horror that were never used on the battlefield in World War II. Only a handful of nations have refused to sign, including North Korea, Iraq (under Saddam Hussein), and Syria. In August 2013, the government of Syria used the nerve gas sarin against suburbs of Damascus

that were under the control of antiregime rebels. The attack killed more than a thousand civilians. Syrian dictator Bashar al-Assad may have used chemical weapons earlier, but this incident was so conspicuous that it could not be ignored.

President Obama proposed to punish the Assad regime for its use of poison gas by launching air strikes. Obama took the unusual step of asking Congress for its approval of the strikes. It seemed quite possible that Congress would vote down such a resolution. In September, however, the government of Russia announced that Syria was willing to sign the Chemical Weapons Convention, a treaty governing chemical weapons, and place its weapons under international control. This initiative was a diplomatic triumph for Russian president Vladimir Putin. The U.S. Senate postponed the vote on the bombing resolution indefinitely.

By October 2013, to the surprise of many, the Assad regime was cooperating with international inspectors. The chemical weapons were removed from Syria to a U.S. ship equipped with special decontamination systems. In August 2014, President Obama announced that the destruction of the weapons was complete. In 2015, however, Assad's forces apparently used chlorine gas to attack rebels. Chlorine has many industrial uses and is not a controlled substance. Employing it as a weapon, though, violates the Chemical Weapons Convention.

16-4c China—The Next Superpower?

A major challenge to the United States may be the growing importance of China. Following President Richard Nixon's historic visit to China in 1972, American diplomatic and economic relations with the Chinese gradually improved. Diplomacy with China focused on cultivating a more pro-Western disposition in the formerly isolationist nation. Relations with China are important in part because until recently, that nation has enjoyed economic growth averaging almost 10 percent a year for more than thirty years in a row. Such growth has turned China into a great power.

Chinese-American Trade Relations China has one of the fastest-growing economies in the world, along with a population of 1.3 billion. Measured in terms of purchasing power, its gross domestic product (GDP) surpassed that of the United States in 2014. In terms of its own currency, China's GDP is *195 times* what it was in 1978, when China implemented reforms to make the economy more market oriented. Never in the history of the world have so many people been lifted out of poverty so quickly.

Chinese President Xi Jinping. Xi has launched a major crackdown on official corruption in China. *Why might the absence of democracy foster corruption among Chinese officials?*

Chinese Exports. China's rapid growth has been fueled in part by an enormous manufacturing export sector. One result is that Americans can buy Chinese products for much less than U.S.-manufactured goods would cost. Toys, electronics, hardware, clothing, and many other items are cheaper than they otherwise would be. The flip side is that the American workers who used to make such products lost their jobs. Studies have shown that workers who lose employment due to foreign competition have a hard time recovering. It is no surprise, therefore, that in the 2016 presidential race, many candidates criticized imports. Donald Trump in particular demanded huge cuts in foreign trade.

China's Currency Holdings. To a considerable extent, instead of buying U.S. products with the dollars it earned, China instead loaded up on U.S. treasuries (and also on U.S. private-sector debt). By the start of 2015, China owned $3,840 billion in foreign obligations, $2,520 billion of it from the United States, and $1,580 billion in U.S. treasuries. Some economists feared that if China were to dump its holdings, the price of treasuries could fall greatly. The result could be much higher interest rates and a recession. Others argued that the effect of such sales would be limited to driving down the value of the dollar, which would help U.S. exports.

In 2015, China entered a *growth recession*. The economy continued to grow, but at a much reduced rate. Chinese imports of commodities such as crude oil and iron ore fell, driving down their prices. One response by the Chinese government was to sell off $510 billion of its foreign currency holdings in 2015, including $292 billion in treasuries. What effects did the sell-off have on the United States? Lower commodity prices did hurt some U.S. producers, but interest rates remained stable. Further, by January 2016, the trade-weighted value of the U.S. dollar hit its highest point in fourteen years. Clearly, any effects of the Chinese sell-off were completely swamped by other factors.

The Issue of Taiwan Although China has not demonstrated any ambition to acquire non-Chinese territory, it has a rather expansive definition of what Chinese territory is. China considers Taiwan, a former Chinese province, to be a legal part of China. In practice, however, since 1949 the island has functioned as an independent nation. The United States has historically supported a free and separate Taiwan and has stated that any reunion of China and Taiwan must come about by peaceful means.

Recent Chinese Nationalism In recent years, China has exhibited nationalist tendencies that have alarmed some of its neighbors. China is engaged in a territorial dispute with Japan over uninhabited islands in the East China Sea. China has also claimed almost all of the uninhabited islands located in the South China Sea, even ones that are a considerable distance from the Chinese mainland. These claims have resulted in military confrontations with the Philippines and Vietnam.

In 2012, President Obama announced a "pivot" to East Asia. The pivot involves shifting naval resources into the region and negotiating enhanced security relationships with area nations. China's response was to accuse the United States of attempting to "contain" China.

Within China itself, nationalism has often taken the form of discrimination against minority nationalities. These include the people of Tibet and also the Uighurs, a Muslim people in the western region of Xinjiang. Both Tibet and Xinjiang have experienced very large inflows of the majority Chinese group, known as *Han Chinese*. Many Tibetans and Uighurs believe that they are becoming oppressed minorities within their own countries. As a result, disturbances have been common.

CRITICAL THINKING

▶ *If we have strong trade relations with a country, does that make it less likely that we would ever go to war with that country? Why or why not?*

AMERICA AT ODDS | Foreign Policy

In 1947, Republican senator Arthur Vandenberg of Michigan announced, "Politics stops at the water's edge." By this, Vandenberg, formerly a fierce isolationist, meant that Republicans and Democrats should cooperate in dealing with such foreign policy issues as the Cold War with the Soviet Union.

Bipartisanship was never complete even in Vandenberg's day, however, and it is much less common today. True, the two major parties are more likely to cooperate over a foreign policy issue than over domestic policy. Nevertheless, Americans are at odds over many foreign policy issues, as reflected in Congress. The following are a few of these issues:

- *In foreign policy, is it best to ally with other nations whenever possible—or should America carefully guard its ability to act alone?*

- *Should the president take complete charge of the foreign policy process, including the use of armed force—or should the president collaborate closely with Congress?*

- *Should the war on terrorism be the central focus of U.S. foreign policy—or should we devote equal energy to managing our relations with rising powers such as China?*

- *Should the United States take a firm line with Russia over Ukraine, or is it more important to head off a new Cold War?*

- *In attempting to promote peace between Israelis and Palestinians, should the United States put most of its pressure on the Palestinians—or should it also pressure the Israelis to, for example, suspend the construction of new Jewish settlements in the West Bank?*

- *Is the recent nuclear arms agreement between Iran and six world powers a blessing—or a catastrophe?*

STUDY TOOLS 16

READY TO STUDY? IN THE BOOK, YOU CAN:

☐ Review what you've read with the following chapter quiz.

☐ Check your answers in Appendix D at the back of the book.

☐ Rip out the Chapter Review Card, which includes key terms and chapter summaries.

ONLINE AT WWW.CENGAGEBRAIN.COM, YOU CAN:

☐ Learn about Afghanistan after Osama bin Laden in a short video.

☐ Explore various online resources in the United Nations and U.S. Department of Defense websites in the Internet Resources tool.

☐ Interact with figures from the text, and watch quick animation clips.

☐ Prepare for tests with quizzes.

☐ Review the key terms with Flash Cards.

FILL-IN

Learning Outcome 16–1

1. The executive departments and other government agencies that are most directly involved in foreign policy include the _____.

Learning Outcome 16–2

2. The nation's founders and the early presidents believed that a policy of _____ was the best way to protect American interests.

3. The _____ was a war of words, warnings, and ideologies between the Soviet Union and the United States that lasted from the late 1940s through the late 1980s.

Learning Outcome 16–3

4. In 2001, supported by a coalition of allies, the U.S. military attacked al Qaeda camps in _____ and the ruling Taliban regime that harbored those terrorists.

5. In 2011, U.S. Navy Seals killed Osama bin Laden in Abbottabad, a city in _____.

Learning Outcome 16–4

6. The 1993 Oslo Accords led to the establishment of the _____ in the occupied territories.

7. With respect to the prospects of nuclear proliferation, American officials are most concerned about recent developments in the countries of _____.

8. The danger exists of a possible future crisis in U.S.-Chinese relations over the status of _____.

MULTIPLE CHOICE

Learning Outcome 16–1

9. The power to declare war belongs to
   a. the president.
   b. Congress.
   c. the Joint Chiefs of Staff.

Learning Outcome 16–2

10. Direct involvement by one country in another country's affairs best describes
    a. political realism.
    b. collective security.
    c. interventionism.

11. Actions taken under the Truman Doctrine and the Marshall Plan marked the beginning of a policy of
    a. containment.
    b. deterrence.
    c. mutually assured destruction.

Learning Outcome 16–3

12. The phrase *weapons of mass destruction* refers to
    a. landmines and cluster munitions.
    b. improvised explosive devices (IEDs).
    c. chemical, biological, and nuclear weapons.

Learning Outcome 16–4

13. For many years after Israel was founded in 1948,
    a. the neighboring Arab states did not accept its legitimacy as a nation.
    b. the only peace treaty that it was able to negotiate was one with Syria.
    c. it lived in peace with its neighbors in the Middle East.

14. During 2010, a sophisticated computer "worm" attacked centrifuges used in _____ uranium enrichment program.
    a. North Korea's
    b. Iran's
    c. Israel's

GOVT
ONLINE

PREPARE FOR TESTS ON
THE STUDYBOARD!

○ CORRECT
○ INCORRECT
○ INCORRECT
○ INCORRECT

**Personalize Quizzes
from Your StudyBits**

**Take Practice
Quizzes by Chapter**

CHAPTER QUIZZES

► Chapter 1
Chapter 2
Chapter 3
Chapter 4

**4LTR
PRESS**

THE DECLARATION OF INDEPENDENCE

IN CONGRESS, JULY 4, 1776

A Declaration by the Representatives of the United States of America, in General Congress assembled. When in the Course of human Events, it becomes necessary for one People to dissolve the Political Bands which have connected them with another, and to assume among the Powers of the Earth, the separate and equal Station to which the Laws of Nature and of Nature's God entitle them, a decent Respect to the Opinions of Mankind requires that they should declare the causes which impel them to the Separation.

We hold these Truths to be self-evident, that all Men are created equal, that they are endowed by their Creator with certain unalienable Rights, that among these are Life, Liberty, and the Pursuit of Happiness—That to secure these Rights, Governments are instituted among Men, deriving their just Powers from the Consent of the Governed, that whenever any Form of Government becomes destructive of these Ends, it is the Right of the People to alter or to abolish it, and to institute new Government, laying its Foundation on such Principles, and organizing its Powers in such Forms, as to them shall seem most likely to effect their Safety and Happiness. Prudence, indeed, will dictate that Governments long established should not be changed for light and transient Causes; and accordingly all Experience hath shewn, that Mankind are more disposed to suffer, while Evils are sufferable, than to right themselves by abolishing the Forms to which they are accustomed. But when a long Train of Abuses and Usurpations, pursuing invariably the same Object, evinces a Design to reduce them under absolute Despotism, it is their Right, it is their Duty, to throw off such Government, and to provide new Guards for their future Security. Such has been the patient Sufferance of these Colonies; and such is now the Necessity which constrains them to alter their former Systems of Government. The History of the present King of Great-Britain is a History of repeated Injuries and Usurpations, all having in direct Object the Establishment of an absolute Tyranny over these States. To prove this, let Facts be submitted to a candid World.

He has refused his Assent to Laws, the most wholesome and necessary for the public Good.

He has forbidden his Governors to pass Laws of immediate and pressing Importance, unless suspended in their Operation till his Assent should be obtained; and when so suspended, he has utterly neglected to attend to them.

He has refused to pass other Laws for the Accommodation of large Districts of People, unless those People would relinquish the Right of Representation in the Legislature, a Right inestimable to them, and formidable to Tyrants only.

He has called together Legislative Bodies at Places unusual, uncomfortable, and distant from the Depository of their Public Records, for the sole Purpose of fatiguing them into Compliance with his Measures.

He has dissolved Representative Houses repeatedly, for opposing with manly Firmness his Invasions on the Rights of the People.

He has refused for a long Time, after such Dissolutions, to cause others to be elected; whereby the Legislative Powers, incapable of Annihilation, have returned to the People at large for their exercise; the State remaining in the mean time exposed to all the Dangers of Invasion from without, and Convulsions within.

He has endeavoured to prevent the Population of these States; for that Purpose obstructing the Laws for Naturalization of Foreigners; refusing to pass others to encourage their Migrations hither, and raising the Conditions of new Appropriations of Lands.

He has obstructed the Administration of Justice, by refusing his Assent to Laws for establishing Judiciary Powers.

He has made Judges dependent on his Will alone, for the Tenure of their offices, and the Amount and payment of their Salaries.

He has erected a Multitude of new Offices, and sent hither Swarms of Officers to harrass our People, and eat out their Substance.

He has kept among us, in Times of Peace, Standing Armies, without the consent of our Legislatures.

He has affected to render the Military independent of, and superior to the Civil Power.

He has combined with others to subject us to a Jurisdiction foreign to our Constitution, and unacknowledged by our Laws; giving his Assent to their Acts of pretended Legislation:

For quartering large Bodies of Armed Troops among us:

For protecting them, by a mock Trial, from Punishment for any Murders which they should commit on the Inhabitants of these States:

For cutting off our Trade with all Parts of the World:

For imposing Taxes on us without our Consent:

For depriving us, in many cases, of the Benefits of Trial by Jury:

For transporting us beyond Seas to be tried for pretended Offences:

For abolishing the free System of English Laws in a neighbouring Province, establishing therein an arbitrary Government, and enlarging its Boundaries, so as to render it at once an Example and fit Instrument for introducing the same absolute Rule into these Colonies:

For taking away our Charters, abolishing our most valuable Laws, and altering fundamentally the Forms of our Governments:

For suspending our own Legislatures, and declaring themselves invested with Power to legislate for us in all Cases whatsoever.

He has abdicated Government here, by declaring us out of his Protection and waging War against us.

He has plundered our Seas, ravaged our Coasts, burnt our towns, and destroyed the Lives of our People.

He is, at this Time, transporting large Armies of foreign Mercenaries to compleat the works of Death, Desolation, and Tyranny, already begun with circumstances of Cruelty and Perfidy, scarcely paralleled in the most barbarous Ages, and totally unworthy the Head of a civilized Nation.

He has constrained our fellow Citizens taken Captive on the high Seas to bear Arms against their Country, to become the Executioners of their Friends and Brethren, or to fall themselves by their Hands.

He has excited domestic Insurrections amongst us, and has endeavoured to bring on the Inhabitants of our Frontiers, the merciless Indian Savages, whose known Rule of Warfare, is an undistinguished Destruction, of all Ages, Sexes and Conditions.

In every state of these Oppressions we have Petitioned for Redress in the most humble Terms: Our repeated Petitions have been answered only by repeated Injury. A Prince, whose Character is thus marked by every act which may define a Tyrant, is unfit to be the Ruler of a free People.

Nor have we been wanting in Attentions to our British Brethren. We have warned them from Time to Time of Attempts by their Legislature to extend an unwarrantable Jurisdiction over us. We have reminded them of the Circumstances of our Emigration and Settlement here. We have appealed to their native Justice and Magnanimity, and we have conjured them by the Ties of our common Kindred to disavow these Usurpations, which, would inevitably interrupt our Connections and Correspondence. They too have been deaf to the Voice of Justice and of Consanguinity. We must, therefore, acquiesce in the Necessity, which denounces our Separation, and hold them, as we hold the rest of Mankind, Enemies in War, in Peace, Friends.

We, therefore, the Representatives of the UNITED STATES OF AMERICA, in General Congress Assembled, appealing to the Supreme Judge of the World for the Rectitude of our Intentions, do, in the Name, and by the Authority of the good People of these Colonies, solemnly Publish and Declare, That these United Colonies are, and of Right ought to be, Free and Independent States; that they are absolved from all Allegiance to the British Crown, and that all political Connection between them and the State of Great-Britain, is and ought to be totally dissolved; and that as Free and Independent States, they have full Power to levy War, conclude Peace, contract Alliances, establish Commerce, and to do all other Acts and Things which Independent States may of right do. And for the support of this declaration, with a firm Reliance on the Protection of divine Providence, we mutually pledge to each other our lives, our Fortunes, and our sacred Honor.

THE CONSTITUTION OF THE UNITED STATES

PREAMBLE

We the People of the United States, in Order to form a more perfect Union, establish Justice, insure domestic Tranquility, provide for the common defence, promote the general Welfare, and secure the Blessings of Liberty to ourselves and our Posterity, do ordain and establish this Constitution for the United States of America.

ARTICLE I

Section 1. All legislative Powers herein granted shall be vested in a Congress of the United States, which shall consist of a Senate and House of Representatives.

Section 2. The House of Representatives shall be composed of Members chosen every second Year by the People of the several States, and the Electors in each State shall have the Qualifications requisite for Electors of the most numerous Branch of the State Legislature.

No Person shall be a Representative who shall not have attained to the Age of twenty five Years, and been seven Years a Citizen of the United States, and who shall not, when elected, be an Inhabitant of that State in which he shall be chosen.

Representatives and direct Taxes shall be apportioned among the several States which may be included within this Union, according to their respective Numbers, which shall be determined by adding to the whole Number of free Persons, including those bound to Service for a Term of Years, and excluding Indians not taxed, three fifths of all other Persons. The actual Enumeration shall be made within three Years after the first Meeting of the Congress of the United States, and within every subsequent Term of ten Years, in such Manner as they shall by Law direct. The Number of Representatives shall not exceed one for every thirty Thousand, but each State shall have at Least one Representative; and until such enumeration shall be made, the State of New Hampshire shall be entitled to chuse three, Massachusetts eight, Rhode Island and Providence Plantations one, Connecticut five, New York six, New Jersey four, Pennsylvania eight, Delaware one, Maryland six, Virginia ten, North Carolina five, South Carolina five, and Georgia three.

When vacancies happen in the Representation from any State, the Executive Authority thereof shall issue Writs of Election to fill such Vacancies.

The House of Representatives shall chuse their Speaker and other Officers; and shall have the sole Power of Impeachment.

Section 3. The Senate of the United States shall be composed of two Senators from each State, chosen by the Legislature thereof, for six Years; and each Senator shall have one Vote.

Immediately after they shall be assembled in Consequence of the first Election, they shall be divided as equally as may be into three Classes. The Seats of the Senators of the first Class shall be vacated at the Expiration of the second Year, of the second Class at the Expiration of the fourth Year, and of the third Class at the Expiration of the sixth Year, so that one third may be chosen every second Year; and if Vacancies happen by Resignation, or otherwise, during the Recess of the Legislature of any State, the Executive thereof may make temporary Appointments until the next Meeting of the Legislature, which shall then fill such Vacancies.

No Person shall be a Senator who shall not have attained to the Age of thirty Years, and been nine Years a Citizen of the United States, and who shall not, when elected, be an Inhabitant of that State for which he shall be chosen.

The Vice President of the United States shall be President of the Senate, but shall have no Vote, unless they be equally divided.

The Senate shall chuse their other Officers, and also a President pro tempore, in the Absence of the Vice President, or when he shall exercise the Office of President of the United States.

The Senate shall have the sole Power to try all Impeachments. When sitting for that Purpose, they shall be on Oath or Affirmation. When the President of the United States is tried, the Chief Justice shall preside: And no Person shall be convicted without the Concurrence of two thirds of the Members present.

Judgment in Cases of Impeachment shall not extend further than to removal from Office, and disqualification to hold and enjoy any Office of honor, Trust, or Profit under the United States: but the Party convicted shall nevertheless be liable and subject to Indictment, Trial, Judgment, and Punishment, according to Law.

Section 4. The Times, Places and Manner of holding Elections for Senators and Representatives, shall be prescribed in each State by the Legislature thereof; but the Congress may at any time by Law make or alter such Regulations, except as to the Places of chusing Senators.

The Congress shall assemble at least once in every Year, and such Meeting shall be on the first Monday in December, unless they shall by Law appoint a different Day.

Section 5. Each House shall be the Judge of the Elections, Returns, and Qualifications of its own Members, and a Majority of each shall constitute a Quorum to do Business; but a smaller Number may adjourn from day to day, and may be authorized to compel the Attendance of absent Members, in such Manner, and under such Penalties as each House may provide.

Each House may determine the Rules of its Proceedings, punish its Members for disorderly Behavior, and, with the Concurrence of two thirds, expel a Member.

Each House shall keep a Journal of its Proceedings, and from time to time publish the same, excepting such Parts as may in their Judgment require Secrecy; and the Yeas and Nays of the Members of either House on any question shall, at the Desire of one fifth of those Present, be entered on the Journal.

Neither House, during the Session of Congress, shall, without the Consent of the other, adjourn for more than three days, nor to any other Place than that in which the two Houses shall be sitting.

Section 6. The Senators and Representatives shall receive a Compensation for their Services, to be ascertained by Law, and paid out of the Treasury of the United States. They shall in all Cases, except Treason, Felony and Breach of the Peace, be privileged from Arrest during their Attendance at the Session of their respective Houses, and in going to and returning from the same; and for any Speech or Debate in either House, they shall not be questioned in any other Place.

No Senator or Representative shall, during the Time for which he was elected, be appointed to any civil Office under the Authority of the United States, which shall have been created, or the Emoluments whereof shall have been increased during such time; and no Person holding any Office under the United States, shall be a Member of either House during his Continuance in Office.

Section 7. All Bills for raising Revenue shall originate in the House of Representatives; but the Senate may propose or concur with Amendments as on other Bills.

Every Bill which shall have passed the House of Representatives and the Senate, shall, before it become a Law, be presented to the President of the United States; If he approve he shall sign it, but if not he shall return it, with his Objections to the House in which it shall have originated, who shall enter the Objections at large on their Journal, and proceed to reconsider it. If after such Reconsideration two thirds of that House shall agree to pass the Bill, it shall be sent together with the Objections, to the other House, by which it shall likewise be reconsidered, and if approved by two thirds of that House, it shall become a Law. But in all such Cases the Votes of both Houses shall be determined by Yeas and Nays, and the Names of the Persons voting for and against the Bill shall be entered on the Journal of each House respectively. If any Bill shall not be returned by the President within ten Days (Sundays excepted) after it shall have been presented to him, the Same shall be a Law, in like Manner as if he had signed it,

unless the Congress by their Adjournment prevent its Return in which Case it shall not be a Law.

Every Order, Resolution, or Vote, to which the Concurrence of the Senate and House of Representatives may be necessary (except on a question of Adjournment) shall be presented to the President of the United States; and before the Same shall take Effect, shall be approved by him, or being disapproved by him, shall be repassed by two thirds of the Senate and House of Representatives, according to the Rules and Limitations prescribed in the Case of a Bill.

Section 8. The Congress shall have Power To lay and collect Taxes, Duties, Imposts and Excises, to pay the Debts and provide for the common Defence and general Welfare of the United States; but all Duties, Imposts and Excises shall be uniform throughout the United States;

To borrow Money on the credit of the United States;

To regulate Commerce with foreign Nations, and among the several States, and with the Indian Tribes;

To establish an uniform Rule of Naturalization, and uniform Laws on the subject of Bankruptcies throughout the United States;

To coin Money, regulate the Value thereof, and of foreign Coin, and fix the Standard of Weights and Measures;

To provide for the Punishment of counterfeiting the Securities and current Coin of the United States;

To establish Post Offices and post Roads;

To promote the Progress of Science and useful Arts, by securing for limited Times to Authors and Inventors the exclusive Right to their respective Writings and Discoveries;

To constitute Tribunals inferior to the supreme Court;

To define and punish Piracies and Felonies committed on the high Seas, and Offenses against the Law of Nations;

To declare War, grant Letters of Marque and Reprisal, and make Rules concerning Captures on Land and Water;

To raise and support Armies, but no Appropriation of Money to that Use shall be for a longer Term than two Years;

To provide and maintain a Navy;

To make Rules for the Government and Regulation of the land and naval Forces;

To provide for calling forth the Militia to execute the Laws of the Union, suppress Insurrections and repel Invasions;

To provide for organizing, arming, and disciplining, the Militia, and for governing such Part of them as may be employed in the Service of the United States, reserving to the States respectively, the Appointment of the Officers, and the Authority of training the Militia according to the discipline prescribed by Congress;

To exercise exclusive Legislation in all Cases whatsoever, over such District (not exceeding ten Miles square) as may, by Cession of particular States, and the Acceptance of Congress, become the Seat of the Government of the United States, and to exercise like Authority over all Places purchased by the Consent of the Legislature of the State in which the Same shall be, for the Erection of Forts, Magazines, Arsenals, dock-Yards, and other needful Buildings;—And

To make all Laws which shall be necessary and proper for carrying into Execution the foregoing Powers, and all other Powers vested by this Constitution in the Government of the United States, or in any Department or Officer thereof.

Section 9.   The Migration or Importation of such Persons as any of the States now existing shall think proper to admit, shall not be prohibited by the Congress prior to the Year one thousand eight hundred and eight, but a Tax or duty may be imposed on such Importation, not exceeding ten dollars for each Person.

The privilege of the Writ of Habeas Corpus shall not be suspended, unless when in Cases of Rebellion or Invasion the public Safety may require it.

No Bill of Attainder or ex post facto Law shall be passed.

No Capitation, or other direct, Tax shall be laid, unless in Proportion to the Census or Enumeration herein before directed to be taken.

No Tax or Duty shall be laid on Articles exported from any State.

No Preference shall be given by any Regulation of Commerce or Revenue to the Ports of one State over those of another: nor shall Vessels bound to, or from, one State be obliged to enter, clear, or pay Duties in another.

No Money shall be drawn from the Treasury, but in Consequence of Appropriations made by Law; and a regular Statement and Account of the Receipts and Expenditures of all public Money shall be published from time to time.

No Title of Nobility shall be granted by the United States: And no Person holding any Office of Profit or Trust under them, shall, without the Consent of the Congress, accept of any present, Emolument, Office, or Title, of any kind whatever, from any King, Prince, or foreign State.

Section 10.   No State shall enter into any Treaty, Alliance, or Confederation; grant Letters of Marque and Reprisal; coin Money; emit Bills of Credit; make any Thing but gold and silver Coin a Tender in Payment of Debts; pass any Bill of Attainder, ex post facto Law, or Law impairing the Obligation of Contracts, or grant any Title of Nobility.

No State shall, without the Consent of the Congress, lay any Imposts or Duties on Imports or Exports, except what may be absolutely necessary for executing its inspection Laws: and the net Produce of all Duties and Imposts, laid by any State on Imports or Exports, shall be for the Use of the Treasury of the United States; and all such Laws shall be subject to the Revision and Controul of the Congress.

No State shall, without the Consent of Congress, lay any Duty of Tonnage, keep Troops, or Ships of War in time of Peace, enter into any Agreement or Compact with another State, or with a foreign Power, or engage in War, unless actually invaded, or in such imminent Danger as will not admit of delay.

ARTICLE II

Section 1.   The executive Power shall be vested in a President of the United States of America. He shall hold his Office during the Term of four Years, and, together with the Vice President, chosen for the same Term, be elected, as follows:

Each State shall appoint, in such Manner as the Legislature thereof may direct, a Number of Electors, equal to the whole Number of Senators and Representatives to which the State may be entitled in the Congress; but no Senator or Representative, or Person holding an Office of Trust or Profit under the United States, shall be appointed an Elector.

The Electors shall meet in their respective States, and vote by Ballot for two Persons, of whom one at least shall not be an Inhabitant of the same State with themselves. And they shall make a List of all the Persons voted for, and of the Number of Votes for each; which List they shall sign and certify, and transmit sealed to the Seat of the Government of the United States, directed to the President of the Senate. The President of the Senate shall, in the Presence of the Senate and House of Representatives, open all the Certificates, and the Votes shall then be counted. The Person having the greatest Number of Votes shall be the President, if such Number be a Majority of the whole Number of Electors appointed; and if there be more than one who have such Majority, and have an equal Number of Votes, then the House of Representatives shall immediately chuse by Ballot one of them for President; and if no Person have a Majority, then from the five highest on the List the said House shall in like Manner chuse the President. But in chusing the President, the Votes shall be taken by States, the Representation from each State having one Vote; A quorum for this Purpose shall consist of a Member or Members from two thirds of the States, and a Majority of all the States shall be necessary to a Choice. In every Case, after the Choice of the President, the Person having the greater Number of Votes of the Electors shall be the Vice President. But if there should remain two or more who have equal Votes, the Senate shall chuse from them by Ballot the Vice President.

The Congress may determine the Time of chusing the Electors, and the Day on which they shall give their Votes; which Day shall be the same throughout the United States.

No person except a natural born Citizen, or a Citizen of the United States, at the time of the Adoption of this Constitution, shall be eligible to the Office of President; neither shall any Person be eligible to that Office who shall not have attained to the Age of thirty five Years, and been fourteen Years a Resident within the United States.

In Case of the Removal of the President from Office, or of his Death, Resignation or Inability to discharge the Powers and Duties of the said Office, the same shall devolve on the Vice President, and the Congress may by Law provide for the Case of Removal, Death, Resignation or Inability, both of the President and Vice President, declaring what Officer shall then act as President, and such Officer shall act accordingly, until the Disability be removed, or a President shall be elected.

The President shall, at stated Times, receive for his Services, a Compensation, which shall neither be increased nor diminished during the Period for which he shall have been elected, and he shall not receive within that Period any other Emolument from the United States, or any of them.

Before he enter on the Execution of his Office, he shall take the following Oath or Affirmation: "I do solemnly swear (or affirm) that I will faithfully execute the Office of President of the United States, and will to the best of my Ability, preserve, protect and defend the Constitution of the United States."

Section 2.   The President shall be Commander in Chief of the Army and Navy of the United States, and of the Militia of the several States, when called into the actual Service of the United States; he may require the Opinion, in writing, of the principal Officer in each of the executive Departments, upon any Subject relating to the Duties of their respective Offices, and he shall have Power to grant Reprieves and Pardons for Offenses against the United States, except in Cases of Impeachment.

He shall have Power, by and with the Advice and Consent of the Senate to make Treaties, provided two thirds of the Senators present concur; and he shall nominate, and by and with the Advice and Consent of the Senate, shall appoint Ambassadors, other public Ministers and Consuls, Judges of the supreme Court, and all other Officers of the United States, whose Appointments are not herein otherwise provided for, and which shall be established by Law; but the Congress may by Law vest the Appointment of such inferior Officers, as they think proper, in the President alone, in the Courts of Law, or in the Heads of Departments.

The President shall have Power to fill up all Vacancies that may happen during the Recess of the Senate, by granting Commissions which shall expire at the End of their next Session.

Section 3.   He shall from time to time give to the Congress Information of the State of the Union, and recommend to their Consideration such Measures as he shall judge necessary and expedient; he may, on extraordinary Occasions, convene both Houses, or either of them, and in Case of Disagreement between them, with Respect to the Time of Adjournment, he may adjourn them to such Time as he shall think proper; he shall receive Ambassadors and other public Ministers; he shall take Care that the Laws be faithfully executed, and shall Commission all the Officers of the United States.

Section 4.   The President, Vice President and all civil Officers of the United States, shall be removed from Office on Impeachment for, and Conviction of, Treason, Bribery, or other high Crimes and Misdemeanors.

ARTICLE III

Section 1.   The judicial Power of the United States, shall be vested in one supreme Court, and in such inferior Courts as the Congress may from time to time ordain and establish. The Judges, both of the supreme and inferior Courts, shall hold their Offices during good Behaviour, and shall, at stated Times, receive for their Services a Compensation, which shall not be diminished during their Continuance in Office.

Section 2.   The judicial Power shall extend to all Cases, in Law and Equity, arising under this Constitution, the Laws of the United States, and Treaties made, or which shall be made, under their Authority;—to all Cases affecting Ambassadors, other public Ministers and Consuls;—to all Cases of admiralty and maritime Jurisdiction;—to Controversies to which the United States shall be a Party;—to Controversies between two or more States;—between a State and Citizens of another State;—between Citizens of different States;—between Citizens of the same State claiming Lands under Grants of different States, and between a State, or the Citizens thereof, and foreign States, Citizens or Subjects.

In all Cases affecting Ambassadors, other public Ministers and Consuls, and those in which a State shall be a Party, the supreme Court shall have original Jurisdiction. In all the other Cases before mentioned, the supreme Court shall have appellate Jurisdiction, both as to Law and Fact, with such Exceptions, and under such Regulations as the Congress shall make.

The Trial of all Crimes, except in Cases of Impeachment, shall be by Jury; and such Trial shall be held in the State where the said Crimes shall have been committed; but when not committed within any State, the Trial shall be at such Place or Places as the Congress may by Law have directed.

Section 3.   Treason against the United States, shall consist only in levying War against them, or, in adhering to their Enemies, giving them Aid and Comfort. No Person shall be convicted of Treason unless on the Testimony of two Witnesses to the same overt Act, or on Confession in open Court.

The Congress shall have Power to declare the Punishment of Treason, but no Attainder of Treason shall work Corruption of Blood, or Forfeiture except during the Life of the Person attainted.

ARTICLE IV

Section 1.   Full Faith and Credit shall be given in each State to the public Acts, Records, and judicial Proceedings of every other State. And the Congress may by general Laws prescribe the Manner in which such Acts, Records and Proceedings shall be proved, and the Effect thereof.

Section 2.   The Citizens of each State shall be entitled to all Privileges and Immunities of Citizens in the several States.

A Person charged in any State with Treason, Felony, or other Crime, who shall flee from Justice, and be found in another State, shall on Demand of the executive Authority of the State from which he fled, be delivered up, to be removed to the State having Jurisdiction of the Crime.

No Person held to Service or Labour in one State, under the Laws thereof, escaping into another, shall, in Consequence of any Law or Regulation therein, be discharged from such Service or Labour, but shall be delivered up on Claim of the Party to whom such Service or Labour may be due.

Section 3.   New States may be admitted by the Congress into this Union; but no new State shall be formed or erected within the Jurisdiction of any other State; nor any State be formed by the Junction of two or more States, or Parts of

States, without the Consent of the Legislatures of the States concerned as well as of the Congress.

The Congress shall have Power to dispose of and make all needful Rules and Regulations respecting the Territory or other Property belonging to the United States; and nothing in this Constitution shall be so construed as to Prejudice any Claims of the United States, or of any particular State.

Section 4. The United States shall guarantee to every State in this Union a Republican Form of Government, and shall protect each of them against Invasion; and on Application of the Legislature, or of the Executive (when the Legislature cannot be convened) against domestic Violence.

ARTICLE V

The Congress, whenever two thirds of both Houses shall deem it necessary, shall propose Amendments to this Constitution, or, on the Application of the Legislatures of two thirds of the several States, shall call a Convention for proposing Amendments, which, in either Case, shall be valid to all Intents and Purposes, as part of this Constitution, when ratified by the Legislatures of three fourths of the several States, or by Conventions in three fourths thereof, as the one or the other Mode of Ratification may be proposed by the Congress; Provided that no Amendment which may be made prior to the Year One thousand eight hundred and eight shall in any Manner affect the first and fourth Clauses in the Ninth Section of the first Article; and that no State, without its Consent, shall be deprived of its equal Suffrage in the Senate.

ARTICLE VI

All Debts contracted and Engagements entered into, before the Adoption of this Constitution shall be as valid against the United States under this Constitution, as under the Confederation.

This Constitution, and the Laws of the United States which shall be made in Pursuance thereof; and all Treaties made, or which shall be made, under the Authority of the United States, shall be the supreme Law of the Land; and the Judges in every State shall be bound thereby, any Thing in the Constitution or Laws of any State to the Contrary notwithstanding.

The Senators and Representatives before mentioned, and the Members of the several State Legislatures, and all executive and judicial Officers, both of the United States and of the several States, shall be bound by Oath or Affirmation, to support this Constitution; but no religious Test shall ever be required as a Qualification to any Office or public Trust under the United States.

ARTICLE VII

The Ratification of the Conventions of nine States shall be sufficient for the Establishment of this Constitution between the States so ratifying the Same.

AMENDMENT I [1791]

Congress shall make no law respecting an establishment of religion, or prohibiting the free exercise thereof; or abridging the freedom of speech, or of the press; or the right of the people peaceably to assemble, and to petition the Government for a redress of grievances.

AMENDMENT II [1791]

A well regulated Militia, being necessary to the security of a free State, the right of the people to keep and bear Arms, shall not be infringed.

AMENDMENT III [1791]

No Soldier shall, in time of peace be quartered in any house, without the consent of the Owner, nor in time of war, but in a manner to be prescribed by law.

AMENDMENT IV [1791]

The right of the people to be secure in their persons, houses, papers, and effects, against unreasonable searches and seizures, shall not be violated, and no Warrants shall issue, but upon probable cause, supported by Oath or affirmation, and particularly describing the place to be searched, and the persons or things to be seized.

AMENDMENT V [1791]

No person shall be held to answer for a capital, or otherwise infamous crime, unless on a presentment or indictment of a Grand Jury, except in cases arising in the land or naval forces, or in the Militia, when in actual service in time of War or public danger; nor shall any person be subject for the same offense to be twice put in jeopardy of life or limb; nor shall be compelled in any criminal case to be a witness against himself, nor be deprived of life, liberty, or property, without due process of law; nor shall private property be taken for public use, without just compensation.

AMENDMENT VI [1791]

In all criminal prosecutions, the accused shall enjoy the right to a speedy and public trial, by an impartial jury of the State and district wherein the crime shall have been committed, which district shall have been previously ascertained by law, and to be informed of the nature and cause of the accusation; to be confronted with the witnesses against him; to have compulsory process for obtaining witnesses in his favor, and to have the Assistance of Counsel for his defence.

AMENDMENT VII [1791]

In Suits at common law, where the value in controversy shall exceed twenty dollars, the right of trial by jury shall be preserved, and no fact tried by a jury, shall be otherwise re-examined in any Court of the United States, than according to the rules of the common law.

AMENDMENT VIII [1791]

Excessive bail shall not be required, nor excessive fines imposed, nor cruel and unusual punishments inflicted.

AMENDMENT IX [1791]

The enumeration in the Constitution, of certain rights, shall not be construed to deny or disparage others retained by the people.

AMENDMENT X [1791]

The powers not delegated to the United States by the Constitution, nor prohibited by it to the States, are reserved to the States respectively, or to the people.

AMENDMENT XI [1795]

The Judicial power of the United States shall not be construed to extend to any suit in law or equity, commenced or prose-cuted against one of the United States by Citizens of another State, or by Citizens or Subjects of any Foreign State.

AMENDMENT XII [1804]

The Electors shall meet in their respective states, and vote by ballot for President and Vice-President, one of whom, at least, shall not be an inhabitant of the same state with themselves; they shall name in their ballots the person voted for as President, and in distinct ballots the per-son voted for as Vice-President, and they shall make dis-tinct lists of all persons voted for as President, and of all persons voted for as Vice-President, and of the number of votes for each, which lists they shall sign and certify, and transmit sealed to the seat of the government of the United States, directed to the President of the Senate;—The President of the Senate shall, in the presence of the Senate and House of Representatives, open all the certificates and the votes shall then be counted;—The person having the greatest number of votes for President, shall be the President, if such number be a majority of the whole number of Electors appointed; and if no person have such majority, then from the persons having the high-est numbers not exceeding three on the list of those voted for as President, the House of Representatives shall choose immediately, by ballot, the President. But in choosing the President, the votes shall be taken by states, the representa-tion from each state having one vote; a quorum for this pur-pose shall consist of a member or members from two-thirds of the states, and a majority of all states shall be necessary

to a choice. And if the House of Representatives shall not choose a President whenever the right of choice shall devolve upon them, before the fourth day of March next following, then the Vice-President shall act as President, as in the case of the death or other constitutional disability of the President.—The person having the greatest number of votes as Vice-President, shall be the Vice-President, if such number be a majority of the whole number of Electors appointed, and if no person have a majority, then from the two highest numbers on the list, the Senate shall choose the Vice-President; a quorum for the purpose shall consist of two-thirds of the whole number of Senators, and a majority of the whole number shall be necessary to a choice. But no person constitutionally ineligible to the office of President shall be eligible to that of Vice-President of the United States.

AMENDMENT XIII [1865]

Section 1. Neither slavery nor involuntary servitude, except as a punishment for crime whereof the party shall have been duly convicted, shall exist within the United States, or any place subject to their jurisdiction.

Section 2. Congress shall have power to enforce this arti-cle by appropriate legislation.

AMENDMENT XIV [1868]

Section 1. All persons born or naturalized in the United States, and subject to the jurisdiction thereof, are citizens of the United States and of the State wherein they reside. No State shall make or enforce any law which shall abridge the privileges or immunities of citizens of the United States; nor shall any State deprive any person of life, liberty, or property, without due process of law; nor deny to any person within its jurisdiction the equal protection of the laws.

Section 2. Representatives shall be apportioned among the several States according to their respective numbers, counting the whole number of persons in each State, excluding Indians not taxed. But when the right to vote at any election for the choice of electors for President and Vice President of the United States, Representatives in Congress, the Executive and Judicial officers of a State, or the members of the Legislature thereof, is denied to any of the male inhabitants of such State, being twenty-one years of age, and citizens of the United States, or in any way abridged, except for participation in rebel-lion, or other crime, the basis of representation therein shall be reduced in the proportion which the number of such male citi-zens shall bear to the whole number of male citizens twenty-one years of age in such State.

Section 3. No person shall be a Senator or Representative in Congress, or elector of President and Vice President, or hold any office, civil or military, under the United States, or under any State, who having previously taken an oath, as a member of Congress, or as an officer of the United States, or as a member of any State legislature, or as an executive or judicial officer of any State, to support the Constitution of the United States, shall have engaged in insurrection or rebellion against the same, or given aid or comfort to the enemies thereof. But Congress may by a vote of two-thirds of each House, remove such disability.

Section 4. The validity of the public debt of the United States, authorized by law, including debts incurred for payment of pensions and bounties for services in suppressing insurrection or rebellion, shall not be questioned. But neither the United States nor any State shall assume or pay any debt or obligation incurred in aid of insurrection or rebellion against the United States, or any claim for the loss or emancipation of any slave; but all such debts, obligations and claims shall be held illegal and void.

Section 5. The Congress shall have power to enforce, by appropriate legislation, the provisions of this article.

AMENDMENT XV [1870]

Section 1. The right of citizens of the United States to vote shall not be denied or abridged by the United States or by any State on account of race, color, or previous condition of servitude.

Section 2. The Congress shall have power to enforce this article by appropriate legislation.

AMENDMENT XVI [1913]

The Congress shall have power to lay and collect taxes on incomes, from whatever source derived, without apportionment among the several States, and without regard to any census or enumeration.

AMENDMENT XVII [1913]

Section 1. The Senate of the United States shall be composed of two Senators from each State, elected by the people thereof, for six years; and each Senator shall have one vote. The electors in each State shall have the qualifications requisite for electors of the most numerous branch of the State legislatures.

Section 2. When vacancies happen in the representation of any State in the Senate, the executive authority of such State shall issue writs of election to fill such vacancies: Provided, That the legislature of any State may empower the executive thereof to make temporary appointments until the people fill the vacancies by election as the legislature may direct.

Section 3. This amendment shall not be so construed as to affect the election or term of any Senator chosen before it becomes valid as part of the Constitution.

AMENDMENT XVIII [1919]

Section 1. After one year from the ratification of this article the manufacture, sale, or transportation of intoxicating liquors within, the importation thereof into, or the exportation thereof from the United States and all territory subject to the jurisdiction thereof for beverage purposes is hereby prohibited.

Section 2. The Congress and the several States shall have concurrent power to enforce this article by appropriate legislation.

Section 3. This article shall be inoperative unless it shall have been ratified as an amendment to the Constitution by the legislatures of the several States, as provided in the Constitution, within seven years from the date of the submission hereof to the States by the Congress.

AMENDMENT XIX [1920]

Section 1. The right of citizens of the United States to vote shall not be denied or abridged by the United States or by any State on account of sex.

Section 2. Congress shall have power to enforce this article by appropriate legislation.

AMENDMENT XX [1933]

Section 1. The terms of the President and Vice President shall end at noon on the 20th day of January, and the terms of Senators and Representatives at noon on the 3d day of January, of the years in which such terms would have ended if this article had not been ratified; and the terms of their successors shall then begin.

Section 2. The Congress shall assemble at least once in every year, and such meeting shall begin at noon on the 3d day of January, unless they shall by law appoint a different day.

Section 3. If, at the time fixed for the beginning of the term of the President, the President elect shall have died, the Vice President elect shall become President. If the President shall not have been chosen before the time fixed for the beginning of his term, or if the President elect shall have failed to qualify, then the Vice President elect shall act as President until a President shall have qualified; and the Congress may by law provide for the case wherein neither a President elect nor a Vice President elect shall have qualified, declaring who shall then act as President, or the manner in which one who is to act shall be selected, and such person shall act accordingly until a President or Vice President shall have qualified.

Section 4. The Congress may by law provide for the case of the death of any of the persons from whom the House of Representatives may choose a President whenever the right of choice shall have devolved upon them, and for the case of the death of any of the persons from whom the Senate may choose a Vice President whenever the right of choice shall have devolved upon them.

Section 5. Sections 1 and 2 shall take effect on the 15th day of October following the ratification of this article.

Section 6. This article shall be inoperative unless it shall have been ratified as an amendment to the Constitution by the legislatures of three-fourths of the several States within seven years from the date of its submission.

AMENDMENT XXI [1933]

Section 1. The eighteenth article of amendment to the Constitution of the United States is hereby repealed.

Section 2. The transportation or importation into any State, Territory, or possession of the United States for delivery or use therein of intoxicating liquors, in violation of the laws thereof, is hereby prohibited.

Section 3. This article shall be inoperative unless it shall have been ratified as an amendment to the Constitution by conventions in the several States, as provided in the Constitution, within seven years from the date of the submission hereof to the States by the Congress.

AMENDMENT XXII [1951]

Section 1. No person shall be elected to the office of the President more than twice, and no person who has held the office of President, or acted as President, for more than two years of a term to which some other person was elected President shall be elected to the office of President more than once. But this Article shall not apply to any person holding the office of President when this Article was proposed by the Congress, and shall not prevent any person who may be holding the office of President, or acting as President, during the term within which this Article becomes operative from holding the office of President or acting as President during the remainder of such term.

Section 2. This article shall be inoperative unless it shall have been ratified as an amendment to the Constitution by the legislatures of three-fourths of the several States within seven years from the date of its submission to the States by the Congress.

AMENDMENT XXIII [1961]

Section 1. The District constituting the seat of Government of the United States shall appoint in such manner as the Congress may direct:

A number of electors of President and Vice President equal to the whole number of Senators and Representatives in Congress to which the District would be entitled if it were a State, but in no event more than the least populous state; they shall be in addition to those appointed by the states, but they shall be considered, for the purposes of the election of President and Vice President, to be electors appointed by a state; and they shall meet in the District and perform such duties as provided by the twelfth article of amendment.

Section 2. The Congress shall have power to enforce this article by appropriate legislation.

AMENDMENT XXIV [1964]

Section 1. The right of citizens of the United States to vote in any primary or other election for President or Vice President, for electors for President or Vice President, or for Senator or Representative in Congress, shall not be denied or abridged by the United States, or any State by reason of failure to pay any poll tax or other tax.

Section 2. The Congress shall have power to enforce this article by appropriate legislation.

AMENDMENT XXV [1967]

Section 1. In case of the removal of the President from office or of his death or resignation, the Vice President shall become President.

Section 2. Whenever there is a vacancy in the office of the Vice President, the President shall nominate a Vice President who shall take office upon confirmation by a majority vote of both Houses of Congress.

Section 3. Whenever the President transmits to the President pro tempore of the Senate and the Speaker of the House of Representatives his written declaration that he is unable to discharge the powers and duties of his office, and until he transmits to them a written declaration to the contrary, such powers and duties shall be discharged by the Vice President as Acting President.

Section 4. Whenever the Vice President and a majority of either the principal officers of the executive departments or of such other body as Congress may by law provide, transmit to the President pro tempore of the Senate and the Speaker of the House of Representatives their written declaration that the President is unable to discharge the powers and duties of his office, the Vice President shall immediately assume the powers and duties of the office as Acting President.

Thereafter, when the President transmits to the President pro tempore of the Senate and the Speaker of the House of Representatives his written declaration that no inability exists, he shall resume the powers and duties of his office unless the Vice President and a majority of either the principal officers of the executive department or of such other body as

Congress may by law provide, transmit within four days to the President pro tempore of the Senate and the Speaker of the House of Representatives their written declaration that the President is unable to discharge the powers and duties of his office. Thereupon Congress shall decide the issue, assembling within forty-eight hours for that purpose if not in session. If the Congress, within twenty-one days after receipt of the latter written declaration, or, if Congress is not in session, within twenty-one days after Congress is required to assemble, determines by two-thirds vote of both Houses that the President is unable to discharge the powers and duties of his office, the Vice President shall continue to discharge the same as Acting President; otherwise, the President shall resume the powers and duties of his office.

AMENDMENT XXVI [1971]

Section 1. The right of citizens of the United States, who are eighteen years of age or older, to vote shall not be denied or abridged by the United States or by any State on account of age.

Section 2. The Congress shall have power to enforce this article by appropriate legislation.

AMENDMENT XXVII [1992]

No law, varying the compensation for the services of the Senators and Representatives, shall take effect, until an election of Representatives shall have intervened.

APPENDIX C

FEDERALIST PAPERS NO. 10 AND NO. 51

The founders completed drafting the U.S. Constitution in 1787. It was then submitted to the thirteen states for ratification, and a major debate ensued. As you read in Chapter 2, on the one side of this debate were the Federalists, who urged that the new Constitution be adopted. On the other side of the debate were the Anti-Federalists, who argued against ratification.

During the course of this debate, three men well known for their Federalist views—Alexander Hamilton, James Madison, and John Jay—wrote a series of essays in which they argued for immediate ratifcation of the Constitution. The essays appeared in the New York City Independent Journal *in October 1787, just a little over a month after the Constitutional Convention adjourned. Later, Hamilton arranged to have the essays collected and published in book form. The articles filled two volumes, both of which were published by May 1788. The essays are often referred to collectively as the* Federalist Papers.

Scholars disagree as to whether the Federalist Papers *had a significant impact on the decision of the states to ratify the Constitution. Nonetheless, many of the essays are masterpieces of political reasoning and have left a lasting imprint on American politics and government. Above all, the* Federalist Papers *shed an important light on what the founders intended when they drafted various constitutional provisions.*

Here we present just two of these essays, Federalist Paper No. 10 *and* Federalist Paper No. 51. *Each essay was written by James Madison, who referred to himself as "Publius." We have annotated each document to clarify the meaning of particular passages. The annotations are set in italics to distinguish them from the original text of the documents.*

#10

Federalist Paper No. 10 is a classic document that is often referred to by teachers of American government. Authored by James Madison, it sets forth Madison's views on factions in politics. The essay was written, in large part, to counter the arguments put forth by the Anti-Federalists that small factions might take control of the government, thus destroying the representative nature of the republican form of government established by the Constitution. The essay opens with a discussion of the "dangerous vice" of factions and the importance of devising a form of government in which this vice will be controlled.

Among the numerous advantages promised by a well-constructed Union, none deserves to be more accurately developed than its tendency to break and control the violence of faction. The friend of popular governments never finds himself so much alarmed for their character and fate as when he contemplates their propensity to this dangerous vice. He will not fail, therefore, to set a due value on any plan which, without violating the principles to which he is attached, provides a proper cure for it. The instability, injustice, and confusion introduced into the public councils have, in truth, been the mortal diseases under which popular governments have everywhere perished, as they continue to be the favorite and fruitful topics from which the adversaries to liberty derive their most specious declamations. The valuable improvements made by the American constitutions on the popular models, both ancient and modern, cannot certainly be too much admired; but it would be an unwarrantable partiality to contend that they have as effectually obviated the danger on this side, as was wished and expected. Complaints are everywhere heard from our most considerate and virtuous citizens, equally the friends of public and private faith and of public and personal liberty, that our governments are too unstable, that the public good is disregarded in the conflicts of rival parties, and that measures are too often decided, not according to the rules of justice and the rights of the minor party, but by the superior force of an interested and overbearing majority. However anxiously we may wish that these complaints had no foundation, the evidence of known facts will not permit us to deny that they are in some degree true. It will be found, indeed, on a candid review of our situation, that some of the distresses under which we labor have been erroneously charged on the operation of our governments; but it will be found, at the same time, that other causes will not alone account for many of our heaviest misfortunes; and, particularly, for that prevailing and increasing distrust of public engagements and alarm for private rights which are echoed from one end of the continent to the other. These must be chiefly, if not wholly, effects of the unsteadiness and injustice with which a factious spirit has tainted our public administration.

In the following paragraph, Madison clarifies for his readers his understanding of what the term faction means.

By a faction I understand a number of citizens, whether amounting to a majority or minority of the whole, who are united and actuated by some common impulse of passion, or of interest, adverse to the rights of other citizens, or the permanent and aggregate interests of the community.

In the following passages, Madison looks at the two methods of curing the "mischiefs of factions." One of these methods is removing the causes of faction. The other is to control the effects of factions.

There are two methods of curing the mischiefs of faction: the one, by removing its causes; the other, by controlling its effects.

There are again two methods of removing the causes of faction: the one, by destroying the liberty which is essential to its existence; the other, by giving to every citizen the same opinions, the same passions, and the same interests.

It could never be more truly said than of the first remedy that it was worse than the disease. Liberty is to faction what air is to fire, an aliment without which it instantly expires. But it could not be a less folly to abolish liberty, which is essential to political life, because it nourishes faction than it would be to wish the annihilation of air, which is essential to animal life, because it imparts to fire its destructive agency.

The second expedient is as impracticable as the first would be unwise. As long as the reason of man continues fallible, and his is at liberty to exercise it, different opinions will be formed. As long as the connection subsists between his reason and his self-love, his opinions and his passions will have a reciprocal influence on each other; and the former will be objects to which the latter will attach themselves. The diversity in the faculties of men, from which the rights of property originate, is not less an insuperable obstacle to a uniformity of interests. The protection of these faculties is the first object of government. From the protection of different and unequal faculties of acquiring property, the possession of different degrees and kinds of property immediately results; and from the influence of these on the sentiments and views of the respective proprietors ensues a division of the society into different interests and parties.

The latent causes of faction are thus sown in the nature of man; and we see them everywhere brought into different degrees of activity, according to the different circumstances of civil society. A zeal for different opinions concerning religion, concerning government, and many other points, as well of speculation as of practice; an attachment to different leaders ambitiously contending for pre-eminence and power; or to persons of other descriptions whose fortunes have been interesting to the human passions, have, in turn, divided mankind into parties, inflamed them with mutual animosity, and rendered them much more disposed to vex and oppress each other than to co-operate for their common good. So strong is this propensity of mankind to fall into mutual animosities that where no substantial occasion presents itself the most frivolous and fanciful distinctions have been sufficient to kindle their unfriendly passions and excite their most violent conflicts. But the most common and durable source of factions has been the various and unequal distribution of property. Those who hold and those who are without property have ever formed distinct interests in society. Those who are creditors, and those who are debtors, fall under a like discrimination. A landed interest, a manufacturing interest, a mercantile interest, a moneyed interest, with many lesser interests, grow up of necessity in civilized nations, and divide them into different classes, actuated by different sentiments and views. The regulation of these various and interfering interests forms the principal task of modern legislation and involves the spirit of party and faction in the necessary and ordinary operations of government.

No man is allowed to be a judge in his own cause, because his interest would certainly bias his judgment, and, not improbably, corrupt his integrity. With equal, nay with greater reason, a body of men are unfit to be both judges and parties at the same time; yet what are many of the most important acts of legislation but so many judicial determinations, not indeed concerning the rights of single persons, but concerning the rights of large bodies of citizens? And what are the different classes of legislators but advocates and parties to the causes which they determine? Is a law proposed concerning private debts? It is a question to which the creditors are parties on one side and the debtors on the other. Justice ought to hold the balance between them. Yet the parties are, and must be, themselves the judges; and the most numerous party, or in other words, the most powerful faction must be expected to prevail. Shall domestic manufacturers be encouraged, and in what degree, by restrictions on foreign manufacturers? Are questions which would be differently decided by the landed and the manufacturing classes, and probably by neither with a sole regard to justice and the public good. The apportionment of taxes on the various descriptions of property is an act which seems to require the most exact impartiality; yet there is, perhaps, no legislative act in which greater opportunity and temptation are given to a predominant party to trample on the rules of justice. Every shilling with which they overburden the inferior number is a shilling saved to their own pockets.

It is in vain to say that enlightened statesmen will be able to adjust these clashing interests and render them all subservient to the public good. Enlightened statesmen will not always be at the helm. Nor, in many cases, can such an adjustment be made at all without taking into view indirect and remote considerations, which will rarely prevail over the immediate interest which one party may find in disregarding the rights of another or the good of the whole.

The inference to which we are brought is that the causes of faction cannot be removed and that relief is only to be sought in the means of controlling its effects.

In the preceding passages, Madison has explored the causes of factions and has concluded that they cannot "be removed" without removing liberty itself, which is one of the causes, or altering human nature. He now turns to a discussion of how the effects of factions might be controlled.

If a faction consists of less than a majority, relief is supplied by the republican principle, which enables the majority to defeat its sinister views by regular vote. It may clog the administration, it may convulse the society; but it will be unable to execute and mask its violence under the forms of the Constitution. When a majority is included in a faction, the form of popular government, on the other hand, enables it to sacrifice to its ruling passion or interest both the public good and the rights of other citizens. To secure the public good and private rights against the danger of such a faction, and at the same time to preserve the spirit and the form of popular government, is then the great object to which our inquiries are directed. Let me add that it is the great desideratum by which alone this form of government can be rescued from the opprobrium under which it has so long labored and be recommended to the esteem and adoption of mankind.

According to Madison, one way of controlling the effects of factions is to make sure that the majority is not able to act in "concert," or jointly, to "carry into effect schemes of oppression."

By what means is this object attainable? Evidently by one of two only. Either the existence of the same passion or interest in a majority at the same time must be prevented, or the majority, having such coexistent passion or interest, must be rendered, by their number and local situation, unable to concert and carry into effect schemes of oppression. If the impulse and the opportunity be suffered to coincide, we well know that neither moral nor religious motives can be relied on as an adequate control. They are not found to be such on the injustice and violence of individuals, and lose their efficacy in proportion to the number combined together, that is, in proportion as their efficacy becomes needful.

From this view of the subject it may be concluded that a pure democracy, by which I mean a society consisting of a small number of citizens, who assemble and administer the government in person, can admit of no cure for the mischiefs of faction. A common passion or interest will, in almost every case, be felt by a majority of the whole; a communication and concert results from the form of government itself; and there is nothing to check the inducements to sacrifice the weaker party or an obnoxious individual. Hence it is that such democracies have ever been spectacles of turbulence and contention; have ever been found incompatible with personal security or the rights of property; and have in general been as short in their lives as they have been violent in their deaths. Theoretic politicians, who have patronized this species of government, have erroneously supposed that by reducing mankind to a perfect equality in their political rights, they would at the same time be perfectly equalized and assimilated in their possessions, their opinions, and their passions.

In the following six paragraphs, Madison sets forth some of the reasons why a republican form of government promises a "cure" for the mischiefs of factions. He begins by clarifying the difference between a republic and a democracy. He then describes how in a large republic, the elected representatives of the people will be large enough in number to guard against factions—the "cabals," or concerted actions, of "a few." On the one hand, representatives will not be so removed from their local districts as to be unacquainted with their constituents' needs. On the other hand, they will not be "unduly attached" to local interests and unfit to understand "great and national objects." Madison concludes that the Constitution "forms a happy combination in this respect."

A republic, by which I mean a government in which the scheme of representation takes place, opens a different prospect and promises the cure for which we are seeking. Let us examine the points in which it varies from pure democracy, and we shall comprehend both the nature of the cure and the efficacy which it must derive from the Union.

The two great points of difference between a democracy and a republic are: first, the delegation of the government, in the latter, to a small number of citizens elected by the rest; secondly, the greater number of citizens and greater sphere of country over which the latter may be extended.

The effect of the first difference is, on the one hand, to refine and enlarge the public views by passing them through the medium of a chosen body of citizens, whose wisdom may best discern the true interest of their country and whose patriotism and love of justice will be least likely to sacrifice it to temporary or partial considerations. Under such a regulation it may well happen that the public voice, pronounced by the representatives of the people, will be more consonant to the public good than if pronounced by the people themselves, convened for the purpose. On the other hand, the effect may be inverted. Men of factious tempers, of local prejudices, or of sinister designs, may, by intrigue, by corruption, or by other means, first obtain the suffrages, and then betray the interests of the people. The question resulting is, whether small or extensive republics are most favorable to the election of proper guardians of the public weal; and it is clearly decided in favor of the latter by two obvious considerations.

In the first place it is to be remarked that however small the republic may be the representatives must be raised to a certain number in order to guard against the cabals of a few; and that however large it may be they must be limited to a certain number in order to guard against the confusion of a multitude. Hence, the number of representatives in the two cases not being in proportion to that of the constituents, and being proportionally greatest in the small republic, it follows that if the proportion of fit characters be not less in the large than in the small republic, the former will present a greater option, and consequently a greater probability of a fit choice.

In the next place, as each representative will be chosen by a greater number of citizens in the large than in the small republic, it will be more difficult for unworthy candidates to practice with success the vicious arts by which elections are too often carried; and the suffrages of the people being more free, will be more likely to center on men who possess the most attractive merit and the most diffusive and established characters.

It must be confessed that in this, as in most other cases, there is a mean, on both sides of which inconveniencies will be found to lie. By enlarging too much the number of electors, you render the representative too little acquainted with all their local circumstances and lesser interests; as by reducing it too much, you render him unduly attached to these, and too little fit to comprehend and pursue great and national objects. The federal Constitution forms a happy combination in this respect; the great and aggregate interests being referred to the national, the local and particular to the State legislatures.

In the remaining passages of this essay, Madison looks at another "point of difference" between a republic and a democracy. Specifically, a republic can encompass a larger territory and a greater number of citizens than a democracy can. This fact, too, argues Madison, will help to control the influence of factions because the interests that draw people together to act in concert are typically at the local level and would be unlikely to affect or dominate the national government. As Madison states, "The influence of factious leaders may kindle a flame within their particular States but will be unable to spread a general conflagration through the other States." Generally, in a large republic, there will be numerous factions, and no particular faction will be able to "pervade the whole body of the Union."

The other point of difference is the greater number of citizens and extent of territory which may be brought within the compass of republican than of democratic government; and it is this circumstance principally which renders factious combinations less to be dreaded in the former than in the latter. The smaller the society, the fewer probably will be the distinct parties and interests composing it; the fewer the distinct parties and interests, the more frequently will a majority be found of the same party; and the smaller the number of individuals composing a majority, and the smaller the compass within which they are placed, the more easily will they concert and execute their plans of oppression. Extend the sphere and you take in a greater variety of parties and interests; you make it less probable that a majority of the whole will have a common motive to invade the rights of other citizens; or if such a common motive exists, it will be more difficult for all who feel it to discover their own strength and to act in unison with each other. Besides other impediments, it may be remarked that, where there is a consciousness of unjust or dishonorable purposes, communication is always checked by distrust in proportion to the number whose concurrence is necessary.

Hence, it clearly appears that the same advantage which a republic has over a democracy in controlling the effects of faction is enjoyed by a large over a small republic—is enjoyed by the Union over the States composing it. Does this advantage consist in the substitution of representatives whose enlightened views and virtuous sentiments render them superior to local prejudices and to schemes of injustice? It will not be denied that the representation of the Union will be most likely to possess these requisite endowments. Does it consist in the greater security afforded by a greater variety of parties, against the event of any one party being able to outnumber and oppress the rest? In an equal degree does the increased variety of parties comprised within the Union increase this security. Does it, in fine, consist in the greater obstacles opposed to the concert and accomplishment of the secret wishes of an unjust and interested majority? Here again the extent of the Union gives it the most palpable advantage.

The influence of factious leaders may kindle a flame within their particular States but will be unable to spread a general conflagration through the other States. A religious sect may degenerate into a political faction in a part of the Confederacy; but the variety of sects dispersed over the entire face of it must secure the national councils against any danger from that source. A rage for paper money, for an abolition of debts, for an equal division of property, or for any other improper or wicked project, will be less apt to pervade the whole body of the Union than a particular member of it, in the same proportion as such a malady is more likely to taint a particular county or district than an entire State.

In the extent and proper structure of the Union, therefore, we behold a republican remedy for the diseases most incident to republican government. And according to the degree of pleasure and pride we feel in being republicans ought to be our zeal in cherishing the spirit and supporting the character of federalists.

Publius
(James Madison)

#51

Federalist Paper No. 51, which was also authored by James Madison, is one of the classics in American political theory. Recall from Chapter 2 that a major concern of the founders was to create a relatively strong national government but one that would not be capable of tyrannizing over the populace. In the following essay, Madison sets forth the theory of "checks and balances." He explains that the new Constitution, by dividing the national government into three branches (executive, legislative, and judicial), offers protection against tyranny.

To what expedient, then, shall we finally resort, for maintaining in practice the necessary partition of power among the several departments as laid down in the Constitution? The only answer that can be given is that as all these exterior provisions are found to be inadequate the defect must be supplied, by so contriving the interior structure of the government as that its several constituent parts may, by their mutual relations, be the means of keeping each other in their proper places. Without presuming to undertake a full development of this important idea I will hazard a few general observations which may perhaps place it in a clearer light, and enable us to form a more correct judgment of the principles and structure of the government planned by the convention.

In the following two paragraphs, Madison explains that to ensure that the powers of government are genuinely separated, it is important that each of the three branches of government (executive, legislative, and judicial) should have a "will of its own." Among other things, this means that persons in one branch should not depend on persons in another branch for the "emoluments annexed to their offices" (pay, perks, and privileges). If they did, then the branches would not be truly independent of one another.

In order to lay a due foundation for that separate and distinct exercise of the different powers of government, which to a certain extent is admitted on all hands to be essential to the preservation of liberty, it is evident that each department should have a will of its own; and consequently should be so constituted that the members of each should have as little agency as possible in the appointment of the members of the others. Were this principle rigorously adhered to, it would require that all the appointments for the supreme executive, legislative, and judiciary magistracies should be drawn from the same fountain of authority, the people, through channels having no communication whatever with one another. Perhaps such a plan of constructing the several departments would be less difficult in practice than it may in contemplation appear. Some difficulties, however, and some additional expense would attend the execution of it. Some deviations, therefore, from the principle must be admitted. In the constitution of the judiciary department in particular, it might be inexpedient to insist rigorously on the principle: first, because peculiar qualifications being essential in the members, the primary consideration ought to be to select that mode of choice which best secures these qualifications; second, because the permanent tenure by which the appointments are held in that department must soon destroy all sense of dependence on the authority conferring them.

It is equally evident that the members of each department should be as little dependent as possible on those of the others for the emoluments annexed to their offices. Were the executive magistrate, or the judges, not independent of the legislature in this particular, their independence in every other would be merely nominal.

One of the striking qualities of the theory of checks and balances as posited by Madison is that it assumes that persons are not angels but driven by personal interests and motives. In the following two paragraphs, which are among the most widely quoted of Madison's writings, he stresses that the division of the government into three branches helps to check personal ambitions. Personal ambitions will naturally arise, but they will be linked to the constitutional powers of each branch. In effect, they will help to keep the three branches separate and thus serve the public interest.

But the great security against a gradual concentration of the several powers in the same department consists in giving to those who administer each department the necessary constitutional means and personal motives to resist encroachments of the others. The provision for defense must in this, as in all other cases, be made commensurate to the danger of attack. Ambition must be made to counteract ambition. The interest of the man must be connected with the constitutional rights of the place. It may be a reflection on human nature that such devices should be necessary to control the abuses of government. But what is government itself but the greatest of all reflections on human nature? If men were angels, no government would be necessary. If angels were to govern men, neither external nor internal controls on government would be necessary. In framing a government which is to be administered by men over men, the great difficulty lies in this: you must first enable the government to control the governed; and

in the next place oblige it to control itself. A dependence on the people is, no doubt, the primary control on the government; but experience has taught mankind the necessity of auxiliary precautions.

This policy of supplying, by opposite and rival interests, the defect of better motives, might be traced through the whole system of human affairs, private as well as public. We see it particularly displayed in all the subordinate distributions of power, where the constant aim is to divide and arrange the several offices in such a manner as that each may be a check on the other—that the private interest of every individual may be a sentinel over the public rights. These inventions of prudence cannot be less requisite in the distribution of the supreme powers of the State.

In the next two paragraphs, Madison first points out that the "legislative authority necessarily predominates" in a republican form of government. The "remedy" for this lack of balance with the other branches of government is to divide the legislative branch into two chambers with "different modes of election and different principles of action."

But it is not possible to give to each department an equal power of self-defense. In republican government, the legislative authority necessarily predominates. The remedy for this inconveniency is to divide the legislature into different branches; and to render them, by different modes of election and different principles of action, as little connected with each other as the nature of their common functions and their common dependence on the society will admit. It may even be necessary to guard against dangerous encroachments by still further precautions. As the weight of the legislative authority requires that it should be thus divided, the weakness of the executive may require, on the other hand, that it should be fortified. An absolute negative on the legislature appears, at first view, to be the natural defense with which the executive magistrate should be armed. But perhaps it would be neither altogether safe nor alone sufficient. On ordinary occasions it might not be exerted with the requisite firmness, and on extraordinary occasions it might be perfidiously abused. May not this defect of an absolute negative be supplied by some qualified connection between this weaker department and the weaker branch of the stronger department, by which the latter may be led to support the constitutional rights of the former, without being too much detached from the rights of its own department?

If the principles on which these observations are founded be just, as I persuade myself they are, and they be applied as a criterion to the several State constitutions, and to the federal Constitution, it will be found that if the latter does not perfectly correspond with them, the former are infinitely less able to bear such a test.

In the remaining passages of this essay, Madison discusses the importance of the division of government powers between the states and the national government. This division of powers, by providing additional checks and balances, offers a "double security" against tyranny.

There are, moreover, two considerations particularly applicable to the federal system of America, which place that system in a very interesting point of view.

First. In a single republic, all the power surrendered by the people is submitted to the administration of a single government; and the usurpations are guarded against by a division of the government into distinct and separate departments. In the compound republic of America, the power surrendered by the people is first divided between two distinct governments, and then the portion allotted to each subdivided among distinct and separate departments. Hence a double security arises to the rights of the people. The different governments will control each other, at the same time that each will be controlled by itself.

Second. It is of great importance in a republic not only to guard the society against the oppression of its rulers, but to guard one part of the society against the injustice of the other part. Different interests necessarily exist in different classes of citizens. If a majority be united by a common interest, the rights of the minority will be insecure. There are but two methods of providing against this evil: the one by creating a will in the community independent of the majority—that is, of the society itself; the other, by comprehending in the society so many separate descriptions of citizens as will render an unjust combination of a majority of the whole very improbable, if not impracticable. The first method prevails in all governments possessing an hereditary or self-appointed authority. This, at best, is but a precarious security; because a power independent of the society may as well espouse the unjust views of the major as the rightful interests of the minor party, and may possibly be turned against both parties. The second method will be exemplified in the federal republic of the United States. Whilst all authority in it will be derived from and dependent on the society, the society itself will be broken into so many parts, interests and classes of citizens, that the rights of individuals, or of the minority, will be in little danger from interested combinations of the majority. In a free government the security for civil rights must be the same as that for religious rights. It consists in the one case in the multiplicity of interests, and in the other in the multiplicity of sects. The degree of security in both cases will depend on the number of interests and sects; and this may be presumed to depend on the extent of country and number of people comprehended under the same government. This view of the subject must particularly recommend a proper federal system to all the sincere and considerate friends of republican government, since it shows that in exact proportion as the territory of the Union may be formed into more circumscribed Confederacies, or States, oppressive combinations of a majority will be facilitated; the best security, under the republican forms, for the rights of every class of citizen, will be diminished; and consequently the stability and independence of some member of the government, the only other security, must be proportionally increased. Justice is the end of government. It is the end of civil society. It ever has been and ever will be pursued until it be obtained, or until liberty be lost in the pursuit. In a society under the forms of which the stronger faction can readily unite and oppress the weaker, anarchy may as truly be said to reign as in a state of nature, where the weaker individual is not secured against the violence of the stronger; and as, in the latter state, even the stronger individuals are prompted, by the uncertainty of their condition, to submit to a government which may protect the weak as well as themselves; so, in the former state, will the more powerful factions or parties be gradually induced, by a like motive, to wish for a government which will protect all parties, the weaker as well as the more powerful. It can be little doubted that if the State of Rhode Island was separated from the Confederacy and left to itself, the insecurity of rights under the popular form of government within such narrow limits would be displayed by such reiterated oppressions of factious majorities that some power altogether independent of the people would soon be called for by the voice of the very factions whose misrule had proved the necessity of it. In the extended republic of the United States, and among the great variety of interests, parties, and sects which it embraces, a coalition of a majority of the whole society could seldom take place on any other principles than those of justice and the general good; whilst there being thus less danger to a minor from the will of a major party, there must be less pretext, also, to provide for the security of the former, by introducing into the government a will not dependent on the latter, or, in other words, a will independent of the society itself. It is no less certain than it is important, notwithstanding the contrary opinions which have been entertained, that the larger the society, provided it lie within a practicable sphere, the more duly capable it will be of self-government. And happily for the *republican cause,* the practicable sphere may be carried to a very great extent by a judicious modification and mixture of the *federal principle.*

Publius
(James Madison)

APPENDIX D

ANSWERS TO CHAPTER QUIZ QUESTIONS

Chapter 1

Fill-In

1. Government (Learning Outcome 1–1)
2. it resolves conflicts, provides public services, and defends the nation and its culture against attacks by other nations (Learning Outcome 1–1)
3. autocracy (Learning Outcome 1–2)
4. representative democracy (Learning Outcome 1–2)
5. life, liberty, and property (Learning Outcome 1–3)
6. equality in voting, individual freedom, equal protection of the law, majority rule and minority rights, and voluntary consent to be governed (Learning Outcome 1–3)
7. conservatives and liberals (Learning Outcome 1–4)
8. conservatives (Learning Outcome 1–4)
9. moderates (Learning Outcome 1–4)
10. Libertarians (Learning Outcome 1–4)

Multiple Choice

11. c. (Learning Outcome 1–1)
12. a. (Learning Outcome 1–1)
13. b. (Learning Outcome 1–2)
14. c. (Learning Outcome 1–2)
15. b. (Learning Outcome 1–3)
16. a. (Learning Outcome 1–3)
17. c. (Learning Outcome 1–4)
18. a. (Learning Outcome 1–4)

Chapter 2

Fill-In

1. Mayflower Compact (Learning Outcome 2–1)
2. imposing taxes on the American colonists and exercising more direct control over colonial trade (Learning Outcome 2–2)
3. Sugar Act, the Stamp Act, and taxes on glass, paint, and lead (Learning Outcome 2–2)
4. Congress of the Confederation (Learning Outcome 2–3)
5. Shays' Rebellion (Learning Outcome 2–3)
6. House of Representatives and the Senate (Learning Outcome 2–4)
7. "Treason, Bribery, or other high Crimes and Misdemeanors" (Learning Outcome 2–4)
8. bill of rights (Learning Outcome 2–4)
9. separation of powers (Learning Outcome 2–5)
10. judicial review (Learning Outcome 2–5)

Multiple Choice

11. c. (Learning Outcome 2–1)
12. b. (Learning Outcome 2–2)
13. b. (Learning Outcome 2–3)
14. a. (Learning Outcome 2–4)
15. a. (Learning Outcome 2–5)

Chapter 3

Fill-In

1. the ability to experiment with innovative policies at the state or local level, and the opportunity for the political and cultural interests of regional groups to be reflected in the laws governing those groups (Learning Outcome 3–1)
2. necessary and proper (Learning Outcome 3–2)
3. full faith and credit (Learning Outcome 3–2)
4. implied powers and national supremacy (Learning Outcome 3–3)
5. the Great Depression (Learning Outcome 3–3)
6. picket-fence (Learning Outcome 3–3)
7. federal mandate (Learning Outcome 3–4)
8. fiscal federalism (Learning Outcome 3–4)
9. threatening to withhold federal highway funds from states that did not comply (Learning Outcome 3–5)
10. No Child Left Behind (Learning Outcome 3–5)

Multiple Choice

11. a. (Learning Outcome 3–1)
12. c. (Learning Outcome 3–1)
13. b. (Learning Outcome 3–2)

14. c. (Learning Outcome 3–2)

15. a. (Learning Outcome 3–3)

16. c. (Learning Outcome 3–4)

17. b. (Learning Outcome 3–5)

Chapter 4

Fill-In

1. due process (Learning Outcome 4–1)

2. (1) be for a clearly secular purpose; (2) neither advance nor inhibit religion in its primary effect; and (3) avoid an "excessive government entanglement with religion" (Learning Outcome 4–2)

3. subversive speech (Learning Outcome 4–2)

4. Libel (Learning Outcome 4–2)

5. preferred-position (Learning Outcome 4–2)

6. "National Security Letters" (Learning Outcome 4–3)

7. *Roe v. Wade* (1973) (Learning Outcome 4–3)

8. Fourth (Learning Outcome 4–4)

9. the *Miranda* warnings (Learning Outcome 4–4)

Multiple Choice

10. b. (Learning Outcome 4–1)

11. b. (Learning Outcome 4–1)

12. c. (Learning Outcome 4–2)

13. a. (Learning Outcome 4–2)

14. b. (Learning Outcome 4–3)

15. a. (Learning Outcome 4–4)

Chapter 5

Fill-In

1. suspect classification (Learning Outcome 5–1)

2. separate-but-equal (Learning Outcome 5–2)

3. race, color, religion, gender, and national origin (Learning Outcome 5–2)

4. full political, economic, and social equality (Learning Outcome 5–3)

5. 77 cents (Learning Outcome 5–3)

6. Latinos (Learning Outcome 5–4)

7. Japanese (Learning Outcome 5–4)

8. Americans with Disabilities Act (Learning Outcome 5–4)

9. that gives special consideration, in jobs and college admissions, to members of groups that have been discriminated against in the past (Learning Outcome 5–5)

10. strict (Learning Outcome 5–5)

Multiple Choice

11. b. (Learning Outcome 5–1)

12. a. (Learning Outcome 5–2)

13. a. (Learning Outcome 5–3)

14. c. (Learning Outcome 5–4)

15. b. (Learning Outcome 5–4)

16. a. (Learning Outcome 5–5)

Chapter 6

Fill-In

1. First (Learning Outcome 6–1)

2. Disturbance (Learning Outcome 6–1)

3. 11.3 (Learning Outcome 6–2)

4. Right-to-work (Learning Outcome 6–2)

5. identity interest group (Learning Outcome 6–2)

6. all of the attempts by organizations or by individuals to influence the passage, defeat, or contents of legislation or to influence the administrative decisions of government (Learning Outcome 6–3)

7. *amicus curiae* briefs (Learning Outcome 6–3)

8. are not coordinated with a candidate's campaign.

9. revolving door (Learning Outcome 6–4)

Multiple Choice

10. b. (Learning Outcome 6–1)

11. c. (Learning Outcome 6–1)

12. a. (Learning Outcome 6–2)

13. c. (Learning Outcome 6–2)

14. b. (Learning Outcome 6–3)

15. c. (Learning Outcome 6–3)

16. c. (Learning Outcome 6–4)

Chapter 7

Fill-In

1. Federalists and the Jeffersonian Republicans (Learning Outcome 7–1)

2. Republican (Learning Outcome 7–1)

3. Republican (Learning Outcomes 7–1)

4. Democrats (Learning Outcomes 7–2)

5. a growing detachment from both major political parties (Learning Outcome 7–2)

6. primary (Learning Outcome 7–3)

7. national convention (Learning Outcome 7–4)

8. Theodore Roosevelt

Multiple Choice

9. a. (Learning Outcome 7–1)

10. c. (Learning Outcome 7–2)

11. b. (Learning Outcome 7–3)

12. c. (Learning Outcome 7–4)

13. b. (Learning Outcome 7–5)

Chapter 8

Fill-In

1. family, schools, churches, the media, opinion leaders, and peer groups (Learning Outcome 8–1)

2. party identification (Learning Outcome 8–2)

3. policy voting (Learning Outcome 8–2)

4. educational attainment, occupation and income, age, gender, religion and ethnic background, and geographic region (Learning Outcome 8–2)

5. the gender gap (Learning Outcome 8–2)

6. each person within the entire population being polled has an equal chance of being chosen (Learning Outcome 8–3)

7. house effect (Learning Outcome 8–3)

8. push poll (Learning Outcome 8–3)

9. owned property (Learning Outcome 8–4)

10. literacy tests, poll taxes, the grandfather clause, and white primaries (Learning Outcome 8–4)

Multiple Choice

11. c. (Learning Outcome 8–1)

12. b. (Learning Outcome 8–1)

13. a. (Learning Outcome 8–2)

14. b. (Learning Outcome 8–3)

15. b. (Learning Outcome 8–4)

16. a. (Learning Outcome 8–4)

Chapter 9

Fill-In

1. who receives the largest popular vote in a state is credited with all that state's electoral votes (Learning Outcome 9–1)

2. 270 (Learning Outcome 9–1)

3. direct (Learning Outcome 9–2)

4. the states moving their primaries to earlier in the year in an effort to make their primaries more prominent in the media and influential in the political process (Learning Outcome 9–2)

5. delegates (Learning Outcome 9–2)

6. opposition (Learning Outcome 9–3)

7. collecting as much information as possible about voters in a database and then filtering out various groups for special attention (Learning Outcome 9–4)

8. federal income tax returns (Learning Outcome 9–5)

9. super PACs (Learning Outcome 9–5)

Multiple Choice

10. a. (Learning Outcome 9–1)

11. b. (Learning Outcome 9–1)

12. a. (Learning Outcome 9–2)

13. c. (Learning Outcome 9–3)

14. c. (Learning Outcome 9–4)

15. b. (Learning Outcome 9–5)

Chapter 10

Fill-In

1. Priming (Learning Outcome 10–1)

2. television (Learning Outcome 10–1)

3. televised comment, lasting for only a few seconds, that captures a thought or a perspective and has an immediate impact on the viewers (Learning Outcome 10–1)

4. they have lost a major share of their advertising revenue to online sites. (Learning Outcome 10–1)

5. John F. Kennedy and Richard Nixon (Learning Outcome 10–2)

6. political candidates' press advisers, who try to convince reporters to give a story or event concerning a candidate a particular interpretation or slant (Learning Outcome 10–2)

7. male, middle-aged, and conservative (Learning Outcome 10–3)

8. talk-show hosts often exaggerate their political biases for effect. Hosts sometimes appear to care more about the entertainment value of their statements than whether they are, strictly speaking, true. No journalistic conventions are observed (Learning Outcome 10–3)

9. losers (Learning Outcome 10–4)

10. the collection, analysis, and dissemination of information online by independent journalists, scholars, political activists, and the general citizenry (Learning Outcome 10–5)

11. net neutrality (Learning Outcome 10–5)

12. gaffe (Learning Outcome 10–5)

Multiple Choice

13. a. (Learning Outcome 10–1)

14. c. (Learning Outcome 10–2)

15. c. (Learning Outcome 10–3)

16. c. (Learning Outcome 10–4)

17. b. (Learning Outcome 10–5)

Chapter 11

Fill-In

1. ten (Learning Outcome 11–1)

2. serve the broad interests of the entire society and act according to his or her perception of national needs (Learning Outcome 11–1)

3. fund-raising ability, franking privileges, professional staffs, lawmaking power, access to the media, and name recognition (Learning Outcome 11–2)

4. preside over sessions of the House, vote in the event of a tie, put questions to a vote, participate in making important committee assignments, and schedule bills for action (Learning Outcome 11–3)

5. cloture (Learning Outcome 11–3)

6. a meeting held by a congressional committee or subcommittee to approve, amend, or redraft a bill (Learning Outcome 11–4)

7. Rules (Learning Outcome 11–4)

8. the federal judiciary and to the cabinet (Learning Outcome 11–5)

9. authorization and appropriation (Learning Outcome 11–6)

Multiple Choice

10. c. (Learning Outcome 11–1)

11. a. (Learning Outcome 11–2)

12. b. (Learning Outcome 11–3)

13. b. (Learning Outcome 11–4)

14. c. (Learning Outcome 11–5)

15. a. (Learning Outcome 11–6)

Chapter 12

Fill-In

1. the legal profession (Learning Outcome 12–1)

2. commander in chief (Learning Outcome 12–2)

3. chief legislator (Learning Outcome 12–2)

4. presidential orders to carry out policies described in laws passed by Congress (Learning Outcome 12–3)

5. War Powers Resolution (Learning Outcome 12–3)

6. an inherent executive power claimed by presidents to withhold information from, or to refuse to appear before, Congress or the courts (Learning Outcome 12–4)

7. the heads of the executive departments and other officials whom the president may choose to appoint (Learning Outcome 12–5)

8. White House Office, the Office of Management and Budget, and the National Security Council (Learning Outcome 12–5)

Multiple Choice

9. c. (Learning Outcome 12–1)

10. c. (Learning Outcome 12–2)

11. a. (Learning Outcome 12–2)

12. a. (Learning Outcome 12–3)

13. a. (Learning Outcome 12–3)

14. b. (Learning Outcome 12–4)

15. c. (Learning Outcome 12–5)

Chapter 13

Fill-In

1. 16 (Learning Outcome 13–1)

2. secretary (Learning Outcome 13–2)

3. Commerce (Learning Outcome 13–2)

4. president; Senate (Learning Outcome 13–3)

5. merit through open, competitive examinations (Learning Outcome 13–3)

6. enabling legislation (Learning Outcome 13–4)

7. a three-way alliance among legislators, bureaucrats, and interest groups to make or preserve policies that benefit their respective interests (Learning Outcome 13–4)

8. reports on gross governmental inefficiency, illegal action, or other wrongdoing (Learning Outcome 13–5)

Multiple Choice

9. b. (Learning Outcome 13–1)

10. a. (Learning Outcome 13–2)

11. c. (Learning Outcome 13–2)

12. b. (Learning Outcome 13–2)

13. c. (Learning Outcome 13–3)

14. b. (Learning Outcome 13–4)

15. a. (Learning Outcome 13–5)

Chapter 14

Fill-In

1. constitutions, statutes, administrative agency rules and regulations, and decisions by courts (Learning Outcome 14–1)
2. the authority of a court to hear and decide a particular case (Learning Outcome 14–2)
3. writ of *certiorari* (Learning Outcome 14–2)
4. oral arguments (Learning Outcome 14–2)
5. concurring (Learning Outcome 14–2)
6. senatorial courtesy (Learning Outcome 14–3)
7. strict construction and originalism (Learning Outcome 14–4)
8. Anthony Kennedy (Learning Outcome 14–4)
9. rewriting a statute to negate a court's ruling, proposing constitutional amendments to reverse Supreme Court decisions, or limiting the jurisdiction of the federal courts (Learning Outcome 14–5)

Multiple Choice

9. b. (Learning Outcome 14–1)
10. b. (Learning Outcome 14–2)
11. a. (Learning Outcome 14–3)
12. a. (Learning Outcome 14–4)
13. b. (Learning Outcome 14–5)

Chapter 15

Fill-In

1. issue identification and agenda setting, policy formulation and adoption, and policy implementation and evaluation (Learning Outcome 15–1)
2. Medicare (Learning Outcome 15–2)
3. all persons obtain health-care insurance from one source or another, or pay a penalty (Learning Outcome 15–2)
4. Canada and Mexico (Learning Outcome 15–3)
5. a rise in sea levels, changes in rainfall patterns, and increases in extreme weather (Learning Outcome 15–3)
6. solar power, hydropower, and wind power (Learning Outcome 15–3)
7. recession (Learning Outcome 15–4)
8. Federal Reserve System (Learning Outcome 15–4)

Multiple Choice

9. c. (Learning Outcome 15–1)
10. b. (Learning Outcome 15–2)
11. a. (Learning Outcome 15–2)
12. c. (Learning Outcome 15–3)
13. b. (Learning Outcome 15–4)
14. c. (Learning Outcome 15–4)

Chapter 16

Fill-In

1. departments of state and defense, and the National Security Council and the Central Intelligence Agency (Learning Outcome 16–1)
2. isolationism (Learning Outcome 16–2)
3. Cold War (Learning Outcome 16–2)
4. Afghanistan (Learning Outcome 16–3)
5. Pakistan (Learning Outcome 16–3)
6. Palestinian Authority (Learning Outcome 16–4)
7. North Korea and Iran (Learning Outcome 16–4)
8. Taiwan (Learning Outcome 16–4)

Multiple Choice

9. b. (Learning Outcome 16–1)
10. c. (Learning Outcome 16–2)
11. a. (Learning Outcome 16–2)
12. c. (Learning Outcome 16–3)
13. a. (Learning Outcome 16–4)
14. b. (Learning Outcome 16–4)

NOTES

Chapter 1

1. The *Levant* is a traditional name for a region that contains—in addition to Syria—Israel, Jordan, Lebanon, and the Palestinian Territories.

2. Harold Laswell, *Politics: Who Gets What, When, and How* (1936; repr., Whitefish, Mont.: Literary Licensing LLC, 2011).

3. As quoted in Mario M. Cuomo and Harold Holzer, *Lincoln on Democracy* (New York: Fordham University Press, 2004), p. 64.

4. From Lincoln's first inaugural address. See Abraham Lincoln, *Axioms and Aphorisms from Abraham Lincoln* (Seattle: CreateSpace, an Amazon company, 2012), p. 26.

5. *Obergefell v. Hodges*, 135 S.Ct. 2071 (2015).

Chapter 2

1. The first *European* settlement in today's United States was St. Augustine, Florida, which was founded on September 8, 1565, by the Spaniard Pedro Menéndez de Ávilés.

2. Archaeologists recently discovered the remains of a colony at Popham Beach, on the southern coast of what is now Maine, that was established at the same time as the colony at Jamestown. The Popham colony disbanded after thirteen months, however, when the leader, after learning that he had inherited property back home, returned—with the other colonists—to England.

3. John Camp, *Out of the Wilderness: The Emergence of an American Identity in Colonial New England* (Middleton, Conn.: Wesleyan University Press, 1990).

4. Ironically, the colonists were in fact protesting a tax reduction. The British government believed that if tea were cheaper, Americans would be more willing to drink it, even though it was still taxed. The Americans viewed the tax reduction as an attempt to trick them into accepting the principle of taxation. If the tea had been expensive, it would have been easy to organize a boycott. Because the tea was cheap, the protesters destroyed it so that no one would be tempted to buy it. (Also, many of the protesters were in the business of smuggling tea, and they would have been put out of business by the cheap competition.)

5. Much of the colonists' fury over British policies was directed personally at King George III, who had ascended the British throne in 1760 at the age of twenty-two, rather than at Britain or British rule *per se.* If you look at the Declaration of Independence in Appendix A, you will note that much of that document focuses on what "He" (George III) has or has not done. George III's lack of political experience, his personality, and his temperament all combined to lend instability to the British government at this crucial point in history.

6. *Thomas Paine: Collected Writings* (New York: Library of America, 1995), p. 36.

7. As quoted in Joseph J. Ellis, *Passionate Sage: The Character and Legacy of John Adams* (1993; repr., New York: W. W. Norton, 2001), p. 104.

8. Locke had coined the phrase "pursuit of happiness" in *An Essay Concerning Human Understanding*. Still, some scholars feel that Locke's influence on the colonists, including Thomas Jefferson, has been exaggerated. For example, Jay Fliegelman states that Jefferson's fascination with the ideas of Homer, Ossian, and Patrick Henry "is of greater significance than his indebtedness to Locke." Jay Fliegelman, *Declaring Independence: Jefferson, Natural Language, and the Culture of Performance* (Stanford, Calif.: Stanford University Press, 1993).

9. Well before the Articles were ratified, many of them had, in fact, already been implemented. The Second Continental Congress and the thirteen states conducted American military, economic, and political affairs according to the standards and form specified later in the Articles of Confederation. See Robert W. Hoffert, *A Politics of Tensions: The Articles of Confederation and American Political Ideas* (Niwot, Colo.: University Press of Colorado, 1992).

10. Shays' Rebellion was not merely a small group of poor farmers. The participants and their supporters represented whole communities, including some of the wealthiest and most influential families of Massachusetts. Leonard L. Richards, *Shays' Rebellion: The American Revolution's Final Battle* (Philadelphia: University of Pennsylvania Press, 2003).

11. Madison, however, was much more "republican" in his views—that is, less of a centralist—than Hamilton. See Lance Banning, *The Sacred Fire of Liberty: James Madison and the Founding of the Federal Republic* (Ithaca, N.Y.: Cornell University Press, 1995).

12. The State House was later named Independence Hall. The East Room was the same room in which the Declaration of Independence had been signed eleven years earlier.

13. Charles A. Beard, *An Economic Interpretation of the Constitution of the United States* (New York: Macmillan, 1913; Mineola, N.Y.: Dover, 2004.

14. In 1961, the Twenty-third Amendment added three additional members to the electoral college to represent the District of Columbia.

15. Morris was partly of French descent, which is why his first name may seem unusual. Note, however, that naming one's child *Gouverneur* was not common at the time in any language, including French.

16. Quoted in J. J. Spengler, "Malthusianism in Late Eighteenth-Century America," *American Economic Review* 25 (1935), p. 705.

17. For further detail on Wood's depiction of the founders' views, see Gordon S. Wood, *Revolutionary Characters: What Made the Founders Different* (New York: Penguin Press, 2006).

18. Some scholarship suggests that the *Federalist Papers* did not play a significant role in bringing about the ratification of the Constitution. Nonetheless, the papers have lasting value as an authoritative explanation of the Constitution.

19. The papers written by the Anti-Federalists are online at www.constitution.org/afp/afp.htm. For essays on the positions, arranged in topical order, of both the Federalists and the Anti-Federalists in the ratification debate, see John P. Kaminski and Richard Leffler, *Federalists and Antifederalists: The Debate over the Ratification of the Constitution,* 2d ed. (Madison, Wis.: Madison House, 1998).

20. The concept of the separation of powers generally is credited to the French political philosopher Montesquieu (1689–1755), who included it in his monumental two-volume work entitled *The Spirit of the Laws,* published in 1748. See Charles de Montesquieu, *The Spirit of the Laws*, ed. Anne M. Cohler, Basia Carolyn Miller, and Harold Samuel Stone (Cambridge: Cambridge University Press, 1989).

21. The Constitution does not explicitly mention the power of judicial review, but the delegates at the Constitutional Convention probably assumed that the courts would have this power. Indeed, Alexander Hamilton, in *Federalist Paper* No. 78, explicitly outlined the concept of judicial review. In any event, whether the founders intended for the courts to exercise this power is a moot point, because in an 1803 decision, *Marbury v. Madison,* the Supreme Court successfully claimed this power for the courts—see Chapter 14.

22. An amendment concerning compensation of members of Congress became the Twenty-seventh Amendment to the Constitution when it was ratified 203 years later, in 1992.

23. The Twenty-first Amendment repealed the Eighteenth Amendment, which had prohibited the manufacture or sale of alcoholic beverages nationwide (Prohibition). Special conventions were necessary because prohibitionist forces controlled legislatures in many states where a majority of the voters supported repeal.

Chapter 3

1. The federal models used by the German and Canadian governments provide interesting comparisons with the U.S. system. See Arthur B. Gunlicks, *The Länder and German Federalism* (Manchester, England: Manchester University Press, 2003); and Jennifer Smith, *Federalism* (Vancouver: University of British Columbia Press, 2004).

2. Text of an address by the president to the National Conference of State Legislatures, Atlanta, Georgia (Washington, D.C.: The White House, Office of the Press Secretary, July 30, 1981).

3. Until the 1960s, U.S. paper currency—known informally as greenbacks—could be redeemed (in peacetime) for an equivalent value in silver. In 1964, the Treasury stopped issuing new silver-backed notes, and in 1968 it halted silver redemption for older notes as well. Today, you can "redeem" an old dollar bill—for a freshly printed one.

4. 133 S.Ct. 2675 (2013).

5. 135 S.Ct. 2584 (2015).

6. An excellent illustration of this principle was President Dwight Eisenhower's disciplining of Arkansas governor Orval Faubus when Faubus refused to allow a Little Rock high school to be desegregated in 1957. Eisenhower federalized the National Guard to enforce the court-ordered desegregation of the school.

7. 5 U.S. 137 (1803).

8. 17 U.S. 316 (1819).

9. 22 U.S. 1 (1824).

10. *Hammer v. Dagenhart,* 247 U.S. 251 (1918). This decision was overturned in *United States v. Darby,* 312 U.S. 100 (1941).

11. *Wickard v. Filburn,* 317 U.S. 111 (1942).

12. *McLain v. Real Estate Board of New Orleans, Inc.,* 444 U.S. 232 (1980).

13. 514 U.S. 549 (1995).

14. *Printz v. United States,* 521 U.S. 898 (1997).

15. *United States v. Morrison,* 529 U.S. 598 (2000).

16. 549 U.S. 497 (2007).

17. 567 U.S. ___ (2012).

18. 132 S.Ct. 2566 (2012).

19. 570 U.S. ___ (2013).

Chapter 4

1. 32 U.S. 243 (1833).

2. *Yamataya v. Fischer,* 189 U.S. 86 (1903).

3. *Reno v. American-Arab Anti-Discrimination Committee,* 325 U.S. 471 (1999).

4. 134 S.Ct. 1811.

5. *Everson v. Board of Education,* 330 U.S. 1 (1947).

6. 370 U.S. 421 (1962).

7. *Stone v. Graham,* 449 U.S. 39 (1980).

8. *Wallace v. Jaffree,* 472 U.S. 38 (1985).

9. See, for example, *Brown v. Gwinnett County School District,* 112 F.3d 1464 (1997).

10. *Santa Fe Independent School District v. Doe,* 530 U.S. 290 (2000).

11. *Epperson v. Arkansas,* 393 U.S. 97 (1968).

12. *Edwards v. Aguillard,* 482 U.S. 578 (1987).

13. *Kitzmiller v. Dover Area School District,* 400 F. Supp.2d 707 (M.D.Pa. 2005).

14. 403 U.S. 602 (1971).

15. In addition, Maine and Vermont have long-standing voucher programs for students in school districts that are too small to support a high school. These vouchers can only be used to attend schools in neighboring public school districts.

16. *Zelman v. Simmons-Harris,* 536 U.S. 639 (2002).

17. *Holmes v. Bush* (Fla.Cir.Ct. 2002). For details about this case, see David Royse, "Judge Rules School Voucher Law Violates Florida Constitution," *USA Today,* August 6, 2002, p. 7D.

18. 98 U.S. 145 (1878).

19. *Police v. City of Newark,* 170 F.3d 359 (3d Cir. 1999).

20. *Equal Employment Opportunity Commission v. Abercrombie & Fitch Stores,* 575 U.S. ___ (2015).

21. 134 S.Ct. 2751 (2014).

22. *Schenck v. United States,* 249 U.S. 47 (1919).

23. The bad tendency test was used later in a famous 1925 case, *Gitlow v. New York* (268 U.S. 652).

24. *Schenck v. United States, op cit.*

25. *Brandenburg v. Ohio,* 395 U.S. 444 (1969).

26. *Liquormart v. Rhode Island,* 517 U.S. 484 (1996).

27. 413 U.S. 15 (1973).

28. *Reno v. American Civil Liberties Union,* 521 U.S. 844 (1997); and *Ashcroft v. American Civil Liberties Union,* 542 U.S. 656 (2004). In *United States v. American Library Association,* 539 U.S. 194 (2003), the Court finally found that the government could require libraries that received certain federal subsidies to install filtering software to prevent minors from viewing pornographic material. The filters could be turned off at adult request. The subsidies were small, however, and about one-third of libraries nationwide rejected them and did not install the software.

29. *Morse v. Frederick,* 551 U.S. 393 (2007).

30. See, for example, *Doe v. University of Michigan,* 721 F.Supp. 852 (1989).

31. *Hazelwood School District v. Kuhlmeier,* 484 U.S. 260 (1988).

32. Brandeis made this statement in a dissenting opinion in *Olmstead v. United States,* 277 U.S. 438 (1928).

33. 381 U.S. 479 (1965). In this case, the Supreme Court found that Connecticut could not ban birth control methods.

34. 410 U.S. 113 (1973). Jane Roe was not the real name of the woman in this case. It is a common legal pseudonym used to protect a party's privacy.

35. See, for example, the Supreme Court's decision in *Lambert v. Wicklund,* 520 U.S. 1169 (1997). The Court held that a Montana law requiring a minor to notify one of her parents before getting an abortion was constitutional.

36. *Schenck v. ProChoice Network,* 519 U.S. 357 (1997); and *Hill v. Colorado,* 530 U.S. 703 (2000).

37. *McCullen v. Coakley,* 573 U.S. ___ (2014).

38. *Stenberg v. Carhart,* 530 U.S. 914 (2000).

39. *Gonzales v. Carhart,* 550 U.S. 124 (2007).

40. *Washington v. Glucksberg,* 521 U.S. 702 (1997).

41. *Gonzales v. Oregon,* 546 U.S. 243 (2006).

42. The state of South Carolina challenged the constitutionality of this act, claiming that the law violated states' rights under the Tenth Amendment. The Supreme Court, however, held that Congress had the authority, under its commerce power, to pass the act because drivers' personal information had become an article of interstate commerce. *Reno v. Condon,* 528 U.S. 141 (2000).

43. *Sorrell v. IMS Health,* 131 S.Ct. 2653 (2011).

44. 372 U.S. 335 (1963).

45. *Mapp v. Ohio,* 367 U.S. 643 (1961).

46. *Riley v. California,* 134 S.Ct. 2473 (2014).

47. 384 U.S. 436 (1966). In 1968, Congress passed legislation including a provision that reinstated the previous rule that statements made by defendants can be used against them as long as the statements were made voluntarily. This provision was never enforced, however, and only in 1999 did a court try to enforce it. The case ultimately came before the Supreme Court, which held that the *Miranda* rights were based on the Constitution and thus could not be overruled by legislative act. See *Dickerson v. United States,* 530 U.S. 428 (2000).

48. *Arizona v. Fulminante,* 499 U.S. 279 (1991).

49. *Davis v. United States,* 512 U.S. 452 (1994).

50. *J.D.B. v. North Carolina,* 131 S.Ct. 2394 (2011).

51. Thomas P. Sullivan, *Police Experiences with Recording Custodial Interrogations* (Chicago: Northwestern University School of Law Center on Wrongful Convictions, Summer 2004), p. 4.

Chapter 5

1. *Michael M. v. Superior Court,* 450 U.S. 464 (1981).

2. See, for example, *Craig v. Boren,* 429 U.S. 190 (1976).

3. *Orr v. Orr,* 440 U.S. 268 (1979).

4. *Mississippi University for Women v. Hogan,* 458 U.S. 718 (1982).

5. 163 U.S. 537 (1896).

6. 347 U.S. 483 (1954).

7. 349 U.S. 294 (1955).

8. *Swann v. Charlotte-Mecklenburg Board of Education,* 402 U.S. 1 (1971).

9. *Keyes v. School District No. 1,* 413 U.S. 189 (1973).

10. *Milliken v. Bradley,* 418 U.S. 717 (1974).

11. *Riddick v. School Board of City of Norfolk,* 627 F.Supp. 814 (E.D.Va. 1984).

12. 570 U.S. ___ (2013).

13. *Ledbetter v. Goodyear Tire & Rubber Co.,* 550 U.S. 618 (2007).

14. Claudia Goldin, "A Grand Gender Convergence: Its Last Chapter," *American Economic Review* 104, no. 4 (2014): 1091–1119.

15. *Oncale v. Sundowner Offshore Services,* 523 U.S. 75 (1998).

16. *Faragher v. City of Boca Raton,* 524 U.S. 775 (1998).

17. The Supreme Court upheld these actions in *Hirabayashi v. United States,* 320 U.S. 81 (1943); and *Korematsu v. United States,* 323 U.S. 214 (1944).

18. Historians in the early and mid-twentieth century gave much smaller figures for the pre-Columbian population—as low as 14 million people for the entire New World. Today, 40 million is considered a conservative estimate, and an estimate of 100 million has much support among demographers. If 100 million is correct, the epidemics that followed the arrival of the Europeans killed one out of every five people alive in the world at that time. See Charles C. Mann, *1491* (New York: Vintage, 2006).

19. *County of Oneida, New York v. Oneida Indian Nation,* 470 U.S. 226 (1985).

20. *Sutton v. United Airlines,* 527 U.S. 471 (1999); and *Toyota v. Williams,* 534 U.S. 184 (2002).

21. *Board of Trustees of the University of Alabama v. Garrett,* 531 U.S. 356 (2001).

22. 539 U.S. 558 (2003).

23. 517 U.S. 620 (1996).

24. 576 U.S. ___ (2015).

25. *Goodridge v. Department of Public Health,* 798 N.E.2d 941 (Mass. 2003).

26. 133 S.Ct. 2675 (2013).

27. *Log Cabin Republicans v. United States,* 716 F.Supp.2d 884 (C.D.Cal. 2010).

28. 438 U.S. 265 (1978).

29. 515 U.S. 200 (1995).

30. 539 U.S. 244 (2003).

31. 539 U.S. 306 (2003).

32. *Parents Involved in Community Schools v. Seattle School District No. 1,* 551 U.S. 701 (2007).

33. 133 S.Ct. 2411 (2013) and 579 U.S. ___ (2016).

34. *Schuette v. Coalition to Defend Affirmative Action,* 134 S.Ct. 1623 (2014).

Chapter 6

1. Marco Werman and Mary Kay Magistad, "China Past Due: Land Rights," Public Radio International (PRI), May 1, 2013 (www.pri.org/stories/2013-05-01/china-past-due-land-rights).

2. David Bicknell Truman, *The Governmental Process: Political Interests and Public Opinion* (Santa Barbara, Calif.: Praeger, 1981). This work is a political science classic.

3. Robert H. Salisbury, *Interests and Institutions: Substance and Structure in American Politics* (Pittsburgh: University of Pittsburgh Press, 1992).

4. Phillip Bradley, ed., *Democracy in America*, Vol. 1 (New York: Knopf, 1980), p. 191.

5. Mancur Olson, *The Logic of Collective Action: Public Goods and the Theory of Groups*, rev. ed. (Cambridge, Mass.: Harvard University Press, 1971).

6. Martin Gilens and Benjamin I. Page, "Testing Theories of American Politics: Elites, Interest Groups, and Average Citizens," *Perspectives on Politics* 12, no. 3 (Fall 2014).

7. 558 U.S. 50 (2010).

8. 132 S.Ct. 2492 (2012).

9. *Caperton v. A. T. Massey Coal Co.*, 556 U.S. 868 (2009).

10. *United States v. Harriss*, 347 U.S. 612 (1954).

Chapter 7

1. Letter to Francis Hopkinson written from Paris while Jefferson was ambassador to France, as cited in John P. Foley, ed., *The Jeffersonian Cyclopedia* (New York: Russell & Russell, 1967), p. 677.

2. The U.S. Senate presents the text of the address at www.access.gpo.gov/congress/senate/farewell/sd106-21.pdf.

3. The association of red with the Republicans and blue with the Democrats is little more than a decade old. The terms *red* and *blue* are derived from the colors used by the major television networks to show the states carried by the Republican and Democratic presidential candidates. This use of colors deliberately reverses a traditional pattern. In most European countries, the right-of-center party uses blue, while the left-of-center party employs red. The use of red originated in the socialist movement, from which most European left-of-center parties descend. From time to time, Republicans have accused Democrats of socialism. U.S. television networks thus assigned red to the Republicans precisely so that the networks would not appear to be endorsing that accusation.

4. Theda Skocpol and Vanessa Williamson, *The Tea Party and the Remaking of Republican Conservatism* (New York: Oxford University Press, 2013).

5. John B. Judis and Ruy Teixeira, *The Emerging Democratic Majority* (New York: Scribner, 2002).

6. Matt Grossmann and David A. Hopkins, "Ideological Republicans and Group Interest Democrats: The Asymmetry of American Party Politics," *Perspectives on Politics* 13, no. 1 (March 2015): 119–139.

7. For an interesting discussion of the pros and cons of patronage from a constitutional perspective, see the majority opinion versus the dissent in the Supreme Court case *Board of County Commissioners v. Umbehr*, 518 U.S. 668 (1996).

8. The term *third party*, although not literally accurate (because sometimes there has been a fourth party, a fifth party, and even more), is commonly used to refer to a minor party.

9. Today, ten states have multimember districts for their state houses, and a handful also have multimember districts for their state senates.

Chapter 8

1. Doris A. Graber, *Mass Media and American Politics*, 9th ed. (Washington, D.C.: CQ Press, 2014).

2. The elections that Gallup predicted incorrectly were usually close ones. In 2004, Gallup reported a statistical tie—49 percent each—between Republican George W. Bush and Democrat John Kerry. In 1976, Gallup falsely predicted that Republican incumbent Gerald Ford would prevail over Democrat Jimmy Carter. In 1948, Gallup wrongly predicted that Republican Thomas Dewey would defeat Democratic incumbent Harry Truman. The 2012 elections, however, may have been Gallup's biggest embarrassment to date. Assuming very low Democratic voter turnout, Gallup had Romney well in the lead throughout October. It corrected its last poll to reflect greater turnout, but it still predicted a Romney victory.

3. John M. Benson, "When Is an Opinion Really an Opinion?" *Public Perspective*, September/October 2001, pp. 40–41.

4. As quoted in Karl G. Feld, "When Push Comes to Shove: A Polling Industry Call to Arms," *Public Perspective*, September/October 2001, p. 38.

5. Pew Research Center for the People and the Press, survey conducted September 21–October 4, 2006 and reported in "Who Votes, Who Doesn't, and Why," released October 28, 2006.

6. *Guinn v. United States*, 238 U.S. 347 (1915).

7. *Smith v. Allwright*, 321 U.S. 649 (1944).

8. *Veasey v. Abbott*, 815 F.3d 958 (2016).

9. For more information on voting systems, see the website of verifiedvoting.org.

10. The argument about the vote-eligible population was first made by Michael P. McDonald and Samuel L. Popkin, "The Myth of the Vanishing Voter," *American Political Science Review*, 95, no. 4 (December 2001), p. 963.

Chapter 9

1. These states award one electoral vote to the candidate who wins the popular vote in a congressional district and an additional two electoral votes to the winner of the statewide popular vote. Other states have considered similar plans.

2. The word *caucus* apparently was first used in the name of a men's club, the Caucus Club of colonial Boston, sometime between 1755 and 1765. (Many early political and government meetings took place in pubs.) We have no certain knowledge of the origin of the word, but it may be from an Algonquin term meaning "elder" or from the Latin name of a drinking vessel.

3. Today, the Democratic and Republican caucuses in the House and Senate (the Republicans now use the term *conference* instead of *caucus*) choose each party's congressional leadership and sometimes discuss legislation and legislative strategy.

4. Due to the customs of the time, none of the candidates could admit that he had made a personal decision to run. All claimed to have entered the race in response to popular demand.

5. Parties cannot use their freedom-of-association rights to practice racial discrimination in state-sponsored elections: *Smith v. Allwright*, 321 U.S. 649 (1944). When racial discrimination is not involved, the parties have regularly won freedom-of-association suits against state governments. Examples are *Tashjian v. Republican Party of Connecticut*, 479 U.S. 208 (1986), and *California Democratic Party v. Jones*, 530 U.S. 567 (2000).

6. In Washington, the state government holds presidential primaries for both parties. The Democratic Party, however, ignores the Democratic primary and chooses its national convention delegates through a caucus/convention system. In 1984, following a dispute with the state of Michigan over primary rules, the state Democratic Party organized a presidential primary election that was run completely by party volunteers. In 2008, after a similar dispute with its state, the Virginia Republican Party chose its candidate for the U.S. Senate at its state party convention instead of through the Virginia primary elections.

7. The case was *California Democratic Party v. Jones*, cited in footnote 5.

8. *Washington State Grange v. Washington State Republican Party et al.*, 552 U.S. 442 (2008).

9. See Marty Cohen, David Karol, Hans Noel, and John Zaller, *The Party Decides: Presidential Nominations Before and After Reform* (Chicago: University of Chicago Press, 2008). This enormously influential work argued that party leaders usually determine primary outcomes. Donald Trump's political career placed this theory into question.

10. These numbers are from the website www.twitteraudit.com. This site calculates which followers of a Twitter account are actual human beings, as opposed to Internet "bots" or other artifacts. Twitter "fakes" are surprisingly common. Among top politicians, the percentage of total followers who are not real people ranges from 36 percent for Trump to 11 percent for Sanders.

11. This act is sometimes referred to as the Federal Election Campaign Act of 1972 because it became effective in that year. The official date of the act, however, is 1971.

12. *Buckley v. Valeo*, 424 U.S. 1 (1976).

13. This figure is from the Center for Responsive Politics.

14. *Colorado Republican Federal Campaign Committee v. Federal Election Commission*, 518 U.S. 604 (1996).

15. Quoted in George Will, "The First Amendment on Trial," *The Washington Post*, December 1, 2002, p. B7.

16. 540 U.S. 93 (2003).

17. 551 U.S. 449 (2007).

18. 558 U.S. 50 (2010).

19. 599 F.3d 686 (D.C.Cir. 2010).

20. 134 S.Ct. 1434.

21. *NAACP v. Alabama*, 357 U.S. 449 (1958).

Chapter 10

1. *Mutual Film Corporation v. Industrial Commission of Ohio*, 236 U.S. 230 (1915).

2. *Joseph Burstyn, Inc. v. Wilson*, 343 U.S. 495 (1952).

3. *Reno v. American Civil Liberties Union*, 521 U.S. 844 (1997).

4. *United States v. Playboy Entertainment Group*, 529 U.S. 803 (2000).

5. Bernard Cohen, *The Press and Foreign Policy* (Princeton, N.J.: Princeton University Press, 1963), p. 81.

6. As quoted in Michael Grunwald, "The Year of Playing Dirtier," *Washington Post*, October 27, 2006, p. A1.

7. John G. Geer, *In Defense of Negativity: Attack Ads in Presidential Campaigns* (Chicago: University of Chicago Press, 2006).

8. The commission's action was upheld by a federal court. See *Perot v. Federal Election Commission*, 97 F.3d 553 (D.C.Cir. 1996).

9. For more details on how political candidates manage news coverage, see Doris A. Graber, *Mass Media and American Politics*, 7th ed. (Washington, D.C.: CQ Press, 2005).

10. For suggestions on how to dissect spin and detect when language is steering one toward a conclusion, see Brooks Jackson and Kathleen Hall Jamieson, *unSpun: Finding Facts in a World of Disinformation* (New York: Random House, 2007).

11. *Red Lion Broadcasting Co. v. FCC*, 395 U.S. 367 (1969).

12. Kathleen Hall Jamieson, *Everything You Think You Know about Politics . . . and Why You're Wrong* (New York: Basic Books, 2000), pp. 187–195.

13. Debra Reddin van Tuyll and Hubert P. van Tuyll, "Political Partisanship," in William David Sloan and Jenn Burleson Mackay, eds., *Media Bias: Finding It, Fixing It* (Jefferson, N.C.: McFarland, 2007), pp. 35–49.

14. Jamieson, *Everything You Think You Know about Politics*, pp. xiii–xiv.

15. The term *podcasting* is used for this type of information delivery because initially podcasts were downloaded onto Apple's iPods.

Chapter 11

1. These states are Alaska, Delaware, Montana, North Dakota, South Dakota, Vermont, and Wyoming.

2. In June 2015, the United States Supreme Court upheld the right of state voters to transfer redistricting to independent commissions. Voters can do this even if the state legislature objects. See *Arizona State Legislature v. Arizona Independent Redistricting Commission*, 576 U.S. _____ (2015).

3. *Baker v. Carr*, 369 U.S. 186 (1962).

4. *Wesberry v. Sanders,* 376 U.S. 1 (1964).

5. See, for example, *Davis v. Bandemer*, 478 U.S. 109 (1986).

6. *Amicus curiae* brief filed by the American Civil Liberties Union (ACLU) in support of the appellants in *Easley v. Cromartie*, 532 U.S. 234 (2001).

7. See, for example, *Shaw v. Reno*, 509 U.S. 630 (1993); *Miller v. Johnson*, 515 U.S. 900 (1995); *Shaw v. Hunt*, 517 U.S. 899 (1996); and *Bush v. Vera*, 517 U.S. 952 (1996).

8. *Easley v. Cromartie*, 532 U.S. 234 (2001).

9. *Powell v. McCormack*, 395 U.S. 486 (1969).

10. Some observers maintain that another reason Congress stays in session longer is the invention of air-conditioning. Until the advent of air-conditioning, no member of Congress wanted to stay in session during the hot and sticky late spring, summer, and early fall months in Washington, D.C.

11. *U.S. Term Limits, Inc. v. Thornton*, 514 U.S. 779 (1995).

12. A term used by Woodrow Wilson in *Congressional Government* (New York: Meridian Books, 1956 [first published in 1885]).

Chapter 12

1. Lyndon B. Johnson, *The Vantage Point: Perspectives of the Presidency, 1963–1969* (New York: Henry Holt & Co., 1971).

2. Four presidents have been Unitarians, members of a church directly descended from the (Protestant) Massachusetts Puritans. Because Unitarianism is not strictly Christian, however, it cannot be called Protestant either. Mitt Romney, if elected in 2012, would have been the first Mormon president. Some may consider the Mormons, or Latter-Day Saints, to be in the Protestant tradition, but their theology differs radically from that of both Protestant and Catholic Christianity.

3. *Ex parte Grossman*, 267 U.S. 87 (1925).

4. *Clinton v. City of New York*, 524 U.S. 417 (1998).

5. Woodrow Wilson, *Constitutional Government in the United States* (1908; repr., Washington, D.C.: Woodrow Wilson Press, 2008), p. 70.

6. The Constitution does not grant the president explicit power to remove from office officials who are not performing satisfactorily or who do not agree with the president. In 1926, however, the Supreme Court prevented Congress from interfering with the president's ability to fire those executive-branch officials whom he had appointed with Senate approval. See *Myers v. United States*, 272 U.S. 52 (1926).

7. Ironically, Lincoln believed that the actions of the president ought to be strictly limited when war powers were not concerned. He therefore left most domestic issues that did not involve the war entirely to Congress. In doing so, Lincoln was true to the ideas of his former party, the Whigs. That party advocated a limited role for the presidency in reaction to the sweeping assumption of authority by President Andrew Jackson, their great opponent. See David Donald's classic essay "Abraham Lincoln: Whig in the White House," in *Lincoln Reconsidered: Essays on the Civil War Era*, 3d ed. (New York: Vintage, 2001), pp. 133–147.

8. Richard E. Neustadt, *Presidential Power: The Politics of Leadership* (New York: John Wiley, 1960), p. 10.

9. As quoted in Richard M. Pious, *The American Presidency* (New York: Basic Books, 1979), pp. 51–52.

10. A phrase coined by Samuel Kernell in *Going Public: New Strategies of Presidential Leadership*, 4th ed. (Washington, D.C.: Congressional Quarterly Press, 2006).

11. Christopher S. Kelley and Bryan W. Marshall, "Assessing Presidential Power: Signing Statements and Veto Threats as Coordinated Strategies," *American Politics Research* 37, no. 3 (May 2009): 508.

12. Congress used its power to declare war in the War of 1812, the Mexican War (1846–1848), the Spanish-American War (1898), and World War I (U.S. involvement lasted from 1916 until 1918) and on six different occasions during World War II (U.S. involvement lasted from 1941 until 1945).

13. As quoted in Thomas E. Cronin, *The State of the Presidency*, 2d ed. (Boston: Little, Brown, 1980), p. 11.

Chapter 13

1. This definition follows the classic model of bureaucracy put forth by German sociologist Max Weber. See Max Weber, *Theory of Social and Economic Organization*, ed. Talcott Parsons (New York: Oxford University Press, 1974).

2. It should be noted that although the president is technically the head of the bureaucracy, the president cannot always control the bureaucracy—as you will read later in this chapter.

3. Maury Gittleman and Brooks Pierce, "Compensation for State and Local Government Workers," *Journal of Economic Perspectives* 26, no. 1 (Winter 2012), pp. 217–242 (www.aeaweb.org/articles.php?doi=10.1257/jep.26.1.217).

4. Chris Edwards, "Reducing the Costs of Federal Worker Pay and Benefits," October 1, 2015 (www.downsizinggovernment.org/federal-worker-pay).

5. Alicia Munnell, Jean-Pierre Aubry, Josh Hurwitz, and Laura Quinby, *Comparing Compensation: State-Local versus Private Sector Workers*, Center for Retirement Research at Boston College, September 2011 (slge.org/publications/comparing-compensation-state-local-versus-private-sectorworkers).

6. Congressional Budget Office, "Comparing the Compensation of Federal and Private-Sector Employees," January 30, 2012 (www.cbo.gov/publication/42921).

7. For an insightful analysis of the policymaking process in Washington, D.C., and the role played by various groups in the process, see Morton H. Halperin and Priscilla A. Clapp, with Arnold Kanter, *Bureaucratic Politics and Foreign Policy*, 2d ed. (Washington, D.C.: The Brookings Institution, 2006). Although the focus of the book is on foreign policy, the analysis applies in many ways to the general policymaking process.

Chapter 14

1. 347 U.S. 483 (1954).

2. See *Plessy v. Ferguson*, 163 U.S. 537 (1896).

3. 558 U.S. 310 (2010).

4. *Austin v. Michigan Chamber of Commerce*, 494 U.S. 652 (1990) and *McConnell v. Federal Election Commission*, 540 U.S. 93 (2003).

5. Although a state's highest court is often referred to as the state supreme court, there are exceptions. In the New York court system, for example, the supreme court is a trial court, and the highest court is called the New York Court of Appeals.

6. Between 1790 and 1891, Congress allowed the Supreme Court almost no discretion over which cases to decide. After 1925, in almost 95 percent of appealed cases the Court could choose whether to hear arguments and issue an opinion. Beginning in October 1988, mandatory review was nearly eliminated.

7. *West Virginia v. EPA* (pending).

8. *United States v. Texas*, 579 U.S. ___ (2016).

9. *Friedrichs v. California Teachers Association*, 578 U.S. ___ (2016).

10. *Whole Woman's Health v. Hellerstedt*, 579 U.S. ___ (2016).

11. 135 S.Ct. 2584 (2015).

12. 347 U.S. 483 (1954).

13. 5 U.S. 137 (1803). The Supreme Court had considered the constitutionality of an act of Congress in *Hylton v. United States*, 3 U.S. 171 (1796), in which Congress's power to levy certain taxes was challenged. That particular act was ruled constitutional, rather than unconstitutional, however, so this first federal exercise of judicial review was not clearly recognized as such. Also, during the decade before the adoption of the federal Constitution, courts in at least eight states had exercised the power of judicial review.

14. *King v. Burwell*, 135 S.Ct. 2480 (2015).

15. 539 U.S. 558 (2003).

16. 135 S.Ct. 2584 (2015).

17. Antonin Scalia, *A Matter of Interpretation: Federal Courts and the Law* (Princeton, N.J.: Princeton University Press, 1997).

18. Letter by Thomas Jefferson to William C. Jarvis, 1820, in Andrew A. Lipscomb and Albert Ellery Bergh, *The Writings of Thomas Jefferson,* Memorial Edition (Washington, D.C.: Thomas Jefferson Memorial Association of the United States, 1904).

19. As quoted in Carl Hulse and David D. Kirkpatrick, "DeLay Says Federal Judiciary Has 'Run Amok,' Adding Congress Is Partly to Blame," *New York Times,* April 8, 2005, p. 5.

Chapter 15

1. Stan Dorn, *Uninsured and Dying Because of It: Updating the Institute of Medicine Analysis on the Impact of Uninsurance on Mortality* (Washington, D.C.: Urban Institute, 2008).

2. *National Federation of Independent Business v. Sebelius,* 132 S.Ct. 2566 (2012).

3. *King v. Burwell,* 135 S.Ct. 2480 (2015).

4. A recent investigation has shown that hydraulic fracturing that takes place deep underground has no effect on underground water sources used for human consumption. The distance is too great. However, contamination *is* possible if the pipes leading down to the fracking are not properly sealed. A second study has linked the underground disposal of wastewater generated by fracking to an increase in the number of small earthquakes. Fracking itself rarely induces quakes.

5. Paul Krugman, "Romer and Bernstein on Stimulus," in the blog *Conscience of a Liberal, New York Times,* January 10, 2009.

Chapter 16

1. *Public Papers of the Presidents of the United States: Harry S. Truman, 1947* (Washington, D.C.: U.S. Government Printing Office, 1963), pp. 176–180.

2. The containment policy was outlined by George F. Kennan, the chief of the policy-planning staff for the Department of State at that time, in an article that appeared in *Foreign Affairs,* July 1947, p. 575. The author's name was given as "X."

3. Antiwar bombings differed from more recent ones: Antiwar bombers made a general practice of phoning in warnings with the goal of preventing casualties. In most cases, the warnings were successful. The right-wing bombers of the 1990s and today's jihadi terrorists, in contrast, clearly have sought to kill as many people as possible.

GLOSSARY

A

adjudicate To render a judicial decision. In administrative law, it is the process in which an administrative law judge hears and decides issues that arise when an agency charges a person or firm with violating a law or regulation enforced by the agency.

administrative law The body of law created by administrative agencies (in the form of rules, regulations, orders, and decisions) in order to carry out their duties and responsibilities.

affirmative action A policy that gives special consideration, in jobs and college admissions, to members of groups that have been discriminated against in the past.

agenda setting The ability to determine which issues are considered important by the public and by politicians.

agents of political socialization People and institutions that influence the political views of others.

Anti-Federalists A political group that opposed the adoption of the Constitution.

appellate court A court having appellate jurisdiction. An appellate court normally does not hear evidence or testimony. Instead, it reviews the transcript of the trial court's proceedings, other records relating to the case, and attorneys' arguments as to why the trial court's decision should or should not stand.

apportionment The distribution of House seats among the states on the basis of their respective populations.

appropriation A part of the congressional budgeting process—the determination of how many dollars will be spent in a given year on a particular government activity.

Articles of Confederation The nation's first constitution, which established a national form of government following the American Revolution. The Articles provided for a confederal form of government in which the central government had few powers.

Australian ballot A secret ballot that is prepared, distributed, and counted by government officials at public expense; used by all states in the United States since 1888.

authority The ability to legitimately exercise power, such as the power to make and enforce laws.

authorization A part of the congressional budgeting process—the creation of the legal basis for government programs.

autocracy A form of government in which the power and authority of the government are in the hands of a single person.

B

biased sample A poll sample that does not accurately represent the population.

bicameral legislature A legislature made up of two chambers, or parts.

bill of attainder A legislative act that inflicts punishment on particular persons or groups without granting them the right to a trial.

Bill of Rights The first ten amendments to the U.S. Constitution. They list the freedoms—such as the freedoms of speech, press, and religion—that a citizen enjoys and that cannot be infringed on by the government.

block grant A federal grant given to a state for a broad area, such as criminal justice or mental-health programs.

bureaucracy A large, complex, hierarchically structured administrative organization that carries out specific functions.

bureaucrat An individual who works in a bureaucracy. As generally used, the term refers to a government employee.

busing The transportation of public school students by bus to schools physically outside their neighborhoods to eliminate school segregation based on residential patterns.

C

cabinet An advisory group selected by the president to assist with decision making. Traditionally, the cabinet has consisted of the heads of the executive departments and other officers whom the president may choose to appoint.

campaign strategy The comprehensive plan developed by a candidate and his or her advisers for winning an election.

capitalism An economic system based on the private ownership of wealth-producing property, free markets, and freedom of contract. The privately owned corporation is the preeminent capitalist institution.

case law The rules of law announced in court decisions. Case law includes the aggregate of reported cases that interpret judicial precedents, statutes, regulations, and constitutional provisions.

categorical grant A federal grant targeted for a specific purpose as defined by federal law.

caucus A meeting held to choose political candidates or delegates.

checks and balances A major principle of American government in which each of the three branches is given the means to check (to restrain or balance) the actions of the others.

chief diplomat The role of the president of the United States in recognizing and interacting with foreign governments.

chief executive The head of the executive branch of government; in the United States, the president.

chief of staff The person who directs the operations of the White House Office and advises the president on important matters.

Children's Health Insurance Program (CHIP) A joint federal–state program that provides health-care insurance for low-income children.

citizen journalism The collection, analysis, and dissemination of information online by independent journalists, scholars, politicians, and the general citizenry.

civil disobedience The deliberate and public act of refusing to obey laws thought to be unjust.

civil law The branch of law that spells out the duties that individuals in society owe to other persons or to their governments, excluding the duty not to commit crimes.

civil liberties Individual rights protected by the Constitution against the powers of the government.

civil rights movement The movement in the 1950s and 1960s, by minorities and concerned whites, to end racial discrimination.

civil rights The rights of all Americans to equal treatment under the law, as provided by the Fourteenth Amendment to the Constitution.

civil service Nonmilitary government employees.

climate change The increase in the average temperature of the Earth's surface over the last half century and its projected continuation; also referred to as *global warming*.

closed primary A primary in which only party members can vote to choose that party's candidates.

cloture A procedure for ending filibusters in the Senate and bringing the matter under consideration to a vote.

coalition An alliance of individuals or groups with a variety of interests and opinions who join together to support all or part of a political party's platform.

coalition An alliance of nations formed to undertake a foreign policy action, particularly a military action. A coalition is often a temporary alliance that dissolves after the action is concluded.

Cold War The war of words, warnings, and ideologies between the Soviet Union and the United States that lasted from the late 1940s through the late 1980s.

colonial empire A group of dependent nations that are under the rule of an imperial power.

commander in chief The supreme commander of a nation's military force.

commerce clause The clause in Article I, Section 8, of the Constitution that gives Congress the power to regulate interstate commerce (commerce involving more than one state).

commercial speech Advertising statements that describe products. Commercial speech receives less protection under the First Amendment than ordinary speech.

common law The body of law developed from judicial decisions in English and U.S. courts, not attributable to a legislature.

competitive federalism A model of federalism in which state and local governments compete for businesses and citizens, who in effect "vote with their feet" by moving to jurisdictions that offer a competitive advantage.

concurrent powers Powers held by both the federal and the state governments in a federal system.

concurring opinion A statement written by a judge or justice who agrees (concurs) with the court's decision, but for reasons different from those in the majority opinion.

confederal system A league of independent sovereign states, joined together by a central government that has only limited powers over them.

confederation A league of independent states that are united only for the purpose of achieving common goals.

conference committee A temporary committee that is formed when the two chambers of Congress pass differing versions of the same bill. The conference committee consists of members from the House and the Senate who work out a compromise bill.

conference In regard to the Supreme Court, a private meeting of the justices in which they present their arguments concerning a case under consideration.

conference report A report submitted by a conference committee after it has drafted a single version of a bill.

congressional district The geographic area that is served by one member in the House of Representatives.

conservatism A set of political beliefs that include a limited role for the national government in helping individuals and in the economic affairs of the nation, as well as support for traditional values and lifestyles.

conservative movement An ideological movement that arose in the 1950s and 1960s and continues to shape conservative beliefs.

Constitutional Convention The convention of delegates from the states that was held in Philadelphia in 1787 for the purpose of amending the Articles of Confederation. In fact, the delegates wrote a new constitution (the U.S. Constitution) that established a federal form of government.

constitutional law Law based on the U.S. Constitution and the constitutions of the various states.

containment A U.S. policy designed to contain the spread of communism by offering military and economic aid to threatened nations.

contempt of court A ruling that a person has disobeyed a court order or has shown disrespect to the court or to a judicial proceeding.

continuing resolution A temporary resolution passed by Congress that enables executive agencies to continue working with the same funding that they had in the previous fiscal year.

cooperative federalism A model of federalism in which the states and the federal government cooperate in solving problems.

Credentials Committee A committee of each national political party that evaluates the claims of national party convention delegates to be the legitimate representatives of their states.

criminal law The branch of law that defines and governs actions that constitute crimes. Generally, criminal law has to do with wrongful actions committed against society for which society demands redress.

cross-cutting requirements Requirements that apply to all federal grants.

Cuban missile crisis A nuclear standoff that occurred in 1962 when the United States learned that the Soviet Union had placed nuclear warheads in Cuba.

D

dealignment Among voters, a growing detachment from both major political parties.

de facto segregation Racial segregation that occurs not as a result of government actions but because of social and economic conditions and residential patterns.

de jure segregation Racial segregation that occurs because of laws or decisions by government agencies.

delegate A person selected to represent the people of one geographic area at a party convention.

democracy A system of government in which the people have ultimate political authority. The word is derived from the Greek demos ("the people") and kratia ("rule").

détente A French word meaning a "relaxation of tensions." Détente characterized the relationship between the United States and the Soviet Union in the 1970s as they attempted to pursue cooperative dealings and arms control.

deterrence A policy of building up military strength for the purpose of discouraging (deterring) military attacks by other nations; the policy that supported the arms race between the United States and the Soviet Union during the Cold War.

devolution The surrender or transfer of powers to local authorities by a central government.

dictatorship A form of government in which absolute power is exercised by an individual or group whose power is not supported by tradition.

diplomat A person who represents one country in dealing with representatives of another country.

direct democracy A system of government in which political decisions are made by the people themselves rather than by elected representatives. This form of government was practiced in some parts of ancient Greece.

direct primary An election held within each of the two major parties—Democratic and Republican—to choose the party's candidates for the general election. Voters choose the candidate directly, rather than through delegates.

direct technique Any method used by an interest group to interact with government officials directly to further the group's goals.

dissenting opinion A statement written by a judge or justice who disagrees with the majority opinion.

diversity of citizenship A basis for federal court jurisdiction over a lawsuit that arises when (1) the parties in the lawsuit live in different states or when one of the parties is a foreign government or a foreign citizen, and (2) the amount in controversy is more than $75,000.

divine right theory The theory that a monarch's right to rule was derived directly from God rather than from the consent of the people.

division of powers A basic principle of federalism established by the U.S. Constitution, by which powers are divided between the national and state governments.

domestic policy Public policy concerning issues within a national unit, such as national policy on health care or the economy.

double jeopardy The prosecution of a person twice for the same criminal offense; prohibited by the Fifth Amendment in all but a few circumstances.

dual federalism A system of government in which the federal and the state governments maintain diverse but sovereign powers.

due process clause The constitutional guarantee, set out in the Fifth and Fourteenth Amendments, that the government will not illegally or arbitrarily deprive a person of life, liberty, or property.

due process of law The requirement that the government use fair, reasonable, and standard procedures whenever it takes any legal action against an individual; required by the Fifth and Fourteenth Amendments.

E

earmark Spending provision inserted into legislation that benefits only a small number of people.

easy-money policy A monetary policy that involves stimulating the economy by expanding the rate of growth of the money supply.

economic policy All actions taken by the national government to address ups and downs in the nation's level of business activity.

electoral college The group of electors who are selected by the voters in each state to officially elect the president and vice president. The number of electors in each state is equal to the number of that state's representatives in both chambers of Congress.

electorate All of the citizens eligible to vote in a given election.

elector In American politics, a member of the electoral college.

electronic media Communication channels that involve electronic transmissions, such as radio, television, and the Internet.

elite theory The belief that the government is controlled by one or more elite groups.

enabling legislation A law enacted by a legislature to establish an administrative agency. Enabling legislation normally specifies the name, purpose, composition, and powers of the agency being created.

entitlement program A government program (such as Social Security) that allows, or entitles, a certain class of people (such as elderly persons) to receive benefits.

entitlement program A government program that provides benefits to all persons who meet specified requirements.

equality A concept that holds, at a minimum, that all people are entitled to equal protection under the law.

equal protection clause Section 1 of the Fourteenth Amendment, which says that no state shall "deny to any person within its jurisdiction the equal protection of the laws."

establishment clause The section of the First Amendment that prohibits Congress from passing laws "respecting an establishment of religion."

exclusionary rule A criminal procedural rule stating that illegally obtained evidence is not admissible in court.

executive agreement A binding international agreement, or pact, that is made between the president and another head of state and that does not require Senate approval.

Executive Office of the President (EOP) A group of staff agencies that assist the president in carrying out major duties.

executive order A presidential order to carry out a policy or policies described in a law passed by Congress.

executive privilege An inherent executive power claimed by presidents to withhold information from, or to refuse to appear before, Congress or the courts. The president can also accord the privilege to other executive officials.

ex post facto law A criminal law that punishes individuals for committing an act that was legal when the act was committed.

expressed powers Constitutional or statutory powers that are expressly provided for by the U.S. Constitution; also called *enumerated powers*.

F

faction A group of individuals forming a cohesive minority.

federalism A system of shared sovereignty between two levels of government—one national and one subnational—occupying the same geographic region.

Federalists A political group, led by Alexander Hamilton and John Adams, that supported the adoption of the Constitution and the creation of a federal form of government.

federal mandate A requirement in federal legislation that forces states and municipalities to comply with certain rules.

Federal Open Market Committee (FOMC) The most important body within the Federal Reserve System; decides how monetary policy should be carried out.

federal question A question that pertains to the U.S. Constitution, acts of Congress, or treaties. A federal question provides a basis for federal court jurisdiction.

federal system A form of government that provides for a division of powers between a central government and several regional governments.

feminism A doctrine advocating full political, economic, and social equality for women.

filibustering The Senate tradition of unlimited debate undertaken for the purpose of preventing action on a bill.

first budget resolution A budget resolution, which is supposed to be passed in May, that sets overall revenue goals and spending targets for the next fiscal year, beginning on October 1.

First Continental Congress A gathering of delegates from twelve of the thirteen colonies, held in 1774 to protest the Coercive Acts.

fiscal federalism The allocation of taxes collected by one level of government (typically the national government) to another level (typically state or local governments).

fiscal policy The use of changes in government expenditures and taxes to alter national economic variables.

fiscal year A twelve-month period that is established for bookkeeping or accounting purposes. The government's fiscal year runs from October 1 through September 30.

foreign policy A systematic and general plan that guides a country's attitudes and actions toward the rest of the world. Foreign policy includes all of the economic, military, commercial, and diplomatic positions and actions that a nation takes in its relationships with other countries.

fracking Technique for extracting oil or natural gas from underground rock by the high-power injection of a mixture of water, sand, and chemicals.

framing An agenda-setting technique that establishes the context of a media report. Framing can mean fitting events into a familiar story or filtering information through preconceived ideas.

free exercise clause The provision of the First Amendment stating that the government cannot pass laws "prohibiting the free exercise" of religion.

fundamental right A basic right of all Americans, such as First Amendment rights. Any law or action that prevents some group of persons from exercising a fundamental right is subject to the *strict scrutiny standard*.

G

gender gap The difference between the percentage of votes cast for a particular candidate by women and the percentage of votes cast for the same candidate by men.

general election A regularly scheduled election to choose the U.S. president, vice president, and senators and representatives in Congress. General elections are held in even-numbered years on the Tuesday after the first Monday in November.

gerrymandering The drawing of a legislative district's boundaries in such a way as to maximize the influence of a certain group or political party.

glass ceiling An invisible but real discriminatory barrier that prevents women and minorities from rising to top positions of power or responsibility.

GOP A nickname for the Republican Party—"grand old party."

government corporation An agency of the government that is run as a business enterprise. Such agencies engage primarily in commercial activities, produce revenues, and require greater flexibility than most government agencies have.

government The individuals and institutions that make society's rules and possess the power and authority to enforce those rules.

grandfather clause A clause in a state law that had the effect of restricting voting rights to those whose ancestors had voted before the 1860s. It was one of the techniques used in the South to prevent African Americans from exercising their right to vote.

Great Compromise A plan for a bicameral legislature in which one chamber would be based on population and the other chamber would represent each state equally. Also known as the Connecticut Compromise.

greenhouse gas A gas that, when released into the atmosphere, traps the sun's heat and slows its release into outer space. Carbon dioxide (CO_2) is a major example.

H

head of state The person who serves as the ceremonial head of a country's government and represents that country to the rest of the world.

house effect In the case of a polling firm, a consistent tendency to report results more favorable to one of the political parties than the results reported by other pollsters.

I

ideology Generally, a system of political ideas that are rooted in religious or philosophical beliefs concerning human nature, society, and government.

imminent lawless action test The current Supreme Court doctrine for assessing the constitutionality of subversive speech. To be illegal, speech must be "directed to inciting . . . imminent lawless action."

implied powers The powers of the federal government that are implied by the expressed powers in the Constitution, particularly in Article I, Section 8.

independent executive agency A federal agency that is not located within a cabinet department.

independent regulatory agency A federal organization that is responsible for creating and implementing rules that regulate private activity and protect the public interest in a particular sector of the economy.

independent expenditure An expenditure for activities that are independent from (not coordinated with) those of a political candidate or a political party.

independent expenditure An expenditure for activities that are independent from (not coordinated with) those of a political candidate or a political party.

indirect technique Any method used by interest groups to influence government officials through third parties, such as voters.

individual mandate In the context of health-care reform, a requirement that all persons obtain health-care insurance from one source or another. Those failing to do so must pay a penalty.

inflation A sustained rise in average prices; equivalent to a decline in the value of the dollar.

inherent powers The powers of the national government that, although not always expressly granted by the Constitution, are necessary to ensure the nation's integrity and survival as a political unit.

institution An ongoing organization that performs certain functions for society.

instructed delegate A representative who deliberately mirrors the views of the majority of his or her constituents.

interest group An organized group of individuals sharing common objectives who actively attempt to influence policymakers.

interstate commerce Trade that involves more than one state.

interventionism Direct involvement by one country in another country's affairs.

iron triangle A three-way alliance among legislators, bureaucrats, and interest groups to make or preserve policies that benefit their respective interests.

ISIS The Islamic State in Iraq and Greater Syria; a terrorist organization that by 2014 had taken over substantial portions of Iraq and Syria. Also known as *ISIL* (the Islamic State in Iraq and the Levant) or the Islamic State.

isolationism A political policy of noninvolvement in world affairs.

issue ad A political advertisement that focuses on a particular issue. Issue ads can be used to support or attack a candidate's position or credibility.

issue networks Groups of individuals or organizations—which consist of legislators and legislative staff members, interest group leaders, bureaucrats, the media, scholars, and other experts—that support particular policy positions on a given issue.

J

judicial review The power of the courts to decide on the constitutionality of legislative enactments and of actions taken by the executive branch.

judiciary The courts, one of the three branches of government in the United States.

jurisdiction The authority of a court to hear and decide a particular case.

justiciable controversy A controversy that is not hypothetical or academic but real and substantial; a requirement that must be satisfied before a court will hear a case. *Justiciable* is pronounced jus-*tish*-a-bul.

K

Keynesian economics An economic theory proposed by British economist John Maynard Keynes that is typically associated with the use of fiscal policy to alter national economic variables.

kitchen cabinet The name given to a president's unofficial advisers. The term was coined during Andrew Jackson's presidency.

L

legislative rule An administrative agency rule that carries the same weight as a statute enacted by a legislature.

***Lemon* test** A three-part test enunciated by the Supreme Court in the 1971 case of *Lemon v. Kurtzman* to determine whether government aid to parochial schools is constitutional.

libel A published report of a falsehood that tends to injure a person's reputation or character.

liberalism A set of political beliefs that include the advocacy of active government, including government intervention to improve the welfare of individuals and to protect civil rights.

libertarianism The belief that government should do as little as possible, not only in the economic sphere, but also in regulating morality and personal behavior.

liberty The freedom of individuals to believe, act, and express themselves as they choose so long as doing so does not infringe on the rights of other individuals in the society.

limited government A form of government based on the principle that the powers of government should be clearly limited either through a written document or through wide public understanding.

literacy test A test given to voters to ensure that they could read and write and thus evaluate political information. This technique was used in many southern states to restrict African American participation in elections.

lobbying All of the attempts by organizations or by individuals to influence the passage, defeat, or contents of legislation or to influence the administrative decisions of government.

lobbyist An individual who handles a particular interest group's lobbying efforts.

M

Madisonian Model The model of government devised by James Madison, in which the powers of the government are separated into three branches: legislative, executive, and judicial.

majoritarianism The belief that public policy is or should be set in accordance with the opinions of a majority of the people.

majority leader The party leader elected by the majority party in the House or in the Senate.

majority party The political party that has more members in the legislature than the opposing party.

malapportionment A condition in which the voting power of citizens in one district is greater than the voting power of citizens in another district.

managed news coverage News coverage that is manipulated (managed) by a campaign manager or political consultant to gain media exposure for a political candidate.

markup session A meeting held by a congressional committee or subcommittee to approve, amend, or redraft a bill.

Marshall Plan A plan providing for U.S. economic assistance to European nations following World War II to help those nations recover from the war. The plan was named after George C. Marshall, secretary of state from 1947 to 1949.

mass media Communication channels, such as newspapers and radio and television broadcasts, through which people can communicate to large audiences.

material incentive A reason to join an interest group—practical benefits such as discounts, subscriptions, or group insurance.

Mayflower Compact A document drawn up by Pilgrim leaders in 1620 on the ship *Mayflower*. The document stated that laws were to be made for the general good of the people.

media Newspapers, magazines, television, radio, the Internet, and any other printed or electronic means of communication.

Medicaid A joint federal–state program that pays for health-care services for low-income persons.

Medicare A federal government program that pays for health-care insurance for Americans aged sixty-five years and over.

minority-majority district A district in which minority groups make up a majority of the population.

minority leader The party leader elected by the minority party in the House or in the Senate.

minority party The political party that has fewer members in the legislature than the opposing party.

***Miranda* warnings** A series of statements informing criminal suspects, on their arrest, of their constitutional rights, such as the right to remain silent and the right to counsel; required by the Supreme Court's 1966 decision in *Miranda v. Arizona*.

moderates Persons whose views fall in the middle of the political spectrum.

monarchy A form of autocracy in which a king, queen, or other aristocrat is the highest authority in the government. Monarchs usually obtain their power through inheritance.

monetary policy Actions taken by the Federal Reserve to change the amount of money in circulation to affect interest rates, credit markets, the rate of inflation, the rate of economic growth, and the rate of unemployment.

Monroe Doctrine A U.S. policy, announced in 1823 by President James Monroe, that the United States would not tolerate foreign intervention in the Western Hemisphere, and in return, we would stay out of European affairs.

moral idealism In foreign policy, the belief that the most important goal is to do what is right. Moral idealists think that it is possible for nations to cooperate as part of a rule-based community.

mutually assured destruction (MAD) A phrase referring to the assumption that if the forces of two nations are capable of destroying each other, neither nation will take a chance on war.

N

national convention The meeting held by each major party every four years to nominate presidential and vice-presidential candidates, write a party platform, and conduct other party business.

national health insurance A program, found in many of the world's economically advanced nations, under which the central government provides basic health-care insurance coverage to everyone in the country.

national party chairperson An individual who serves as a political party's administrative head at the national level and directs the work of the party's national committee.

national party committee The political party leaders who direct party business during the four years between the national party conventions, organize the next national convention, and plan how to support the party's candidate in the next presidential election.

National Security Council (NSC) A council that advises the president on domestic and foreign matters concerning the safety and defense of the nation.

natural rights Rights that are not bestowed by governments but are inherent within every man, woman, and child by virtue of the fact that he or she is a human being.

necessary and proper clause Article I, Section 8, Clause 18, of the Constitution, which gives Congress the power to make all laws "necessary and proper" for the federal government to carry out its responsibilities; also called the *elastic clause*.

negative political advertising Political advertising undertaken for the purpose of discrediting a candidate in voters' eyes. Attack ads are one form of negative political advertising.

neutral competency The application of technical skills to jobs without regard to political issues.

neutrality The position of not being aligned with either side in a dispute or conflict, such as a war.

New Deal The policies ushered in by the Roosevelt administration in 1933 in an attempt to bring the United States out of the Great Depression.

new federalism A plan to limit the federal government's role in regulating state governments and to give the states increased power in deciding how they should spend government revenues.

nominating convention An official meeting of a political party to choose its candidates. Nominating conventions at the state and local levels also select delegates to represent the citizens of their geographic areas at a higher-level party convention.

nuclear option Changing Senate rules—in particular, rules that require a supermajority—by simple majority vote. Also known as the *constitutional option*.

O

obscenity Indecency or offensiveness in speech, expression, behavior, or appearance.

Office of Management and Budget (OMB) An agency in the Executive Office of the President that has the primary duty of assisting the president in preparing and supervising the administration of the federal budget.

"one person, one vote" rule A rule, or principle, requiring that congressional districts have equal populations so that one person's vote counts as much as another's vote.

open primary A primary in which voters can vote for a party's candidates regardless of whether they belong to the party.

opinion A written statement by a court expressing the reasons for its decision in a case.

opposition research The attempt to learn damaging information about an opponent in a political campaign.

oral argument A spoken argument presented to a judge in person by an attorney on behalf of her or his client.

Oslo Accords The first agreement signed between Israel and the PLO; led to the establishment of the Palestinian Authority in the occupied territories.

P

Palestine Liberation Organization (PLO) An organization formed in 1964 to represent the Palestinian people. The PLO has a long history of terrorism but for some years has functioned primarily as a political party.

parliament The national legislative body in countries governed by a parliamentary system, such as Britain and Canada.

partisan politics Political actions or decisions that benefit a particular party.

party activist A party member who helps to organize and oversee party functions and planning during and between campaigns, and may even become a candidate for office.

party identifier A person who identifies himself or herself as being a supporter of a particular political party.

party platform The document drawn up by each party at its national convention that outlines the policies and positions of the party.

party ticket A list of a political party's candidates for various offices. In national elections, the party ticket consists of the presidential and vice-presidential candidates.

patronage A system of rewarding the party faithful and workers with government jobs or contracts.

patronage The practice by which elected officials give government jobs to individuals who helped them gain office.

peer group Associates, often close in age to one another; may include friends, classmates, co-workers, club members, or religious group members.

personal attack ad A negative political advertisement that attacks a candidate's character.

picket-fence federalism A model of federalism in which specific policies and programs are administered by all levels of government—national, state, and local.

pluralist theory A theory that views politics as a contest among various interest groups—at all levels of government—to gain benefits for their members.

pocket veto A special type of veto power used by the chief executive after the legislature has adjourned. Bills that are not signed die after a specified period of time.

podcasting The distribution of audio or video files to personal computers or mobile devices such as smartphones.

police powers The powers of a government body that enable it to create laws for the protection of the health, safety, welfare, and morals of the people. In the United States, most police powers are reserved to the states.

policymaking process The procedures involved in identifying an issue and then getting it on the political agenda; formulating, adopting, and implementing a policy with regard to the issue; and then evaluating the results of the policy.

political action committee (PAC) A committee that is established by a corporation, labor union, or special interest group to raise funds and make campaign contributions on the establishing organization's behalf.

political advertising Advertising undertaken by or on behalf of a political candidate to familiarize voters with the candidate and his or her views on campaign issues; advertising for or against policy issues.

political consultant A professional political adviser who, for a fee, works on an area of a candidate's campaign. Political consultants include campaign managers, pollsters, media advisers, and "get-out-the- vote" organizers.

political culture The set of ideas, values, and attitudes about government and the political process held by a community or a nation.

political party A group of individuals who organize to win elections, operate the government, and determine policy.

political realism In foreign policy, the belief that nations are inevitably selfish and that we should seek to protect our national security, regardless of moral arguments.

political socialization The learning process through which most people acquire their political attitudes, opinions, beliefs, and knowledge.

politics The process of resolving conflicts over how society should use its scarce resources and who should receive various benefits, such as public health care and public higher education.

poll tax A fee of several dollars that had to be paid before a person could vote. This device was used in some southern states to discourage African Americans and low-income whites from voting.

poll watcher A representative from one of the political parties who is allowed to monitor a polling place to make sure that the election is run fairly and that fraud doesn't occur.

power The ability to influence the behavior of others, usually through the use of force, persuasion, or rewards.

precedent A court decision that furnishes an example or authority for deciding subsequent cases involving identical or similar facts and legal issues.

precinct A political district within a city, such as a block or a neighborhood, or a rural portion of a county; the smallest voting district at the local level.

preemption A doctrine rooted in the supremacy clause of the Constitution that provides that national laws or regulations governing a certain area take precedence over conflicting state laws or regulations governing that same area.

press secretary A member of the White House staff who holds news conferences for reporters and makes public statements for the president.

primary A preliminary election held for the purpose of choosing a party's final candidate.

primary election An election in which voters choose the candidates of their party, who will then run in the general election.

primary source of law A source of law that establishes the law. Primary sources of law include constitutions, statutes, administrative agency rules and regulations, and decisions rendered by the courts.

priming An agenda-setting technique in which a media outlet promotes specific facts or ideas that may affect the public's thinking on related topics.

print media Communication channels that consist of printed materials, such as newspapers and magazines.

privatization The transfer of the task of providing services traditionally provided by government to the private sector.

probable cause Cause for believing that there is a substantial likelihood that a person has committed or is about to commit a crime.

progressivism Today, an alternative, more popular term for the set of political beliefs also known as liberalism.

public-interest group An interest group formed for the purpose of working for the "public good." Examples are the American Civil Liberties Union and Common Cause.

public debt The total amount of money that the national government owes as a result of borrowing; also called the *national debt*.

public opinion poll A survey of the public's opinion on a particular topic at a particular moment.

public opinion The views of the citizenry about politics, public issues, and public policies; a complex collection of opinions held by many people on issues in the public arena.

public services Essential services that individuals cannot provide for themselves, such as building and maintaining roads, establishing welfare programs, operating public schools, and preserving national parks.

purposive incentive A reason to join an interest group—satisfaction resulting from working for a cause in which one believes.

push poll A campaign tactic used to feed false or misleading information to potential voters, under the guise of taking an opinion poll, with the intent to "push" voters away from one candidate and toward another.

Q

quota system A policy under which a specific number of jobs, promotions, or other types of placements, such as university admissions, are given to members of selected groups.

R

random sample In the context of opinion polling, a sample in which each person within the entire population being polled has an equal chance of being chosen.

rating system A system by which a particular interest group evaluates (rates) the performance of legislators based on how often the legislators have voted with the group's position on particular issues.

rational basis test A test (also known as the *ordinary scrutiny standard*) used by the Supreme Court to decide whether a discriminatory law violates the equal protection clause of the Constitution. It is used only when there is no classification—such as race or gender—that would require a higher level of scrutiny.

realignment A process in which the popular support for and relative strength of the parties shift and the parties are reestablished with different coalitions of supporters.

recession A period in which the level of economic activity falls; usually defined as two or more quarters of economic decline.

renewable energy Energy from technologies that do not rely on extracted resources, such as oil and coal, that can run out.

representative democracy A form of democracy in which the will of the majority is expressed through groups of individuals elected by the people to act as their representatives.

republic Essentially, a representative system in which there is no king or queen and the people are sovereign.

reverse discrimination Discrimination against those who have no minority status.

right-to-work laws Laws that ban unions from collecting dues or other fees from workers whom they represent but who have not actually joined the union.

rulemaking The process undertaken by an administrative agency when formally proposing, evaluating, and adopting a new regulation.

rule of law A basic principle of government that requires those who govern to act in accordance with established law.

Rules Committee A standing committee in the House of Representatives that provides special rules governing how particular bills will be considered and debated by the House. The Rules Committee normally proposes time limits on debate for any bill.

S

sample In the context of opinion polling, a group of people selected to represent the population being studied.

sampling error In the context of opinion polling, the difference between what the sample results show and what the true results would have been had everybody in the relevant population been interviewed.

school voucher An educational certificate, provided by a government, that allows a student to use public funds to pay for a private or a public school chosen by the student or his or her parents.

secession The act of formally withdrawing from membership in an alliance; the withdrawal of a state from the federal Union.

second budget resolution A budget resolution, which is supposed to be passed in September, that sets "binding" limits on taxes and spending for the next fiscal year.

Second Continental Congress The congress of the colonies that met in 1775 to assume the powers of a central government and to establish an army.

seditious speech Speech that urges resistance to lawful authority or that advocates the overthrow of a government.

self-incrimination Providing damaging information or testimony against oneself in court.

senatorial courtesy A practice that allows a senator of the president's party to veto the president's nominee to a federal court judgeship within the senator's state.

separate-but-equal doctrine A Supreme Court doctrine holding that the equal protection clause of the Fourteenth Amendment did not forbid racial segregation as long as the facilities for blacks were equal to those for whites.

separation of powers The principle of dividing governmental powers among the legislative, executive, and judicial branches of government.

sexual harassment Unwanted physical contact, verbal conduct, or abuse of a sexual nature that interferes with a recipient's job performance, creates a hostile environment, or carries with it an implicit or explicit threat of adverse employment consequences.

Shays' Rebellion A rebellion of angry farmers in western Massachusetts in 1786, led by former Revolutionary War captain Daniel Shays.

signing statement A written statement, appended to a bill at the time the president signs it into law, indicating how the president interprets that legislation.

sit-in A tactic of nonviolent civil disobedience. Demonstrators enter a business, college building, or other public place and remain seated until they are forcibly removed or until their demands are met.

slander The public utterance (speaking) of a statement that holds a person up for contempt, ridicule, or hatred.

social conflict Disagreements among people in a society over what the society's priorities should be.

social contract A voluntary agreement among individuals to create a government and to give that government adequate power to secure the mutual protection and welfare of all individuals.

socialism A political ideology, often critical of capitalism, that lies to the left of liberalism on the traditional political spectrum. Socialists are scarce in the United States but common in many other countries.

soft money Campaign contributions not regulated by federal law, such as some contributions that are made to political parties instead of to particular candidates.

solidarity Mutual agreement among the members of a particular group.

solidary incentive A reason to join an interest group—pleasure in associating with like-minded individuals.

Solid South A term used to describe the tendency of the southern states to vote Democratic after the Civil War.

sound bite A televised comment, lasting for only a few seconds, that captures a thought or a perspective and has an immediate impact on viewers.

Soviet bloc The group of Eastern European nations that fell under the control of the Soviet Union following World War II.

Speaker of the House The presiding officer in the House of Representatives. The Speaker is a member of the majority party and is the most powerful member of the House.

special election An election that is held at the state or local level when the voters must decide an issue before the next general election or when vacancies occur by reason of death or resignation.

spin A reporter's slant on, or interpretation of, a particular event or action.

spin doctor A political candidate's press adviser who tries to convince reporters to give a story or event concerning the candidate a particular "spin" (interpretation, or slant).

standing committee A permanent committee in Congress that deals with legislation concerning a particular area, such as agriculture or foreign relations.

standing to sue The requirement that an individual must have a sufficient stake in a controversy before he or she can bring a lawsuit. The party bringing the suit must demonstrate that he or she has either been harmed or been threatened with a harm.

stare decisis A common law doctrine under which judges normally are obligated to follow the precedents established by prior court decisions. Pronounced *ster*-ay dih-*si*-sis.

statutory law The body of law enacted by legislatures (as opposed to constitutional law, administrative law, or case law).

straw poll A nonscientific poll in which there is no way to ensure that the opinions expressed are representative of the larger population.

strict scrutiny standard A standard under which a law or action must be necessary to promote a compelling state interest and must be narrowly tailored to meet that interest.

subcommittee A division of a larger committee that deals with a particular part of the committee's policy area. Most standing committees have several subcommittees.

suffrage The right to vote; the franchise.

supremacy clause Article VI, Clause 2, of the Constitution, which makes the Constitution and federal laws superior to all conflicting state and local laws.

suspect classification A classification, such as race, that provides the basis for a discriminatory law. Any law based on a suspect classification is subject to strict scrutiny by the courts, meaning that the law must be justified by a compelling state interest.

symbolic speech The expression of beliefs, opinions, or ideas through forms other than verbal speech or print; speech involving actions and other nonverbal expressions.

T

Tea Party movement A grassroots conservative movement that arose in 2009 after Barack Obama became president. The movement opposes big government and current levels of taxation, and also rejects political compromise.

third party In the United States, any party other than the two major parties (Republican and Democratic).

three-fifths compromise A compromise reached during the Constitutional Convention by which three-fifths of all slaves were to be counted for purposes of representation in the House of Representatives.

trade organization An association formed by members of a particular industry, such as oil or trucking industries, to develop common standards and goals for the industry. Trade organizations, as interest groups, lobby government for legislation or regulations that specifically benefit their members.

treaty A formal agreement between the governments of two or more countries.

trial court A court in which trials are held and testimony is taken.

trustee A representative who tries to serve the broad interests of the entire society and not just the narrow interests of his or her constituents.

two-party system A political system in which two strong and established parties compete for political offices.

tyranny The arbitrary or unrestrained exercise of power by an oppressive individual or government.

U

unemployment The state of not having a job when actively seeking one.

unicameral legislature A legislature with only one chamber.

unitary system A centralized governmental system in which local or subdivisional governments exercise only those powers given to them by the central government.

V

veto A Latin word meaning "I forbid"; the refusal by an official, such as the president of the United States or a state governor, to sign a bill into law.

veto power A constitutional power that enables the chief executive (president or governor) to reject legislation and return it to the legislature with reasons for the rejection. This either prevents or delays the bill from becoming law.

vote-eligible population The number of people who are actually eligible to vote in an American election.

voting-age population The number of people residing in the United States who are at least eighteen years old.

W

ward A local unit of a political party's organization, consisting of a division or district within a city.

Watergate scandal A scandal involving an illegal break-in at the Democratic National Committee offices in 1972 by members of President Richard Nixon's reelection campaign staff.

weapons of mass destruction Chemical, biological, and nuclear weapons that can inflict massive casualties.

whip A member of Congress who assists the majority or minority leader in the House or in the Senate in managing the party's legislative program.

whistleblower In the context of government employment, someone who "blows the whistle" (reports to authorities or the press) on gross governmental inefficiency, illegal action, or other wrongdoing.

White House Office The personal office of the president. White House Office personnel handle the president's political needs and manage the media, among other duties.

white primary A primary election in which African Americans were prohibited from voting. The practice was banned by the Supreme Court in 1944.

winner-take-all system A system in which the candidate who receives the most votes wins. In contrast, proportional systems allocate votes to multiple winners.

writ of *certiorari* An order from a higher court asking a lower court for the record of a case. *Certiorari* is pronounced sur-shee-uh-*rah*-ree.

writ of *habeas corpus* An order that requires an official to bring a specified prisoner into court and explain to the judge why the person is being held in jail.

INDEX

Equal employment opportunity programs, 117–118
Equality
    defined, 13
    as political value, 13
    in voting, 11
Equal Pay Act, 109
Equal protection clause
    affirmative action and, 118
    defined, 100
    gays and lesbians, 116
    intermediate scrutiny standard, 101
    ordinary scrutiny, 101
    original intention of, 101–102
    racial gerrymandering, 242
    rational basis test, 101
    separate-but-equal doctrine, 102
    strict scrutiny standard, 100
Equal Rights Amendment, 46, 108
Espionage Act, 84, 91, 304
Establishment clause, 77, 79–90
Ethiopia, 50
Ethnicity
    distribution of US population by, 15–16
    voting behavior and, 175–176
European Union (EU)
    austerity program, 370
    as confederal system, 51
    Grexit and Brexit, 370
    refugee crisis, 370
    terrorist attacks, 370
Eurozone, 370
Euthanasia, 88
Everson v. Board of Education, 77
Every Student Succeeds Act, 68, 107
Evolution
    vs. creationism, 80–81
    vs. intelligent design, 80–81
Exacting scrutiny, 101
Executive agreements, 359
    defined, 277
    presidential use of, 277
Executive branch. *See also* President of United States
    authority of, and Constitution, 39
    bureaucracy as part of, 290
    checks and balances and, 43–44
    organization of, 280–281
    separation of powers, 43
Executive departments, 281. *See also* specific departments
    list of each with duties, 293
    organization of, 293, 294
    president's cabinet, 280–281
    types of structures, 294
Executive memorandums, 276
Executive Office of the President, 281–282
Executive orders, 275–276
Executive privilege, 280
Exports, of China, 375
Export taxes, 38–39, 55
Ex post facto law, 74
Expressed powers, 54, 60
Expression, freedom of, 83–87. *See also* Speech, freedom of

F

Facebook, 83, 206, 219, 230
FactCheck, 229
Faction, 41, 133
Fairness doctrine, talk radio and, 226
False Claims Act, 304
Family, formation of political opinion and, 170

Fannie Mae (Federal National Mortgage Association), 297
Farm bill, 339
Farm Bureau, 130
Farm subsidies, 123, 130
Fast-track authority, 270
Faubus, Orval, 103
Federal Assault Weapons Ban, 73
Federal budget
    appropriation, 257
    authorization, 257
    budget deficit (*See* Public debt)
    budgeting process, 257–259
    by category, 293
    cost of maintaining government, 291–292
    debt ceiling issue, 258–259
    defense spending, 292
    earmarks, 243
    entitlement programs, 257
    pork barrel spending, 243
    projections of, 258
    public debt and, 351–352
    social program spending, 292
    steps in process, 256–259
Federal budget deficit. *See* Public debt
Federal Bureau of Investigation (FBI)
    Apple and customer privacy, 306–307
    National Security Letters, 91
Federal Communications Commission (FCC)
    creation of, 296
    fairness doctrine, 226
    principle duties of, 297
Federal court system, 316–319
    appellate courts (courts of appeal), 317
    assessing role of, 328–330
    court procedures, 315–316
    diversity of citizenship, 315
    ideology and, 325–328
    judicial appointments, 319–322
    jurisdiction, 315
    organization of, 316
    as policymakers, 322–328
    senatorial courtesy, 320
    trial courts (U.S. district courts), 316–317
    U.S. Supreme Court, 318–319
Federal Deposit Insurance Corporation, principal duties of, 297
Federal Election Campaign Act, 207–208
Federal Election Commission (FEC), 208, 232
Federal Election Commission v. Wisconsin Right to Life Inc., 209–210
Federal government. *See also* Federalism
    bankruptcy and private corporations, 297–298
    federal spending as anticyclical, 68
    organization of, 293–298
        executive departments, 293
        government corporations, 296–298
        independent executive agencies, 295–296
        independent regulatory agencies, 296, 297
        overview of, 293
    size of, 12
    term of, 51

Federal grants
    block, 67
    categorical, 66–67
    to control states, 68
    cross-cutting requirements, 67
    land-grant colleges and, 66
    minimum drinking age and, 68
    No Child Left Behind and, 68
    state budgets and, 67
Federal Home Loan Mortgage Corporation (Freddie Mac), 297
Federal Housing Finance Agency, 298
Federalism, 48–69. *See also* National government
    advantages of, 51–52
    alternatives to, 51
    Canadian vs. American, 53
    characteristics of, 50–51
    compared to unitary system, 51
    competitive, 68–69
    concurrent powers, 58
    confederal system, 51
    cooperative, 62–63
    defined, 50
    disadvantages of, 52–54
    division of powers, 54–59
    dual, 61–62
    federal mandate, 64
    fiscal side of, 66–69
        competitive federalism, 68–69
        cost of federal mandates, 68
        federal grants, 66–67
        fiscal federalism, 66
    George W. Bush Administration and, 65
    horizontal, 57
    interstate relations, 57–58
    minimum drinking age and, 68
    nation-centered, 63
    picket-fence federalism, 63
    politics of, 64–65
    preemption, 63
    as principle of Constitution, 42–43
    state-centered, 63
    struggle for supremacy and, 59–63
    subcultures and, 52
    supremacy clause, 59
    supremacy of national government
        Civil War, 61
        cooperative federalism, 62–63
        dual federalism, 61–62
        early Supreme Court decisions, 59–60
        struggle for, 59–63
    today, 63–66
        economic cycles and, 68
        health-care reform, 65
        immigration, 65
        new federalism, 63–64
        shifting boundary between federal and state authority, 64–65
        Supreme Court and, 64
Federalist Gazette of the United States, 223
Federalist Papers, 40, 41, 324, 328
Federalists, 50, 196
    defined, 39
    as first political party, 146–147
    ratification of Constitution, 40–41
Federal lands, 55, 56

Federal Lands Freedom Act, 56
Federal mandates
    cost of, 68
    defined, 64
    examples of, 66
Federal National Mortgage Association (Fannie Mae), 297
Federal Open Market Committee (FOMC), 347
Federal question, 315
Federal Register, 306
Federal Regulation of Lobbying Act, 139
Federal Reserve System (Fed)
    easy-money policy, 347
    overview of, 346–347
    principal duties of, 297
    tight-money policy, 347
Federal system. *See also* Federalism
    defined, 42, 50
    other countries that have, 51
    of United States, 50–54
Federal tax system, 349–351
    as progressive system, 349–350
    taxes under George W. Bush, 350
    tax loopholes, 350
Federal Trade Commission (FTC)
    adjudication by, 300
    creation of, 290, 300
    principal duties of, 297
Federal Trade Commission Act, 290, 300
Feingold, Russell, 209
Felman, Jim, 335
Felons, voting, 188, 190
Feminist movement, 108
Fifteenth Amendment, 102, 105, 185, 186
Fifth Amendment
    double jeopardy, 92
    due process, 92
    recording confessions, 95
    right to privacy, 87
    self-incrimination, 92
    text of, 75
Filibuster, 237, 250–251
Fillmore, Millard, 323
Film, First Amendment and, 219
Financial crisis of 2008, regulation and, 289
Fines, 93
Finland, 178
Fiorina, Carly, 200
First Amendment, 77–87
    campaign self-financing, 208
    freedom of expression, 83–87
    freedom of religion, 27, 77–83
    freedom of speech, 83–87
    interest groups and, 124
    issue-oriented group and, 209
    media and, 219
    right to freedom of association, 197
    right to petition government, 124
    right to privacy, 87
    text of, 75
First budget resolution, 258
First Continental Congress, 30
First Gulf War, as background to invasion of Iraq in 2003, 366
First Lady, 283
Fiscal federalism, 66–69
Fiscal policy
    defined, 348
    federal tax system and, 349–351
    Keynesian economics, 348–349
    president's control over, 275

Fiscal year, 257
Fisher v. U. Texas, 118
501(c)4 committee, 211–212
501(c)4 organizations, 137
527 committee, 211–212
527 organization, 137
Food and Drug Administration (FDA)
   Avandia and, 289
   regulation by, 290
Food stamps, 134, 339
   federal budget spent on, 292
Ford, Gerald, 285
   pardon of Nixon, 270, 271
Foreign Intelligence Surveillance
     Court (FISC), 3, 92,
     316–317
Foreign policy, 357–376
   Cabinet and, 359–360
   Central Intelligence Agency
     (CIA), 360
   Congress powers and, 360
   Defense Department, 359–360
   defined, 358
   history of, 360–364
     Cold War, 362–364
     containment, 362
     Cuban missile crisis, 363
     interventionism, 361
     isolationism, 361
     Monroe Doctrine, 3610
     neutrality, 3610
     post-cold war, 364
     Truman Doctrine and
       Marshall Plan, 362
     World Wars, 361–362
   Iran as emerging nuclear threat,
     373–374
   Israeli-Palestinian conflict,
     369–372
   makers of, 358–360
   moral idealism, 358, 361
   National Security Council and,
     360
   North Korea's nuclear program,
     372–373
   Obama on, 263
   political realism, 358
   presidential power in, 276–278,
     358–359
   State Department and, 359
   terrorism, 364–366
   weapons of mass destruction,
     372–374
Fourteenth Amendment, 328
   equal protection clause
     defined, 100
     intermediate scrutiny
       standard, 101
     ordinary scrutiny, 101
     original intention of,
       101–102
     rational basis test, 101
     strict scrutiny standard, 100
   gender discrimination, 108
   incorporating Bill of Rights
     into, 76
   Native Americans, 114
   persons covered by, 76–77
   sodomy laws, 116
Fourth Amendment
   exclusionary rule, 93–94
   NSA collecting metadata, 91
   probable cause, 92
   right to privacy, 87
   text of, 75
   unreasonable search and seizure,
     92
   warrants, 92

Fox News, 223, 228
Fracking, 344–345
Framing, 221
France
   anti-immigration politics in
     Europe, 178
   health care spending, 339
   Seven Years' War, 28–29
   as unitary system, 51
   voter turnout, 185
   World War II, 362
Franklin, Benjamin, 36
Fraud, e-fraud, 306
Freddie Mac (Federal Home Loan
     Mortgage Corporation),
     297
Freedom(s)
   of assembly, 75
   of association, 197
   of expression, 83–87
   individual, 11
   of petition, 75
   of the press, 75, 218, 219
   of religion, 75, 77–83
   of speech, 75, 83–87
Freedom Caucus, 247
Freedom House, 8
Freedom of Information Act (FOIA),
     89, 305
Free exercise clause, 77, 82–83
Free markets, 14
Free rider problem, 127
Free Soil Party, 163, 164
French and Indian War, 28–29
Front loading, 200
Full faith and credit clause, 57–58
Fulton, Robert, 60
Fundamental Orders of Connecticut,
     27
Fundamental rights, 76
   defined, 100
   strict scrutiny standard and, 100

G

Gaddafi, Muammar, 263, 368
Gallup, George, 179
Gallup Organization, founding of,
     179
Gambling, Native American
     operations, 115
Garland, Merrick, 256, 322
Gay Activist Alliance, 116
Gay Liberation Front, 116
Gays
   changing attitude toward,
     116–117
   changing legal landscape, 116
   civil rights of, 18, 116–117, 326
   "Don't ask, don't tell" policy, 117
   in military, 117
   same-sex marriage, 57–58, 117, 326
Gaza Strip War, 371–372
Geer, John, 224
Gender
   intermediate-scrutiny standard,
     101
   voting behavior and, 175
   wage discrimination, 109
Gender discrimination, 108
Gender gap, 175
General election, 194
General fund budget, 67
General Services Administration
   formation of, 296
   principle duties of, 296
Geographic region, voting behavior
     and, 176–177

George III, King (England), 29, 30
Georgia, Russian attack on, 357
Germany, 50
   aging population in, 16
   anti-immigration politics in
     Europe, 178
   austerity program, 370
   Berlin Wall, 364
   end of Cold War, 364
   refugee crisis, 370
   voter turnout, 185
   World War II, 362
Gerry, Elbridge, 239
Gerrymandering
   after 2010 census, 240–241
   racial, 241–242
Gibbons, Thomas, 60
Gibbons v. Ogden, 60
Gideon v. Wainwright, 77, 93
Gilens, Martin, 128
Gingrich, Newt, 210
Ginsburg, Ruth Bader, 88, 109, 322
Gitlow v. New York, 77
Glass ceiling, 109
Global warming
   debate on, 343–344
Going public strategy, 273
Goldwater, Barry, 18, 224
Google, 230, 231
Google+, 219
GOP (grand old party), 149
Gorbachev, Mikhail, 364
Gore, Al
   election of 2000, 165
     popular vote, 150
   as vice president, 284
Government
   access to, and interest groups,
     127–128
   aristocracy, 9
   authority of, 5
   autocracy, 7
   capitalism and, 14
   coalition, 45
   cost of maintaining, 291–292
   defending nation and culture,
     6–7
   defined, 5
   dictatorship, 7–8
   direct democracy, 8–9
   limited, 10, 42
     vs. effective, 44
   managing economy, 6
   minority, 45
   monarchy, 7
   need for, 4
   online, 305–306
   plutocracy, 10
   power of, 5
   principles of, in Constitution
     checks and balances, 43–44
     federalism, 42–43
     limited government, 42
     popular sovereignty, 42
     separation of powers, 43
   privatization, 305
   providing public service, 5–6
   representative, 10–11
   representative democracy, 9
   resolving conflicts, 5
   salary for workers, 299
   size of, 12
   in sunshine, 305
   theocracy, 10
   types of, 7–10
Government corporations
   defined, 296
   list of selected, 297

Government Performance and
     Results Act, 304
Government regulation. *See*
     Regulation/regulatory
     agencies
Graber, Doris A., 171
Graham, Larry, 130
Grandfather clause, 102, 186
Grand jury, 75, 76
Grassroots organizing, 137
Gratz v. Bollinger, 118
Great Britain. *See also* England;
     United Kingdom
   American independence from,
     28–31
   ban on Trump, 78
   Brexit, 370
   coalition government, 45
   Cold War and, 362–364
   fusion of powers, 45
   health care spending, 339
   Irish Republic Army and peace
     process, 365
   Parliament, 10
   parliamentary system, 9, 45
   Seven Years' War, 28–29
   terrorist bombings in London's
     transportation system,
     365
   as unitary system, 51
   World War II, 362
Great Charter, 10
Great Compromise, 37–38, 238
Great Depression
   cooperative federalism and, 62
   Farm Bureau and fair prices
     during, 130
   federalism in Canada vs. U.S.
     during, 53
   formation of public opinion, 171
   Keynes on, 348
   presidential power to regulate
     economy, 274
   Republican and Democratic
     Parties, 149
Great Recession
   deficit spending to fight, 352
   Fannie Mae and Freddie Mac,
     297
   federalism and, 68
   formation of public opinion, 171
   Keynesian economics and,
     348–349
   public debt and, 352
   regulation and financial crisis,
     289
   state and federal spending
     during, 68
   unemployment during, 6
Great Society, 62, 66
Greece
   direct democracy and, 8
   Grexit, 370
Greenhouse gas emissions, 64, 343
Green Party, 163–164, 165
Greenpeace USA, 134
Grexit, 370
Griswold v. Connecticut, 77, 87
Grossmann, Matt, 156
Ground game, 206
Growth recession, 375
Grutter v. Bollinger, 118
Guam, 238, 361
Guinn v. United States, 186
Gun control
   Brady Handgun Violence
     Prevention Act, 64
   Gun-Free School Zones Act, 64

obscenity and, 85–86
online advertising revenues, 230, 231
podcasting news, 231
political campaigns and, 204–207, 206, 231–234
   candidates' 24/7 exposure, 233
   controlling netroots, 233
   fundraising on, 205–206
   microtargeting, 206
   Obama's campaign, 206–207
   online fundraising, 233
   rise of Internet campaign, 233
   support for local organizing, 206–207
   targeting supporters, 206
public opinion polls and, 179
revenge porn, 90
shaping public opinion, 171
usage of, by consumers, 230
Internet Corporation for Assigned Names and Numbers (ICANN), 220
Internment camps, 113
Inter-Services Intelligence (ISI), 368
Interstate commerce, 62
defined, 38
regulated by Congress, 38, 54, 63
supremacy of national government and, 60
Interstate Commerce Commission (ICC), 296
Interstate compacts, 58
Interventionism, 361
Intolerable Acts, 29
Investigatory stops, 99
Invisible primary, 199
Iran
   Council of Guardians, 10
   Islamic government in, 10
   nuclear weapons and, 373–374
   Obama and nuclear deal with, 277
   as oil exporter, 342
   religious intolerance in, 79
   as theocracy, 10
   United States involvement and, 263
Iraq
   First Gulf War, 366
   ISIS and, 278, 369
   Kuwait invaded by, 366
   as oil exporter, 342
   rise and fall of insurgency, 367
   weapons of mass destruction thought to be in, 366–367
   WMD inspections, 366–367
Iraq War
   authorization of armed forces in, 277
   federal budget spent on, 292
   First Gulf War background, 366
   invasion of, 367
   Obama and, 368
   President Bush and, 277
   public opinion of, 14
   rise and fall of insurgency, 367
   withdrawal, 367
Ireland, Irish Republic Army and peace process England, 365
Irish Republican Army, 365
Iron triangle, 250
   policymaking and, 337
ISIS (Islamic State)
   attacks in Iraq and Syria, 278

compromising freedom and privacy to fight, 3
self-radicalized terrorists, 365–366
United States involvement and, 263
ISIS (Islamic State in Iraq and Greater Syria)
   air strikes against, 369
   attacks on Iraq, 369
   rise of, 369
Islam, government based on, 10
Islam, Yusuf, 78
Isolationism, 361
Israel, 365
   conflict with Palestinians, 369–372
   Gaza Strip War, 371–372
   negotiations with, 371–372
   as unitary system, 51
Issue ads, 136–137
   defined, 223
   effectiveness of, 224
Issue campaigns, 209
Issue identification, 336–337
Issue networks, 250, 302–303
Issue-oriented parties, 163–164
Italy, 362
   voter turnout, 185
Iyengar, Shanto, 224

J

Jackson, Andrew, 27, 61, 272
   Democrats and, 148
   election of 1824, 196
   election of 1828, 147
   kitchen cabinet, 281
Jamestown colony, 26
Jamieson, Kathleen Hall, 228, 229
Japan
   aging population in, 16
   nuclear crisis in, 345
   Pearl Harbor attacked by, 362
   as unitary system, 51
   voter turnout, 185
   World War II, 362
Japanese Americans, 113
Jay, John, 40
Jefferson, Thomas, 27, 32, 59, 84, 223, 272, 328
   Constitutional Convention and, 36
   Declaration of Independence, 31–32
   election of 1796, 147
   election of 1800, 147, 196
   election of 1804, 147
   establishment clause, 78, 79
   on political parties, 146
   on slavery, 40
   wall of separation, 78, 79
Jeffersonian Republicans, 147–148, 196
Jeffords, James M., 328
Jews, voting behavior, 175
Jim Crow laws, 102
Job Corps, 62
John, King (England), 10
Johnson, Andrew
   impeachment, 255
   vetoes by, 271
Johnson, Lyndon B., 18, 62, 264, 284
   affirmative action, 117
   block grants, 67
   daisy girl ad, 224
   election of 1964, 150
      percentage of votes for, 280

Great Society, 66
   Medicare and Medicaid, 18
Joint Chiefs of Staff, 359–360
Jolie, Angelina, 171
Jordan, 371
Judicial activism, 324–325
Judicial branch
   authority of, and Constitution, 39
   checks and balances and, 43–44
   judicial review, 44
   separation of powers, 43
Judicial restraint, 324–325
Judicial review, 44, 59
   defined, 324
   power of, 324
Judiciary, 311–330
   broad language and, 323–324
   checks and balances, 324, 330
   defined, 312
   electing judges, 311
   federal court system, 316–319
   federal judicial appointments, 319–322
   ideology and, 325–328
   jurisdiction, 314–315
   origins and sources of American law, 312–316
   power of judicial review, 324
   standing to sue, 315
Judis, John, 155
Jurisdiction, 314–315
Jury trials, 93
   common law tradition, 312–313
   impartial jury, 77
   right to, 75
Justice, Department of, 281, 294, 295
Justiciable controversy, 315

K

Kagan, Elena, 322, 326, 1090
Kaine, Tim, 284
Kasich, John, 200, 266
   election of 2016
      Twitter followers, 206
Kelly, Megyn, 111, 228
Kennedy, Anthony, 326, 327, 328
Kennedy, Jacqueline, 284
Kennedy, John F., 265, 266
   election of 1960, television debates, 204, 224
Kerry, John, 266
   as secretary of state, 359
Keynes, John Maynard, 348–349
Keynesian economics, 348–349
Kim Jong Il, 373
Kim Jong-un, 8, 373
King, Martin Luther, Jr., 104, 105
King Caucus, 196
King v. Burwell, 326
Kirk, Mark, 256
Kitchen cabinet, 281
Klopfer v. North Carolina, 77
Koch, Charles, 157, 209, 210
Koch, David, 157, 210
Korean War, 277, 363
Kosovo, 364
Krugman, Paul, 177
Ku Klux Klan, 102, 103
Kurds, 367
Kuwait, invaded by Iraq, 366

L

Labor, Department of, 281, 295
Labor interest groups, 130–132
Labor unions. *See* Unions

Lady Gaga, 171
Land-grant colleges, 66
Landon, Alfred, 178
Land seizure, in China and India, 125
Landslide election, 279–280
Lasswell, Harold, 5
The Late Show, 226
Latino, 112. *See also* Hispanics
Latter-Day Saints, 82
Law enforcement
   bias debate, 99, 106–107
   online privacy versus, 306–307
Lawrence v. Texas, 116, 326, 328
Law(s)
   administrative, 313–314
   case, 314
   civil, 314
   common law tradition, 312–313
   constitutional, 313
   criminal, 314
   due process of, 76
   election laws favoring two-party system, 161
   equal protection of, 11
   ex post facto law, 74
   Jim Crow, 102
   legislative process, 251–254
   primary sources of, 313–314
   rule of law, 42
   rule of precedent, 312
   sodomy, 116
   sources of, 313–314
   statutory, 313
   steps in bill becoming a law, 251–254
   sunshine, 305
League of Nations, 361–362
Lebanon, 371
Ledbetter, Lily, 109
Lee, Richard Henry, 31
Legislation
   enabling, 300
   supermajority to pass important legislation, 237
   by Supreme Court, 328, 329
Legislative branch
   checks and balances and, 43–44
   separation of powers, 43
Legislative process, 251–254
Legislative rules, 300
Legislature
   bicameral, 37
   unicameral, 32
Lemon test, 81
Lemon v. Kurtzman, 81
Leoni, Téa, 226
Le Pen, Marine, 178
Lesbians
   changing attitude toward, 116–117
   civil rights of, 18, 116–117, 326
   "Don't ask, don't tell" policy, 117
   in military, 117
   same-sex marriage, 57–58, 117, 326
Lewinsky, Monica, 280
Lexington, Battle of, 30
Libel, 85
Liberalism/liberals
   bias in media, 228
   big government and, 18
   civil rights movement, 18
   defined, 16
   progressives and, 19
   replacing Justice Scalia, 322
   roots of, 18
   size of government, 12

Voting Rights Act, 104–105, 186, 187, 241–242
   weakening of, 106
Vouchers, school, 81–82

W

Wage discrimination, 109
Wallace, George, 164
Wallace, Henry, 164
Wall of separation, 78, 79
Wall Street Journal, 221, 223
War, Congressional power to declare, 267, 276, 360
War, Department of, original size of, 290
Ward, 159
War on terrorism. *See also* September 11, 2001 terrorist attacks
   FBI and Apple privacy issue, 307
   openness of government afterwards, 305
   presidential power and, 280
   U.S. response to 9/11, 366
War Powers Resolution, 277, 360
Warrants, 92
   NSA and, 91
Warren, Earl, 103, 321, 324–325
Warren, Rick, 171
Warren Court, 324–325

Washington, George, 27, 30, 32, 34, 36, 196, 274
   farewell address, 146
   on political parties, 146
   powers of president under, 272
   president's role in foreign affairs and, 276–277
   on slavery, 40
Washington, Kerry, 226
Washington Post, 221, 222, 230
Watergate scandal, 270, 280
Weapons of mass destruction
   Iran as emerging threat, 373–374
   North Korea's nuclear program, 372–373
Web. *See* Internet
Webster, Daniel, 148
Welfare
   cooperative federalism and, 62–63
   picket-fence federalism, 63
   reform, as devolution, 64, 65
   spending on, 292
Wentworth, Alexandra, 229
West, Lindy, 111
West Germany, Berlin Wall, 364
Whig Party, 148–149, 196
Whips, 248
Whistle-Blower Protection act, 304
Whistleblowers, 303–304
White House, 264

White House chief of staff, 282
White House Office, 282–283
White primary, 102, 186
Whitman, Meg, 193
Whole Woman's Health v. Hellerstedt, 89
WikiLeaks, 91
Wilkow, Andrew, 227
Williamson, Vanessa, 152–153
William the Conqueror, 312
Wilson, Woodrow, 108, 149, 266, 272, 280
   election of 1912, 164–165
   moral idealism and, 361
   neutrality policy, 361
   on presidential powers, 272
Wind power, 345
Windsor, United States v., 117
Winner-take-all system, 162, 195
Wolf v. Colorado, 77
Women
   civil rights of, 107–110
     feminist movement, 108
     World War I and, 107–108
   in federal office, 109
   feminist movement, 108
   glass ceiling, 109
   in politics today, 109
   sexual harassment, 109–110
   voting behavior and, 175
   voting rights, 107–108, 186
   wage discrimination, 109

World War I and women's rights, 107–108
Wood, Gordon S., 40
Workplace
   religious practices in, 82–83
   sexual harassment, 109–110
   women in, 109
World Trade Center. *See also* September 11, 2001 terrorist attacks
   terrorist attack on, in 2001, 365
World War I
   clear and present danger, 84
   neutrality policy, 361
   women's rights and, 107–108
World War II
   attack on Pearl Harbor, 362
   dropping atomic bomb, 278, 362
   formation of public opinion, 171
Write-in candidate, 196
Writ of *certiorari,* 318
Writ of *habeas corpus,* 74

X

Xinjiang, 375–376

Y

Yellen, Janet, 348
Yeltsin, Boris, 364
Yom Kippur War, 370

CHAPTER 1 LEARNING OUTCOMES / KEY TERMS

1-1 **Explain what is meant by the terms** *politics* **and** *government.* Resolving conflicts over how society should use its scarce resources and who should receive various benefits is the essence of **politics. Government**—the individuals and **institutions** that make society's rules and possess the **power** and **authority** to enforce those rules—resolves **social conflicts,** provides **public services,** and defends the nation and its culture against attacks by other nations.

authority The ability to legitimately exercise power, such as the power to make and enforce laws.

government The individuals and institutions that make society's rules and possess the power and authority to enforce those rules.

institution An ongoing organization that performs certain functions for society.

politics The process of resolving conflicts over how society should use its scarce resources and who should receive various benefits, such as public health care and public higher education.

power The ability to influence the behavior of others, usually through the use of force, persuasion, or rewards.

public services Essential services that individuals cannot provide for themselves, such as building and maintaining roads, establishing welfare programs, operating public schools, and preserving national parks.

social conflict Disagreements among people in a society over what the society's priorities should be.

1-2 **Identify the various types of government systems.** Authoritarian rule by an individual is called **autocracy.** In a **monarchy,** a king, queen, or other aristocrat usually obtains power through inheritance. A **dictatorship** is authoritarian rule by an individual or group whose power is not supported by tradition. **Democracy** is a system of government in which supreme political authority rests with the people. One modern institution with some of the characteristics of **direct democracy** is the ballot proposal. In a **representative democracy,** the will of the people is expressed through groups of individuals elected by the people to act as their representatives. Other forms of government include aristocracy, plutocracy, and theocracy.

autocracy A form of government in which the power and authority of the government are in the hands of a single person.

democracy A system of government in which the people have ultimate political authority. The word is derived from the Greek *demos* ("the people") and *kratia* ("rule").

dictatorship A form of government in which absolute power is exercised by an individual or group whose power is not supported by tradition.

direct democracy A system of government in which political decisions are made by the people themselves rather than by elected representatives. This form of government was practiced in some parts of ancient Greece.

divine right theory The theory that a monarch's right to rule was derived directly from God rather than from the consent of the people.

monarchy A form of autocracy in which a king, queen, or other aristocrat is the highest authority in the government. Monarchs usually obtain their power through inheritance.

parliament The national legislative body in countries governed by a parliamentary system, such as Britain and Canada.

representative democracy A form of democracy in which the will of the majority is expressed through groups of individuals elected by the people to act as their representatives.

republic Essentially, a representative democracy in which there is no king or queen and the people are sovereign.

1-3 **Summarize some of the basic principles of American democracy and basic American political values.** In writing the U.S. Constitution, the framers incorporated two basic principles of government that had evolved in England: **limited government** and representative government. Our democracy resulted from a type of **social contract** among early Americans to create and abide by a set of governing rules. American democracy is based on several principles, including equality in voting, individual freedom, equal protection of the law, majority rule and minority rights, and collective voluntary consent to be governed. The rights to **liberty, equality,** and property are fundamental political values shared by most Americans. Differences among Americans in interpreting these values underlie the division between the Democratic and Republican parties, as well as the **Tea Party movement.**

capitalism An economic system based on the private ownership of wealth-producing property, free markets, and freedom of contract. The privately owned corporation is the preeminent capitalist institution.

equality A concept that holds, at a minimum, that all people are entitled to equal protection under the law.

liberty The freedom of individuals to believe, act, and express themselves as they choose so long as doing so does not infringe on the rights of other individuals in the society.

limited government A form of government based on the principle that the powers of government should be clearly limited either through a written document or through wide public understanding.

natural rights Rights that are not bestowed by governments but are inherent within every man, woman, and child by virtue of the fact that he or she is a human being.

political culture The set of ideas, values, and attitudes about government and the political process held by a community or a nation.

social contract A voluntary agreement among individuals to create a government and to give that government adequate power to secure the mutual protection and welfare of all individuals.

Tea Party movement A grassroots conservative movement that arose in 2009 after Barack Obama became president. The movement opposes big government and current levels of taxation, and also rejects political compromise.

1-4 **Define common American ideological positions, such as "conservatism" and "liberalism."** The emergence of the **conservative movement** in the 1950s and 1960s was essential to the development of modern American **conservatism.** Conservatives believe that individuals and families should take responsibility for their own economic circumstances, and they place a high value on the principle of order, on family values, and on patriotism. Conservatism includes those who want society and the government to reflect traditional religious values. While tracing its roots to the New Deal programs of Franklin D. Roosevelt, American **liberalism** took its modern form in the 1960s. Support for minority rights of all kinds became an important part of liberal ideology. Liberals, or **progressives,** argue that big government is a necessary tool for promoting the common welfare, and strongly favor the separation of church and state. Liberals identify with the Democratic Party, and conservatives typically identify themselves politically as Republicans. People whose views fall in the middle of the traditional political spectrum are generally called **moderates.** Many Americans have opinions that do not fit neatly under the liberal or conservative label. Some Americans, for example, are both economic progressives and social conservatives. The **ideology** of **socialism** has few adherents in the United States. **Libertarianism,** on the other hand, has unusually strong support.

FIGURE 1–3   THE TRADITIONAL POLITICAL SPECTRUM

LEFT · CENTER · RIGHT

Socialist · Liberal · Moderate · Conservative · Libertarian

Democrats · Republicans

conservatism A set of political beliefs that include a limited role for the national government in helping individuals and in the economic affairs of the nation, as well as support for traditional values and lifestyles.

conservative movement An ideological movement that arose in the 1950s and 1960s and continues to shape conservative beliefs.

ideology Generally, a system of political ideas that are rooted in religious or philosophical beliefs concerning human nature, society, and government.

liberalism A set of political beliefs that include the advocacy of active government, including government intervention to improve the welfare of individuals and to protect civil rights.

libertarianism The belief that government should do as little as possible, not only in the economic sphere, but also in regulating morality and personal behavior.

moderates Persons whose views fall in the middle of the political spectrum.

progressivism Today, an alternative, more popular term for the set of political beliefs also known as liberalism.

socialism A political ideology, often critical of capitalism, that lies to the left of liberalism on the traditional political spectrum. Socialists are scarce in the United States but common in many other countries.

CHAPTER 2 LEARNING OUTCOMES / KEY TERMS

2-1 **Point out some of the influences on the American political tradition in the colonial years.** American politics owes much to the English political tradition, but the colonists derived most of their understanding of limited government and representative government from their own experiences. In 1620, the Pilgrims drew up the **Mayflower Compact,** in which they set up a government and promised to obey its laws.

Other colonies, in turn, established fundamental governing rules and principles that were later expressed in the U.S. Constitution and **Bill of Rights.** Colonial leaders became familiar with the practical problems of governing. They learned how to build coalitions among groups with diverse interests and how to make compromises.

Bill of Rights The first ten amendments to the U.S. Constitution. They list the freedoms—such as the freedoms of speech, press, and religion— that a citizen enjoys and that cannot be infringed on by the government.

Mayflower Compact A document drawn up by Pilgrim leaders in 1620 on the ship *Mayflower.* The document stated that laws were to be made for the general good of the people.

2-2 **Explain why the American colonies rebelled against Britain.** After the Seven Years' War, the British government decided to pay its war debts and to finance the defense of its North American empire by imposing taxes on the colonists. The colonists protested, and Britain responded with a series of repressive measures. The colonists established the **First Continental Congress** and sent a petition to King George III to explain their

grievances. The congress also called for a continued boycott of British goods and required each colony to establish an army. Soon after British soldiers fought colonial citizen soldiers in the first battles of the American Revolution in 1775, delegates gathered for the **Second Continental Congress,** which assumed the powers of a central government. The congress adopted the Declaration of Independence on July 4, 1776.

First Continental Congress A gathering of delegates from twelve of the thirteen colonies, held in 1774 to protest the Coercive Acts.

Second Continental Congress The congress of the colonies that met in 1775 to assume the powers of a central government and to establish an army.

unicameral legislature A legislature with only one chamber.

2-3 **Describe the structure of government established by the Articles of Confederation and some of the strengths and weaknesses of the Articles.** The **Articles of Confederation** established the Congress of the Confederation as the central governing body. It was a **unicameral legislature** in which each state had one vote. Congress had several powers, including the power to declare war, to enter into treaties, and to settle disputes among the states under certain circumstances. Nevertheless, the central government created

by the Articles was weak. Congress could not force the states to meet military quotas. It could not regulate trade or agreements between the states or with other nations. Disruptions such as **Shays' Rebellion** frightened political and business leaders and persuaded more and more Americans that a true national government had to be created. Congress called on the states to send delegates to a meeting in Philadelphia in 1787 that became the **Constitutional Convention.**

Articles of Confederation The nation's first national constitution, which established a national form of government following the American Revolution. The Articles provided for a confederal form of government in which the central government had few powers.

confederation A league of independent states that are united only for the purpose of achieving common goals.

Constitutional Convention The convention of delegates from the states that was held in Philadelphia in 1787 for the purpose of amending the Articles of Confederation. In fact, the delegates wrote a new constitution (the U.S. Constitution) that established a federal form of government.

Shays' Rebellion A rebellion of angry farmers in western Massachusetts in 1786, led by former Revolutionary War captain Daniel Shays.

2-4 **List the major compromises made by the delegates at the Constitutional Convention, and discuss the Federalist and Anti-Federalist positions on ratifying the Constitution.** Delegates resolved the small-state/large-state controversy over representation in Congress with the **Great Compromise,** which established a **bicameral legislature.** The **three-fifths compromise** settled a deadlock on how slaves would be counted to determine representation in the House of Representatives. The delegates also agreed that Congress could prohibit the importation of slaves beginning in 1808. The South agreed to let Congress have the power to regulate both

interstate commerce and commerce with other nations in exchange for a ban on export taxes. Other actions taken at the convention included the creation of an independent executive and the establishment of the United States Supreme Court. The battle over ratification was fought between the **Federalists,** who favored a strong central government and the new Constitution, and the **Anti-Federalists,** who argued that the Constitution would lead to aristocratic **tyranny** or an overly powerful central government that would limit personal freedom. To gain support for ratification, the Federalists promised to add a bill of rights to the Constitution.

Anti-Federalists A political group that opposed the adoption of the Constitution.

bicameral legislature A legislature made up of two chambers, or parts.

faction A group of persons forming a cohesive minority.

Federalists A political group, led by Alexander Hamilton and John Adams, that supported the adoption of the Constitution and the creation of a federal form of government.

Great Compromise A plan for a bicameral legislature in which one chamber would be based on population and the other chamber would represent each state equally. Also known as the Connecticut Compromise.

interstate commerce Trade that involves more than one state.

three-fifths compromise A compromise reached during the Constitutional Convention by which three-fifths of all slaves were to be counted for purposes of representation in the House of Representatives.

tyranny The arbitrary or unrestrained exercise of power by an oppressive individual or government.

2-5 **Summarize the Constitution's major principles of government, and describe how the Constitution can be amended.** The Constitution incorporated the principles of limited government, popular sovereignty, and the **rule of law.** A **federal system,** in which the national government shares sovereign powers with the state governments, was established. **Separation of powers** and a system of **checks and balances** ensure that no one branch—legislative, executive, or judicial—can exercise exclusive control. An amendment to the Constitution can be proposed either by a two-thirds vote in each chamber of Congress or by a national convention called at the request of

FIGURE 2–6   THE PROCESS OF AMENDING THE CONSTITUTION

How is it that the president has no role in amending the Constitution?

AN AMENDMENT CAN BE PROPOSED BY . . .	AN AMENDMENT CAN BE RATIFIED BY . . .
A two-thirds vote in both houses of Congress	Three-fourths of state legislatures
A vote at a national constitutional convention called by Congress at the request of two-thirds of state legislatures	Three-fourths of states at special conventions

Traditional   Used once (21st Amendment)   Never used

two-thirds of the state legislatures. Ratification of an amendment requires either approval by three-fourths of the state legislatures or by three-fourths of the states in special conventions.

checks and balances A major principle of American government in which each of the three branches is given the means to check (to restrain or balance) the actions of the others.

commerce clause The clause in Article I, Section 8, of the Constitution that gives Congress the power to regulate interstate commerce (commerce involving more than one state).

federal system A form of government that provides for a division of powers between a central government and several regional governments.

Madisonian Model The model of government devised by James Madison, in which the powers of the government are separated into three branches: legislative, executive, and judicial.

rule of law A basic principle of government that requires those who govern to act in accordance with established law.

separation of powers The principle of dividing governmental powers among the legislative, the executive, and the judicial branches of government.

veto power A constitutional power that enables the chief executive (president or governor) to reject legislation and return it to the legislature with reasons for the rejection. This either prevents or delays the bill from becoming law.

CHAPTER 3 LEARNING OUTCOMES / KEY TERMS

3-1 **Explain what federalism means, how federalism differs from other systems of government, and why it exists in the United States.** Government powers in a federal system are divided between a national government and subnational governments. The powers of both levels of government are specified and limited. Alternatives to **federalism** include a **unitary system,** in which subnational governments exercise only those powers given to them by the national government, and a **confederal system,** in which the national government exists and operates only at the direction of the subnational governments. The Articles of Confederation failed because they did not allow for a sufficiently strong central government, but the framers of the Constitution were fearful of a too-powerful central government. The appeal of federalism was that it retained state powers and local traditions while establishing a strong national government capable of handling common problems.

confederal system A league of independent sovereign states, joined together by a central government that has only limited powers over them.

federalism A system of shared sovereignty between two levels of government—one national and one subnational—occupying the same geographic region.

unitary system A centralized governmental system in which local or subdivisional governments exercise only those powers given to them by the central government.

3-2 **Indicate how the Constitution divides governing powers in our federal system.** The national government possesses three types of powers: **expressed, implied,** and **inherent.** The Constitution expressly enumerates twenty-seven powers that Congress may exercise, while the **necessary and proper clause** is the basis for implied powers. The national government also enjoys certain inherent powers—powers that governments must have simply to ensure the nation's integrity and survival. In addition, the Constitution expressly prohibits the national government from undertaking certain actions. The Tenth Amendment states that powers that are not delegated to the national government by the Constitution nor prohibited to the states are "reserved" to the states or to the people. In principle, each state has **police powers**—the ability to regulate its internal affairs and to enact whatever laws are necessary to protect the health, safety, welfare, and morals of its people. The Constitution also contains provisions, such as the full faith and credit clause, relating to interstate relations. **Concurrent powers** can be exercised by both the state governments and the federal government. The **supremacy clause** asserts that national government power takes precedence over any conflicting state action.

concurrent powers Powers held by both the federal and the state governments in a federal system.

division of powers A basic principle of federalism established by the U.S. Constitution, by which powers are divided between the national and state governments.

expressed powers Constitutional or statutory powers that are expressly provided for by the U.S. Constitution; also called *enumerated powers*.

implied powers The powers of the federal government that are implied by the expressed powers in the Constitution, particularly in Article I, Section 8.

inherent powers The powers of the national government that, although not always expressly granted by the Constitution, are necessary to ensure the nation's integrity and survival as a political unit.

necessary and proper clause Article I, Section 8, Clause 18, of the Constitution, which gives Congress the power to make all laws "necessary and proper" for the federal government to carry out its responsibilities; also called the *elastic clause*.

police powers The powers of a government body that enable it to create laws for the protection of the health, safety, welfare, and morals of the people. In the United States, most police powers are reserved to the states.

supremacy clause Article VI, Clause 2, of the Constitution, which makes the Constitution and federal laws superior to all conflicting state and local laws.

3-3 **Summarize the evolution of federal-state relationships in the United States over time.** The United States Supreme Court, in *McCulloch v. Maryland* (1819) and *Gibbons v. Ogden* (1824), played a key role in establishing the constitutional foundations for the supremacy of the national government. An increase in the political power of the national government was also a result of the South's defeat in the Civil War. The relationship between the states and the national government has evolved through several stages. The model of **dual federalism,** which prevailed after the Civil War until the 1930s, assumes that the states and the national government are more or less equals, with each level of government having separate and distinct functions and responsibilities. The model of **cooperative federalism,** which views the national and state governments as complementary parts of a single governmental mechanism, grew out of the need to solve the pressing national problems caused by the Great Depression. The 1960s and 1970s saw an even greater expansion of the national government's role in domestic policy, but the massive social programs undertaken during this period also resulted in greater involvement by state and local governments. The model in which every level of government is involved in implementing a policy is sometimes referred to as **picket-fence federalism.**

cooperative federalism A model of federalism in which the states and the federal government cooperate in solving problems.

dual federalism A system of government in which the federal and the state governments maintain diverse but sovereign powers.

New Deal The policies ushered in by the Roosevelt administration in 1933 in an attempt to bring the United States out of the Great Depression.

picket-fence federalism A model of federalism in which specific policies and programs are administered by all levels of government—national, state, and local.

preemption A doctrine rooted in the supremacy clause of the Constitution that provides that national laws or regulations governing a certain area take precedence over conflicting state laws or regulations governing that same area.

secession The act of formally withdrawing from membership in an alliance; the withdrawal of a state from the federal Union.

3-4 **Describe developments in federalism in recent years.** Starting in the 1970s, several administrations favored a shift from nation-centered federalism to state-centered federalism. One of the goals of the **"new federalism"** was to return to the states certain powers that had been exercised by the national government since the 1930s—a process called **devolution.** The federal government and the states seem to be in a constant tug-of-war over federal regulations, federal programs, and federal demands on the states. In the last several years, Supreme Court decisions regarding state immigration laws, health-care reform, and voting rights have affected the shape of our federal system. The politics of federalism include controversies surrounding **federal mandates.**

devolution The surrender or transfer of powers to local authorities by a central government.

federal mandate A requirement in federal legislation that forces states and municipalities to comply with certain rules.

new federalism A plan to limit the federal government's role in regulating state governments and to give the states increased power in deciding how they should spend government revenues.

3-5 **Explain what is meant by the term** *fiscal federalism.* To help the states pay for some of the costs associated with implementing national policies, the national government gives back some of the tax dollars it collects to the states—in the form of **categorical** and **block grants.** States have come to depend on this process of **fiscal federalism** as an important source of revenue. By giving or withholding federal grant dollars, the federal government has been able to exercise control over matters that traditionally have been under the control of state governments. Sometimes state and local governments engage in **competitive federalism** by offering lower taxes or more services to attract businesses and citizens.

block grant A federal grant given to a state for a broad area, such as criminal justice or mental-health programs.

categorical grant A federal grant targeted for a specific purpose as defined by federal law.

competitive federalism A model of federalism in which state and local governments compete for businesses and citizens, who in effect "vote with their feet" by moving to jurisdictions that offer a competitive advantage.

cross-cutting requirements Requirements that apply to all federal grants.

fiscal federalism The allocation of taxes collected by one level of government (typically the national government) to another level (typically state or local governments).

4-1 **Define the term *civil liberties,* explain how civil liberties differ from civil rights, and state the constitutional basis for our civil liberties. Civil liberties** are legal and constitutional rights that protect citizens from government actions. Civil rights specify what the government *must* do. Civil liberties set forth what the government *cannot* do. Many of our liberties were added by the Bill of Rights, ratified in 1791. The United States Supreme Court has used the **due process clause** to incorporate most of the protections guaranteed by the Bill of Rights into the liberties protected from state government actions under the Fourteenth Amendment.

TABLE 4—2 INCORPORATING THE BILL OF RIGHTS INTO THE FOURTEENTH AMENDMENT

Year	Issue	Amendment Involved	Court Case
1925	Freedom of speech	I	*Gitlow v. New York,* 268 U.S. 652.
1931	Freedom of the press	I	*Near v. Minnesota,* 283 U.S. 697.
1932	Right to a lawyer in capital punishment cases	VI	*Powell v. Alabama,* 287 U.S. 45.
1937	Freedom of assembly and right to petition	I	*De Jonge v. Oregon,* 299 U.S. 353.
1940	Freedom of religion	I	*Cantwell v. Connecticut,* 310 U.S. 296.
1947	Separation of church and state	I	*Everson v. Board of Education,* 330 U.S. 1.
1948	Right to a public trial	VI	*In re Oliver,* 333 U.S. 257.
1949	No unreasonable searches and seizures	IV	*Wolf v. Colorado,* 338 U.S. 25.
1961	Exclusionary rule (See "The Rights of the Accused" section later in this chapter.)	IV	*Mapp v. Ohio,* 367 U.S. 643.
1962	No cruel and unusual punishments	VIII	*Robinson v. California,* 370 U.S. 660.
1963	Right to a lawyer in all criminal felony cases	VI	*Gideon v. Wainwright,* 372 U.S. 335.
1964	No compulsory self-incrimination	V	*Malloy v. Hogan,* 378 U.S. 1.
1965	Right to privacy	Various	*Griswold v. Connecticut,* 381 U.S. 479.
1966	Right to an impartial jury	VI	*Parker v. Gladden,* 385 U.S. 363.
1967	Right to a speedy trial	VI	*Klopfer v. North Carolina,* 386 U.S. 213.
1969	No double jeopardy	V	*Benton v. Maryland,* 395 U.S. 784.
1982	Right to refuse to quarter soldiers	III	*Engblom v. Carey,* 677 F.2d 957 (2d Cir.)
2010	Right to bear arms	II	*McDonald v. Chicago,* 561 U.S. 3025.

bill of attainder A legislative act that inflicts punishment on particular persons or groups without granting them the right to a trial.

civil liberties Individual rights protected by the Constitution against the powers of the government.

due process clause The constitutional guarantee, set out in the Fifth and Fourteenth Amendments, that the government will not illegally or arbitrarily deprive a person of life, liberty, or property.

due process of law The requirement that the government use fair, reasonable, and standard procedures whenever it takes any legal action against an individual; required by the Fifth and Fourteenth Amendments.

***ex post facto* law** A criminal law that punishes individuals for committing an act that was legal when the act was committed.

writ of *habeas corpus* An order that requires an official to bring a specified prisoner into court and explain to the judge why the person is being held in jail.

4-2 **List the religious freedoms guaranteed by the First Amendment, and explain how the courts have interpreted and applied these freedoms.** The First Amendment prohibits Congress from passing laws "respecting an establishment of religion, or prohibiting the free exercise thereof." Issues involving the **establishment clause** include prayer in the public schools, the teaching of evolution versus creationism or intelligent design, and government aid to parochial schools. The Supreme Court has ruled that public schools cannot sponsor religious activities and has held unconstitutional state laws forbidding the teaching of evolution in the schools. Some aid to parochial schools has been held to violate the establishment clause, while other forms of aid have been held permissible. In its interpretation of the **free exercise clause,** the Court has ruled consistently that the right to hold any religious belief is absolute. The right to practice one's beliefs may have some limits. Title VII of the 1964 Civil Rights Act, however, bolstered free exercise of religion in the workplace.

establishment clause The section of the First Amendment that prohibits Congress from passing laws "respecting an establishment of religion."

free exercise clause The provision of the First Amendment stating that the government cannot pass laws "prohibiting the free exercise" of religion.

***Lemon* test** A three-part test enunciated by the Supreme Court in the 1971 case of *Lemon v. Kurtzman* to determine whether government aid to parochial schools is constitutional.

school voucher An educational certificate, provided by a government, that allows a student to use public funds to pay for a private or a public school chosen by the student or his or her parents.

4-3 Describe how freedom of speech is protected by the First Amendment, and show how the courts have implemented this freedom. Although the Supreme Court has zealously safeguarded the right to free speech, including **symbolic speech,** under the First Amendment, at times it has imposed limits on speech in the interests of protecting other rights. These rights include security against harm to one's person or reputation, the need for public order, and the need to preserve the government. The current standard for evaluating the legality of speech opposing the government is the **imminent lawless action test.** The First Amendment freedom of the press generally protects the right to publish a wide range of opinions and information. Over the years, the Court has developed various guidelines and doctrines to use in deciding whether freedom of expression can be restrained.

commercial speech Advertising statements that describe products. Commercial speech receives less protection under the First Amendment than ordinary speech.

imminent lawless action test The current Supreme Court doctrine for assessing the constitutionality of subversive speech. To be illegal, speech must be "directed to inciting . . . imminent lawless action."

libel A published report of a falsehood that tends to injure a person's reputation or character.

obscenity Indecency or offensiveness in speech, expression, behavior, or appearance.

seditious speech Speech that urges resistance to lawful authority or that advocates the overthrow of a government.

slander The public utterance (speaking) of a statement that holds a person up for contempt, ridicule, or hatred.

symbolic speech The expression of beliefs, opinions, or ideas through forms other than verbal speech or print; speech involving actions and other nonverbal expressions.

4-4 Discuss why Americans are increasingly concerned about privacy rights. The Supreme Court has held that a right to privacy is implied by other constitutional rights guaranteed in the Bill of Rights. The nature and scope of this right, however, are not always clear. In 1973, the Court held that the right to privacy is broad enough to encompass a woman's decision to terminate a pregnancy, though the right is not absolute throughout pregnancy. Since that decision, the Court has upheld some restrictive state laws requiring certain actions prior to abortions. Privacy issues have also been raised in the context of physician-assisted suicide; several states now allow the practice. A concern among Americans in recent years is that their personal information could be collected by organizations that use the data improperly, and some laws have been passed to protect the privacy rights of individuals. Since the terrorist attacks of September 11, 2001, the news media and Congress have debated how the United States can strengthen national security while still protecting civil liberties, particularly the right to privacy. The USA Patriot Act, the revelations regarding the NSA's collection of metadata, programs such as PRISM, and the tapping of foreign leaders' phones have all been part of the ongoing discussion. The 2015 USA Freedom Act sought to limit some aspects of data collection by the government.

4-5 Summarize how the Constitution and the Bill of Rights protect the rights of accused persons. Constitutional safeguards include the Fourth Amendment protection from unreasonable searches and seizures and the requirement that no warrant for a search or an arrest be issued without **probable cause;** the Fifth Amendment prohibition against **double jeopardy** and the protection against **self-incrimination;** the Sixth Amendment guarantees of a speedy trial, a trial by jury, a public trial, the right to confront witnesses, and the right to counsel at various stages in some criminal proceedings; and the Eighth Amendment prohibitions against excessive bail and fines and against cruel and unusual punishments. The Constitution also provides for the **writ of habeas corpus**—an order requiring that an official bring a specified prisoner into court and explain to the judge why the person is being held in jail.

double jeopardy The prosecution of a person twice for the same criminal offense; prohibited by the Fifth Amendment in all but a few circumstances.

exclusionary rule A criminal procedural rule stating that illegally obtained evidence is not admissible in court.

***Miranda* warnings** A series of statements informing criminal suspects, on their arrest, of their constitutional rights, such as the right to remain silent and the right to counsel; required by the Supreme Court's 1966 decision in *Miranda v. Arizona*.

probable cause Cause for believing that there is a substantial likelihood that a person has committed or is about to commit a crime.

self-incrimination Providing damaging information or testimony against oneself in court.

5-1 **Explain the constitutional basis for our civil rights and for laws prohibiting discrimination. Civil rights** are the rights of all Americans to equal treatment under the law. The **equal protection clause** of the Fourteenth Amendment has been interpreted by the courts to mean that states may not discriminate unreasonably against a particular group or class of individuals. The amendment also provides a legal basis for federal civil rights legislation. The U.S. Supreme Court has developed various standards for determining whether the equal protection clause has been violated. A law based on a **suspect classification,** for example, is subject to the **strict scrutiny standard.**

civil rights The rights of all Americans to equal treatment under the law, as provided by the Fourteenth Amendment to the Constitution.

equal protection clause Section 1 of the Fourteenth Amendment, which states that no state shall "deny to any person within its jurisdiction the equal protection of the laws."

fundamental right A basic right of all Americans, such as First Amendment rights. Any law or action that prevents some group of persons from exercising a fundamental right is subject to the *strict scrutiny standard.*

rational basis test A test (also known as the *ordinary scrutiny standard*) used by the Supreme Court to decide whether a discriminatory law violates the equal protection clause of the Constitution. It is used only when there is no classification—such as race or gender—that would require a higher level of scrutiny.

strict scrutiny standard A standard under which a law or action must be necessary to promote a compelling state interest and must be narrowly tailored to meet that interest.

suspect classification A classification, such as race, that provides the basis for a discriminatory law. Any law based on a suspect classification is subject to strict scrutiny by the courts, meaning that the law must be justified by a compelling state interest.

5-2 **Discuss the reasons for the civil rights movement and the changes it caused in American politics and government.** The equal protection clause was originally intended to protect the newly freed slaves from discrimination after the Civil War. By the late 1880s, however, southern states had begun to pass a series of segregation laws. In 1896, the Supreme Court established the **separate-but-equal doctrine,** which was used to justify segregation for nearly sixty years. In 1954, the Court held that segregation by race in public education was unconstitutional. One year later, the arrest of Rosa Parks for violating local segregation laws spurred a boycott of the bus system in Montgomery, Alabama. The protest was led by the Reverend Dr. Martin Luther King, Jr. In 1956, a federal court prohibited the segregation of buses in Montgomery, marking the beginning of the **civil rights movement.** Civil rights protesters in the 1960s applied the tactic of nonviolent **civil disobedience** in actions throughout the South. As the civil rights movement demonstrated its strength, Congress passed a series of civil rights laws, including the Civil Rights Act of 1964, the Voting Rights Act of 1965, and the Civil Rights Act of 1968. Today, the percentages of voting-age blacks and whites registered to vote are nearly equal. Political participation by African Americans has increased, as has the number of African American elected officials. African Americans continue to struggle for income and educational parity with whites.

busing The transportation of public school students by bus to schools physically outside their neighborhoods to eliminate school segregation based on residential patterns.

civil disobedience The deliberate and public act of refusing to obey laws thought to be unjust.

civil rights movement The movement in the 1950s and 1960s, by minorities and concerned whites, to end racial discrimination.

de facto **segregation** Racial segregation that occurs not as a result of government actions but because of social and economic conditions and residential patterns.

de jure **segregation** Racial segregation that occurs because of laws or decisions by government agencies.

separate-but-equal doctrine A Supreme Court doctrine holding that the equal protection clause of the Fourteenth Amendment did not forbid racial segregation as long as the facilities for blacks were equal to those for whites.

sit-in A tactic of nonviolent civil disobedience. Demonstrators enter a business, college building, or other public place and remain seated until they are forcibly removed or until their demands are met.

5-3 **Describe the political and economic achievements of women in this country over time, and identify some obstacles to equality that women continue to face.** The struggle of women for equal treatment initially focused on **suffrage.** In 1920, the Nineteenth Amendment was ratified, granting voting rights to women. **Feminism** shaped a new movement that began in the 1960s. Congress and state legislatures enacted measures to provide equal rights for women, and the courts accepted the argument that gender discrimination violates the equal protection clause. Although women remain underrepresented in politics, increasingly women have gained power as public officials. In spite of federal legislation to promote equal treatment of women in the workplace, women continue to face various forms of discrimination, including the **glass ceiling.** The prohibition of gender discrimination has been extended to prohibit **sexual harassment.**

feminism A doctrine advocating full political, economic, and social equality for women.

glass ceiling An invisible but real discriminatory barrier that prevents women and minorities from rising to top positions of power or responsibility.

sexual harassment Unwanted physical contact, verbal conduct, or abuse of a sexual nature that interferes with a recipient's job performance, creates a hostile environment, or carries with it an implicit or explicit threat of adverse employment consequences.

suffrage The right to vote; the franchise.

5-4 **Summarize the struggles for equality that other groups in America have experienced.** Latinos constitute the largest ethnic minority in the United States. Economically, Latino households are often members of this country's working poor. Immigration reform has been an important issue for many Latinos. Following the 2014 elections, Hispanic representation in Congress was at a new high. Asian Americans suffered from discriminatory treatment in the late 1800s and early 1900s, and again during World War II. Today, Asian Americans lead other minority groups in median income and median education. Native Americans had no civil rights under U.S. laws until 1924. Beginning in the 1960s, some American Indians formed organizations to strike back at the U.S. government and to reclaim their heritage, including their lands. Persons with disabilities first became a political force in the 1970s. The Americans with Disabilities Act (ADA) of 1990 is the most significant legislation protecting the rights of this group of Americans. In the decades following the 1969 Stonewall Inn incident, laws and court decisions protecting the rights of gay men and lesbians have reflected changing social attitudes. In 2015, the Supreme Court ruled that the Constitution guarantees a right to same-sex marriage in every state.

5-5 **Explain what affirmative action is and why it has been so controversial. Affirmative action** programs have been tested in court cases involving claims of **reverse discrimination.** Some states have banned affirmative action or replaced it with alternative policies.

FIGURE 5–1 **PERSONS IN POVERTY IN THE UNITED STATES BY RACE AND HISPANIC ORIGIN**

Blacks, Hispanics, and American Indians are more likely than whites or Asians to have incomes below the poverty line. *Why are children substantially more likely than adults to live in families with incomes below the poverty line?*

Source: The 2010 Census.

affirmative action A policy that gives special consideration, in jobs and college admissions, to members of groups that have been discriminated against in the past.

quota system A policy under which a specific number of jobs, promotions, or other types of placements, such as university admissions, are given to members of selected groups.

reverse discrimination Discrimination against those who have no minority status.

6-1 **Explain what an interest group is, why interest groups form, and how interest groups function in American politics.** An **interest group** is an organized group of people sharing common objectives who actively attempt to influence government policymakers through direct and indirect methods. The right to form interest groups and to lobby the government is protected by the First Amendment. Interest groups may form—and existing groups may become more politically active—when the government expands its scope of activities. Interest groups also come into existence in response to a perceived threat to a group's interests, or they can form in reaction to the creation of other groups. **Purposive incentives, solidary incentives,** and **material incentives** are among the reasons people join interest groups. Interest groups (a) help bridge the gap between citizens and government; (b) help raise public awareness and inspire action on various issues; (c) provide public officials with specialized information that may be useful in making policy choices; and (d) serve as another check on public officials. The **pluralist theory** of American democracy views politics as a contest among various interest groups to gain benefits for their members. Two other theories to describe American democracy are **majoritarianism** and **elite theory.** Although both interest groups and political parties are groups of people joined together for political purposes, they differ in several ways.

elite theory The belief that the government is controlled by one or more elite groups.

free rider problem The difficulty that exists when individuals can enjoy the outcome of an interest group's efforts without having to contribute, such as by becoming members of the group.

interest group An organized group of individuals sharing common objectives who actively attempt to influence policymakers.

majoritarianism The belief that public policy is or should be set in accordance with the opinions of a majority of the people.

material incentive A reason to join an interest group—practical benefits such as discounts, subscriptions, or group insurance.

pluralist theory A theory that views politics as a contest among various interest groups—at all levels of government—to gain benefits for their members.

purposive incentive A reason to join an interest group—satisfaction resulting from working for a cause in which one believes.

solidary incentive A reason to join an interest group—pleasure in associating with like-minded individuals.

6-2 **Identify the various types of interest groups.** The most common interest groups are those that promote private interests. Business has long been well organized for effective action. Hundreds of business groups operate at all levels of government, and there are also umbrella organizations, including the U.S. Chamber of Commerce, that represent business interests. **Trade organizations** support policies that benefit specific industries. Producers of various specific farm commodities have formed organizations to promote their own interests, and many groups work for general agricultural interests. Interest groups representing labor have been some of the most influential groups in the nation's history. While the strength and political power of labor unions have waned in the past several decades, more than one-third of all public-sector workers are union members. Most professions that require advanced education or specialized training have organizations to protect and promote their interests. Other types of groups include **public-interest groups,** which are formed with the broader goal of working for the "public good." In reality, however, all lobbying groups represent special interests. Groups organized for the protection of consumer rights were very active in the 1960s and 1970s, and some are still active today. Americans who share the same race, ethnicity, gender, or other characteristic often have important common interests and form identity interest groups. Some interest groups, including environmental and religious groups, promote a shared political perspective or ideology. Numerous interest groups focus on a single issue. Efforts by state and local governments to lobby the federal government have escalated in recent years.

public-interest group An interest group formed for the purpose of working for the "public good." Examples are the American Civil Liberties Union and Common Cause.

right-to-work laws Laws that ban unions from collecting dues or other fees from workers whom they represent but who have not actually joined the union.

trade organization An association formed by members of a particular industry, such as the oil industry or the trucking industry, to develop common standards and goals for the industry. Trade organizations, as interest groups, lobby government for legislation or regulations that specifically benefit their members.

6-3 **Discuss how the activities of interest groups help to shape government policymaking.** Interest groups use a variety of strategies to steer policies in ways beneficial to their interests. Sometimes, they attempt to influence policymakers directly, but at other times they try to exert indirect influence on policymakers by shaping public opinion. **Lobbying** and providing election support are two important **direct techniques** used by interest groups. Groups also try to influence public policy through the general public. **Indirect techniques** include advertising, **rating systems,** issue advocacy through **independent expenditures,** mobilizing constituents, going to court, and organizing demonstrations.

TABLE 6–5	DIRECT LOBBYING TECHNIQUES
Technique	**Description**
Making Personal Contacts with Key Legislators	A lobbyist's personal contacts with key legislators or other government officials—in their offices, in the halls of Congress, or on social occasions such as dinners, boating expeditions, and the like—comprise one of the most effective direct lobbying techniques.
Providing Expertise and Research Results for Legislators	Lobbyists often have knowledge and expertise that are useful in drafting legislation, and this expertise can be a major strength for an interest group. Harried members of Congress cannot possibly be experts on everything they vote on and therefore eagerly seek information to help them make up their minds.
Offering "Expert" Testimony before Congressional Committees	Lobbyists often provide "expert" testimony before congressional committees for or against proposed legislation. Each expert offers as much evidence as possible to support her or his position.
Providing Legal Advice to Legislators	Many lobbyists assist legislators in drafting legislation or prospective regulations. Lobbyists are a source of ideas and sometimes offer legal advice on specific details.
Following Up on Legislation	Because executive agencies responsible for carrying out legislation can often change the scope of the new law, lobbyists may also try to influence the bureaucrats who implement the policy.

direct technique Any method used by an interest group to interact with government officials directly to further the group's goals.

independent expenditure An expenditure for activities that are independent from (not coordinated with) those of a political candidate or a political party.

indirect technique Any method used by interest groups to influence government officials through third parties, such as voters.

lobbying All of the attempts by organizations or by individuals to influence the passage, defeat, or contents of legislation or to influence the administrative decisions of government.

lobbyist An individual who handles a particular interest group's lobbying efforts.

political action committee (PAC) A committee that is established by a corporation, labor union, or special interest group to raise funds and make campaign contributions on the establishing organization's behalf.

rating system A system by which a particular interest group evaluates (rates) the performance of legislators based on how often the legislators have voted with the group's position on particular issues.

6-4 **Describe how interest groups are regulated by government.** In spite of legislation designed to reduce the "revolving door" syndrome, it remains common for those who leave positions with the federal government to become **lobbyists** or consultants for the interest groups they helped to regulate. The Lobbying Disclosure Act of 1995 reformed a 1946 law in several ways, particularly by creating stricter definitions of who is a lobbyist. In the wake of lobbying scandals in the early 2000s, additional lobbying reform efforts were undertaken. The Honest Leadership and Open Government Act of 2007 increased lobbying disclosure requirements and placed further restrictions on the receipt of gifts and travel by members of Congress paid for by lobbyists and the organizations they represent.

CHAPTER 7 LEARNING OUTCOMES / KEY TERMS

7-1 Summarize the origins and development of the two-party system in the United States. After the Constitution was ratified, the Federalist Party supported a strong central government that would encourage the development of commerce and manufacturing. The party's opponents, Jefferson's Republicans, favored a more limited role for government. After suffering electoral defeats in the early 1800s, the Federalists went out of existence, resulting in a **realignment** of the party system. In the mid-1820s, Jefferson's Republicans split into two groups—the Democrats and the National Republicans (later the Whig Party). As the Democrats and Whigs competed for the presidency during the 1840s and 1850s, the **two-party system** as we know it today emerged. By the mid-1850s, most northern Whigs were absorbed into the new Republican Party, which opposed the extension of slavery. After the Civil War, the Republicans and Democrats were roughly even in strength, although the Republicans were more successful in presidential contests. After the realigning election of 1896, many Americans viewed the **GOP** as the party that knew how to manage the nation's economy, and it remained dominant in national politics until the Great Depression. The election of 1932 brought Franklin D. Roosevelt to the presidency and the Democrats back to power at the national level. In the 1960s, however, conservative Democrats did not like the direction in which their party seemed to be taking them, and over time most of them became Republican voters. The result of this "rolling realignment" was that by 2000, the two major parties were fairly evenly matched.

GOP A nickname for the Republican Party—"grand old party."

political party A group of individuals who organize to win elections, operate the government, and determine policy.

realignment A process in which the popular support for and relative strength of the parties shift and the parties are reestablished with different coalitions of supporters.

7-2 Describe the current status of the two major parties. A key characteristic of recent politics has been the extreme partisanship of party activists and members of Congress. The rolling realignment after the elections of 1968 resulted in parties that were much more homogeneous. By 2009, the most conservative Democrat in the House was to the left of the most moderate Republican. Ideological uniformity has made it easier for the parties to maintain discipline in Congress. Political polarization grew even more severe after the 2010 elections. Many of the new Republican members of Congress were pledged to the Tea Party philosophy of no-compromise conservatism. Also significant is the number of independent voters, contributing to a potential **dealignment** in the party system.

dealignment Among voters, a growing detachment from both major political parties.

7-3 Explain how political parties function in our democratic system. Political parties link the people's policy preferences to actual government policies. They recruit and nominate candidates for political office, coordinate campaigns, and take care of a number of tasks that are essential to the smooth functioning of the electoral process. Parties also help educate the public about important political issues. Parties coordinate policy among the various branches and levels of government, and balance the competing interests of those who support the party. In government, the **minority party** checks the actions of the party in power.

coalition An alliance of individuals or groups with a variety of interests and opinions who join together to support all or part of a political party's platform.

majority party The political party that has more members in the legislature than the opposing party.

minority party The political party that has fewer members in the legislature than the opposing party.

primary A preliminary election held for the purpose of choosing a party's final candidate.

7-4 Discuss the structure of American political parties. 7 The party in the **electorate** consists of **party identifiers** and **party activists.** Each party is decentralized, with national, state, and local organizations. Delegates to the **national convention** nominate the party's presidential and vice-presidential candidates, and they adopt the **party platform.** The national party organization includes a **national party committee,** a **national party chairperson,** and congressional campaign committees. The party in government consists of all of the party's candidates who have won elections and now hold public office. The party in government helps to organize the government's agenda by convincing its own party members in office to vote for its policies.

electorate All of the citizens eligible to vote in a given election.

national convention The meeting held by each major party every four years to nominate presidential and vice-presidential candidates, write a party platform, and conduct other party business.

national party chairperson An individual who serves as a political party's administrative head at the national level and directs the work of the party's national committee.

national party committee The political party leaders who direct party business during the four years between the national party conventions, organize the next national convention, and plan how to support the party's candidate in the next presidential election.

party activist A party member who helps to organize and oversee party functions and planning during and between campaigns, and may even become a candidate for office.

party identifier A person who identifies himself or herself as being a supporter of a particular political party.

party platform The document drawn up by each party at its national convention that outlines the policies and positions of the party.

party ticket A list of a political party's candidates for various offices. In national elections, the party ticket consists of the presidential and vice-presidential candidates.

patronage A system of rewarding the party faithful and workers with government jobs or contracts.

precinct A political district within a city, such as a block or a neighborhood, or a rural portion of a county; the smallest voting district at the local level.

solidarity Mutual agreement among the members of a particular group.

ward A local unit of a political party's organization, consisting of a division or district within a city.

7-5 **Describe the different types of third parties and how they function in the American political system.** The United States has a two-party system in which the Democrats and the Republicans dominate national politics. American election laws and the rules governing campaign financing tend to favor the major parties. There are also institutional barriers, such as single-member legislative districts and the electoral college system, that prevent **third parties** from enjoying electoral success. There are different kinds of third parties. An issue-oriented party is formed to promote a particular cause or timely issue. An ideological party supports a particular political doctrine or a set of beliefs. A splinter party develops out of a split within a major party, which may be part of an attempt to elect a specific person. Third parties have brought many issues to the public's attention and can influence election outcomes. Third parties also provide a voice for voters who are frustrated with the Republican and Democratic parties.

TABLE 7–1 THE MOST SUCCESSFUL THIRD-PARTY PRESIDENTIAL CAMPAIGNS SINCE 1865

This table includes all third-party candidates winning more than 5 percent of the popular vote or any electoral votes since 1865. It does not count "unfaithful electors" in the electoral college who did not vote for the candidate to whom they were pledged.

Year	Third Party	Third-Party Presidential Candidate	Percent of the Popular Vote	Electoral Votes	Winning Presidential Candidate and Party
1892	Populist	James Weaver	8.5%	22	Grover Cleveland (D)
1912	Progressive	Theodore Roosevelt	27.4	88	Woodrow Wilson (D)
	Socialist	Eugene Debs	6.0	—	
1924	Progressive	Robert LaFollette	16.6	13	Calvin Coolidge (R)
1948	States' Rights	Strom Thurmond	2.4	39	Harry Truman (D)
1960	Independent Democrat	Harry Byrd	0.4	15*	John F. Kennedy (D)
1968	American Independent	George Wallace	13.5	46	Richard Nixon (R)
1980	National Union	John Anderson	6.6	—	Ronald Reagan (R)
1992	Independent	Ross Perot	18.9	—	Bill Clinton (D)
1996	Reform	Ross Perot	8.4	—	Bill Clinton (D)

*Byrd received fifteen electoral votes from unpledged electors in Alabama and Mississippi.
Source: Dave Leip's Atlas of U.S. Presidential Elections at www.uselectionatlas.org.

---

third party In the United States, any party other than the two major parties (Republican and Democratic).

two-party system A political system in which two strong and established parties compete for political offices.

8-1 Describe the political socialization process. Most people acquire their political attitudes, opinions, beliefs, and knowledge through a complex learning process called **political socialization.** Most political socialization is informal. The strong early influence of the family later gives way to the multiple influences of schools, churches, the **media,** opinion leaders, major life events, **peer groups,** and economic status and occupation. People and institutions that influence the political views of others are called **agents of political socialization.**

agents of political socialization People and institutions that influence the political views of others.

media Newspapers, magazines, television, radio, the Internet, and any other printed or electronic means of communication.

peer group Associates, often close in age to one another; may include friends, classmates, co-workers, club members, or religious group members.

political socialization The learning process through which most people acquire their political attitudes, opinions, beliefs, and knowledge.

public opinion The views of the citizenry about politics, public issues, and public policies; a complex collection of opinions held by many people on issues in the public arena.

8-2 Discuss the different factors that affect voter choices. For established voters, party identification is one of the most important and lasting predictors of how a person will vote. Voters' choices often depend on the perceived character of the candidates rather than on their qualifications or policy positions. When people vote for candidates who share their positions on particular issues, they are engaging in policy voting. Historically, economic issues have had the strongest influence on voters' choices. Socioeconomic factors, including educational attainment, occupation and income, age, gender, religion, ethnic background, and geographic region, also influence how people vote. Ideology is another indicator of voting behavior.

gender gap The difference between the percentage of votes cast for a particular candidate by women and the percentage of votes cast for the same candidate by men.

Solid South A term used to describe the tendency of the southern states to vote Democratic after the Civil War.

8-3 Explain how public opinion polls are conducted, problems with polls, and how they are used in the political process. A **public opinion poll** is a survey of the **public's opinion** on a particular topic at a particular moment, as measured through the use of **samples.** Early polling efforts often relied on **straw polls.** The opinions expressed in straw polls, however, usually represent an atypical subgroup of the population, or a **biased sample.** Over time, more scientific polling techniques were developed. Today, polling is used extensively by political candidates and policymakers. Polls can be quite accurate when conducted properly. In-person surveys have been replaced by telephone interviews, often with prerecorded messages that solicit responses. Some pollsters specialize in Internet surveys. To achieve the most accurate results possible, pollsters use **random samples,** in which each person within the entire population being polled has an equal chance of being chosen. A properly drawn random sample will be representative of the population as a whole, though responses of various groups are sometimes weighted in an effort to achieve representativeness. Public opinion polls are fundamentally statistical. The true result of a poll is not a single figure, but a range of probabilities. All polls contain a **sampling error.** Polling firms often use differing models that contribute to a **house effect.** Problems with polls can stem from the way questions are worded, and polls often reduce complex issues to questions that simply call for "yes" or "no" answers. Moreover, polls of voter preferences cannot reflect rapid shifts in public opinion unless they are taken frequently. Many journalists base their political coverage during campaigns almost exclusively on poll findings, and media companies often report only the polls conducted by their affiliated pollsters. A tactic used in some political campaigns is a **push poll,** which asks "fake" polling questions that are designed to "push" voters toward one candidate or another.

biased sample A poll sample that does not accurately represent the population.

house effect In the case of a polling firm, a consistent tendency to report results more favorable to one of the political parties than the results reported by other pollsters.

public opinion poll A survey of the public's opinion on a particular topic at a particular moment.

push poll A campaign tactic used to feed false or misleading information to potential voters, under the guise of taking an opinion poll, with the intent to "push" voters away from one candidate and toward another.

random sample In the context of opinion polling, a sample in which each person within the entire population being polled has an equal chance of being chosen.

sample In the context of opinion polling, a group of people selected to represent the population being studied.

sampling error In the context of opinion polling, the difference between what the sample results show and what the true results would have been had everybody in the relevant population been interviewed.

straw poll A nonscientific poll in which there is no way to ensure that the opinions expressed are representative of the larger population.

8-4 **Indicate some of the factors that affect voter turnout, and discuss what has been done to improve voter turnout and voting procedures.** The Fifteenth Amendment to the Constitution (1870) guaranteed suffrage to African American males. Yet, for many decades, African Americans were effectively denied the ability to exercise their voting rights. Today, devices used to restrict voting rights, such as the **poll tax, literacy tests,** the **grandfather clause,** and **white primaries,** are explicitly prohibited by constitutional amendments, by the Voting Rights Act of 1965, or by court decisions. The Nineteenth Amendment (1920) gave women the right to vote, and the Twenty-sixth Amendment (1971) reduced the minimum voting age to eighteen. Some restrictions on voting rights, such as registration, residency, and citizenship requirements, still exist. Most states also do not permit prison inmates or felons to vote. Attempts to improve voter turnout and voting procedures include simplifying the voter-registration process, conducting voting by mail, updating voting equipment, and allowing early voting. In recent years, a number of states have passed laws that may have the effect of making it harder to vote, not easier. Voter turnout is affected by several factors, including educational attainment, income level, age, and minority status.

FIGURE 8—4 VOTER TURNOUT AROUND THE WORLD

This list excludes nations that do not have free elections, based on ratings from Freedom House. It includes all free nations with an economy (nominal GDP) of at least $1 trillion.

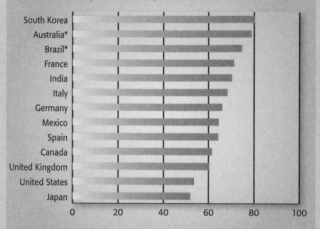

*In these countries, those who do not vote are required to pay a fine.
Source: International Institute for Democracy and Electoral Assistance. (Presidential votes in nations with presidential systems. Based on voting-age population, which depresses the percentages.)

grandfather clause A clause in a state law that had the effect of restricting voting rights to those whose ancestors had voted before the 1860s. It was one of the techniques used in the South to prevent African Americans from exercising their right to vote.

literacy test A test given to voters to ensure that they could read and write and thus evaluate political information. This technique was used in many southern states to restrict African American participation in elections.

poll tax A fee of several dollars that had to be paid before a person could vote. This device was used in some southern states to discourage African Americans and low-income whites from voting.

vote-eligible population The number of people who are actually eligible to vote in an American election.

voting-age population The number of people residing in the United States who are at least eighteen years old.

white primary A primary election in which African Americans were prohibited from voting. The practice was banned by the Supreme Court in 1944.

CHAPTER 9 LEARNING OUTCOMES / KEY TERMS

9-1 **Explain how elections are held and how the electoral college functions in presidential elections.** During **general elections,** voters decide who will be the U.S. president, vice president, and members of Congress. An election board supervises the voting process in each precinct. **Poll watchers** from each of the two major parties typically monitor the polling place as well. Citizens do not vote directly for the president and vice president. Instead, they vote for **electors** who will cast their ballots in the **electoral college.** Each state has as many electoral votes as it has U.S. senators and representatives. There are also three electors from the District of Columbia. The electoral college system is primarily a **winner-take-all system** because, in nearly all states, the candidate who receives the most popular votes in the state is credited with all of that state's electoral votes. To be elected through this system, a candidate must receive at least 270 electoral votes, a majority of the 538 electoral votes available.

FIGURE 9–1   STATE ELECTORAL VOTES IN 2016

The size of each state reflects the number of electoral votes that state has, following the changes required by the 2010 census. The colors show which party the state voted for in the 2016 presidential elections: red for Republican, blue for Democratic. A candidate must win 270 electoral votes to be elected president.

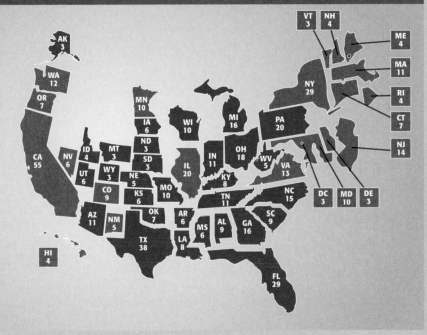

Australian ballot A secret ballot that is prepared, distributed, and counted by government officials at public expense; used by all states in the United States since 1888.

elector A member of the electoral college.

electoral college The group of electors who are selected by the voters in each state to officially elect the president and vice president. The number of electors in each state is equal to the number of that state's representatives in both chambers of Congress.

general election A regularly scheduled election to choose the U.S. president, vice president, and senators and representatives in Congress. General elections are held in even-numbered years on the Tuesday after the first Monday in November.

poll watcher A representative from one of the political parties who is allowed to monitor a polling place to make sure that the election is run fairly and that fraud doesn't occur.

special election An election that is held at the state or local level when the voters must decide an issue before the next general election or when vacancies occur by reason of death or resignation.

winner-take-all system A system in which the candidate who receives the most votes wins. In contrast, proportional systems allocate votes to multiple winners.

9-2 **Discuss how candidates are nominated.** The methods used by political parties to nominate candidates have changed over time and have included **caucuses** and **nominating conventions.** Today, candidates who win **primary elections** go on to compete against the candidates from other parties in the general election. In variations of **closed** or **open direct primaries,** voters cast their ballots directly for candidates. The elections that nominate candidates for Congress and for state or local offices are almost always direct primaries. Most of the states hold presidential primaries, which are indirect primaries used to choose **delegates** to the national nominating conventions. In some states, delegates are chosen through a caucus/convention system. Each political party holds a national convention at which delegates adopt the party platform and nominate the party's presidential and vice-presidential candidates.

9 Campaigns and Elections

CHAPTER REVIEW / KEY TERMS

CHAPTER 9 LEARNING OUTCOMES / KEY TERMS

caucus A meeting held to choose political candidates or delegates.

closed primary A primary in which only party members can vote to choose that party's candidates.

Credentials Committee A committee of each national political party that evaluates the claims of national party convention delegates to be the legitimate representatives of their states.

delegate A person selected to represent the people of one geographic area at a party convention.

direct primary An election held within each of the two major parties—Democratic and Republican—to choose the party's candidates for the general election. Voters choose the candidate directly, rather than through delegates.

nominating convention An official meeting of a political party to choose its candidates. Nominating conventions at the state and local levels also select delegates to represent the citizens of their geographic areas at a higher-level party convention.

open primary A primary in which voters can vote for a party's candidates regardless of whether they belong to the party.

primary election An election in which voters choose the candidates of their party, who will then run in the general election.

9-3 Indicate what is involved in launching a political campaign today, and describe the structure and functions of a campaign organization. To run a successful campaign, a candidate's campaign staff must be able to raise funds, get media coverage, produce and pay for political ads, schedule the candidate's time effectively with constituent groups and potential supporters, convey the candidate's position on the issues, conduct **opposition research,** and persuade the voters to go to the polls. Political party organizations are no longer as important as they once were in providing campaign services. Candidates now turn to **political consultants** who specialize in a particular area of the campaign such as conducting polls or developing the candidate's advertising. Most candidates have a campaign manager who coordinates and plans the **campaign strategy.**

campaign strategy The comprehensive plan developed by a candidate and his or her advisers for winning an election.

opposition research The attempt to learn damaging information about an opponent in a political campaign.

political consultant A professional political adviser who, for a fee, works on an area of a candidate's campaign. Political consultants include campaign managers, pollsters, media advisers, and "get-out-the-vote" organizers.

9-4 Describe how the Internet has transformed political campaigns. Today, the ability to make effective use of social media and the Internet is essential to a candidate. In 2008, Barack Obama gained an edge on his rivals in part because of his superior use of new technologies, and his 2012 campaign was even more sophisticated. Obama took Internet fund-raising to a new level. Microtargeting, a technique that involves collecting as much information as possible about voters in a database and then filtering out various groups for special attention, was pioneered by the George W. Bush campaign in 2004. In 2012, Obama's microtargeting operation vastly outperformed Mitt Romney's. Obama also took Web-based organizing to a new level. By 2012, the Obama campaign was able to create active local support groups in towns and counties across the country.

9-5 Summarize the current laws that regulate campaign financing and the role of money in modern political campaigns. The modern campaign is an expensive undertaking. Campaign-financing laws enacted in the 1970s provided public funding for presidential primaries and general elections, limited individual and group contributions to candidates, and created the Federal Election Commission. Beginning in 2004, leading Democratic and Republican presidential candidates were refusing public funding for the primaries because they could raise much more money without it. By 2012, the public financing of presidential campaigns was effectively over. The Bipartisan Campaign Reform Act of 2002 addressed the increasing use of **soft money** and **independent expenditures** to a certain extent. Several court decisions, however, have altered the rules of campaign financing. Notable consequences of these rulings include the rise of super PACs and fewer restrictions on wealthy individuals who wish to spend significant amounts of money during political campaigns. Another campaign-finance issue arose after the creation of a new kind of organization, known as the 501c, which has the ability to spend money during campaigns and to conceal the identity of its donors.

independent expenditure An expenditure for activities that are independent from (not coordinated with) those of a political candidate or a political party.

WWW.CENGAGEBRAIN.COM

CHAPTER REVIEW

CHAPTER 10 LEARNING OUTCOMES / KEY TERMS

10-1 **Explain the role of the media in a democracy.** What the media say and do has an impact on what Americans think about political issues, but the media also reflect what Americans think about politics. While the new media based on the Internet are becoming increasingly important, the traditional media—radio, television, and print—remain important to American politics and government. By helping to determine what people will talk and think about, the media play a role in setting the political agenda. Two techniques of **agenda setting** are **priming** and **framing.** Of all the media, television still has the greatest impact on most Americans, but the medium of television imposes constraints on how political issues are presented. Television reporting relies extensively on visual elements, and stories may be communicated in only a **sound bite.**

agenda setting The ability to determine which issues are considered important by the public and by politicians.

electronic media Communication channels that involve electronic transmissions, such as radio, television, and the Internet.

framing An agenda-setting technique that establishes the context of a media report. Framing can mean fitting events into a familiar story or filtering information through preconceived ideas.

mass media Communication channels, such as newspapers and radio and television broadcasts, through which people can communicate to large audiences.

priming An agenda-setting technique in which a media outlet promotes specific facts or ideas that may affect the public's thinking on related topics.

print media Communication channels that consist of printed materials, such as newspapers and magazines.

sound bite A televised comment, lasting for only a few seconds, that captures a thought or a perspective and has an immediate impact on viewers.

10-2 **Summarize how television influences the conduct of political campaigns.** Candidates for political office spend a great deal of time and money cultivating a TV presence through political ads, debates, and general news coverage. Televised **political advertising** consumes at least half of the total budget for a major political campaign. **Negative political advertising,** including **personal attack ads** and **issue ads,** is frequently used. Televised debates are a feature of presidential campaigns. They provide an opportunity for voters to find out how candidates differ on issues and allow candidates to capitalize on the power of television to improve their images or point out the failings of their opponents. Candidates' campaigns have become increasingly sophisticated in **managing news coverage.** Press advisers often try to convince reporters to give a story or event a **spin** that is favorable to the candidate.

issue ad A political advertisement that focuses on a particular issue. Issue ads can be used to support or attack a candidate's position or credibility.

managed news coverage News coverage that is manipulated (managed) by a campaign manager or political consultant to gain media exposure for a political candidate.

negative political advertising Political advertising undertaken for the purpose of discrediting a candidate in voters' eyes. Attack ads are one form of negative political advertising.

personal attack ad A negative political advertisement that attacks a candidate's character.

political advertising Advertising undertaken by or on behalf of a political candidate to familiarize voters with the candidate and his or her views on campaign issues; advertising for or against policy issues.

spin A reporter's slant on, or interpretation of, a particular event or action.

spin doctor A political candidate's press adviser who tries to convince reporters to give a story or event concerning the candidate a particular "spin" (interpretation, or slant).

10-3 **Explain why talk radio has been described as the Wild West of the media.** Talk-show hosts do not attempt to hide their political biases; if anything, they exaggerate them for effect. Sometimes, hosts appear to care more about the entertainment value of their statements than whether they are, strictly speaking, true. No journalistic conventions are observed. Those who think that talk radio is good for the country argue that talk shows, taken together, provide a great populist forum. Others fear that talk shows empower fringe groups, perhaps magnifying their rage.

10-4 **Describe types of media bias and explain how such bias affects the political process.** Relatively few Americans believe that the news media are unbiased in their reporting, and there has been a notable decline in the public's confidence in news media in recent years. Nevertheless, the public does believe that the press is successful in fulfilling its role as a watchdog. While the majority of Americans think that the media reflect a bias in either a liberal or a conservative direction, it is a media bias against losers that may play a significant role in shaping presidential campaigns and elections. The media use the winner–loser framework to describe events throughout the campaigns. Today's news culture is in the midst of change. News organizations are redefining their purpose and looking for special niches in which to build their audiences. For some, the niche is hyperlocalism; for others, it is personal commentary. In many ways, news organizations have begun to base their appeal more on how they cover the news and less on what they cover. Narrowcasting has also become important on television.

10-5 **Indicate the extent to which the Internet is reshaping news and political campaigns.** The Internet is a major source of information. Almost every major news organization, both print and broadcast, delivers news online. In addition, there has been a veritable explosion of **citizen journalism** in recent years. Blogs are offered by independent journalists, scholars, political activists, and the citizenry at large. **Podcasting** is another form of news distribution. The Internet is an inexpensive way for candidates to contact, recruit, and mobilize supporters, as well as to disseminate information about their positions on issues. Candidates hire Web managers to create well-designed campaign websites to attract viewers, manage their e-mails, and track their credit-card contributions. The Web manager also hires bloggers to promote the candidate's views, arranges for podcasting of campaign information, and hires staff to monitor the Web for news about the candidates and to track the online publications of netroots groups. Citizen videos have also changed the traditional campaign. Comments a candidate makes may be caught on camera by someone with a cell phone or digital camera and published on the Internet for all to see. Many politicians have experienced the dangers of 24/7 exposure.

FIGURE 10–1   ADVERTISING REVENUES: ONLINE VERSUS THE NEWSPAPER INDUSTRY, 2001–2016

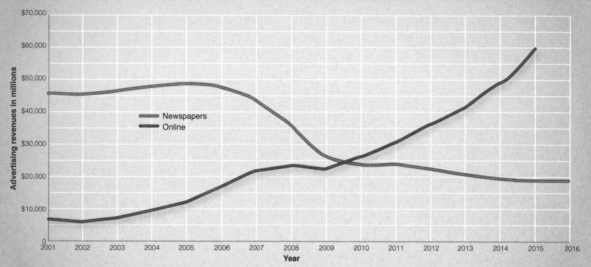

Sources: The Interactive Advertising Bureau and authors' calculations. Numbers are for the United States only.

citizen journalism The collection, analysis, and dissemination of information online by independent journalists, scholars, politicians, and the general citizenry.

podcasting The distribution of audio or video files to personal computers or mobile devices such as smartphones.

CHAPTER REVIEW

11-1 Explain how seats in the House of Representatives are apportioned among the states. The Constitution provides for the **apportionment** of House seats among the states on the basis of their respective populations, though each state is guaranteed at least one seat. Every ten years, the 435 House seats are reapportioned based on the outcome of the census. Each representative to the House is elected by voters in a **congressional district.** Within each state, districts must contain, as nearly as possible, equal numbers of people. This principle is known as the **"one person, one vote" rule. Gerrymandering** occurs when a district's boundaries are drawn to maximize the influence of a certain group or political party.

apportionment The distribution of House seats among the states on the basis of their respective populations.

congressional district The geographic area that is served by one member in the House of Representatives.

earmark Spending provision inserted into legislation that benefits only a small number of people.

gerrymandering The drawing of a legislative district's boundaries in such a way as to maximize the influence of a certain group or political party.

instructed delegate A representative who deliberately mirrors the views of the majority of his or her constituents.

malapportionment A condition in which the voting power of citizens in one district is greater than the voting power of citizens in another district.

minority-majority district A district in which minority groups make up a majority of the population.

"one person, one vote" rule A rule, or principle, requiring that congressional districts have equal populations so that one person's vote counts as much as another's vote.

trustee A representative who tries to serve the broad interests of the entire society and not just the narrow interests of his or her constituents.

11-2 Describe the power of incumbency. If legislators choose to run for reelection, they enjoy several advantages over their opponents, including name recognition, access to the media, and lawmaking power. Members of Congress also have administrative staffs in Washington, D.C., and in their home districts. A key advantage is their fund-raising ability. Most incumbent members of Congress have a much larger network of contacts, donors, and lobbyists than their challengers have. While incumbents who run are usually reelected, there have been occasional periods of some turbulence when fewer incumbents than usual won reelection.

11-3 Identify the key leadership positions in Congress, describe the committee system, and indicate some important differences between the House of Representatives and the Senate. The Constitution provides for the presiding officers of both the House and the Senate, and each chamber has added other leadership positions. The majority party in each chamber chooses the major officers of that chamber, selects committee chairpersons, and has a majority on all committees. Chief among the leaders in the House of Representatives is the **Speaker of the House,** who has a great deal of power. Other leaders include the **majority and minority leaders** and the **whips.** The vice president of the United States is the president of the Senate, and senators elect the president pro tempore ("pro tem"). The real power in the Senate is held by the majority and minority leaders, and their whips. The committee system is a way to provide for specialization, or a division of legislative labor. Much of the work of legislating is performed by the **standing committees** and their **subcommittees** in the House and the Senate. A **conference committee** is formed for the purpose of achieving agreement between the House and Senate on the wording of a legislative act. With its larger size, the House needs more rules and more formality than the Senate. The House **Rules Committee** proposes time limits on debate for most bills. The Senate normally permits extended debate. The use of unlimited debate to obstruct legislation is called **filibustering,** which may be ended by invoking **cloture.** There are other important differences between the House and the Senate as well. The Senate, for example, has the power of "advice and consent" on presidential appointments and treaties.

cloture A procedure for ending filibusters in the Senate and bringing the matter under consideration to a vote.

conference committee A temporary committee that consists of members from the House and the Senate who work out a compromise bill.

filibustering The Senate tradition of unlimited debate undertaken for the purpose of preventing action on a bill.

majority leader The party leader elected by the majority party in the House or in the Senate.

minority leader The party leader elected by the minority party in the House or in the Senate.

Rules Committee A standing committee in the House that provides special rules governing how particular bills will be considered and debated.

Speaker of the House The presiding officer in the House of Representatives. A member of the majority party who is the most powerful member of the House.

standing committee A permanent committee in Congress that deals with legislation concerning a particular area, such as agriculture or foreign relations.

subcommittee A division of a larger committee that deals with a particular part of the committee's policy area.

whip A member of Congress who assists the majority or minority leader in managing the party's legislative program.

11-4 Summarize the specific steps in the lawmaking process. After a bill is introduced, it is sent to the appropriate standing committee. A committee chairperson will typically send the bill on to a subcommittee, where public hearings may be held. After a **markup session,** the bill goes to the full committee for further action. After a bill is reported to the chamber, it is scheduled for floor debate. If, after votes are taken on the legislation, the House and Senate have passed differing versions of the same bill, a conference committee is formed to produce a compromise bill. A **conference report** is submitted to each chamber. If the bill is approved by both chambers, it is ready for action by the president.

conference report A report submitted by a conference committee after it has drafted a single version of a bill.

markup session A meeting held by a congressional committee or subcommittee to approve, amend, or redraft a bill.

pocket veto A special type of veto power used by the president after the legislature has adjourned.

11-5 Identify Congress's oversight functions, and explain how Congress fulfills them. Congress oversees the departments and agencies of the executive branch, and can rein in the power of the bureaucracy by choosing not to provide the money necessary for the bureaucracy to function. Congress also has the authority to investigate the actions of the executive branch, the need for certain legislation, and even the actions of its own members. Congress has the power to impeach federal officials and remove them from office. The Senate either confirms or fails to confirm the president's nominees for federal judgeships and top executive branch officers.

nuclear option Changing Senate rules—in particular, rules that require a supermajority—by simple majority vote. Also known as the *constitutional option*.

11-6 Indicate what is involved in the congressional budgeting process. The budgeting process, which involves **authorization** and **appropriation,** begins when the president submits a proposed federal budget for the next **fiscal year.** In the **first budget resolution,** Congress sets overall revenue goals and spending targets. The **second budget resolution** sets "binding" limits on taxes and spending. When Congress is unable to pass a complete budget by October 1, it usually passes **continuing resolutions,** which enable executive agencies to keep on doing whatever they were doing the previous year with the same amount of funding. **Entitlement programs** operate under open-ended budget authorizations.

appropriation The determination of how many dollars will be spent in a given year on a particular government activity.

authorization The creation of the legal basis for government programs.

continuing resolution A temporary resolution that enables executive agencies to continue working with the same funding that they had in the previous fiscal year.

entitlement program A government program (such as Social Security) that allows, or entitles, a certain class of people (such as elderly persons) to receive benefits.

first budget resolution A budget resolution, which is supposed to be passed in May, that sets overall revenue goals and spending targets for the next fiscal year, beginning on October 1.

fiscal year A twelve-month period (from October 1 through September 30, for the U.S. government) that is established for bookkeeping or accounting purposes.

second budget resolution A budget resolution, which is supposed to be passed in September, that sets "binding" limits on taxes and spending for the next fiscal year.

CHAPTER 12 LEARNING OUTCOMES / KEY TERMS

12-1 **List the constitutional requirements for becoming president.** Article II of the Constitution sets forth relatively few requirements for becoming president. A person must be a natural-born citizen, at least thirty-five years of age, and a resident within the United States for at least fourteen years.

12-2 **Explain the roles that a president adopts while in office.** In the course of exercising his or her powers, the president performs a variety of roles. The president is the nation's **chief executive**—the head of the executive branch— and enforces laws and federal court decisions. The president leads the nation's armed forces as **commander in chief.** As **head of state,** the president performs ceremonial activities as a personal symbol of the nation. As **chief diplomat,** the president directs U.S. foreign policy and is the nation's most important representative in dealing with foreign governments. The president has become the chief legislator, informing Congress about the condition of the country and recommending legislative measures. As political party leader, the president chooses the chairperson of his or her party's national committee, attends party fund-raisers, and exerts influence within the party by using presidential appointment powers and engaging in the practice of **patronage.**

chief diplomat The role of the president of the United States in recognizing and interacting with foreign governments.

chief executive The head of the executive branch of government; in the United States, the president.

commander in chief The supreme commander of a nation's military force.

diplomat A person who represents one country in dealing with representatives of another country.

head of state The person who serves as the ceremonial head of a country's government and represents that country to the rest of the world.

patronage The practice by which elected officials give government jobs to individuals who helped them gain office.

12-3 **Indicate the scope of presidential powers.** The Constitution gives the president specific powers, such as the power to make **treaties,** to grant reprieves and pardons, and to **veto** bills passed by Congress. The president also has inherent powers—powers that are necessary to carry out the specific constitutional duties of the presidency. Several presidents have greatly expanded the powers of the office. The president, for example, is now expected to develop a legislative program. The president's political skills, the ability to persuade others, and the strategy of "going public" all play a role in determining legislative success. The president's executive authority has been expanded by the use of **executive orders** and **signing statements,** and the ability to make **executive agreements** has enhanced presidential power in foreign affairs. As commander in chief, the president can respond quickly to a military threat without waiting for congressional action, and since 1945, the president has been responsible for deciding if and when to use nuclear weapons.

executive agreement A binding international agreement, or pact, that is made between the president and another head of state and that does not require Senate approval.

executive order A presidential order to carry out a policy or policies described in a law passed by Congress.

signing statement A written statement, appended to a bill at the time the president signs it into law, indicating how the president interprets that legislation.

treaty A formal agreement between the governments of two or more countries.

veto A Latin word meaning "I forbid"; the refusal by an official, such as the president of the United States or a state governor, to sign a bill into law.

12-4 **Describe advantages enjoyed by Congress and by the president in their institutional relationship.** Congress has the advantage over the president in the areas of legislative authorization, the regulation of foreign and interstate commerce, and some budgetary matters. The president has the advantage over Congress in dealing with a national crisis, in setting foreign policy, and in influencing public opinion. The relationship between Congress and the president is affected by their different constituencies and election cycles, and the fact that the president is limited to two terms in office. Their relationship is also affected when government is divided, with at least one house of Congress controlled by a different party than the White House.

executive privilege An inherent executive power claimed by presidents to withhold information from, or to refuse to appear before, Congress or the courts. The president can also accord the privilege to other executive officials.

Watergate scandal A scandal involving an illegal break-in at the Democratic National Committee offices in 1972 by members of President Richard Nixon's reelection campaign staff.

12-5 **Discuss the organization of the executive branch and the role of cabinet members in presidential administrations.** The heads of the executive departments are members of the president's **cabinet.** The president may add other officials to the cabinet as well. In general, presidents don't rely heavily on the advice of the formal cabinet. Department heads are often more responsive to the wishes of their own staffs, to their own political ambitions, or to obtaining resources for their departments than they are to the presidents they serve. Since 1939, top advisers and assistants in the **Executive Office of the President (EOP)** have helped the president carry out major duties. Some of the most important staff agencies in the EOP are the **White House Office,** which is headed by the **chief of staff** and includes the **press secretary;** the **Office of Management and Budget;** and the **National Security Council.** In recent years, the responsibilities of the vice president have grown immensely, and the vice president has become one of the most important of the president's advisers.

TABLE 12–3	THE EXECUTIVE OFFICE OF THE PRESIDENT AS OF 2016
Agency	
Council of Economic Advisers	
Council on Environmental Quality	
Executive Residence	
National Security Council	
Office of Administration	
Office of Management and Budget	
Office of National Drug Control Policy	
Office of Science and Technology Policy	
Office of the U.S. Trade Representative	
Office of the Vice President	
White House Office	

Source: www.whitehouse.gov.

cabinet An advisory group selected by the president to assist with decision making. Traditionally, the cabinet has consisted of the heads of the executive departments and other officers whom the president may choose to appoint.

chief of staff The person who directs the operations of the White House Office and advises the president on important matters.

Executive Office of the President (EOP) A group of staff agencies that assist the president in carrying out major duties.

kitchen cabinet The name given to a president's unofficial advisers. The term was coined during Andrew Jackson's presidency.

National Security Council (NSC) A council that advises the president on domestic and foreign matters concerning the safety and defense of the nation.

Office of Management and Budget (OMB) An agency in the Executive Office of the President that has the primary duty of assisting the president in preparing and supervising the administration of the federal budget.

press secretary A member of the White House staff who holds news conferences for reporters and makes public statements for the president.

White House Office The personal office of the president. White House Office personnel handle the president's political needs and manage the media, among other duties.

CHAPTER 13 LEARNING OUTCOMES / KEY TERMS

13-1 **Describe the size and functions of the U.S. bureaucracy and the major components of federal spending.** A **bureaucracy** is a large, complex administrative organization that is structured hierarchically. In the federal government, the bureaucracy is part of the executive branch, and its head is the president of the United States. The federal bureaucracy exists because Congress, over time, has delegated certain tasks to specialists. The three levels of government employ about 16 percent of the civilian labor force. Over half of the federal budget consists of various social programs. Defense spending, including veterans' benefits, also accounts for a significant amount of total federal spending. Other categories of spending include military and economic foreign aid, as well as interest on the national debt.

bureaucracy A large, complex, hierarchically structured administrative organization that carries out specific functions.

bureaucrat An individual who works in a bureaucracy. As generally used, the term refers to a government employee.

13-2 **Discuss the structure and basic components of the federal bureaucracy.** The fifteen executive departments are the major service organizations of the federal government. Each department was created by Congress as the perceived need for it arose, and each manages a specific policy area. Department heads are appointed by the president and confirmed by the Senate. Each department includes several subagencies. **Independent executive agencies** have a single function. Sometimes agencies are kept independent because of the sensitive nature of their functions, but at other times, Congress creates independent agencies to protect them from **partisan politics.** There are more than two hundred independent executive agencies. An **independent regulatory agency** is responsible for a specific type of policy. Its function is to create and implement rules that regulate private activity and protect the public interest in a particular sector of the economy. **Government corporations** are businesses owned by the government. They provide a service that could be handled by the private sector, and they charge for their services. A number of intermediate forms of organization exist that fall between a government corporation and a private one.

government corporation An agency of the government that is run as a business enterprise. Such agencies engage primarily in commercial activities, produce revenues, and require greater flexibility than most government agencies have.

independent executive agency A federal agency that is not located within a cabinet department.

independent regulatory agency A federal organization that is responsible for creating and implementing rules that regulate private activity and protect the public interest in a particular sector of the economy.

partisan politics Political actions or decisions that benefit a particular party.

13-3 **Describe how the federal civil service was established and how bureaucrats get their jobs.** Federal **bureaucrats** holding top-level positions are appointed by the president and confirmed by the Senate. The list of positions that are filled by appointments is published after each presidential election in a book that summarizes about eight thousand jobs. The rank-and-file bureaucrats—the rest of the federal bureaucracy—are part of the **civil service.** They obtain their jobs through the Office of Personnel Management (OPM). The OPM recruits, interviews, and tests potential government workers and makes recommendations to individual agencies as to which persons meet relevant standards. The Civil Service Reform Act of 1883 established the principle of government employment on the basis of merit through open, competitive examinations.

civil service Nonmilitary government employees.

13-4 **Explain how regulatory agencies make rules and how issue networks affect policymaking in government.** Regulatory agencies are sometimes regarded as the fourth branch of government. **Enabling legislation** makes the regulatory agency a potent organization. Agencies make **legislative rules** that are as legally binding as laws passed by Congress. When they are engaging in **rulemaking,** agencies must follow certain procedural requirements and must also make sure that their rules are based on substantial evidence. Bureaucrats in federal agencies are expected to exhibit **neutral competency,** which means that they are supposed to apply their technical skills to their jobs without regard to political issues. In reality, however, each independent agency and each executive department is interested in its own survival and expansion. **Iron triangles** are well established in almost every part of the bureaucracy. In some policy areas, there are less structured relationships among experts who have strong opinions and interests regarding the direction of policy. These **issue networks** are able to exert a great deal of influence on legislators and bureaucratic agencies.

FIGURE 13–6   ISSUE NETWORK: THE ENVIRONMENT

Executive Departments and Agencies
• Environmental Protection Agency
• Agriculture Department
• Energy Department
• Department of the Interior
• National Oceanic and Atmospheric Admin.
• Bureau of Land Management
• Army Corps of Engineers

Key Congressional Committees
• **Senate**
Appropriations, Energy and Natural Resources, Environment and Public Works, Finance, Commerce, Science, and Transportation
• **House of Representatives**
Agriculture, Appropriations, Natural Resources, Transportation and Infrastructure

Selected Interest Groups
• **Environmental Groups**
Environmental Defense, Friends of the Earth, National Audubon Society, Clean Water Action, National Wildlife Federation, The Ocean Conservancy, American Forests
• **Industry Groups**
Citizens for a Sound Economy, Edison Electric Institute, U.S. Chamber of Commerce, National Food Processors Association, International Wood Products Association, National Mining Association, American Resort Development Association

adjudicate To render a judicial decision. In administrative law, it is the process in which an administrative law judge hears and decides issues that arise when an agency charges a person or firm with violating a law or regulation enforced by the agency.

enabling legislation A law enacted by a legislature to establish an administrative agency. Enabling legislation normally specifies the name, purpose, composition, and powers of the agency being created.

iron triangle A three-way alliance among legislators, bureaucrats, and interest groups to make or preserve policies that benefit their respective interests.

issue networks Groups of individuals or organizations—which consist of legislators and legislative staff members, interest group leaders, bureaucrats, the media, scholars, and other experts—that support particular policy positions on a given issue.

legislative rule An administrative agency rule that carries the same weight as a statute enacted by a legislature.

neutral competency The application of technical skills to jobs without regard to political issues.

rulemaking The process undertaken by an administrative agency when formally proposing, evaluating, and adopting a new regulation.

13-5 **Identify some of the ways in which the government has attempted to curb waste and improve efficiency in the bureaucracy.** To encourage federal employees to report gross governmental inefficiency or wrongdoing, Congress has passed laws to protect **whistleblowers** and to make cash rewards to them. To improve efficiency, almost every federal agency has had to describe its goals and identify methods for evaluating how well those goals are met. President Obama created the position of a chief performance officer who works with other economic officials in an attempt to increase efficiency and eliminate waste in government. Other ideas for reforming government bureaucracies include pay-for-performance plans, **privatization,** and using the Internet to let citizens file forms and apply for services online.

privatization The transfer of the task of providing services traditionally provided by government to the private sector.

whistleblower In the context of government employment, someone who "blows the whistle" (reports to authorities or the press) on gross governmental inefficiency, illegal action, or other wrongdoing.

CHAPTER 14 LEARNING OUTCOMES / KEY TERMS

14-1 Summarize the origins of the American legal system and the basic sources of American law. The American legal system evolved from the **common law** tradition that developed in England. The practice of deciding new cases with reference to **precedents (stare decisis)** became a cornerstone of the American judicial system. Various **primary sources of law** provide the basis for **constitutional law, statutory law, administrative law,** and **case law.** Civil law spells out the duties that individuals in society owe to other persons or to their governments. **Criminal law** has to do with wrongs committed against the public as a whole. A court must have **jurisdiction** to hear and decide a particular case. A **federal question** provides a basis for federal court jurisdiction. Federal courts can also hear **diversity-of-citizenship** cases. To bring a lawsuit before a court, a person must have **standing to sue,** and the issue must be a **justiciable controversy.** The courts have also established procedural rules that apply in all cases.

administrative law The body of law created by administrative agencies (in the form of rules, regulations, orders, and decisions) in order to carry out their duties and responsibilities.

case law The rules of law announced in court decisions. Case law includes the aggregate of reported cases that interpret judicial precedents, statutes, regulations, and constitutional provisions.

civil law The branch of law that spells out the duties that individuals in society owe to other persons or to their governments, excluding the duty not to commit crimes.

common law The body of law developed from judicial decisions in English and U.S. courts, not attributable to a legislature.

constitutional law Law based on the U.S. Constitution and the constitutions of the various states.

contempt of court A ruling that a person has disobeyed a court order or has shown disrespect to the court or to a judicial proceeding.

criminal law The branch of law that defines and governs actions that constitute crimes. Generally, criminal law has to do with wrongful actions committed against society for which society demands redress.

diversity of citizenship A basis for federal court jurisdiction over a lawsuit that arises when (1) the parties in the lawsuit live in different states or when one of the parties is a foreign government or a foreign citizen, and (2) the amount in controversy is more than $75,000.

federal question A question that pertains to the U.S. Constitution, acts of Congress, or treaties. A federal question provides a basis for federal court jurisdiction.

judiciary The courts; one of the three branches of government in the United States.

jurisdiction The authority of a court to hear and decide a particular case.

justiciable controversy A controversy that is not hypothetical or academic but real and substantial; a requirement that must be satisfied before a court will hear a case. *Justiciable* is pronounced jus-*tish*-a-bul.

precedent A court decision that furnishes an example or authority for deciding subsequent cases involving identical or similar facts and legal issues.

primary source of law A source of law that establishes the law. Primary sources of law include constitutions, statutes, administrative agency rules and regulations, and decisions rendered by the courts.

stare decisis A common law doctrine under which judges normally are obligated to follow the precedents established by prior court decisions. Pronounced *ster*-ay dih-*si*-sis.

statutory law The body of law enacted by legislatures (as opposed to constitutional law, administrative law, or case law).

standing to sue The requirement that an individual must have a sufficient stake in a controversy before he or she can bring a lawsuit. The party bringing the suit must demonstrate that he or she has either been harmed or been threatened with a harm.

trial court A court in which trials are held and testimony is taken.

14-2 Delineate the structure of the federal court system. The U.S. district courts are **trial courts**—the courts in which cases involving federal laws begin. There is at least one federal district court in every state, and there is one in the District of Columbia. The U.S. courts of appeals are **appellate courts** that hear cases on review from the U.S. district courts located within their respective judicial circuits. Some federal administrative agency decisions may also be appealed to these courts. The Court of Appeals for the Federal Circuit has national jurisdiction over certain types of cases. The United States Supreme Court has some original jurisdiction, but most of its work is as an appellate court. The Supreme Court may take appeals of decisions made by the U.S. courts of appeals as well as appeals of cases decided in the state courts when federal questions are at issue. To bring a case before the Supreme Court, a party may request that the Court issue a **writ of *certiorari*.** If the Court grants "cert," it will typically hear **oral arguments.** The justices will then discuss the case in **conference.** When the Court has reached a decision, the justices explain their reasoning in written **opinions.**

appellate court A court having appellate jurisdiction. An appellate court normally does not hear evidence or testimony but reviews the transcript of the trial court's proceedings, other records relating to the case, and attorneys' arguments as to why the trial court's decision should or should not stand.

concurring opinion A statement written by a judge or justice who agrees (concurs) with the court's decision, but for reasons different from those in the majority opinion.

conference In regard to the Supreme Court, a private meeting of the justices in which they present their arguments concerning a case under consideration.

dissenting opinion A statement written by a judge or justice who disagrees with the majority opinion.

opinion A written statement by a court expressing the reasons for its decision in a case.

oral argument A spoken argument presented to a judge in person by an attorney on behalf of her or his client.

writ of *certiorari* An order from a higher court asking a lower court for the record of a case. *Certiorari* is pronounced sur-shee-uh-*rah*-ree.

14-3 **Say how federal judges are appointed.** Federal judges are appointed by the president with the advice and consent of the Senate. They receive lifetime appointments. The Senate Judiciary Committee holds hearings on judicial nominees and makes its recommendations to the Senate, where it takes a majority vote to confirm nominations. **Senatorial courtesy** gives home-state senators of the president's party influence over the president's choice of nominees for district courts (and, to a lesser extent, the U.S. courts of appeals). The process of nominating and confirming federal judges often involves political debate and controversy.

senatorial courtesy A practice that allows a senator of the president's party to veto the president's nominee to a federal court judgeship within the senator's state.

14-4 **Explain how the federal courts make policy, and describe the role of ideology and judicial philosophies in judicial decision making.** It is unavoidable that judges influence or even establish policy when they interpret and apply the law, because the law does not always provide clear answers to questions that come before the courts. Federal judges can also decide on the constitutionality of laws or actions undertaken by the other branches of government through the power of **judicial review.** Generally, activist judges believe that the courts should actively use their powers to check the other two branches of government to ensure that they do not exceed their authority. Restraintist judges generally assume that the courts should defer to the decisions of the other branches. Neither judicial activism nor judicial restraint is necessarily linked to a particular political ideology. There are numerous examples of ideology affecting Supreme Court decisions. Judicial decision making, however, can be complex. How much weight is given to the factors that may be taken into account when deciding cases depends, in part, on the approaches justices take toward the interpretation of laws and the Constitution. Important judicial philosophies include originalism, textualism, and modernism.

judicial review The power of the courts to decide on the constitutionality of legislative enactments and of actions taken by the executive branch.

14-5 **Identify some of the criticisms of the federal courts and some of the checks on the power of the courts.** Policymaking by unelected judges has important implications in a democracy. Critics, especially on the political right, frequently accuse the **judiciary** of "legislating from the bench." There are several checks on the courts, however, including judicial traditions and doctrines, the judiciary's lack of enforcement powers, and potential congressional actions in response to court decisions. The American public continues to have a fairly high regard for the federal judiciary.

CHAPTER 15 LEARNING OUTCOMES / KEY TERMS

15-1 **Explain what domestic policy is, and summarize the steps in the policymaking process.** Domestic policy consists of public policy concerning issues within a national unit. The **policymaking process** involves several phases. Identifying a problem that can be solved politically (issue identification) and getting the issue on the political agenda **(agenda setting)** begin the process. The second stage involves the formulation and adoption of specific plans for achieving a particular goal. The final stages of the process focus on the implementation of the policy and evaluating its success. Each phase of the policymaking process involves interactions among various individuals and groups.

agenda setting In policymaking, getting an issue on the political agenda to be addressed by Congress; part of the first stage of the policymaking process.

domestic policy Public policy concerning issues within a national unit, such as national policy concerning health care or the economy.

policymaking process The procedures involved in getting an issue on the political agenda; formulating, adopting, and implementing a policy with regard to the issue; and then evaluating the results of the policy.

15-2 **Discuss the issue of health-care funding and recent legislation on universal health insurance.** Most federal spending on health care is accounted for by two **entitlement programs, Medicaid** and **Medicare.** Medicare is the government's second-largest domestic spending program. In some countries, the government is responsible for providing basic health-care insurance to everyone through **national health insurance.** The plan that the United States has adopted relies on private insurance companies. Under the Patient Protection and Affordable Care Act, signed into law in 2010 by President Obama, employer-provided health insurance continues, and a new health insurance marketplace allows small businesses and individuals to shop for plans. The legislation also includes an **individual** **mandate**—most individuals are required to obtain coverage or pay an income tax penalty. One immediate change was that young people could remain covered by their parents' insurance until they turn twenty-six, but the most important provisions of the new law were not to take effect until 2014, when subsidies were available to help citizens purchase health-care insurance if they were not covered by Medicare, Medicaid, or an employer's plan. Conservatives were opposed to the Affordable Care Act, but repeated attempts by Republicans in the House to repeal Obamacare were ineffectual. The roll-out of the federal health insurance exchange in 2013 did not go smoothly but by April 2014, the end of the sign-up period, 8 million Americans had obtained insurance policies through the state and federal exchanges.

Children's Health Insurance Program (CHIP) A joint federal–state program that provides health-care insurance for low-income children.

entitlement program A government program that provides benefits to all persons who meet specified requirements.

individual mandate In the context of health-care reform, a requirement that all persons obtain health-care insurance from one source or another. Those failing to do so must pay a penalty.

Medicaid A joint federal–state program that pays for health-care services for low-income persons.

Medicare A federal government program that pays for health-care insurance for Americans aged sixty-five years and over.

national health insurance A program, found in many of the world's economically advanced nations, under which the central government provides basic health-care insurance coverage to everyone in the country.

15-3 **Summarize the issues of energy independence, climate change, and alternative energy sources.** In 2016, our nation imported 45 percent of its petroleum supply. Fortunately, friendly neighbors, Canada and Mexico, supply 45 percent of those imports. Most climatologists believe that **climate change** is the result of human activities, especially the release of **greenhouse gases** into the atmosphere. The predicted outcomes of climate change vary, and attitudes toward it have become highly politicized. The issues of U.S. energy security and climate change raise the question of whether we can develop new energy sources. Due, in part, to new techniques, such as **fracking,** there has recently been an increase in supplies of natural gas and oil. Nuclear power does not contribute to global warming; a key obstacle to the construction of new nuclear power plants, however, is cost. There are also concerns about the possible dangers of storing spent nuclear fuel. **Renewable energy** technologies, such as solar power and wind energy, continue to be developed.

climate change The increase in the average temperature of the Earth's surface over the last half century and its projected continuation; also referred to more generally as *global warming*.

fracking Technique for extracting oil or natural gas from underground rock by the high-power injection of a mixture of water, sand, and chemicals.

greenhouse gas A gas that, when released into the atmosphere, traps the sun's heat and slows its release into outer space. Carbon dioxide (CO_2) is a major example.

renewable energy Energy from technologies that do not rely on extracted resources, such as oil and coal, that can run out.

15-4 **Describe the two major areas of economic policymaking, and discuss the issue of the public debt.** Economic **policy** consists of all actions taken by the government to address the ups and downs in the nation's level of business activity. The national government has two main tools to smooth the business cycle and to reduce **unemployment** and **inflation.** **Monetary policy** is under the control of the Federal Reserve System (the Fed), an independent regulatory agency. The Fed and its **Federal Open Market Committee** make decisions about monetary policy several times each year. In periods of recession and high unemployment, the Fed pursues an **easy-money**

policy. In periods of rising inflation, the Fed adopts a tight-money policy. **Fiscal policy,** associated with **Keynesian economics,** involves the use of changes in government spending or taxes to stimulate or curb economic activity. The government raises money to pay its expenses through taxes levied on business and personal income and through borrowing. When the government spends more than it receives, it borrows to finance the shortfall. Every time there is a federal government deficit, there is an increase in the total accumulated **public debt.** The federal budget deficit has gone down in recent years.

FIGURE 15–4   THE NET PUBLIC DEBT AS A PERCENTAGE OF THE GROSS DOMESTIC PRODUCT (GDP)

Percentages from 2016 onwards are projections

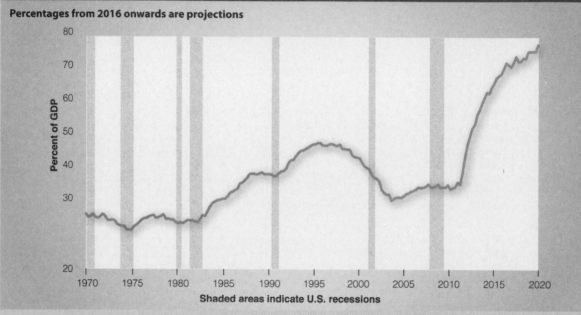

Source: research.stlouisfed.org and the Congressional Budget Office.

easy-money policy A monetary policy that involves stimulating the economy by expanding the rate of growth of the money supply.

economic policy All actions taken by the national government to address ups and downs in the nation's level of business activity.

Federal Open Market Committee (FOMC) The most important body within the Federal Reserve System; decides how monetary policy should be carried out.

fiscal policy The use of changes in government expenditures and taxes to alter national economic variables.

inflation A sustained rise in average prices; equivalent to a decline in the value of the dollar.

Keynesian economics An economic theory proposed by British economist John Maynard Keynes that is typically associated with the use of fiscal policy to alter national economic variables.

monetary policy Actions taken by the Federal Reserve to change the amount of money in circulation to affect interest rates, credit markets, the rate of inflation, the rate of economic growth, and the rate of unemployment.

public debt The total amount of money that the national government owes as a result of borrowing; also called the *national debt*.

recession A period in which the level of economic activity falls; usually defined as two or more quarters of economic decline.

unemployment The state of not having a job when actively seeking one.